Beyond The Dreams of Avarice.
The Very Wealthy in Modern Britain

William D. Rubinstein

EER

Edward Everett Root, Publishers, Brighton, 2022.

EER

Edward Everett Root, Publishers, Co. Ltd.,

Atlas Chambers, 33 West Street, Brighton, Sussex, BN1 2RE, England.

Full details of our overseas agents in America, Australia, China, Europe, Japan,
and how to order our books are given on our website.

www.eerpublishing.com

edwardeverettroot@yahoo.co.uk

Beyond The Dreams of Avarice. The Very Wealthy in Modern Britain

ISBN: 978-1-912224-32-6 Hardback
ISBN: 978-1-912224-34-0 eBook

First published in Great Britain in 2022.

Design and typesetting by Pageset Limited, High Wycombe, Bucks.

Contents

About the Author   vi

Introduction   vii

Chapter 1: The Richest Landowners in the UK in 1880–1895   1

Chapter 2: Large Personal Fortunes of landowners and the
            Businessmen Who Owned the Most Land   85

Chapter 3: The Largest Estates Left in the UK, 1809–1899   101

Chapter 4: The Largest Estates Left in the UK, 1900–1949   178

Chapter 5: The Largest Estates Left in the UK, 1950–1979   277

Chapter 6: Wealth in Contemporary Britain   301

A Note on Sources   306

Index   307

About the Author

William D. Rubinstein was born in New York, and was educated at Swarthmore College and at Johns Hopkins University. He has held Chairs of History at Deakin University near Melbourne, Australia and at the University of Wales. He has published widely on modern British history and many other topics. Many of his books have been published by *EER*. He is a Fellow of the Australian Academy of the Humanities, of the Australian Academy of the Social Sciences, and of the Royal Historical Society of the UK.

Available now from *EER* are his works:

Churchill, The Contradictions of Greatness.

Elites and the Wealthy in Modern British History. Essays in Social and Economic History. New extended edition.

Men Of Property. The Very Wealthy in Britain Since The Industrial Revolution. New updated edition.

Who Were The Rich? Five volumes covering 1809–69. Further volumes in preparation.

Unsolved Historical Mysteries. Answers To Outstanding Historical Puzzles.

• A major new study of *Hitler, The Mentality of Evil* by Professor Rubinstein will be published by *EER* in 2022.

Introduction.
Part One – The Wealthiest Landowners.

This book examines the lives and careers of Britain's wealthiest people and families from the mid-eighteenth century, with an emphasis on the nineteenth and twentieth centuries.

The first part of this work examines the richest landowners. This can be done with a surprising degree of accuracy for the later nineteenth century, in contrast to the periods before or since. In 1872 Parliament commissioned an official register of all landowners in the United Kingdom, *The Return of Owners of Land,* which was published in several parts between 1872 and 1875. The only part of the United Kingdom excluded from this survey was London. It was arranged by county, and gave the name, address, acreage in that county, and gross annual income from their land, for every landowner, London excepted.

In 1883 John Bateman collated all of this data, and produced a seminal, comprehensive guide to Britain's largest landowners at that time, *The Great Landowners of Great Britain and Ireland.* This listed, in alphabetical order, all landowners – London excluded – who owned 3,000 or more acres or had a gross annual income from their land of £3,000 p.a. (per annum) or more, together with some biographical information on every such person, such as his education, chief place of residence, political offices held, and so on. This included many revisions of the data in the original *Return,* and is regarded as the authoritative guidebook to Britain's landed elite in the late Victorian period. The work was reprinted in 1971 by Leicester University Press and The Humanities Press in the USA, with an Introduction by Professor David Spring of Johns Hopkins University.

The task of providing similar data on the great London landowners was in large measure undertaken by Professor Peter H. Lindert, in his article "Who Owned Victorian England?: The Debate Over Landed Wealth and Inequality," which appeared in the *Agricultural History Review,* Volume 61, Number 4, Fall 1987, pp. 25-51. Working from an unpublished study of landowners in London carried out by the London County Council in 1892-1895, he produced a list of London's landowners with the highest incomes from their London lands. There are many *caveats* in the use of this source, although the two highest incomes belonged, just as one might expect, to the Duke of Westminster and the Duke of Bedford. For each such landowner on his list (pp. 47-48), Lindert gives his total London acreage, and two figures for the income of each, "Assessed Annual Rental Value (Real Estate), and "Estimated Annual Land value (Site Only)," with the former figure in most cases being much higher than the latter. For instance, the Duke of Westminster was credited with owning 475,566 acres of London land, with his income for the first category being £423,787 p.a., and, for the second category, £189,611 p.a. In my work, the second, lower figure has been taken as the more likely to be accurate for London landowners included in this study.

The first part of this book consists of biographical information on the thirty-five wealthiest landowners, from the mid/late eighteenth century to the present, with information about the successive holders of each peerage or other main owner of their land, in descending order of gross annual income. Wherever possible, the probate valuation of the landowner and many of his or her close relatives is given. Until 1925, this valuation was that of the value of the gross unsettled personalty of the person in question, that is, of the non-landed component of his estate left at death. From 1926, the probate records also include the valuation of the settled land (i.e., land held in settlement, which the apparent owner could not sell without many complications) which the landowner owned.

A rough rule of thumb is that, prior to 1914, a pound was worth about 120 times what it is today, and say 60 times what it is today in the period c. 1914-1960 or so. Thus, an estate of £500,000 left in 1900 was worth about £60 million today. But even this does not capture the full extent of the vast increase in land values which has taken place in Britain since the 1960s, and especially since the 1990s. The market value of land was usually taken to be about thirty times its gross annual income, so that a landowner whose total landed income in Bateman was given as say £80,000 was about £2.4 million – if it came on the market. 120 times this is about £288 million today. But it is clear that the market value of this land today would in many cases be vastly higher, possibly in the billions in London and the south-east of England. Another consideration is that the wealth of Britain's wealthiest persons showed a sharp decline between about 1940 and 1965, as unprecedented rates of taxation hit the wealthy. Someone leaving £1 million in 1950 would probably have been among the 200 or so richest people in Britain, while today this figure would be exceeded by the wealth of every single homeowner of many streets in London's posher areas and suburbs, and many living elsewhere.

Some preliminary conclusions may be drawn from the biographies and statistics set out here. Most of the great aristocratic landed fortunes date from the Reformation, the Elizabethan period, and the age of "Old Corruption" in the eighteenth century. The fortunes of the very wealthiest were almost always enhanced by good luck – fortunate marriages, fortunate inheritances, fortunate political alliances, fortunate ownership of land which could be exploited for profit. Possibly not a single one of the wealthiest landowners here made their money after the early nineteenth century, a topic which will be discussed later in this book. Some did most certainly exploit the opportunities their particular landed holdings gave them – many London real property owners, beginning with the Dukes of Westminster, many owners of coal mines, or holdings such as slate quarries in the case of the Barons Penrhyn, over and above their purely agricultural holdings. As the offices they held plainly shows, they were the dominant political elite until the late nineteenth century.

Until comparatively recently, most married endogenously, that is, to women of other aristocratic families. This has been changing – although not entirely – recently, just as it has been with the wives of the two current younger Royal Princes.

In terms of education, the majority attended Eton, with Westminster School until the early nineteenth century, and Harrow and a number of other leading public school the runners up, followed by Oxford and (probably trailing) Cambridge.

Until the Second World War, a military career was the default occupation of many of the heirs to the great landed estates, and this, too, has been changing recently to "real" careers in such fields as investments and accountancy. There has plainly been an exodus from senior political positions in Parliament of the great landowners and their close relatives, so that very few members even of right-wing Tory Cabinets come from this background. This trend has accelerated since the early twentieth century. Since 1999 only ninety-two hereditary peers now have seats in the Lords. It also appears that fewer and fewer from landed backgrounds would want a political career, perhaps wisely.

Chapter 1: The Richest Landowners in the UK in 1880–95

1. Leveson-Gower – Dukes of Sutherland and Earls of Ellesmere – £212,957 p.a.

Becoming a great landowner generally entailed a family history of fortunate inheritances, fortunate marriages, and the fortunate development of one's own land. In the nineteenth century, George Granville Leveson-Gower (generally pronounced "Looson-Gore"), 1st Duke of Sutherland (1758-1833) was the most fortunate of all. In real terms, he was almost certainly the wealthiest landowner in modern British history, the lucky beneficiary of three separate sources of great wealth. He was the oldest surviving son of Sir Granville Leveson-Gower, 1st Marquess of Stafford (1721-1803), himself the grandson of the 1st Duke of Kingston-upon-Hull, and known as Earl Gower from 1754 until 1786, when he was created 1st Marquess of Stafford. Educated at Westminster School and at Christ Church, Oxford, he served in several Cabinets, as Lord Privy Seal and Lord President of the Council. He was "one of the largest landowners" (*Oxford Dictionary of National Biography*) in Staffordshire and Shropshire, and very active in developing coal mines on his properties, as well as canals, as was, even more famously, his brother-in-law Francis Egerton, 3rd Duke of Bridgewater, widely known as the "Canal Duke." The first Duke of Sutherland's mother was his father's second wife, Lady Louisa Egerton (1723-61), daughter of Scroop Egerton, 1st Duke of Bridgewater (1681-1744).

In 1883 the Duke of Sutherland owned 1,358,545 acres of land worth £141,667 p.a. in Sutherlandshire (1,176,454 acres/£56,937 p.a.); Ross-shire (149,999 acres/p.a.); Shropshire (17,495 acres/£40,418 p.a.); Staffordshire (12,744 acres/p.a.); and the North Riding (1853 acres/£2,323 p.a.), and the Earl of Ellesmere owned 13,222 acres worth £71,290 p.a. in Lancashire (10,080 acres/£55,421 p.a.); and smaller amounts in Cheshire, Northamptonshire, and Staffordshire (3,142 acres/£15,869 p.a.)

The first Duke of Sutherland (1758-1833) was born in London and was educated at Westminster School, in France, and at Christ Church, Oxford. He entered the House of Commons at the age of twenty in a family pocket borough, and, in 1788, was given a peerage while his father was still alive as Baron Gower of Stittenham. From 1790 until 1792 he served as Ambassador to France, just as the French Revolution was about to enter its most destructive phase. In 1785 he married- and became the beneficiary of his second source of great wealth- Lady Elizabeth Sutherland (1765-1839), nineteenth Countess of Sutherland, a peer in her own right, which was possible with some ancient Scottish peerages. She was the owner of more than half of the land in Sutherlandshire and a major portion of Ross-shire, amounting to well over one million acres, which her husband acquired upon their marriage. Her husband, who had no obvious Scottish ancestry, liked his new role as a Highland Chief, but "actively disliked the sound of bagpipes" (*ODNB*). In 1803, his father, the Marquess of Stafford died, and he inherited his father's vast property and wealth.

In the same year, he also acquired, by inheritance, the third source of his enormous wealth, when Francis Egerton, 3rd Duke of Bridgewater (1783-1803) died childless, leaving his vast properties to Sutherland for his lifetime but, after his death, to Sutherland's half-brother (the son of his father's third wife) Francis Leveson-Gower (later Egerton) (1800-57), who, in 1846, was created 1st Earl of Ellesmere.

The Duke of Bridgewater was the owner of land and property in Lancashire and elsewhere on a grand scale, but is more famous, as noted, as the "Canal Duke," with a penchant amounting to a near mania, for building canals. The most famous canal he constructed was the one from Manchester to Liverpool which, just before the coming of the railways, carried most of the export trade from the Cotton Capitol of England to its major commercial seaport, and was probably the most lucrative business in Britain.

These three separate inheritances made Leveson-Gower the richest man in Britain and almost certainly the richest landowner of the nineteenth century. In 1833, just before his death, he was created 1st Duke of Sutherland. His residences included Cleveland House and Stafford House (now called Lancaster House, and the scene of international conferences) in London, Trentham Hall in Staffordshire, and Dunrobin Castle in Sutherlandshire. The total value of his wealth at death is difficult to ascertain, but he left at least £1.4 million in personalty. The component of his estate probated in the Prerogative Court of Canterbury was assessed at "Upper Value," i.e., over £1 million, with another £350,000 probated in the Prerogative Court of York, and a further £74,499 in Scotland. With his land (not included in these figures), he was probably worth £7-8 million in all, quite possibly an underestimate.

Sutherland was described by Charles Grenville as the "Leviathan of Wealth," while the *Quarterly Review* stated that his was "a single estate certainly not in these days equalled in the British Empire." When Queen Victoria visited the second Duke at Sutherland House, his main London residence, a few years after his death, she noted that she had gone "from my house to his palace."

Sutherland was a pro-Reform Whig and a notable art collector who was one of the first to open his art collection to the public, but today he is famous – or infamous – for one thing, the "Highland Clearances." This was the replacement, by landowners, of common fields in northern Scotland with more profitable sheep runs, and with land tenure similar to the highly successful agriculture of England. Although the "Clearances" began before the Duke (and Duchess) of Sutherland instituted them on their Highland properties, they have been blamed for their apparently inhuman aspects. Many of the inhabitants emigrated to Canada or became tenant farmers on the Duke's properties; the effects of the "Clearances" are still deplored in many circles in Scotland.

The first Duke's eldest son George Leveson-Gower, 2nd Duke of Sutherland (1786-1861) succeeded to the property of the Marquess of Stafford and of the Countess of Sutherland, but not to the property of the Duke of Bridgewater. He was educated at Eton and Christ Church, Oxford, and became an M.P. in 1808 at twenty-two, and then succeeded to the dukedom in 1833. He left "Under £1 million" in personalty. He was married to Lady Harriet, daughter of the 6th Earl of Carlisle, and fathered many children; according to wikipedia, "A very large proportion of today's aristocracy are descended" from him. But his younger half-brother Francis (1800-57) inherited the Duke of Bridgewater's properties and, as noted, was in 1846 created the 1st Earl of Ellesmere. He was educated at Eton and Christ Church, Oxford, became an M.P. and, rather unusually, a writer and patron of the arts of note, producing the first translation into English of Goethe's *Faust,* and donating the famous Chandos Portrait of Shakespeare to the National Gallery as its first acquisition. He was also President of the Royal Geographical Society, and Ellesmere

Island in Canada is named for him. He left £410,000 in personalty at his death. The two peerages, Sutherland and Ellesmere, were then held by different persons until 1963, when they were jointly inherited by the 6th Duke of Sutherland. Another brother of the first Duke of Sutherland, Granville Leveson-Gower (1773-1846) was created 1st Earl Granville in 1833. An M.P. and long-serving Ambassador to France and Russia, he left £160,000, but owned little or no land.

George, 3rd Duke of Sutherland (1828-92) inherited the title from his father and was educated at Eton and, unusually, at King's College, London; he was a Patron of thirteen Anglican livings. In 1888, only four months after the death of his first wife – it was *de rigueur* to wait a year before remarrying – he married his mistress, Mary Caroline Blair, after her husband had died mysteriously. The Duke then tried to disinherit his legal heirs and leave all his property to her; she was found guilty of destroying relevant documents and was imprisoned for six weeks as a result. Despite this, she was given a substantial settlement by the Duke's family, and left £470,000 when she died in 1912. The third Duke left £1,275,089 in personalty when he died. In 1886, *Walford's County Families* stated that the residences of the Duke of Sutherland were Lillies Hall, Newport, Shropshire; Trentham Hall, Stoke-on-Trent, Staffordshire; Dunrobin Castle, Sutherlandshire; Tarbat, Ross-shire; and Stafford House SW; the residences of his relative the Earl of Ellesmere were listed as Worsley Hall, Manchester; the Manor House, Brackley, Northamptonshire; Stretchworth Park, Newmarket, Suffolk; and Bridgewater House SW. The third Duke's eldest son, Cromartie, 4th Duke of Sutherland (1851-1913) was educated at Eton and became a military officer. Although he became so worried about the supposed decline in the value of his estates that he moved many of his assets to Canada, he still managed to leave £1,220,906 in personalty.

The dukedom then passed to his eldest son, George, 5th Duke (1888-1963), also educated at Eton. He served as a junior minister in the Tory governments of the 1920s, and, from 1933 to 1936, was the first President of the British Film Institute. Despite the extraordinarily high levels of taxation which existed after 1914, he left £365,545, of which £185,545 was in land. He died childless, and, under the complex rules of succession determining these peerages, the Earldom of Sutherland (not the Dukedom) came to his niece, Elizabeth, 24th Countess of Sutherland (1929-2019), while the Dukedom of Sutherland was inherited by his distant relative John Sutherland Egerton, 5th Earl of Ellesmere, who, as a result, also became the 6th Duke of Sutherland (1915-2000). He was educated at Eton and at Trinity College, Cambridge, and spent four years during the Second World War as a P.O.W. in German hands. To pay death duties, he was forced to sell many of his family art works, but still remained very wealthy. He also died childless, and both titles passed to his cousin Francis, 7th Duke of Sutherland (b. 1940), who was educated at Eton and at the Royal Agricultural College, Cirencester. Like his predecessor, he was also forced to sell an Old Master owned by his family, Titian's *Diana and Actaeon*, which he sold to the National Gallery in 2008 for a cool £50 million. In 2009 the *Sunday Times Rich List* estimated his wealth at £480 million, and, in its 2020 *Rich List*, at £585 million, making him the 240th wealthiest person in Britain. In 2001, the Duke of Sutherland owned 12,000 acres of land, worth £72 million (Cahill, p. 107).

His heir, James, Marquess of Stafford (b. 1975), was educated at Eton, Edinburgh University, and at the Cass Business School. As with many of the wealthiest aristocratic landowners of the nineteenth century, the Dukes of Sutherland are still immensely wealthy, despite decades of paying taxes pegged at astronomical levels, although most have been overtaken at the very top of the wealth tree by new men and families.

2. Grosvenor – Dukes of Westminster – £228,605 p.a.

The origins of the phenomenally lucrative Grosvenor estates in London are well known. In 1677 a twelve year old (*sic*) heiress, Mary Davies married Sir Thomas Grosvenor, 3rd Bt. (1655-1700). She had inherited the Manor of Ebury, consisting of 500 acres of undeveloped land west of the settled areas of central London, and comprising small farms, market gardens, and vacant, marshy fields. Its development for housing and shops did not begin at all until the 1720s, while what is now Belgravia was not developed until the 1820s. According to John Bateman's *Great Landowners* (p. 472), "an uncle of the compiler [i.e., of John Bateman] tells him that he shot snipe on it within a mile of Belgrave Square in 1822; now [1883] the land is leased by the square foot." Sir Thomas Grosvenor, 3rd Bt. was an M.P. for Chester and a landowner in Cheshire. He built Eaton Hall in Cheshire, the Grosvenor family mansion. Mary Davies was the daughter of a scrivener (a clerk or notary) who had inherited "swampy meals" (marshlands) west of London. Clearly, they could not imagine that their descendant two hundred years later would be made a duke, on the basis of being one of the very richest men in Britain.

In 1883 the Duke of Westminster owned 19,794 acres of land outside of London worth £38,994 p.a. in Cheshire (15,138 acres/£32,387 p.a.); Flintshire (3,621 acres/£4,355 p.a.) and smaller amounts in Denbighshire and Buckinghamshire. He also owned 496 acres of land in London, with an Estimated Annual Land Value (Site Only) in 1892-95 of £189,611 p.a. and an Assessed Annual Rental Value (Real Estate) of £423,787 p.a.

The acreage and annual income of land in London was excluded from the *Return of Owners of Land* of 1872-75 and thus from John Bateman's *Great Landowners*. We do, however, have statistics from 1892-95 for the greatest London landowners, compiled by Professor Peter Lindert, and published in his article "Who Owned Victorian England?: The Debate Over Landed Wealth and Inequality," in the *Agricultural History Review*, Vol. 61 (1987), pp. 25-49. His figures are estimates made from maps drawn up at the time by the London County Council. Two different sets of estimates were made at the time, and are both given in the tables in Lindert's article, for "Assessed Annual Rental Value (Real Estate)," and for "Estimated Annual Land Value (Site Only)." For the Grosvenor estates in London, these figures were given, respectively (p. 47), as £423,787 and £189,611. No further information is given in Lindert's article about how the two figures were determined, which are only estimates based on maps and the average values found in the areas covered by the maps, not actual rental figures as in the *Return of Owners of Land*.

In this present work, the lower figure has been taken as the basis of the annual incomes of the major London landowners, although the higher figure will also be given. If the higher figure is actually the more accurate, it will be seen that in the 1890s the Duke of Westminster had an annual income (including his lands outside of London) of £462,000 a year, an incredible figure, which takes no account of his income from non-landed sources. Assuming that the total wealth value of his landed income was about thirty times its annual income – the usual figure for agricultural land, but one which may or may not be relevant for London real estate – Westminster's total landed wealth was around £13.9 million, which is actually very close to the figures (£13.5-£14 million) often given as the total value of his land and property; the higher figure thus may be accurate for the Duke of Westminster as well, presumably, as for all the other major owners of land in central London. We simply don't know. Even accepting the lower income figure as valid suggests that in the 1880s-1890s the Duke of Westminster enjoyed an annual landed income of £228,605 p.a., the highest of any British landowner after the Duke of Sutherland's lands were divided between his two sons after he died.

The Grosvenor holdings in London consisted of three components, about 100 acres in Mayfair bordering on Park Lane and Oxford Street, and 200 acres in Belgravia and Pimlico. Mayfair and Belgravia were developed as residences for the rich and for the British elite; Pimlico – much of which was sold after the death of the second Duke in 1953 to pay for death duties – was slightly more downmarket, although still very affluent. By the mid-late nineteenth century, probably most of the political and economic elite in London lived in either Mayfair or Belgravia, with their famous squares and fashionable streets, in town houses whose sites were owned by the Duke of Westminster (or other fortunate London landowners) and rented out to residents on short (typically seven or fourteen year) leases, or long-term (ninety-nine year) leases, with the renter paying an annual ground rent, but the whole of the property reverting to the Duke at the end of the lease. (A number of great aristocrats continued to live in or near St. James's Square.) The value of these properties was continually rising and rising; as critics of British landownership regularly noted, the Duke of Westminster and the other great London landowners became wealthier and wealthier without lifting a finger through investment, innovation, or sales, unlike any and every business entrepreneur. Also in contrast to any and all businesses, the value of this land would continue to grow not only through Booms but also through Depressions- unless London was suddenly deserted- with no fear of bankruptcy or indebtedness.

Much of the Grosvenor land in London was developed under Robert Grosvenor (1767-1845), the son of Richard Grosvenor, 1st Earl Grosvenor (1731-1802). He was educated at Westminster School and then at Harrow, and at Trinity College, Cambridge. He served as an M.P. from 1788 until 1802, when he was known as Viscount Belgrave (he personally gave the name "Belgravia" to that part of his London land, which was not known as that before), and then succeeded to his father's earldom. He served as a junior minister in 1789-91. In 1794 he married Lady Eleanor (1770-1846), the daughter of the first Earl of Wilton. From the mid-1820s, he employed the architect Thomas Cundy (1790-1867) and the famous builder Thomas Cubitt (1788-1855) to construct many of the houses on his property. Cubitt himself died a millionaire. He also served as Mayor of Chester in 1807-8 and rebuilt Eaton Hall near Eccleston, Cheshire as his mansion there (for which Eaton Square is named). He was given an elevation in the peerage in 1831 to become the 1st Marquess of Westminster – it is curious that he was allowed to take such a grandiose title – and was made a Knight of the Garter in 1841. Westminster was a lifelong Whig and Reformer, and was also known for his successful stable of racehorses. He left £410,000 in personalty at his death, including £60,000 in the York Prerogative Court.

The Marquess had three sons of note. The eldest, Richard, succeeded as the second Marquess. His second son, Thomas Grosvenor, later Egerton (1799-1882) was allowed to succeed by special remainder as the second Earl of Wilton, following the death of his grandfather. In 1883 the Earl of Wilton owned 9,871 acres worth £27,338 p.a., chiefly in Lancashire. He left £230,365 in personalty at his death. The Marquess's third son, Robert Grosvenor (1801-93), who was educated at Westminster School and at Christ Church, Oxford, was a Whig M.P. from 1822 until 1857, when he was created 1st Baron Ebury. He was famous as an extreme Evangelical Anglican, who in 1855 introduced into Parliament the *Sunday Trading Bill,* which would have forced shops to close on Sunday. It proved so unpopular that it was withdrawn. He left £147,048.

The 1st Marquess was succeeded by his eldest son Richard Grosvenor, 2nd Marquess of Westminster (1795-1869), who was educated at Westminster School and at Christ Church, Oxford.

He served as an M.P. from 1830 until he succeeded as a peer in 1846, and was a junior minister from 1850-1852, but made no real mark in politics. Regarded as a model landlord, he was made a Knight of the Garter in 1857. In 1819 he married Lady Elizabeth, daughter of the 1st Duke of Sutherland, thus uniting the two wealthiest aristocratic families. They had thirteen children, of whom the last to die, Lady Theodora Grosvenor (later Guest), a well-known author and benefactress, lived until 1924. He left £800,000 in personalty.

His eldest surviving son, Hugh Lupus Grosvenor (1825-99) succeeded him as the 3rd Marquess. He was educated at Eton and Balliol College, Oxford and became an M.P. at twenty-two. He married his cousin, Lady Constance Leveson-Gower. Originally opposed to the Gladstone government, he was reconciled to him and, in Gladstone's 1874 Resignation Honours, was created 1st Duke of Westminster, the last non-royal duke to be created in Britain. (Winston Churchill was allegedly offered a dukedom sometime before he retired in 1955 – he was supposedly to have become Duke of London – but declined the honour.) Like his relatives, he was famous for his racing stable, with his famous horse *Bend Or* winning the Derby in 1880. He was something of a radical, serving as President of the RSPCA and associated with Gladstone in opposing the atrocities carried out by the Turks against the Armenians. At Eaton Hall, which was rebuilt for him by Alfred Waterhouse, he installed a carillon of twenty-eight bells which sounded every quarter hour, night and day; this did not endear him to his guests. He left £594,229 in personalty, in addition to his vast holdings in London property and in land in Cheshire and elsewhere.

His younger brother Richard de Aquila Grosvenor (1837-1912), who was educated at Westminster School and at Trinity College, Cambridge, was a Liberal M.P. from 1861 until 1886, and served as Parliamentary Secretary to the Treasury (i.e., the Chief Whip) in W.E. Gladstone's 1880-85 government, probably the most important political office held by the Grosvenors in the nineteenth century. Like many other Liberal aristocrats and men of wealth, he left the Liberal Party when Gladstone advocated Home Rule for Ireland in 1886 and joined the Liberal Unionists. In 1886 he was created 1st Baron Stalbridge. Although he served as Chairman of the London and North Western Railway for many years, unlike the members of his family who were astronomically wealthy, he was relatively poor, and left only £5864 at his death. He was the grandfather of Elspeth Huxley (1907-97), the writer and broadcaster.

The first Duke of Westminster was succeeded by his grandson Hugh, 2nd Duke of Westminster (1879-1953), widely known as "Bend Or," after his grandfather's horse. He was the son of Victor, Earl Grosvenor (1853-84), who died at thirty-one, and his wife Lady Sibell (d. 1929), daughter of the 9th Earl of Scarborough. The 2nd Duke was educated at Eton, and had a distinguished war record in the Boer War and World War One. That, however, basically exhausts the list of his merits; he represented the embodiment of the worst features of the "idle rich." He owned two yachts and travelled from Eaton Hall to London on a private train, at the same time as seventeen Rolls-Royces independently brought along with what else he packed for the trip. He was married four times, and had a string of mistresses (whom he treated generously), the first of whom was Michelle "Coco" Chanel, the famous fashion designer. In politics, he was an extreme right-wing anti-semite. In 1931, disliking the political stance of his brother-in-law William Lygon, Earl Beauchamp, the Leader of the Liberal Party in the House of Lords, he "exposed [him] as a homosexual to the King and Queen," reportedly hoping "to ruin the Liberal Party through him." He then sent Beauchamp a note saying, "Dear Bugger-in-Law, You got what you deserved. Westminster." (Beauchamp died in New York in 1939. He had seven children in a conventional marriage, and is depicted as Lord Marchmain in Evelyn Waugh's *Brideshead Revisited*.)

Westminster tore down Grosvenor House on Park Lane in the mid-1920s. His addresses are given in *Who Was Who* as Bourdon House, Baker Street W., and Eaton Hall. When he died in 1953, the probate records stated that he left £10,703,656, one of the largest estates ever probated in Britain up to that time. Of that sum, £5,000,000 represented settled land (and not only personalty, as Cahill (p. 151) states). As Cahill notes, the real value of his wealth was much higher than this; we know this since his heirs paid over £14 million in death duties, more than the total alleged value of his estate. Westminster apparently had literally vast amounts in various kinds of property in Canada and South Africa, which he concealed and managed astutely. Probably the main casualty of the astronomical levels- up to 98 per cent- of death duties he actually had to pay was that he had to sell off much of his Pimlico estate, leaving him with only the ground rents of Mayfair and Belgravia for his heirs to fall back on, among his London properties. There is a biography of the second Duke by Leslie Field, *The Golden Duke of Westminster* (1983).

The second Duke had two surviving daughters but no surviving son, and the peerage next passed to his cousin William Grosvenor, 3rd Duke of Westminster (1894-1963). Sadly, he was born with brain damage, and lived in Bath with a carer. He enjoyed only the most minimal benefits of his family inheritance, and left only £15,287 at his death. He was unmarried and childless, and the title passed to another cousin (by a different father), Gerald, 4th Duke of Westminster (1907-67). He was educated at Sandhurst, and had a military career: he was severely wounded in the leg in 1944. He did serve as High Sheriff of Cheshire in 1959, but held the title for only three years. Possibly his most notable act as Duke was to tear down Waterhouse's Eaton Hall and replace it with a far smaller but more modern house. He left £5,489,000 at his death, again representing only a fraction of his real wealth. He was succeeded by his brother Robert, 5th Duke of Westminster (1910-79), who was educated at Eton, and also had a career as an army officer. Before he succeeded to the peerage, he served as Tory M.P. for Fermanagh and South Tyrone (the family owned land in Northern Ireland, as well as elsewhere in Britain) from 1955 until 1964, and was responsible for the Adoption Act of 1964. He was succeeded by his son Gerald, 6th Duke of Westminster (1951-2016), who was educated at Harrow and at Sandhurst, served as a major-general in the Army, and was a businessman who tremendously expanded the enterprises in which the family was engaged. He was also notable for the range of charities and good causes with which he was involved. He was also regarded, throughout his time as Duke, as one of the very richest men in Britain. In the first edition of the *Sunday Times Rich List*, in 1989, he was stated to be the second richest man in the country, with a fortune of £3.2 billion, behind only the Queen. In the last *Rich List* before his death, in 2016, he was stated to be worth £9.35 billion, the sixth richest person in the UK. He actually left the remarkable sum of £616,400,000 for probate.

His unexpected death at sixty-five brought the title to his son Hugh, 7th Duke of Westminster (b. 1991), who is descended from the Romanovs via his mother, and was educated at Mostyn House School; Ellesmere College; and at Newcastle University, where he obtained a Management degree. In the 2020 *Rich List*, his wealth was put at £10,295,000,000, the tenth largest private fortune in the UK, and by far the largest held by an old-line landed aristocrat, with the Earl Cadogan's £6.8 billion fortune being the next largest, in eighteenth place, amidst the plethora of internet tycoons and former Russians. The present Duke was also the richest person in the world aged under thirty. The Dukes of Westminster have also added very considerably to their holdings of agricultural land, in 2001 owning, according to Kevin Cahill, no less than 129,300 acres of land, far more than in 1883. Although the Duke of Bedford had a higher income in the 1880-99 period than the Duke of Westminster, Westminster has been ranked here above Bedford because he had certainly (as it were) overtaken him in the twentieth century.

3. Russell – Dukes of Bedford – £265,379 p.a.

The Dukes of Bedford owe their rise into the aristocracy to Sir John Russell (c. 1485-1565), a major advisor to Kings Henry VIII and Edward VI. As a reward, he was given the area around Covent Garden in London and lands near Tiverton in Devon. He was created Baron Russell in 1539 and Earl of Bedford in 1551. His descendant, William, 5th Earl of Bedford (1616-1700) made the right political choices and supported the House of Orange during and after the Glorious Revolution, and in 1694 was created 1st Duke of Bedford and Marquess of Tavistock, the courtesy title by which his heir has been known ever since. He also benefitted by inheriting more land in central London, in what is now Bloomsbury, from the Wriothesley family, Earls of Southampton, of whom the 3rd Earl (1573-1624) was the dedicatee of Shakespeare's two long poems. The mother of the 1st Duke of Bedford, Lady Catherine Brydges, daughter of Giles, 3rd Baron Chandos.

In 1883 the Duke of Bedford owned 86,335 acres worth £141,793 p.a., outside of London, in Bedfordshire (32,269 acres/£45,687 p.a.); Devonshire (22,607 acres/£45,907 p.a.); Cambridgeshire (18,800 acres/ £34,325 p.a.); Northamptonshire (3,414 acres/£4,049 p.a.), and smaller amounts of land in Dorset, Buckinghamshire, Huntingdonshire, Cornwall, Hampshire, Hertfordshire, and Lincolnshire. In London, in 1892-95 he owned 249 acres with an Assessed Rental Value (Real Estate) of £339,458 and an Estimated Annual Land Value (Site Only) of £123,586.

Although the income figure credited above to the Duke of Bedford is slightly larger than that credited to the Duke Of Westminster, Westminster was almost certainly wealthier and has been ranked second, ahead of Bedford.

The Duke was educated at Magdalen College, Oxford. The title then went through several holders down the generations, when it was inherited by Francis Russell, 5th Duke of Bedford (1765-1802), who was the son of the Marquess of Tavistock (1739-67), and the grandson of the fourth Duke. His mother was Lady Elizabeth (1739-68), daughter of William Keppel, 2nd Earl of Albermarle. Educated at Westminster School and at Trinity College, Cambridge, he was a noted agricultural improver, and became known for his model farms. More importantly, he developed the Bloomsbury site owned by his family in central London, using James Burton and Thomas Cubitt to construct Bloomsbury Square, Russell Square, Tavistock Square, and the other housing developments of the area. The elites and very wealthy did not flock to these houses as they did to the Duke of Westminster's similar developments in Mayfair and Belgravia, but they proved very lucrative. He also further increased the stateliness of Woburn Abbey in Bedfordshire, his palatial country house. Like many members of his family, his was, perhaps surprisingly, a political radical and a supporter of Charles James Fox. The 5th Duke had two illegitimate children, but no legitimate male heir, and at his death the title passed to his brother John Russell, 6th Duke of Bedford (1766-1839).

The 6th Duke of Bedford was educated at Westminster School and served as an M.P. from 1790 until he succeeded to the title in 1802. He continued his father's political stance as a radical Foxite Whig, and was married twice. With his first wife, whom he married in 1786, (Hon.) Georgiana Byng (c. 1768-1801), daughter of the 4th Baron Torrington, he had three sons. In 1803 he remarried Lady Georgiana (1781-1853), the daughter of the 4th Duke of Gordon, he had five sons and five daughters. Her sons included an admiral, a general, and an Anglican vicar. His second wife was noted as a patroness of the arts, and she had what has been described as a "longstanding liaison" with Sir Edwin Landseer, the artist.

The Duke's sons with his first wife are worthy of note. His eldest son Francis (1788-1861) succeeded as the 7th Duke of Bedford. His second son, Lord George William Russell (1710-1846), has an entry in the *ODNB* as an "army officer and diplomatist," and served as Ambassador to Prussia from 1835 till 1841. His third son became the most famous of all, Lord John Russell (1792-1878), one of the most important political figures in nineteenth century Britain, who introduced the Great Reform Act into Parliament, and served as Whig-Liberal Prime Minister from 1846-52 and in 1865-6. In 1861 he was created 1st Earl Russell. His eldest son, known as Viscount Amberley, predeceased him in 1876; his wife (1842-74) also died young. Amberley was the father of the world-famous philosopher and political activist Bertrand Russell (1872-1970), later 3rd Earl Russell, who won the Nobel Prize in Literature in 1950. Bertrand Russell's maternal grandmother, who helped to raise him, Henrietta Dillon-Lee, Baroness Stanley of Alderley, was, when she was a young woman, very friendly with the widow of the "Young Pretender," that is, the widow of "Bonnie Prince Charlie," Charles Edward Stuart, who invaded England in 1745. There was thus a direct connection, between two persons who knew each other, between the last gasp of the Reformation in England and anti-Vietnam War agitation in the 1960s.

The 6th Duke of Bedford left £250,000 in personalty when he died. He was succeeded by his son Francis, 7th Duke of Bedford (1788-1861), who was also educated at Westminster School and at Trinity College, Cambridge. He sat in the Commons from 1809 until he was given a peerage in his own right at Baron Howland of Streatham in 1833. He left £600,000 in personalty at his death, and was succeeded by his son William, 8th Duke of Bedford (1809-72, left £600,000 in personalty), educated at Eton and Christ Church, Oxford and also an M.P., from 1832 to 1841. He died unmarried, and was succeeded by his cousin, Francis, 9th Duke of Bedford (1819-91), who was an officer in the Scots Guards and served as Lord-Lieutenant of Bedfordshire. He was also an M.P., from 1847 until 1872, was Patron of 25 Livings, and was President of the Royal Agricultural Society. In 1844, he married Lady Elizabeth Sackville-West, daughter of the 5th Earl De la Warr. She served as Mistress of the Robes to Queen Victoria. According to this Duke's entry in the *ODNB*, "over £1 million was added to the ducal revenues in his time by fines exacted on the leases falling due upon his Bloomsbury estate." Like his forebears he was a Liberal, but, like very many in the landed aristocracy, became a Liberal Unionist in 1886 in protest against Gladstone's Irish Home Rule Bill. In 1891 he committed suicide by shooting himself through the heart, while "temporarily insane," at his residence at 81 Eaton Square. This was presumably not because of financial concerns, since he left £230,970 in personalty, and had residences at Woburn Abbey; at Oakley House, Bedford; at Endsleigh House in Tavistock; at Norris Castle at East Cowes; and at his Mayfair townhouse. It does perhaps suggest that the Bedfords became prone to depression and unfortunate behaviour, as will be seen below.

He was succeeded by his eldest son George, 10th Duke of Bedford (1852-93), educated at Balliol College, Oxford, and also a Liberal M.P., from 1873 to 1885. In 1876 he married Lady Adeline, daughter of Charles, 3rd Earl Somers, but left no legitimate children, although he had an illegitimate daughter by an Indian woman. He died of diabetes at only forty-one, leaving £335,603 in personalty. He was succeeded by his brother Herbrand, 11th Duke of Bedford (1858-1940), who was educated at home and at Balliol College, Oxford. He served from 1884 until 1888 as Aide-de-

Camp to the Viceroy of India, and, in 1888, married Mary DuCurroy (1865-1937), the daughter of (Revd.) Walter Tribe, Archdeacon of Lahore. He was offered a junior ministerial position by Lord Salisbury in 1900, but declined, noting that he did not wish to participate in Westminster politics. But he did serve as Lord Lieutenant of Middlesex from 1898 until 1926 and also served as the first Mayor of Holborn in 1900-01. As well, he was Chairman of the Bedfordshire County Council from 1895 until 1928. His real interest lay in a range of zoological and other natural history bodies. He was President of the Zoological Society from 1899 until 1936, and had a well-known and important private zoo at Woburn, his country house. He built the aquarium at the London Zoo, and donated the only known living specimens of Przheralsky's Horse, the only known wild horse, to the London Zoo, as well as the only known surviving specimen of Pére David's Deer. He opened the Whipsnade Zoo in 1931 to breed wild animals. He was also President of the Imperial Cancer Research Fund from 1910-36, and was made a K.G. in 1902. His wife, Mary Tribe, most unusually became a nurse and a surgeon's assistant, and, remarkably, gained a pilot's license in 1933, becoming known as the "Flying Duchess." She was made a D.B.E. in 1928. but died in a plane crash in 1937. When the Duke died in 1940, he left £4,651,371, of which £3,239,130 was in settled land. This was the largest estate left in Britain in the decade 1940-49. The deficiencies of his character are noted below.

In 1913 he agreed to sell the Covent Garden estate for £2 million to the business speculator Harry Mallaby-Deeley. It is unclear why he did this. (There has always been a much-repeated rumour that the Duke invested this money in Imperial Czarist bonds, and lost everything four years later; this is almost certainly untrue). In the 1920s, and possibly before, his houses and apartments in Bloomsbury became the favoured residences of the "Bloomsbury Group" of bohemian and unorthodox writers, artists, and intellectuals, which included Virginia Woolf, Lytton Strachey, E. M. Forster, and John Maynard Keynes. Many of its male members had graduated from Cambridge. Lytton Strachey lived at 51 Gordon Square, where a plaque now commemorates the fact that this and the immediate surrounding area, was their home territory. Most came from upper middle class, or even elite, backgrounds, but found Mayfair and Belgravia highly inappropriate. During the 1920s, the term "Bloomsbury" became a metonymy for nonconformist writers and artists leading an unorthodox lifestyle in London, similar to the meaning connoted by "Greenwich Village" in New York. By the 1930s, the term "Hampstead," with its connotation of earnest social democrats and political radicals, rather replaced "Bloomsbury" in the popular mind, although the fame of the "Bloomsbury Group" has ensured that something of its renown still remain, such as in Bloomsbury Publishing, whose premises are in Bedford Square. The astronomical cost of housing in central London means, however, that few struggling writers, artists, or actors can today afford to live there. Whether the Duke of Bedford encouraged this kind of fame coming to his property – or was even more than vaguely aware of it – is unclear.

The 11th Duke was succeeded by his only son Hastings William Sackville, 12th Duke of Bedford (1888-1953), who was educated at Eton and Balliol College, Oxford. He experienced what has been described as a "lonely" childhood; his *ODNB* entry states that his father was "forbidding, aloof, and autocratic," while his mother, the "Flying Duchess," was "deaf, short-tempered, and dismissive of anything short of perfection." At Oxford (where he graduated with a Fourth in History) he became a strong and lifelong Evangelical Christian. In 1912, he briefly joined the Middlesex Regiment, but soon resigned, and refused to rejoin it at the start of the First World War. As a result, his father disinherited him, and the two did not speak for twenty years. During that War, he became a helper at a camp near Portsmouth, his bad eyesight keeping him out of the Army. After the War he had a highly controversial political career, becoming a member of several extreme right-wing and pro-fascist parties and movements. He became President of the openly anti-semitic "British People's Party," and met with Oswald Mosley and other right-wing extremists. In June 1942, in a speech in the House of Lords, he attacked Winston Churchill and "the attempt by moneylending financiers and big business monopolists to destroy the relatively sane financial system of the Axis Powers." Made in wartime, at a time when Britain's back was still against the wall, his remarks led to demands for his internment – if, indeed, his remarks were not actually treasonous – but he, like the Duke of Westminster and other extreme right-wing aristocrats, was left alone by the Churchill government. His son later stated that "My father was the loneliest man I have ever known," and that he was "incapable of giving or receiving love," and was "utterly self-centred and opinionated." His wife Louisa (1893-1960), the daughter of Robert Whitwell, an Oxford don, separated from him in 1935, and brought a well-publicised lawsuit in which she sued him for the restoration of conjugal rights, describing the Duke as "the most cold, mean, and conceited person" she had known. In 1939 he disinherited his son and heir following the son's unsuitable marriage. In 1953 the Duke died of gunshot wounds, aged sixty-four, which were stated by the Coroner to be "self-inflicted," but which his son believed was suicide. The Duke was still enormously wealthy, leaving £5,792,253, of which £4,990,000 was in settled land, one of the very largest estates left in Britain in the 1950s. This figure – like that for the estate of the second Duke of Westminster, who also died in 1953 – is certainly an understatement of his actual wealthy, since his heirs had to pay £14 million in death duties, suggesting that he was actually worth £15-£20 million or even more.

His son and successor, John, 13th Duke of Bedford (1917-2002), was of a totally different character, and became well-known to the general public. He was educated by "tutors and maids" (*ODNB*) and later stated that he didn't know that his father was the millionaire heir to a dukedom. His father gave him almost nothing. In 1938 his first job was as a rent collector in Stepney. His father then cut him off entirely when he married an older woman, Clare Holloway (1903-45), the divorced wife of an army officer. He joined the Coldstream Guards, but was invalided out in 1940, and worked as a reporter on the *Daily Telegraph*. In 1953 he became the 13th Duke of Bedford, and was faced with paying off the colossal death duties levied on his father's estate. Two years later, he opened the family stately home, Woburn Abbey, to tourists and, with the help of Jimmy Chipperfield, of Chipperfield's Circus, opened Woburn Safari Park and Zoo, the first of its kind. His mass-market experiment paid off, Woburn attracting half a million paying visitors a year. He was married twice more, the third time, in 1960, to the divorced French television producer Nicole Milinaire. The Duke frequently appeared on television and wrote a (ghosted) well-known memoir, *A Silver-Plated Spoon* (1959) and other works. He and his wife became tax exiles in Monaco, and later lived in Santa Fe, New Mexico, where he died. A greater contrast with his father is difficult to imagine.

There have been two more Dukes of Bedford since then, (Henry) Robin Ian, 14th Duke (1940-2003), and Andrew, 15th Duke (b. 1962). Robin held the title for only seven months, was a stockbroker, and became known as the presenter of the BBC television show *Country House*. His son Andrew, educated at Harrow and Harvard, still retains Woburn Abbey which continues to hold one of the greatest art collections in private hands. In 2017 he was said to be worth £685 million, and still owns 185 buildings in Bloomsbury, many of which are rented to London University. In the 2020 *Sunday Times Rich List,* the present Duke was said to be worth £750 million, the 188th largest fortune in the UK. In 2001 he was credited by Kevin Cahill with owning 23,020 acres of land. His family is another example of an old, senior aristocratic dynasty which has prospered in today's world, although not perhaps at the very top.

4. (Montagu Douglas) Scott, Dukes of Buccleuch and Queensberry – £231,163 p.a.

One of the very wealthiest landed aristocrats, the Dukes of Buccleuch (generally pronounced "Ba-clue") and Queensberry was of royal descent, and combined great landed wealth in both Scotland and England.

In 1883 the Duke of Buccleuch and Queensberry owned 406,108 acres worth £217,163 p.a. in Dumfriesshire (254,179 acres/£95,239 p.a.); Roxburghshire (104,461 acres/£39,457 p.a.); Selkirk (60,428 acres/£19,828 p.a.); Northamptonshire (17,965 acres/£26,531 p.a.); Midlothian (3,436 acres/£16,328 p.a.); Warwickshire (6,881 acres/ £12,567 p.a.), and seven other counties, including Surrey (7 acres/£708 p.a.). In addition, he received an annual income of £4091 from "minerals," and another £10,601 p.a. from Granton Harbour in Edinburgh.

All of the recent holders of this title were educated in England, almost always at Eton and Oxford, indicative of how the traditional Scottish aristocracy became anglicised into the English aristocracy. Anna Scott (1651-1732), the daughter of Francis Scott, 2nd Earl of Buccleuch, was created a duchess in 1663; her title was confirmed in 1687. Making a woman a duchess in her own right was very unusual, and was the result of a complex series of manoeuvrings by her family as she was the only heiress to a great Scottish estate. In 1665 she married James Crofts (1649-85), the illegitimate son of King Charles II and Lucy Walter, who in 1663 was created 1st Duke of Monmouth. When he married the Duchess of Buccleuch, he changed his surname to "Scott," her surname. As an illegitimate son he was ineligible to succeed to the Throne, which passed to Charles II's brother James II, a Roman Catholic. In 1685 Monmouth launched "Monmouth's Rebellion," aimed at deposing James II and placing himself on the Throne as a Protestant King. It was unsuccessful, and Monmouth was executed. Three years later, William III of Orange launched a successful invasion of England, deposed James II and placed himself and his wife Mary II on the Throne as Protestant monarchs. Had Monmouth succeeded in his rebellion, the Royal Family might today be named "Scott" rather than "Windsor."

Despite his treason, his widow was confirmed as Duchess of Buccleuch in 1687; she married, secondly, the 3rd Baron Cornwallis. The dukedom passed to her grandson Francis Scott, 2nd Duke of Buccleuch (1695-1751), the son of the Earl of Dalkeith. The second Duke was educated at Eton, received a D.C.L. degree from Oxford, and was a Fellow of the Royal Society, all indicating his anglicised background. The title now passed to Henry Scott, 3rd Duke of Buccleuch and also 5th Duke of Queensberry (1746-1812), the grandson of the previous Duke. He was educated at Eton, but was more closely associated with Scotland than some of his predecessors. It was during his time as Duke that the Buccleuchs became very wealthy. In 1767 he married Lady Elizabeth Montagu, the daughter of George, 1st Duke of Montagu, and, in 1810, two years prior to his death, he inherited much of the wealth of his second cousin once removed, William Douglas, 4th Duke of Queensberry (1725-1810), known as "Old Q" and for his many mistresses and habitual gambling. Queensberry was one of the very richest men in Britain, leaving "Upper Value" (i.e., above £1 million) in personalty when he died. He was unmarried, and left his vast wealth both to the Duke of Buccleuch (who inherited his dukedom) and to another relative, the Earl of Wemyss.

The 3rd Duke of Buccleuch was more closely connected with Scotland than some other holders of the title, serving as a Governor of the Royal Bank of Scotland from 1777-1812 (Adam Smith had been his tutor), and as a Joint Founder of the Royal Society of Edinburgh. He held the posts of Lord Lieutenants of both Haddingtonshire and Midlothian, and was a lifelong friend of Sir Walter Scott. Like other holders of his title, his chief stately home was Dalkeith Palace (*sic* – a Palace, not merely a House) in Midlothian, in which the family resided until 1914.

He was succeeded for only seven years by his son Charles William, 4th Duke of Buccleuch and 6th Duke of Queensberry (1772-1819), who was educated at Eton and Christ Church, Oxford, and served as an M.P. from 1793 until 1807, when he was created (in his father's lifetime) Baron Scott of Tyndale, enabling him to sit in the Lords. He was a noted cricketer and also apparently a poet of note, who in 1813 was offered the Poet Laureateship, which he declined, and which went instead to Robert Southey. He was succeeded for sixty-five years by his son Walter Francis, 5th Duke of Buccleuch and 7th Duke of Queensberry (1806-84), who was educated at Eton and St. John's College, Cambridge. He had a significant political career, and held the posts of Lord Privy Seal from 1842-6 and of Lord President of the Council in 1846 in Sir Robert Peel's Tory government, but remained a Conservative and did not agree with Peel's move towards the Whig/Liberals. The 5th Duke was very wealthy, leaving £475,000 in personalty in England and £435,319 in personalty in Scotland, a total of £910,369. His son and successor, William, 6th Duke of Buccleuch and 8th Duke of Queensberry (1831-1914), whose mother was Lady Charlotte Thynne, daughter of the 2nd Marquess of Bath, was educated at Eton and Christ Church, Oxford, and served in the House of Commons (as the "Earl of Dalkeith") in 1853-68 and 1874-80 as a Conservative M.P. In 1886, his residences were given in one reference work, apart from Dalkeith, as Montagu House, Richmond, Surrey; Boughton Hall, Kettering; Drumlanrig Castle, Thornhill, Dumfriesshire; The Lodge, Langholm, Dumfriesshire; Bowhill, Selkirk; and Montagu House, Whitehall, W., which must have been rather confusing as to just where the Duke and his family might be. He was also very wealthy, leaving £1,159,442 in Scotland and £205,626 in England, a total of £1,365,068.

His heir – becoming heir to the dukedom after his elder brother was killed in a hunting accident – was John, 7th Duke of Buccleuch and 9th Duke of Queensberry (1864-1935). Originally a Royal Navy officer, he served as a Conservative M.P. from 1895 until 1905. In 1893 he married Lady Margaret, daughter of the 4th Earl of Bradford. The best known of his many children was his daughter Lady Alice (1901-2004 – she lived to be 103), who married Prince Henry, Duke of Gloucester (1900-74), the third son of King George V (who served as Governor-General of Australia from 1945-47), and thus married into the Royal Family. The 7th Duke left £551,295 when he died. His son Walter, 8th Duke of Buccleuch and 10th Duke of Queensberry (1894-1973), was educated at Eton and Christ Church, Oxford, and was a military officer as well as a Conservative M.P. from 1923-35, when he succeeded to the title. As was the case with other senior landed aristocrats, he was pro-Nazi and pro-Appeasement, and actually attended Hitler's 50th Birthday celebrations in Germany, which must have embarrassed his Royal relatives.

His son and heir, Walter, 9th Duke of Buccleuch and 11th Duke of Queensberry (1923-2007), was educated at Christ Church, Oxford, served as a Conservative M.P., was M.P. for Edinburgh North from 1960-73, and held office as a junior minister in 1961-64. In his lifetime, he was known as the largest private landowner in Britain, said to own 280,000 acres. His son, the 10th Duke of Buccleuch and 12th Duke of Queensberry (b. 1954), was educated at Eton and Oxford, and was a Page of Honour to the Queen from 1967-73. He has served as President of the National Trust of Scotland, and as Deputy Chairman of ITV. He is Lord Lieutenant of Roxburghshire, and was Lord High Commissioner to the General Assembly of the Church of Scotland in 2018-2019. He still owns a remarkable art collection. In the 2020 *Sunday Times Rich List,* he was credited with being worth £253 million, the 508th wealthiest person in the UK. In 2001, Kevin Cahill estimated his landholding as 270,700 acres.

5. Cavendish – Dukes of Devonshire £180,750 p.a.

One of the most famous and politically significant of the great landed aristocratic dynasties, the family of Cavendish, Dukes of Devonshire began their upward ascent in the fourteenth century, and received an earldom (as 1st Earl of Devonshire) in 1618. They were made dukes in 1694, for – as in many other cases – strongly supporting William III and Mary II against James II during the "Glorious Revolution." One curious oddity of their title is that, although Dukes of Devonshire, they do not own a single acre of land in that county, let alone enough to have taken it as their title. One theory is that the scribe drawing up their patent of nobility wrote "Devonshire" instead of "Derbyshire," although there has been an Earl of Derby since the twelfth century. In any case, they became one of the greatest of all landed families, and were close to the centres of power for many centuries.

In 1883 the Duke of Devonshire owned 198,572 acres worth £180,750 p.a., in Derbyshire (89,462 acres/ £89,557 p.a.); the West Riding, Yorkshire (19,239 acres/ £16,718 p.a.); Lancashire (12,681 acres/£12,494 p.a.); Sussex (11,062 acres/£14,881 p.a.); Co. Cork (32,550 acres/£19,326 p.a.); Co. Waterford (27,483 acres/£15,000 p.a.), and smaller amounts of land in Somerset, Lincolnshire; Cumberland; Middlesex (524 acres/£3,079 p.a.); Nottinghamshire; Staffordshire; Cheshire; and Co. Tipperary.

By the late eighteenth century, William, 5th Duke of Devonshire (1748-1811) was one of the most significant figures in the aristocratic world. The son of William, 4th Duke of Devonshire (1720-64), who served as Prime Minister in 1756-7, and Lady Charlotte Boyle, daughter of Richard Boyle, 3rd Earl of Burlington and the 6th Baroness Clifford, he did not attend a public school, but inherited the dukedom in 1764, when his annual landed income was estimated at £36,000 p.a. He owned seven aristocratic residences – Chatsworth and Hardwick hall in Derbyshire; Lismore Castle in Co. Waterford; Londesborough House and Bolton Abbey in Yorkshire; Chiswick House, Middlesex; and Devonshire House and Burlington House in Piccadilly. By the end of his life, his annual income had risen, according to one source, to £125,000 p.a. He served as Lord High Treasurer of Ireland and as Lord Lieutenant of Derbyshire, but declined Cabinet posts. He is best remembered for his first wife, Lady Georgiana Spencer (1757-1806), the daughter of John, 1st Earl Spencer, who he married in 1774. She was and is well-known, and has been the subject of books and films like *The Duchess.* She is famous for her friendship with famous artists like Gainsborough and Reynolds, and also for her circle of demi-monde figures, the "Devonshire House Set," satirized in Sheridan's *School* for *Scandal.* She is said to have invented women's "hair towers," and the "picture hats" depicted in so many aristocratic portraits, and had an important unofficial role in politics. In 1809, after her death, the Duke married Lady Elizabeth Hervey (1757-1824), daughter of the 4th Earl of Bristol. She had already lived in a *menage à trois* with the Duke and the Duchess. The Duke had several illegitimate children, including two by his second wife before his first wife's death, among them (Admiral) Sir Augustus Clifford, 1st Bt. (1788-1877). He is also known for developing the town of Buxton. He left £300,000 in personalty at his death, but also large debts.

He was succeeded by his son by Lady Georgiana, William, 6th Duke of Devonshire (1790-1858), who was born in Paris, where his father was briefly Ambassador, and was educated at Harrow and Trinity College, Cambridge. He inherited the vast wealth of the dukedom when he was twenty-one. He never married, and was known as the "Bachelor Duke." Like most of his family before 1886, he was pro-Whig, and served as Lord Chamberlain of the Household in 1827-28 and 1830-34. He is best remembered as employing Joseph Paxton as head gardener at Chatsworth, and for building the remarkable 277-foot-long glass-walled conservatory there, It was heated by coal fires to produce near-tropical temperatures, and was the model for the Crystal Palace in London and, indeed, for a component of modern architecture, as well as for all heated conservatories. He helped to establish the Royal Botanic Gardens at Kew and was President of the Royal Horticultural Society from 1838 until his death. The "Cavendish banana" is named for him. He left £500,000 in personalty.

As he was unmarried, the title and property passed to a relative, William, 7th Duke of Devonshire (1808-91), the grandson of the 4th Duke of Devonshire; his father, Lord William Cavendish, was killed in a carriage accident in 1812. The 7th Duke was educated at Eton and Trinity College, Cambridge, and showed considerable intelligence, graduating as Second Wrangler and Smith's Prizeman in Mathematics. In 1829 he married (Hon.) Blanche (1812-40), daughter of George, 6th Earl of Carlisle. Although he served as an M.P. from 1829-34, and was Lord Lieutenant of Lancashire and of Derbyshire, he never held a Cabinet post, but is remembered for his academic and scientific role. He endowed the famous Cavendish Laboratory at Cambridge, and also endowed the Cavendish Professorship of Physics at Cambridge, whose holders have included a succession of scientific luminaries. The first five holders of this Professorship were James Clerk Maxwell, Lord Rayleigh, J.J. Thompson, Ernest Rutherford, and W.L. Bragg, the last four of whom won the Nobel Prize. The Duke served as Chancellor of Cambridge University (1861-91), London University (1836-56), and the Victoria University of Manchester (1880-91), and was President of the Royal Agricultural Society. He was also the Patron of forty livings in the Anglican Church. He left £1,782,239 in personalty at his death.

He was succeeded by his son Spencer Compton Cavendish, 8th Duke of Devonshire (1833-1908), in terms of political service the best-known member of the Cavendish family in modern times. He was educated at Trinity College, Cambridge, and served in the Commons from 1857 until he inherited the dukedom in 1891. In the Commons he was known by his courtesy title, the Marquess of Hartington, and is usually known by this name in political histories. He held a variety of Cabinet posts, including Chief Secretary for Ireland (1871-74), Secretary of State for India (1880-82), Secretary for War (1882-85), and Lord President of the Council (1895-1903). Originally a Whig/Liberal, like other members of his family, he served as Leader of the Liberal Party in the House of Commons from 1875-80, and was asked by the Queen to become Liberal Prime Minister in 1880, but had to give way to Gladstone. In 1886, like many other Liberal aristocrats, he quit the Liberal Party in opposition to Gladstone's Irish Home Rule proposals, and became Leader of the newly-formed Liberal Unionist Party from 1886-1903. One reason for his dislike of Gladstone's Irish policies probably stemmed from the fact that his younger brother, Lord Frederick Cavendish (1838-82), Chief Secretary for Ireland, was assassinated by Fenian extremists in Phoenix Park, Dublin, in 1882. He was also blamed for the death of General Charles Gordon in Khartoum in 1885. From 1895 until 1903 he served as Lord President of the Council under Lord Salisbury, the Conservative Party leader, but opposed Joseph Chamberlain's proposals for

Tariff Reform in 1903. Hartington did not marry until 1892, when he was fifty-nine. He then married Louisa, widow of the 7th Duke of Manchester. For many years he lived with his mistress, Catherine "Skittles" Walters. He was also very wealthy, leaving £1,164,961 in personalty, as well as vast amounts of land.

The title then came to Victor, 9th Duke of Devonshire (1868-1938), the son of the 8th Duke's younger brother Lord Edward Cavendish. He was educated at Eton and Trinity College, Cambridge, and served as an M.P. from 1891 to 1908, when he succeeded his uncle. In the Commons, he was known as Lord Victor Cavendish. He served in a variety of Government posts, including Secretary of State for the Colonies in 1922-24 (he was the last Duke to serve in a British Cabinet, although some have served as junior ministers). From 1916 until 1921 he served as Governor-General of Canada, and was apparently regarded as a success in the post. In 1892 he married Lady Evelyn FitzMaurice (1870-1960), daughter of Henry, 5th Marquess of Lansdowne, also a major politician of that time. They had two sons and six daughters. In 1920, their daughter Lady Dorothy Cavendish (1900-66) married Harold Macmillan (1894-1986), the future Prime Minister. After her death she became well-known for her lengthy affair with Robert Boothby, another Conservative politician and a truly shady character, to whom, remarkably, Macmillan gave a life peerage in 1958.

The Duke's son Lord Charles Cavendish (1896-1981) married – again remarkably – Adele Astaire (1896-1981), the dancer and actress sister of Fred Astaire. The 9th Duke was also faced with vastly higher rates of death duties and lower revenues from his agricultural lands. He sold many priceless manuscripts and rare books owned by the family to Henry Huntington, the California millionaire, including several Shakespeare First Folios and rare Quartos. In 1920, Devonshire House, the family's famous mansion of Piccadilly, was vacated, and the building was demolished and replaced by an office bloc in 1924. The 9th Duke left only £112,209 when he died, although it is unclear if this includes the value of his land. The family remained and remains very wealthy, although the kind of princely lifestyle lived by Dukes before 1914 is now impossible, and probably undesirable.

His son and successor, Edward, 10th Duke of Devonshire (1895-1950), was also educated at Eton and Trinity College, Cambridge and served as an M.P. from 1923 until he inherited the title in 1938. He was a career army officer, serving as a captain in World War One, and retiring as a Lieutenant-Colonel in 1935. He served as a junior minister in Churchill's Wartime government, and was a company director after the War. In 1817 he married Lady Mary Gascoyne-Cecil, the granddaughter of Lord Salisbury the Prime Minister. The 10th Duke died at only fifty-five. His eldest son, William Cavendish, Marquess of Hartington (1917-44) was, shortly before his death, married to Kathleen Kennedy, the daughter of Joseph Kennedy, American Ambassador to Britain and the sister of the future President John F. Kennedy. In September 1944, as an officer in the British Army, Lord Hartington was shot dead by a German sniper during the Allied campaign in Belgium, aged twenty-six. The 10th Duke left £796.473 when he died, although, like many of his landed contemporaries, he was apparently worth far more, as the family had to pay death duties estimated at £7 million, requiring the sale of Old Master artworks and agricultural land.

His younger son, Andrew, 11th Duke of Devonshire (1920-2004) was also educated at Eton and Trinity College, Cambridge and was married to Deborah Mitford (1920-2014), one of the "Mitford Sisters." He had an unusual political career, having held government office as a Minister of State from 1960-64, appointed by his uncle Harold Macmillan, although he later joined the

Social Democratic Party, and, still later, the United Kingdom Independence Party (UKIP). He served as a captain during the Second World War and was noted as a racehorse owner and art collector. The family had evidently recovered much of his wealth, and he was ranked as the seventy-third richest man in Britain on the 2004 *Sunday Times Rich List*. The present duke is Peregrine, 12th Duke of Devonshire (b. 1944). He was educated at Eton and Exeter College, Oxford. He served as Chairman of the Ascot racecourse from 1998 till 2008, and was a Trustee of the Wallace Collection. The Cavendishes, like many old aristocratic families, had recovered much of its wealth in the astronomic boom in land prices and lower rates of taxation, in the 2020 *Sunday Time Rich List* the Duke was ranked as the 161st richest man in the UK, said to be worth no less than £895 million.

6. Percy – Dukes of Northumberland – £176,048 p.a.

Although the Dukes of Northumberland, among the greatest landowners in the north of England, have the surname of "Percy," a time-honoured name among major aristocrats in the Middle Ages and early modern period, the current family has only a remote connection with the ancient Percies. The most famous member of the former aristocratic family was probably Sir Henry Percy, depicted as "Harry Hotspur" in Shakespeare's *Henry IV Part I*. The present dukedom dates only from 1766, when it was created for the third time by King George III for Sir Hugh Smithson, 4th Bt. (1714-86). In 1750 he had changed his surname to "Percy," having married, in 1740, the daughter of Algernon Seymour, 7th Duke of Somerset (1684-1750), the son of Lady Elizabeth Percy (1667-1722), the last surviving child of Joscelyn Percy, 11th Earl of Northumberland (1644-70), last of the ancient Percy aristocrats.

Thus, although his surname became "Percy," the first Duke of Northumberland of the present creation was not a blood relative of his Medieval namesakes. The first Duke was also created Earl of Egremont and Baron Lovaine, and his second son Earl of Beverley. A closer inspection of his background shows that he was the son of one Langdale Smithson (d.c. 1682), whose grandfather was a haberdasher in Cheapside in London, who bought a country estate and obtained a baronetcy in 1663 for supporting Charles II in the Civil War. The first Duke inherited the baronetcy from his grandfather. He had the good fortune to inherit more property from various cousins, and became an M.P. He then hit the jackpot bigtime by, as noted, marrying the heiress to the vast Percy property, now without a male heir, became a Royal favourite, was made Lord Lieutenant of Northumberland and a Knight of the Garter, and raised the Percy income from £8,000 p.a.to £50,000 p.a. by astute investment in coal mines. The fact that he controlled seven seats in Parliament also eased his upward ascent, and he held a variety of government posts, such as Lord Lieutenant of Ireland from 1763 to 1765. Curiously enough, his original name of "Smithson" is today arguably better known than his later name of "Percy," as his illegitimate son James Smithson (1764-1829) founded, in his will, the world-famous Smithsonian Institution in Washington D.C.

In 1883 the Duke of Northumberland owned 186,397 acres worth £176,048 p.a., in Northumberland (181,616 acres/£161,874 p.a.); Surrey (3765 acres/ £6697 p.a.); Middlesex (882 acres/£7,226 p.a.); and Co. Durham (134 acres/£251 p.a.).

His son and heir Hugh Percy, 2nd Duke of Northumberland (1742-1817) was educated at Eton and St. John's College, Cambridge, despite becoming an army officer in 1759 at the age of sixteen. In 1762, aged nineteen or twenty, he became a Lieutenant-Colonel in the 111th Foot and in the Grenadier Guards, and, the following year, was also elected an M.P. while still a serving officer. He fought with some distinction in the British army during the American Revolution and, in July 1775 was appointed a Major-General in the American Army and, in September 1775, aged thirty-three, a Major-General in the home army. He returned to England in 1777, inherited the dukedom in 1786, and was made a full General in 1793. Like his father, he became Lord Lieutenant of Northumberland, and increased the family income, again mainly through colliery royalties, to £80,000 p.a. He was married twice: first, in 1764, to Lady Anne, daughter of John, 3rd Earl of Bute, whom he divorced, citing her adultery, in 1779, and with whom he had no children; and, secondly, also in 1779, to his sister-in-law Frances (1752-1820), daughter of Peter Burrell of Langley Park, Beckenham, Kent, with whom he had three children. The second Duke left £660,000 in personalty at his death.

His son, Hugh, 3rd Duke of Northumberland (1785-1847), was educated at Eton and St. John's College, Cambridge. He served as an M.P., from 1806, when he was twenty-one, until 1812, when he was given a peerage, although his father was still alive, as Baron Percy. In 1812 he attempted to gain emancipation for the slaves (not accomplished by Parliament until 1834), but was otherwise known as an anti-Catholic Tory. In 1829-30 he served, apparently effectively, as Lord Lieutenant of Ireland. In 1817, he married Lady Charlotte (d. 1866), daughter of Edward Clive, 1st Earl of Powis, but died without children. He served in the usual range of senior positions, and was Chancellor of Cambridge University from 1840 until 1847. He helped to fund the Church Building Society and also was significant in allowing football to be played by his tenants, increasing its popularity.

At this time, the Dukes of Northumberland had three main residences. Alnwick Castle in Northumberland had belonged to the older Percy family, and was inherited by the newly-created dukes. It was remodelled by Anthony Salvin for £320,000 between 1854 and 1865, and is still owned by the family. Syon House, in Isleworth in west London, was built in 1547 and acquired by the 9th Earl of Northumberland of the old Percy family in 1594. It was rebuilt by Robert Adam and its 200-acre site by "Capability" Brown in the mid-nineteenth century. In the 3rd Duke's time, the chief London mansion of the family was Northumberland House, occupying a large site adjacent to Trafalgar Square in central London. Built in about 1605, it included a picture gallery 106 feet long, and many other princely features. By the mid-nineteenth century, however, it was the last remaining aristocratic mansion in central London, all the other owners having deserted the area for Mayfair, Belgravia, and other venues to the west. The Metropolitan Board of Works also wanted to acquire the site, wreck the House, and put a major road there linking Trafalgar Square with the Thames. In 1866 the 5th Duke sold the building to the Board of Works for £500,000. It was demolished in 1874, and Northumberland Avenue was put through on its former site.

The 3rd Duke died in 1847, leaving £320,000 in personalty. His nearest male relative and successor was Algernon, 5th Duke of Northumberland (1792-1865), the second son of the 2nd Duke. He did not attend a public school or university, but entered the Royal Navy at twelve, became a captain at twenty-two, and then went on half-pay in 1815 at twenty-three; this did not prevent him from becoming a full Admiral in 1862. In 1816 he was created Baron Prudhoe, and, in 1852, he served as First Lord of the Admiralty in Lord Derby's "Who? Who?" Tory government. The 5th Duke was known for his financing of various scholarly projects. He travelled extensively in Africa – before he became a Duke – and served as President of what became the Royal National Lifeboat Institution from 1851 to his death. Prudhoe Bay in Alaska is named for him. He was also known for his philanthropy. In 1842, aged forty-nine, he married Lady Eleanor (d. 1911), daughter of the 2nd Marquess of Westminster. He left £500,000 in personalty at his death. Like the previous Duke, he died childless, and the title came to his cousin, George, 5th Duke of Northumberland (1778-1867), who held the title for only two years. He was the son of Algernon Percy, 1st Earl of Beverley (1750-1830), the second son of the 1st Duke. His brothers included (Rt. Revd.) Hugh Percy, Bishop of Rochester and then of Carlisle (1784-1856), and (Hon.) Henry Percy (1785-1825), a military officer who served as ADC to the Duke of Wellington, and carried the Waterloo Dispatch, announcing the defeat of Napoleon, to the Prince Regent in London. Educated at Eton and St. John's College, Cambridge, he served as an M.P. from 1799 to 1830 before succeeding to his father's earldom, and held a number of ministerial posts, such as Captain of the Yeomen of the Guards under Peel, from 1841-46. In 1801 he married (Hon.) Louisa (1781-1848), daughter of James Stuart-Wortley-Mackenzie, son of the 3rd Earl of Bute, and had a large family. He left £350,000 in personalty.

His son and successor, Percy Algernon, 6th Duke of Northumberland (1810-99) was educated at Eton, and then entered the Grenadier Guards. He served as an M.P. from 1831-2 and then in 1852-65, and held junior posts in the Conservative government of 1858-9 and was Lord Privy Seal in Disraeli's Cabinet in 1878-80. In 1848 he married Louisa (1813-90), daughter of Henry Drummond (1786-1860), a banker who funded the Drummond Professorship of Political Economy at All Souls College, Oxford, but who is better known as one of the leaders of the so-called Catholic Apostolic Church (or "Irvingites") a peculiar sect founded in 1831, whose members, often from wealthy or aristocratic backgrounds, regarded themselves as successors to the Twelve Apostles. (They were mainly breakaways from the Anglican Church, not from Roman Catholicism, despite their title). The 6th Duke gave ten per cent of his income – about £20,000 per year – to the new Church, allowing them to fund missionary activities and to build the prominent Church of Christ the King in Gordon Square, near London University. It was the 6th Duke who sold Northumberland House to the Metropolitan Board of Works. In 1886, his residences were listed as Syon House and Alnwick Castle, and also Albery Park, Guildford, Surrey, and 2 Grosvenor Place S.W., near Hyde Park Corner. Possibly because of his annual gifts to his Church, he left less in personalty than any other holder of the title, £90,889.

His son and successor, Henry, 7th Duke of Northumberland (1846-1918) was educated at Christ Church, Oxford, and served as an M.P. from 1868 till 1885. In 1887 he was called up to the House of Lords as Baron Lovaine, in his father's lifetime. He served as Treasurer of the Household from 1874-5, and was Chairman of the National Union of Conservative Associations from 1879 until 1883. The Duke was Chancellor of Durham University and was Lord High Steward at the Coronation of King George V in 1911. In 1868 he married Lady Edith Campbell, daughter of George, 6th Duke of Argyll. They had thirteen children. One of his younger sons, Lord Eustace Percy (1887-1958), served in the Cabinet as President of the Board of Trade from 1924-29 and as Minister Without Portfolio in 1935-6. He was the author, in 1945, of the "Percy Report" on higher technological education, and in 1953 was created 1st Baron Percy of Newcastle. Like his father, the 7th Duke was a member of the Catholic Apostolic Church, and was regarded by his sons as a stern upholder of that sect. The 7th Duke left £950,000 in personalty.

His eldest son, Alan, 8th Duke of Northumberland (1880-1930), was educated at Eton and Christ Church, Oxford. He served in the Grenadier Guards during the Boer War, and, in the 1911-14 period, argued for conscription in Britain and expected war with Germany. During the

War, he acted as an "official eyewitness," and served as a Lieutenant Colonel and member of the Directorate of Military Operations. He was also strongly opposed to the strategies offered by the generals and to David Lloyd George as war leader. Just after the War, and like many other senior landed aristocrats, he moved sharply to the extreme right, producing such works as *International Revolutionary Propaganda* (1920) and *The Conspiracy Against the British Empire* (1921), led from Moscow and which included the IRA, colonial agitators, and British socialists. Returning to the mainstream earlier than most, he rejoined the Conservative Party in 1922 (when they held office in their own right for the first time since 1905) and served as President of the Conservative National Union in 1924, and bought the right-wing Fleet Street newspaper the *Morning Post* from Lord Rothermere. Unlike his father, he was a conforming Anglican, and served as Chairman of the House of Laymen of the York Archdiocese of the Church of England from 1919-23. He was President of the Royal Institution of Naval Architects and served in other ceremonial roles. He died at only fifty, leaving no less than £2,500,000, of which £2,100,000 was the value of his land.

His son and successor, Henry, 10th Duke of Northumberland (1912-40), educated at Eton, served as a junior minister in 1935. He was an army officer during the Second World War, and was killed at Dunkirk in 1940, aged only twenty-eight and unmarried. He left £1,802,079. He was succeeded by his brother Hugh, 11th Duke of Northumberland (1914-88), who was also educated at Eton and Christ Church, Oxford, and also served as a captain during the Second World War. In 1946 he married Lady Elizabeth Montagu-Douglas-Scott, daughter of the 8th Duke of Buccleuch. He had briefly served as a junior minister in the Churchill "Caretaker" government of 1945, and was Lord Steward of the Household from 1973 until his death. He held a variety of distinguished posts, such as Chairman of the Medical Research Council from 1967-77; Chancellor of Newcastle University from 1964 until his death; and President of the Wildfowl Trust and other conservation bodies. By the time of his death his family wealth had increased significantly, and he left £17,291,957. He was succeeded by his eldest son, Henry, 11th Duke of Northumberland (1953-95), who was educated at Eton and Christ Church, Oxford. He died unmarried at forty-two, and was succeeded by his brother, the present title holder, Ralph, 12th Duke of Northumberland (b. 1956), educated at Eton and Oxford, and a professional land agent. The family is now richer than ever; on the 2020 *Sunday Times Rich List*, the present Duke was listed as the 300th richest person in the UK, worth £445 million. In 2002 he was credited by Kevin Cahill with owning 132,000 acres of land.

7. Stanley (or Smith-Stanley) – Earls of Derby £163,273 p.a.

The largest landowners in Lancashire at the time of the *Return of Owners of Land*, where they were often known as the "Kings of Lancashire," the Stanleys, Earl of Derby, were among the oldest of the great landowner families and also among the richest. Their title, Earls of Derby, is a reference to West Derby in Lancashire, adjacent to Liverpool, not to the town of Derby or the county of Derbyshire. In fact, the family did not own a single acre of land in Derbyshire and had no connection with that county. They are also the first non-ducal family on our list. Given their prominence, wealth, and political importance, which included a nineteenth century Prime Minister, they could certainly have procured a Dukedom, but apparently did not wish to be so elevated.

The first Stanley to become Earl of Derby was given the title in 1485 by King Henry VII for supporting him at Bosworth. By the mid-eighteenth century, there had been ten holders of the Earldom, with Edward, 11th Earl of Derby (1689-1776) succeeding a distant relative, James, 10th

Earl of Derby, in 1736. He was the son of Sir Thomas Stanley, 4th Bt. (d. 1714), from another branch of the family. The 11th Earl served as an M.P. from 1727 until 1736, when he succeeded to the peerage. He was head of the Lancashire Militia at the time of the invasion of Britain by "Bonnie Prince Charlie," in 1745, and served as Lord Lieutenant of Lancashire in 1741-57 and 1771-76. In 1714, he married Elizabeth, daughter of Robert Hesketh, a local landowner. Their daughter, Lady Charlotte Stanley, was married to (General) John Burgoyne, who surrendered to the Americans at the Battle of Saratoga in 1777. He was also a playwright of note. The Earl's eldest son James, Lord Strange (1716-71) married Lucy, the daughter of Hugh Smith of Weald Hall, Essex, and as a result changed his surname to "Smith-Stanley," by which the family was known for several generations. Lord Strange died before his father, and the title passed to his son Edward Smith-Stanley (1752-1834), 12th Earl of Derby, who was educated at Eton and Trinity College, Cambridge. He served as an M.P. from 1774-76, and then succeeded to the earldom.

In 1883 the Earl of Derby owned 68,942 acres worth £163,273 p.a., in Lancashire (57,000 acres/£156,735 p.a.); Cheshire (9,500 acres/ £6,460 p.a.); Flintshire (92 acres/£78 p.a.). Bateman states that they owned 950 acres in Kent and 1400 in Surrey, whose income was "unstated," but there is no record of this in the original *Return of Owners of Land,* where they are credited with owning 35 acres/£54 p.a. in Kent, but nothing in Surrey.

When he held the title, the Industrial Revolution took full flight, and the Stanleys, with their vast holdings in industrial Lancashire, including many lucrative coal fields, and substantial properties in and near Liverpool, England's most important commercial port, became astronomically wealthy. It was in another field, however, that the 12th Earl made a permanent mark, as a very important pioneer of modern horseracing. "The Oaks" is named for his estate "The Oaks" in Carshalton. He then won a coin toss for naming a race for colts. He won, and the race has been known as "The Derby" ever since. He gave his name as well to the best-known American horserace, the "Kentucky Derby" (pronounced "durby," not "darby"). In 1774 the 12th Earl married Lady Elizabeth (1751-97), daughter of the 6th Duke of Hamilton, and the mother of the next Earl. She later had an affair with John Sackville, 3rd Duke of Dorset, and left the Earl, who refused to grant a divorce. Soon after her death, he married Elizabeth Farren, a well-known actress, and fathered a daughter.

At his death in 1834, he was succeeded by his son Edward Smith-Stanley, 13th Earl of Derby (1775-1851), who was known from 1776 until 1832 as "Lord Stanley." He lived mainly at Knowsley Hall near Liverpool, until recently the family's main seat. Educated at Eton and Trinity College, Cambridge, and a colonel in the local militia, he served as an M.P. from 1796 until 1832, when he was created Baron Stanley of Bickerstaffe in the lifetime of his father; two years later, he succeeded to the earldom. The 13th Earl was a well-known naturalist who had 1272 rare birds and 345 mammals at Knowsley and was President of the Linnean Society from 1828-33. He left £144,000 in personalty at his death.

In 1798 he married his cousin, Charlotte (d. 1817), daughter of (Revd.) Geoffrey Hornby, who served as High Sheriff of Lancashire in 1774-5. The 13th Earl was succeeded by the most politically important holder of the title in modern times, Edward Geoffrey Smith-Stanley, 14th Earl of Derby (1799-1869). Although known today only to historians of Victorian England (and not very well known at that), he had a most remarkable career. Educated at Eton and Christ Church, Oxford and a strong Evangelical Anglican, he was elected an M.P. in 1822, serving until 1844, when he was called up to the Lords as Baron Stanley of Bickerstaffe, and then succeeded to the earldom in 1851. He was very highly regarded and served in a variety of senior positions.

More importantly, he was responsible for a remarkable number of major changes and innovations. Originally a Whig, he served from 1830-33 as Chief Secretary for Ireland (in the Cabinet from 1831), and then served as Secretary for the Colonies from 1833-34. In the former post, he initiated the system of National Education for Ireland; in the latter, he was chiefly responsible for abolishing slavery throughout the British Empire. In the mid-1840s he became a Tory, and served as a member of Sir Robert Peel's Cabinet from 1841 to 1845 as Colonial Secretary. He opposed the Repeal of the Corn Laws in 1846, and became Leader of the "Protectionist" (i.e., pro-tariff) sector of the Conservative Party, serving as Leader of the Tories from 1846-68, longer than any other major party Leader. He became Prime Minister three times, always as the head of a minority government. His first administration, in 1852, is known as the "Who? Who?" government," after the reaction of the old and deaf Duke of Wellington, when its list of Cabinet ministers was read out to him. Most were obscure and had never held office before. The most notable was Derby's Chancellor of the Exchequer, Benjamin Disraeli, whose entry into Cabinet politics was made possible by Derby. Derby's second government, in 1858-9, is notable for abolishing the East India Company and replacing it with direct British rule in India, and also for enacting "Jewish emancipation," the right of professing Jews elected to Parliament to take the oath of office stating "so help me God," rather than swear "on the true faith of a Christian," as was the case before. His third ministry, in 1866-8, was especially notable for passing the 1867 Reform Act, which extended the vote to the urban working classes. This was a most remarkable record, and yet few among even well-informed persons know much – or anything – about it. In 1825, he married (Hon.) Emma (1805-76), daughter of Richard Bootle-Wilbraham, a Lancashire landowner who had been created Baron Skelmersdale in 1828.

The 14th Earl died in 1869, leaving £250,000 in personalty. He was succeeded by his son Edward, 15th Earl of Derby (1826-93), who was educated at Eton (which he disliked), Rugby (which he liked), and at Trinity College, Cambridge, where he was a member of the secret society, the "Cambridge Apostles." He served as an M.P. from 1848 until he inherited the earldom in 1869. He held junior office under his father as Prime Minister in 1852, then served as the first Secretary of State for India in 1858-59, and as Foreign Minister in 1866-68, when he spelled out for the first time that Britain would not enter into any official alliances with any European state, "splendid isolation." In Disraeli's Cabinet, he served as Foreign Minister from 1874-78, but became a Liberal after about 1880, serving as Colonial Secretary under Gladstone from 1882-85. He was among the many Liberal landed aristocrats who became Liberal Unionists in 1886, and served as the Leader of the Party in the Lords from 1886 to 1891. In 1862 there occurred the most bizarre incident in his political career, when the Greek government unofficially offered to make him King of Greece following the deposition of King Otto, a German. A bachelor until 1870, in that year he married Lady Mary, the daughter of the 5th Earl De La Warr and the widow of the second Marquess of Salisbury. They had no children, and the title passed to his brother. The 15th Earl died in 1893, leaving the enormous sum of £1,935,554 in personalty.

His son and successor, Frederick, 16th Earl of Derby (1841-1908), was educated at Eton and then at Sandhurst, and became a captain in the Grenadier Guards. He served as a Conservative M.P. from 1865-86, when he was created Baron Stanley of Preston, the title by which he was known until he succeeded his brother as Earl in 1893. In Tory Cabinets, he held a variety of positions, including Secretary for War (1878-80), Colonial Secretary (1885-6), and President of the Board of Trade (1886-8). He is best known for his appointment as Governor-General of

Canada from 1886 until he succeeded to the earldom in 1893. In that post, he was very popular and created a number of important precedents about the powers of the Governor-General. His most important contribution to Canadian (later North American) culture was donating the Stanley Cup, which is awarded to the winner of the Playoffs in the National Hockey League, long regarded as Canada's national sport. In 1864 he married Lady Constance (1840-1922), daughter of the 4th Earl of Clarendon. In 1886 his residences were listed in one standard reference book as Knowsley in Lancashire; Fairhill, Tunbridge, Kent; Holwood near Beckenham, Kent; and 33 St. James's Square. The 16th Earl left £917,350 in personalty.

His son Edward, 17th Earl of Derby (1865-1948), was educated at Wellington, and then became an army officer in the Grenadier Guards. He served in the Boer War as, among other roles, Private Secretary to Lord Roberts, the British Commander. From 1892 until 1905 he was a Conservative M.P., his background and competence marking him out for early promotion. He was a junior minister under Salisbury and Balfour, and from 1903-05 sat In Arthur Balfour's Cabinet as Postmaster-General. During the First World War he was the initiator of the "Derby Scheme" to increase voluntary enlistments (before conscription was enacted), and served as Secretary for War under Lloyd George from 1916 till April 1918. Many regarded him as the wrong man for the job, with Haig writing in his Diary that Derby "bear[s] the mark of the last man who sat on him," apparently the first use of that well-known phrase. He served with more distinction as Ambassador to France from 1918-1920, at the time of the Versailles Conference, and later held Cabinet office again as Secretary for War from 1922-24. He was known for his large stable and importance at the turf. In 1899 he married Lady Alice (1864-1957), daughter of the 7th Duke of Manchester.

They had two sons. The younger, Oliver Stanley (1896-1950, left £149,113), who was educated at Eton, was a Conservative M.P. from 1924 until his death. He served in National Government Cabinets in the 1930s, at times with his elder brother as his fellow Cabinet minister, most notably as President of the Board of Trade from 1937-40, and then as Secretary for War in 1940. In the Churchill Wartime Coalition, he served as Secretary for the Colonies in 1942-45. His sudden death at only fifty-four, shortly before the Tories regained office, was a considerable blow to them. There has been speculation that, in 1951, Stanley would have become Chancellor of the Exchequer rather than R.A Butler, and quite possibly rising to Prime Minister in the late 1950s. Instead, he is known (if at all) only to historians. His father, the 17th Earl of Derby, was one of the wealthiest men in Britain, and left £3,217,839 when he died in 1948, one of the largest estates of its time, of which £1,280,000 was the value of his land.

The title then passed to his grandson, Edward, 18th Earl of Derby (1918-94). He was the son of Lord Stanley (1894-1938, left £2,209,864), the eldest son of the 17th Earl, who, like his brother described above, was a Conservative M.P. during the interwar years, and briefly served in the Cabinet alongside his brother as Secretary of State for the Dominions in 1938, when he died, aged forty-four. He had married (Hon.) Sybil Cadogan (1893-1969), the daughter of Viscount Chelsea. The 18th Earl was educated at Eton and Magdalen College, Oxford, and served as a major in the Grenadier Guards during the Second World War. He was Lord Lieutenant of Lancashire from 1951-68 but was one of the first holders of the earldom in many generations not to serve in Parliament or pursue a political career. Faced with paying the huge death duties on his grandfather's estate, he was also a prominent racehorse owner and opened the Knowsley Safari Park in 1971. He was also a director of Grenada Television. In 1948 he married Isabel Milles-Lade, the granddaughter of the 1st Baron Sondes, but had no children. At his death, he managed to leave £48,630,312, a sum which would a few decades earlier have seemed incredible, but which represented assets that had grown enormously from the vast increase in land values and stock prices, and lower rates of taxation. His successor was his nephew Edward, 19th Earl of Derby (b. 1962), who was educated at Eton and at the Royal Agricultural College, Cirencester, and who has pursued a career as a merchant banker and financier. He is the Chairman of institutions ranging from the Royal Liverpool Philharmonic Society to the Rugby Football League Association. He was not listed on the *Sunday Times Rich List* for 2020, meaning that its compilers believed his personal wealth to be less than £120 million, the minimum sum needed to appear among the thousand richest persons in Britain. According to Kevin Cahill, in 2001 the Earl still owned 27,000 acres of land.

8. (Cavendish-) Bentinck, Dukes of Portland £161,376 p.a.

The origins of the Dukedom of Portland date to just after the Glorious Revolution of 1688-89, and not before. William Bentinck (1649-1709), the son of a Dutch baron, became a close friend, confidante, and right-hand man of William of Orange. Bentinck was instrumental in arranging his marriage to the future Queen Mary II, and in securing support for William's invasion of England and his ascendancy to the throne as William III, jointly with his wife, Mary II. As a result, in 1689 he was created Earl (not Duke) of Portland, and received lands in Ireland. In 1678 he married as his first wife Ann, daughter of Sir Edward Villiers (d. 1688) and sister of Edward Villiers, 1st Earl of Jersey. The Dukes of Portland descend from her. In 1700, after her death, he married Jane, daughter of Sir John Temple and widow of the 3rd Baron Berkeley.

The current Earl of Portland, who inherited the title in 1990 after the last Duke of Portland died without male heirs, are descended from her. As with many other of the wealthiest aristocratic families, the Bentincks, Duke of Portland accumulated land and property by fortunate marriages and inheritances over many generations. Their landholdings in 1883 were quite miscellaneous, centring in Nottinghamshire and Northumberland, but also including lands in other English counties and large holdings in Scotland. In addition, they owned 151 acres of prime London land, in Marylebone, which included Portland Place and Great Portland Street. By the late nineteenth century, their main stately home was Welbeck Abbey near Worksop, Nottinghamshire, in the so-called "Dukeries," near where other senior aristocrats also had country houses. In the eighteenth century, their main country residence was Bulstrode Park, near Gerrard's Cross in Buckinghamshire, which the family sold to the 11th Duke of Somerset in 1811. It still exists, and was last sold to a private purchaser in 2016 for £18 million.

In 1883 the Duke of Portland owned 183,199 acres worth £88,350 p.a, outside of London, in Nottinghamshire (43,036 acres/£35,752 p.a.); Northumberland (12,337 acres/ £10,477 p.a.); Derbyshire (8,074 acres/£9,643 p.a.); Ayrshire (17,244 acres/£19,671 p.a.); and Caithness (101,000 acres/£10,400 p.a.). In addition, they had smaller holdings in Lincolnshire, Norfolk, Worcestershire, and Buckinghamshire, and received £9,570 p.a. from "mines," whose location was unstated. In London, they owned 151 acres in 1892-94, with an Estimated Annual Land Value (Site Only) of £53,456 p.a., and an Assessed Annual Rental Value (Real Estate) of £145,144 p.a.

The 1st Earl of Portland was succeeded by his son Henry Bentinck (1682-1726), who served as a Whig M.P. from 1705 until he inherited the Earldom in 1709. In 1716 he was created 1st Duke of Portland. In 1704 he married Lady Elizabeth, daughter of Wriothesley Noel, 2nd Earl of Gainsborough, an heiress with a dowry of £60,000. He inherited vast wealth from her family and from other relatives. He was one of the original subscribers to the Royal Academy of Music in 1719 and, in 1721, was appointed Governor of Jamaica, a position whose salary was very high, possibly because so many of its holders died there, as he did in 1726. He was succeeded by his son William Bentinck, 2nd Duke of Portland (1709-62), who, in 1734, married Lady Margaret, daughter of Edward Harley, 2nd Earl of Oxford and Mortimer, another heiress.

He was succeeded by his son, the most politically significant holder of the title, William Cavendish-Bentinck, 3rd Duke of Portland (1738-1809), who also inherited vast properties from his maternal grandmother, the daughter of John Holles, 1st Duke of Newcastle. Known as the "Marquess of Titchfield," his courtesy title, for much of his career, the Duke was educated at Westminster School and Christ Church, Oxford – the first of his line to be educated in the conventional upper class manner – and was elected an M.P. in 1761 before succeeding his father in the dukedom the following year. In 1766 he married Lady Dorothy (1750-94), the daughter of William, 4th Duke of Devonshire, and fathered a large family. One of his younger sons, Lord Charles, was the ancestor of Queen Elizabeth the Queen Mother, and hence of the present Queen. As a result of his marriage he added "Cavendish" to his surname. He held a variety of senior Cabinet posts, and was twice Prime Minister, in 1783 and 1807-09. A moderate Whig who was acceptable to most factions in the party, he also held the positions of Lord Lieutenant of Ireland (1782), Home Secretary (1794-1806), and Lord President of the Council (1806-7). He was also the head of the Royal Academy of Music, and supported cultural figures including Handel. He was also the owner of the famous Portland Vase. The Duke died in debt, owing £52,000, despite his great income, necessitating the sale of Bulstrode Park.

His son and heir was William, 4th Duke of Portland (1768-1854), who was educated at Westminster School and at Christ Church, Oxford. He served as an M.P. from 1790 until he succeeded to the title in 1809. He was Lord Privy Seal and Lord President of the Council in the government of George Canning (his brother-in-law) in 1827-28, and was Lord Lieutenant of Middlesex from 1794 till 1841. In 1795 he married Henrietta (d. 1844), daughter and heiress of (Major General) John Scott, a wealthy Scottish landowner, and added his surname to his own, being known as "Cavendish-Scott-Bentinck." He left £980,000 in personalty at his death, in addition to his lands. His eldest surviving son, (William) John, 5th Duke of Portland (1800-79), was one of his more unusual aristocrats of his day; his entry in the *ODNB* defines him as a "recluse." He was educated at home rather than at a public school and then became a captain in the Life Guards, as well as a Tory M.P. for two years, 1824-26. He then spent huge amounts on building vast underground chambers at Welbeck Abbey, his main country house, including an underground "great hall" 160 feet by 63 feet and a huge underground library. These were equipped with a hydraulic lift which could carry twenty persons at a time, a curious construction for a recluse. His tenants were required to ignore him if any saw him – one was sacked for tipping his hat to the Duke – and he handled all of his business by post, rather than meet a commercial or professional man. He was unmarried, but apparently fathered three illegitimate children. After his death, a woman claimed that she was his daughter, and that he had been living a double life as a London upholsterer named Thomas Charles Druce, who had died in 1864. This claim was dismissed by the Court, although it would hardly be made unless it seemed plausible. Despite his vast expenditures, he remained one of the wealthiest men in Britain, leaving £1,500,000 in personalty in England, and another £85,084 in personalty in Scotland. In addition, his younger brother Lord Henry Bentinck (1804-70) left £500,000 in personalty.

He was succeeded by a somewhat distant cousin, William Cavendish-Bentinck (1857-1943), 6th Duke of Portland, who held the title for sixty-four years. He was the son of (Lt. Gen.) Arthur Cavendish-Bentinck, the son of Lord Charles Bentinck, a younger son of the third Duke, the Prime Minister. The 6th Duke's grandmother was the niece of the Duke of Wellington. His half-sister – the daughter of his father by the father's second wife – was, implausibly, Lady Ottoline Morrell (*nee* Cavendish-Bentinck, 1873-1938), the Bloomsbury Group literary figure. He was educated at Eton and became a military officer. He inherited the title when he was twenty-two, and served as Master of the Horse in the Tory governments of 1886-92 and 1895-1905. In 1913 he hosted Crown Prince Francis-Ferdinand, the heir to the Austrian throne, at Welbeck Abbey, when a gun accidentally discharged and its bullet came within a few feet of the Crown Prince. A few feet to one side, and two World Wars might never have occurred. In 1889 the Duke married Anna (1863-1954), the daughter of Thomas Dallas-Yorke, and had two sons and a daughter. She was a Vice-President of the RSPCA. He left £210,916. In 1886 (when he was the Patron of thirteen livings in the Church of England), his residences were listed as Welbeck Abbey, Nottinghamshire; Bolsover Castle, Derby; Fullarton House near Troon, Ayrshire; Langwell in Caithness; and 13 Grosvenor Place, S.W. (Previously the London residence of the Dukes was Hertford House.) He was also a member of seven clubs in London and elsewhere. He was succeeded by his son William, 7th Duke of Portland (1893-1977). He was educated at Eton and served as a Tory M.P. from 1922 till 1943, holding junior ministerial posts in 1928-29 and 1931. He was Lord Lieutenant of Nottinghamshire from 1939-62. He left £4,391,478.

He died without male heirs, and the title passed to a distant relative, Ferdinand, 8th Duke of Portland (1888-1980), the great-great grandson of the 3rd Duke. He was educated at Eton, at the Royal Military College at Sandhurst, and in Germany, and was severely wounded in the First World War. After working for Vickers in the 1920s, he settled in Kenya from about 1927, and served as Speaker of the Kenya Legislative Council from 1955-60. He also died without a male heir, leaving only £30,016 in England, and the title passed to his brother Victor, 9th Duke of Portland (1897-1990). He was educated at Wellington, served in the Grenadier Guards in the First World War, and had a distinguished career as a career diplomat and Foreign Office official. He served as HM Ambassador to Poland from 1945-47, and was Chairman of the Joint Intelligence Committee of the Chiefs of Staff from 1939-45. He left £352,414. The only address listed for him in *Who's Who* was 21 Carlyle Square, S.W.3. He also died without a male heir, and the title of Duke of Portland became extinct. However, the older, separate title of Earl of Portland remained in use, representing the split in the family dating back for centuries. This title now came to the 9th Duke's very distant kinsman Henry Noel Bentinck, 11th Earl of Portland (1919-97), who from 1952-1955 had worked on a sheep station in Tasmania, and later worked as the producer of the BBC radio programme *Today*. The present holder of the Earldom, Timothy Bentinck, 12th Earl of Portland (b. 1953), was educated at Harrow and at the University of East Anglia. He is a well-known actor in the West End, in films, and on radio, and is nationally known as David Archer in the long-running popular BBC radio drama, *The Archers*.

At stages between 1879 and 1899, the Duke of Portland's lucrative London properties in Marylebone were inherited by Frederick George Ellis, 7th Baron Howard de Walden (1830-99), who left £74,233 in personalty. His son and heir, Thomas Evelyn Scott-Ellis, 8th Baron Howard de Walden (1880-1946), left £1,248,490. He was educated at Eton and Sandhurst. His extremely interesting and varied career is examined in an entry in the *ODNB*. The Howard de Walden estate currently consists of 120 acres, containing 800 house and building sites, and includes such celebrated, and lucrative, properties as Harley Street, the venue of the upmarket medical profession.

9. Crichton-Stuart, Marquesses of Bute, £151,135 p.a.

An unusual Scottish noble family in that most of its income derived not from Scotland but from Glamorganshire – specifically, from Cardiff, which was developed as a major city by John, 2nd Marquess (1793-1848).

The family descends from John Stuart (1360-1449), Sheriff of Bute. They became peers in 1603 when James Stuart (d. 1710) was made 1st Earl of Bute. John Stuart, 3rd Earl of Bute (1703-92) served as Prime Minister under George III in 1762-3. He was born in Edinburgh and educated at Eton and at the Universities of Groningen and Leiden. In 1751 he became tutor to the future King George III (who became King in 1760), and is regarded by historians as the last Royal Favourite to become Prime Minister, as well as the first Tory since Governments were first headed by Prime Ministers under Sir Robert Walpole.

Bute was a Scottish Representative Peer for most of the period between 1741 and 1780, when he retired, not a British peer. Like many of his successors, he was known for his artistic taste, and had Robert Adam rebuild his country house at Luton Hoo, Bedfordshire. His son John Stuart, 4th Earl of Bute (1744-1814) gained the family's land in south Wales when he married Hon. Charlotte Windsor, the granddaughter of the 7th Earl of Pembroke, whose lands he inherited. In 1794 he was elevated to become 1st Marquess of Bute in the peerage of Great Britain, enabling him automatically to sit in the House of Lords. His son John Crichton-Stuart, 2nd Marquess of Bute (1793-1848) succeeded him. His son, John, 3rd Marquess of Bute (1847-1900) caused a great scandal by becoming a Roman Catholic. Described in his entry in the *ODNB* as a "benefactor and patron of architecture," he greatly developed Cardiff in south Wales, part of his Welsh inheritance. In part as a result, he was very wealthy, and left £1,142,247 in personalty. Because of his conversion, the family has remained Roman Catholic ever since. His son John, 4th Marquess of Bute (1881-1947), educated at Harrow, was forced to sell off large parts of Cardiff to pay for his father's death duties. His son, John, 5th Marquess (1907-56) still had means enough to purchase the archipelago of St. Kilda in the Outer Hebrides and present it to the National Trust as a bird sanctuary.

His son John, 6th Marquess (1933-93), educated at Ampleforth and at Cambridge, was described in his entry in the *ODNB* as a "benefactor and patron of the arts." In 1966, again to pay death duties, he gave his impressive mansion at 6 Charlotte Square in Edinburgh, known as Bute House, to the Government, to use as the Official Residence of the Secretary of State for Scotland. It was used for this purpose from 1970 until 1999, and since 1999 has been used as the Official Residence of the First Minister of Scotland, currently Nicola Sturgeon. Quite different was his son and successor, John Colum Crichton-Stuart, 7th Marquess (1958-2021), a successful racing car driver under the name "Johnny Dumfries," who won the 1988 24 Hour Le Mans Race. John, 8th Marquess of Bute (b. 1989) is the current holder of the title. The family is still very rich, and has been included on the *Sunday Times Rich List*. Their family seat is Mount Stuart, Rothesay, on the Isle of Bute.

In 1883 the Marquess of Bute owned 116,668 acres worth £151,135 p.a., in Glamorganshire (21,402 acres/ £100,000 p.a.); Ayrshire (43,734 acres/£22,756 p.a.; Bute 29,279 acres/£19,574 p.a.; Wigtown 20,157 acres/£2,936 p.a., with smaller amounts in five other counties, and another £2,506 p.a. for minerals.

10. Fitzwilliam (or Wentworth-Fitzwilliam), Earls Fitzwilliam £138,801 p.a.

The Earls Fitzwilliam became one of the very wealthiest of landed aristocrats based mainly on their holdings in Yorkshire, which included some of the most lucrative and important coal seams in England. They also inherited lands in Co. Wicklow in Ireland, but were not major landowners elsewhere in England or Ireland. Their main residence was Wentworth Wodehouse in the unlikely venue of Rotherham in Yorkshire. It is believed to be the largest house in Britain, with a facade 606 feet long, and containing 365 rooms, one for every day of the year. It is said that guests were given confetti to scatter before coming to dinner in the Dining Hall, so that they could find their way back through the mansion's five miles of corridors. It was built in the early eighteenth century and expanded by Charles, 2nd Marquess of Rockingham, the Prime Minister, whose sister married the 3rd Earl Fitzwilliam, who later inherited Rockingham's property.

Rockingham employed Humphry Repton, the landscape gardener, to set out its gardens. In 1912, Lord Fitzwilliam hosted King George V and the Royal Family for four days at Wentworth Wodehouse, along with most of the landed aristocracy of the north of England and the Archbishop of Canterbury; the house and grounds were also thrown open to the general public, and 40,000 people came for the event. There is a recent lively history of the Earls Fitzwilliam by Catherine Bailey, *Black Diamonds: The Rise and Fall of an English Dynasty* (2008) – coal was often known as "black diamonds." From 1629 until 1833 there was also a Viscount Fitzwilliam, an Irish peerage. The two families were unrelated.

In 1883 the Earl Fitzwilliam owned 115,743 acres worth £138,801 p.a., in Yorkshire (22,192 acres/£87,406 p.a.); Co. Wicklow (89,891 acres/£46,444 p.a.), in addition to smaller holdings in Northamptonshire, Cambridgeshire, Derbyshire, Huntingdonshire, Lincolnshire, Co. Kildare, and Co. Wexford.

Our family first joined the aristocracy in 1620, when William Fitzwilliam (d. 1643) was created 1st Baron Fitzwilliam in the Irish peerage. This was rather unusual, as the family had no real connections with Ireland, despite its possibly Irish-sounding surname. It became wealthy in the 16th century via a London alderman, who bought lands in and near Peterborough in Northamptonshire. His grandson, William, 3rd Baron Fitzwilliam (1643-1719), was M.P. for Peterborough from 1667-79 and in 1681. He owned around 20,000 acres in that area, and married an heiress, Anne Cremor, who brought him lands worth £1,200 p.a. He is thought to have had an income of about £3,000 p.a. at his death. In 1716, he was created 1st Earl Fitzwilliam and Viscount Milton, again in the Irish peerage, apparently for bringing pro-government M.P.s for Northamptonshire into Parliament. The Irish peerage did not give him an automatic seat in the Lords. His son, John, 2nd Earl Fitzwilliam (c. 1685-1728), was a pro-Whig M.P. from 1710-28. He lived at Milton Hall near Peterborough, served as Lord Lieutenant of Peterborough and, again, had no obvious connection with Ireland.

It was in the next generation that this family really reached the top. William, 3rd Earl Fitzwilliam (1719-56), son of the 2nd Earl, was educated at Eton and was elected as an M.P. in 1741, aged twenty-one. Eleven months later, in 1742, he was given a Great Britain peerage as Baron Fitzwilliam; in 1746 he was made Earl Fitzwilliam in the Great Britain peerage, with an automatic seat in the House of Lords. In between, in 1744, he had married Lady Anne Wentworth, daughter of the 1st Marquess of Rockingham. Her brother, Charles, 2nd Marquess of Rockingham (1730-82), was Prime Minister in 1765-6 and in 1782, and was the enormously wealthy owner of Wentworth Wodehouse and vast landed properties. He died without direct heirs, and left all of his holdings to his sister and her descendants, thus transforming a fairly run-of-the-mill aristocrat to one of the richest in the country, their wealth growing on a daily basis as coal became "king" during the Industrial Revolution. The 3rd Earl (i.e., the 1st of the Great Britain peerage) died aged only thirty-six, and was succeeded by his son William, 4th Earl Fitzwilliam (1748-1833). The 3rd Earl had many children, several of whom also made fortunate marriages. His daughter Lady Charlotte (1746-1833) married Thomas Dundas, 1st Baron Dundas (1741-1820), who commissioned the first practical steamboat, aptly named the *Charlotte Dundas*.

Their son Lawrence Dundas (1766-1839) became the 1st Marquess of Zetland. The 4th Earl, who was educated at Eton, was a highly regarded Whig political figure, who became a Tory because of his opposition to supporters of the French Revolution, and served as Lord Lieutenant of Ireland in 1794-5 and Lord President of the Council in 1794 and 1806. Between 1795 and 1806 he was in opposition to both party groupings and in 1819 was dismissed as Lord Lieutenant of Yorkshire because of his opposition to the "Peterloo Massacre," at which fifteen protesters were killed by the local militia. In 1782 he inherited Lord Rockingham's vast wealth, consisting of about 60,000 acres. He was said to have an annual income in the 1780s of £60,000 p.a., which grew, according to accounts, to £115,000 p.a. by 1827. His coal mines produced 122,000 tons of coal by that date, and were among the largest in Britain. He was also known as an excellent landlord, who cared for his tenants in distress. In 1770 he married Lady Charlotte (d. 1822), the daughter of William Ponsonby, 2nd Earl of Bessborough. The 4th Earl left £180,000 in personalty when he died.

His son and successor was Charles, 5th Earl Fitzwilliam (1786-1857), who was educated at Eton, and served as a Whig M.P. from 1806-33. He was a strong Evangelical Anglican, who was known for his pro-Free Trade views, and for his sympathy for Protestant Dissenters, Roman Catholics, and for Parliamentary Reform. He served three periods as President of the Royal Statistical Society and in 1831-32 was the inaugural President of the British Association for the Advancement of Science. In 1806 he married his cousin (Hon.) Mary Dundas, daughter of Thomas, 1st Baron Dundas; they had thirteen children. He left £250,000 in personalty at his death. His successor was his younger son William, 6th Earl Fitzwilliam (1815-1902), who became the heir when his elder brother Charles Wentworth-Fitzwilliam, Viscount Milton (1812-35) died young. The 6th Earl was educated at Eton and Trinity College, Cambridge, served as an M.P. in 1837-41 and 1846-57, and was Lord Lieutenant of the West Riding of Yorkshire from 1857 till 1892. In 1838 he married Lady Frances, daughter of George Douglas, 17th Earl of Morton, and had fourteen children. A Patron of twenty-nine Anglican livings, his London residence was at 4 Grosvenor Square, now the Italian Embassy. In the 6th Earl's time, Britain reached its zenith as an industrial and manufacturing nation, and his coal mines and other industrial works generated enormous profits, as did his agricultural lands. At his death he left £2,590,271 in personalty, of which £162,534 was in Ireland, one of the very largest fortunes left by any landed aristocrat, a figure which did not include his settled land.

His eldest son William Wentworth-Fitzwilliam, Viscount Milton (1839-77) who was educated at Eton and Trinity College, Cambridge, served as an M.P. from 1865-62. He was an epileptic who was also an explorer in northern Canada. In 1867 he married Laura, daughter of Lord Charles Beauclerk, son of the 8th Duke of St. Albans, but died in Rouen in 1877. The 6th Earl was therefore succeeded by Viscount Milton's son William Wentworth-Fitzwilliam, 7th Earl Fitzwilliam (1872-1943), who was born, implausibly, in Point de Meuron, Ontario, when his father lived in

Canada. The 7th Earl was accused of being a "changeling," swapped at birth for another male baby "to purge the family of epilepsy"; needless to say, there is no evidence for this claim, and he was educated at Eton and Trinity College, Cambridge, served as a Tory M.P. from 1895 till 1902, and was Lord Mayor of Sheffield in 1909-10. In the 1890s, he served as Aide-de-camp to Lord Lansdowne, the Viceroy of India, and he also served as an officer in the Boer War and World War One. He remained very wealthy, employing 2000 men in his coal mines, and had many other profitable interests. Despite high rates of taxation and the Depression, he left £1,320,969 at his death. In 1896 he married his relative Lady Maud (1877-1967), daughter of Lawrence Dundas, 1st Marquess of Zetland. She was known for her work for animal charities, and was President of the Association for the Prevention of Cruelty to Pit Ponies. The 7th Earl's London residence was 10 Chesterfield Street in Mayfair, now the Bahamas High Commission.

His only son (William) Peter Wentworth-Fitzwilliam, 8th Earl Fitzwilliam (1910-48), was educated at Eton and then served, during the Second World War, was an officer in the Commandos and in the Special Operations Executive, winning a DSO. In 1933 he married Olive, daughter of (Rt. Revd.) Benjamin Plunket, Bishop of Tuam. They had one daughter, but no sons. She was an alcoholic, and he was apparently seeking a divorce at the time of his death. In May 1948 he was killed in a plane crash along with Kathleen Kennedy Cavendish, the Marchioness of Hartington, (the sister of John F. Kennedy), with whom he was romantically linked. In 1946 Emmanuel ['Manny'] Shinwell, the Labour MP and Minister of Mines, began mining coal in the gardens and lands surrounding Wentworth Woodhouse in lieu of paying death duties, a move which sparked anger across the political spectrum, and was widely seen as representing "class war" by the new Labour government. The 8th Earl still managed to leave £711,704, a very considerable amount at the time. With no direct male heir, the title now passed to a sixty-five year old cousin, Eric Wentworth-Fitzwilliam, 9th Earl Fitzwilliam (1883-1948), who was educated at Eton. He had no children, and died only four years later, leaving £94,227. His successor was yet another distant cousin, Thomas Wentworth-Fitzwilliam, 10th Earl Fitzwilliam (1904-79), who was educated at Eton and Magdalene College, Cambridge. He was President of the Peterborough Conservative Association. Although he had two daughters, there were no more male heirs, and the Earldom became extinct. Nevertheless, he left £11,776,401. Much of the family property, however, passed to Lady Juliet Tadgell, the only child of the 8th Earl. She was stated to be worth £45 million on one recent *Rich List*, but does not appear on the 2020 *Sunday Times Rich List*.

11. Portman – Viscount Portman £126,324 p.a.

The Portmans were significant landowners in the West Country, especially in Somerset, but make this list on the basis of their prime real estate in central London, which, in the 1890s, had the third highest Assessed Annual Rental Value (Real Estate) of any London landowners. They owned 227 acres of land in Marylebone, bounded by Oxford Street to the south, Edgware Road to the west, Crawford Street to the north, and Manchester Square to the east, and including upmarket locations such as Bryanston Square and Portman Square.

The London land was given by King Henry VIII to Sir William Portman, Lord Chief Justice (c. 1497-1557) in 1533 but, as with the prime residential areas of London owned by other wealthy aristocrats like the Duke of Westminster, not developed until much later, in this case until the mid-eighteenth century at the earliest, remaining fields and market gardens until then. In the 1760s, Henry Portman (c. 1739-96) began to develop his holdings as superior housing and also shops and businesses along Oxford Street. Portman Square was developed in 1764. Many of his London properties built later were constructed by the architect James Thompson Parkinson (1780-1859).

It is notable that the family, although wealthy and respectable on the basis of their landowning in the south-west of England, did not receive a title of any kind until 1837, when Edward Berkeley Portman became 1st Baron Portman. Henry Portman, of Orchard Portman, Somerset, was educated at New College, Oxford, but never sat in Parliament or had any direct connections with London. His son Edward Berkeley Portman (1771-1823), who was educated at St. John's College, Cambridge, served as M.P. for Boroughbridge 1802-6 and for Dorset from 1806-23, and was High Sheriff of Dorset in 1798-9. He left £80,000 in personalty at his death. With his first wife, Lucy (1778-1812), daughter of (Revd.) Thomas Whitby of Cresswell Hall, Staffordshire, he was the father of Edward Berkeley Portman, who secured the family's peerage.

In 1883 Viscount Portman owned 33,891 acres of land outside of London, in Somerset (24,339 acres/£35,557 p.a.); Dorset (7,798 acres/£9,478 p.a.); and Devon (1,754 acres/£937 p.a.). In 1892-94, they owned 227 acres of land in London, with an Assessed Annual Rental Value (Real Estate) of £218,768 p.a. and an Estimated Annual Land Value (Site Only) of £80,352 p.a.

Edward Berkeley Portman, 1st Viscount Portman (1799-1888) was educated at Eton and at Christ Church, Oxford, where he graduated with a First. He served as a Liberal M.P. for Dorset from 1823-32, and then for Marylebone from 1832-33. Four years later, in 1837, he was created 1st Baron Portman, and, many years later in 1873, 1st Viscount Portman. Despite his London wealth, he was mainly known as a breeder of Devon cattle, was President of the Royal Agricultural Society three times, and served as Lord Lieutenant of Somerset from 1839 to 1864. Indeed, his entry in the *ODNB* does not mention his London real estate or connections. In 1827 he married Lady Emma Lascelles (1809-65), daughter of Henry, 2nd Earl of Harewood. She served as Lady of the Bedchamber from 1837-51. Their eldest son succeeded at the 2nd Viscount. A younger son, Maurice Berkeley Portman (1833-88) became a member of the Canadian Parliament, while his brother Edwin Berkeley Portman (1830-1921), educated at Rugby and Balliol College, Oxford, became a barrister and a Tory M.P. from 1885 to 1892. The 1st Viscount Portman left £244,092 in personalty at his death.

He was succeeded by his son William Henry, 2nd Viscount Portman (1829-1919), who lived to be ninety. He was educated at Eton and at Merton College, Oxford, and served as a Liberal M.P. from 1852-85. Like many other Liberal aristocrats, he then joined the Liberal Unionists, and succeeded to the title in 1888. The family was now richer than ever: many of the Marylebone properties had been leased out long before for 99 years. These progressively came up for renewal in the 2nd Viscount's time and were re-leased for vastly more. He was said to have had an income of £100,000 a year. His addresses were given in *Who's Who* as Blandford, Dorset; Wentworth Lodge, Boscombe, Hampshire; and at 22 Portman Square, and he built a new family mansion at Bryanston, Dorset. He apparently spent much of his time at his rural properties, where he was Master of the Fox Hounds of the Portman Hunt and a colonel in the West Somerset Yeomanry. In 1855 he married Mary Selina (d. 1899), granddaughter of the 5th Earl Fitzwilliam. They had two daughters and six sons, a fact of some importance, as four of the sons succeeded to the title. At his death in 1919 he left £816,650 in personalty.

Henry, 3rd Viscount Portman (1860-1923), the eldest son, was educated at Eton and Christ Church, Oxford, and in 1901 married the Dowager Countess of Portarlington, the granddaughter of the 1st Marquess of Ailsa. They had one daughter, but no sons. He died only four years

31

after his father, leaving £615,088 in personalty. He was succeeded by his younger brother Claude, 4th Viscount Portman (1864-1929), who was educated at Eton, and lived at Buxted Park, Sussex (which is now an upmarket hotel). He died only seven years after succeeding, leaving £466,805, of which £404,458 was in settled land, clearly an underestimate of its real value. He did leave a son, Edward, 5th Baron Portman (1898-1942), who was educated at Eton and Sandhurst, and served as a lieutenant in the First World War. Like his father, he was a Master of the Fox Hounds, He married (Hon.) Sybil, daughter of the 3rd Baron Penrhyn, and left £465,075, of which £359,371 was in settled land. He lived at Staple Fitzpaine Manor in Taunton. The 4th Viscount had two daughters, but no sons, so the title reverted to another son of the 2nd Viscount, Seymour, 6th Viscount Portman (1868-1946). Little can be found about his career. He lived at Durweston, Blandford, Dorset, and was unmarried. He held the title for only four years, before dying and leaving £135,023. Now, a fourth son of the 2nd Viscount succeeded, something he could hardly have expected when young, Gerald, 7th Viscount Portman (1875-1948). He was also educated at Eton, and then at Sandhurst, and served as ADC to the Viceroy of India in 1901 and as an officer during the First World War. Although his address was given as The Manor, Healing, Lincolnshire, he was also a Master of the Fox Hounds in the Portman Hunt in the south-west. In 1902 he married Dorothy, daughter of Sir Robert Sheffield, 5th Bt. They had two sons, ensuring that a subsequent generation would succeed to the title. When he died, he left the remarkable sum of £4,493,306, of which £4,249,000 was in settled land. This was the third largest estate left in Britain in the decade 1940-49.

He was succeeded by his son Gerald, 8th Viscount Portman (1903-67), who was educated at Eton and Sandhurst, and served as a captain in the Second World War. He was a director of Alliance Assurance. Although he was married twice, he had no children, and left £1,308,186 at his death. The viscountcy then came to his nephew, Edward, 9th Viscount Portman (1934-99), the son of the younger son of the 7th Viscount. He was educated at Canford School, and gave his occupation in *Who's Who* as a "farmer". His address was Clock Mill, Clifford, Herefordshire. He was given considerable media publicity when he alleged that the famous solicitor Lord Goodman stole £10 million from his family trust fund, diverting much of it to the Labour Party. This allegation was apparently untrue. He died at sixty-five, and was succeeded by the present peer, Christopher, 10th Viscount Portman (b. 1958), who was educated at Marlborough. In *Who's Who*, he gives his hobbies as "molecular nanotechnology" and "computer science," and was director of BioQPharma of San Francisco, and is the Chairman of Portman Settled Estates.

Despite the many and heavy rounds of death duties the family has had to pay, they remain extraordinarily wealthy, with the astronomical rise in property values in London and elsewhere outweighing whatever they lost by many times. In the 2020 *Sunday Times Rich List* Lord Portman is stated to be the 67th richest person in Britain, worth £2.05 billion. Assuming that the probate valuation of the 7th Viscount in 1948- £4.5 million- is correct and that the *Rich List* estimate is correct, this represents a growth in his family's wealth of over 450 times (*not* 450 per cent) in seventy-two years. The present Viscount's heir is his son Luke Henry Portman, born in 1984.

12. Ward, Earls of Dudley £123,176 p.a.

The main source of the great wealth of the Earls of Dudley may be inferred from the enormous difference between their acreage owned and their annual income. This was the product of the vast mineral deposits they owned in Staffordshire and Worcestershire, which included two hundred iron and coal mines and iron and steel works.

Their main country house was Witley Court in Droitwich, Worcestershire, which they purchased from Lord Foley in 1837 and greatly enlarged. It was so grand that Queen Adelaide, the widow of William IV, lived there between 1843 and 1846. High taxation and the declining wealth of the Dudleys forced them to sell it in 1920, to Sir Herbert Smith, a Kidderminster carpet manufacturer. Probably the most notable event there since that time occurred in 1967, when Procul Harum recorded the video of their famous track "A Whiter Shade of Pale" there, when the place was largely abandoned. The main London house of the Dudleys was Dudley House, at 100 Park Lane, built in 1829. Also in 1920, it was sold to the millionaire South African "Randlord" Sir Joseph Robinson. Unlike so many Mayfair mansions of the aristocracy, however, it still exists, pretty much as it was in Edwardian times. Although it is owned by the Grosvenor Estates, it is currently rented to the brother of the Emir of Qatar.

In 1883 the Earl of Dudley owned 25,554 acres worth £123,176 p.a., in Worcestershire (14,698 acres/£48,545 p.a.); Staffordshire (4,730 acres/ £68,460 p.a.); Merionethshire (4,472 acres/ £3,114 p.a.); Roxburghshire (1,086 acres/£2,825 p.a.); and Shropshire (568 acres/£232 p.a.).

Although the Dudley peerage goes back to the Middle Ages, the first member of the Ward family to be ennobled was Humble (sic) Ward (c. 1614-70), the son of a wealthy London goldsmith, who married Frances Sutton (d. 1697), the granddaughter of the 5th Baron Dudley of a previous creation. Ward paid off his extensive debts, and inherited his property. He was High Sheriff of Staffordshire in 1658 and was created 1st Baron Ward in 1658. His wife later succeeded her grandfather as 6th Baroness Dudley. The Ward barony then descended its holder in the mid-eighteenth-century being John Ward, 6th Baron Ward (1704-74), who succeeded his cousin in 1740. He was educated at King's College, Cambridge and served as Tory M.P. from 1727-34. In 1763 he was created 1st Viscount Dudley and Ward. He was succeeded by his son by his first marriage, John Ward, 2nd Viscount Dudley and Ward (1725-88), who was educated at Oriel College, Oxford and served as a Tory M.P. from 1754-74, when he inherited the peerage. He had an illegitimate daughter, but no sons. At his death, the title passed to his half-brother (his father's son with his second wife), William Ward, 3rd Viscount Dudley and Ward (1750-1823), who was educated at Eton and Oriel College, Oxford, and also served as an M.P. from 1780-88.

His only son and successor, John William Ward, 4th Viscount Dudley and Ward (1781-1833), was educated by private tutors and then at Edinburgh University and at Oriel and Corpus Christi College, Oxford. He served as an M.P. from 1802 until 1823, when he succeeded to the title. A Whig, then a Canningite Tory, and finally an opponent of the 1832 Great Reform Act, he served as Foreign Minister in 1827-28. He was regarded as highly intelligent, and, in 1829, opened one of the earliest railways in the Country in his coalfields in Staffordshire. He was said to have had an income of £120,000 p.a., and also owned plantations and slaves in Jamaica. He was increasingly depressed, which he blamed on the beatings he received from his harsh father. The 4th Viscount was unmarried, but apparently fathered a child with Lady Lyndhurst, the wife of the Lord Chancellor. According to the *ODNB*, his diaries, destroyed after his death, "contained pornographic descriptions of his remorseless but joyless sexual exploits with women 'both in high and low life'" (*ODNB*, citing Greville's *Memoirs*). According to a contemporary, he "died insane," leaving £350,000 in personalty.

He was succeeded by his second cousin, (Revd.) William Henry Ward, 10th Baron Ward (1781-1835), who was educated at Queen's College, Cambridge, and held the title for only two years. An Anglican clergyman, he married Amelia, daughter of William Gooch Pillans, and lived at Himley Hall, Staffordshire. After his death at fifty-four, his son inherited the title. This was William Ward, 11th Baron Ward and later 1st Earl of Dudley (1817-85). He was educated at Eton and at Christ Church and Trinity College, Oxford, and was a noted cricketer. He held no political offices, but restored Worcester Cathedral, and was a Trustee of the National Gallery and the National Portrait Gallery. In 1837, Witley Court was bought for him, and he enjoyed an ever-larger income from his coal and land. Despite having held no senior political posts, in 1860 he was created 1st Earl of Dudley of a new creation. At his death, he left £1,026,325 in personalty. In 1851, as his second wife, he married Georgiana (1846-1929), daughter of Sir Thomas Moncrieff, 7th Bt. Her sister Harriet married Sir Charles Mordaunt, 10th Bt. (1836-97) and, as Lady Mordaunt, became involved in a celebrated divorce case in which she admitted adultery with Viscount Cole, Sir Frederick Johnstone, and the Prince of Wales, who was kept out of the proceedings only with difficulty.

His son and successor was William Ward, 2nd Earl of Dudley (1867-1932). He was educated at Eton and served as a junior minister in Lord Salisbury's government of 1895-1902 and, from 1902-5, served as Lord Lieutenant for Ireland. His Vice-Regal progress was described in James Joyce's *Ulysses*. From 1908 till 1911 he was Governor-General of Australia, and was unpopular with the Australian Labor Party, one of the first socialist parties to hold power. In Australia, his wife Rachel *nee* Gurney (1868-1920) founded the Bush Nursing Scheme to place trained nurses in remote rural places, a forerunner of the famous Flying Doctor Service. In 1920, she drowned while bathing in Ireland. The 2nd Earl was also a military officer who served in the Boer War and as a lieutenant-colonel in the First World War, where he assisted the Anzacs with the ill-fated campaign at Gallipoli. In 1886 his residences were given in a standard reference work as Witley Court and Dudley House, Park Lane, and also Himley Court in Dudley, Worcestershire and Ednam in Kelso, and he was a Patron of fourteen Anglican livings. His income had already apparently started to decline, and he left £403,687, of which £400,000 was in settled land. The well-known actress Rachel Ward is his great-granddaughter.

The title then came to his son William, 3rd Earl of Dudley (1894-1969), who was educated at Eton and Christ Church, Oxford, and served as a captain during the First World War, when he was wounded and won the MC. He was a Conservative M.P. from 1921-24 and in 1931-32, when he inherited the earldom, and served as a junior minister in 1921-23. He took an active role in business life, serving as President of the Iron and Steel Federation in 1935-36, and of the Birmingham Chamber of Commerce in 1937-39. He was married three times, the first, in 1919, to Lady Millicent, the daughter of the 4th Duke of Sutherland, who died in 1930, and the third time, in 1961, to Princess Grace Radziwill. He became known for strongly opposing homosexual law reform in the Lords in 1967. He is also said to have fathered a daughter, in 1923, with Venetia Stanley, the wife of the former Cabinet minister E.S. Montagu. Mandy Rice-Davies, known for her role in the Profumo scandal, claimed that when she was seventeen, in 1961, the Earl proposed to her. In his later years he lived in the Bahamas, and left only £14,278 in England.

His son and heir, William, 4th Earl of Dudley (1920-2013) was educated at Eton and Christ Church, Oxford, and served in the Second World War, in which he was wounded. He acted as Aide-de-Camp to Field Marshal Lord Wavell, Viceroy of India, in 1942-43. He was married twice, first, in 1946, to Stella Carcano y Morra, the daughter of the Argentinian Ambassador to Britain (divorced 1960), and secondly to the actress Maurine Swanson (1932-2011), who later became involved in a number of libel suits over claims that she had an affair with the fashionable London-based osteopath Stephen Ward, a major figure in the Profumo Scandal. The 4th earl was succeeded by the present title-holder, David, 5th Earl of Dudley (b. 1947), who was educated at Eton and Christ Church, Oxford, and lives in France. His heir is his half-brother (Hon.) Leander Ward. The family owned only 2000 acres in 2001, according to Kevin Cahill, and are not listed on the 2020 *Sunday Times Rich List*.

13. Paget, Marquesses of Anglesey £110,598 p.a.

One of the lesser known of the richest landed aristocratic families – except for one titleholder, who was the Number Two man at Waterloo – the progenitor of today's Anglesey peerage was William Paget, 1st Baron Paget (1506-63), an M.P. from 1529-63, who was a key adviser to King Henry VIII, and benefitted from the King's largesse through gifts of land often confiscated from the Catholic Church. He was created Baron Paget in 1563 and was given extensive lands at Cannock Chase and Burton Abbey in Staffordshire, and Beaudesart, Staffordshire, one of their principal country houses. It will be seen from the landed acreages in 1883 that this family's lands in Staffordshire and Derbyshire contained extensive coal and other mineral deposits, the main source of their wealth. Despite their title as Marquesses, the family did not own lands in Anglesey until much later.

In 1883 the Marquess of Anglesey owned 29,737 acres worth £110,598 p.a., in Staffordshire (17,441 acres/£91,304 p.a.); Anglesey (9,620 acres/£9,784 p.a.); Derbyshire (1,559 acres/£8,696 p.a.); and Dorset (1,117 acres/£814 p.a.)

The Pagets continued generation after generation until the time of Henry Paget, 8th Baron Paget and 1st Earl of Uxbridge (1663-1743). He was the son of William, 7th Baron Paget (1637-1713), a diplomat who was Ambassador to Austria and to the Ottoman Empire, and of France Pierrepont, granddaughter of Robert Pierrepont, 1st Earl of Kingston-upon-Hull. The 8th Baron was an M.P. from 1695 till 1712, in his father's lifetime, when he was created 1st Baron Burton, along with eleven others in order to give the Tories a majority in the Lords. He had served as a Lord Commissioner of the Treasury in 1710-11 and as Captain, Yeoman of the Guards from 1711-15. His son, Thomas Catesby Paget (1689-1742), educated at Trinity College, Oxford, was an M.P. from 1715-27 and married (Hon.) Elizabeth, daughter of John, 1st Earl of Bridgewater. He died a year before his father, who was succeeded as 2nd Earl of Uxbridge and 8th Baron Paget by Thomas's son Henry Paget (1719-69), educated at St. John's College, Oxford. In his brief biography in the *ODNB*, he was described as a "miser," who inherited, apart from his family's holdings, the "immense wealth" of one Peter Walter, "the well-known usurer," who had been Steward to the 1st Earl. The 2nd Earl never married, and the earldom became extinct, although the barony was inherited by a distant relative.

This was Henry Bayly (later Paget) (1744-1812), 9th Baron Paget and later 1st Earl of Uxbridge of the second creation. He was the son of Sir Nicholas Bayley, 2nd Bt. (1709-82), of Plâs Newydd, Anglesey, an M.P. and Lord Lieutenant of Anglesey. Through him, the Anglesey connections and lands came to the Pagets. His mother was the daughter of (Brigadier General) Thomas Paget. In 1769 Henry Bayly became 10th Baron Paget, and changed his surname to "Paget" the following year. In 1784 he was created 1st Earl of Uxbridge of the second creation. He served as Lord Lieutenant of Anglesey from 1782 and of Staffordshire in 1801-12. He had a residence at Surbiton Place near London, as well as at Plâs Newydd, and left £150,000 in personalty at his death. In

1775, he married Jane (c. 1747-1817), daughter of (Very Revd.) Arthur Champagne, Dean of Clonmacnoise, in the Church of Ireland, from a Huguenot family that had settled there. They had numerous children, among them a General and a Vice-Admiral, but one stood out above all for his military prowess.

His eldest son was Henry William Paget, 2nd Earl of Uxbridge and, from July 1815, 1st Marquess of Anglesey, who was born in 1768 and died in 1854. He was educated at Westminster School and at Christ Church, Oxford, and served as an M.P. from 1790-1804 and 1806-10. In 1792 he raised the Stafford Volunteers to fight in France, and served as their lieutenant-colonel commandant in 1794. In 1795 he joined the regular army as an officer – despite still being an M.P. – and rose through the ranks from Lieutenant to Major-General in 1802. He fought in Spain under Sir John Moore, and then, in 1815, commanded the cavalry as second-in-command to Wellington at Quatre Bras on 16 June 1815 and at Waterloo two days later. At the great battle, his leg was blown off by canon fire, at which he reputedly said to the Iron Duke that "By God, sir, I've lost my leg!," to which Wellington replied "By God, sir, you have!" Paget's relations with Wellington were by no means totally pleasant. In 1809 Paget had eloped with the wife of Wellington's brother, Lord Cowley, leading to his wife divorcing him and his marrying Lady Cowley. According to a probably apocryphal story, Paget's leg was later exhibited as a tourist attraction in Waterloo, Belgium. Because of the great victory, Paget was created 1st Marquess of Anglesey on 4 July 1815 and made a full general in 1819. It is interesting to note that aristocrats and others of high birth were able to lead the British to their greatest ever military victory at Waterloo (which was won, as Wellington famously put it, "on the playing fields of Eton"), but the public school-educated officers a century later are widely accused of being incompetent butchers in the Great War.

Anglesey then had a political career, serving as Master General of the Ordnance in 1827-28 and in 1846-52, and as Lord Lieutenant of Ireland in 1828 and 1830-33, some of this time under Wellington as Prime Minister. In Ireland, he was a considerable reformer, and introduced state aided education for 400,000 Irish children previously without schooling. In 1795 he married Lady Caroline Villiers (1774-1835), daughter of the 4th Earl of Jersey, with whom he had eight children. As noted, in 1809 he eloped with Lady Charlotte, the daughter of Charles, 1st Earl Cadogan and the wife of Henry Wellesley, 1st Baron Cowley, Wellington's brother. Lady Charlotte's brother challenged Paget to a duel, which took place on Wimbledon Common, with shots being fired but none hitting their presumed targets. In 1810 he married Lady Charlotte, and had ten more children, but was ostracised from High Society for many years. Among his many children were Lord George Paget (1818-80), who was second in command to Lord Cardigan at the Charge of the Light Brigade in 1854, and Lady Adelaide Cadogan (1820-90 – she married a Cadogan) who wrote the first book on the card game *Patience* in about 1870. Anglesey was made a Field Marshal in 1846, and – despite losing his leg in battle – died at eighty-six in 1854, leaving £140,000 in personalty. Although his income from land and minerals was said to have averaged over £76,000 p.a. in the period 1809-35, he also accumulated huge debts, which made his wealth much less than otherwise.

His son and heir, Henry, 2nd Marquess of Anglesey (1797-1869) was educated at Westminster and served as an M.P. in 1830-32, when he was called to the Lords in his father's lifetime as Baron Paget. He served in junior ministerial posts from 1837-41, but did not have a distinguished political career. Although his family was extremely wealthy, like his father he ran up massive debts, and was said to have owed £110,000 in 1833 and £60,000 in 1842. He left only £40,000 in personalty when he died. The 2nd Marquess was married three times, first to Eleanor (d. 1828), the granddaughter of the 5th Duke of Argyll, and secondly to Henrietta (d. 1844), the daughter of Sir Charles Bagot. He was succeeded by his eldest son (the son of Eleanor), Henry, 3rd Marquess of Anglesey (1821-80), who was educated at Westminster and served as an M.P. from 1854-57. In 1845 he married Sophia, daughter of James Eversfield, and left £60,000 in personalty. He had no children, and was succeeded by his half-brother also named Henry, 4th Marquess of Anglesey (1835-98). His education could not be traced in any source, and he appears not to have had much of a career, although he was a J.P. and D.L. of Anglesey and a D.L. of Staffordshire. His addresses in 1886 were given as Beaudesert Park near Rugeley and Plâs Newydd in Anglesey; he apparently had no London residence. He was married three times. In the 1930s the famous artist Rex Whistler painted scenes on canvas in the rooms at Plâs Newydd, which was made over to the National Trust in 1976. The 4th Marquess must, however, have been a more astute financial manager than his forebears, as he left £535,95 in personalty.

His son and heir, Henry, 5th Marquess of Anglesey (1875-1905), was – in a negative sense – one of the more colourful holders of the title. Educated at Eton, he was known for his lavish parties, his posing in flamboyant and bizarre costumes (photographs of which can be seen on his wikipedia site) and cross-dressing, and on squandering the fortune he inherited. He had his own theatre company which he installed in the chapel at Plâs Newydd. In 1901 he attended Conan Doyle's stage adaptation of Sherlock Holmes at a London theatre. While there, jewellery worth £50,000 was stolen from his rooms at the Walsingham House Hotel, where he was living. He successfully enlisted he author Arthur Conan Doyle's assistance to find the thief, Paget's French valet, who was arrested at Dover and jailed for five years. The jewellery was never recovered. In 1898 he married his cousin Lilian (1876-1962), daughter of Sir George Chetwynd, 4th Bt. Their marriage was annulled in 1900 on the grounds of non-consummation. It seems apparent that the Marquess was gay, and his life has been discussed in histories of homosexuality in Britain. Worst of all, he was a spendthrift on a grand scale, and ran up debts of no less than £544,000. He died in Monte Carlo at only twenty-nine, leaving no estate which could be traced in the probate records. The title now passed to a cousin, Henry, 6th Marquess of Anglesey (1885-1947), the son of Lord Alexander Paget and (Hon.) Hester, daughter of the 2nd Viscount Combermere. He was educated at Eton and Sandhurst, and lived a much more conventional lifestyle, serving as a captain in the Royal Horse Guards, and holding the position of Lord Chamberlain to Queen Mary from 1922. He also evidently restored the depleted family fortune, since he left £1,158,167 when he died, of which £1,050,209 was the value of his land.

His son and successor George, 7th Marquess of Anglesey (1922-2013) was educated at Eton and served as a major in the Italian campaign during World War Two. He was a distinguished historian, the author of the well-known biography of his forebear, *One Leg: The Life and Letters of the 1st Marquess of Anglesey* (1961), and also of an eight-volume history *History of the British Cavalry, 1816-1919*, published between 1973 and 1997. He was Lord Lieutenant of Gwynedd from 1983-89, and served in a wide variety of public bodies. He was President of the Anglesey Conservative Association from 1948-83, of the National Museum of Wales from 1962-68, and of the Ancient Monuments Commission from 1979-84, among many others. He was married to Dame Shirley Paget (*nee* Morgan, 1924-2017), who grew up in New Jersey, and served as President of the National Federation of Women's Institutes, 1966-69 and as Chairman of the Broadcasting Complaints Commission, 1987-91. She was made as DBE in 1983. The 7th Marquess was succeeded by the present title holder, Charles, 8th Marquess of Anglesey, who was born in 1950 and educated at

Eton, Exeter College, Oxford, and Sussex University, from which he obtained a D. Phil. The 7th Marquess was estimated to own about 8,000 acres in Anglesey in 2001, although the extent of his landholdings elsewhere is unclear. The present Marquess does not appear on the 2020 *Sunday Times Rich List*.

Many of the Pagets had distinguished careers as army or navy officers, and, as seen, several had rather unusual careers. One of the most unusual careers was that of Almeric Paget, later 1st Baron Queenborough (1861-1949). He was the sixth son of Lord Alfred Paget, the 5th son of the 1st Marquess of Anglesey. He was educated at Harrow and Corpus Christi College, Cambridge, but then lived in the United States of America from 1881 till 1901, where he was, successively, a cattle rancher in Iowa (and a friend of future President Theodore Roosevelt), a real estate agent in St. Paul, Minnesota, and then the chairman of coal and steel companies in New York, where he married Pauline Whitney (d. 1916), of the immensely wealthy Whitney family of Wall Street. He returned to England in 1907, serving as High Sheriff of Suffolk in 1907, and as a Tory M.P. from January 1910 until 1917. During the First World War, he established the Almeric Page Massage Corps, which hired one hundred masseuses to give massages to wounded soldiers. In 1918 he was given a peerage as 1st Baron Queenborough, and was Treasurer of the League of Nations Union from 1920 until 1936. He resigned from this post when the Soviet Union, which he bitterly hated, was admitted to the League. He was a strong supporter of Franco and extolled the virtues of Hitler. In 1935 he wrote an article claiming that a conspiracy of Freemasons and Communists was trying to take over the world. This did not prevent him from serving as President of the National Union of Conservative and Unionist Associations in 1928-29 and again in 1940-41, when Britain was at war with Hitler. In 1921 he married as his second wife an American woman, Edith Starr Miller, described in one source as a "conspiracy theorist and anti-Mormon agitator," who was the author of books with titles like *Occult Theocracy*. They separated in 1932. He was also a keen yachtsman, and served as Commodore of the Royal Thames Yacht Club. He left £255,276. His daughter Olive, later Winn and then Lady Baillie (1899-1974, left £4,360,976) in 1926 bought Leeds Castle, Kent from the estate of Cornelius Wykeham-Martin (1855-1924) for £180,000, restoring it and eventually presenting it to the National Trust, although many remain confused by the fact that this very popular stately home is located near Maidstone, Kent, rather than in Yorkshire, as its name suggests.

14. Vane, Dukes of Cleveland/Barons Barnard – £97,398 p.a.

William Harry Vane, 1st Duke of Cleveland (1766-1842) was descended, on his mother's side, from Barbara Palmer (*nee* Villiers), the mistress of Charles II, who was made Duchess of Cleveland of the first creation by the King. The first Duke's father was Henry Vane, 2nd Earl of Darlington (1726-92), while his mother was Margaret Lowther, sister of James Lowther, 1st Earl of Lonsdale. Inheriting from both parents, the first Duke of Cleveland of the newest creation became the owner of vast amounts of lucrative land scattered throughout England, adding to his holdings by inheriting from the enormously wealthy Countess of Bath, who died in 1808. His main residence was Raby Castle in Staindrop, Co. Durham.

In 1883 the Duke of Cleveland owned 104,194 acres of land scattered in eleven counties worth £97,398 p.a., with their most important holdings being in Co. Durham (55,837 acres/ £29,219 p.a.); Shropshire (25,604 acres/ £32,605 p.a.); Sussex (6,025/£6,491 p.a.); and Somerset (4,784 acres/ £8,062 p.a.)

The first Duke was known from birth as Viscount Barnard, and was educated at Christ Church, Oxford. In 1827 he was created Marquess of Cleveland and, in 1833, Duke of Cleveland. In 1787 he married his cousin, Lady Catherine Powlett, daughter of Harry Powlett, 6th and last Duke of Bolton. He served as an M.P. and was given his dukedom in part as a reward for supporting the Great Reform Act of 1832. At the time of his death in 1842 he was certainly one of the very richest men in England. He left £1,000,000 "within province," i.e., in the Prerogative Court of Canterbury, a figure which did not include his land. According to his entry in the *Oxford Dictionary of National Biography*, he "left almost £1million in addition to around £1,250,000 in consols [government stock] and plate and jewellery to the value of a further £1 million." His country mansions included Raby Castle and Newton House in Yorkshire, as well as Cleveland House, located at 9 St. James's Square in central London, where he died. Cleveland House, adjacent to Duke of York Street on the north side of the Square. Cleveland House was owned by the Dukes of Cleveland until 1894, when it was pulled down.

The first Duke was succeeded by his eldest son Henry Vane, 2nd Duke of Cleveland (1788-1864), a career army officer who joined the British Army in 1815 and rose to be a full general in 1863. He also served as an M.P. before succeeding to the title and, like his father, was created a Knight of the Garter. He left £800,000 in personalty at his death. Dying childless, he was briefly succeeded by his younger brother William John Vane, 3rd Duke of Cleveland (1792-1864), who died eight months later, leaving £180,000 in personalty. He had lived at Dowham Hall, Suffolk before inheriting the title. The peerage then passed to the third son of the first Duke, Harry, 4th Duke of Cleveland (1803-91), who changed his surname to "Poulett" upon inheriting property from his grandmother. Educated at Eton and Oriel College, Oxford, he was a diplomat and a prominent M.P. The Cleveland wealth continued to grow during his lifetime; he left £1,449,242 in personalty (in addition to all his land) when he died, one of the very largest estates of that time. He was a Patron of 22 livings in the Church of England, and added Battle Abbey, Sussex to his other residences. Like his brothers, he left no clear heir; in 1892 the Committee of Privileges of the House of Lords decided that the Dukedom of Cleveland had become extinct with his death, but that a distant relative, Henry De Vere Vane (1854-1918) had succeeded to one of the Duke's lesser titles, as the 9th Baron Barnard. He was educated at Eton and at BNC, Oxford, and was a civil servant at the Charity Commission before inheriting Raby Castle and the Duke's other landed property. He was also a prominent Freemason. Lord Barnard sold Cleveland House and lived at 20 Belgrave Square in Belgravia. Despite inheriting great wealth he left only £130,000.

The title then passed to his surviving son, Christopher Vane, 10th Baron Barnard (1888-1964), educated at Eton and Trinity College, Cambridge, who was an army officer and landowner at Raby Castle, and served as Lord Lieutenant of Co. Durham. He left £438,021 when he died, (a figure which included his land and his personalty), a sum consistent with the very high rates of taxation which existed for most of his time as a peer, but before land values started escalating astronomically. His son and successor (Henry) John Vane, 11th Baron Barnard (1923-2016) was educated at Eton, but then took an M.Sc. degree in Management Studies at Durham University Business School. Like his father, he was prominent in local politics in Co. Durham, serving as a County councillor. He was widely admired by locals, to whom he was known as "The Boss." He was able to retain Raby Castle and its 60,000 acres of surrounding land, including extensive grouse moors, as well as an estate in Somerset, and left no less than £94 million when he died. The title and property then passed to his son Henry Vane, 11th Baron Barnard (b. 1959), who was educated at Eton, at Edinburgh University (B.Sc.), and at Durham University, where he received an MBA in 1994. The Vanes have managed to remain extraordinarily wealthy despite being little known to the general public, probably because in recent times they had little to do with London and steered clear of national politics or (unlike Charles II) scandal.

15. Hill, Marquesses of Downshire – £96,398 p.a.

"Downshire" is a reference to Co. Down in Ulster, where the Marquesses were major landowners throughout the nineteenth century, although they also owned lands in England. Their main residences were Hillsborough Castle, Co. Down and Easthampstead Park in Wokingham, Berkshire. They also had a London residence at 24 Belgrave Square. Hillsborough Castle, built by the first Marquess, remained in the family until 1922, when it was sold to the British government. From 1924 until 1973 it was the official residence of the Governor of Northern Ireland; since then, it has been the official residence of the Secretary of State for Northern Ireland and of the Queen and members of the Royal Family when visiting Northern Ireland. It was also the venue of, and gave its name to, the controversial Anglo-Irish Agreement of 1985.

In 1883 the Marquess of Downshire owned 120,189 acres worth £91,691 p.a., of which 116,621 acres worth £91,522 p.a. was in Ireland, especially in Co. Down (78,051 acres/£73, 378 p.a.); Wicklow (15,766 acres/ £5, 018 p.a.); and King's County (13,679 acres/£7,261 p.a.) The remainder of his land was in England, in Berkshire (5,287 acres/£4,853 p.a.) and Suffolk (281 acres/ £316 p.a.).

Much of the landed estate of this family was accumulated by Wills Hill, 1st Marquess of Downshire (1718-93), the son of Trevor Hill, 1st Viscount Hillsborough (1693-1742). Until he received a U.K. peerage, he was an Irish peer, and able to sit in the British House of Commons. He held a variety of major offices, including Comptroller of the Household (1754-56) and Secretary of State for the Colonies (1768-72), at a crucial time when opposition to British rule of the American colonies was growing. Hill was staunchly opposed to an and all concessions to the American colonists, thus contributing to the outbreak of the American Revolution in 1775. He was created Earl of Hillsborough in 1751 and Marquess of Downshire in 1789, both Irish peerages. In 1756 he was also created 1st Baron Harwich in the peerage of Great Britain, enabling him to sit in the House of Lords. Downshire inherited much land, but also acquired many more acres through his marriage to Lady Margaret, daughter of the Earl of Kildare, and through inheritance from distant relatives. Although he had debts estimated at £70,000, by the time of his death he was one of the greatest landowners in northern Ireland.

Her was succeeded by his eldest son, Arthur Hill, 2nd Marquess of Downshire (1763-1801), educated at Magdalen College, Oxford, who served as a British M.P. and was a Deputy Lieutenant of Berkshire, where he owned lands. For reasons which are unclear, he committed suicide in 1801 at the age of forty-eight. The career of his son and heir, Arthur, 3rd Marquess of Downshire (1788-1845), showed that the family had moved closer to the English aristocracy. He was born in London, was educated at Eton and at Christ Church, Oxford, and married Lady Mary, daughter of the Earl of Listowel. But somewhat surprisingly – and despite the fact that he was an Anglican – he was a strong supporter of the Gaelic language and was President of the Ulster Gaelic Society. His eldest son Arthur, 4th Marquess of Downshire (1812-68) was also educated at Eton and Christ Church, Oxford, and divided his time between Co. Down (of which was an M.P. and High Sheriff) and Easthampstead Park in Berkshire. He left £50,000 in personalty in England. His eldest surviving son, Arthur, 5th Marquess of Downshire (1844-74) died at the age of only twenty-nine, leaving £140,000 in personalty in England. He was succeeded by Arthur, 6th Marquess of Downshire (1871-1918), who was educated at Eton. He married Katherine ("Kitty") Hare (1872-1959), granddaughter of the Earl of Listowel. In 1899, Kitty became friendly with Joseph Laycock (later Brigadier-General Sir Joseph Laycock, 1867-1952), the grandson of Christian Allhusen, a millionaire chemical manufacturer in Gateshead, and had an affair with him, leading in 1902 to Downshire obtaining a divorce. Laycock married her, but was also having an affair with Daisy Greville, Countess of Warwick. Downshire married twice more before dying at forty-six in 1918, leaving £135,540. The sixth Marquess was a well-liked eccentric, and served as the chief of Wokingham's voluntary fire service.

He was succeeded by his son Arthur, 7th Marquess of Downshire (1894-1989), who was educated at Eton. He served with the British Red Cross during World War One. During his period as Marquess, most of the family's extensive Irish lands were sold off. This began in his father's time, when the 1903 Irish Land Act forced the sale of much of his land to tenants. As noted, after Northern Ireland came into existence, the British government purchased Hillsborough Castle. In *Who's Who*, his only address was given as 81 Onslow Square, SW7. He died at ninety-four, leaving £122,355. As he was childless, the title then came to Arthur, 8th Marquess of Downshire (1929-2003), a grandson of the sixth Marquess. He was educated at Eton, but, most remarkably, became a chartered clerk from 1950 to 1955, and then a chartered accountant. When he succeeded to the peerage, he still retained the Easthampstead estate in Berkshire. He had also inherited the Trumbull Papers, 368 volumes of manuscripts collected by Sir William Trumbull (1639-1716), British Ambassador to France and to the Ottoman Empire, which contained letters from Donne, Dryden, and Alexander Pope among many others. He sold the Papers to the British Library for £2.5 million. In 1970, he had purchased the Clifton estate in North Yorkshire, whose stately home, Clifton Castle, had been built in 1802. He thus re-established his family as successful landowners in Yorkshire.

He was succeeded by his son, Arthur, 9th Marquess (b. 1959), who was educated at Eton, and then at the Royal Agricultural College in Cirencester, and at the Central London Polytechnic. Like his father, he is a chartered accountant as well as a businessman and a farmer. Little known to the general public, the Downshires made a successful transformation as great landowners in northern Ireland to professionals and significant landowners in Yorkshire.

16. Manners, Dukes of Rutland – £97,486 p.a.

The Manners family, Dukes of Rutland, are very old. The family first received a peerage in 1525 when Thomas Manners (c. 1488-1543) was created Earl of Rutland. In 1703 the ninth Earl of Rutland was created Duke of Rutland and Marquess of Granby by Queen Anne. Many pubs in England are named "The Marquess of Granby," in honour of John Manners, Marquess of Granby (1721-70), eldest son of the third Duke, who was a notable soldier in the Seven Years' War, but who died before his father and never succeeded to the dukedom. For over 500 years the family's principal seat has been Belvoir Castle near Grantham, Leicestershire. John Manners, 1st Duke of Rutland of the present creation (there were two previous creations of unrelated families) was born in 1638 and died in 1711. He received his dukedom mainly for supporting the Glorious Revolution in 1688 and backing Queen Anne as Sovereign. He is probably best known for obtaining what might be termed a "quasi-divorce" from his first wife, Lady Anne Pierrepont, daughter of Henry,

1st Marquess of Dorchester, a "separation from bed and board" in 1663, made official by an Act of Parliament in 1667, very unusual at the time, which was debated in the House of Lords. King Charles II, who attended these sessions, famously said that the debates were "as good as a play." The Duke was challenged to a duel by his father-in-law, which he declined. The Duke was married twice more; the 2nd Duke was the son of his third wife, Lady Catherine (d. 1773), daughter of Baptist Noel, 3rd Viscount Campden.

In 1883 the Duke of Rutland owned 70,137 acres worth £97,486 p.a. in Leicestershire (30,188 acres/£46,241 p.a.); Derbyshire (27,069 acres/£31,170 p.a.); Cambridgeshire (6,585 acres/£9,505 p.a.); Lincolnshire (2,837 acres/£4,757 p.a.), and smaller amounts in Suffolk, Nottinghamshire, and Rutland, from which their title derives (764 acres/£1,248 p.a.).

The Dukes who held the title in the period covered in this work begin with John Henry Manners, 5th Duke of Rutland (1778-1857), the son of Charles, 4th Duke of Rutland (1754-87), who died at only thirty-three, and of Lady Mary, daughter of Charles, 4th Duke of Beaufort, who was known as the "Beautiful Duchess," and was painted four times by Reynolds. He was educated at Ealing School near London, at Harrow, and at Trinity College, Cambridge (M.A. 1797), and served as High Steward of Cambridge from 1800-1835. Like many others in the high aristocracy, he was created a K.G., in 1803. The 5th Duke was best known as a racehorse breeder and owner, who owned the Cheveley Stud Park at Newmarket and won the Derby in 1828. He was a well-known sporting figure, who was depicted as "the Duke" in Disraeli's *Coningsby*. He married Lady Elizabeth, daughter of Frederick, 5th Earl of Carlisle, and served as Lord Lieutenant of Leicestershire for fifty-eight years, from 1799 until 1857. He is also known for twice rebuilding Belvoir Castle, the first time in the early nineteenth century by James Wyatt in Gothic Revival style. In 1816 a disastrous fire almost consumed the building, in which paintings by Titian, Rubens, and Van Dyck, among others, were destroyed. Belvoir Castle was then rebuilt by Sir James Thornton in the same style. It is said that the English "afternoon tea" was pioneered at Belvoir, to fill in the gap between lunch and dinner. The Castle is still owned by the Dukes, and was recently used as a substitute for Windsor Castle in the second series of *The Crown*. He left £100,000 in personalty, besides his land.

He was succeeded by his eldest son Charles, 6th Duke of Rutland (1815-88), known until his father's death as the Marquess of Granby. He was educated at Eton and Trinity College, Cambridge – these dukes favoured Cambridge rather than Oxford – and served as an M.P. from 1837 until he succeeded to the title. From 1848 until 1851 he was one of the "Triumvirate" which led the pro-Protectionist Tory Party in Parliament after the pro-Free Trade Conservatives under Sir Robert Peel left the party over the repeal of the Corn Laws, the other member of the Triumvirate being Disraeli and J.C. Herries, although he never held a Cabinet post. The 6th duke was a Patron of 23 livings in the Anglican Church. He died unmarried, leaving £109,952 in personalty, and caused a scandal when the terms of his will were announced, when he left his yacht *Lufra* to Frances, Lady Miles (1827-1908), apparently his mistress, the wife of Sir Philip Miles, 2nd Bt. She was a renowned Society beauty, widely known as the "Venus of Miles." He was then succeeded in the dukedom by his younger brother John, 7th Duke of Rutland (1818-1906), in political terms probably the best-known member of the family in modern times. Known as Lord John Manners for most of his career, he was also educated at Eton and Trinity College, Cambridge, and was a famous "Tory radical," wanting to unite the aristocracy and the working classes against the capitalist industrialists. A volume of poetry he published in 1841 contained the oft-quoted line,

"Let wealth and commerce die, but leave us still our old nobility!" Manners was the leader of "Young England," a group which advocated Tory radicalism and saw Disraeli as its hero. Manners was significant in securing reforms which favoured the industrial working classes such as the "Ten Hours Act" of 1847. He served in many Tory Cabinets between 1852 and 1892, and was Postmaster-General under Disraeli in 1874-80. Created a K.G. in 1891, he died in 1906 at the age of eighty-seven, leaving £99,596 in personalty. In *Who's Who*, he stated that he owned 62,000 acres of land, probably an underestimate.

The 7th Duke was succeeded by his son Henry, 8th Duke of Rutland (1852-1925) who, like his forebears, was educated at Eton and Trinity College, Cambridge. He served as an M.P. from 1888-95, and was married to Violet (d. 1937), the daughter of (Col.) (Hon.) Charles Lindsay, son of the 24th Earl of Crawford. He had four surviving children, including three daughters. His two youngest daughters were allegedly fathered by other men, Lady Violet (1888-1971) by Montagu Corry, Lord Rowton, Disraeli's private secretary, and Lady Diana (1892-1986) by Henry Cust, a well-known Tory journalist and M.P. Lady Diana was married to Duff Cooper, 1st Viscount Norwich, the famous political figure. Cust was also rumoured to have had a "relationship" with one of his servant girls, who was, most remarkably, Margaret Thatcher's grandmother – small world!

The 8th Duke stated in *Who's Who* that he owned 18,000 acres of land which, if true, shows that much of the land held by the family in the previous generation had been sold off, and might also explain how he left £930,737 in personalty, far more than his forebears. In the late nineteenth century, his addresses given in standard reference works included Belvoir Castle; Haddon Hall, in Bakewell, Derbyshire; Longshawe in Sheffield; and Cheveley Park near Newmarket, while his London residence was Bute House, Campden Hill, owned by the Duke between 1865 and 1888. His only surviving son, John Henry, 9th Duke (1886-1940) was also educated at Eton and Trinity College, Cambridge and joined the Diplomatic Service. During the First World War, according to Catherine Bailey's biography, *The Secret Rooms* (2012), while he served as an officer in a Leicestershire regiment, his mother pulled strings with Lord Kitchener and Sir John French to keep him from actual fighting on the Western Front and he "spent the rest of his life ashamed and his final years locked away trying to erase his past." He married Kathleen Tennant, the granddaughter of the Scottish multi-millionaire Sir Charles Tennant, Bt., and the niece of Margot Tennant, the famous wife of the Liberal Prime Minister H.H. Asquith. The Duke was also a highly regarded expert on Medieval art. His London residence was at 5 Audley Square. He was still extremely wealthy, leaving £562, 693.

His son and successor, Charles, 10th Duke of Rutland (1919-99), again educated at Eton and Trinity College, Cambridge, served as a captain in the Grenadier Guards in the Second World War, and was Chairman of the Leicestershire County Council. His residences included Belvoir Castle and Haddon Hall, a mansion built in the Middle Ages, near Bakewell, Derbyshire. He was also Chairman of Rutland Hotels Ltd. He was succeeded by his son David, 11th Duke of Rutland (b. 1959), educated at Stanbridge Earls School in Hampshire, a now closed-down school for students with special needs. The present Duke was noted as a strong United Kingdom Independenc y (UKIP) supporter. In the 2020 *Sunday Times Rich List,* he was credited with a fortune of £146 million, the 837th biggest fortune in Britain. This shows that the Dukes of Rutland have managed to remain extremely wealthy, but are relatively far less wealthy in comparative terms than in the nineteenth century, and are not in the billionaire super-rich class. The present Duke married

Emma Watkins, described as the daughter of a Welsh farmer from Knighton, Powys, rather than the daughter of a duke or an earl. Times have changed.

17. Hamilton (-Russell), Viscounts Boyne – £88,364 p.a.

Gustavus Hamilton (1642-1723) was a relative of James Hamilton, 1st Earl of Abercorn; he was named after the Swedish King Gustavus Adolphus, for whom his father had fought in the Thirty Years' War. Ever since, all holders of the Boyne viscountcy have been named Gustavus. He was educated at Trinity College, Dublin. In 1689 he was appointed a colonel in the army of William of Orange; he fought at the Battle of the Boyne in 1690, won by William of Orange who later became King William III, joint Sovereign of Britain with Queen Mary II. William defeated the forces of the deposed King James II, making permanent (until the twentieth century) the Protestant Ascendancy in Ireland. Gustavus then sat as an M.P. in the Irish House of Commons; in 1715 he was made Baron Hamilton of Stackallan, and, in 1717, Viscount Boyne in the Irish peerage. His grandson Gustavus, 2nd Viscount Boyne (1710-46) was educated at Westminster School, served as a British M.P. in 1736-41, and was a member of the Society of Dilettanti.

In 1883 Viscount Boyne owned 30,205 acres of land worth £88,364 p.a. in Co. Durham (18,023 acres/£76,885 p.a.); Shropshire (8,424 acres/ £8,014 p.a.); North Riding (439 acres/ £235 p.a.); Radnorshire (580 acres/ £258 p.a.); Co. Meath (2,739 acres; £2,972 p.a.).

By the nineteenth century, the Boynes might have remained obscure Irish peers, not terribly wealthy by English standards. In the 1820s, however, Gustavus Hamilton, 7th Viscount Boyne (1798-1872) married Emma Russell (1809-70), the daughter of Matthew Russell (1765-1822) of Brancepeth Castle, Co. Durham, from whom the subsequent line of Viscounts Boyne descend. Matthew Russell was the son of William Russell (c. 1734-1817), an enormously wealthy colliery owner and merchant in Co. Durham, who had purchased Brancepeth Castle in 1796 for £75,000. He was "said to be worth half a million," and left £280,000 in personalty when he died. His son Matthew Russell, who was educated at Oxford, served as M.P. for Saltash from 1802-22, and left £200,000 in personalty when he died. His property passed to his son William Russell (1798-1850), also an M.P., who was educated at Eton and Cambridge, and died unmarried. William's vast property then came to his sister Emma, the wife of the 7th Viscount Boyne, who changed his surname from "Hamilton" to "Hamilton-Russell," and has remained the main source of the wealth of the Viscounts Boyne ever since. This fortunate marriage also explains why, in 1883, an Irish peer owned only 2,739 acres of land in Ireland, compared with 27,000 in England, chiefly in Co. Durham. Matthew Russell was married to Elizabeth Tennyson, the aunt of the poet laureate Alfred, Lord Tennyson. Brancepeth Castle, five miles from Durham, remained the chief seat of the Boynes until the time of the 8th Viscount, who succeeded in 1907 and died in 1942.

Gustavus, 7th Viscount, who was educated at Eton and at Trinity College, Oxford, died in 1872, leaving £70,000 in personalty. He had been given a British peerage, as Baron Brancepeth, in 1866. He was succeeded by his son Gustavus Hamilton-Russell, 8th Viscount Boyne (1830-1907). The 8th Viscount was educated at Eton, and married the daughter of the 2nd Earl of Eldon, the son of famously reactionary and very wealthy Lord Chancellor (q.v.), who served between 1807 and 1827, and who had been born in Newcastle-upon-Tyne. Apart from Brancepeth Castle, his residences were at Burwarton House at Bridgnorth, Shropshire; Stackwell House, Co. Meath; and 16 Grosvenor Gardens, S.W. Burwarton House was built for the 6th Viscount Boyne, to designs by Anthony Salvin. It is still owned by the family, and has been altered several times.

The 8th Viscount remained very wealthy, and left £668,763 in personalty when he died. His son and successor, Gustavus, 9th Viscount Boyne (1864-1942), was educated at Eton and Magdalene College, Cambridge. he married a daughter of the 5th Earl of Harewood and left £416,796 when he died. In *Who's Who* he stated that his addresses were Burwarton House in Shropshire and Belgrave House in Belgrave Square, S.W.1. The title then passed to his grandson Gustavus, 10th Viscount Boyne (1931-95), who was educated at Eton, Sandhurst, and at the Royal Agricultural College, Cirencester. He was a Director of the National Westminster Bank from 1976 to 1990, and Deputy Chairman (1975-82) of the Telford Development Corporation. A Tory, he served as a Lord-in-Waiting from 1981-95, and was Lord Lieutenant of Shropshire in 1994-95. His son and successor, Gustavus, 11th Viscount Boyne (b. 1965), was educated at Harrow and at the Royal Agricultural College, Cirencester.

18. Wyndham – Barons Leconfield and Earls of and Barons Egremont – £88,112 p.a.

The Leconfields/Egremonts are among the most colourful and interesting of the great landed families. George Wyndham, 1st Baron Leconfield (1787-1869) was the illegitimate son of George O'Brien Wyndham, 3rd Earl of Egremont (1751-1837), a truly larger than life character. Educated at Westminster School, at Eton, and at Christ Church, Oxford, among other things he allegedly had fifteen mistresses and more than forty illegitimate children. His mistress Rosalie Duthé, a "French courtesan" has been described as "the first officially recorded dumb blonde" (Johanna Pitman, *On Blondes* (2004), p. 129). Egremont, who sat in the Lords for sixty-five years, from 1772 until 1837, was the owner of Petworth House in Sussex and of Egremont Castle in Cumberland. He was known as a notable Patron of the Arts, employing Turner, Constable, and John Flaxman, the sculptor, and for the humane treatment of his Irish peasants on his estates there, and also for creating a model farm and introducing many agricultural improvements. He left £250,000 in personalty "within province," i.e. of the Prerogative Court of Canterbury, in the southern two-thirds of England, when he died, having given vast amounts to charity. In 1802 he married Leconfield's mother, Elizabeth Ilive (1769-1822). This was after Lord Leconfield was born, too late to allow his son to inherit the earldom, which went to Egremont's nephew, George Wyndham, 4th Earl of Egremont (1786-1845), although the unentailed portion of the third earl's estate came to his son, who also inherited from the fourth Earl at his death in 1845.

In 1883 Lord Leconfield owned 109,935 acres worth £88,112 p.a., in Sussex (30,221 acres/£29,688 p.a.); Yorkshire (24,733 acres/£31,019 p.a.; Cumberland (11,147 acres/£6,742 p.a.); Co. Clare (37,292 acres/£15,699 p.a.); Co. Limerick (6,269 acres/£4,820 p.a.); Co. Tipperary (273 acres/£144 p.a.).

The first Baron Leconfield served in the Royal Navy from 1799 until he transferred to the Army in 1802, and was Lieutenant-Colonel commanding the 20th Light Dragoons at the Siege of Ciudad Rodrigo in 1812. After inheriting vast amounts of landed property, he was given a peerage as 1st Baron Leconfield (a family estate in Yorkshire) in 1859, and left £250,000 in personalty when he died. Like his father, he was a notably humane Irish landlord during the Famine. His grandson, George Wyndham (1863-1913), was a famous late Victorian and Edwardian journal editor and Tory politician. The Leconfield title was inherited by Henry Wyndham, 2nd Baron Leconfield (1830-1901), who was educated at Eton and Christ Church, Oxford. He served as a Captain in the Lifeguards and as an M.P. before inheriting the peerage in 1869. A Patron of 23 livings in the Anglican Church, he married Lady Constance Primrose (d. 1939), the sister of

Archibald Primrose, 5th Earl of Rosebery, Prime Minister in 1894-95. His daughter Lady Maud Wyndham was the mother of Henry Vincent Yorke (1905-73), a novelist of some note who used the pseudonym "Henry Green." This Lord Leconfield had a London residence at 9 Chesterfield gardens, W., and left no less than £1,803,959 when he died.

Charles Wyndham, 3rd Baron Leconfield (1872-1952), an army officer in the Boer War and the First World War – he was Hon. Colonel of the 98th Surrey and Sussex Yeomanry – was Lord Lieutenant of Sussex from 1917 to 1949, and was a Master of the Foxhounds from 1901 to 1942. He owned Petworth and also Cockermouth Castle in Cumberland, and was the owner of Scalfell Pike, the tallest peak in England. Despite massive taxation, he was still remarkably wealthy, and left £2,136,439 when he died, of which £1,796,951 was in settled land, a very considerable sum for someone who owned no land in London. He was succeeded by his brother Hugh Archibald, 4th Baron Leconfield (1877-1963, left £41,983), educated at Eton and New College, Oxford, who was an historian of note, the author of *The Atlantic and Slavery* (1935) and *Britain in the World* (1944) and other works, and was a Fellow of the Royal Historical Society. His London address was 3 Wyndham House, Sloane Square, SW 1.

He was briefly succeeded by a son of the second Baron, Edward, 5th Baron Leconfield (1883-1967), educated at Eton and Oxford, a professional army officer who was wounded, mentioned in despatches, and received the DSO during the First World War, retiring from the Army as a Colonel in 1926. He was a "substantial landowner at Edmonthorpe, Leicestershire," according to the *ODNB*'s entry on his son, and lived at 34 Hereford House, North Row, Park Lane, W.1. His son and successor, John Edward Reginald Wyndham, 6th Baron Leconfield and 1st Baron Egremont (1920-72), was educated at Eton and Trinity College, Cambridge. He was a civil servant from 1940-1946, and then worked at the Conservative Research Department from 1947 to 1952. He became well known as the Private Secretary to Harold Macmillan, when he was a minister in the Churchill wartime Cabinet and later, when Macmillan served as Prime Minister, from 1957 to 1963. In 1963 he received an hereditary peerage in his own right (while his father, Lord Leconfield was still alive) as 1st Baron Egremont, thus reviving the title of his colourful ancestor. He wrote a notable family history, *Wyndham and Children First* (1968), and was a Trustee of the Wallace Collection and High Sheriff of Sussex in 1960. His addresses were given as Petworth; Cockermouth Castle; and 62 Chester Square, SW 1. Egremont died at only fifty-two, leaving £1,576,519, mainly in settled land, although he had to donate many of the very valuable art works at Petworth to the National Trust in lieu of death duties. The present 7th Baron Leconfield and 2nd Baron Egremont, John (b. 1948), who is well-known as the historian and biographer Max Egremont, was born in 1948, and attended Eton and Christ Church, Oxford. He wrote noted biographies of his relatives Wilfrid Scawen Blunt and George Wyndham, of Arthur Balfour, Sir Edward Spiers, and of Siegfried Sassoon, was a Trustee of the Wallace Collection and of the British Museum, and was a member of the Royal Commission on Historical Manuscripts from 1989 to 2001. He is married to the garden designer Caroline Nelson. In 2008, he was credited by a newspaper with being worth £48 million, but he did not appear among the one thousand richest persons in the 2020 *Sunday Times Rich List*.

19. Cust – Barons (and Earls) Brownlow – £86,426 p.a.

The Cust family had been gentry and lawyers in Lincolnshire, when Sir Richard Cust, 1st Bt. (1622-1700) was created a baronet in 1677. His great-grandson, Sir John Cust, 3rd Bt. (1718-70), who was educated at Eton and Corpus Christi College, Cambridge, was a barrister who served as an M.P. from 1743 until 1770, and was Speaker of the House of Commons from 1761 until 1768. He inherited Belton House, near Grantham, Lincolnshire, from his mother, as well as other property. Belton House was the principal residence of the Brownlows until 1984, when it was sold to the National Trust, which also purchased 1317 acres of land from the family for £8 million. The third baronet was succeeded by his son, Sir Brownlow Cust, 4th Bt. (1744-1807), who was educated at Eton and Corpus Christi College, Cambridge, and served as an M.P. from 1766 until 1776. In that year he was created 1st Baron Brownlow, "Brownlow" being a reference to his grandmother Anne Brownlow, Lady Cust, who was the heiress of John Brownlow, 1st Viscount Tyrconnel (1690-1754), from whom Belton House and other property was inherited. His eldest son, Sir John Cust, 5th Bt. and 2nd Baron Brownlow (1779-1853), also educated at Eton and then at Trinity College, Cambridge, served as an M.P. from 1802 to 1807, when he inherited the peerage. He also served as Lord Lieutenant of Lincolnshire from 1809 to 1852. In 1815 he was created 1st Earl Brownlow and Viscount Alford. Like his father he inherited much property, in his case form his first two wives (he was married three times), as well as compensation of £10,058 following the abolition of slavery on his estates in British Guiana.

His titles then came to his grandson, Sir John William Egerton-Cust, 6th Bt. and 2nd Earl Brownlow (1842-67), the son of (Hon.) John Hume Egerton Cust and Lady Marianne, daughter of the second Marquess of Northampton. He was educated at Eton. In 1853 he added "Egerton" to his surname, after inheriting more property from John Egerton, 3rd Earl of Bridgewater. In 1883 the Earl Brownlow owned 58,335 acres worth £86,426 p.a., in Shropshire (20,233 acres worth £29,717 p.a.); Lincolnshire (11,652 acres/ £20,457 p.a.); Buckinghamshire (11,785 acres/£15,450 p.a.); Hertfordshire (8,551 acres/£12,760 p.a.), and smaller amounts of land in Bedfordshire; Yorkshire, North Riding; Co. Durham; Berwickshire; and Flintshire.

The 2nd Earl Brownlow died unmarried at the age of only twenty-five, leaving £160,000 in personalty. He was succeeded by his brother Adelbert Wellington Brownlow-Cust, 3rd Earl Brownlow (1844-1921). He was also educated at Eton, serving briefly (1866-7) as an M.P. before he inherited the peerage. He served as a junior minister in Tory governments between 1865 and 1892, most importantly as Under-Secretary of State for War from 1889 till 1892. He also had a long career as an officer in the Volunteers, and was an Aide-de-Camp to Queen Victoria and to King Edward VII and George V. He served as Lord Lieutenant of Lincolnshire from 1867 until his death fifty-four years later. He married Lady Adelaide, daughter of Henry, 18th Earl of Shrewsbury, but died childless. By successive fortunate inheritances and marriages, the Brownlows had become extremely wealthy, and he left no less than £1,295,984 at his death. His residences included Belton House, and also Ashridge Park, Berkhamstead, and 3 Carlton Terrace, S.W.

Without a direct male heir the earldom became extinct with his death, but the Brownlow barony passed to his second cousin Adelbert Salusbury Cockayne-Cust, 5th Baron Brownlow (1867-1927). He was educated at Eton and was an army officer from 1888 until 1908, and also served in France during World War One. He served as Governor of Trinidad in 1894-5, as Mayor of Grantham in 1924-5, and was Organising Secretary of the Royal National Lifeboat Institution. Like his predecessor, he was very wealthy, leaving £746,047 at his death. He was succeeded by his son Peregrine, 6th Baron Brownlow (1899-1978), who was educated at Eton and Sandhurst. He had a varied career, which included an appointment as Principal Private Secretary to Lord Beaverbrook as Minister of Aircraft Production in 1940 and then as a Squadron Leader in the

RAF during the War. He had been Personal Lord in Waiting to King Edward VIII in 1936, Lord Lieutenant of Lincolnshire, 1936-50, and Mayor of Grantham, 1934-5. Despite the high rates of taxation existing for much of his life, he managed to leave no less than £3,524,587 at his death.

His son and successor, Edward, 7th Baron Brownlow (b. 1936) was also educated at Eton and married Shirlie (*sic*), daughter of John Yeomans of The Manor Fram, Croome, Worcestershire, described as "eloping with the farmer's daughter," which caused his father to decline to speak with him for ten years. He became an insurance broker, a member of Lloyd's and Chairman of Harris & Dixon (Underwriting Agencies) Ltd. He was also High Sheriff of Lincolnshire in 1978-79. After selling Belton House in 1984, he has lived at St. Peter in Jersey. Despite having to sell the family mansion, Lord Brownlow is still extremely wealthy, and was credited in the *Sunday Times Rich List* for 2020 with being worth £247 million, the 521st richest person in Britain; his wealth increased by £7 million between 2019 and 2020. His son and heir, (Hon.) Peregrine Cust, was born in 1974.

20. Sir Richard Wallace, 1st Bt. – £85,737 p.a.

In 1883 Sir Richard Wallace, 1st Bt. owned 72,307 acres worth £85,737 p.a., in Suffolk (11,224 acres/ £11,253 p.a.); Cambridgeshire (25 acres/ £295 p.a.); Co. Antrim (58,365 acres/£67,945 p.a.); and Co. Down (2,693 acres/£6,244 p.a.).

Sir Richard Wallace, 1st Bt. (1818-90) is one of the most unusual of the very greatest landowners of 1883. His name at birth was Richard Jackson, and was apparently – but not definitely – the illegitimate son of Richard Seymour-Conway, Viscount Beauchamp, and later 4th Marquess of Hertford (1800-70), and (on his birth certificate) a Mrs. Agnes Jackson, who has been identified as Agnes Wallace, the daughter of Sir Thomas Wallace of Craigie, Ayrshire. At that time, however, she was married to a Samuel Bickley, a Lloyd's insurance broker, with whom she had four children. As Viscount Beauchamp was an eighteen year old student at Oxford at the time, it has been argued that his father was actually Francis Seymour-Conway, 3rd Marquess of Hertford (1777-1842), and that the fourth Marquess was actually his brother. (J.F. Burus, "The Life and Work of Sir Richard Wallace, Bt., M.P.," in *Lisburn Historical Society Journal*, Vol. 3, Part 2 (1980).) He was given the surname "Jackson" at birth. At six, he was sent to Paris to live with his alleged father and his grandmother, Maria Seymour-Conway, Marchioness of Hertford (c. 1770-1856), who was herself believed to be the illegitimate daughter of William, 4th Duke of Queensberry (1725-1810), known as "Old Q," a multi-millionaire aristocrat (see also the Dukes of Buccleuch and Queensberry, above). In Paris, the future Sir Richard led a privileged life, took the surname of "Wallace" by which he is known, and fathered a son by Amélie-Julie Castlenau (1819-97), the daughter of a French army officer, whom he later married.

From about 1843 he also became secretary to the fourth Marquess of Hertford, as well as his salesroom buying agent. Together, they began a buying spree of Old Master works of art on a grand scale. When the fourth Marquess died in 1870 (leaving £500,000 in personalty), Wallace succeeded to the unentailed portion of his landed estates, as well as to three town houses in London and two in Paris. He was notable for assisting the French victims of the Franco-Prussian War of 1870-71, for which he received a baronetcy. In the 1870s he moved his vast art collection to Hertford House in Manchester Square in London, and served as a Conservative M.P. for Lisburn in Ireland, where he had an estate. He spent his last years in Paris, dying in 1890, and leaving £1,226,353 in personalty in England. When his widow died in 1897, leaving £752,473 in personalty in England, she left Hertford House (where she lived) and its entire contents to the Nation. Thus, this unusual Anglo-French landowner is today among the most famous people included in this discussion, for his townhouse and its contents comprise the Wallace Collection in Manchester Square, arguably the greatest art collection ever assembled in one or two lifetimes, certainly in modern England. The Collection includes Frans Hals' *The Laughing Cavalier*, Fragonard's *Lady With a Swing*; Poussin's *A Dance to the Music of Time*, two Rembrandts, four Van Dycks, eight Watteaus and Canalettos, nine Rubens, and so on, as well as armour, jewellery, silver plate, and furniture. The Wallace Collection is visited by most educated tourists to London. It is also one of only two aristocratic townhouses in central London still kept more or less as it was in the nineteenth century, the Duke of Wellington's Apsley House being the other. (A number of others, such as Dudley House at 100 Park Lane, still stand with the same frontage, but are now used as embassies or corporate headquarters.) What became of his 72,307 acres of land in Britain, including his main country house at Sudbourn Hall, Suffolk, is unclear. At some stage after his death, Sudbourn Hall was purchased by the father of Kenneth Clark, the famous art historian and television presenter; his father was a multi-millionaire member of the families which owned Coats & Clark Sewing Thread, of Paisley in Scotland. Sir Richard Wallace had four children in France with his French wife; they presumably inherited his lands, although this is unclear.

Meanwhile, his father's family was not left destitute. In 1883 Francis, 5th Marquess of Hertford (1812-84) owned 12,289 acres worth £18,392 p.a., chiefly in Warwickshire, where his stately home, Ragley Hall at Alcester, is situated. The fifth Marquess left £213,992 in personalty when he died; George, 7th Marquess (1871-1940) left £166,972. The present title holder is Henry, 9th Marquess (b. 1958).

21. Anderson-Pelham – Earls of Yarborough – £84,649 p.a.

One of the least known and most obscure of the great landowners, the Earl of Yarborough have been great landowners in Lincolnshire for several generations, their country house being Brocklesby Park at Ulceby, Lincolnshire, rebuilt in 1898 after a fire. In 1883 the Earl of Yarborough owned 56,893 acres worth £84,649 p.a. in Lincolnshire (56,893 acres/£84,000 p.a.) and Berkshire (98 acres/ £649 p.a.).

Charles Anderson-Pelham (1749-1823), educated at Eton, was an M.P. from 1768 until 1794 – he was first elected for a family pocket borough at nineteen. He was said to be "one of the richest commoners in England" (*History of Parliament*) and was pro-Whig, as were succeeding members of his family until the 1880s. He was created 1st Baron Yarborough in 1794, although – like most subsequent holders of the peerage – he held no government office. His son Charles Anderson-Pelham (1781-1846), educated at Eton and Trinity College, Cambridge, was an M.P. from 1803 until 1823, when he succeeded to the barony. In 1837 he was made 1st Earl of Yarborough. He also inherited from his wife, Henrietta, heiress of her grandfather Sir Thomas Worsley, 6th Bt. of Appledurcombe, Isle of Wight. He was the founder of the Royal Yacht Squadron at Cowes, Isle of Wight. His son, Charles, 2nd Earl of Yarborough (1809-62), educated at Eton, also served as a pro-Whig M.P., from 1831 until 1846, when he succeeded to the title. In Parliament he was known by his courtesy title Lord Worsley. He was well-liked by his tenants and neighbours, and became known as "Yarborough the Good." Apart from Brocklesby Park, he had a residence at 17 Arlington Street, Mayfair. He left £140,000 in personalty at his death.

His son and successor, Charles, 3rd Earl of Yarborough (1835-75), was educated at Eton and also served as an M.P. from 1857-62 before succeeding to the title. He was a Lieutenant-Colonel in the Lincolnshire Militia, and left £180,000 in personalty when he died at forty. His son and successor, Charles, 4th Earl of Yarborough (1859-1936) was much longer lived. Also educated at Eton and Trinity College, Cambridge, he was a Liberal in politics until the Home Rule Crisis of the 1880s, when like many other Liberal aristocrats, he became a Liberal Unionist and then a Conservative. He was the only Yarborough peer to hold a government office of any kind, serving as Captain, Gentleman at Arms (Chief Whip in the House of Lords) from 1890-92, in Lord Salisbury's government. He was made a Privy Councillor in 1890, and was, much later in 1935, made a Knight of the Garter. He was also Lord-Lieutenant of Lincolnshire from 1921-36, a Patron of seventeen Anglican livings, and a prominent Freemason. In his entry in *Who's Who*, he stated that he "owned about 50,000 acres in Lincolnshire." He was very wealthy, leaving £778,879 when he died, of which his land was valued at £529,297. His eldest son Charles (1887-1914) was killed in action in Flanders, and he was succeeded by his younger son Sackville, 5th Earl of Yarborough (1888-1948). He was also educated at Eton and at Trinity College, Cambridge, and served in the First World War as a captain; he received the M.C. and was mentioned in despatches. He left £442,533 when he died, of which £330,000 was the value of his land. The title then passed to another brother, Marcus, 5th Earl of Yarborough (1893-1966), similarly educated at Eton and Trinity College, Cambridge, who also received an agricultural diploma from Oxford. He served as an officer in both World Wars.

His son, John, 7th Earl of Yarborough (1920-91), educated at Eton and at Trinity College, Cambridge, was a major-general in the Grenadier Guards and a long-serving official in the British Legion. He contested Grimsby as a Conservative at the 1955 General Election, and was High Sheriff of Lincolnshire in 1964. The title is currently held by his son, Charles, 8th Earl of Yarborough (b. 1963), who served as High Sheriff of Lincolnshire in 2014-2015. Around 2013 he converted to Islam, and has been known since then as Abdul Mateen Pelham.

22. Gordon-Lennox, Dukes of Richmond, Gordon, and Lennox – £79,683 p.a.

In 1883 the Duke of Richmond, Gordon, and Lennox owned 286,411 acres worth £79,683 p.a., in Banffshire (159,952 acres/£23,841 p.a.); Aberdeenshire (69,660 acres/£24,747 p.a.); Inverness-shire (27,409 acres/£1,182 p.a.); Elgin (12,271 acres/£10,618 p.a.); Sussex (17,117 acres/£19,283 p.a.); Yorkshire, North Riding (2 acres/£12 p.a.).

Charles Lennox, 1st Duke of Richmond and 1st Duke of Lennox (1677-1723) was another illegitimate son of King Charles II, the "Merry Monarch," in his case with the French-born Louise de Kérouaille, whom Charles made Duchess of Portsmouth. The new Duke's surname was apparently invented by the King, and the titles he was given had previously been held by the Royal Stuarts in Scotland. The 1st Duke of the new creation was also a nobleman in the French nobility, when his mother was granted a French title, and was Lord High Admiral of Scotland. He was also an early patron of cricket, and helped to develop the game into its modern form. His family has always been associated with sport: the land near his country house, Goodwood House near Chichester in Sussex, later became a famous racetrack. In 1692, he married Anne (d. 1722), daughter of Francis Brudenell, Lord Brudenell, who was the son of Robert Brudenell, 3rd Earl of Cardigan. His title, Duke of Richmond (in Surrey), was given to several places in the British Empire, including Richmond County in New York City, New York, more popularly known as Staten Island.

The 1st Duke's eldest son and successor, Charles Lennox, and Duke of Richmond and

Lennox (1701-50), known from 1701-23 by his courtesy title the Earl of March, served as an M.P. from 1722-23, when he succeeded to the dukedom. In 1719 he married the wealthy (Hon.) Sarah Cadogan (1705-51), daughter of the Earl of Cardigan, when the Duke was aged only eighteen. He married her to pay-off a gambling debt. After his marriage ceremony he went on the Grand Tour and, according to a popular story, was reluctant to meet his new bride again, but went to the theatre and asked who a striking young woman was, to which he was given the reply "You must be a stranger in London not to know the toast of the town, the beautiful Lady March." The marriage was actually a great success, with the future Duchess serving as a Lady of the Bedchamber to Queen Caroline. She was one of twenty-one Society ladies whose petition led to the establishment of the London Foundling Hospital. They had twelve surviving children. In 1999, the BBC presented a miniseries on the lives of three of their daughters, called *The Aristocrats*. The second Duke was – like his father – a noted cricket player, and had his own team of players. He served as Lord of the Bedchamber from 1717 till his death and as master of the Horse from 1735 until his death, as well as Mayor of Chichester in 1735-6. His campaign against smuggling in Sussex led to the execution of thirty-five smugglers.

Charles Lennox, 3rd Duke of Richmond and Gordon (1735-1806), his son and heir, was educated at Westminster School and Leiden University, and had a tremendously varied career. He was a significant career soldier, joining the 2nd Foot Guards as an ensign in 1752, and rising to Major General in 1761, General in 1782, and Field Marshal in 1796. He was also very active in political and official life, serving as Ambassador to France in 1765, and also serving as a Cabinet minister under the Whigs in 1765-6 and under Pitt the younger in 1784-95, when he was Master-General of the Ordnance. Despite his background, he was a political radical, almost an extreme radical, who supported the American Revolution, was pro-Irish, calling for the two islands to be joined together by a "union of hearts"- a phrase that entered the political language- and in 1780 actually called for manhood suffrage and annually elected Parliaments. The 3rd Duke built the famous racetrack at Goodwood, near his country house, and was a patron of artists including Stubbs and Reynolds. Apart from Goodwood House, he also had a residence, Richmond House, in Whitehall, now rebuilt as an important, architecturally-distinguished Government building (the original building was destroyed in a fire in 1710 and has been rebuilt several times). In 1757 he married Lady Mary Bruce (d. 1796), the daughter of the 3rd Earl of Ailesbury, but had no surviving children. He did, however, have three illegitimate daughters by his mistress Mrs. Mary Bennett (1765-1845) and another illegitimate daughter by the Viscountess de Cambis. Mary, of his daughters with Mary Bennett, married William Light (1786-1839), the founder of Adelaide, Australia.

He was succeeded by his nephew, Charles Lennox, 4th Duke of Richmond and Gordon (1764-1819), the son of (General) Lord George Lennox, son of the 2nd Duke of Richmond and Lady Louisa, daughter of William Kerr, 4th Marquess of Lothian. He joined the Army in 1787 as a captain. Like many members of his family, he was notable in the cricket world; he was a founder of the Marylebone Cricket Club, helped to pay for the purchase of Lord's Cricket Ground. A colourful character, he fought two (indecisive) duels, one with Frederick, Prince of Wales. He served as an M.P. from 1790-1806, and was Lord Lieutenant of Ireland in 1807-13. Later, he served briefly as Governor-General of Canada, from 1818-19. In 1789 he married Lady Charlotte Gordon (1768-1842) and fathered fourteen children. He served with Wellington and the British forces in Brussels in 1815. His wife held a ball, just before Waterloo, for British officers in Belgium, which appeared in Thackeray's *Vanity Fair* and in Byron's poem *Childe Harold's Pilgrimage*. The 4th Duke died in Canada when he was bitten in the hand by a fox and developed hydrophobia. In 1836 his widow inherited much of the estates of her brother, the last Duke of Gordon, and the 5th Duke changed his surname to "Gordon-Lennox."

His son and successor Charles Gordon-Lennox, 5th Duke of Richmond and Lennox (1791-1860) was educated at Westminster School and at Trinity College, Dublin, presumably because his father was Lord Lieutenant of Ireland. He was also a military officer and served in the Peninsular War, where he was severely wounded. The 5th Duke served as an M.P. from 1812 until 1819, and was one of the major leaders of the "Ultra Tories," opposed to Catholic Emancipation and other measures of reform. Nevertheless, and surprisingly, he fell out with the Duke of Wellington and his Cabinet and joined Earl Grey's Whig government which passed the Great Reform Act; his improbable switch in parties is mentioned in all political histories of the period. He was rewarded by holding the Cabinet post of Postmaster-General from 1830-34. As noted, in 1836 he added "Gordon" to his surname. In 1817 he married Lady Charlotte Paget (1797-1874), daughter of the 1st Marquess of Anglesey, and had eight children. He left £120,000 in personalty when he died.

He was succeeded by his son Charles Gordon-Lennox, 6th Duke of Richmond and Lennox (1818-1903), who was educated at Westminster School and at Christ Church, Oxford. Like his forebears, he was an Army officer, and had a notable career in politics, serving as an M.P. in 1841-60 and holding Cabinet posts in Conservative governments as President of the Board of Trade 1867-8 and 1885, and as Lord President of the Council in Disraeli's government of 1874-80, when he was also Leader of the House of Lords in 1874-5. In 1876, he was created Duke of Gordon and Earl of Kintora, from his maternal grandfather's title, and thus held three Dukedoms simultaneously. In 1843 he married Frances, daughter of Algernon Greville. He died in 1903, leaving £353,573 in personalty. His son and heir, Charles, 7th Duke of Richmond and Lennox and 2nd Duke of Gordon (1845-1928), was educated at Eton and also served as an Army officer and as an M.P. from 1869 until 1886. He fought in the Boer War and was married as his first wife to Amy (1847-79), daughter of Percy Ricardo (1820-92), a member of the very wealthy family of David Ricardo, the famous economist and very wealthy stockbroker; the family was of Jewish descent, but had married Anglicans for several generations. They had three sons and two daughters. In 1886 the Duke had three residences, Goodwood House near Chichester; Gordon Castle in Morayshire; and 49 Belgrave Square in Belgravia. He left £312,830.

His son Charles, 8th Duke of Richmond and Lennox and 3rd Duke of Gordon (1870-1935) was also an army officer and served as ADC to Lord Roberts in South Africa during the Boer War. In 1893 he married Hilda Brassey (1872-1971), the granddaughter of the great railway and engineering contractor Thomas Brassey (1805-70), who left £3.2 million, and was thus the second Duke of his family to marry into the business and professional wealth elite, rather than into the landed aristocracy. He held the dukedom for only seven years, before leaving only £17,450, and was succeeded by his son Frederick, 9th Duke of Richmond and Lennox and 4th Duke of Gordon (1904-89), who was educated conventionally at Eton and Christ Church, Oxford, but then became professionally interested in motor racing, and was apprenticed to Bentley Motors – surely the first duke in history to be apprenticed to a business firm. He served as a Flight-Lieutenant in World War Two, and spent much of his career reinvigorating Goodwood, both as a racetrack and as a track for motor racing, and was Vice-President of the Royal Automobile Club (RAC) for many years. In order to pay the extensive death duties on his father's landed estates, he was forced to sell the family's Scottish properties, and his residences were given in *Who's Who* as Carne's Sear near Goodwood and 29 Hyde Park Street, W2. He left £700,814. He was married to Elizabeth Grace Hudson (1900-92), the daughter of an Anglican clergyman. They had two sons. The younger, Lord Nicholas Lennox (1931-2004) was Ambassador to Spain, 1984-89. His elder son, Charles Henry, 10th Duke of Richmond and Lennox and 5th Duke of Gordon (1929-2017), was educated at Eton and at Temple College, and had a career as a chartered accountant. He was a prominent Anglican layman, serving as a Church Commissioner from 1963-76, was Chancellor of Sussex University 1985-98, and was Lord Lieutenant of West Sussex, 1990-94.

His heir, Charles, 11th Duke of Richmond and Lennox and 6th Duke of Gordon (b. 1955), was educated at Eton and is a well-known film and still photographer, who helped to film *Barry Lyndon* for Stanley Kubrick. He has developed Goodwood further, and was the founder of the Goodwood Festival of Speed. On the 2020 *Sunday Times Rich List,* he was credited with being the 537th wealthiest person in Britain, worth £228 million, striking evidence of the vast rise in the wealth of those aristocrats who managed to hold on to even some of their land, and develop other interests. In 2001 he was stated by Kevin Cahill to own about 12,000 acres, in Sussex.

23. Legge, Earls of Dartmouth – £78,522 p.a.

The Earls of Dartmouth owned lands throughout the country. Given the high ratio of annual income to their acreage outside of London, much of their lands in the West Riding and Staffordshire must have had coal and other mineral deposits, while their lands in and near London must have had a considerable rental income. For unknown reasons, the maps giving the locations of London's large landowners in the 1890s does not include the Earl of Dartmouth, but his London holdings were apparently in Kentish Town, and at Aldersgate, Charterhouse Square, Old Jewry, and adjacent areas in the City of London. Their main country house was at Partshull Hall, near Wolverhampton; the family acquired it in 1848. The Earls of Dartmouth are not as widely known as some other families discussed here, although their peerage dates back to 1682.

In 1883 the Earl of Dartmouth owned 19,518 acres worth £58,657 p.a. in the West Riding (8,024 acres/£20,520 p.a.); Staffordshire (7,316 acres/ £16,356 p.a.); Buckinghamshire (2,195 acres/£4,700 p.a.); Shropshire (1,096 acres/£2,711 p.a.); Kent (391 acres/£10,470 p.a.); Middlesex (42 acres/£3,350 p.a.); and Sussex (454 acres/£550 p.a.). In 1892-95 he also owned 421 acres in London, worth £50,826 p.a. (Assessed Annual Rental Value Real Estate) and £21,165 p.a. (Estimated Annual Land Value-Site Only).

William Legge (1608-70) was an important figure in the English Civil War, who supported the Restoration and was given a number of important offices, including Lieutenant-General of the Ordnance, as well as lands in Co. Louth and at the Minories in London. He declined an earldom. His wife, Elisabeth Washington (c. 1616-88) was the niece of the ancestor of the first American President. Their son George Legge, 1st Baron Dartmouth (c. 1647-91) was a distinguished Admiral and supporter of the Stuarts, who was appointed the first Admiral of the Fleet by James II. He was imprisoned in the Tower by William III in 1691, where he died. He had held numerous senior appointments under Charles II and was made 1st Baron Dartmouth in 1682. He had been educated at Westminster School and at King's College, Cambridge, and also received lands from the King, at Bromley and at Lewisham in Kent. His only son, William Legge, 1st Earl of Dartmouth (1672-1750), was also educated at Westminster and at King's College, Cambridge, and served as Secretary of State for the Southern Department and Lord Privy Seal. In 1711 he was elevated to became 1st

Earl of Dartmouth and Viscount Lewisham. Unlike his father, he made the right choice in 1714, supporting the Hanoverian Succession. He married, in 1700, Lady Anne Finch, the daughter of Heneage Finch, 2nd Earl of Aylesford. Their younger son, Hon.) Henry Bilson-Legge (1708-64) was Private Secretary to Sir Robert Walpole, and served as Chancellor of the Exchequer three times between 1754 and 1761. His wife, (Hon.) Mary Stawell (1726-80), the daughter of Edward, 4th Baron Stawell, inherited his lands, and was created Baroness Stawell in her own right in 1760.

The 1st Earl's eldest son, George Legge, Viscount Lewisham (c. 1703-32) predeceased his father, and the title passed to his son William Legge, 2nd Earl of Dartmouth (1731-1801). He was educated at Trinity College, Oxford and served as Secretary of State for the Colonies from 1772-75. He was famous for his charity, and served as Vice-President of the London Foundling Hospital. Dartmouth College, the famous tertiary institution in New Hampshire, USA, founded in 1769, was named in his honour in the hopes of receiving his largesse (which apparently was not forthcoming). In 1755 he married Frances, the daughter of Sir Charles Nicoll. Several of his sons enjoyed successful careers, including his younger sons (Rt. Revd.) (Hon.) Edward Legge (1756-1827, Bishop of Oxford 1816-27, and (Admiral) Arthur Kaye Legge (1766-1835). His eldest son, George Legge, 3rd Earl of Dartmouth (1755-1810), who was educated at Eton and Christ Church, Oxford. He was an M.P. from 1778-84, and was called to the House of Lords in 1801, in his father's lifetime, as Baron Dartmouth. He served in Addington's Cabinet and for many years as Lord Chamberlain. In 1782 he married his relative Lady Frances Finch (1761-1838), daughter of Heneage, 3rd Earl of Aylesford; they had fifteen children.

His son and heir, William, 4th Earl of Dartmouth (1784-1853), was educated at Eton and Christ Church, Oxford, and served as a Major in the Staffordshire Militia. He served briefly as an M.P. in 1810 before succeeding to the peerage. He was married twice. With his first wife, Lady Frances Chetwynd-Talbot (d. 1823), the daughter of the 2nd Earl Talbot, he had one son, who succeeded him. With his second wife, (Hon.) Frances (d. 1849), daughter of George, 5th Viscount Barrington, he had six daughters and six sons, the most notable of whom was (Hon.) Augustus Legge (1839-1913), who was Bishop of Lichfield from 1891 to his death. In 1848, the Earl gave up Sandwell House, the family's main residence, near Birmingham, for Patshull House, at Pattingham near Wolverhampton, Staffordshire, which had been built in 1730. He left £130,000 in personalty.

His son William Walter, 5th Earl of Dartmouth (1823-91), was also educated at Eton and Christ Church, Oxford, and later served as Lord-Lieutenant of Staffordshire. He served as an M.P. in 1849-53, and then succeeded to the title. He helped to found Dartmouth Park in West Bromwich. In 1846 he married Lady Augusta Finch (1822-1900), daughter of Heneage, 5th Earl of Aylesford, yet another marriage between these two families; they had two sons and four daughters. He was a Patron of eight livings; his wife was a noted philanthropist in the West Midlands, with an entry in the *ODNB* as a "philanthropist." In 1886, his residences were Paishull Hall, and also Woodsome Hall in Huddersfield, and 40 Grosvenor Square. He left £119,811 in personalty.

The Earl's younger son, Sir Henry Charles Legge (1852-1924, left £50,040), was Equerry to the Royal Household from 1893-1920. His elder brother, William, 6th Earl of Dartmouth (1851-1936), was also educated at Eton and Christ Church, Oxford, and served as a Major in the Volunteers. Like other members of his family, he was a noted cricketer, and later served as a Conservative M.P. from 1878 till 1891, when he succeeded to the title. He held the posts of Vice-Chamberlain of the Household in 1885-86 and 1886-91, and was an Alderman of the Staffordshire County Council and Lord-Lieutenant of Staffordshire from 1891 till 1927. In 1879 he married Lady Mary Coke (d. 1920), daughter of Thomas Coke, 2nd Earl of Leicester; they had three sons and two daughters. The 6th Earl was still extremely wealthy, and left £784,322, of which £661,100 was in settled land. His eldest son, William Legge, 7th Earl of Dartmouth (1881-1958), also educated at Eton and Christ Church, Oxford, was a member of the London County Council (L.C.C.) from 1907, and a Conservative M.P. from 1910-18. During the First World War, he served, chiefly in Palestine, as a Major and Acting Lieutenant-Colonel. He also served as Acting Lord Great Chamberlain from 1928-36 and as High Bailiff of Westminster from 1930-42. In 1905, he married Lady Ruperta Wynn-Carrington (1883-1963), daughter of Charles, 1st Marquess of Lincolnshire. They had one son, who was killed in 1942 at El Alamein, and five daughters. Despite paying massive death duties on his father's estate, he was still substantially wealthy, leaving £467,398, of which £289,920 was in settled land, at a time of greatly diminished large fortunes, especially among the traditional landed aristocracy. As he had no surviving son, the title passed to his younger brother, Humphry Legge, 8th Earl of Dartmouth (1888-1962). His career was remarkably different from those of his forebears. The only education listed for him in *Who's Who* was on the naval training ship *HMS Britannia* at Dartmouth; he then served as a Commander in the Royal Navy during the First World War. He then became a professional police officer, rising to become Chief Constable of Berkshire from 1932 till 1953. His wife also came from a rather non-traditional background. In 1923 he married Roma, daughter of Sir Ernest Horlick, 2nd Bt., President of Horlicks Ltd., the malted milk powder manufacturers, whose father had received a baronetcy chiefly for his milk flavouring. The 8th Earl left much less than his brother, £103,591, of which £30,869 was in land.

The two most recent holders of the title also branched out from their ancestors' traditional profiles. The son of the 9th Earl, Gerald, 9th Earl of Dartmouth (1924-97) was educated at Eton and, in 1948, married Raine McCorquodale, the daughter of Dame Barbara Cartland (divorced 1976). He was a banker and financier, and a Director of the Rea Brothers Group PLC, the City merchant bank. He was also Chairman of the Royal Choral Society 1973-92, and of the Anglo-Brazilian Society from 1975 till 1994. His son and heir, William Legge, 10th Earl of Dartmouth (b. 1949), was educated at Eton and Christ Church, Oxford, and then at the Harvard Business School, and was a chartered accountant. He served as a Member of the European Parliament from 2009 until 2019, but was also Deputy-Chairman of UKIP in 2016-18.

24. Grant-Ogilvie, Earls of Seafield – £78,227 p.a.
In 1883 the Earl of Seafield owned 305,930 acres worth £78,227 p.a. in Inverness-shire (160,224 acres/£19,895 p.a.); Elgin (96,760 acres/£23,154 p.a.); and Banffshire (48,946 acres/£35,178 p.a.)

The Ogilvys (as they were then known) had been significant landowners in the north of Scotland for generations, and had been made Earls of Findlater in the Scottish peerage in 1638. James Ogilvy, 4th Earl of Findlater (1663-1730) was given a second Scottish earldom, as the 1st Earl of Seafield, in 1701. A noted lawyer, he served as Solicitor-General for Scotland in 1693-1702 and as Lord Chancellor of Scotland from 1702-8, among other senior offices. A supporter of the Act of Union, he served as a Scottish Representative Peer in the Westminster Parliament at various times between 1707 and 1730. In 1687, he married Anne, daughter of Sir William Dunbar, Bt. Their son James, 2nd Earl of Seafield (d.1764) married Lady Elizabeth Hay, daughter of Thomas Hay, 7th Earl of Kinnoul. The title then passed to their son James, 3rd Earl of Seafield (c. 1714-70), who established linen and bleaching works on his land, and married Lady Mary Murray (1720-

95), daughter of James Murray, 1st Duke of Atholl. Their son James Ogilvy, 4th Earl of Seafield (1750-1811) was educated at Christ Church, Oxford (where he was known as Baron Deskfoord or Deskford), and was a noted landscape and garden architect and designer. Although in 1779 he married Christina, daughter of Sir Joseph Murray, Count of Melgum and Lieutenant-General in the Army of the Holy Roman Empire, he was widely regarded as a homosexual, and was forced to live abroad for much of his life. He was buried in a tomb with his male partner, Johann Fischer (1773-1860). As he had no children, the Earldom of Seafield passed to his second cousin, while the Earldom of Findlater, which the family still held, became dormant.

His second cousin and successor, Sir Lewis Grant-Ogilvy, 9th Bt. (1767-1840: "Ogilvy" in his surname was thereafter often spelled "Ogilvie"), 5th Earl of Seafield, was an hereditary baronet, the son of Sir James Grant, 8th Bt. (1738-1811) and Jean Duff (1746-1805). He was educated at Edinburgh High School and then at Westminster School, and then read Law at Edinburgh University and at Lincoln's Inn. He served as an M.P. from 1790-96, when he became permanently "mentally deranged," and his younger brother and successor took over the administration of his estate. This was (Col.) Sir Francis William Ogilvie-Grant, 9th Bt. and 6th Earl of Seafield (1778-1853), a professional military officer who was known as the largest planter of trees in Britain, responsible for planting no fewer than 31 million trees on his properties. He served as a Tory M.P. from 1802-1840, and then as a Scottish Representative Peer from 1841 until his death. He and his successors were also Chiefs of the Clan Grant.

The 6th Earl had four successors in quick order. John, 7th Earl of Seafield (1815-81) served in the Royal Navy and was then a Scottish Representative Peer from 1853-58, when he was created Baron Strathspey in the United Kingdom peerage, giving him an automatic seat in the Lords. His main residences were Cullen House in Banffshire and Castle Grant in Strathspey, also in Morayshire. Rather strangely, he disentailed his lands, meaning that the successors to his peerages would not necessarily inherit the Seafield lands. They continued to be separately inherited until 1946. In 1850 he married (Hon.) Caroline Stuart (d. 1911), and left £159,106 in personalty. He was then succeeded for only four years by his son Ian, 8th Earl of Seafield (1851-84), who was educated at Eton and, like other members of his family, was an Elder of the Church of Scotland. He was unmarried, and after his death of heart disease at only thirty-three, leaving £156,286 in personalty, the title passed to his uncle, James, 9th Earl of Seafield (1817-88) an army officer who served as a Conservative M.P. from 1868-74. As he did not inherit the Strathspey peerage, it was recreated for him as Baron Strathspey of the second creation in 1884, giving him an automatic seat in the Lords. He left only £1,840 in personalty. His son and heir, Francis, 10th Earl of Seafield (1847-88) served in the Royal Navy, and then moved to New Zealand, where he lived for the rest of his life. He held the title for only six months before dying at forty-one, leaving nothing in Britain.

His son and heir, James, 11th Earl of Seafield (1876-1915) was born and educated in New Zealand, at private schools there. In 1898 he married Mary, daughter of Dr. Joseph Townend of Christchurch, New Zealand. The Earl served as an officer in the Boer War and as a Captain during the First World War. In 1915, he died of wounds received in the fighting at Flanders. His Scottish peerage was one in which a daughter could succeed in the absence of a son, and his title went to his only child, Nina Ogilvie-Grant (later Ogilvie-Grant-Studley-Herbert), 12th Countess of Seafield (1906-69). In 1930 she married Derek Studley-Herbert (divorced 1957, died 1960). In 1930 she had acted as one of the godparents of Anthony Armstrong-Jones, later the Earl of Snowdon. The Countess was said in the popular press to have been the second wealthiest woman in Britain, after the Queen, a claim which appears exaggerated, based largely on the assertion that she allegedly inherited $30 million from Mrs. Joseph H. Townend of New Zealand, her step-grandmother. During the 1920s she had also been linked in the popular press with the Prince of Wales, then the most eligible bachelor in Britain, before his infatuation with Mrs. Simpson. Her son and successor, Ian, 13th Earl of Seafield (b. 1939), was educated at Eton and has been married twice, his second wife being Leila, daughter of Mahmoud Refaat of Cairo. He lives at Cullen House. In 2001 he still owned 101,000 acres of land, according to the research of Kevin Cahill, and about 84,000 acres in 2008, according to *The Scotsman* newspaper.

25. Herbert, Earls of Pembroke and Montgomery – £77,720 p.a.

The title "Earl of Pembroke" has been created ten different times since 1138. The tenth and current creation occurred in 1551 for William Herbert, 1st Earl of Pembroke (1501-1570), a major political figure during the reigns of Edward VI, Mary I, and Elizabeth I, who was married to the sister of Catherine Parr, Henry VIII's sixth wife. According to John Aubrey, he could "neither read nor write," but "had a stamp for his name." His grandson, William Herbert, 3rd Earl of Pembroke (1580-1630), was Chancellor of Oxford University, co-founder of Pembroke College, Oxford, and served as Lord Chamberlain from 1615 till 1625. He and his brother Philip Herbert, 1st Earl of Montgomery (1584-1650), remain universally known as the "incomparable pair of brothers" to whom Shakespeare's First Folio was dedicated in 1623. The two earldoms became merged in 1630, when Philip Herbert, 1st Earl of Montgomery, succeeded as 4th Earl of Pembroke; the two titles have been held by a single successor ever since. From the late eighteenth century, the family owned considerable acreage in Wiltshire and also in Ireland, especially in Co. Dublin, where they owned Pembroke Township, adjacent to the City of Dublin, whose rental income, as will be seen above, was exceptionally high compared to its acreage. For over four hundred years, their main country house has been Wilton House near Salisbury, Wiltshire. It is still occupied by the current Earl, who employs a staff of 140 on his 14,000 acre estate.

In 1883, the Earl of Pembroke and Montgomery owned 44,806 acres worth £77,720 p.a., in Wiltshire (42,244 acres/£40,500 p.a.); Westmorland (230 acres/£57 p.a.); Co. Dublin (2,301 acres/£35,586 p.a.); and Co. Wicklow (230 acres/£1,577 p.a.).

George Herbert, 11th Earl of Pembroke (1759-1827), was the son of Henry, 10th Earl of Pembroke (1734-94) and Lady Elizabeth (1737-1831), daughter of Charles Spencer, 3rd Duke of Marlborough. He was educated at Harrow, and became an army officer who was active in the French Revolutionary Wars. He was promoted to Lieutenant-General in 1802, and to General in 1812. Already wealthy, he became richer still when he inherited Pembroke Township near Dublin from his grandmother, the daughter of the 5th Earl Fitzwilliam. He also had a political career, serving as an M.P. from 1780-84 and in 1788-94, when he succeeded to the Earldom, and was Vice-Chamberlain of the Household and, later, Governor of Guernsey. At his death, he left £600,000 in personalty, a very large sum. The Earl was married twice: first, in 1787, to Elizabeth (d. 1793), daughter of Topham Beauclerk, and, secondly, to the Countess Catherine Vorontsova, the daughter of a Russian aristocrat. His eldest son and successor was the product of his first marriage. With his second marriage, he was the father of Sidney Herbert, 1st Baron Herbert of Lea (1810-61). Sidney Herbert was educated at Harrow and at Oriel College, Oxford, and served as an M.P. from 1832 until 1861, when he received a peerage. He served in Cabinets under Peel and Palmerston as Secretary of State for the Colonies in 1855 and as Secretary of State for

War in1845-6, 1852-4, 1855, and 1859-61, and is best known for asking Florence Nightingale to organise nurses to treat the British soldiers in Crimea, the beginning of her worldwide renown. Lord Herbert also ran the family estates while his half-brother, the 12th Earl, lived abroad. In 1846 he married Elizabeth à Court-Repington (1822-1911); several of their children were notable. His eldest son Sidney Herbert (1853-1913) succeeded as the 14th Earl of Pembroke. Their daughter Mary (1849-1935) married the famous Austrian theologian Baron Friedrich von Hugel. Their son Sir Michael Herbert (1857-1904) served as British Ambassador to the United States in 1888-93. Lord Herbert of Lea died of Bright's Disease at the age of only fifty-one, leaving £160,000 in personalty. Had he lived, it is quite possible that he might have become Prime Minister.

The 11th Earl's eldest son was Robert Herbert, 12th Earl of Pembroke (1791-1862), who was educated at Harrow and at Christ Church, Oxford. In 1814 at Palermo, Sicily he made a secret marriage with Princess Ottavia Spinelli (1779-1857) of the Sicilian aristocracy, to which his father, the Earl, took great exception, and convinced the Sicilian authorities to dissolve the marriage – it was annulled in 1819 – and imprison his son, who escaped. The Princess lived in London until her death, and was awarded compensation of £800 p.a. (later raised to £5,000 p.a.). Neither ever married again. The 12th Earl then lived in Paris, where he fathered seven illegitimate children with two mistresses; as noted, his half-brother Lord Herbert of Lea, ran his estates in the U.K. The 12th Earl died in Paris in 1862, leaving £120,000 in personalty in Britain. As he had no sons, the title passed to George Herbert, 12th Earl of Pembroke (1850-95), the son of Lord Herbert of Lea. He was educated at Eton and served in 1874-5 as Under-Secretary of State for War in Disraeli's government. He founded the Pembroke Technical School near Dublin. His entry in the *ODNB* defines him as a "travel writer." He spent much of his life travelling through Europe, and was on a voyage in the south Pacific when his ship was wrecked near Fiji; in 1872 he co-authored an account of this, *South Sea Bubbles*. In 1874 he married Lady Gertrude Chetwynd-Talbot (1840-1906), the daughter of Henry, 13th Earl of Shrewsbury. Like his father, he died young, leaving £268,296 in personalty. He had no children, and was succeeded by his brother Sidney Herbert, 14th Earl of Pembroke (1853-1913). He was educated at Eton and at Christ Church, Oxford. He served as an M.P. in 1877-85 and 1886-95, and was a junior minister under Lord Salisbury and A.J. Balfour. He was widely regarded as the handsomest man in Parliament. Like other members of his family, he was a noted cricketer, and was President of the MCC in 1896. In 1877 he married Lady Beatrix, daughter of George, 2nd Earl of Durham. The sister of these two Earls, Lady Elizabeth Maud Herbert (1851-1933) was married to Sir Hubert Parry (1848-1918), the famous composer, whose best-known work is the renowned hymn *Jerusalem*, based on the poem by William Blake. The 14th Earl left £243,890 in personalty.

There have been four further holders of the title. Reginald, 15th Earl of Pembroke (1880-1960), the son of the 14th Earl, was educated at Eton and Sandhurst, and served as a Major in the First World War, and in the Foreign Office during the Second World War. In 1904 he married Lady Beatrice Paget, daughter of the Marquess of Anglesey. He left £329,459, of which £300,000 was in land. His son and successor, Sidney, 16th Earl of Pembroke (1906-69), was educated at Eton and Pembroke College, Oxford. He served in the Second World War, and was an Equerry to the Duke of Kent, as well as a Trustee of the National Gallery and the National Portrait Gallery. In 1936 he married Lady Mary, the daughter of the Marchioness of Linlithgow. He left £88,978, of course a great under-statement of his true wealth. His son Henry, 17th Earl of Pembroke (1939-2003) was educated at Eton and Oxford, but his son and successor, William, 18th Earl of Pembroke (b.

1978), was educated at Bryanston School and then at Sheffield Hallam University. He became a product designer with Conran and Partners, and is the manager of the Wilton Estates. In 2001, he was stated by Kevin Cahill to own 14,000 acres in Wiltshire and another 14,000 in the Republic of Ireland. In the 2020 *Sunday Times Rich List,* the Duke of Pembroke was said to be worth £149 million.

26. Murray, Earls of Mansfield – £77,006 p.a.

In 1883 the Earl of Mansfield owned 49,074 acres worth £42,968 p.a. in Perthshire (31,197 acres/£34,738 p.a.); Dumfries-shire (14,342 acres/ £13,389 p.a.); Cheshire (224 acres/£3,110 p.a.); and Clackmannanshire (1,705 acres/£1,751 p.a.). They also had the income of "coal rented at £1,886" p.a. In addition, in 1892-95 he owned 207 acres in London worth £132,210 p.a. in Assessed Annual Rental Value (Real Estate) and £34,738 p.a. in Estimated Annual Land Value (Site Only).

The famous judge David Murray, 1st Earl of Mansfield (1705-93) received this family's first English peerage, but he was already a member of the Scottish aristocracy. He was born at Scone Palace, Perthshire, the third son of David Murray, 5th Viscount of Stormont (1665-1746), who were already large landowners in Scotland. The family had been strongly associated with the Jacobite Pretenders, and Mansfield was attacked, during the first half of his career, as a secret Jacobite, a charge he had repeatedly to deny. He was educated in Perth, Scotland, and then at Westminster School and at Christ Church, Oxford. At Oxford, he won a Latin poetry prize just ahead of William Pitt, his lifelong rival and political opponent. He was called to the bar at Lincoln's Inn in 1730, and became one of the leading barristers of his time. Murray became an M.P. in 1742, and was immediately made Solicitor-General, a post he held until 1754, and he was in effect the Leader of the House of Commons. He then became Attorney-General for England and Wales in 1754-56, briefly Chancellor of the Exchequer in 1757, and Lord Chief Justice of the King's Bench from 1756 till 1788, and a member of the Cabinet – a combination obviously impermissible in later times. In 1756 he was given a peerage as Baron Mansfield, named for the town in Nottinghamshire, although he had no connection with it, possibly as a tribute to his wife's family.

As a judge, Mansfield was a very significant legal reformer and a major influence on the evolution of English law. His decision in Somersett's (*sic*) Case in 1772 helped to outlaw slavery in England, and he had a mulatto illegitimate niece, Dido Elizabeth Belle. In 1776 he was made Earl of Mansfield and, most unusually, was given a second earldom, also as Earl of Mansfield, in 1792. This was apparently done so that his Scottish relatives could inherit his English peerage, something that was apparently not permitted at the time. At his death at eighty-eight in 1793, he was said to have been enormously wealthy, a product of inheriting lands in Scotland, and of having a vast income from earnings at the bar and from lucrative office-holding for many years. From 1754 he owned Kenwood House on Hampstead Heath, now a well-known art museum, which his family continued to own until 1925. In 1738 he married Lady Elizabeth Finch (1704-84), daughter of Daniel Finch, 2nd Earl of Nottingham, but died without children. He was buried in Westminster Abbey.

At his death, the two Earldoms passed to different people. One passed to his nephew, David Murray, 7th Viscount of Stormont and 2nd Earl of Mansfield (1727-96), and the other, most unusually, to his wife, (Hon.) Louisa Cathcart (1758-1843), daughter of Charles, 9th Baron

Cathcart, who also became the 2nd Countess of Mansfield, of a different creation. The nephew was the son of David, 6th Viscount of Stormont, and was educated at Westminster School and at Christ Church, Oxford. He was helped throughout his career by his uncle, who regarded him as his *de facto* son, and became a diplomat, who served as Ambassador to Saxony-Poland, to Austria, and to France. From 1763 until 1793 he was a Scottish Representative Peer (as Viscount of Stormont) he then inherited his uncle's earldom. He served under Lord North and other Prime Ministers as Secretary of State for the Northern Department and Leader of the Lords from 1779-82, as Lord President of the Council in 1783 and 1794-96, and as Lord Justice General 1778-95. Known as a learned man, and Chancellor of Marischal College, Aberdeen from 1793, in 1759 he married Henrietta (d. 1766), the daughter of Graf Heinrich von Bunau and, secondly in 1776, (Hon.) Louisa Cathcart, who inherited the "other" Earldom of Mansfield when his uncle died. His second marriage produced a son, David, 3rd Earl of Mansfield (1777-1840), was educated at Westminster School and at Christ Church, Oxford, and was a career army officer. He served as Lord-Lieutenant of Clackmannanshire from 1803. In 1797, he married Frederica (1774-1860), daughter of (Rt. Revd.) William Markham, Archbishop of York. He left £229,430 in personalty at his death.

His son William, 4th Earl of Mansfield (1806-98) was educated at Westminster School, and was a Tory M.P. from 1830-1840, serving as a Lord of the Treasury (a government Whip) in 1834-5. He was also three times Lord High Commissioner to the General Assembly of the Church of Scotland. He inherited his father's earldom in 1840, and his grandmother's second earldom when she died in 1843. Like many holders of this title, he was made a Knight of the Thistle. In 1829 he married Louisa (d. 1837), the daughter of Cuthbert Ellison (1783-1860), a wealthy banker in Newcastle-upon-Tyne and an M.P. who left £180,000. In 1886, his residences were given as Scone Palace, Perth; Comlongan Castle, Dumfries; Schaw Park, Clackmannan; and Kenwood House in Hampstead. He left £137,243 in personalty. His only son predeceased him in 1893, and he was succeeded by his grandson William, 5th Earl of Mansfield (1860-1906), who was educated at Eton and at Sandhurst, and was a Captain in the Grenadier Guards. He died at forty-six, leaving £132,220 in personalty. He had no sons, and was succeeded by his brother Alan, 6th Earl of Mansfield (1864-1935), who was educated at Charterhouse and at Sandhurst, and was a Lieutenant in the Black Watch, 1886-94 and Gentleman usher of the Green Rod from 1895 to 1917. In 1899 he married Margaret (d. 1933), daughter of (Rear-Admiral) Sir Malcolm MacGregor, 4th Bt., and left £496,087 at his death. In 1925, however, he sold Kenwood House to Edward Guinness, 1st Earl of Iveagh, of the brewery family, one of the very richest men in Britain (he left £13.5 million at his death), who donated it, and its great art collection, to the Nation when he died in 1927.

There have been three holders of the title since 1935. Mungo, 7th Earl of Mansfield (1900-71), the son of the 6th Earl, was educated at Christ Church, Oxford, and was a Unionist M.P. from 1931 to 1935 and Lord-Lieutenant of Perthshire. He held a remarkably wide number of positions, and was a noted ornithologist as well as Chairman of the Edinburgh Board of the Royal Insurance Company. In 1928 he married Dorothea (d. 1985), daughter of Sir Lancelot Carnegie. He served as Lord High Commissioner to the Church of Scotland in 1961-2. His son William, 8th Earl of Mansfield (1930-2015), was educated at Eton and Christ Church, Oxford, and served with the Scots Guards in Malaya, 1949-50. He was a barrister of the Inner Temple, and practiced from 1958-71. After succeeding to the title, he served as a British Delegate to the European Parliament, 1973-75, and a junior minister in the Thatcher government from 1979 to 1984. In 1955 he married Pamela Foster. His son, Alexander, 8th Earl of Mansfield (b. 1956), was educated at Eton and at

Magdalene College, Cambridge, and was a Member of the Scottish Council of the Historic Houses Association from 1993-2007. In 2001 he owned 33,800 acres in Britain and Ireland, according to the research of Kevin Cahill.

27. Howard (later Fitzalan-Howard), Dukes of Norfolk – £75,596 p.a.

Among the best-known of senior landed aristocratic families in Britain, the Dukes of Norfolk are the Premier Duke (as the oldest ducal title-holder is known) in the English peerage, and are always Earl Marshals of England. They are also among the best-known Roman Catholic families in Britain, as Recusants- pre-Reformation Catholics who never became Anglicans- rather than recent converts. Like many very old peerages, the title has been re-created several times, the first time in 1397, and the present Dukedom dating from 1483. In that year John Howard (c. 1425-85), a descendant of King John and of King Edward I, and also a strong supporter of the Yorkists during the War of the Roses, was given a dukedom. He was a leading supporter of King Richard III, and was killed at Bosworth in 1485. He was also the great-grandfather of Anne Boleyn and the great-great-grandfather of Queen Elizabeth I. Through various travails of forfeiting the Dukedom and then having it restored, the title continued to Edward Howard, 9th Duke of Norfolk (1685-1777), the first of the more recent dukes to be considered here. The family owned much land in Sussex and in and near Sheffield in Yorkshire (sold in the 1950s), as well as – it is believed – ten acres in London, although this holding does not appear in Peter Lindert's list of London landowners in 1892-94.

He was the brother of the previous title-holder, Thomas Howard, 8th Duke of Norfolk (1683-1732). Their family was well-known as strict Roman Catholics at a time when that carried severe penalties and social ostracism. The 9th Duke took part in the Jacobite Rising of 1715, when the "Old Pretender" invaded Scotland and then northern England, and was fortunate not to be executed for treason. His wife Mary *nee* Blount (c. 1712-73) also came from a notable Recusant family. Dying childless, the title passed to his second cousin, Charles Howard, 10th Duke of Norfolk (1720-86), who was educated on the Continent. He lived quietly at his estate at Deepdene in Surrey, and wrote several pamphlets advocating toleration for Catholics; he was widely regarded as eccentric. In 1739, he married Catherine (1718-84), the daughter of John Brockholes, of a Lancashire Recusant family.

Their only son, Charles Howard, 11th Duke of Norfolk (1746-1815) was educated by Catholic tutors. He was married twice, and had five children by his mistress Mary Gibbon, a relative of the historian, whom he may have secretly married. He also had another illegitimate son by another mistress, Sir William Woods (1785-1842), who held the post of Garter King of Arms from 1838 until his death. (Woods himself had two mistresses and six illegitimate children.) The 11th Duke spent much of his wealth rebuilding Arundel Castle, the family's famous stately home in Sussex. In 1780, the 11th Duke gave up his family's Catholicism and became an Anglican. He served as an M.P. from 1780 until 1784 and was a government Whip. A political radical, at a political dinner held in a London tavern in 1798, he proposed a toast to "Our Sovereign's health – the majesty of the people." Unsurprisingly, this did not please George III, who stripped him of the various offices he held. At his death, the 11th Duke left £140,000 in personalty "within province" (i.e., within the Archdiocese of Canterbury, the southern two-thirds of England).

He had no legitimate children, and the title then passed to his third cousin, Bernard Edward Howard, 12th Duke of Norfolk (1765-1842) who was the son of Henry Howard (1713-87), a land agent and, remarkably, in employment as a wine merchant in Glossop, Derbyshire. A Roman Catholic, the 12th Duke was educated at the English College at Douai in France. He sat in the Lords from 1829, when Catholics were first allowed to sit in Parliament, and was appointed a Knight of the Garter in 1834, probably the first professing Catholic to be appointed to that rank since 1688. His marriage to Lady Elizabeth Belasyse (1770-1819), the daughter of Henry, 2nd Earl of Fauconberg, ended in divorce in 1794 caused by her adultery with the second Earl of Lucan. He left £180,000 in personalty at his death. Before their divorce, they produced a son, Henry Charles Howard, 13th Duke of Norfolk (1791-1856). In 1814 he married Lady Charlotte Leveson-Gower (1788-1870), the daughter of the astronomically wealthy George, 1st Duke of Sutherland. As noted, in 1829 Catholics were finally permitted to sit in Parliament, and the 13th Duke – then known by his courtesy title of the Earl of Surrey – was the first professing Catholic to be elected to the House of Commons and to take his oath as an M.P. since the Reformation, serving as M.P. for Horsham from 1829-32; he sat for other seats from 1832 until 1841, when he was summoned to the House of Lords via one of his father's minor titles, as Baron Maltravers. A staunch Whig, he served in Whig governments from 1846 until 1854. Not well-liked – Thomas Creevy called him "odious" – he left £100,000 "within province" at his death. His younger son, Lord Eustace Howard (1818-83, left £118,325), an M.P. from 1852-68 and a junior minister, was created Baron Howard of Glossop in 1869.

His eldest son Thomas Fitzalan-Howard, 14th Duke of Norfolk (1815-60) was educated at Trinity College, Cambridge without taking a degree (prior to 1872, non-Anglicans could matriculate at Cambridge but not graduate), and served as a Captain in the Guards. He was a Whig M.P. from 1837-52, but resigned from his original seat at Arundel in protest at the Ecclesiastical Titles Act of 1851 (repealed in 1871), which forbade non-Anglican clergymen from using a placename in their official titles, a deliberately anti-Catholic law, perhaps the last such to be passed. No one was ever prosecuted under this Act, and the head of the Roman Catholic Church in England was known as the Archbishop of Westminster, in apparent violation of the Act. In 1839 he married Augusta (1821-86), the daughter of (Admiral) Sir Edmund Lyons (1790-1858), later 1st Baron Lyons, the British Ambassador to Greece. The 15th Duke added "Fitzalan-" to his surname, possibly taken from one of his minor titles, Lord Fitzalan; it has remained part of the family surname ever since. He was close to many Catholic intellectuals, especially the French Count de Montalembert and John Henry Newman, and became a major Catholic philanthropist. At his death at the age of only forty-five, he left £90,000 in personalty, less than one might expect, probably because of his generous charitable donations. He and his wife had many children.

Their younger son Sir Edmund Fitzalan-Howard, 1st Viscount FitzAlan of Derwent, created a viscount in 1921 (1853-1947, left £69,777), served as the last Governor-General of Ireland, in 1921-22, and the first Roman Catholic to hold that post. Their oldest son, Henry Fitzalan-Howard, 15th Duke of Norfolk (1847-1917) was educated at the Oratory School in Birmingham. His career illustrates the increasing acceptability of Catholics in the mainstream of British public life, and their increasing acceptance by the Anglican Establishment. He inherited the title at thirteen, and served as Postmaster-General in Lord Salisbury's Tory Cabinet in 1895-1900. He resigned to fight in the Boer War. He served as the first Lord Mayor of Sheffield in 1895-97 – the Duke had landed property in that area – as Mayor of Westminster in 1899-1900, and as the first Chancellor of Sheffield University. Although he was a Catholic, as Earl Marshal he organised the funeral of Queen Victoria. He used his influence to make John Henry Newman a Cardinal, and was an amateur church builder of some note. In 1886 he had four residences: Arundel Castle in Sussex; The Farm, Sheffield; Derwent Hall, in Bakewell, Derbyshire; and Norfolk House at 31 St. James's Square, which was built in 1754 and replaced by an office block in 1938. The 15th Duke was married twice – first, in 1877, to Lady Flora (1854-1902), daughter of Charles Abney-Hastings, 1st Baron Donington, and secondly, in 1904, to (Hon.) Gwendolen (1877-1945), daughter of Marmaduke, 11th Lord Herries, the mother of his son and heir. At his death, he left £300,000 in personalty.

His son and heir was the well-known Bernard Marmaduke Fitzalan-Howard, 16th Duke of Norfolk (1908-75), who was often in the public eye in the age of radio and television in his role as Earl Marshal. He inherited the Dukedom at nine, and was educated at the Oratory School, and served as a Major in the Royal Sussex Regiment. He was wounded in World War Two. From 1941 until 1945 he was Joint Parliamentary Secretary to the Ministry of Agriculture in the wartime Coalition government, along with Tom Williams (later Baron Williams of Barnburgh, 1888-1967), a Labour M.P. who began working as a coalminer at the age of eleven. The Duke oversaw the Coronation of George VI and Elizabeth II, the State Funeral of Sir Winston Churchill, and the Investiture of Prince Charles as Prince of Wales. He also acted, rather incongruously, as Manager of the MCC cricketing tour of Australia in 1962-63. In 1937, he married (Hon.) Lavinia Strutt (1916-95), the daughter of Algernon Strutt, 3rd Baron Belper, a descendant of Edward Strutt, 1st Baron Belper, a cotton manufacturer and the first industrialist to receive a peerage, in 1856. The Duchess remained an Anglican and did not convert to Catholicism. The Duke was regarded as perhaps the leading Catholic layman in Britain, and was connected with many Catholic charities and institutions. He left £3,536,537 when he died. His widow left £4,117,746.

As the 15th Duke had four daughters but no sons, the title then passed to his second cousin once removed, Miles Francis Stapleton Fitzalan-Howard, 17th Duke of Norfolk (1915-2002). He also inherited the titles of 4th Baron Howard of Glossop from his father and 12th Baron Beaumont from his mother. He was the son of Bernard, 3rd Baron Howard of Glossop (1885-1972) and of Mona Stapleton, 11th Baroness Beaumont (1894-1971) in her own right. He was educated at Ampleforth College and at Christ Church, Oxford, and was a career army officer, serving as a Captain during World War Two (and awarded an M.C.), rising to Colonel in 1958, retiring in 1965. He served as Chief of the British Mission to the Soviet Forces in Germany in 1957 and as Director of Service Intelligence in the Ministry of Defence, 1966-67. As a leading Catholic layman – although disagreeing with the Church on birth control – he represented the Queen at Papal Investitures and funerals. In 1949 he married Anne Constable-Maxwell (1927-2013). His son, the present title holder, Edward William Fitzalan-Howard, 18th Duke of Norfolk (b. 1956) was educated at Ampleforth College and at Lincoln College, Oxford, and was a company director. In 1987 he married Georgina, daughter of Jack Gore. They have three sons and two daughters.

In 1883 the Duke of Norfolk owned 49,866 acres worth £5,596 p.a. in Yorkshire, West Riding (19,440 acres/£39,897 p.a.); Sussex (21,346 acres/£39,897 p.a.); Norfolk (4,460 acres/£5,095 p.a.); Surrey (3,172 acres/£2,247 p.a.); Derbyshire (1,274 acres/£493 p.a.), with smaller holdings in Suffolk, Stafford, and Nottinghamshire. In 2001, Duke of Norfolk was said to own about 46,000 acres. Arundel Castle is still their chief residence.

28. Edwardes, Barons Kensington – £75,588 p.a.

In 1883, Lord Kensington owned 7,471 acres worth £5399 p.a. in Pembrokeshire (6,537 acres/£4,974 p.a.), and smaller amounts in Radnor, Cardiganshire, and Carmarthenshire. In addition, in 1892-94 he owned 172 acres in London, worth £148,401 p.a. in Assessed Annual Rental Value (Real Estate) and £70,209 p.a. in Estimated Annual Land Value (Site Only).

The Edwardes family, who became the Barons Kensington, were a landed family in Wales in a relatively minor way who, most fortunately, in 1783 inherited about 250 acres of land in west London from their relatives, the Rich family. Their London property included Holland House, but at the time mainly consisted of market gardens and farmer's fields. During the nineteenth century this land was developed into the area bounded by Earls Court Road, Cromwell Road, and Old Brompton Road, and also extending north of Kensington High Street. It included Edwardes Square and the squares and streets around Earls Court and Lexham Gardens, as well as other residential property in the area. (See *Survey of London, Vol. 42: Kensington Square to Earls Court* (1986), Chapter XVI.) If this holding had been kept intact today and Lord Kensington still owned its ground rents, he would be a multi-billionaire, but, unfortunately for them it was sold off during the nineteenth century. In 1892-94 it consisted of about 172 acres, rather than the 250 the family inherited a century earlier. In 1902-03, most of this was sold to Sir Edward Guinness, Lord Iveagh, for £565,000. At his death in 1930, it was purchased by Sir John Ellerman, Britain's richest man, who then sold it on to Metropolitan Ground Rents, a property company, for £1,000,000. The Barons Kensington appear in this discussion because of their London lands, rather than for their agricultural acreage, which was much less extensive than the other landowners surveyed here.

William Edwardes, 1st Baron Kensington (c. 1711-1801), was the son of Francis Edwardes (d. 1725), a Welsh M.P. from 1722 until his death. He was the son of Lady Elizabeth Rich, the heiress of Edward Henry Rich, 7th Earl of Warwick and 4th Earl of Holland (1697-1721), from whom the London properties were inherited. He was an M.P. from 1747 until 1801 (except for 1784-86), fifty-two years. Edwardes was married twice, the second time to Elizabeth, daughter of William Warren of Longridge, Lancashire. In 1776 he was created 1st Baron Kensington, rather strangely in the Irish peerage, although he had no known interests or property in Ireland, presumably with the intention of allowing him to sit in the House of Commons (Irish peers could be elected to the House of Commons; probably the best known was Lord Palmerston, the Prime Minister.) He was the "Father of the House" of Commons when he died at the age of ninety. His son, William Edwardes, 2nd Baron Kensington (1777-1852), born when his father was sixty-six, and married to his second wife, was educated by private tutors, and was a Whig M.P. from 1802-18. He served as a Lord of the Admiralty in 1806-07. In 1797 he married Dorothy, daughter of Richard Thomas, and had nine children. Edwardes Square, on his property in west London, was named in his honour. He was said to have been a spendthrift who owed £270,000 at his death. His son William Edwardes, 3rd Baron Kensington (1801-72), entered the Royal Navy at thirteen in 1814 and became a Captain, retiring in 1827. He was then Lord Lieutenant of Pembrokeshire. In 1833, he married Laura, the daughter of Cuthbert Ellison, a wealthy colliery owner and M.P. in Newcastle-upon-Tyne. He left £25,000 in personalty, a very low sum, given his background.

His son and successor, William, 4th Baron Kensington (1835-96) was educated at Eton and was a Lieutenant in the Coldstream Guards before becoming a Liberal M.P., serving from 1868 until 1885. In 1886 he was awarded a British peerage (as Baron Kensington), giving him an automatic seat in the Lords. He held a number of junior ministerial positions in Liberal governments, including Comptroller of the Household, 1880-85; Lord-in-Waiting, 1886; and

Captain, Yeomen of the Guards (the government's Chief Whip in the Lords), 1892-94, when he was one of relatively few hereditary peers who continued to support the Liberal Party. He had a fatal heart attack in 1896 while hunting. In 1867 he married Grace, daughter of Robert Johnstone-Douglas. In 1886 his residences were listed at St. Brides in Pembroke and 69 Grosvenor Street in Mayfair. He left £57,889 in personalty at his death. His elder son, William, 5th Baron Kensington (1868-1900) was educated at Eton and became an army officer. He died of wounds received in the Boer War in 1900 at the age of thirty-two. He left £813,951 in personalty, suggesting that the family's wealth had been made over to him as likely to avoid death duties for many years, or that the lucrative sales of the family's properties in London were completed in the brief time that he held the title. He was unmarried, and the title passed to his brother Hugh, 6th Baron Kensington (1873-1938), who was also a career army officer, serving in the Boer War and in the First World War in the Dardanelles and the Middle East. In 1903, he married Mabel (d. 1934), the daughter of George Pilkington (1840-1925, left £177,012) of the famous glass manufacturing firm in St. Helens, Lancashire. The 6th Earl left only £9,228.

His son, William, 7th Baron Kensington (1904-81) was educated at Eton and Sandhurst and served as a Lieutenant-Colonel in the Indian Army. After his retirement, he moved to Rhodesia (later Zimbabwe), where he was a farmer. He left £280,502 in England at his death. His heirs have continued to live in southern Africa. The 7th Baron was unmarried, and the title passed to his nephew, Hugh, 8th Baron Kensington (1933-2018), the son of (Hon.) Hugh Owen Edwardes (d. 1937), the younger son of the 6th Baron. He was educated at Eton, and was a farmer in Natal, South Africa. The title then passed to his son William, 9th Baron Kensington (b. 1964), who was educated in Natal, South Africa, and lives there as a farmer. The Edwardes family thus today has no ostensible connections with Kensington in London or with Wales.

29. Pelham-Holles, later Pelham-Clinton, Dukes of Newcastle – £74,547 p.a.

During the mid-eighteenth century, the Duke of Newcastle and his relatives were synonymous with the so-called Whig Oligarchy, especially during the long Whig ascendancy in Parliament under Sir Robert Walpole (1676-1745), and his two Pelham successors, Thomas Pelham-Holles, 1st Duke of Newcastle (1693-1768) and his younger brother Henry Pelham (1694-1754), who were Prime Ministers for much of the period between 1743 and 1762, and were powerful leaders in Parliament for much of the time between the defeat of the "Old Pretender" in 1715 and the period following the accession of George III in 1760. The Dukes of Newcastle owned much land in Nottinghamshire, with its lucrative collieries. Their main country house, Clumber Park near Worksop, was demolished in 1938 after being damaged in fires; the estate itself was acquired in 1946 by the National Trust. During the eighteenth century the Dukes also had lands in Sussex, where they had great political influence and "owned" many seats in the House of Commons.

In 1883, the Duke of Newcastle owned 25,547 acres worth £74,547 p.a., in Nottinghamshire (34,467 acres/£73,098 p.a.); Derbyshire (827 acres/£1,124 p.a.); Yorkshire West Riding (237 acres/£307 p.a.); and Lincolnshire (16 acres/£18 p.a.).

The title of Duke of Newcastle has been created several times. In 1694 John Holles, 4th earl of Clare (1662-1711) was created Duke of Newcastle-upon-Tyne. He was the son of Gilbert Holles, 3rd Earl of Clare (1633-89) and Grace Pierrepont, the daughter of (Hon.) William Pierrepont and granddaughter of the 1st Earl of Kingston-upon-Hull. Holles was elected an M.P. in 1689, but became a member of the House of Lords only two days later when his father died and he succeeded as 4th Earl of Clare. In 1690 he married Lady Margaret Cavendish (1661-1715), the daughter of Henry Cavendish, 2nd Duke of Newcastle-upon-Tyne of a previous creation. Her father died in 1691 without a surviving son, meaning that there was no longer a Duke of Newcastle. In 1694, John Holles was elevated in the peerage to become 1st Duke of Newcastle-upon-Tyne of a new creation. Holles and his wife had only one child, a daughter, Lady Henrietta Cavendish Holles (1694-1755), who married the 2nd Earl of Oxford and Mortimer. Holles died at forty-nine of injuries he received when he fell off of a horse. He had purchased much of the land in what is today Marylebone, later sold by the family; Holles Street is named for him.

At his death, most of his property came to his nephew, Thomas Pelham-Holles (1693-1768), the son of Thomas Pelham, 1st Baron Pelham (1653-1712), an M.P. from 1678 until 1705, and of Lady Grace Holles, sister of John Holles, 1st Duke of Newcastle-upon-Tyne. He was educated at Westminster School and at Clare College, Cambridge. In 1715, probably as a result of his opposing the Jacobites, he was created 1st Duke of Newcastle-under-Lyne. Conveniently, England has two cities named Newcastle, and the new Duke's title was taken from the smaller of the two. The new Duke served as Lord Chamberlain of the Household from 1717 till 1724, and then, in the Cabinet, as Secretary of State for the Southern Department for thirty years, from 1724 until 1754. He then became Prime Minister in 1754-56 and 1757-62, when he was replaced by Lord Bute. He finally held the post of Lord Privy Seal from 1765 until his death. He was one of a number of aristocrats who formed the Royal Academy of Music and brought Handel to England. In 1717 he married Lady Henrietta Godolphin (1701-76), daughter of the 2nd Earl of Godolphin, and granddaughter of the great Duke of Marlborough. His younger brother, Henry Pelham (1694-1754), who was educated at Westminster School, King's College, Cambridge, and Hart Hall, Oxford, was an M.P. from 1717 until 1754, and held the posts of Prime Minister and Chancellor of the Exchequer from 1743 until his death. In 1726 he married Lady Catherine Manners, the daughter of John Manners, 2nd Duke of Rutland, and had four daughters. As Prime Minister, his government is still remembered for two pieces of legislation, both enacted in 1753, the Jewish Naturalisation Act (the so-called "Jew Bill"), which allowed professing Jews to be naturalised as British subjects, and the Clandestine Marriage Act, which made a formal ceremony of marriage a requirement for a marriage to be valid, and set the legal minimum age for a marriage to be valid.

The first Duke of Newcastle-under-Lyne was childless, and he was succeeded by special remainder as the 2nd Duke by his nephew, Henry Fiennes Clinton, later Pelham-Clinton, 2nd Duke of Newcastle (1720-94). He was the son of Henry Clinton, 7th Earl of Lincoln (1684-1728) and Lucy, daughter of Thomas Pelham, 1st Baron Pelham, and was educated at Eton and Clare College, Cambridge. He made the Grand Tour with Horace Walpole, his close friend, with whom, as a famously handsome man, he was rumoured to have had a homosexual relationship. Nevertheless, in 1744 he married his cousin Catherine Pelham (1727-60), the daughter of his uncle Henry Pelham, the Prime Minister, and had four sons. Both the Duke of Newcastle and his brother Henry Pelham regarded him as their heir, and he became 2nd Duke of Newcastle by special remainder after the death of his uncle. He had already become 9th Earl of Lincoln following the death of his brother in 1730. As the Pelhams were among the most powerful men in Britain, the 2nd Duke was showered with lucrative posts during this period, the zenith of "Old Corruption," official positions which had few real duties, but paid their holders enormous salaries or incomes. His extraordinarily long list of such positions included Controller of Customs of the Port of London from 1749 until his death; Master of the Jewel Office; Cofferer of the Household;

and Auditor of the Exchequer. In addition, he was a Gentleman of the King's Bedchamber; Lord Lieutenant of Cambridgeshire and of Nottinghamshire; and High Steward of Westminster from 1759 until his death. In 1752, he was also made a Knight of the Garter. Although his relatives were leaders of the Whigs, he was a Tory supporter of William Pitt, which led to family tensions.

As his older sons had predeceased him, he was very briefly succeeded by his younger son Thomas Pelham-Clinton, 3rd Duke of Newcastle (1752-95), who held the dukedom from February 1794 until May 1795. It is believed that he was educated at the Academy of Angers in France, and then became a military officer, rising to Major-General in 1787. He served during the American Revolutionary War as Aide-de-Camp to his relative, General Sir Henry Clinton. In 1782 he secretly married Lady Anna Maria Stanhope (1760-1834), daughter of William, 2nd Earl of Harrington, a match which did not please his father, who placed his properties in trust during his lifetime for the 3rd Duke's son. He died suddenly of an emetic he had taken for whooping cough. He was succeeded by his son Henry Pelham-Clinton, 5th Duke of Newcastle (1785-1851), who was educated at Eton, where he became a lifelong foe of irreligion and a champion of the Anglican Establishment, later donating the Newcastle Scholarship, a prize for the best written examinations in Divinity and Classics at Eton. In 1807 he married Georgiana (1789-1822), the daughter of Edward Miller Mundy (1756-1822), a landowner and M.P.; according to the Duke's entry in the *ODNB*, she brought with her a dowry of £190,000 and an income of £12,000 p.a., a claim which seems implausible, as Mundy had children, including sons, by three wives and left only £16,000 when he died. The Duke became one of the most visible of "Ultra-Tories," utterly opposed to the parliamentary Reform Act of 1832 or to other changes in the Constitution. He was one of only twenty-two peers to vote against the Third Reading of the Reform Act. As a result, he became wildly unpopular with the radical mob, and one of properties, Nottingham Castle, was burned to the ground. In 1832, he gave William E. Gladstone his first seat in Parliament, at Newark, which he controlled. Gladstone was then the "rising hope of those stern and unbending Tories," in Macaulay's famous phrase; presumably the Duke would have been utterly appalled to learn that Gladstone would later become the radical leader of the Liberal Party. According to the *ODNB*, the Duke also "narrowly escaped being buried alive when in a coma." The claim made by the author of his entry in the *ODNB*, that the Duke "gained the reputation of representing all that was worst about the British aristocracy," is, of course, a matter of opinion.

His son, Henry Pelham-Clinton, 5th Duke of Newcastle (1811-64) was educated at Eton and Christ Church, Oxford, and served as an M.P. from 1832-51, when he succeeded to the Dukedom. He was a lifelong friend and colleague of Gladstone, and was the only holder of the title after the eighteenth century to hold senior political office. He served (under Peel) as First Commissioner of Woods and Forests, 1841-46 and as Chief Secretary for Ireland in 1846. He then joined the Peelites, and served as Secretary for War and the Colonies 1852-54 and then as Secretary for War and as Secretary at War 1854-5 under Lord Aberdeen at the start of the Crimean War. He resigned from this post "in disgrace" (*ODNB*) because of the incompetence of the British expedition to Crimea at the start of the War. Under Lord Palmerston, he re-emerged as Secretary for the Colonies from 1859-64. At this time he visited the United States and Canada, and was a Manager of the Canterbury Association which colonised New Zealand. In 1832, he married Lady Susan Hamilton (1814-89), daughter of Alexander Hamilton, 10th Duke of Hamilton, but they were divorced in 1850, when the Duchess eloped with Horatio, Lord Hamilton, and had an illegitimate child with him. Three of his five children also had unorthodox private lives. His daughter Lady Susan

Pelham-Clinton (1839-75), the wife of Lord Adolphus Vane-Tempest, became the mistress of the Prince of Wales (later Edward VII); his son Lord Arthur Pelham-Clinton (1840-70?) apparently committed suicide as a result of a homosexual scandal involving him and two cross-dressing friends, although some believe that he fled abroad and lived out his life under a false identity; his son Lord Albert Pelham-Clinton (1845-84) was also divorced, a very rare occurrence at the time. The 5th Duke left £250,000 in personalty at his death.

His son, Henry Pelham-Clinton, 6th Duke of Newcastle (1834-79), was educated at Eton and at Christ Church, Oxford, and served as an M.P. from 1857-59. He was known as a leading Freemason. But he was also an addicted gambler, who fled from Britain in 1860 to escape gambling debts of £230,000. In Paris, however, in 1861 he was fortunate to marry Henrietta Hope (1843-1913), the daughter of the banker Henry Thomas Hope (1808-62), of Deepdene, Surrey, an M.P. and art patron who came from the very wealthy Anglo-Dutch banking family, and who was the owner, among other things, of the Hope diamond. He paid off the Duke's gambling debts and settled £50,000 p.a. on the couple, according to reports. (He left £300,000 in personalty when he died.) The Duke died at forty-five, leaving only £1,500 in personalty in England. His widow re-married, in 1880, (Revd.) Thomas Hohler (d. 1892). The 6th Duke had two sons who succeeded him. Henry Pelham-Clinton, 7th Duke of Newcastle (1864-1928) was educated at Eton and at Magdalen College, Oxford. He was in poor health, and took little part in public life, although he was a member of the London School Board from 1894 till 1897. He was known as an Anglo-Catholic enthusiast, and was the Patron of ten Anglican livings. He managed to restore much of the family fortunes, and left £1,000,000 when he died. He rebuilt Clumber House and its architecturally distinguished St. Mary the Virgin Chapel. In 1886 his addresses were given as Clumber House; Worksop Manor, Nottinghamshire; and 14 Westbourne Terrace, London, W. In 1889 he married Kathleen (d. 1955, left £79,476), daughter of (Major) Henry Augustus Candy, and the daughter of the 3rd Baron Rossmore; they had no children.

The 7th Duke was succeeded by his brother, Henry Pelham-Clinton- Hope (1866-1941: he added "Hope" to his surname in 1894 after inheriting from his Hope relatives). He was educated at Eton and at Trinity Hall, Cambridge, and had the kind of dissolute life associated with some of his recent relatives. Initially an army officer, in 1894 he married Mary, daughter of William Yohe, an American actress. He was declared bankrupt in 1896, although having inherited some of the Hope fortune a few years earlier. One item of his inheritance was the Hope diamond, which he sold in 1902 to pay his debts. His actress wife left him for an American army officer, and they were divorced in 1902. In 1904 he married Olive (d. 1912), daughter of George Horatio Thompson, a banker of Melbourne, Australia. His entry in *Who's Who* stated that he owned "about 35,600 acres," but he left only £9,615 when he died.

His son and successor, Henry Pelham-Clinton-Hope, 9th Duke of Newcastle (1907-88), was educated at Eton and Madgalen College, Oxford. He joined the Royal Auxiliary Air Force in 1936 and was a Squadron Leader in World War Two. He was married three times and divorced twice; from 1948, he lived mainly in Southern Rhodesia. He was still very wealthy, leaving £3,163,807 at his death on 4 November 1988. He had two daughters but no son, and, at his death, was succeeded by his third cousin, Edward Pelham-Clinton, 10th Duke of Newcastle (1920-88). He was educated at Eton and at Trinity College, Oxford, served as a Captain in the Royal Artillery during the Second World War, and was Deputy Keeper of the Royal Scottish Museum in Edinburgh. He was the Deputy Editor of the six volume *The Moths and Butterflies of Great Britain and Ireland,* a subject on which he was an acknowledged expert. His principal residence when he inherited the title was Furzeleigh House in Axminster. Sadly, he did not enjoy the title for long, dying on 25 December 1988, only eight weeks after inheriting the Dukedom. He was also very wealthy at his death, and left £2,222,203.

He was unmarried; there were no male heirs to the Dukedom, which became extinct after 273 years. For his other title, 17th Earl of Lincoln, however, an heir was found, a tenth (*sic*) cousin, one Edward Horace Fiennes-Clinton (1913-2001), an Australian engineer who lived in Bunbury, Western Australia. He had worked as a boilermaker, a welder's assistant, and as a butcher at the Kalgoorlie Gold Mines, and learned of his good fortune from a telephone call made to him by a reporter on the *Daily Telegraph* newspaper. This extraordinary rags-to-riches story became well-known in Australia, and was mentioned on *Neighbours*, a popular Australian television soap opera. The 18th Earl of Lincoln, as he had become, was succeeded by his grandson Robert Edward Fiennes-Clinton (b. 1972), who lives in Perth, Western Australia, and is a Fellow of the Royal Zoological Society. He was educated at the Pinjarra High School in Pinjarra, eighty-six kilometers south of Perth, a school where a substantial percentage of the students are Australian Aborigines. The vicissitudes of the ducal Newcastle family and their relatives are nothing if not remarkable.

30. Bertie, later Drummond-Burrell, then Drummond-Willoughby, and then Heathcote-Drummond-Willoughby, Barons Willoughby de Eresby and Earls of Ancaster – £74,006 p.a.

In 1883, the Baroness Willoughby de Eresby owned 132,220 acres worth £74,006 p.a., in Lincolnshire (24,696 acres/£36,530 p.a.); Caernarvonshire (30,391 acres/£7,966 p.a.); Perthshire (76,837 acres/£28,955 p.a.); and Denbighshire (296 acres/£555 p.a.). In addition, in 1883 Lord Aveland owned 31,275 acres worth £46,894 p.a. in Lincolnshire (17,637 acres/£27,082 p.a.); Rutland (13,633 acres/£19,797 p.a.; and very small amounts in Derbyshire and Huntingdonshire.) These totals have not been counted with the acreage/rental for Lord Willoughby de Eresby. If the two are totalled, however, in 1883 the family owned 163,495 acres worth £120,900 p.a., which of course are very high sums.

One of the very oldest of existing peerages, the Barons Willoughby de Eresby were first given their title in 1313 when Robert de Willoughby (1260-1317) was given a peerage. The present peer is the twenty-eighth in the long line of title holders. It is one of the few English peerages which can be inherited by a woman, which has happened six times, and it has gone through several abeyances as well as changes of surname and promotions, to the Earldom of Lindsey in 1614 and to the Dukedom of Ancaster in 1715, which have since become extinct. Given its age and acreage, it is surprisingly obscure, and many well-informed people have probably never heard of it. No holder of this title since the Middle Ages has an entry in the *Oxford Dictionary of National Biography*, even the 1st Earl of Ancaster, who was promoted from Baron to Earl in 1892. The 132,220 acres of land owned in 1883 by Clementina, 24th Baroness Willoughby de Eresby in her own right were located in Lincolnshire, Perthshire, and in two counties in Wales. The two traditional country houses owned by them are Grimsthorpe Castle near Bourne in Lincolnshire, owned by the family since 1516, and Drummond Castle in Perthshire, owned by the family since the time of the 22nd Baron in the early nineteenth century.

The first holder of the title to be considered here is Priscilla Bertie, 21st Baroness Willoughby de Eresby (1761-1828), who secured the title after it was held in abeyance from 1779 to 1780. In

1779 she married Peter Burrell (1754-1820), an M.P. from 1776 until 1796, when he was created 1st Baron Gwydyr (*sic*). The Burrells were proverbial for their good luck and fortunate marriages, with the family fortune founded by his grandfather, also a Peter Burrell (1692-1756), a merchant and government contractor who was an M.P. from 1722 till 1756. The Baroness inherited a good deal of property from her father, Peregrine, 3rd Duke of Ancaster (1714-78), with whose death the dukedom became extinct but the barony was inherited by his daughter. Peter Burrell was said by Farington to have had an income of £18,000 p.a., and left £120,000 in personalty when he died. He is, and is best remembered as one of the main founders of what is now the Metropolitan Cricket Club, the MCC. The Baroness left £100,000 in personalty in her own right when she died. Burrell left £100,000 in personalty when he died.

Her son, Peter Robert Burrell, 2nd Baron Gwydyr and 22nd Baron Willoughby de Eresby (1782-1865) was educated at Eton and at St. John's College, Cambridge, and was called to the bar at Lincoln's Inn in 1774. He inherited the position of Deputy Lord Great Chamberlain from his father, and held the Crown at the Coronation of Queen Victoria in 1838. He served as a Whig M.P. from 1812 to 1820. He was a patron of the explorer of Australia Peter Allan Cunningham, who discovered what he termed the Gwydir (*sic*) River in New South Wales. In 1807 Burrell married Sarah Drummond (1796-1865), the daughter of James Drummond, 11th Earl of Perth. His son and heir, Alberic (or Abyric, *sic*) Drummond Willoughby (as he was known), 3rd Baron Gwydyr and 23rd Baron Willoughby de Eresby (1821-70), held the title for only five years. He was educated at Eton and Trinity College, Cambridge, and was a J.P. and D.L. of Lincolnshire. He died unmarried and left £70,000 in personalty.

The titles then fell into abeyance for a year. The Gwydyr peerage was inherited by a cousin, but the Willoughby de Eresby peerage was inherited by the daughter of the 22nd Baron and sister of the 23rd Baron, Clementina Elizabeth *nee* Burrell-Drummond, later Heathcote-Drummond-Willoughby, 24th Baroness Willoughby de Eresby in her own right (1809-88). In 1827 she married Sir Gilbert Heathcote, 5th Bt. (1795-1867), a major landowner who was educated at Westminster School and at Trinity College, Cambridge and served as a Liberal M.P. from 1820 until 1856. In that year he was created 1st Baron Aveland. They had two children, a son who succeeded to the titles, and a daughter, Clementina (d. 1922) who married (Vice-Admiral) Sir George Tryon (1832-93) and was the mother of George Tryon, 1st Baron Tryon (1871-1940). The Baroness served as Joint Great Chamberlain from 1870 until her death. She left £207,269 in personalty at her death.

Her son, who inherited the titles of both his mother and father, was Gilbert Henry Heathcote-Drummond-Willoughby, 25th Baron Willoughby de Eresby and 2nd Baron Aveland (1830-1910). He was educated at Harrow and at Trinity College, Cambridge and was a Conservative M.P. from 1852 until 1867, when he inherited his father's title and sat in the House of Lords. He added the names Willoughby and Drummond to his surname in 1872. He served as Joint Lord Great Chamberlain from 1871 till 1901. In 1892 he was made an earl, taking the title of 1st Earl of Ancaster, a revival of a title his family held in the Middle Ages. In 1863 he married Lady Evelyn Gordon (d. 1921), daughter of Charles Gordon, 10th Marquess of Huntly. They had four sons and six daughters. He left £150,000 in personalty.

His son and successor Gilbert Heathcote-Drummond-Willoughby, 2nd Earl of Ancaster, 3rd Baron Aveland, and 26th Baron Willoughby de Eresby (1867-1951), was educated at Eton and Trinity College, Cambridge. He also served as a Conservative M.P., from 1894 until 1910, and as Lord Great Chamberlain, from 1937 till 1950. In 1921-23 he held the position of Parliamentary

Secretary to the Minister of Agriculture. He was Lord Lieutenant of Rutland from 1921 till 1951 and Chairman of the Rutland County Council from 1922 until 1937. In 1905 he married the American Eloise (d. 1953), daughter of W.L. Breese of New York. He had two residences, Grimsthorpe in Lincolnshire and Drummond Castle, Crieff, in Perth. He left £485,927, of which £253,580 was in settled land. His son and heir, Gilbert James Heathcote-Drummond-Willoughby, 3rd Earl of Ancaster, 4th Baron Aveland, and 27th Baron Willoughby de Eresby (1907-83), was educated at Eton and Magdalene, Cambridge. He served as a Conservative M.P from 1933 until 1950, a year before he succeeded to his father's titles. In the Second World War he served as a Major in the Royal Artillery; he was wounded and mentioned in despatches. He held the post of Lord Great Chamberlain from 1950 till 1952. In 1933 he married (Hon.) Nancy Astor (d. 1975, left £353,656), daughter of Waldorf Astor, 2nd Viscount Astor (1879-1952, left £974,725), of the famous and very wealthy Anglo-American family. At his death he left £1,468,694. He was succeeded by his daughter, (Nancy) Jane Heathcote-Drummond-Willoughby, 28th Baroness Willoughby de Eresby, who was born in 1934, and is unmarried. From 1994-2004, she was a Trustee of the National Portrait Gallery.

31. Hamilton, later Douglas-Hamilton, Dukes of Hamilton, later Hamilton and Brandon – £73,636 p.a.

In 1883 the Duke of Hamilton and Brandon owned 157,386 acres worth £73,636 p.a., in Buteshire (102,386 acres/£18,702 p.a.); Lanarkshire (45,731 acres/£38,702 p.a.); Linlithgowshire (3,694 acres/£7,445 p.a.); Suffolk (4,939 acres/£8,017 p.a.); Stirlingshire (810 acres/£911 p.a.); and Berkshire (2 acres/£120 p.a.). His income was "exclusive of a mineral rent of £67,000 [p.a.]," according to Bateman.

The Dukes of Hamilton and Brandon were great landowners in the Scottish Lowlands, especially in Lanarkshire, in the area in and around Glasgow. They also owned extremely lucrative coal mines in this area, at a time when "Coal was King." James Hamilton, 1st Duke of Hamilton (1606-49) was the son of James Hamilton, 2nd Marquess of Hamilton (1589-1625) and Lady Anne (c. 1588-1647), the daughter of James, 7th Earl of Glencairn. He was educated at Exeter College, Oxford. He fought in Germany during the Thirty Years' War. Charles I made him his chief advisor on Scottish affairs, and Hamilton became closely involved in the bitter hostility between the factions there, the Covenanters and the followers of the King. In 1649, he was defeated by Cromwell at the Battle of Preston and executed. In 1643 he was created 1st Duke of Hamilton in the Scottish peerage. In 1622 he married Margaret Feilding, daughter of William, Viscount Feilding. He was aged fifteen and she aged nine at the time of their marriage. Hamilton was known as "Captain Luckless." They were given a United Kingdom dukedom, with an automatic seat in the House of Lords, in 1711, when James Hamilton, 4th Duke of Hamilton (1658-1712) was created 1st Duke of Brandon in the peerage of Great Britain. He had played an important role in bringing about the Act of Union in 1707. In 1712 he fought a famous duel over an inheritance with Charles, Lord Mohun in Hyde Park, at which both men were mortally wounded.

Douglas Hamilton, 8th Duke of Hamilton and 5th Duke of Brandon (1756-99) was the son of James Hamilton, 6th Duke of Hamilton and 4th Duke of Brandon (1724-58) and Elizabeth Gunning (1733-90), from an Irish gentry family, a favourite of George III whom he created Baroness Hamilton of Hameldon (*sic*) in her own right in 1776. She later remarried John Campbell, 5th Duke of Argyll. The 8th Duke of Hamilton was educated at Eton, and succeeded his elder brother, James, 7th Duke of Hamilton (1755-69), who died at fourteen. In 1778 he married Elizabeth (1757-1837), the daughter of Peter Burrell and the sister of the 1st Baron Gwydyr. He was involved in many extra-marital affairs, and had several illegitimate children, but no legitimate ones. They were divorced in 1794; she later remarried the 1st Marquess of Exeter. The title then passed to his uncle, Archibald Hamilton, 9th Duke of Hamilton and 6th Duke of Brandon (1740-1819). He was the younger son of James Hamilton, 5th Duke of Hamilton (1703-43), and was educated at Eton, served as an M.P. from 1768 until 1772, and was Lord-Lieutenant of Lanarkshire. In 1744 he inherited the estates of Charles, 2nd Earl of Macclesfield. The 9th Duke was a very successful patron of the turf; his horses won the St. Leger Stakes seven times. In 1765 he married Lady Harriet Stewart (d. 1768), the daughter of Alexander Stewart, 6th Earl of Galloway.

His son and successor was Alexander Hamilton, 10th Duke of Hamilton and 7th Duke of Brandon (1767-1852). From 1864 until 1895, the Dukes of Hamilton were also Dukes of Châtelherault in the French aristocracy, a title granted them by Napoleon III. He was educated at Harrow and at Christ Church, Oxford, and lived as a young man in Italy, where he gained a passion for collecting art works. He was then a Colonel in the Lanarkshire Militia, and was a Whig M.P. from 1802-06, when he was called to the House of Lords in one of his father's subsidiary titles, Baron Dutton. He served as Ambassador to Russia in 1806-07, and also developed a liking for Napoleon Bonaparte, rare among British aristocrats. He held many posts which accorded with his rank, from Lord Lieutenant of Lanarkshire from 1802-52 to Trustee of the British Museum, 1834-52. He was Lord High Steward at the Coronations of William IV in 1831 and Queen Victoria in 1838. In 1810, he married Susan Beckford (1786-1859), the daughter of William Thomas Beckford (1760-1840), the art collector and author of *Vathek,* and Lady Mary Gordon, the daughter of Charles Gordon, 9th Earl of Aboyne. They had a son, who succeeded him, and a daughter, who married the 5th Duke of Newcastle. The Duke was a Grand Master Freemason, a well-known dandy, and a great art collector, who owned Da Vinci's *Laughing Boy* and other important art works. He was also a collector of Egyptian mummies, and arranged to have his own body mummified and placed in a sarcophagus of the Ptolemaic period, where it remains, although its place of burial was moved after his death. He left £126,704 in personalty at his death. In 1882, thirty years after his death, his collection of antiquities, paintings, and manuscripts was sold for £397,562, an extraordinary sum.

His son and successor, William Hamilton (later Douglas-Hamilton), 11th Duke of Hamilton and 8th Duke of Brandon (1811-63), was educated at Eton and Christ Church, Oxford. He held a number of official posts in Britain, and was Lord Lieutenant of Lanarkshire from 1852 until his death. In 1843, however, he married Princess Marie Amélie (1817-88), daughter of the Grand Duke of Baden and of Stéphanie de Beauharnais, the adopted daughter of Napoleon I, and lived for much of his life in Paris and in Baden. In France, he and his wife were close friends of Napoleon III. They had a son and a daughter, Lady Mary Hamilton, who married Albert I of Monaco, and is an ancestress of the ruling house of Monaco. In London, the Duke lived in a house at 22 Arlington Street in St. James's (now known as Wimborne House) which he had purchased from the Duke of Beaufort for £60,000, a remarkable sum. He died suddenly at fifty-two, leaving £419,980 in personalty. His son William Douglas-Hamilton, 12th Duke of Hamilton and 9th Duke of Brandon (1845-95), was educated at Eton and at Christ Church, Oxford, where he took up boxing and was noted for his rudeness. In 1873 he married Lady Mary Montagu (1854-

1934), daughter of William Montagu, 7th Duke of Manchester, and had one daughter but no sons. He was the Patron of sixteen Anglican Livings. In 1886, his residences were listed at Hamilton Palace, Glasgow; Brodrick Castle, Isle of Arran; Easton Park, Wickham Market, Suffolk; and 12 Hill Street, Mayfair. The 12th Duke died at Algiers, and left £312,890 in personalty in Britain, although he also is said to have had many debts. Under the terms of his family settlement, some of his lands went to a relative, the Duchess of Montrose, rather than to the next title-holder.

There were no close male relatives of the 12th Duke, and the title came to a fourth cousin, Alfred Douglas-Hamilton, 13th Duke of Hamilton and 10th Duke of Brandon (1862-1940), the son of (Captain) Charles Douglas-Hamilton (1808-73), a great-grandson of the 4th Duke of Hamilton. He served in the Royal Navy, where he was noted as (for the time) an incredible swimmer and diver. Just before he left the Royal Navy in 1895, he contracted a rare tropical disease which partially paralysed him; he was partially disabled for the rest of his life. In 1901, however, he married Nina (1878-1951), the daughter of Robert Poore, a landowner, and had four sons and three daughters. His wife was a noted champion of animal welfare, a founder of the Animal Defence and Anti-Vivisection Society, and has an entry in the *ODNB* as an "animal welfare activist." He left £187,353; his widow left £115,018, both very large sums at the time.

His son Douglas Douglas-Hamilton, 14th Duke of Hamilton and 11th Duke of Brandon (1903-73), is best known for being the man that Adolf Hitler's deputy Rudolph Hess intended to meet on his flight from Germany to Scotland in May 1941, with the aim of making peace between Germany and Britain. The Duke had met Hess (and Hermann Goering) at the 1936 Olympics in Berlin, but was just as mystified as everyone else when Hess landed on his estate. Apart from this, the 14th Duke led a colourful and varied life. He was educated at Eton and at Balliol College, Oxford, and became an amateur boxer of note, winning the Scottish Amateur Middleweight championship. He served as a Conservative M.P. from 1930 until he succeeded to the Dukedom in 1940. In 1935, in order to find out at first-hand about working-class life, he joined a trade union and worked as a coalminer under the name of "Mr. Hamilton." He was also well-known as a pioneering aviator, and was Chief Pilot in 1933 on the expedition to fly over Mt. Everest, which showed the need for cockpit pressurisation. He served in the Royal Auxiliary Air Force from 1927, and in World War Two was a Fighter Commander who was mentioned in despatches. He also served in a wide variety of other roles, as Lord Commissioner of the Household from 1940-64, as Chancellor of St. Andrews University, 1948-73, and four times as Lord Commissioner to the General Assembly of the Church of Scotland. In 1937 he married Lady Elizabeth Percy (1916-2008), daughter of Alan Percy, 8th Duke of Northumberland. At his death he left £3,156,085. He has an entry in the *ODNB*, which describes him as a "boxer, aviator, politician." Their eldest son succeeded as the 15th Duke. His younger brother, Lord James Douglas-Hamilton, Baron Selkirk of Douglas (b. 1942), who was educated at Eton and at Balliol College, Oxford, was a Conservative M.P. from February 1974 until 1997, when he was given a life peerage. He served as a junior minister in the Conservative governments between 1987 and 1997, and was a member of the Scottish Parliament from 1999 until 2007.

The title next passed to his son Angus Douglas-Hamilton, 15th Duke of Hamilton and 12th Duke of Brandon (1938-2010), who was educated at Eton and at Balliol College, Oxford. He was a page boy at the 1953 Coronation, was a Flight Lieutenant in the RAF and a test-pilot for Scottish Aviation, and is, like his grandmother, interested in animal welfare. He was married three times; his successor's mother was his first wife, Sarah, daughter of (Major) Sir Walter Scott, 4th

Bt. They were divorced in 1987. His successor, his son Alexander Douglas-Hamilton, 16th Duke of Hamilton and 13th Duke of Brandon (b. 1978), was educated at Gordonstoun School. In 2011 he married the interior designer Sophie (b. 1976), the daughter of Hubert Rutherford. In 2001 the Duke of Hamilton owned about 5,200 acres in East Lothian, according to Kevin Cahill.

32. Duff, later Carnegie, Earls, later Dukes of Fife – £72,563 p.a.

In 1883 the Earl of Fife owned 249,220 acres worth £72,563 p.a., in Aberdeenshire (135,829 acres/£16,240 p.a.); Banff (72,432 acres/£36,379 p.a.); and Elgin (40,959 acres/£18,693 p.a., and other lands in Elgon, acreage unstated, worth £1,251 p.a.).

Although the Earls, later Dukes of Fife sound as if they can be traced back to Clan leaders in the Middle Ages, their first peerage title dates from only 1735, and was based in large part on the wealth accumulated by a merchant in Banffshire. In 1889, the Earl of Fife married into the Royal Family and received a dukedom. Their landed holdings were mainly in the north of Scotland: in all, in 1883 they owned nearly 250,000 acres.

William Duff, 1st Earl of Fife (1696-1763) was the son of William Duff (d. 1722), a wealthy merchant and landowner in Braco, Banffshire. He served as an M.P. from 1727 until 1734, when he stood down in favour of his brother, and, in 1735, was created 1st Baron Braco (*sic*) in the Irish peerage – although he had no known links with Ireland. A major political force in the north of Scotland, he was elevated in the peerage to become Earl of Fife and Viscount Macduff, again in the Irish peerage. (To be granted the title of "Macduff," he had to prove that he was related to Lord Macduff, the Thane of Fife, which he did.) He was married twice: first, in 1719, to Lady Jane Forbes (d. 1720), the daughter of James Ogilvy, 4th Earl of Findlater and 1st Earl of Seafield, the widow of Hugh Forbes; following her death after only a year of marriage, he remarried Jean Grant, daughter of Sir James Grant, 6th Bt., M.P., from whom the subsequent peers descend. He was succeeded by his son James Duff, 2nd Earl of Fife (1727-1809), who was educated at Edinburgh University, and served as an M.P. from 1754 until 1790, which, as an Irish peer, he was able to do. In 1793 he was created 1st Baron Fife in the peerage of Great Britain, giving him an automatic seat in the Lords. In 1759 he married Lady Dorothy Sinclair, daughter of Alexander Sinclair, 9th Earl of Caithness. They had no children, although Lord Fife had three illegitimate children by a local girl, Margaret Adam; their son Sir James Duff (1753-1839) became a well-known general in the Army and helped to put down the Irish Rebellion of 1798; he has an entry in the *ODNB* as an "army officer." The 2nd Earl was known as an agricultural improver, who assisted his tenants in bad times.

As the 2nd Earl had no sons, his titles passed to his brother, Alexander Duff, 3rd Earl of Fife (1731-1811). He was an advocate, admitted to the Scots bar in 1754. In 1775 he married Mary Skene (b. c. 1735) daughter of George Skene of Skene, Aberdeenshire. In 1788 she eloped with her cousin George Skene, whose address was, ironically, Scotland Yard (then a residential area in London), who was executed for forgery in 1812; Alexander divorced her in 1812, although she had been considered unfit to raise his children before then, who were taken from her care. Her date of death could not be traced. The 3rd Earl held the peerage for only two years. He had two sons, the 4th Earl and (General) (Hon.) Sir Alexander Duff (1778-1851), Commander of the 88th Foot from 1798-1810, who was active in India, Egypt, and at the Siege of Buenos Aires in 1806, and was the father of the 5th Earl. Alexander's elder son James Duff, 4th Earl of Fife (1776-1857), another very colourful member of this family. He was educated at Westminster School and at Christ Church, Oxford, and read for the bar at Lincoln's Inn, but wasn't called. He then fought for the Allies in Europe during the Napoleonic War and was appointed a Major-General in the Spanish army, and was severely wounded at the Siege of Cadiz in 1810, and assisted José de San Martin, the" Liberator of Argentina." Back in England, he served as a Canningite Tory M.P. from 1818 till 1827, and as a Lord of the Bedchamber from 1819-21 and 1827-35, as well as Lord Lieutenant of Banffshire from 1813-56. He was also Grand Master of the Freemasons from 1814-16. In 1827 he was created 1st Baron Fife in the peerage of Great Britain, giving him a seat in the House of Lords. In 1799 he married Maria (1775-1805), daughter of John Manners M.P. (1730-92) of Grantham Grange, Lincolnshire, the illegitimate son of Lord John Manners, younger son of John, 2nd Duke of Rutland, and of Louisa Tollemache, 7the Countess Dysart (1745-1840). The 4th Earl's wife died of rabies in 1805 after being bitten by her pet dog, who, unbeknownst to them was rabid.

The 4th Earl died without children, and the title passed to his nephew James Duff, 5th Earl of Fife (1814-79), the son of his brother General Sir Alexander Duff and of Ann (d. 1859), daughter of James Stein of Kilbagie. He served as a Liberal M.P. from 1837 till 1857, when he was created 1st Baron Skene in the British peerage, his uncle's British peerages having become extinct with his death. He was Lord Lieutenant of Banffshire and Morayshire. In 1816 he married Lady Agnes Hay (1829-69), daughter of William Hay, 18th Earl of Erroll and of Lady Elizabeth FitzClarence, illegitimate daughter of King William IV, a fact which gave him and his offspring a quasi-Royal stamp. His probate valuation could not be traced in any probate record. His only son Alexander Duff, 6th Earl of Fife and 1st Duke of Fife (1849-1912) was educated at Eton, and served as a Liberal M.P. from 1874-79, when he succeeded his father; he served as Captain, Gentlemen at Arms under W.E.Gladstone in 1880-81. In 1885 he was made 1st Earl of Fife in the United Kingdom peerage. In 1889 he married Princess Louisa (1867-1931), the eldest daughter of the Prince of Wales, later Edward VII, and the sister of the future King George V. As a result, in that year he was created 1st Duke of Fife; in 1900 his daughter and successor was made the heiress to his Dukedom by special remainder. He served as Lord High Constable at the Coronations of 1902 and 1911, and as Lord Lieutenant of Elginshire from 1872 until 1902. From 1900 until his death he held the seemingly anomalous post of Lord Lieutenant of the City of London. The Duke had been active as an investor in the British South Africa Company and other business enterprises. In 1912, he went with his family on a sea voyage in his yacht. Off the coast of Morocco, they were shipwrecked, and were in the water when rescued; they had then to walk four miles to the nearest town, Tangier. As a result, the Duke contracted pleurisy, and died a few weeks later, at Aswan in Egypt. He was a wealthy man, and left £1,000,000. In 1886, he is listed as having had eight residences, six in Scotland, including Duff House and Eden House in Banff, and East Sheen Lodge, Surrey, and 4 Cavendish Square W. His widow, who was known as a recluse, died at her home in Portman Square in 1931.

The Dukedom then came, most unusually, to a woman, Princess Alexandra, 2nd Duchess of Fife (1891-1959), the elder of his two daughters. In 1905, when her father was on the Throne, she was given the title of Princess Royal, and was allowed to use "H.R.H." as part of her title. In 1910 she was secretly engaged for some time to Prince Christopher of Greece and Denmark, but, in 1913, married her first cousin once removed, Prince Arthur of Connaught (1883-1938), the son of Prince Arthur, Duke of Connaught and Strathearn (1850-1942), Queen Victoria's third son. He was educated at Eton and Sandhurst, served in the Boer War and World War one, and was Governor-General of South Africa in 1920-24. They had one child, a son, Alastair, Duke of Connaught and Strathearn (1914-43), who died at twenty-eight "of exposure," in Ottawa, Canada, as the brief reports about his death, made during the War, put it. Many years later, more emerged about his death, which occurred when he "fell out of a window when drunk, and perished of hypothermia overnight." During both World Wars, the Duchess worked as a trained nurse, a vocation which she enjoyed and at which she was successful; she won a nursing prize for a paper she wrote about the treatment of eclampsia. Although her husband had been wealthy, she lost a good deal of money in 1923 as an executor, responsible in part for his debts, of Lord Farquhar, her husband's former business partner, who turned out to be bankrupt and in debt. She spent the rest of her life at her residence at 64 Avenue Road, St. John's Wood, and left £86,217.

As she had no surviving children, the title passed to her nephew, James Carnegie, 3rd Duke of Fife (1929-2015), the son of Charles Carnegie, 11the Earl of Southesk (1893-1992) and of Princess Maud (1893-1945), the Duchess's younger sister. The 3rd Duke was educated at Gordonstoun and at the Royal Agricultural College, Cirencester, and served with the Scots Guards in Malaya in 1948-50. He was a Vice-Patron of the British Olympic Association, and an amateur racing car driver. In 1992 he succeeded his father as the 12th Earl of Southesk and Chief of the Clan Carnegie. In the early 1990s, a sample of the Duke's DNA was used to prove that bones found buried in Russia belonged to his relative Czar Nicholas II and his family, murdered by the Bolsheviks in 1918, which were then properly buried by the new Russian government. In 1956, he married (Hon.) Caroline Dewar (b. 1934), the daughter of Henry Dewar, 3rd Baron Forteviot (1906-93), of Dewar's, the whisky distillers. They were divorced in 1966. Their son, David Carnegie, 4th Duke of Fife (and 13th Earl of Southesk) (b. 1961), was educated at Eton and at Pembroke College, Cambridge, and later at the Royal Agricultural College, Cirencester, and later gained an MBA degree at the University of Edinburgh. He worked as a stockbroker in London, and more recently, as an investment banker and accountant in Edinburgh, and lives at Kinnaird Castle in Angus. In 1987 he married Caroline (b. 1961), daughter of Martin Brian Bunting, and has three sons. According to Kevin Cahill, in 2001 the Duke of Fife owned only 1500 acres of agricultural land, a tiny fraction of what his ancestors owned in the nineteenth century.

33. Lambton, Earls of Durham – £71,671 p.a.

In 1883 the Earl of Durham owned 30,471 acres worth £71,671 p.a. in Co. Durham (14,664 acres/£63,929 p.a.) and Northumberland (15,807 acres/£7,742 p.a.).

The Lambton family emerged in the early eighteenth century as large-scale and very wealthy land and colliery owners, especially in Co. Durham, where their coal deposits were among the most lucrative of any colliery owners in Britain. They were not titled, nor members of any stratum in Society above the gentry class, much before then. (There is a family history by John Colville, *Those Lambtons! A Most Unusual Family* (1988).) The first Earl's father, William Henry Lambton (1764-1797) was already wealthy, and had been educated at Eton and Trinity College, Cambridge. He served in Parliament as a radical M.P. for Durham city from 1787 until his death at only thirty-one, when his son, the 1st Earl, was only five. He married into the aristocracy, his wife – the mother of the 1st Earl of Durham – being Lady Anne Villiers (1772-1832), daughter of George Villiers, 1st Earl of Jersey (1735-1805), whose family had been ennobled only recently. John George Lambton, 1st Earl of Jersey (1792-1840) was educated at Eton, and became an M.P. in 1813, at the age of twenty-one, serving until he was given a peerage in 1828. Because of the success of his coal mines during the Industrial Revolution, he was extremely wealthy. Thomas Creevy famously stated that Lambton had told him that "a man might jog on" with an annual income of £40,000; Creevy then called him "King Jog." Lambton suffered from chronic insomnia, and in 1822 also told Creevy that "it was damned hard that a man with £80,000 a year can't sleep." Lambton was also notorious for his mood swings, and was described as "sullen, silent, and sulky" by Lord Palmerston, who also witnessed his rages and temper tantrums at Cabinet meetings and elsewhere.

Lambton was widely known as "Radical Jack," and was a champion of many radical causes. He protested against the so-called "Peterloo Massacre," and was one of the drafters of the Reform Bill of 1832. In 1828 he was created 1st Baron Durham, and, in 1833, 1st Earl of Durham. From 1830-33, he served as Lord Privy Seal in the Cabinet of Earl Grey (his father-in-law), and was Ambassador to Russia from 1835-37. He is most famous, however, for his time as Governor-in-Chief of British North America (i.e., Canada), from 1838 to 1839. He recommended the merger of Upper and Lower (French-speaking Quebec) Canada, and issued his famous *Report*, which paved the way for some degree of self-rule and, eventually, for the self-governing Dominions of the British Empire. Never in good health, he died in 1840 at the age of forty-eight, leaving £250,000 in personalty. In 1812, at Gretna, he had married Henrietta (Harriet) Cholmondeley (d. 1815), illegitimate daughter of George, 1st Marquess of Cholmondeley, with whom he had three daughters before her death only three years later. In 1816, he married Lady Louisa Grey (1797-1841), daughter of Charles Grey, 2nd Earl Grey (164-1845), later Prime Minister, with whom he had two sons, one of whom died young, and three daughters.

His surviving son and successor was (George) D'Arcy Lambton, 2nd Earl of Durham (1828-79), who was educated at Trinity College, Cambridge. He inherited his father's Earldom at eleven, but did not have a political career, although he was Lord Lieutenant of County Durham from 1854 until his death. He was chiefly known as a breeder of racehorses. In 1876, his right eye had to be removed when his son Charles accidentally shot him at a shooting party. In 1854, he married Lady Beatrix Hamilton (1835-71), daughter of James, 1st Duke of Abercorn (1811-85). They had eight sons and five daughters. His eldest sons were two twins, who succeeded him in the peerage. His third son was (Admiral of the Fleet) Sir Hedworth Lambton, who changed his surname to "Meux" in 1911 (1856-1929), a well-known naval officer, especially during the Boer War, and a Conservative M.P. 1916-18, who left £910,466, an enormous amount for a younger son. Much of his wealth was the product of a totally unexpected inheritance. In 1910, shortly before her death, he was introduced to Valerie Susie Meux (*nee* Langdon, 1852-1910), the daughter of a butcher, a music hall actress who had eloped with Sir Henry Meux, 3rd Bt. (1856-1910), a wealthy member of the Meux family of brewers, who had left £696,823 (she left £204,151). He gave her a vivid account of his highly-regarded naval actions during the Boer War. She was so impressed that she made him her heir, although they had never met before and were unrelated; to gain this inheritance – of which as a Lambton and an Admiral he was hardly in dire need – he had to change his surname to "Meux," which he did in 1911, probably to the chagrin of the Meux family. The 2nd Earl's fifth son, George Lambton (1860-1945, left £87,553) was a famous racehorse trainer, with an entry in the *ODNB*, who was one of the first to expose the doping of horses. His daughter Ann [Nancy] Lambton (1912-2008), was a recognised "orientalist and Persianist" (*ODNB*), who was internationally known as an expert on Iran, and gave advice on Iranian affairs to the Foreign Office. Her grandfather, the 2nd Earl, died at the age of fifty-one in 1879, leaving £500,000 in personalty.

As noted, the eldest male offspring of the 2nd Earl were twin boys. Under the peerage laws of inheritance, the elder inherited the title, even if born only a few minutes before his brother. In this case, both succeeded to the peerage, although the younger twin held the title for less than five months. The elder twin, John Lambton, 3rd Earl of Durham (1855-1928). He was educated at Eton and served as a Lieutenant-Colonel in the Coldstream Guards. He was Lord Lieutenant of Co. Durham from 1884 until 1928, and Chancellor of Durham University from 1919 until 1928. In 1882, he married Ethel (1860-1931), daughter of Henry Beilby William Milner (d. 1876, left £90,000), the son of Sir William Milner, 4th Bt. (1779-1855), of a Leeds cloth manufacturing family who had moved into the gentry. Unfortunately, his wife was confined to a mental institution for most of her married life, and they had no children. The 3rd Earl had an illegitimate son, John R.H. Rudge (b. 1892) with Letitia ["Letty"] Rudge (1861-1923), later known as Letty Lind. They could not marry, as the Earl could not divorce his wife if she was confined to an asylum. In *Who Was Who*, his addresses were given as 39 Grosvenor Square; Lambton Castle, Durham; and Harraton House, Newmarket. He is credited in that work with being the "owner of about 30,500 acres." He left £1,543,698, of which £1,126,618 was in settled land. The 3rd Earl died on 18 September 1928, and was succeeded by his twin brother, who held the title only until 31 January 1929. Frederick, 4th Earl of Durham (1855-1929), was educated at Eton, and served in the Coldstream Guards from 1874-1880. In 1879 he married his second cousin once removed, Beatrix Bulteel (1859-1937, left £5,279), the daughter of John Bulteel, from a Devon gentry family who had married into the Barings, the great merchant bankers. They had three sons and three daughters. Their daughter Lady Lilian Lambton (1881-1966) married Charles Douglas-Home, 13th Earl of Home (1873-1951), and was the mother of Sir Alec Douglas-Home, 14th Earl of Home, later Baron Home of the Hirsel (1903-95), Prime Minister in 1963-4, and Foreign Minister 1960-63 and 1970-74. The 4th Earl of Durham served as a Liberal M.P. from 1880-85, and later as a Liberal Unionist M.P. from 1900-1910. Like his brother, he was also very wealthy, leaving £1,326,100, of which £909,030 was in settled land.

The 4th Earl's son and successor was John Lambton, 5th Earl of Durham (1884-1970), who was educated at Eton and served in the First World War, in which he was wounded. He was an amateur jockey, and donated the Pershaw Monument – a structure on Pershaw Hill in Sunderland, built in 1844 in the style of an ancient Greek temple – to the National Trust. He was married twice. His first wife, whom he married in 1919, was Diana Farquhar (1901-24), daughter of Granville Farquhar. They had two sons before her very early death. Their eldest son, John Roderick Lambton, Viscount Lambton (1920-41), committed suicide at the age of twenty by shooting himself. The younger son, Anthony Lambton (1922-2006) disclaimed the Earldom when he inherited it in 1970, and became a well-known Tory politician. In 1931 the 5th Earl married Hermione (1906-90, left £1,729,402), the daughter of Sir George Bullough, 1st Bt. (1870-1939, left £710,037), described in one source as a "late Victorian playboy." He was the son of John Bullough (1836-91), a millionaire (he left £1,228,184) textile machinery manufacturer (Howard & Bullough) in Leicester. They had one son, John George Lambton (1932-2012).

His surviving son, Anthony Lambton, inherited the title of 6th Earl of Durham on 4 February 1970, and disclaimed it – as was now possible – on 23 February 1970, in order to stay in the House of Commons. He was educated at Harrow, and served in World War Two, but was invalided out because of a chronic eye ailment (he always wore dark glasses) and worked for the duration of the War in a factory in Wallsend. He was elected a Conservative M.P. in 1950, serving until he resigned in May 1973. After serving as a very junior minister during the 1950s, he was appointed Parliamentary Under-Secretary for Defence (RAF) by Edward Heath when Heath unexpectedly won the 1970 election. Lambton was unpopular, despite his competence, because of his bad temper and inability to suffer fools, a chip off the block of his ancestor the 1st Earl. Although he had disclaimed his peerage, he continued to be known as Lord Lambton. In May 1973 the *News of the World* newspaper exposed his liaisons with prostitutes, while the investigating police found cannabis in his home. The fact that he was a minister for the RAF raised the possibility of his being blackmailed by a hostile power. He was forced to leave politics, and spent much of the rest of his life in Siena, Italy, where he died. There, he wrote two novels and a well-regarded biography of *The Mountbattens* (1989). In 1942 he had married Belinda ("Blindy") Blew-Jones, the daughter of (Col.) Douglas Blew-Jones and of Violet Birkin, the sister of Freda Dudley Ward (1894-1983), the mistress of the Prince of Wales (later Edward VIII) before he met Mrs. Wallis Simpson. (The two were first introduced by Freda Ward.) She remained with him despite his scandal. They had five daughters, one of whom is the broadcaster Lady Lucinda Lambton (b. 1943), and a son and successor. Lord Lambton left £11,800,306 in England when he died. His only son, Edward Lambton, 7th Earl of Durham (b. 1961), was a musician, a member of the band "Pearl TN," where he was known as Ned Lambton. He has been married three times and divorced twice. His first wife, the mother of his heir, was Christobel McEwan, the granddaughter of Sir John McEwan. In 1897 Lambton stood for Parliament for the Referendum Party, but received only 3.4 per cent of the vote. In 2001, the Earl of Durham owned 9,500 acres in Co. Durham, according to Kevin Cahill, only a fraction of what they owned in the nineteenth century.

34. Lowther, Earls of Lonsdale – £71,333 p.a.

In 1883, the Earl of Lonsdale owned 68,065 acres worth £71,333 p.a., in Cumberland (28,228 acres/£42,818 p.a.); Westmorland (39,229 acres/£27,141 p.a.); Rutland (493 acres/£1,251 p.a.); and Lancashire (115 acres/£123 p.a.).

Sir John Lowther, 1st Bt. (1605-75), the first member of this family to be granted an hereditary title, was created a baronet in 1638. Apart from being a large-scale landowner in Westmorland and Cumberland, in part in the Lake District, he served as M.P. for Westmorland from 1629 until 1640. A Royalist during the Civil War, after the Restoration he was again elected an M.P., this time for Cumberland, from 1660 until his death. Lowther was also a very successful businessman who was widely regarded as unscrupulous, and was said to have left £80,000 at his death, an enormous sum at the time.

In 1696 Sir John Lowther (1655-1700), a barrister and M.P. who served as Lord Privy Seal from 1699 until his death the following year, was created 1st Viscount Lonsdale. This title became extinct in 1751. However, in 1784 his descendant Sir James Lowther, 5th Bt. (1736-1802) was created 1st Earl of Lonsdale. As he had no children, in 1797 he was also created 1st Viscount Lonsdale, with a special remainder to his third cousin Sir William Lowther, 2nd Bt. of a different baronetcy. The 1st Earl of Lonsdale was educated at Peterhouse, Cambridge, and served as an M.P. from 1757 until 1784. He was regarded – almost certainly without reason – as "the richest commoner in England," said to be worth £2 million, which included lands in Westmorland and Cumberland, and a plantation in Barbados, as well as collieries, and the harbour of Whitehaven, Cumberland. He controlled eight "pocket boroughs" in the north of England, and in 1781 secured the election of William Pitt the younger for one of his seats, Appleby. A colourful but unpopular character known as "Wicked Jimmy," he employed as his solicitor John Wordsworth, the father of the poet, to whom he owed £4,000 but failed to pay him during the Earl's lifetime. In 1792 he fought an inconclusive duel with a captain in the Guards.

His third cousin and successor, Sir William Lowther, 2nd Bt., later 2nd Viscount Lonsdale and 1st Earl of Lonsdale (1757-1844), was, confusingly, the son of another Lowther baronet, (Revd.) Sir William Lowther, 1st Bt. (1707-88), Rector of Swiillington, Yorkshire, and of Anne Zouch (1723-59), daughter of (Revd.) Charles Zouch. He was educated at Westminster School and at Trinity College, Cambridge, and served as a Tory M.P. from 1780 until 1802, when he succeeded his third cousin by special remainder, becoming the 2nd Viscount Lonsdale and one of the richest men in the north of England. In 1781 he had married Lady Augusta Fane (1761-1838), the daughter of John Fane, 9th Earl of Westmorland. In 1807 the Viscount was created 1st Earl of Lonsdale of a new creation and was Lord Lieutenant of Westmorland and Cumberland from 1802 until his death. He also rebuilt Lowther Hall, the main family seat, and was regarded as enjoying an income of nearly £100,000 a year, from his lands, collieries, and Whitehaven harbour. He is best known today as the patron of William Wordsworth and secured the poet the nominal but paid position of Collector of Stamps for Westmorland, which allowed him to write poetry untroubled by financial worries. According to his entry in the ODNB, he left £200,000 in personalty at his death; according to the PCC probate records, he left £100,000 "within province," i.e., the Archdiocese of Canterbury. Confusingly, he had a younger brother, Sir John Lowther, 1st Bt. (1759-1844), who was also a long-serving M.P. and was created a baronet.

His son and successor, William Lowther, 2nd Earl of Lonsdale (1787-1872) was educated at Harrow and at Trinity College, Cambridge, and served as an M.P. from 1808 until 1841, when he was summoned to the Lords in one of his father's minor titles, Baron Lowther; from 1844, he was Earl of Lonsdale. He held many offices in Tory governments from 1809 until 1852, including First Commissioner of Woods and Forests, 1828-30, under Wellington; Postmaster General, with a seat in the Cabinet, 1841-45, under Peel; and Lord President of the Council, with a seat in the Cabinet, in 1852 under Derby. He was also Lord Lieutenant of Cumberland and Westmorland from 1844 until 1868. The 2nd Earl never married, but fathered two daughters and a son by three different women, all of them French or Italian opera singers or dancers. His son Francis William Lowther (1841-1908) left £269,580. Francis was the father of Claude Lowther (1870-1929), the owner of Herstmonceux Castle in Sussex, a well-known right-wing Conservative M.P. from 1900-06 and from December 1910 until 1922; he left £100,554. The 2nd Earl appears to have been the wealthiest member of his family and left £700,000 in personalty at his death in 1872.

His brother (Hon.) Henry Cecil Lowther (1790-1867), an army officer and a well-known cricketer, was an M.P. from 1812 to his death, and was the "Father of the House" (the longest-serving M.P.) from 1862 until 1867. Another important member of the Lowther family was James Lowther, 1st Viscount Ullswater (1855-1949), the son of (Hon.) William Lowther M.P. (1871-1912, left £92,742), the grandson of the 1st Earl of Lonsdale, and of Charlotte (d. 1908), daughter of the judge James Parke, 1st Baron Wensleydale (1782-1868). He was educated at Eton; King's College London; and Trinity College, Cambridge, and became a barrister of the Inner Temple. In 1883-85 and 1886-1917, he served as an M.P., and, from 1905 until 1921, was Speaker of the House of Commons. In 1917 he presided over the Speaker's Conference, which led to full manhood suffrage and to the granting of the vote to women over thirty. He was made a Viscount in 1921, and left £229,079 when he died at ninety-four. He is also well-known for the advice he gave to new M.P.s about to speak in Parliament for the first time: "Stand up, Speak up, Shut up."

As the 2nd Earl had no legitimate sons, the title passed to his nephew, Henry Lowther, 3rd Earl of Lonsdale (1818-76), the eldest son of (Hon.) Henry Cecil Lowther and Lady Lucy Sherard (1792-1848), the daughter of Philip Sherard, 5th Earl of Harborough (1767-1807). He was educated at Westminster School and at Trinity College, Cambridge, and served as an M.P. from 1847 until he inherited the peerage in 1872. In 1852 he had married Emily (d. 1917), the daughter of St. George Caulfeild (*sic*). He held the title for only four years when he suddenly died, leaving £140,000. Unusually, his three sons succeeded him in turn. His eldest son St. George Lowther, 4th Earl of Lonsdale (1855-82), was educated at Eton, and was a Colonel in the Militia. He was a successful racehorse owner, but died at twenty-seven, possibly of alcoholism. In 1878 he married (Hon.) Constance (1859-1917, left £107,635), daughter of Sidney Herbert, Baron Herbert of Lea (1810-61), the son of George, 11th Earl of Pembroke (*q.v.*). In 1885, she remarried Frederick, 2nd Marquess of Ripon (1852-1923, left £596,291). The 4th Earl's only child was his daughter Lady (Gladys) Juliet Lowther (later Duff and then Trevor, 1881-1965), who left £46,799. He was succeeded by his brother Hugh Lowther, 5th Earl of Lonsdale (1857-1944), a larger-than-life figure known as "the Yellow Earl," for the colour he favoured. He was educated at Eton, but left at twelve to follow sporting pursuits. He was known for his immaculate dress, and travelled in a special train. A renowned sportsman, he donated the Lonsdale Belt for boxing champions, and was the actual author of the standard "Marquess of Queensberry Rules" used ever since. He was the first President of the Automobile Association, and in 1895 entertained Kaiser Wilhelm II at Lowther Castle. In 1888 he went on an expedition to explore northern Canada and Alaska, and nearly died. In 1878 he married Lady Grace (1854-1941, left £8711), daughter of Charles Gordon, 10th Marquess of Huntly; they were unable to have children after she fell from a horse. In 1886 the Earl had an affair with the married actress Violet Cameron (1862-1919), with whom he had an illegitimate daughter. Despite this, in 1886 he was listed in one reference work as being the Patron of 32 Anglican livings. A notorious spendthrift, he was forced to sell Whitehaven Castle in 1921 and to move out of Lowther Castle in 1935. In 1947, after his death, the contents of Lowther Castle were auctioned off, in one of the largest aristocratic sales of its time. In 1886, his residences were listed as Lowther Castle, Penrith; Whitehaven Castle; Barley-Thorpe, Oakham; and 14 Carlton Terrace. A biography has been written about the 5th Earl, *The Yellow Earl* (1965), by Douglas Sutherland. He left £130,840 at his death, of which £102,042 was in settled land.

As the 5th Earl had no sons, the title passed to the third son of the 3rd Earl, Lancelot, 6th Earl of Lonsdale (1867-1953), who gained the title sixty-two years after the death of his father. He was educated at Malvern College and at Magdalene College, Cambridge, and served as a Captain in the Middle East during the First World War, in which he was twice mentioned in despatches. He was a Deputy MFH. The 6th Earl was married, first, to Sophia Gwendolin Sheffield (1869-1921, left £1,147), the daughter of Sir Robert Sheffield, 5th Bt. (1824-86, left £19,574), and, secondly, in 1923, to Sybil (d. 1966, left £29,887), the daughter of (Major General) Feetham. His elder son Anthony, Viscount Lowther (1896-1949, left £2,969) predeceased him, and the title passed to his grandson. It would appear that the 6th Earl restored much of the family fortune after his brother had greatly diminished it. He left £1,067,489 at his death, an enormous sum in 1953, of which £726,687 was in settled land.

The next holder of the title was James Lowther, 7th Earl of Lonsdale (1922-2006), the son of Anthony, Viscount Lowther and of Muriel Farrar (1896-1968, left £9,263), the daughter of Sir

Herbert Farrar, 1st Bt., a Bedford-born South African "Randlord" who left £80,559 in England and, according to a memoir by a relative, was worth £8 million in South Africa, chiefly as the head of East Rand Proprietary Mines. The 7th Earl was educated at Eton, and briefly attended Cambridge, reading Mechanical Engineering, when he was drafted and sent to Oxford to study tank engineering. He served in the Royal Armoured Corps, and was wounded at Caen. He did his best to improve the family fortunes still further, which included selling off Whitehaven harbour and much land, and taking the roof off of Lowther Castle, leaving it "a romantic ruin." He was a strong supporter of conservation efforts in the Lake District, and was Chairman of Border Television from 1985 to 1990. He appeared in the 2006 *Sunday Times Rich List* as worth £80 million. He was married four times, the first time in 1945 to Tuppina Bennet (divorced 1954; d. 1984), the mother of the present Earl. In all, the 7th Earl had four sons and four daughters. A few days before he died, he set up the Lonsdale Settled Estates, which, according to his eldest son, with whom he did not get on, "disinherited [him] in all but name." The eldest son, Hugh, 8th Earl of Lonsdale (b. 1949), was educated at Eton and has been married three times, but has no children; his heir is his half-brother (Hon.) William Lowther (b. 1957). Very little is given in any source about the present Earl, but it is known that he is the owner of 5,000 acres in Westmorland, certainly far less than the family owned in the nineteenth century.

35. Pennant, later Douglas-Pennant, Barons Penrhyn – £71,018 p.a.

In 1883 Lord Penrhyn owned 49,548 acres worth £71,018 p.a. in Caernarvonshire (41,348 acres/£62,622 p.a.); Northamptonshire (5,377 acres/£7,409 p.a.); Denbighshire (2,625 acres/£750 p.a.); Kent (121 acres/£67 p.a.); and Buckinghamshire (77 acres/£170 p.a.).

The wealth of the Douglas-Pennants began with the Pennant family, who were major plantation owners in Jamaica, and British officials there, for several generations. Its wealth was then completely altered in the late eighteenth and early nineteenth centuries, when they basically cornered the market in slate quarrying in Caernarvonshire, where they enjoyed a virtual monopoly of this product, used in building, roofing, and for many other purposes. The man who was most responsible for this was Richard Pennant, 1st Baron Penrhyn (1737-1808), who was the son of John Pennant (d. 1782), a Liverpool merchant, and of Bonella (d.1763), daughter of John Hodges of Jamaica, a plantation owner there. He was related to many influential Britons in Jamaica: his great-grandfather was Chief Justice there, and another Jamaica relative, Henry Dawkins (d. 1814) left £150,000 in England. Pennant was educated at Newcome's Academy in Hackney, and then at Trinity College, Cambridge. From 1761 until 1790 he served as an M.P.; from 1767 until 1790 as one of Liverpool's M.P.s. In 1790 he was made 1st Baron Penrhyn in the Irish peerage, enabling him to continue to sit in the House of Commons, despite the fact that he had no connection with Ireland and never again sat in the Commons.

He owned the Penrhyn estate in north Wales, and was the owner of six plantations in Jamaica and of 600 slaves. In Parliament, he was one of the few overt defenders of slavery. In 1765, he married Anne (1745-1816), the daughter of (General) Hugh Warburton (1695-1771), his father's business partner, from whom he acquired most of his north Wales property. Probably seeing the writing on the wall in terms of Jamaica plantations, he used much of his income to advance the slate quarrying business, opening up this mountainous part of north Wales, previously almost inaccessible. In 1801 he built a little-known early horse-drawn railway to carry his slate out of the Welsh hills. He was allegedly in debt when he died, but his widow left £120,000 in personalty "within province," i.e. in the Canterbury Archdiocese. They had no sons, and his property, apart from what his wife inherited, came to two people, his second cousin Henry Dawkins (later Dawkins-Pennant, 1764-1840), who left no less than £600,000 in personalty "within province" when he died, and to their daughter Juliana (1808-42), who married Edward Gordon Douglas (later Douglas-Pennant, 1800-86), who in 1866 was made 1st Baron Penrhyn of a new creation. The slate quarrying business expanded enormously; by the late nineteenth century, his quarries were employing 3,000 workers.

Edward Gordon Douglas-Pennant (*nee* Douglas), 1st Baron Penrhyn of the new creation (1800-86), was the son of (Hon.) John Douglas (1756-1818), the son of James Douglas, 14th Earl of Morton (1702-68) and of Lady Frances Lascelles (1762-1817), daughter of Edward Lascelles, 1st Earl of Harewood (1740-1820); the Lascelles. like the Pennants, were major plantation owners in Jamaica. He joined the Grenadier Guards in 1815, and retired in 1846 as a Colonel. In 1833, he married Juliana (d. 1842), the daughter of the 1st Baron Penrhyn of the previous creation; they had two sons and three daughters. After her death, in 1846 he remarried Lady Maria (1818-1912, left £56,911), daughter of Henry FitzRoy, 5th Duke of Grafton. In 1841, he added "Pennant" to his surname. He served as a Conservative M.P. from 1841 until 1866. In that year, he was created 1st Baron Penrhyn of the new creation. He built a "model town" for his workmen, but, in 1868, sacked eighty of his workers who failed to vote for his son at a Parliamentary election. He served as Lord Lieutenant of Caernarvonshire. In 1886, his residences were Penrhyn Castle, Bangor; Woken Park, Stony Stratford, Buckinghamshire; and Mortimer House, Halkin Street, W. He was, of course, very wealthy, and left £761,880 in personalty at his death.

His son and successor, George Douglas-Pennant, 2nd Baron Penrhyn (1836-1907) was educated at Eton and at Christ Church, Oxford. He was an officer in the local volunteers, but was mainly involved in running the family slate quarries. As well, he served as a Conservative M.P. for Caernarvonshire in 1866-68 and 1874-80. Between 1897 and 1903, as an opponent of trade unions, he was involved in much labour strife with the trade unions of men in his quarries which became nationally known, and twice closed his quarries rather than accede to their demands. There were two major strikes in his quarries, in 1900 and 1903, the latter of which was known as the "Great Strike." In 1903 he successfully sued William John Parry (1842-1927), the head of the North Wales Quarrymen's Union, for libel, for an article in *Clarion,* and won £500. Lord Penrhyn and his family were increasingly seen as wealthy English outsiders by the Welsh working class of the area. He was married, first in 1860, to Pamela (1839-69, left £600), daughter of Sir Charles Rushout, 2nd Bt., with whom he had a son and six daughters; and, secondly in 1875, to Gertrude (d. 1940, left £17,457)), daughter of (Revd.) Henry Glynne, a niece of Prime Minister Gladstone, with whom he had two sons, both of whom were killed in the First World War, and six more daughters. He was a racehorse owner and MFH, and rebuilt Penrhyn Castle. He remained very wealthy, and left £596,424 in personalty at his death. His son and successor, Edward Douglas-Pennant, 3rd Baron Penrhyn (1864-1927), was educated at Eton, and served as an officer in the Life Guards and as a Major during the Boer War. He was a Conservative M.P. from 1895 until 1900. In 1887, he married (Hon.) Blanche (1865-1944, left £48,111), daughter of Charles FitzRoy, 3rd Baron Southampton. His eldest son Alan was killed in 1914 in the First World War, and he was succeeded by his younger son. He remained very wealthy during his lifetime, and left £1,112,135 at his death, of which £400,000 was in settled land.

His younger son, Hugh Douglas-Pennant, 4th Baron Penrhyn (1894-1949), was educated at

Eton and Sandhurst, and was an officer in the First World War. He served as Lord Lieutenant of Caernarvonshire from 1933 until 1941. In 1922, he married (Hon.) Sybil (later the wife of Denzil, 6th Earl Fortescue; she d. 1985, leaving £64,288), daughter of Henry Hardinge, 3rd Baron Hardinge, but they had no children, and were divorced in 1941. He also remained very wealthy, and left £892,944 at his death, a vast amount during the post-war time of astronomical tax rates, of which £500,000 was in settled land. The title now came to a distant relative, Frank Douglas-Pennant, 5th Baron Penrhyn (1865-1967- *sic*: he lived to 101), the son of the 1st Baron's second son, a man who theoretically could have met Charles Dickens, who died in 1870, and also could have attended a Beatles concert. At his death he was the oldest ever hereditary peer. He was the son of (Lt. Col.) (Hon.) Archibald Douglas-Pennnat (d. 1884, left £59,790) and of (Hon.) Harriet Hardinge (d. 1942, left £35,114), daughter of Robert Hardinge, 2nd Baron Gifford. He was educated at Eton and at Sandhurst, and served as an officer in the Boer War and the First World War. Unlike his predecessors, he did not leave an enormous amount at his death, £40,682. He was married twice; his surviving son and successor was the son of his second wife, Alice (d. 1965, left £19,772), daughter of Sir William Charles Cooper, 3rd Bt. (1851-1925).

His son Malcolm Douglas-Pennant, 7th Baron Penrhyn (1908-2003), was educated at Eton and at Sandhurst, was an army officer in India and Burma, and fought in North Africa with the Free French. In 1954 he married Elizabeth (d. 2002), daughter of (Brigadier) Sir Percy Laurie (1880-1962), Assistant Commissioner of the Metropolitan Police, 1933-36. They had two daughters but no son, and the title passed to his nephew, Simon Douglas-Pennant, 7th Baron Penrhyn (b. 1938), who was the son of (Hon.) (Major) Nigel Douglas-Pennant (1909-2000), a son of Frank, 5th Baron Penrhyn, and of Margaret (d. 1938, shortly after her son was born), daughter of Thomas George Kirkham. He was educated at Eton and at Clare College, Cambridge, and was a noted cricketer. From 1990-1998 he was a director of Brintons Ltd., carpet manufacturers of Kidderminster. In 1963 he married Josephine, daughter of Robert Upcott. They have two sons and two daughters. The family apparently no longer owns any substantial amount of land. In 1951 the 5th Baron donated his entire holding in Caernarvonshire, nearly 37,000 acres, to the National Trust, the largest single gift of land to that body. (Kevin Cahill, p. 307).

Chapter 2: Large Personal Fortunes of landowners and the Businessmen Who Owned the Most Land

A number of substantial landowners, but not at the very top in terms of gross annual income, left extraordinarily high amounts for probate when they died. Four such men, in particular, left estates so large that they deserve a separate discussion.

1. Andrew Montagu (1815-95) – £1,997,099.

This figure was apparently revised upwards in the probate records, by a handwritten emendation, to £2,005,000. Andrew Montagu was a great untitled landowner who, in 1883, owned 27,265 acres worth £53,034 p.a. in Yorkshire, West Riding (20,700 acres/£35,234 p.a.); Nottinghamshire (3,254 acres/£12,200 p.a.); Cornwall (2657 acres/£3495 p.a.); Northumberland (648 acres/£2,100 p.a.); and Devonshire (6 acres/£5).

He was born Andrew Fountayne Wilson, the son of Richard Fountayne Wilson (1783-1847) of Merton Hall near Doncaster, whose ancestors were merchants in Leeds. His father was (Rt. Revd.) Christopher Wilson, Bishop of Bristol from 1783 to 1792. The father was educated at Eton and at Trinity College, Cambridge. He left £100,000 at his death. The M.P.'s wife – Andrew Montagu's mother – was Sophie (1785-1861, left £12,000), the daughter of George Osbaldeston, an M.P. from 1783 to 1790, and the brother of "Squire" Osbaldeston, the famous sportsman. Andrew changed his surname to Montagu in 1826, upon inheriting the property of Frederick Montagu. He married Nancy Isabella Lé Lacheur (b. 1825), of a Huguenot family. They had one son, Andrew Montagu (1853-84), who predeceased him. His brother James Montagu (1819-91, left £196,949) also predeceased him. The only political office held by Andrew Montagu was that of High Sheriff of Yorkshire, in 1853-4. He was also a Patron of one living. In the 1850s, a keen Tory, Montagu paid off Benjamin Disraeli's many debts, in exchange for holding a mortgage on Hughenden, Disraeli's country house. Disraeli was able to buy back this mortgage shortly before his death in 1881. In 1886, Andrew Montagu's residences were given as Melton Park, Doncaster and Papplewick, Nottingham. At his death, his address was given as Inganthorpe Hall, Wetherby, Leeds, Yorkshire. His main heir was apparently his nephew, the son of his brother James, (Capt.) Frederick James Osbaldeston Montagu (1878-1957), who left £218,045. How Andrew Montagu became so wealthy is rather mysterious, but he must have owned urban property in or near Leeds, Doncaster, and Nottingham, as well coal and other minerals. Very little is known about his business activities.

2. Wentworth Blackett Beaumont, 1st Baron Allendale (1829-1907) – £3,234,807.

In 1883 Wentworth Blackett Beaumont owned 24,098 acres worth £34,670 p.a. in Northumberland (14,279 acres/£15,076 p.a.); Yorkshire, West Riding (9,015 acres/£16,634 p.a.); and Co. Durham

(804 acres/£960 p.a.).

Wentworth Beaumont, later 1st Baron Allendale, was the son of Thomas Beaumont (1792-1848, left £335,000), a land and mine owner, chiefly in Northumberland. He served as an "advanced Liberal" M.P. from 1818 until 1837. He was from an already wealthy family, and had attended Eton and St. John's College, Cambridge. Allendale's mother was Henrietta (d. 1861, left £60,000), the daughter of John Atkinson of Maple Hayes, Staffordshire. Allendale was educated at Harrow and at St. John's College, Cambridge. He served as a Liberal M.P. from 1852 until 1885, and from 1886 until 1892, one of the few substantial landowners who did not become Liberal Unionists in 1886. In 1906, he was created 1st Baron Allendale. He was a Patron of nine livings. He was married twice: first, in 1856, to Lady Margaret (d.1888, left £2209), the daughter of Ulick de Burgh, 1st Marquess of Clanricarde (q.v., below) and (Hon.) Harriet, the daughter of George Canning, the Prime Minister, with whom he had three sons and three daughters. In 1891 he remarried Edith (d. 1927, left £51,647), the daughter of (Lt. Gen.) Henry Meade-Hamilton and the widow of (Major-Gen.) Sir George Pomeroy-Colley. He was succeeded by his eldest son, Wentworth Beaumont, 2nd Baron Allendale (1860-1923), educated at Eton and at Trinity College, Cambridge, who served as a Liberal M.P. from 1895 until 1907, when he succeeded to the peerage. In 1911, he was created 1st Viscount Allendale. He served in the Liberal governments of the time as Captain, Yeoman of the Guards (Chief Whip in the House of Lords), 1907-11, and as a Lord-in-Waiting, 1911-16. At his death in 1923, he left £2,006,770.

It seems clear that the 1st Baron Allendale received a vast income from colliery and other mines on his lands in the West Riding and in Northumberland (he sat for two Northumberland seats in Parliament), as well as from his agricultural land, and possibly his urban property. If he had any other large sources of income, they could not be traced. His personalty left in 1907, over £3 million, was one of the largest personal estates ever left by a British landowner up to that time.

3. Hubert George de Burgh-Canning, 2nd Marquess of Clanricarde (1832-1916) – £2,742,662 – includes £242,662 left in Ireland.

In 1883, the Marquess of Clanricarde owned 58,826 acres worth £24,358 p.a. in Co. Galway.

Lord Clanricarde was the son of Ulick John de Burgh, 1st Marquess of Clanricarde in the Irish peerage (1807-74, left £67,178 in personalty), who was created 1st Baron Somerhill in the UK peerage in 1798. He was the son of (General) John de Burgh, 13th Earl of Clanricarde (1744-1808). The 1st Marquess was a significant political figure, who served as Ambassador to Russia in 1838-40 and served in the Liberal Cabinet as Postmaster-General from 1846-52 and in the Tory Cabinet as Lord Privy Seal in 1858. His wife – the mother of the 2nd Marquess – was (Hon.) Harriet Cannng (1804-76, left £60,000), the daughter of Prime Minister George Canning. According to his entry in the ODNB, the 1st Marquess also had "various mistresses" and "an apparently unlimited number of Illegitimate children." His daughter, Lady Margaret de Burgh, married the 1st Baron Allendale (q.v.), the previous entry. His son, the 2nd Marquess of Clanricarde, was educated at Harrow, and served as an M.P. for Co. Galway from 1867-71. He also served as an attaché at Turin from 1852-63.

To this day, Clanricarde has a reputation in Ireland as one of the worst Irish landlords. A story in The Irish News, 29 November 2014, headlined "Ruthless Landlord and Miser," claims that "no name is held in more bitter memory" than his, as an absentee landlord in London, who never visited Ireland, evicted hundreds of tenants who, through crop failure, were unable to pay their rent, without mercy. This may be something of an exaggeration, as his addresses were listed in 1886 in one reference work as Portumna Castle, Galway and The Albany in Piccadilly. The sources of Clanricarde's very great personal wealth is not entirely clear. He is known to have inherited from his wife's brother Charles Canning, 1st Earl Canning (1812-62, left £250,000 in personalty), Governor-General of India 1854-57 (during the "Indian Mutiny"), and then the first Viceroy of India, 1858-62. Clanricarde was unmarried. His title as Marquess became extinct, but his previous title as Earl of Clanricarde passed to his relative the Earl of Sligo. Much of his wealth was inherited by his great-nephew, the Earl of Harewood. The next holder of this title to die after Clanricarde, Ulick, 5th Earl of Harewood (1846-1929), left £386,010.

4. William Tollemache, 9th Earl of Dysart (1859-1935) – £2,104,312.
This figure was apparently revised upwards in the probate records, by a handwritten emendation, to £2,375,000. In 1883 the Earl of Dysart owned 27,190 acres worth £44,500 p.a., in Lincolnshire (18,025 acres/£9,077 p.a.); Leicestershire (8420 acres/£11,631 p.a.); Surrey (723 acres; £3,768 p.a.); and Rutland (22 acres/£24).

The Earldom of Dysart is a Scottish title. Despite this, the 9th Earl did not own a single acre in Scotland, and his residences were given in one reference work as Ham Hall, Petersham, Surrey and Buckminster Park, Grantham. His only public office was as Lord Lieutenant of Rutland, 1881-1906. The Earl, who was partially blind, was musical, and was President of the London Wagner Society from 1884 to 1895. He was the son of William Tollemache, Lord Huntingtower (d. 1872), who left only £300, and Catherine Elizabeth Burke (d. 1896, left £37,312). His father also produced ten illegitimate sons and daughters. His father was the son of Lionel Tollemache, 8th Earl of Dysart (1794-1878), an enormously wealthy landowner, who left £1,700,000 in personalty. After the death of his grandfather, his estate was kept in trust for twenty-one years, and its trustees greatly increased the value of the family's holdings in the Ham and Petersham area of south London through property development, clearly a source of Lord Dysart's wealth. In 1885, he married Cecilia (1861-1917, left £12,677), daughter of George Onslow Newton. They had no children and were permanently separated from the 1900s on. Lord Dysart's peerage came to his niece Wenefryde Scott, 10th Countess of Dysart (1889-1975) – as with some old Scottish peerages, a female could succeed to the title – who left £329,974.

Post-1750 Businessmen Who Became Substantial (£25,000 + in gross annual landed income) Landowners By 1883.

This section discusses all of the post-1750 British businessmen – merchants, bankers, industrialists – who, themselves or their families, became great landowners. The criterion for inclusion here is having a gross annual landed income of £25,000 or more, by the businessman himself, or by the close members of his family. In most cases, the families listed here do include several related members who each appear in John Bateman's Great Landowners of Great Britain and Ireland, rather than a single individual, as with the wealthy landed aristocrats discussed above. Many other wealthy businessmen, apart from those listed here, appear in Bateman at lower levels of acreage and income, although certainly the great majority of wealthy businessmen active in Britain between 1750 and 1883 owned little or no land. The businessmen who are discussed here appear in descending order of their gross annual landed income.

1. Samuel Jones Loyd, 1st Baron Overstone (1796-1883), Banker in Manchester and in the City of London – £58,098 p.a., and his son-in-law (Brigadier-General) Sir Robert Loyd-Lindsay (*nee* Lindsay), 1st Baron Wantage – £26,492 p.a. = £84,590 p.a.

In 1883, Lord Overstone owned 30,849 acres worth £58,098 p.a., in Northamptonshire (15,045 acres/£30,679 p.a.); Warwickshire (4,460 acres/£7, 54 p.a.); Buckinghamshire (5, 072 acres/£8,849 p.a.); Cambridgeshire (2,402 acres/£4,135 p.a.); Huntingdonshire (1,712 acres/£2,946 p.a.); Leicestershire (1,276 acres/£2,064 p.a.); and five other counties. In 1883, Sir Robert Loyd-Lindsay owned 20,528 acres worth £26,492 p.a., in Berkshire.

One of the most remarkable, but too little known, businessmen in Victorian Britain was the great banker Samuel Jones Loyd, 1st Baron Overstone (1796-1883). He was the son of (Revd.) Lewis Loyd (1767-1858), a Unitarian minister and later a banker, and of Sarah, daughter of John Jones, a Manchester banker. His father gave up the ministry after he married, becoming a partner in his father-in-law's bank, later known as Jones, Loyd & Co. It became one of the largest private banks in the country, with offices in the City of London and in Manchester, and Lewis Loyd became very wealthy, leaving £800,000 when he died. He had already begun the process of acquiring agricultural land, having bought Overstone Park, with 15,000 acres of land, near Northampton, from which his son later took his peerage title, as well as land in Berkshire. Lord Overstone was born in an apartment over the bank's premises at 42 Lothbury in the City of London. His birth was registered with the Unitarians, but he was brought up as an Anglican, enabling him to attend Eton and Trinity College, Cambridge. He became a partner in the family bank in 1816, and served as a Liberal M.P. from 1819 till 1826. In 1829 he married Harriet (1799-1864), the daughter of Ichabod Wright, a prominent Nottingham banker. They had one child, a daughter, Harriet Sarah, who married Sir Robert Loyd-Lindsay (*q.v.*, below). Jones, Loyd & Co. prospered under his direction; between 1817 and 1848 he earned £563,000 from his share of the bank's profits. He was known for being very conservative in his banking practices.

In 1849, in recognition of his leading place as a banker and as a former M.P., he was given a peerage, as 1st Baron Overstone, one of the earliest businessmen to be ennobled. Jones, Loyd & Co. was later absorbed by other banks, and is a remote ancestor of NatWest. Overstone had a major role in shaping the Bank Charter Act of 1844. He was an art collector of note, and a Trustee of the National Gallery and other institutions. From the 1850s onwards he was chiefly a landowner rather than a banker. He rebuilt Overstone Park in Northamptonshire. Today, sadly, it is an abandoned ruin. In London he lived at 2 Carlton Gardens. At his death, he left the extraordinary sum of £2,118,048 in personalty, and land which was valued at £3,114,262, for a total of £5,232,310, making him surely one of the dozen richest men in Britain when he died. His landed income, given in Bateman as £58,098 p.a., meant that he was one of the sixty or so wealthiest landowners in Britain, based on their landed income, among the richest landed aristocrats whose families had taken generations to build up their landed wealth. Although he is well-known to historians of banking – three volumes of his correspondence was edited by D.P. O'Brien and published in 1971 – he is surprisingly little known to most historians of Victorian Britain.

His daughter Harriet Sarah Loyd, later Lady Wantage (1837-1920), who left £768,587 at her death, married her husband in 1858. She was very influential in the Ladies' Committee of the British Red Cross, founded in part by her husband. She was a noted philanthropist, and gave £150,000 to Reading University College. Her husband, Sir Robert James Loyd-Lindsay (*nee*

Lindsay), 1st Baron Wantage (1832-1901), was a descendant of the Earl of Balcarres, was the son of (Lt. Gen.) James Lindsay (1793-1955), and of Anne (c. 1803-94), the daughter of Sir Coutts Trotter, 1st Bt., a prominent banker, like his father-in-law. He was educated at Eton, and joined the Scots Fusilier Guards, serving in the Crimean War, for which he received the V.C., and retired as a Brigadier-General. He served as an Equerry to the Prince of Wales, and added "Loyd-" to his name upon his marriage. Most of the landed acreage he owned came as gifts from his father-in-law. Although he served as a Tory M.P. from 1865 till 1885, he is best known as a founder and the first Chairman of the National Society for Aid to the Sick and Wounded, later known as the British Red Cross. In 1885 he was created 1st Baron Wantage and was Lord Lieutenant of Berkshire. Although he inherited Overstone Park, his main residences were Lockinge House, Wantage, Berkshire and 2 Carlton Gardens. He remained influential in the Anglican Church and in army circles. At his death, he left only £21,671 in personalty. His widow erected an enormous pillar in his honour at The Ridgeway, Oxfordshire. As they had no children, their titles died with them, much of Lady Wantage's property came to a distant cousin, Arthur Thomas Loyd (1882-1944), who left £1,157,484.

2. The Baring Family – Merchant bankers in the City of London – £72,283 p.a. In 1883, four members of the Baring family were listed in Bateman.
Louisa, Lady Ashburton (1827-1903, left £285,588) owned 33,294 acres worth £6002 p.a. in Devon, Cornwall, Hampshire, and Ross-shire; Alexander Hugh Baring, 4th Baron Ashburton (1835-89, left £200,017) owned 36,772 acres worth £6,685 p.a. in Herefordshire, Hampshire, Wiltshire, Essex, and Somerset; Thomas George Baring, 1st Earl of Northbrook (1826-1904, left £246,698) owned 10,059 acres worth £12,710 p.a. in Hampshire and Kent; and William Henry Baring (1819-1906, left £84,875) owned 8,878 acres worth £6,886 p.a. in Hampshire and Wiltshire.

One of the most famous and powerful families in the City of London, the Barings produced more than twenty members with entries in the Oxford Dictionary of National Biography, and were influential politicians as well as merchant bankers. Philip Ziegler's The Sixth Great Power: Barings 1762-1929 (1988) charts the history of this major dynasty. The Barings were Lutherans, originally from Groningen, then in the Holy Roman Empire and now in the Netherlands, who later moved to Bremen, in northern Germany. Johann Baring (1697-1748) was apprenticed to wool merchants in Exeter, and became a successful wool merchant. His two sons, Francis and John Baring, moved to London in 1762, and founded the John & Francis Baring Bank, later known as the Baring Bank. Francis (1740-1810) became a key financial advisor to William Pitt, and became Sir Francis Baring, 1st Bt. He left £250,000 in personalty, although his entry in the Oxford Dictionary of National Biography states that he left £606,000, a figure which probably includes his lands. The Baring Bank specialised in financing American securities, and developed many links with the United States. It also took over the famous and extremely wealthy Amsterdam bank of Hope & Co., founded by a British banker. During most of the nineteenth century, the Baring Bank was seen as one of the two most important City merchant banks, together with the Rothschild's merchant bank. The two banks were often seen as rivals, although the Rothschilds never invested directly in America, and were probably wealthier. In 1890, Barings, which had overinvested in Argentina, crashed and almost went bankrupt, but were saved by a consortium of City financiers. The Bank did famously go into liquidation in 1995. Because the Barings were always Protestants, and later Anglicans, their *entré* into the senior ranks of the Establishment was easier than that of the Rothschilds. The Barings were given no fewer than five hereditary peerages over the years – Ashburton, Northbrook, Cromer, Revelstoke, and Howick of Glendale, and remained very wealthy. In 1929, John, 2nd Baron Revelstoke (1863-1929) left £2,558,779, an enormous sum.

The Barings also bought very substantial amounts of land, as shown by the five family members listed in Bateman. Louisa, Lady Ashburton was the daughter of James Stewart-Mackenzie (d. 1843). In 1858 she married, as his second wife, William Bingham Baring, 2nd Baron Ashburton (1799-1864, left £180,000). She was well known in artistic and cultural circles, and was a famous philanthropist. Her main residence was Melchet Park, at Romsey, Hampshire. Alexander Hugh Baring, 4th Baron Ashburton was educated at Harrow and at Christ Church, Oxford, and served as an M.P. from 1857-67. He was the son of Francis, 3rd Baron Ashburton (1800-68, left £250,000), and was a noted art collector. His main residences were at The Grange, Alresford, Hampshire; Langham Hall, Dedham, Essex; and at Bath House, 82 Piccadilly. Thomas George Baring, 1st Earl of Northbrook (1826-1904), was the son of Francis Baring, 1st Baron Northbrook (1796-1866, left £16,000) was educated at Christ Church, Oxford, was an M.P. from 1847-66. He held a variety of senior posts, including Viceroy of India from 1872 till 1876, and First Lord of the Admiralty from 1880-85. He was made an Earl in 1876. His main residence was at Stratton Park, Micheldever, Hampshire. William Henry Baring, the son of William Baring (d. 1820), was a J.P. for Hampshire and lived at Norman Court, near Salisbury, Wiltshire. In 1844 he married Elizabeth, the daughter of Charles Hammersley, another major banker in the City of London.

3. William Joseph Denison and Sir Albert Denison Conyngham, 1st Baron Londesborough – Banker in the City of London; younger son of a landed aristocrat – £67,876 p.a.

In 1883, Lord Londesborough owned 52,655 acres worth £67,876 p.a. in Yorkshire.

The case of William Denison and Lord Londesborough is one of the more ambiguous examples of businessmen becoming landowners. William Joseph Denison (1770-1849) was a banker at Lombard Street in the City of London, and one of the richest men in Britain, leaving "Upper Value," i.e., above £1 million, and much land. He served as a Whig M.P for thirty-eight years between 1796 and his death. His sister Elizabeth (d. 1861) married Henry Conyngham, 1st Marquess Conyngham (1766-1832). Their third son was Sir Albert Denison Conyngham (1805-60, left £180,000 in personalty), who was educated at Eton and was a career diplomat in British embassies in Europe. He served as the first President of the British Archaeological Association, and was a Whig M.P. in 1835-41 and 1847-50. When Denison died in 1849, he left the whole of his vast fortune to Albert Conyngham, although he was the younger son of a peer. Conyngham changed his name in 1849 to "Denison," and in 1850 was created 1st Baron Londesborough. He became one of the larger landowners in Britain, with a residence at Londesborough Lodge near Scarborough. His eldest son William Denison (1834-1900, left £347,283 in personalty) in 1887 was created 1st Earl of Londesborough.

4. The Baird Family – Ironmasters at Gartsherrie, Lanarkshire – £58,487 p.a.

In 1883, five members of the Baird family were listed in Bateman. Sir Alexander Baird, 1st Bt. (1849-1920, left £285,805) owned 11,018 acres worth £12,630 p.a. in Kincardineshire, Inverness-shire, Forfarshire, and Perthshire; George Alexander Baird (1861-93, left £846,052) owned 23,141 acres worth £23,199 p.a. in Aberdeenshire; John Baird (1852-1900, left £63,560) owned 68,000 acres worth £5,800 p.a. in Inverness-shire and Lancashire; Isabella (*nee* Hay, d. 1904, left £43,956), the widow of James Baird (1802-76, left £1,190,869), owned 19,599 acres worth £8,043 p.a. in Ayrshire; and William Baird (1898-1918, left £654,461), owned 3575 acres worth £8,815 p.a. in Fifeshire.

The Baird ironmastery fortunes was founded by some of the eight sons of Alexander Baird (1765-1833) and Jean Moffat (1768-1851) at Gartsherrie in Lanarkshire. It grew into what was probably the largest firm of ironmasters in Scotland. They were also colliery owners. The family was noted as extremely strict adherents of the Church of Scotland, who turned off all of their blast furnaces on Sundays. By the 1860s, they employed around 10,000 workers. Several of the brothers became extremely wealthy. William Baird (1796-1864) left £2,000,000; his brother James Baird (1802-76), a Tory M.P. from 1851 till 1857, left £1,200,000. The family produced many descendants, including Sir John Lawrence Baird, 1st Viscount Stonehaven (1874-1941), Governor-General of Australia from 1925-30; Peter Thorneycroft, Baron Thorneycroft (1909-94, left £533,232), Tory Chancellor of the Exchequer 1957-8; and William Whitelaw, 1st Viscount Whitelaw (1918-99), Tory Home Secretary 1979-83.

5. Sir Robert Peel, 1st Bt. (1750-1830) – Calico printer at Bury, Lancashire – £57,648 p.a., and his descendants.

In 1883, seven members of the Peel family were listed in Bateman. Edmund Peel (1826-1903, left £59,849 in personalty) owned 8466 acres worth £15,270 p.a. in Flintshire, Norfolk, Denbighshire, and Montgomeryshire; Jonathan Peel (1806-85, left £46,041 in personalty) owned 3019 p.a. worth £7,086 p.a. in Lancashire and Yorkshire; Sir Robert Peel, 3rd Bt. (1822-95, left £9,569 in personalty) owned 9,923 acres worth £24,532 p.a. in Staffordshire, Warwickshire, and Lancashire; William Peel (1803-83, left £62,723 in personalty) owned £3,197 acres worth £3,113 p.a. in Carmarthenshire; Arthur Wellesley Peel (1829-1912, left £128,176 in personalty) owned 2,226 acres worth £3,020 p.a. in Bedfordshire and Hertfordshire; William Croughton Peel (1870-1957), left £32,197) owned 2,415 acres worth £2,468 p.a. in three counties; and Xavier De Castanos Royds Peel (1808-85, left £5,450 in personalty) owned 2,460 acres worth £2,159 p.a. in two counties.

Because the second Sir Robert Peel became Prime Minister, the Peels are among the most famous families listed here, and were one of the few to earn their wealth in a purely industrial trade during the Industrial Revolution, as opposed to mercantile activity, finance, retailing, etc. Sir Robert Peel, 1st Bt. (1750-1830), the son of a yeoman farmer, became a calico printer at Bury, Lancashire, about eight miles from Manchester, in partnership with the man who became his father-in-law, William Yates. Their firm, Peel, Yates & Co. became enormously successful, one of the most successful cotton firms in the Industrial Revolution, and Peel became extremely wealthy, leaving "Upper Value" in personalty (i.e., an estate worth over £1 million, apart from his land) at his death. In 1784 his firm already employed 6800 workers. Unlike many industrialists, who were radical in politics and Non-conformist in religion, Peel was a "Church and King" Tory and a loyal Anglican. He served as the Tory M.P. for Tamworth from 1790 until 1820. During the 1790s he was already rich enough to purchase the 4,000 acre Fazley estate near Tamworth, Staffordshire, and lived in his country house there, Drayton Manor. In 1800 he was given a baronetcy. He was an important M.P., responsible for enacting several significant pieces of legislation, such as the Cotton Mills and Factory Act of 1817.

His eldest son, Sir Robert Peel, 2nd Bt. (1788-1850) was, of course, even more famous. He was educated at Harrow and at Christ Church, Oxford, where he was the first student ever to obtain a Double First in Classics and Mathematics. He served as a Tory M.P. from 1809 till 1850, and held a variety of senior offices, including Home Secretary in 1822-27 and 1828-30, and Prime Minister in 1834-35 and 1841-46, and played a distinguished role in the offices he held, reforming the Metropolitan Police (later known as the "Peelers" in his honour), carrying Roman Catholic "emancipation," and finally repealing the Corn Laws, which led to his splitting the Tory Party, and taking with him a group of liberal Tories, including William E. Gladstone, who later joined the Liberal party. In 1820 Peel married Julia, daughter of (General) Sir John Floyd, 1st Bt. His residences were Drayton Manor, and 12 Stanhope Street and 4 Whitehall Gardens in London. He died from injuries he received when he fell from a horse, and left £400,000 in personalty. Peel had few if any direct connections with his father's calico printing firm, and was chiefly a landowner.

In 1883 his successor, Sir Robert Peel, 3rd Bt. (1822-95, left £9569 in personalty), was educated at Harrow and Christ Church, Oxford, and served as a "Peelite" M.P. from 1850-86. He was a diplomat and served as Chief Secretary for Ireland from 1841 till 1846. He owned valuable lands in Staffordshire, Warwickshire, and Lincolnshire, with his Staffordshire land of 6453 acres worth £17,044 p.a., suggesting that they held lucrative coal mines.

The other Peels listed in Bateman were smaller landowners, and less wealthy, the most prominent being Arthur Wellesley Peel (1829-1912, left £128,176), who was educated at Eton and Balliol College, Oxford, and was an M.P. from 1865 until 1895, when he was created 1st Viscount Peel. He served as Speaker of the House of Commons from 1884-95; his country residence was at Sandy Lodge, Bedfordshire.

His son, William Robert Wellesley Peel (1867-1937, left £82,711), was educated at Harrow and Balliol College, Oxford, and served in British Cabinets as Secretary of State for India, First Commissioner of Works, and Lord Privy Seal, between 1922 and 1931. In 1929 he was created 1st Earl Peel. He is best remembered as the head of the Peel Commission of 1936-37, which was the first official body to recommend the partitioning of the Palestine Mandate between a Jewish and an Arab state, a forerunner to the creation of the State of Israel in 1948.

6. James Morrison (1789-1857) – Retail merchant and merchant banker in the City of London – £53,740 p.a., and his five sons, Charles, Walter, Alfred, George, and Frank Morrison

In 1883, Charles Morrison (1817-1909) owned 75,732 acres worth £31,439 p.a., in Argyllshire (67,000 acres/£16,439 p.a.); Berkshire (6987 acres/£12,206 p.a.); Suffolk (811 acres/£1,513 p.a.), and smaller amounts in Oxfordshire and Essex. Walter Morrison (1836-1921) owned 13,853 acres worth £4,511 p.a., in Yorkshire West Riding (13,705 acres/£4,371 p.a.); and Herefordshire (148 acres/£140 p.a.). Alfred Morrison (1821-97) owned 8,184 acres worth £6,571 p.a., in Wiltshire (7,704/£6,195 p.a.); and Dorset (480 acres/£376 p.a.). George Morrison (1839-84) owned 6,233 acres worth £7,470 p.a., in Buckinghamshire (3,070 acres/£5,308 p.a.); Wiltshire (2,647 acres/£1,356 p.a.); and Oxfordshire (516 acres/£806 p.a.). Frank Morrison (1823-1904) owned 2,913 acres worth £3,754 p.a. in Kent.

The origin of the vast landed acreage owned by the five Morrison brothers was their father, James Morrison (1789-1857), one of the most remarkable businessmen of nineteenth century Britain. He was the grandson of a Scot who settled in Hampshire, and the son of Joseph

Morrison (d.1804), an innkeeper in Middle Wallop, Hampshire, and his wife, Sarah Barnard (d. 1803) of Shapwick, Somerset. James was employed as a teenager as a shopman at Todd & Co., wholesale haberdashers of Fore Street in the City of London. He did well, and became a Partner in 1814 at the same time as he "married the boss's daughter," Mary Anne Todd (1795-1887), the daughter of John Todd. At her death in 1887 she left £617,364. James Morrison reorganised the firm, becoming one of the earliest retailers to "buy 'em cheap and pile 'em high," relying on large-scale turnovers with low profit margins on the goods sold. The Fore Street Warehouse, as it was known, specialised in selling linen, towelling, and ribbons. It bought goods cheaply and directly from distressed and bankrupt companies, avoiding middlemen, and also imported these goods from abroad. The Fore Street Warehouse, located near the Barbican, continued until 1940, when it was destroyed in the Blitz and not reopened. Morrison became spectacularly successful, and was known as the "Napoleon of Shopkeepers." He then became a leading merchant banker as the head of Morrison, Cryder & Co, founded in 1831, specialising in American investments. A radical Liberal, he served as a Liberal M.P. from 1830 till 1837, and was one of the founders of the Reform Club. He became a great art collector, with a major collection of Old Masters, and bought land on a grand scale. He had residences at Fonthill in Wiltshire; at Basildon Park, in Berkshire; in the island of Islay in Scotland, and in London at 95 Upper Harley Street. At his death, his personal estate was probated at "Above £1 million," and is usually estimated as worth in all between £4 and 6 million, making him one of the very richest men in the UK. There is a biography of James Morrison by Caroline Dakers, *A Genius For Money* (2011).

Morrison's land was divided among his five sons. The oldest son was Charles Morrison (1817-1909), who was educated privately in London and Geneva, and then at the University of Edinburgh and at Trinity College, Cambridge. He was mainly a merchant banker (Morrison, Sons & Co.), in partnership with his brother Alfred, at 62 Moorgate Street in The City of London, as well as a partner in the Fore Street Warehouse. His merchant bank was known for lending money to British aristocrats, and for building railways in France and the US. This firm was wound up in the 1850s; he then became an independent merchant banker, specialising in South American securities. A virtual recluse who lived at Basildon Park in Berkshire, and unmarried, he greatly expanded the wealth he inherited from his father. Apart from the 75,732 acres worth £31,434 p.a. he owned in five counties, at his death at ninety-two he left the extraordinary sum of £10,939,298, the largest sum left for probate in British history up to that time. When it was announced, the vastness of his wealth came as a complete surprise to even well-informed businessmen in the City of London. He left much of his land and his wealth to his nephew Hugh Morrison M.P. (1868-1931), the son of his brother Alfred Morrison.

Alfred Morrison (1821-97) was educated at Edinburgh University and at Trinity College, Cambridge, and inherited Fonthill, Wiltshire from his father. Alfred built up what has been described as "the most remarkable gathering of historical autographs" ever assembled, a collection which included the last letter written by Mary Queen of Scots, and 115 letters written by Nelson to Lady Hamilton. In London he lived at 16 Carlton House Terrace. In 1866 he married Mabel (1847-1933, left £110,473), daughter of (Revd.) Robert Chermside. Apart from his lands in Wiltshire and Dorset, he left £869,175 in personalty. Their son Hugh Morrison (1868-1931, left £1,856,418), was a Conservative M.P. from 1918-23 and 1924 until 1931. Hugh's son John Granville Morrison (1906-96) was also a Conservative M.P., from 1942 until 1965, when he was made 1st Baron Margadale, one of the last hereditary peerages to be created, and the first ever gained by the Morrisons, despite their great wealth and political service.

Walter Morrison (1836-1921), another brother, was educated at Eton and at Balliol College, Oxford. His main residences were at Malham Tarn near Settle in the North Riding and at 77 Cromwell Road in London. He was a friend of intellectuals and writers, including J.S. Mill, Darwin, and Charles Kingsley, and served as a Liberal M.P. from 1861 till 1874, and then as a Liberal Unionist M.P. from 1886-92 and 1895-1900. He was an active financier and was Chairman of the Central Argentine Railway and of the Craven Bank. He was an active patron of archaeology in the Middle East. Apart from his lands in Yorkshire and Herefordshire, he left £2,000,000 in personalty. Another brother was Frank Morrison (1823-1904), of Hole Park, Cranbrook, Kent and 8 Cromwell Houses, SW, who, in 1854, was married to Harriet (d. 1909, left £470,408), daughter of James Murray Grant of Glenmoriston, Scotland. Frank left £546,031, apart from his lands. The final brother was George Morrison (1839-84), of Hampworth Lodge, Salisbury, Wiltshire, who was educated at Balliol College, Oxford, and left £331,724 in personalty. Low profit margins on linen and ribbons did indeed prove profitable.

7. Guest, Barons and Viscounts Wimborne – ironmasters at Dowlais, Merthyr Tydfil, Glamorganshire – £46,856 p.a.

In 1883 Lord Wimborne owned 83,539 acres worth £46,856 p.a. in Ross-shire (60,000 acres/£1,180 p.a.); Dorset (17,400 acres/£17,543 p.a.); Glamorganshire (5,820 acres/£7,979 p.a.); Broconshire 5,820/£145 p.a.); and Hampshire (9 acres/£9 p.a.).

The Guest family is a classic example of rapid upward social mobility based on great industrial wealth. Thomas Guest (1718-1807), the son of a farmer, was a partner in the Dowlais Iron Works in Merthyr Tydfil, Glamorganshire, a town later synonymous with Industrial Britain, including its worst features. His son Sir Josiah James Guest, 1st Bt. (1785-1852), who was educated at Bridgnorth Grammar School and at Monmouth School, expanded the Dowlais ironworks, so that they became the largest in the world. He had trained on the factory floor, and boasted that he could roll a bar of steel as well as his workmen. He served as an M.P. for Honiton from 1826 until 1831, and then for Merthyr Tydfil from 1832 until his death. After a brief first marriage – his wife died less than a year after they were married – in 1833 he married into the high aristocracy, to Lady Charlotte Bertie (1812-95), the daughter of the 9th Earl of Albermarle. She was a notable figure in her own right, and has an entry in the *ODNB* as a patron of Welsh literature and the translator of the Mabinogion. Sir Josiah left £500,000 in personalty at his death, plus much land. Their son Ivor Bertie Guest (1835-1914), educated at Harrow and Trinity College, Cambridge, was a Liberal party supporter who married Lady Cornelia Spencer-Churchill (1847-1927), the daughter of the 7th Duke of Marlborough, a close relative of Winston Churchill. On 1883 he owned 83,539 acres worth £46,856 p.a. in Wales, Scotland, and England, his Glamorganshire lands being very lucrative through their mineral deposits. In 1880 he was created 1st Baron Wimborne. In 1886 he owned five residences, including Canford Manor, Wimborne, Dorset; Dowlais House, Merthyr Tydfil, Glamorganshire; and 22 Arlington Street, Mayfair, which became known as Wimborne House. He was also a Patron of six livings.

A number of other members of his family became political figures. His eldest son, Ivor Churchill Guest (1873-1939, left £408,398), who was educated at Eton and Trinity College, Cambridge, served as a Conservative M.P. from 1900 until 1906 and then, as a supporter of Free Trade, as a Liberal M.P. from 1906 until 1910. After succeeding his father as Lord Wimborne, he served in the very difficult position as Lord Lieutenant of Ireland from 1915 until 1918. In 1910, during his father's lifetime, he was created 1st Baron Ashby St. Ledger, in order to increase Liberal strength in the Lords, and, in 1918, he was created 1st Viscount Wimborne. His brother Frederick Edward Guest (1875-1937, left £89,999), M.P., was Chief Whip in 1917-21. The 1st Viscount's son Ivor Guest, 2nd Viscount Wimborne (1903-67), served as a Conservative M.P. in 1935-39, and left £1,921,431. In 1900 the 1st Baron Wimborne sold the family firm, which merged with a prominent steel manufacturers in Birmingham, to become Guest and Keen. It later became known as Guest, Keen, and Nettlefolds (or GKN) and still exists and flourishes as a major industrial firm in automotives and aerospace. The rise of the Guest family from obscure farmers to part of the high aristocracy within a century or so indicates what a great deal of money – and good fortune – could do in British society.

8. Matheson – Merchants in Hong Kong and in the City of London – £46,807 p.a.

In 1883 Sir Alexander Matheson, 1st Bt. owned 220,663 acres worth £26,461 p.a. in Ross-shire (220,663 acres/£23,223 p.a.); and Inverness-shire (230 acres/£3,238 p.a.), and Mary, Lady Matheson owned 424,560 acres worth £20,346 p.a. in Ross-shire (406,070 acres/£17,676 acres/£2,670 p.a.).

Jardine Matheson, the most famous of the "Tai Pan" ("great manager," i.e., leading businessmen) concerns in Hong Kong, was founded in 1832 by two Scotsmen, William Jardine (1784-1843, left £140,000 in personalty), and James Matheson (later Sir James, 1st Bt., 1796-1878). It was originally based in Canton, but moved in 1844 to the new British colony at Hong Kong. It grew enormously after 1834, when the East India Company lost its monopoly of trading in China. As well as dealing in "legitimate" goods such as tea and silk, it notoriously sold opium to the Chinese. Sir James Matheson was born in Sutherlandshire, and went to the Far East around 1820, forming Jardine Matheson in 1832. He returned to London in 1842, and served as a Liberal M.P. from 1843 until 1868. In 1851 he was created a baronet. In the City of London, he formed a separate and leading mercantile and financial firm, Matheson & Co. In 1843 he married Mary Jane (d. 1896, left £20,346), daughter of Michael Percival, the illegitimate son of Spencer Perceval, the Prime Minister. He then bought large amounts of land in northern Scotland. Within one generation he became one of the largest landowners in Scotland. In 1883 this land was owned by his widow. At his death, he left £194,685 in personalty, of which £25,000 was in England.

Sir James died without children, and his nephew Alexander Matheson (later Sir Alexander, 1st Bt., 1805-86) became head of the firm. He had lived in the Far East from the 1830s, and was chiefly responsible for convincing the British government to conduct the First Opium War in 1841, and for taking possession of Hong Kong in 1842. In 1847 he returned to England, heading Matheson & Co. in the City of London, and serving as an M.P. from 1847 until 1884. Like his uncle he purchased vast amounts of land in northern Scotland, and was responsible for building many of the railways in northern Scotland. In 1882 he also received a baronetcy. At the time of his death his residences included Ardross Castle, Alness, Ross-shire, two other houses in Scotland, and 38 Hill Street, Mayfair. He left £643,760 in personalty at his death. He was succeeded in turn by four of his sons: Sir Kenneth James Matheson, 2nd Bt. (1854-1920), who was educated at Harrow and Christ Church, Oxford, and left £106,204); Sir Alexander Percival Matheson, 3rd Bt. (1861-1929), educated at Harrow, who left only £371 in Britain; Sir Roderick Matheson, 4th Bt. (1861-1944, left £23,778); and Sir Torquhil Matheson, 5th Bt. (1871-1963, left £18,021). In the

1880s Sir Alexander moved to Western Australia, where he established a wholesale business in the goldfields. He served as a Member of the Western Australia Legislative Council (1897-1901), and as a Senator for Western Australia in the Australian Parliament (1901-06). Sir Torquhil, who was educated at Eton, was a distinguished soldier, and a Major General during the First World War. He was knighted in 1921 and inherited the baronetcy in 1944. By that point the family had no clear-cut connection with the Hong Kong firm.

9. Crawshay and Bailey, Barons Glanusk – Ironmasters at Cyfarthfa, Merthyr Tydfil, Glamorganshire, and ironmasters and colliery owners at Nant-y-Glo, Monmouthshire – £38,447 p.a.

In 1883 Crawshay Bailey (1789-1872) owned 13,649 acres worth £12,888 p.a. in Monmouthshire (4,078 acres/£6,432 p.a.); Glamorganshire (5,343 acres/£4,533 p.a.); Brecon, Essex, Carmarthenshire, and Herefordshire; his brother Sir Joseph Russell Bailey, 2nd Bt., later 1st Baron Glanusk owned 28,308 acres worth £25,559 p.a. in Breconshire (21,979 acres/£19,367 p.a.); Herefordshire (4,838 acres/£4,803 p.a.); and Buckinghamshire, Radnor, Monmouthshire, and Suffolk.

The founder of this business and landed dynasty was Richard Crawshay (1739-1810), the son of a farmer in Yorkshire, who was apprenticed to an iron merchant in Upper Thames Street in London and took over the firm, becoming the largest iron merchant in the country. He used his capital to buy out the iron mines at Cyfarthfa in Merthyr Tydfil in 1786, and poured large amounts of money into this venture, making it the largest ironworks in the world. At his death in 1810, he left "Upper Value" – i.e., above £1 million – and was one of the richest men in Britain. His son William Crawshay (1764-1834) left £700,000. William's two sons were William Crawshay (1788-1867), who left the vast sum of £2,000,000, and Robert Thompson Crawshay (1817-79), who left a mere £1,200,000. The Crawshays do not appear as large landowners in Bateman, but are included here because Richard Crawshay's sister Susannah married a John Bailey of Wakefield, and their offspring became large-scale landowners.

John Bailey's son Sir Joseph Bailey, 1st Bt. (1783-1858), who left £600,000 in personalty, developed the iron and coal fields at Nant-y-Glo, Monmouthshire. He served as an M.P. from 1835 till 1847, and was created a baronet in 1852. He purchased large amounts of land, chiefly in Wales.

His grandson, who succeeded him, Sir Joseph Russell Bailey, 2nd Bt. (1840-1906), who left £104,553 in personalty, was created 1st Baron Glanusk in 1899. John Bailey's other son, Crawshay Bailey (1789-1872), who left £160,000 in personalty, was the joint proprietor of the Nant-y-Glo mines, and also became a large landowner, also chiefly in Wales. His successors were Joseph Bailey, 2nd Baron Glanusk (1864-1928), who left £77,469, and then Wilfred Bailey, 3rd Baron Glanusk (1891-1948), who left £454,781. The Crawshay mines were taken over by GKN in 1902. Sir Joseph Bailey, 1st Bt.'s son-in-law was Sir Benjamin Hall, 1st Bt. (1802-67, left £25,000 in personalty), was a civil engineer and an M.P. from 1831 until 1858, when he was created 1st Baron Llanover. From 1855 until 1858 he served as First Commissioner of Works, and oversaw the building of the new British Parliament. It is widely believed that "Big Ben," the Clock Tower, takes its famous nickname from Hall, a tall man.

10. Goldsmid – Bullion brokers and financiers in the City of London – £35,580 p.a.

In 1883 Sir Julian Goldsmid, 3rd Bt. (1838-96) owned 14,273 acres worth £35,580 p.a. in Kent (6,530 acres/£8,000 p.a.); Gloucestershire (4,770 acres/£4,700 p.a.); Hampshire (1,800 acres/£1,600 p.a.); Berkshire (980 acres/£1,280 p.a.); and Sussex (193 acres/£20,000 p.a.).

The Goldsmids were enormously wealthy City of London bullion brokers and financiers of Dutch-Jewish background. Aaron Goldsmid (d. 1782) came from Amsterdam to London around 1763, operating as a merchant and financier. His son Abraham Goldsmid (c. 1756-1810) and his brother Benjamin Goldsmid (c. 1753-1808) were also merchants and financiers in transactions between Britain and Europe; Abraham was also a stockbroker. Another brother, Asher Goldsmid (1751-1822, left £50,000) was a partner with Abraham Mocatta as bullion brokers, and was closely connected with the Bank of England and the East India Company. Several of the family experienced financial difficulties as well as anti-semitic and anti-foreign prejudice. Asher's son Isaac Lyon Goldsmid (later Sir Isaac, 1st Bt., 1778-1859) joined the firm of Mocatta and Goldsmid, bullion brokers. He was also a highly successful stockbroker, railway financier, and loan broker to foreign governments. Sir Isaac was one of the most visible and influential Anglo-Jewish leaders of his day, and was prominent in securing the passage of the Jewish Disabilities Bill of 1858, which allowed professing Jews to sit in Parliament. As well, he was a founder of the non-denominational University College London, and of the Reform Club. In 1841 he was made a baronet, the first professing Jew to receive an hereditary title in Britain, and was also a Baron of Portugal. At his death, he left "£1,000,000 and upwards" in personalty, as well as much land. In 1849, Goldsmid purchased Somerhill House near Tonbridge, Kent, built in 1613, the second largest country house in the county after Knole House, Sevenoaks, which remained in the family until 1981.

Sir Isaac's son Sir Francis Henry Goldsmid, 2nd Bt. (1808-78) was the first professing Jew to become a barrister, and the first to become a Queen's Counsel. He served as an M.P. from 1860 until his death, and was also active in beginning the first Reform synagogue in Britain. He left £1,000,000 at his death. His nephew and successor, Sir Julian Goldsmid, 3rd Bt. (1838-96), the son of Frederick David Goldsmid (d. 1866, left £400,000) also became a barrister and served as an M.P. from 1866-68 and 1870-80. He owned the Whiteknight Estate in Berkshire, and left £982,772 in personalty at his death. In 1886, his residences were given as Somerhill, Tonbridge; the Villa Fiorentina, Cannes, France; and 105 Piccadilly, Mayfair. He had no sons, and the baronetcy became extinct, but it was revived in 1934 for his cousin Sir Osmond d'Avigdor-Goldsmid, 1st Bt. (1877-1940, left £148,866), who was educated at Harrow and at Trinity College, Cambridge, and was President of the Board of Deputies of British Jews in 1926-33, when the Anglo-Jewish community was said to be led by a "Cousinhood" of wealthy, highly assimilated families who had been educated at leading public schools and at Oxbridge. The family has been known ever since as d'Avigdor-Goldsmid.

11. Rothschild – Merchant bankers in the City of London, £28,901 p.a.

In 1883 Sir Nathaniel Mayer Rothschild, 2nd Bt. (1840-1915), later 1st Baron Rothschild, owned 15,378 acres worth £28,901 p.a., in Buckinghamshire (9,959 acres/£17,216 p.a.); Hertfordshire (2,939 acres/£5,413 p.a.); Northamptonshire (1,772 acres/£2,817 p.a.); Middlesex (620 acres/£3,356 p.a.); and Bedfordshire (88 acres/£99 p.a.).

Probably the most famous of all City of London financial dynasties, and regarded as the leading family of the Anglo-Jewish community, the English Rothschilds were founded by Frankfurt-born Nathan Mayer Rothschild (1777-1836), who, already fairly prosperous, came to

Manchester in 1798 as a cotton goods exporter. He settled in London in 1806; his sister Judith made a fortunate marriage with (Sir) Moses Montefiore (1784-1885), a wealthy insurance broker and stockbroker in the City. Like Goldsmid, Rothschild became a leading bullion broker, and then, more famously, a leading merchant banker. At his death at fifty-eight he was certainly one of the richest men in Britain, and left "Upper Value," for probate, i.e., over £1 million, and possibly as much as £3.5 million. His relative, Sir Nathaniel Mayer Rothschild, 2nd Bt., was the son of Austrian Baron Lionel de Rothschild (1808-79, left £2.7 million in Britain), and succeeded his uncle, Sir Anthony Nathaniel Rothschild,1st Bt. (1810-76, left £1,800,000 in personalty) as 2nd Baronet. He was educated at Trinity College, Cambridge, where he was a friend of the Prince of Wales, and the joined the family bank, becoming its head in 1879. He was well-known for helping to finance the building of the Suez Canal, and as a close friend of Benjamin Disraeli. He served as a Liberal M.P. from 1865 till 1885, when he was created 1st Baron Rothschild, the first professing Jew to be given a peerage. Rothschild joined the Liberal Unionist party in 1886. His family had accumulated substantial amounts of rural land, with his major country house being at Tring Park in Buckinghamshire; he also owned Gunnersbury Park in Acton. As well, he owned a great London mansion, Rothschild House, at 148 Piccadilly. He suffered from little overt anti-semitism, and was accepted as a pillar of High Society. He left £2.5 million in personalty at his death. His relative Baron Ferdinand de Rothschild (1839-98, left £1,488,129 in personalty) built the famous Waddesdon Manor in 1877-83, now one of the most visited of country mansions. He is unlisted in Bateman, which is based on *The Return of the Owners of Land of 1872-75*, before Baron Ferdinand had purchased land on a grand scale.

12. Hanbury – Tinplate manufacturers at Pontypool, Monmouthshire, £27,781 p.a.

In 1883 John Capel Hanbury(1853-1921) owned 10,973 acres worth £27,787 p.a. in Monmouthshire (10,210 acres/£20,660 p.a.) and Glamorganshire (763 acres/£7,127 p.a.).

In the eighteenth century, Hanbury's ancestors founded the tinplate industry in Wales, that is, the rolling of thin sheets of iron and coating them with tin, which continued at their works at Pontypool. His father, Capel Hanbury-Leigh (1777-1861) left £100,000 in personalty, and served as Lord-Lieutenant of Monmouthshire. Our man resumed the name "Hanbury" in 1864. He served as High Sheriff of Monmouthshire in 1878, but was not involved in public life at the national level. He left £272,693 in personalty.

13. Gladstone – Import-export merchants in Liverpool, slave plantation owners in Demerara, and later proprietors of mercantile houses in India, £27,347 p.a.

In 1883 William Ewart Gladstone (1809-98) owned 6,918 acres worth £18,173 p.a. in Flintshire (6,908 acres/£17,565 p.a.) and Lancashire (10 acres/£608 p.a.), and Sir Thomas Gladstone, 2nd Bt. (1804-89) owned 45,062 acres worth £9,174 p.a. in Kincardineshire.

The father of the famous nineteenth century Prime Minister and political leader of the Liberal party was John Gladstone (*nee* Gladstones, and later Sir Thomas, 1st Bt., 1764-1851), who became a very wealthy import-export merchant in Liverpool, and one of the largest owners of slaves in England, his plantations situated at Demerara, receiving £109,000 in compensation when the slaves were emancipated in 1834.He later developed important commercial interests in India. He served as an M.P. from 1818-27, and was given a baronetcy in 1846. Sir John purchased the Fasque estate in Aberdeenshire in 1829, and became a large-scale landowner. He left £745,679 in personalty at his death. His eldest son, Sir Thomas Gladstone, 2nd Bt. (1804-89, left £254,079 in personalty), was educated at Eton and Christ Church, Oxford. His renowned younger brother William Ewart Gladstone (1809-98, left £59,507 in personalty) was also educated at Eton and Christ Church, Oxford, and served as an M.P. from 1832 until his death. His remarkable career cannot be examined here, other than to say that he served as Prime Minister four times (1868-74, 1880-85, 1886, and 1892-94), as well as Chancellor of the Exchequer under another Prime Minister in 1852-55 and 1859-66. Gladstone began, in Macaulay's famous phrase, as "the rising hope of those stern and unbending Tories," and moved steadily to the left during his enormously long career; his rivalry with Disraeli is legendary. In 1886, Sir Thomas Gladstone lived at Fasque, Aberdeenshire, and William E. Gladstone at Hawarden Castle, Flintshire, although for part of that year he was also resident at 10 Downing Street.

14. Thellusson, Barons Rendlesham – Bankers in the City of London and plantation owners in the West Indies – £25,024 p.a.

In 1883 Frederick William Brook Thellusson, 5th Baron Rendlesham owned 24,028 acres worth £25,024 p.a. in Suffolk (19,869 acres /£19,275 p.a.); Hertfordshire (3,696 acres/£5,500 p.a.); and Ayrshire (190 acres/£249 p.a.).

The progenitor of this family in England was Peter Thellusson (1735-97), a French Huguenot merchant who moved to Geneva, and then came to London in 1762, where he became a leading banker and a Director of the Bank of England. He was also an extensive plantation and slave owner in the West Indies. He is also known for his unusual will, which stipulated that almost the whole of his wealth at death, estimated at £600,000, not be distributed to his relatives but gather interest for four generations, when, having grown enormously, it could be distributed to his living descendants. This was outlawed by the Accumulations Act of 1800. It is believed that Dickens's fictional case of Jarndyce v. Jarndyce in Bleak House was based on Thellusson's will. He had already bought substantial lands in Yorkshire. His son Peter Isaac Thellusson (1761-1808), who was educated at Harrow, was also a leading banker in the City of London, and served as an M.P. from 1787 till 1808. In 1806, he was given an Irish peerage, as 1st Baron Rendlesham, allowing him to continue to sit in the House of Commons. He left an estimated £400,000 at his death. Frederick William Brook Thellusson, 5th Baron Rendlesham (1840-1911) was educated at Eton and Christ Church, Oxford, and sat as a Conservative M.P. from 1874 till 1885. In 1886 his main residence was Rendlesham Hall in Woodbridge, Suffolk. He left £174,148 in personalty.

A number of very wealthy businessmen continued to purchase agricultural land or urban property on a large scale during the first sixty years of the twentieth century, although we do not have the kind of precise statistics which exist for the late nineteenth century. Probably the greatest businessman who became a property accumulator was Sir John Ellerman, 1st Bt. (1862-1933), the mysterious shipowner and financier who was Britain's richest man, leaving the extraordinary sum of £36.7 million at his death. (Ellerman's career will be examined in the second part of this work.) After the First World War, and with many traditional London property owners struggling with inflation and much higher rates of taxation and death duties, Ellerman went on a London property spending spree possibly without parallel in modern history. In 1920 he purchased a portion of the Covent Garden estate from the Duke of Bedford. In 1925 he purchased twenty-one acres of Marylebone, including his properties on Great Portland Street, from Lord Howard de Walden for £3 million. In 1929 he bought fourteen acres in Chelsea, with 500 house properties, from the Cadogan and Hans Place estates. Also in 1929, he acquired eighty-two acres of freehold land in South Kensington from Lord Iveagh's Trustees, with 1,150 house properties and 200 blocks of flats. He also is known to have owned extensive properties in the City of London. By the early 1930s, he was almost certainly among the three or four most extensive owners of London properties. In contrast, Ellerman owned no agricultural lands at all, and quickly sold a small Scottish property he had purchased as part of a wider business deal. Nor did Ellerman own a country house or mansion; his residences consisted of a mansion on South Audley Street in Mayfair and a house overlooking the sea in Eastbourne, Sussex.

Chapter 3: The Largest Estates Left in the UK, 1809–1899

This section presents biographical information about all persons leaving millionaire estates through 1949, and all half-millionaire estates through 1879, with this chapter setting out all such estates from 1809 through 1859. The unexpected date of 1809 is the first year in which the probate valuation of those probated in the Prerogative Court of Canterbury (PCC), the main probate court in England and Wales, included all of that person's personalty, that is, his or her personal property, as opposed to their land. As noted in the previous section, these valuation figures did not include any land owned by this person, and conclusions about the wealthiest landowners have to be drawn from other sources, as was previously discussed. This section will be divided into twenty year segments, although the earliest includes only estates probated between 1809 and 1819. Millionaire estates will be listed first, in chronological order, followed by half-millionaire estates.

1809–1819

This period includes the latter phases of the Napoleonic Wars, the great victory at Waterloo, and both the post-war period of unemployment, as well as the great growth in the British economy as Britain experienced the fruits of the Commercial and Industrial Revolutions.

As will be seen below, many of the largest non-landed fortunes were in unexpected fields, with London – as always – the principal centre of wealth-making. As noted, throughout the nineteenth century, it was probably the case that a pound was worth about 120 times more than it is worth today, so that a fortune of £500,000 was worth around £60 million. However, it seems apparent that this greatly understates the actual rise in values of property and other commodities, so that a fortune of £500,000 was actually worth hundreds of millions, even billions, of pounds today, given the wealth levels of their equivalents today in the recent and current "Rich Lists."

The limitations on what wealth could buy should also be kept in mind: no amount of money could buy an aspirin tablet or an antibiotic, and no millionaire could procure an x-ray, undergo an operation or medical procedure with an anaesthetic, eat many fruits or vegetables out of season, or send an urgent message from London to Edinburgh in less than (at least) three or four days. Most of the people on our list would have been helpless in their private lives without an army of domestic servants who were paid virtually nothing. If one could change places with the wealthy people listed here, one would be very likely to want to return the twenty-first century as quickly as possible.

1. (Hon.) Henry Cavendish (1731-1810) – left "Upper Value," i.e., an estate of over £1 million. Landed fortune; also a famous scientist.
(Hon.) Henry Cavendish was the eldest son of Lord Charles Cavendish (1704-83), the third son

of William Cavendish, 2nd Duke of Devonshire (1672-1729). His mother, Lady Anne (d. 1733), was the daughter of Henry Grey, 1st Duke of Kent (1671-1741). He was educated at the Hackney Academy and at Peterhouse, Cambridge, and was unmarried. He was a famous scientist, who discovered hydrogen, and made important discoveries about electricity and other subjects. Cavendish is known to have inherited £160,000 from his father, but appears to have become a millionaire by reinvesting his wealth and income. He was well-known as a reclusive eccentric, who avoided the company of both women and men, apart from other scientists, and spent little, other than on his scientific interests, unlike other members of his powerful political and landed family. In his entry in the *ODNB*, he was termed "the most important natural philosopher [i.e., scientist] of eighteenth century Britain." He lived at Great Marlborough Street, Middlesex, and later owned residences in Bedford Square, Hampstead, and Clapham Common, and also owned some landed estates.

2. Richard Crawshay (1739-1810) – left "Upper Value," i.e., an estate of over £1 million. Ironmaster at Cyfarthfa, Glamorganshire.

One of the most important ironmasters of the Industrial Revolution, his career and family were discussed in the previous section, as Number 8 of businessmen who purchased the most land. Prior to becoming an ironmaster, he was an iron merchant and dealer in cast iron wares at George Yard, Upper Thames Street in the City of London. He was known as a "devout" Anglican. He allegedly came to London from Yorkshire with five pounds in his pocket, and is the subject of a chapter in Samuel Smiles' *Lives of the Engineers* (1862).

3. William Douglas, 4th Duke of Queensberry (1725-1810) – left "Upper Value," i.e., an estate of over £1 million. Landed fortune.

A notorious rake and gambler – who may have increased his wealth via gambling, as well as from horse racing – and known as "Old Q," he was the son of William Douglas, 2nd Earl of March (1694-1731), and then succeeded a relative, Charles, 3rd Duke of Queensberry (1698-1778). He was educated at Winchester and was unmarried, with a string of mistresses, he devoted his life to "the pursuit of pleasure," but somehow managed to live till he was eighty-five. He was one of the largest landowners in Britain. After his death, his lands came to the Duke of Buccleuch and Queensberry, and to the Earl of Wemyss and March, while much of his personalty came to his illegitimate daughter, Maria Fagnani, (c. 1770-1856), the wife of the 3rd Marquess of Hertford (1777-1842). He was a Scottish Representative Peer from 1761-86, and was then given an English peerage, as Baron Douglas of Amesbury, enabling him to automatically sit in the Lords. He had residences at 138 Piccadilly, at Richmond, and at an estate in Peebleshire.

4. Philip Rundell (1746-1827) – left "Above £1 million." A goldsmith (Rundell, Bridge & Rundell) at Ludgate Hill in the City of London.

Rundell's firm was, from 1804, "the Principal Royal Goldsmith and Jewellers." He was the son of Richard Rundell (1709-76), a successful victualler and malstster in Bath; his mother, Ann Ditcher (1710-59), was the niece of a leading surgeon in Bath. He was apprenticed at fourteen to a jeweller in Bath, came to London, where he worked for William Pickett, a goldsmith at Ludgate Hill, and later became his partner. For most of his life he lived "over the shop" at 32 Ludgate Hill, but later lived near Regent's Park. His great wealth must have derived from making jewellery and other precious items for the aristocracy and for the government and civic elite in London. He was unmarried, but left a legacy to his mistress, Mrs. Elizabeth Wartridge. Most of his wealth was inherited by his great-nephew Joseph Neeld (1789-1856), who became an M.P., and left £250,000 in personalty. Rundell was very famous in his day, and has an entry in the *ODNB*.

5. Robert Jones (Unknown-1808) – left £500,000. A brandy merchant at Little Tower Street and at St. Mary Hill in the City of London.

Virtually nothing could be traced of the life or career of Robert Jones, an extremely wealthy brandy merchant in the City of London, or how he became so wealthy in an occupation where he must have had hundreds of competitors. His common surname makes research about him difficult, and little is known about his career. He may have specialised in types of brandy and liquor not otherwise available or highly prized, but this is unclear. He was unmarried, but left significant amounts to Anglican charities. Nothing could be learned about his parentage or early life. His firm, Robert Jones, Mardell, continued until 1817. Although he died in July 1808, his will was not probated until the following year.

6. William Lygon, 1st Earl Beauchamp (1747-1816) – left £760,000. Landowner.

His surname at birth was Pyndar, and he was a commoner, who inherited lands from several relatives. His father, Reginald Pyndar, later Lygon (1712-88), was a landowner. The future Earl was educated at Christ Church, Oxford, and served as a Tory M.P. from 1775 until 1806. In 1806 he was created 1st Baron Beauchamp, and was made 1st Earl Beauchamp in 1815, when he claimed to have an annual income of £40,000, and is said to have paid £10,000 to the Prince Regent's Privy Purse to secure the title. He was distantly related to a previous Earl Beauchamp of the fifteenth century. In 1883 his successor owned 10,624 acres worth £17,789 p.a., chiefly in Worcestershire. His main residence was Madresfield Court, near Great Malvern.

7. Hugh Percy, 2nd Duke of Northumberland (1742-1817) – left £660,000. Landowner.

The Dukes of Northumberland, including the 2nd Duke, are discussed in the section on the wealthiest landowners above. He was educated at Eton and at St. John's College, Cambridge, and was created 1st Baron Percy in 1776, during his father's lifetime, so that he could sit in the Lords. His half-brother, his father's illegitimate son, James Smithson (1764-1829), left his £120,000 estate to found what is now the Smithsonian Institution in Washington D.C.

8. John Baker (1735-1818) – left £500,000. He inherited from his father, who was a wealthy silk weaver at Spitalfields, and then a "wealthy sleeping partner" in Truman's Brewery at Brick Lane, Spitalfields, London.

Another virtually unknown wealth holder in London during the Regency period, of whose career little is known. It is unclear if he was actively engaged in trade. His father, John Baker, died in 1783. The name of his mother is unknown, but one source states that she was the daughter of the wealthy brewer Sir Benjamin Truman (c. 1700-80). He established almshouses and other charities, some of which still exist. His sister, Elizabeth Baker (c. 1725-1809) left £150,000. He was unmarried, and lived at 80 Lower Grosvenor Street, Middlesex.

9. Charles Boone (1729-1819) – left £500,000. Probably an East India Company fortune, inherited from his father.

In addition, his first wife's grandfather was Sir Ambrose Crowley, the pioneering ironmaster. Charles Boone was the son of Charles Boone (1684-1735) of Lee Place, Kent, who was Governor of Bombay 1715-22, a Director of the East India Company 1729-35, and of the Bank of England, as well as an M.P. This was almost certainly the main source of Boone's wealth. He was educated at Eton and Trinity College, Cambridge, and served as a Tory M.P. from 1757 until 1784. Our man's brother Thomas Boone (c. 1730-1812) was Royal Governor of New Jersey and of South Carolina, and has an entry in the *ODNB*. As noted, our man's first wife was the daughter of an important early ironmaster. Our man lived at Berkeley Square, Middlesex, and at Lee Place, Kent. Much of his wealth came to his daughter Harriet (d. 1837), who married Sir William Drummond (c. 1770-1829), M.P., who has an entry in the *ODNB* as a "classical scholar and diplomatist."

10. John Tunno (1746-1819) – left £500,000. A merchant (Tunno & Loughnan) of New Broad Street and Old Jewry, City of London.

Tunno was born in Berwickshire and a merchant and underwriter, mainly trading with America. He had lived in South Carolina before the American Revolution, and then re-established himself as a merchant in London after American independence. His father George Tunno (1722-1802) had also been a merchant in South Carolina. Tunno may also have been involved in slave trading, although this isn't certain. Our man's son Edward Rose Tunno (1794-1863), a barrister who was educated at Harrow and Cambridge, was an M.P. from 1826-32.

11. Jesse Russell (1743-1820) – left £500,000. A soap maker at Goodman's Yard, Minories, Middlesex (adjacent to the City of London).

Jesse Russell was the son of John Russell (d. 1765), also a soap manufacturer, of Holborn, Middlesex, and was indentured at sixteen to a "joiner" in London. How a soap manufacturer in the Minories accumulated £500,000 is a mystery, although he may have had government contracts. Little is known about his career. His son Jesse Watts Russell (1786-1875) was an M.P. who married the daughter of David Pike Watts (d. 1816), a wealthy merchant who left £160,000.

12. Edward John Hollond (*sic*) (1750-1821) – left £600,000. An East India Company fortune.

Hollond was the son of (Major) John Hollond, an East India Company official and the Commander of Ft. William in Bengal. His mother, Sophia (c. 1723-60), the daughter of Randall Fowke, was allegedly imprisoned in the "Black Hole of Calcutta." Hollond served in the East India Company at Madras from 1789, and was Governor of Fort St. George and Acting President of British India from 1790. When he returned to England, he was regarded as an enormously wealthy "Nabob," as was his twin brother William Hollond (1750-1836), who left £1,000,000. As with many East India Company officials who became very wealthy, just how he made his wealth is unclear, and there is little about him in any source. In England, he lived at Devonshire Place, Middlesex. He was unmarried, but left legacies to his two daughters, who were "living with Mrs. Pope," and were possibly Anglo-Indians.

13. (Revd.) Peter Beauvoir (1736-1821) – left £800,000. Unclear. His father was a "wealthy East India merchant," which is probably the source of his wealth.

Our man owned what is now De Beauvoir Town in Hackney. Beauvoir was the son of Osmond Beauvoir (1680-1757), as noted an East India merchant, whose addresses are given as Downham

Hall, Essex, and previously of Holborn and Bedford Row, Middlesex. Our man was educated at Queen's College, Cambridge, and became an Anglican clergyman in 1760. One source states that the family had become wealthy "through a combination of piracy, sharp trading, and land expropriation" on Guernsey. He was unmarried, dying at eighty-five, and his property came to a relative, Richard Benyon (1760-1854), of Englefield House, Berkshire, who left £300,000. He was an M.P. from 1802-12. The family changed its name to "Benyon de Beauvoir." It remained wealthy and influential, with a descendant, Richard Benyon (b. 1960), serving as a Conservative M.P. since 2005.

14. Henry Hope (c. 1784-1821) – left £500,000. A merchant banker and merchant in the City of London.

A member of the famous Hope family, merchant bankers in Amsterdam, and later in the City of London, who were probably the leading British merchant bankers before the Barings and the Rothschilds. He was the son of John William Hope (1757-1813), merchant banker of Amsterdam and later of Harley Street, Middlesex. Despite his wealthy connections, little or nothing could be learned about our man, who was apparently unmarried, and lived at Harley Street, and at Southampton Row, Bloomsbury – the latter may have been a business address.

15. George Whittingstall (1755-1822) – left £500,000. A brewer at Watford, Hertfordshire, and probably a grain contractor there.

He was the son of Henry Whittingstall (1712-80), a corn miller at Shillington, Bedfordshire. He purchased two breweries in Watford in 1781 and 1790, and also bought fifteen pubs there. He probably also held lucrative grain contracts during the Napoleonic Wars. He had three brothers, and was unmarried, and how he accumulated a fortune of the size he left is rather mysterious, as there would have been dozens of small brewers in or near London. His relatives were also extremely wealthy: his sister Elizabeth Whittingstall (1751-1825, *q.v.*) left £600,000. He left much of his wealth to a distant cousin Edmund Fearnley, who added "-Whittingstall" to his surname.

16. Thomas Coutts (1735-1822) – left £600,000. One of the founders of the famous bank on the Strand in central London, which still exists, and is said to be the bank used by the Queen and the Royal Family.

Thomas Coutts was born in Edinburgh, and was sent to London by his father, a banker and merchant in Edinburgh, to work with his brother James (1733-78), a banker and M.P. for Edinburgh. Our man became Senior Partner in 1775, serving until his death. His first wife was a servant employed by his brother, with whom he had three daughters, all of whom married into the aristocracy. After her death he married Harriet Mellon (1777-1837), a former actress who became the Managing Partner in his bank after his death, almost certainly the first woman to head a major business in British history, and who left £600,000. His daughter with his first wife was the celebrated Angela Burdett-Coutts (1814-1906), the famous philanthropist and friend of Charles Dickens. In 1871 she was given a peerage in her own right as Baroness Burdett-Coutts, and was the first woman to be made a Freeman of the City of London. Thomas Coutts lived at 1 Stratton Street, Mayfair, and had a villa in Highgate, but did not own a country estate.

17. David Ricardo (1772-1823) – left £500,000. A stockbroker and loan contractor in the City of London, and also a major and renowned economist.

David Ricardo was born in the City of London, the son of a Jewish stockbroker in London. He was given an Orthodox Jewish education, but later married a Quaker lady and became a Unitarian. He served as a Whig M.P. from 1819 until his death, and presumably took the required Anglican oath when elected. He became a clerk on the Stock Exchange at fourteen, and became a very wealthy stockbroker and loan contractor, and, despite having no formal education, became a prolific writer on economics, with his *Works and Correspondence* published in eleven collected volumes between 1951 and 1973. With Thomas Malthus, he gave economics its title of "the dismal science," for maintaining that rates of profits always declined. He had three sons and five daughters, many of whom married into the aristocracy and landed gentry. Many of his descendants were army officers and typical members of the upper classes. He died at fifty-one of an ear infection. He lived at Upper Brook Street, Grosvenor Square, and also had a country estate at Gatcombe Park, Gloucestershire.

18. John Julius Angerstein (1735-1823) – left £500,000. A Lloyd's insurance broker and loan contractor during the Napoleonic Wars in the City of London.

John Angerstein was born in St. Petersburg, Russia. His background is very mysterious. He is usually believed to be the illegitimate son of Andrew Poulett Thompson (1711-95), a British Russia merchant, later a Russia merchant at Austin Friars in the City of London. His mother was probably a Swedish lady, Eva, daughter of Johann Andersson Angerstein, although rumour has it that his mother was actually Empress Catherine the Great. He came to London around 1749 and worked for Poulett Thompson. In 1790-96 he served as Chairman of Lloyd's of London. He owned much land in London – such as Angerstein's Wharf and other areas in Dockland, and rural property in Lincolnshire and elsewhere. He lived at Woodlands, Blackheath, Kent, and at 103 Pall Mall, St. James's. Despite his surname, there is no evidence that he had any Jewish, German, or Russian ancestry – unless his mother was the Russian Empress!

19. John Sowerby (1746-1823) – left £500,000. An insurance broker at Hatton Street in the City of London, and a "warehouseman" at Cheapside, City of London.

Described in one source as "a wealthy merchant of Hatton Gardens," Sowerby was a native of Cummersdale near Carlisle, and said to have been the son of a farm labourer, who allegedly came to London with the proverbial "pound or two" in his pocket, he became a wealthy insurance broker and merchant, although just how he amassed half a million pounds starting with nothing remains very unclear. He purchased an estate at Putteridgebury, Hertfordshire in 1788 (now owned by the University of Bedfordshire), and served as High Sheriff of Hertfordshire in 1796-7. His grandson George Sowerby (1832-88) is listed in Bateman as a considerable landowner in four counties.

20. John William Egerton, 7th Earl of Bridgewater (1753-1823) – left £700,000. A landowner and a General in the Army.

The 7th Earl of Bridgewater was the son of (Rt. Revd.) John Egerton, Bishop of Durham (1721-87), who was the brother of the enormously wealthy Francis Egerton, 3rd Duke of Bridgewater (1726-1803), the "canal duke." Our man inherited Bridgewater's minor title as Earl of Bridgewater. He was educated at Eton and Christ Church, Oxford, and had a career as a professional army officer; he was made a general in 1812. He was regarded as one of the very richest men in Britain, with Faringdon claiming in 1803 that he was the fourth richest man in the country. His title came to his brother, Francis Egerton, 8th Earl of Bridgewater (1756-1829), but, in 1883, his lands were apparently owned by the Earl of Brownlow (No. 18 on the list of wealthiest landowners, above) and Lord Egerton of Tatton. The 8th Earl has an entry in the *ODNB* as a "collector of manuscripts and patron of learning," and donated the Egerton Manuscripts to the British Museum. Our man lived at Albermarle Street, Middlesex, and at Ashridge Park, Hertfordshire.

21. Abraham Montefiore (1788-1824) – left £500,000. Stockbroker and insurance broker in the City of London.

Abraham Montefiore was the son of Joseph Elias Montefiore (1759-1804), an "Italian merchant" in London of Sephardic background. His first wife was, unusually, not Jewish, but his second wife, whom he married in 1815, was Henrietta (1791-1866, left £400,000), the sister of the millionaire merchant banker Nathan Rothschild (1777-1836), a connection which, obviously, greatly assisted his business career. He became the stockbroker to the Rothschilds, and was also a major insurance broker in the City of London. His brother Sir Moses Montefiore (1784-1885, left £374,421) was the acknowledged leader of the Anglo-Jewish community until his death at the age of 101. The Montefiores, together with the Rothschilds, Goldsmids, Mocattas, and other wealthy London Jewish families, were known as "the Cousinhood," and were regarded as the leaders and spokesmen for the Anglo-Jewish community down to the Second World War. Chaim Bermant's *The Cousinhood* (1971) is an excellent account of this group.

22. Elizabeth Whittingstall (1751-1825) – left £600,000. Brewery and grain contracting fortune at Watford, Hertfordshire.

The sister of George Whittingstall (1755-1822), No. 15 above, who inherited much of his wealth. She was one of the very wealthiest women in Britain, but almost nothing is known about her life. She was unmarried. She is known to have left much of her wealth to Edmund Fearnley (see above), and to have established almshouses in Hitchin, Hertfordshire. She lived in Watford.

23. Harriet, Lady Holland (1739-1825) – left £500,000. Chiefly a landowner.

She inherited land from her father and from her first husband, and also from her second husband, Sir Nathaniel Holland, 1st Bt., (1735-1811), a fashionable portrait painter. She was the daughter of Sir Cecil Bisshopp (*sic*), 6th Bt. (1700-78), a landowner of Parham Park, Sussex, and an M.P. between 1727 and 1768. Her mother (Hon.) Ann Boscawen (c. 1703-49) was the daughter of the 1st Viscount Falmouth, a leading landowner in Cornwall. She was married, first in 1766, to Thomas Drummer (c. 1739-81), a wealthy landowner and M.P., and, secondly in 1783, to Sir Nathaniel Holland, 1st Bt. (1735-1811), a well-known portrait painter and also an M.P. from 1790 until his death, who left £250,000. Her wealth apparently came to her nephew Robert Brudenell, 6th Earl of Cardigan (d. 1837), who left £350,000 in personalty. Her sisters also married well, with her sister Catherine marrying Charles Jenkinson, 1st Earl of Liverpool (d. 1809, left £200,000 in personalty), the father of the Prime Minister. She lived at Cranbury, near Winchester, Hampshire, and at The Terrace, Piccadilly.

24. John James Stephens (1747-1826) – left £600,000. A glass manufacturer at Lisbon, Portugal.

This very unusual fortune was founded by his brother William Stephens (1731-1803), who came to Lisbon, Portugal, became a favourite of the Portuguese Royal Family, and was given a monopoly on the manufacturing of glass there at the Royal Glass factory, plus exemption from taxation. Our man, who was born in Exeter, took over the firm, and became extremely wealthy. He came from a good family, and was educated at Christ's Hospital in London. He apparently lived in Lisbon for most of his life, and did not have an English address. Much of his wealth came to his cousin's son Stephens Lyne-Stephens (1801-60), who left £700,000. There is a history of this unusual fortune by Jenifer Roberts, *Glass: The Strange History of the Lyne-Stephens Fortune* (2003).

25. Thomas Leyland (1752-1827) – left £800,000. Shipowner and banker in Liverpool.

Little is known of his background, but in Liverpool he was engaged extensively in the slave trade, importing 22,655 slaves to America. From about 1822 he was a banker in Liverpool, in partnership with his nephew, as Leyland & Bullin, and was also an extensive landowner. One account states that he got his start by winning £20,000 in a lottery. He had no children, his wealth coming to Christopher Bullin (later Leyland, c. 1791-1849), who left £600,000 in personalty. Our man was regarded as one of the very wealthiest men in Liverpool, and was said to have been worth £1.5 million. He lived at Walton Hall, Walton-on-the-Hill, Lancashire.

26. Henry Davidson (1771-1827) – left £500,000. A West India merchant in the City of London.

He also owned plantations and slaves in the West Indies, and lands in Scotland. Henry Davidson was the son of Duncan Davidson (1733-99), a wealthy West Indies merchant in the City of London, an M.P. from 1790-96, and a landowner in Scotland. Our man became a partner in his father's firm in 1793, and was the head of the firm of Davidson, Graham & Co., of Lime Street Square in the City of London, and owned plantations and slaves in Jamaica and Grenada, as well as an estate in Ross-shire. He lived at Bedford Square, and the at Cavendish Square, and at Hampstead, and had a country house at Tulloch Castle, Ross-shire. His son Duncan Davidson (1800-81) was an M.P. from 1826-32.

27. Charles Talbot, 15th Earl of Shrewsbury (1753-1827) – left £500,000 in personalty. Landowner.

An extensive landowner in Staffordshire, Cheshire, and other counties. In 1883 his successor as Earl owned 35,729 acres worth £62,382 p.a., the high income compared with his acreage suggesting that he owned coal mines or urban property. Our man succeeded his uncle, George Talbot, 14th Earl of Shrewsbury (d. 1787), and attended University College, Oxford, despite being a Roman Catholic, as were most of his family. He was regarded as the "head of the Roman Catholics in England," but his religion debarred him from participating in English politics. His chief residences were at Heythrop Park, Oxfordshire, at Alton Abbey, Staffordshire, and at Stanhope Street, Middlesex.

28. George Augustus Herbert, 11th Earl of Pembroke and 8th Earl of Montgomery (1759-1827) – left £600,000. Landowner, chiefly in Wiltshire and Co. Dublin.

The Earls of Pembroke and Montgomery are discussed above, as some of the wealthiest landowners. Unusually, they owned much land in Wiltshire and also in Co. Dublin, where in 1883 they were the owners of 2,301 acres with an annual income of £35,586 p.a., presumably in a lucrative part of the Irish capital. The 11th Earl of Pembroke was the son of Henry, 10th earl (1734-94), a lieutenant-general in the Army, and Lady Elizabeth Spencer (1737-1831), the daughter of the 3rd Duke of Marlborough. He was educated at Harrow. He was a lieutenant-general in the Army, and an M.P. between 1780 and 1796. He was known for investing heavily in agricultural improvements, and was said to have tripled his rent rolls as a result. His son Sidney Herbert, 1st Baron Herbert of Lea (1810-61) was a well-known Cabinet minister, best remembered for sending Florence Nightingale to Crimea.

1820–1839

During this period, Britain experienced strong growth as "the workshop of the world," and also the world's financial and commercial centre, with both London – especially the City of London – and the industrial north growing rapidly in population and as business entrepots. In 1832, the membership of the House of Commons was reformed, giving greater powers to the middle classes. In 1834 slavery was abolished, and in 1846 the Corn laws were repealed, ushering in the era of Free Trade. Some of the largest fortunes left in this period were achieved by beneficiaries of the Industrial Revolution, but perhaps not as many as one might have supposed. As before, millionaires are listed first, followed by those leaving personal estates of £500,000 or more.

1. Sir Robert Peel, 1st Bt. (1750-1830) – left "Upper Value," i.e., above £1 million. A calico printer and cotton manufacturer at Bury near Manchester, Lancashire.
The father of the Prime Minister, Sir Robert Peel, 2nd Bt. (1788-1850, left £400,000 in personalty), the first Sir Robert Peel was the son of Robert Peel (1723-95), a successful cotton printer at Blackburn, who is said to have left £140,000. Sir Robert attended Blackburn Grammar School, was apprenticed to a local warehouseman (later his father-in-law), and expanded the family firm. With Richard Arkwright, he was probably the wealthiest early cotton manufacturer. His firm (Peel, Yates & Co.) employed no less than 15,000 workers by 1803. He served as a Tory M.P. from 1790-1820, and, as examined in the previous section, became an extensive landowner. He was created a baronet in 1803. His eldest son, the future Prime Minister, attended Harrow – where he was a friend of Lord Byron the poet – and Christ Church, Oxford. The first baronet purchased Drayton Manor near Tamworth in the 1790s, where he lived until his death.

2. George Granville Leveson-Gower, 2nd Marquess of Stafford and 1st Duke of Sutherland (1758-1833) – left "Upper Value," i.e., above £ million. Landowner.
Probably the richest British landed aristocrat in real terms in modern times, the life of the 1st Duke of Sutherland, and his remarkable good fortune, are set out in the previous section. The son of the 1st Marquess of Stafford, and educated at Westminster School and at Christ Church, Oxford, our man inherited vast holdings in Staffordshire and elsewhere from his father. He then married the Countess of Sutherland in her own right, becoming a major landowner in Scotland, and then he inherited the Duke of Bridgewater's lands and other property, including the Manchester-Liverpool Canal, possibly the most lucrative business in the country. He was created 1st Duke of Sutherland just before his death in 1833. His eldest son, George, 2nd Duke of Sutherland (1786-1861) left

£1,136,820 in personalty. His younger son Francis Leveson-Gower, later Egerton (1800-1857, left £400,000 in personalty) inherited the Duke of Bridgewater's former property, and was created 1st Earl of Ellesmere. The main residences of the 1st Duke were Cleveland House and Stafford House in Mayfair and Dunrobin Castle in Sutherlandshire.

3. William Hollond (*sic*) (1750-1836) – left £1,000,000. A member of the Bengal Civil Service.
The twin brother of Edward John Hollond (1750-1821) above, who left £600,000, William Hollond was the son of (Major) Richard Hollond (c. 1700-51), Commander of the East India Company's troops in Bengal, and was born at Calcutta. Although he was educated at Cheam School in England, his early career was spent in India, where he became a Writer with the East India Company and Chief of the Dacca Council of Revenue. He returned to England in 1783. As with many of the fortunes of the East India "Nabobs," just how he made his enormous wealth is unclear, and there is virtually nothing in any source about his career in India. His addresses were given in the probate records as "formerly of Highnam Court, Gloucestershire and then of West Horsley Place, Surrey, and [42] Grosvenor Square, Middlesex." He had eleven children, several of whom left considerable fortunes.

4. Nathan Mayer Rothschild (1777-1836) – left "Upper Value," i.e., above £1 million. A merchant banker and financier in the City of London.
Born in Frankfurt (where he died at age fifty-seven of septicaemia from an infection), he was the founder of the English branch of the illustrious merchant banking family. Rothschild came to England in 1798 and operated as a bullion broker and commission agent in cotton before becoming a merchant banker with financial links to most European states, at 2 New Court, St. Swithin's Lane, City of London, the famous address of N.M. Rothschild & Co. He is estimated to have left about £3.5 million at his death, in addition to much land – see the previous section. His family was at the centre of the wealthy Anglo-Jewish "Cousinhood," with many of his relatives certainly millionaires. His main residences were at 107 Piccadilly and at Gunnersbury Park near Acton, Middlesex.

5. Robert Holford (1758-1838) – left "Upper Value," i.e., over £1 million. Inherited from his father, a Senior Master in Chancery and a Governor of the New River Company, of London.
Holford was the son of Peter Holford (1719-1804) of Lincoln's Inn Fields and Westonbirt, Gloucestershire, who was a Master in Chancery from 1750 until his death, fifty-four years, and was a Governor of the New River Company, which supplied much of London's water; Peter Holford died "immensely rich." Our man was educated at Westminster School and at St. John's College, Cambridge, and was a barrister of Lincoln's Inn. Despite this, he does not appear to have practiced as a barrister or had an occupation. His addresses were given in the probate records as "Lincoln's Inn Fields and of [Niton,] Isle of Wight." He was unmarried, his chief heir being his nephew Sir Robert Stayner Holford, 1st Bt. (1808-92, left £422,433 in personalty), a landowner who in 1883 owned 16,319 acres worth £21,277 p.a. in Gloucestershire and elsewhere. Sir Robert, a Tory M.P. from 1854-72, has an entry in the *ODNB* as an "art and plant collector." He formed the botanical collection at Westonbirt House and built the great mansion, Dorchester House, in Park Lane, which was torn down in 1929 to build the Dorchester Hotel.

6. Jane Innes (1748-1839) – left £1,042,667, of which £800,000 was left in England and the rest in Scotland. Inherited a banking fortune in Edinburgh from her brother.

Jane Innes was the daughter of George Innes (1704-52), Cashier to the Royal Bank of Scotland and Receive of lands and Rents in Scotland. She inherited from her brother Gilbert Innes(1751-1832), who left £140,000 in personalty, and also inherited land from other relatives. She was unmarried, and little is known about her life. She was said to have had the highest income of any commoner in Scotland, around £22,500 p.a. Her addresses were given in the probate records as "formerly of Piccadilly Place, Edinburgh, and then of Stow, Midlothian."

7. Thomas Allen (1757-1830) – left £500,000. An urban landowner in London.

Thomas Allen was the Lord of the Manor of Finchley in north London, and the owner of urban land in London. An ancestor bought this land in 1622. Almost nothing could be learned about his career, and it is difficult to see how he could have accumulated £500,000, as Finchley had not yet been developed. He must have had other sources of income, but these could not be traced. He lived at Henrietta Street, Cavendish Square, and he also had a residence at Bibsworth, Finchley.

8. Andrew Strahan (1750-1831) – left £800,000. The "King's Printer," with premises in the City of London.

Andrew Strahan was the son of William Strahan (1715-85), a famous and important Edinburgh-born printer, who produced Dr. Johnson's *Dictionary,* works by Gibbon, David Hume, Adam Smith, and served as an M.P. from 1774-84. Our man became the "King's Printer," the official printer of all government documents, from 1785 until his death. He lived at 10 Little New Street, Gough Square, near Fleet Street, in the City of London. He also served as an M.P., from 1797 until 1820. His heirs were his nephews, the Spottiswoode brothers, who also became well-known printers.

9. Henrique Teixera de Sampayo, Count de Povia (1774-1834) – left £600,000. First a merchant in London, then a banker in Lisbon.

The Count de Povia was regarded as the richest man in Portugal. He was the son of a merchant in Lisbon, and amassed a fortune as a merchant in London, providing goods to the British and Portuguese armies fighting Napoleon. He then returned to Lisbon, where he was a founder of what became the Bank of Portugal. A Roman Catholic, he was created a Baron of Portugal in 1818 and a Count in 1823. His total assets, including those in Portugal, must have been far greater than the very large estate he left in England.

10. William Gosling (1765-1834) – left £600,000. Banker in the City of London.

William Gosling was the son of Robert Gosling (1739-94), a banker in London, and became the head of Goslings & Sharpe, a leading bank, of 19 Fleet Street, City of London. His family remained very wealthy throughout the nineteenth century. Despite their wealth, little has been written about this family. He lived at 5 Portland Place, Middlesex, and also had a residence at Roehampton Grove, Putney.

11. William Crawshay (1764-1834) – left £700,000. Ironmaster at Cyfarthfa, Glamorganshire, and an iron merchant in the City of London.

William Crawshay was the son of the millionaire ironmaster Richard Crawshay (1739-1810, *q.v.*).

William Crawshay entered his father's firm as a young man, and became its sole proprietor and was known as "the Iron King." Most of his career, however, was spent as an iron merchant for his firm at George Yard in the City of London. He was also a considerable landowner in south Wales. His main residence was at Stoke Newington, Middlesex. After his death, his business was headed by his son William Crawshay (1788-1867), who left £2 million.

12. Alexander Adair (1742-1834) – left £700,000. Army Agent at Pall Mall, Middlesex.

The son of the commander of an East India Company's ship, Alexander Adair became an Army Agent at Pall Mall. An "army agent" received and invested the incomes of salaries and other sources for army officers, and contracted for military supplies. Most of his wealth must have been generated during the Napoleonic Wars. In 1799/1800 he had an income of £14,000, one of the larger business incomes of the time – he presumably got to keep much of the interest on the officers' incomes he received. His great-nephew Sir Robert Shafto Adair, M.P. (1811-86) was created 1st Baron Waveney in 1873.

13. Sir Charles Flower, 1st Bt. (1763-1834) – left £500,000. Provision merchant in the City of London.

The son of a cheesemonger in the Minories, our man became a provision merchant, also at the Minories and later at Finsbury Square, and made "a large fortune by provision contracting during the Napoleonic Wars, providing meat, cheese, and other foods and commodities to British troops." He served as Lord Mayor of London in 1808-9, and was created a baronet in 1809 as a result. He lived at Russell Square and had country residences in Essex and Oxfordshire.

14. Jonathan Peel (1752-1834) – left £600,000. Calico printer and cotton manufacturer at Accrington, Lancashire.

The brother of the millionaire Sir Robert Peel, 1st Bt. (1750-1830), he operated separately from other members of his family, at Accrington, Lancashire. He also had a large family, many of whom remained very wealthy. His address when he died was Accrington House, Lancashire.

15. William Thwaytes (1748-1834) – left £700,000. Tea and produce importer and merchant in the City of London.

William Thwaytes was the son of a tenant farmer in Westmorland. He began in London as a clerk with Davidson & Newman, "grocers, tea merchants, and confectioners," of 44-46 Fenchurch Street, City of London, and became a partner in 1777 and its sole owner in 1799. It was his company's tea which was thrown into the harbour of Boston, Massachusetts in 1775 during the "Boston Tea Party," which helped to trigger the American Revolution. His firm also imported and dealt in foods, sugar, and confectionery as well as tea, and he owned a share in a plantation in Jamaica. In 1817, at the age of sixty-nine, he married his housekeeper Ann Hook, who inherited £500,000 from him. She died in 1866, leaving £500,000 in personalty. He apparently lived on the premises of his firm at Fenchurch Street.

16. Neil Malcolm (1769-1837) – left £500,000. A planter and merchant in Jamaica, and then a merchant in London.

He was also a major landowner in Scotland and elsewhere. Neil Malcolm was the son of another

Neil Malcolm (1736-1802), a planter in Jamaica and a landowner in Scotland, who lived mainly in London in later life. Our man was a major plantation owner and slave owner in Jamaica, and then lived in London from no later than 1799, where he was apparently a merchant. He was also the 12th Laird of Poltalloch, Argyllshire. In 1883 his son John Malcolm (1805-93, left £413,047 in personalty) owned 835,611 acres worth £24,989 p.a., mainly in Argyllshire, but also in several English counties. His son John Wingfield Malcolm (1833-1902, left £360,172 in personalty), a long-time Tory M.P., was created 1st Baron Malcolm of Poltalloch in 1896. Our man had residences at Hanover Square, Middlesex, at Lamb Abbey, Kent, and at Poltalloch, Argyllshire.

17. Susannah Houblon Newton (1753-1837) – left £500,000. Inherited landed wealth, and also inherited from her husband, a merchant and a banker in London.

She was born in Berkshire, the daughter of John Archer (1716-1800), a landowner in Berkshire and Essex, who lived in St. James's Square, Middlesex, and in Bath. Her mother Lady Mary Fitzwilliam (c. 1718-76) was the daughter of John, 2nd Earl Fitzwilliam. In 1770 she married John Houblon (1736-83), whose family were French Huguenots who migrated to England, and were among the founders of the Bank of England, as well as being Portuguese merchants in London. Her husband had been educated at Harrow and at Cambridge. She added "Newton" to her name upon inheriting the lands of her uncle Michael Newton (d. 1803) of Culversthorpe, Lincolnshire. Her descendants were significant landowners in Essex and Lincolnshire. She was among the wealthiest women in England in her own right. The Houblon-Newton Scholarship, offered by the Huguenot Society, is named for her.

18. John Scott, 1st Earl of Eldon (1751-1838) – left £700,000. Lord Chancellor from 1806-27, and held other political and judicial offices.

The famous, or notorious, Lord Chancellor for twenty-six years, renowned for his extreme opposition to reform and notorious for his tendency to delay judicial decisions. The son of William Scott (1696-1776), a coal shipper in Newcastle-upon-Tyne, and educated at Newcastle-upon-Tyne Royal Grammar School, and at University College, Oxford, and called to the bar at the Middle Temple, Eldon became a K.C. in 1783, and amassed a fortune from his legal practice and as a judge and then as Lord Chancellor for nearly forty years. Apart from his personal wealth, he became a large-scale landowner, especially in Co. Durham. He served as an M.P. from 1793 until 1799, when he was created 1st Baron Eldon, and then 1st Earl of Eldon in 1821. He almost certainly amassed the largest fortune of any legal figure of his time, and became notorious in pro-reform circles. His brother William Scott, 1st Baron Stowell (1745-1836, left £250,000), was also a judge. Eldon lived at 6 Bedford Square, Middlesex, as well as at Eldon, Co. Durham and at Encombe, Dorset.

19. Henry Hewetson (1755-1838) – left £500,000. A 'gold and silver laceman" at King Street, Covent Garden, Middlesex.

The son of a yeoman farmer in Westmorland, he was apprenticed to his uncle Richard Hewetson, a "gold and silver laceman" in Covent Garden, and then became his partner. He became "laceman to His Majesty." He apparently manufactured and sold high-class lace goods embroidered with gold and silver, and "prospered as a result of the boom in uniforms during the Napoleonic Wars." The very large size of his estate suggests that he had other sources of wealth. His addresses were given as 5 Upper Belgrave Place, Middlesex, at The Grange, Worth, Sussex, and at Turnham Green, Middlesex.

20. Harriot (*sic*) Beauclerk, Duchess of St. Albans (1777-1837) – left £600,000. An actress, who married Thomas Coutts the banker, and later the Duke of St. Albans.

A truly extraordinary career. She was born Harriot Mellon, whose father was said to have been a lieutenant in the Madras Infantry, although there is no real evidence for this. Her mother was "an Irish wardrobe keeper" in a company of "strolling players." She became an actress from the age of ten, and later met Thomas Coutts (1737-1822, *q.v.*, above), the extremely wealthy proprietor of Coutts's Bank, inheriting his fortune and becoming a Partner in his bank, probably the first woman in Britain to hold such a position. After his death she married William Beauclerk, 9th Duke of St. Albans (1801-49), who was twenty-four years younger than her. He was the poorest of the British dukes. She left most of her wealth to her step-granddaughter Angela Burdett-Coutts, later Baroness Burdett-Coutts (1814-1906), the famous philanthropist. Our lady lived at 80 Piccadilly, Middlesex, and at Holly Grove, Highgate, Middlesex.

1840–1859

In these years Britain probably reached its relative economic zenith, when it had fully industrialised but before its great rivals, the United States and Germany, had become major industrial powers. Britain was at relative peace, apart from the Crimean War of the 1850s. In 1858 the East India Company was abolished, and replaced by the British Crown in India, headed by a Viceroy. Also in 1858, the Principal Probate Registry at Somerset House replaced the network of ecclesiastical probate courts, making possible truly comprehensive listings of all persons who left large estates in England and Wales.

1. William Henry Vane, 1st Duke of Cleveland and 3rd Earl of Burlington (1766-1842) – left £1,000,000. Landowner.

Listed above as one of the wealthiest of British landowners in 1883, when his successor owned 104,194 acres worth £97,398 p.a., he was the son of Henry Vane, 2nd Earl of Burlington (1726-92) and Margaret Lowther (1733-1806), the sister of James Lowther, 1st Earl of Lonsdale, and educated at Christ Church, Oxford, our man was a Whig M.P. from 1789 until 1792, when he succeeded his father as 3rd Earl. In 1827 he was created 1st Marquess of Cleveland, and, in 1833, 1st Duke of Cleveland, it is said for giving his support to the Great Reform Act of 1832. His son and successor, Harry, 2nd Duke of Cleveland, left £800,000 in personalty when he died in 1864. Our man was noted as a sportsman and patron of the turf. He lived at Raby Castle near Darlington, Co. Durham – where he was a large land and colliery owner – and at Cleveland House, 19 St. James's Square, Middlesex.

2. Richard Arkwright (1755-1843) – left "over £1 million." A cotton manufacturer, chiefly at Cromford near Matlock, Derbyshire.

The son of Sir Richard Arkwright (1732-92), inventor of the spinning frame, who had been a cotton manufacturer at Cromford, was said to have been worth £500,000, and was one of the first manufacturers to be knighted. He was, along with Sir Robert Peel, 1st Bt., the first cotton manufacturer to become a millionaire. At his death, he was said to have been the "richest commoner in England," and to be the largest single owner of government stock (consols). He was said to have left £3,250,000 at his death, although there is no direct evidence for this. He was baptised as a Presbyterian in Bolton, Lancashire, but was an Anglican in later life. Arkwright was also a considerable landowner, with his main residence at Willersley Castle near Matlock, Derbyshire, and owning other residences in Leicestershire and Derbyshire.

3. Philip John Miles (1779-1845) – left "Upper Value," i.e., above £1 million. A West Indies merchant and banker in Bristol and a large-scale plantation owner in the West Indies.
The son of William Miles (1728-1803), a plantation owner and merchant in the West Indies, and then a major merchant in Bristol, who was Mayor of Bristol in 1780-1, Philip John Miles was probably the richest man in Bristol, and one of the largest slave owners in Britain, receiving £41,000 in compensation when the slaves were emancipated in 1834. He was a merchant in Bristol, and head of Miles Bank (later Miles, Harford & Co.) of Corn Street, Bristol. He purchased Leigh Court, Abbots Leigh near Bristol, and was a considerable landowner. He served as an "unswerving Tory" M.P. between 1820 and 1837. His grandson, George Francis (Frank) Miles (1852-91), was accused by Thomas Toughill of being "Jack the Ripper," in Toughill's *The Ripper Code* (2009). Although Philip Miles has an entry in the *ODNB*, he is virtually unknown today, despite his great wealth.

4. William Joseph Denison (1769-1849) – left "Upper Value," i.e., above £1 million. A banker in the City of London.
William Joseph Denison was the son of Joseph Denison (c. 1726-1806), a wealthy merchant and banker in the City of London. He succeeded his father as the head of Denison, Heywood & Kennard, of Lombard Street in the City of London, one of the leading City banks of its day. He was baptised as a Non-conformist, but was an Anglican in later life. As noted in the previous section on businessmen who became large-scale landowners, he was unmarried, and left almost all of his great wealth – estimated by some as up to £3 million – to his nephew Lord Albert Conyngham (later Denison), who was created 1st Baron Londesborough, and became a great landowner, in 1883 owning 52,655 acres worth £67,876 p.a. Our man was also a Whig M.P. between 1796 and his death, a total of thirty-eight years.

5. Thomas Cubitt (1788-1855) – left "Upper value," i.e., above £1 million. A builder in London.
The celebrated builder was born near Norwich, the son of a carpenter, and trained as a carpenter. He set up as a builder in Holborn before 1810, and became the most famous and successful London builder of his time, constructing most of Belgravia and Pimlico for the Grosvenors, and heading many other building projects throughout the capital. His son George Cubitt (1828-1917, left £42,168), a Tory M.P. from 1860-92, was created 1st Baron Ashcombe in 1892; he was the great-grandfather of Camilla Parker-Bowles. Our man lived at Denbies near Dorking and at Belgrave Square, Middlesex. Hermione Hobhouse's *Thomas Cubitt: Master Builder* (1971) is a biography.

6. James Morrison (1789-1857) – Left "Above £1 million." Wholesale and retail merchant and merchant banker in the City of London.
The son of an innkeeper in Hampshire who left £600, James Morrison became one of the very richest men in Britain. He worked as a haberdasher in a "menial" capacity, and then married the daughter of his employer, Mary Ann Todd (1795-1887, left £617,364). Morrison then became a

wholesale and retail merchant in the City of London, pioneering the technique of selling items cheaply for a rapid turnover, at the Fore Street Warehouse. From this, he then became a leading merchant banker, specialising in American finance, and a very large-scale landowner (see the previous section). Morrison served as a Whig/Liberal M.P. from 1830 until 1847. All of his sons were extremely wealthy, with his eldest son Charles Morrison (1819-1909), who left £10,936,667, being probably the third richest man in Britain. Morrison lived at Upper Harley Street, Middlesex, and at Basildon Park near Reading. Caroline Dakers, *A Genius For Money* (2011) is a major biography of this remarkable entrepreneur.

7. Sir Isaac Lyon Goldsmid, 1st Bt. (1778-1859) – left £1,000,000. Bullion broker and stockbroker in the City of London.

The son of Asher Goldsmid (c. 1751-1822), a bullion broker in the City of London, our man's firm, Mocatta & Goldsmid, of Threadneedle Street in the City of London, became bullion brokers to the Bank of England and to the East India Company. He was also a stockbroker, a major investor in railways, and a large-scale landowner (see previous section). In 1841 he was created a baronet, the first professing Jew to receive an hereditary title in Britain, and was also a Baron of Portugal. Goldsmid was a notable figure in the "emancipation of the Jews," the drive to grant equal rights to professing Jews. He lived at St. John's Lodge in Regent's Park, Middlesex.

8. William Hobson (1732-1840) – left £500,000. A major builder in London, and a brickmaker in Shadwell and Dalston, etc.

William Hobson was the son of James Hobson (d. 1782), described on our man's marriage license in 1779 as a "bricklayer," but also a Citizen of London, of Shad Thames, Southwark. He was baptised and married as a Quaker, but was disowned by them in 1801 and died as an Anglican. He was apprenticed to his father at fifteen, and then became a major, large-scale builder, chiefly in London, operating from Stamford Hill. He rebuilt St. Luke's Hospital, and constructed several London docks, Newgate Prison, and the Martello Towers on the south coast of England. He also owned two brickworks, as well as chalk pits in Kent, and had an interest in a brewery in Clerkenwell. He lived at Markfield, Tottenham, Middlesex.

9. Charles George Perceval, 2nd Baron Arden (Irish peerage) and 1st Baron Arden (UK peerage) – left £700,000. Placeman and beneficiary of "Old Corruption," and landowner.

Lord Arden was one of the richest beneficiaries of "Old Corruption," the holding of public offices with few duties but astronomical salaries, which was abolished during the Age of Reform. He was the third son of John Perceval, 2nd Earl of Egmont (1711-70), who served as First Lord of the Admiralty in 1763-6, and was educated at Harrow and at Trinity College, Cambridge. His wealth derived chiefly from holding the sinecure positions of Registrar of the Court of Admiralty and of the Court of Delegates for fifty (!) years, from 1790 until his death. In 1798 alone he earned £8,000 in fees from these posts. He also became a landowner. In addition, he served as a Tory M.P. from 1780 until 1802, when he was created 1st Baron Arden in the UK peerage. He had previously inherited the Irish barony of Arden from his mother, Lady Catherine Compton, daughter of the 8th Earl of Northampton, who was created 1st Baroness Arden (Irish peerage). As Lord Arden, he also held a variety of government posts, including Lord of the Admiralty from 1783-1801. His career was doubtless helped by the fact that his brother was Spencer Perceval (1762-1812), the assassinated Prime Minister. Known as "the arch sinecurist," Lord Arden lived at Lohort Castle, Co. Cork, and at Arden, Warwickshire.

10. Hugh Hammersley (c. 1775-1840) – left £500,000. Banker at Pall Mall, Middlesex.
The son of Thomas Hammersley (d. 1812), a banker at 76 Pall Mall, Middlesex, Hugh Hammersley was probably educated at Eton – there is some doubt about this – and joined his father's bank, becoming its sole partner. Situated at 69 Pall Mall, it was a leading private bank for the wealthy of the West End; the Prince of Wales was a client. The bank apparently ran downhill in the later part of his time as its head, and was apparently almost bankrupt at the time of his death. His high probate valuation may thus be an exaggeration of his actual financial situation. He apparently lived on the premises of his bank on Pall Mall, the only address known for him in later life.

11. George Hay Dawkins Pennant (1764-1840) – left £600,000. A slave and plantation owner in the West Indies and a slate manufacturer in Wales and a landowner.
Born George Hay Dawkins, the son of Henry Dawkins (1728-1814), a wealthy Jamaica plantation owner and landowner in England, who was a member of the Jamaica Assembly and an M.P. in Britain, and who left £150,000 in personalty. He changed his surname to "Pennant" upon inheriting the property of his cousin Richard Pennant, 1st Baron Penrhyn (Irish peerage), a Whig M.P., landowner, and major developer of the slate industry in Wales (see previous section). Our man served as a Tory M.P. between 1814 and 1830. He apparently never lived in the West Indies, his residences being at Penrhyn Castle, Caernarvonshire, and at 56 Portland Place, Middlesex. His son-in-law Lord Penrhyn, who inherited most of his property, in 1883 owned 49,548 acres worth £71,018 p.a., mainly in Caernarvonshire.

12. Charles Duncombe, 1st Baron Feversham (1764-1841) – left £900,000. Landowner.
Charles Duncombe was the son of Charles Slingsby Duncombe (1739-1803), a major landowner in the North Riding. He was educated at Harrow, and served as a Tory M.P. between 1790 and 1826, when he was created 1st Baron Feversham. In 1883 his successor the Earl of Feversham owned 39,312 acres worth £34,328 p.a. in the North Riding. Explaining our man's personal estate of £900,000 is difficult, as he appears to have owned land only in the remote and purely agricultural North Riding, with no evidence of his owning minerals or urban property. He was a noted art collector who owned many Old Master works. His main residence was at Duncombe Park near Helmsley in the North Riding. His descendants have remained very wealthy, with the Earl of Feversham (who died in 2010) leaving £46 million.

13. Joseph Somes (1787-1845) – left £500,000. Shipowner in London.
Joseph Somes was the son of Samuel Somes (1758-1816), a shipowner and victualler of Mile End Road, Middlesex. He worked as a ship's captain from 1805 until 1818 and then became a shipowner. By the 1830s he was regarded as the largest shipowner in England. He was also a shipbuilder, was a Governor of the New Zealand Company, and in 1834 helped to found *Lloyd's Register of Shipping*. His addresses were at New Grove, Mile End Road, Middlesex and at Broad Street, Ratcliff, Stepney, and he also had a residence at Park Street, Grosvenor Square, Middlesex.

14. Samuel Mills (1769-1847) – left £500,000. Silk manufacturer at Milk Street near

Cheapside in the City of London.

Samuel Mills was the son of Benjamin Mills (c. 1738-91), Upper Bailiff (i.e., Chairman) of the Weavers' Company in the City of London in 1780-81. Very little is known about his career, or how he became so wealthy, although he may probably made much of his wealth through funeral mourning. He was a leading silk manufacturer (Mills & Remington) at 11 Milk Street near Cheapside, City of London. He had previously had premises near Finsbury Square. He was also a considerable landowner, with holdings in six counties. Baptised as an Anglican, he was a prominent Congregationalist in later life. His descendants remained extremely wealthy into the twentieth century, with his great-grandson Joseph Trueman Mills (1836-1924) leaving no less than £4,100,000, one of the largest estates of its time. Samuel Mills lived at 20 Russell Square, Middlesex, and also had two residences in Hertfordshire.

15. Sir John Smyth, 4th Bt. (1776-1849) – left £500,000. Landowner and colliery owner.

Sir John Smyth, 4th Bt. was the son of Thomas Smyth (1740-1800), a landowner of Stapleton, Gloucestershire. He succeeded his elder brother as the 4th baronet. He was educated at Worcester College, Oxford. He was a substantial landowner in Somerset and Gloucestershire, as well as owning coal mines there, and may also have had Bristol mercantile connections, although how he amassed £500,000 is unclear. His main residence was at Ashton Court, Ashton, Somerset, although he also had residences in Wiltshire, Gloucestershire, and Wiltshire. He was unmarried, and his property came to his sister's grandson Sir John Grenville Smyth (ne Upton, 1836-1901, left £412,071 in personalty), who was created a baronet in 1859.

16. Sir Samuel Scott, 2nd Bt. (1772-1849) – left £700,000. Banker at Cavendish Square, Middlesex.

Sir Samuel Scott, 2nd Bt. was the son of Sir Claude Scott, 1st Bt. (1742-183), a wealthy banker in Westminster who was an M.P. in 1806 and 1809-12, who was created a baronet in 1819. Our man was a merchant in the City and then became a leading banker at 26 Holles Street, Cavendish Square and then at 1 Cavendish Square. He served as a Tory M.P. between 1802 and 1832. His bank catered mainly for the wealthy of the West End. His family remained very wealthy throughout the nineteenth century. Scott's main residence was at Sandridge Park near Bromley, Kent.

17. Christopher Leyland (c. 1771-1849) – left £600,000. Banker in Liverpool.

Christopher Leyland was the son of Christopher Bullin, a merchant in Staffordshire. He changed his name to "Leyland" after inheriting part of the estate of his wealthy uncle Thomas Leyland (1732-1827, q.v.). Our man was the head of Leyland, Bullin & Co., one of the leading banks in Liverpool, and was regarded as one of the richest men in Europe – according to newspaper reports said to be worth between £5 and £7 million, an obvious exaggeration. He lived at Upper Parliament Street, Liverpool, and had a residence at Malpas, Cheshire. He was unmarried, and his wealth came to his sister Dorothy (1779-1856), who was married to John Naylor, who were the ancestors of the wealthy Naylor-Leyland family.

18. Thomas Thistlethwayte (1779-1850) – left £500,000.

A landowner in Hampshire, although his very large personal estate meant that he must have had other sources of income which could not be traced. He was the son of Robert Thistlethwayte

(1755-1802), a landowner and M.P. Our man served as a Tory M.P. in 1806-7, and lived at Southwick Park near Portsmouth and at Norman Court, Hampshire. In 1883 his son Thomas owned 8,084 acres in Hampshire with an income of £9,929 p.a. in 1883.

19. Lionel Lyde (1775-1853) – left £500,000. Banker in Bristol.

He was the son of Lionel Ames (1739-1821), a wealthy banker of Corn Street, Bristol, who left £120,000 and was Mayor of Bristol in 1788-89. Our man attended Clare College, Cambridge, and became a barrister of Lincoln's Inn (called 1807). He changed his surname to "Lyde" in 1791 when he succeeded to the property of his uncle, Sir Lionel Lyde, 1st Bt. (1724-91), Governor of the Bank of England. Our man had residences at Regent Street in London and in Clifton, Bristol. He was a Unitarian at birth, but died an Anglican.

20. James Ewing (1784-1852) – left £500,000. Apparently an East India Company fortune.

Little is known about the background of James Ewing apart from the fact that he was born in Dublin and apparently attended Westminster School in London. He arrived in India in 1801 as a "writer" (i.e., a clerk) and rose to become the Officiating Judge at Dacca and Patna. How he became so wealthy is unclear, as it is with so many East India Company fortunes – in many cases, the mystery is almost certainly deliberate. He served as a Tory M.P. in 1830-31, and lived at Park Crescent, Portland Place, Middlesex.

21. Sir Josiah John Guest, 1st Bt. (1785-1852) – left £500,000. Ironmaster at Merthyr Tydfil, Glamorganshire.

The son of Thomas Guest (1748-1807), the part-owner of the Dowlais Mines in south Wales, he became its head and expanded the firm to become "the largest ironworks in the world." He was also a large-scale landowner. In 1883 his son and successor, who was created Lord Wimborne, owned 83,539 acres worth £46,856 p.a. Our man lived at Dowlais House, Merthyr Tydfil and at Canford Manor, Wimborne, Dorset.

22. Henry Peyto Verney, 16th Baron Willoughby de Broke (1773-1852) – left £500,000. Landowner.

The 16th Lord Willoughby de Broke was the scion of a peerage dating from 1491. In 1883 his successor owned 18,145 acres worth £23,915 p.a. He was thus not really among the very largest landowners in Britain, and how our man became so wealthy is unclear. He was educated at Oriel College, Oxford, and lived at Compton Verney near Kineton, Warwickshire. In 1920 his successor the 19th Lord Willoughby de Broke (1869-1923, left £156,066), the famous right-wing activist, was forced to sell Compton Verney because of high taxation and low agricultural rentals.

23. James Foster (1786-1853) – left £700,000. Ironmaster at Stourbridge, Staffordshire.

The son of an ironmaster of Stourbridge, Henry Foster, who left £2,500 in 1793, he enlarged the family firm to become one of the biggest ironmasters in Britain, employing 5,000 workers in Staffordshire. He was also the Chairman of a bank in the Black Country, and was a pioneering locomotive builder with his partner John Raistrick. His family remained very rich: his nephew and heir, William Orme Foster (1814-99) left £2,587,681 plus much land. Our man lived at Stourton Castle near Stourbridge.

24. Arthur Wellesley, 1st Duke of Wellington (1769-1852) – left £500,000. Field Marshal and Prime Minister.

The 'Iron Duke' himself, the third son of an Irish earl, the Earl of Mornington, the great soldier was educated at Eton (whose "playing fields" were allegedly the cause of his great victory at Waterloo), and became wealthy mainly through being granted £500,000 by the British government and £100,000 by foreign governments for defeating Napoleon. He also received a large salary as a Field Marshal, and as a Cabinet minister for seventeen years, including spells as Prime Minister in 1828-30 and 1834. His London residence, Apsley House, is a famous tourist site, and he also had a country house at Strathfield Saye in Hampshire.

25. William Henry Cavendish-Bentinck-Scott, 4th Duke of Portland (1768-1854) – left £980,000. A landowner.

The family of the Dukes of Portland were discussed above, as one of the wealthiest of landed dynasties. In 1883 his successor owned 183,199 acres worth £88,350 p.a., plus another £19,750 p.a. from "mines," in many counties. The 4th Duke was the son of William, 3rd Duke of Portland (1738-1809), and was educated at Westminster School and at Christ Church, Oxford. He served as a Whig and later Tory M.P. from 1790 until 1809, when he became a member of the Lords, and thus sat in Parliament for a total of sixty-four years. He profited from extensive coal mines in Nottinghamshire and Northumberland. His main residence was Welbeck Abbey, Nottinghamshire, and he also had houses at Bolsover Castle, Derbyshire and at 18 Cavendish Square, Middlesex.

26. Edward Wigan (1785-1854) – left £500,000. A hop merchant at Southwark, Surrey.

Edward Wigan was the son of another Edward Wigan (1758-1814), a silversmith and goldsmith in Cheapside, City of London. Little is known of our man's career, but he probably became wealthy by supplying hops to the leading firms of London brewers. His daughter Helen (1819-91) married (Revd.) James Spurrell (1815-92), a relative of the Watney brewing family, who left £581,743. Our man's nephew, Sir Frederick Wigan, 1st Bt. (1827-1907), who left £530,570, was created a baronet in 1898. Our man's main business premises was located at Duke Street, Southwark, Surrey; he lived some distance away, at Highbury Terrace, Islington.

27. William Thompson (1793-1854) – left £976,000. An ironmaster in South Wales, and then an iron merchant in the City of London, where he had multiple interests.

William Thompson was the son of James Thompson (1749-1841), a yeoman farmer of Kendal, Westmorland. He was sent by his wealthy uncle to Charterhouse School in London, and was then employed by his uncle, a partner of Richard Crawshay, the famous ironmaster of Cyfarthfa, south Wales. He then became an iron merchant in London, a partner with his father-in-law Samuel Homfray (d. 1822, left £100,000). Thompson also had many other business interests in London, as a shipowner, insurance broker, and dock proprietor, and served as Lord Mayor of London in 1828-29. As well, he became a considerable landowner in Westmorland, where he lived, and had a residence at 12 Whitehall Place, Middlesex.

28. John Hardy (1773-1855) – left £550,000. An ironmaster at Low Moor, Bradford, and also a successful barrister.

John Hardy's career was highly unusual. He was the son of John Hardy (1744-1806), the owner of the Low Moor Iron Works near Bradford, and was educated at Pembroke College, Cambridge. He then became a barrister of the Middle Temple (called 1799), and had a highly successful career on the Northern Circuit, becoming Recorder of Leeds from 1806-34, apparently while heading his family's iron works. His son Gathorne Hardy (1814-1906, left £274,099) was a Tory M.P. from 1856-78, served as Home Secretary in 1867-8, and was created 1st Viscount Cranbrook in 1878 and 1st Earl of Cranbrook in 1892.

29. Samuel Gurney (1786-1856) – left £800,000. Banker and bill discounter in the City of London.

A famous Quaker banker, Samuel Gurney was the son of John Gurney (1749-1809), a banker in Norwich. He had no formal education past the age of fourteen, when he began working in the counting house of his relative Joseph Fry, the Quaker tea dealer. Gurney then became a leading banker and bill discounter (Overend & Gurney) at Lombard Street in the City of London. It grew to become one of the City's largest financial institutions. Gurney was at the centre of the "Quaker Cousinhood" of wealthy businessmen and reformers. He lived at Ham House, Upton, Essex. In 1866, a decade after his death, his bank crashed, setting off a major international financial panic.

30. Henry Kemble (1787-1857) – left £500,000. A tea broker in the City of London.

The son of Edward Kemble (d. 1812), a tea broker in the City of London and a member of its Common Council for many years, Henry Kemble was a successful tea broker at 52 Watling Street in the City of London, and a director of the Equitable Assurance Company. He had inherited much of his wealth from his brother and partner Edward Kemble (1792-1857), who had died a few months earlier, leaving £400,000. He lived at Grove Hill, Camberwell, Surrey. It is difficult to see what distinguished his firm from the dozens of other London firms of tea brokers which were far less successful.

31. George Frederick Muntz (1794-1857) – left £600,000. A metal manufacturer and metal merchant in Birmingham.

Muntz's family was apparently of German or Polish descent. He was baptised as an Anglican. He was the son of Philip Frederick Muntz (1752-1811), a metal merchant in Birmingham. Our man entered the family business at thirteen, and made a fortune manufacturing "Muntz Metal," a compound of copper and zinc used in shipbuilding, and was also a merchant in Birmingham. He was a well-known Radical Liberal M.P. from 1840 until his death, and, as an M.P., initiated the perforation of postage stamps, something which, apparently, no one had thought of before. He lived at Lea Hall, Handsworth, and at Umberslade Hall, Solihull, Warwickshire.

32. Richard Lee (1765-1857) – left £600,000. West India merchant in the City of London and in Middlesex.

Richard Lee was the son of Robert Cooper Lee (1735-94), Crown Solicitor of Jamaica, and then a barrister in London, who owned two plantations in Jamaica. He presumably became wealthy through owning plantations in the West Indies, and was also a merchant in London, but his great wealth may have been the result of his living to be ninety-one, dying unmarried, having reinvested most of his income for many decades. He lived at Weymouth Street, Portland Place, Middlesex and at Calverley Park, Tunbridge Wells, Kent.

33. Sir Edward Buxton, 2nd Bt. (1812-58) – left £500,000. A brewer at Spitalfields, Middlesex.
The son of Sir Thomas Fowell Buxton, 1st Bt. (1786-1845, left £250,000), a brewer at Spitalfields, of Northrepps, Norfolk, our man inherited his father's baronetcy. He was a partner in Truman, Hanbury & Co., a leading brewery firm. Educated at Trinity College, Cambridge, he was registered as a Quaker at birth, but was later an Anglican. He served as a Liberal M.P. from 1847-52 and from 1857 until his death at the age of forty-five. He lived at Colne House, Cromer, Norfolk, and at Upper Grosvenor Street, Middlesex.

34. William Spencer Cavendish, 6th Duke of Devonshire (1790-1858) – left £500,000.
One of the greatest of British landowners (see previous section), in 1883 his successor owned 198,572 acres worth £180,750 p.a. The Duke was educated at Harrow and at Trinity College, Cambridge. He sat in the House of Lords from 1811, after the death of his father William, 5th Duke of Devonshire (1748-1811, left £300,000). He was a patron of Joseph Paxton, who built the enormous Conservatory at Chatsworth, Derbyshire, one of his stately homes, along with Hardwick Hall, Derbyshire and Devonshire House, Piccadilly, Middlesex.

35. Lewis Loyd (1768-1858) – left £800,000. A banker at Manchester and then in the City of London.
The son of a farmer in Carmarthenshire, Lewis Loyd was educated at a Presbyterian school, and then became a Unitarian minister. He later became a banker in Manchester (Jones, Loyd & Co.), after marrying the daughter of John Jones, a Manchester banker. Loyd then moved to London, where he became a leading banker at 43 Lothbury in the City of London. His son, Samuel Jones Loyd, 1st Baron Overstone (1796-1883), was one of the richest bankers in Britain and a great landowner (see previous section). Lewis Loyd lived at Grosvenor Square, Middlesex and at Overstone, near Northampton.

36. Michael Williams (1785-1858) – left £500,000. Copper smelter and banker in Cornwall.
The son of John Williams (1753-1841), a banker and mine owner in Cornwall who left only £6,000, Michael Williams was the leading copper and tin smelter in Cornwall, as well as a partner in the Cornish Bank in Truro, and Chairman of the Cornish Railway Company from 1854 until his death. He also served as a Liberal M.P. from 1853 until his death. Originally a Methodist, he was later an Anglican. He had several residences in Cornwall, including Scorrier House, Truro.

37. Quintin Dick (1777-1858) – left £900,000. East India Company fortune and mercantile wealth in Dublin.
Known for his "vulgar greed," Dick appears to have inherited most of his wealth from his father Samuel Dick (c. 1733-1802), a wealthy merchant and owner of East India Company stock in Dublin. Our man was educated at Trinity College, Dublin, and was a barrister of both King's Inn, Dublin, and of Lincoln's Inn in London. He served as an M.P. in the Irish Parliament from 1800-02, and in the Westminster Parliament from 1803 until 1852. He does not appear to have been active in trade, but seems to have reinvested his wealth until his death at ninety-one. He was known as a fierce anti-Catholic member of the Church of Ireland, and is depicted as Ormsby in Disraeli's *Coningsby*.

38. Sir Joseph Bailey, 1st Bt. (1783-1858) – left £600,000. An ironmaster in South Wales.

The nephew of the millionaire ironmaster at Cyfarthfa, Richard Crawshay (d. 1810, *q.v.*), and the son of a small farmer in Yorkshire, in 1811 Bailey opened the Nant-y-Glo Ironworks in south Wales, which became one of the largest in Britain. He served as a Conservative M.P. from 1835 until his death, and was made a baronet in 1852. His grandson and successor, Sir Joseph Bailey, 2nd Bt. (1840-1906, left £104,553), in 1899 was created 1st Baron Glanusk, named for our man's country house, Glanusk Park in Brecon. He also had a residence at 26 Belgrave Square, Middlesex.

1860-1869

During this period, Britain's economy and world-wide commercial reach continued to grow and expand. Britain still remained the leading economic power in the world, both in manufacturing and in finance, and was at the head of a world-wide empire. But it now received challenges from several quarters. After its unification by Bismarck in 1871, Germany grew into the leading political, military, and economic state on the Continent. An even more formidable challenge appeared in America, where, after reunifying the nation and freeing the slaves in the Civil War, the United States was transforming itself into an economic super-power – one which was, fortunately, a long-term ally of Britain rather than an enemy. In the late nineteenth century America also produced businessmen whose fortunes dwarfed anything seen in Britain or elsewhere, such as Rockefeller, Morgan, Vanderbilt, and Carnegie. Britain also expanded its electorate, with working-class men gaining the vote in the 1867 Reform Act. As before, everyone who left £500,000 or more in personalty (land is not included in the valuation figures) in Britain is listed here, in chronological order, with millionaires listed first and then half-millionaires.

1. George Granville Sutherland-Leveson-Gower, 2nd Duke of Sutherland (1786-1861) – left £1,136,820. Landowner.

The son of the 1st Duke of Sutherland, probably modern Britain's richest landowner (see the previous section), the 2nd Duke was educated at Harrow and at Christ Church, Oxford. He inherited most of his father's enormous wealth, although his younger brother, later created the 1st Earl of Ellesmere, inherited the portion of his father's wealth inherited from the Duke of Bridgwater. Our man served as an M.P. from 1808 until 1820, when he was summoned to the Lords as Baron Gower, and succeeded to the Dukedom in 1833. His residences included Trentham Hall, Staffordshire; Dunrobin Castle, Sutherlandshire; and Stafford House in St. James's. When Queen Victoria visited Sutherland House for the first time, she remarked to the Duke that "she had come from her house to your palace."

2. Duncan Dunbar (1804-62) – left £1,000,000. Shipowner in London.

The son of Duncan Dunbar (1764-1825), a Scottish-born wine merchant in Limehouse who became a substantial shipowner, our Duncan Dunbar eventually owned the largest fleet of ships in the world, a total of forty-three vessels at the peak of his business, which traded especially with India and Australia. He was Deputy-Chairman of Lloyd's Registry in 1857-61 and also Chairman of the London Chartered Bank of Australia. His business premises were at Fore Street, Limehouse, Middlesex; he lived at 50 Porchester Terrace, Bayswater.

3. Hudson Gurney (1775-1864) – left £1,100,000. A banker in Norwich and a brewer in London.

The son of a wealthy banker and brewer in Norwich, Richard Gurney (1742-1811, left £125,000), our man was a partner in Gurney's Bank in Norwich and in Perkins' Brewery at Bermondsey, London. Originally a Quaker, he was disowned by them in 1803 for giving money to fund military activities against Napoleon. He served as an M.P. from 1812-32. Gurney built up a library of 10-15,000 books, and was a noted archaeologist. He lived at Keswick Hall near Norwich, Norfolk and in St. James's Square, Westminster.

4. Richard Thornton (1776-1865) – left £2,800,000. Insurance broker and hemp and East India merchant in the City of London.

One of the very wealthiest men in mid-Victorian Britain, Richard Thornton was the son of a yeoman farmer in Yorkshire. He attended Christ's Hospital in London and was then apprenticed to his uncle, a hop merchant in Southwark. He then became wealthy by importing hemp from Russia during the Napoleonic Wars. Thornton was also a large-scale insurance broker, and an East India merchant, operating from Old Swan Wharf, London Bridge, in the City of London. Unmarried, he left his fortune to five illegitimate children, and to two nephews, one of whom, Richard Thornton West (d. 1878), left £1,000,000. Thornton lived at Cannon Hill near Merton, Surrey.

5. William Crawshay (1788-1867) – left "under £2 million." An ironmaster at Cyfarthfa, Glamorganshire.

The second son of the wealthy ironmaster William Crawshay (1764-1834) who left £700,000 (*q.v.*), our man became head of the great Cyfarthfa ironworks, where "his will was law" (*ODNB*), and was known for his "commanding personality" (*ODNB*). He also owned coal mines, and lived at Caversham Park near Reading, Berkshire, and at Cyfarthfa Castle, Glamorganshire. His family gradually lost its dominance as ironmasters, but remained very wealthy.

6. Sir William Abdy, 7th Bt. (1778-1868) – left £1,000,000. Probably a landowner and urban property owner in London.

The source of his great wealth is not easy to explain. His father, Sir William Abdy, 6th Bt. (1732-1803), a captain in the Royal Navy, left £20,000 in personalty. Our man was educated at Eton and at Christ Church, Oxford. In 1883 his successor owned 3121 acres worth £8710 p.a. in three counties, of which 48 acres worth £5500 p.a. was in Surrey, probably consisting of docks or commercial property. He also owned other properties in London. In addition, he owned plantations in the West Indies and received £13,000 in compensation when his slaves were emancipated. But just how he became a millionaire remains a mystery. He lived in Hill Street, Berkeley Square, Mayfair.

7. Samuel Eyres (1793-1868) – left £1,200,000. A woollen manufacturer in Leeds.

The son of William Eyres (d. 1837), a woollen manufacturer in Leeds, our man became probably the richest woollen manufacturer in Leeds, at Wellington Street, Leeds, but little is known about his career. His great-granddaughter married Bolton Monsell, later Eyres-Monsell (1881-1969), 1st Viscount Monsell, a Tory Cabinet minister. Our man lived at Armley, Leeds.

8. Sir Benjamin Lee Guinness, 1st Bt. (1798-1868) – left £1,160,000. A brewer in Dublin,

head of the famous brewing firm, and almost certainly the richest businessman in Ireland. He was the son of Arthur Guinness (1768-1855), a wealthy brewer in Dublin. A member of the Protestant Church of Ireland, our man gave £150,000 to restore St. Patrick's Anglican Church in Dublin. He served as a Tory M.P. in 1865-68 and as the first Lord Mayor of Dublin in 1851-52, and was created a baronet in 1867. His eldest son Sir Arthur Guinness (1840-1915, left £738,344) was created 1st Baron Ardilaun, and his younger son, Sir Edward Guinness (1847-1927) was created 1st Earl of Iveagh and left £12.5 million, the largest estate left in the UK up to that time. Our man lived at 80 St. Stephen's Green, Dublin, and at 27 Norfolk Street, Park Lane, Mayfair.

9. William Henry Forman (1794-1869) – left £1,100,000. An ironmaster in Glamorganshire and an iron merchant in the City of London.

The son of William Forman (1767-1829, left £130,000), an ironmaster at Doncaster and then a wine merchant in London, this little-known millionaire became head of a leading ironworks in Glamorganshire and then a Partner in Thompson, Forman & Sons, iron merchants at Upper Thames Street and then at Queen Street, Cheapside, in the City of London. He continued to be a major shareholder in the Tredegar Ironworks. He lived at Pippbrook House, Dorking, Kent.

10. Samuel Scott (1807-69) – £1,400,000. Banker in Mayfair, London.

The younger son of the wealthy private banker Sir Samuel Scott, 2nd Bt. (1770-1849, q.v.), who left £700,000, he carried on the family bank at 1 Cavendish Square, Middlesex, a highly successful but little-known private bank, which was absorbed by Parr's Bank in 1894. Its clientele included many of the very rich of Mayfair. Scott was also a large landowner in Scotland and Kent. He lived at Sandridge Park, Bromley, Kent, and at Cavendish Square, Middlesex.

11. Thomas Fielden (1791-1869) – left £1,300,000. A cotton manufacturer at Todmorden, West Riding.

The fifth son of a tenant farmer turned small cotton manufacturer at Todmorden, in the West Riding nineteen miles from Manchester, he became a partner in Fielden Brothers, one of the most successful cotton manufacturing firms in Britain. He managed the company's Manchester warehouse. His parents had been Quakers, but he died an Anglican. He lived at Wellfield, Crumpsall near Manchester.

12. Thomas Cotterell (1780-1860) – left £800,000. Tea broker in Birmingham.

The son of Clement Cotterell (1746-1812), a hardware merchant in Birmingham who developed an export business shipping to America, Thomas Cotterell was listed as a "retired tea broker" in the 1851 Census, and was also an American merchant, with a branch in New York. He apparently was also mainly an exporter of tea to the United States. His nephew William Scholefield (1809-67) was the first Mayor of Birmingham. Cotterell lived at 63 Camden Street, Birmingham, and had a London residence in Islington.

13. Seth Smith (1791-1860) – left £500,000. A builder in London.

The partner of Thomas Cubitt (q.v.), the millionaire builder of the Grosvenor estate and other sites in London, Seth Smith's early years are obscure. After working with Cubitt, he apparently developed his own independent building and construction business, which built the famous

"Pantechnicon" warehouse for storing furniture near Belgrave Square. Widely claimed to be fireproof, it burned to the ground in 1874. Smith lived at 33 Eaton Square, Middlesex.

14. Stephens (*sic*) Lyne-Stephens (1801-60) – left £700,000. Glass manufacturers in Portugal.
The son of the half-millionaire John Lyne-Stephens who left £600,000 in 1826, Lyne-Stephens' family enjoyed a monopoly on the manufacture of glass in Portugal, and became extremely wealthy. He was educated at Trinity College, Cambridge. In 1845 he married Yolanda Duvernay (1812-94, left £602,046), a star ballerina in Paris, and served briefly as an M.P. in 1830-31. He was apparently not active in trade. He lived at Roehampton, Surrey and at Lyndford Hall near Norwich.

15. Joseph Tasker (1797-1861) – left £500,000. Probably a financier in London; inherited building wealth.
The source of Joseph Tasker's great wealth is somewhat unclear. He inherited from his wealthy father John Tasker (c. 1736-1816, left £140,000), a builder and architect in London, and was in his career apparently a very successful investor in Latin America, working from London, and a Director of the United Mexican Mining Association. Tasker was a leading Roman Catholic layman and philanthropist; his daughter Helen, Countess Tasker (1824-88, left £301,255) was made a countess of the Vatican nobility for her own philanthropy. Our man lived at Middleton Hall, Brentwood, Essex and at Marylebone Road, Middlesex.

16. Alexander Henry (c. 1783-1862) – left £700,000. A textile export merchant in Manchester.
Born in Co. Down, Ireland, Alexander Henry became a cotton and woollen export merchant and commission merchant in Manchester, and also owned warehouses in five other cities. He was mainly engaged in exporting to America, where he had spent time as a young man, and was said to have crossed the Atlantic thirty times. He served as a Liberal M.P. from 1843 till 1852. He lived at Woodlands near Manchester, and also had a residence at 56 St. James's Street, Middlesex.

17. Thomas Mills (1794-1862) – left £500,000. Silk manufacturer in the City of London.
The son of Samuel Mills, noted above, who left £500,000 in 1847, a very wealthy silk manufacturer at Finsbury Square in the City of London, Thomas Mills was apprenticed to his father in 1808, but was then educated at Queen's College, Cambridge (matriculated 1815), and then became a barrister of the Inner Temple (called 1832). He served as a Liberal M.P. from 1852 until his death. It is unlikely that he was actively engaged in trade. His family remained extremely wealthy into the twentieth century. He lived at Tolmers Park near Hertford and at 20 Russell Square, Middlesex.

18. Alexander Baird (1799-1862) – left £694,631. Ironmaster and coal owner in Lanarkshire.
One of the Baird brothers whose firm, William Baird & Co., was the largest producer of pig iron in the world, employing 10,000 workers, and also a major owner of coal mines. The firm had its headquarters in Glasgow. He was the son of Alexander Baird (1765-1833), a farmer who had founded the business. Our man appears to have headed the Glasgow office of the firm. He lived in Glasgow and at Urie, Kincardineshire.

19. William Beckett (1784-1863) – left £700,000. Banker in Leeds.
The younger son of Sir John Beckett, 1st Bt. (1743-1826, left £60,000), a woollen manufacturer

and founder of the bank, who was created a baronet in 1813, and of Mary (1749-1833), the daughter of the Bishop of Bristol, he was the head of the largest bank in Leeds, Beckett & Co. His family remained very wealthy. His nephew Sir Edmund Beckett, 1st Baron Grimthorpe (1816-1905) left no less than £2,121,686. Our man lived at Kirkstall Grange, Leeds, and at 18 Upper Brook Street in Mayfair.

20. Edward Loyd (1780-1863) – left £600,000. Banker in Manchester and in the City of London.

The brother of Lewis Loyd (1767-1858, *q.v.*), who left £500,000, and the uncle of the astronomically wealthy Samuel Jones Loyd, 1st baron Overstone (1796-1883), Edward Loyd was a partner in the family bank, first in Manchester and then at 43 Lothbury in the City of London. He lived at Comber House near Croydon, Surrey. This Loyd family, it should be noted, had no connection with Lloyd's Bank or with Lloyd's of London, the insurance institution.

21. Samuel George Smith (1789-1863) – left £500,000. Banker in the City of London.

A member of the well-known banking family who headed Smith, Payne & Co. of Lombard Street in the City of London, he was the son of Samuel Smith (1754-1834), a banker of London and an M.P. from 1788 till 1812. The bank had been founded in Nottingham, and then relocated to London. Lord Carrington was a member of this family. Our man's son Samuel George Smith (1822-1900) left £1,571,644. Our man lived at Sacombe Park, Ware, Hertfordshire.

22. Joshua Bates (1788-1864) – left £700,000. Merchant banker in the City of London.

Born in Massachusetts, where his father Joshua Bates (1755-1804) was a leading merchant and a colonel in the American Revolutionary army, our man also became a leading merchant and shipowner in Boston, Massachusetts, but came to the UK around 1818 and became a Partner in Baring Brothers of Bishopsgate Street in the City of London, the great merchant bank which invested heavily in American securities and businesses. Bates was naturalised in 1843. He lived at Arlington Street, St. James's.

23. Sir William Brown, 1st Bt. (1784-1864) – left £900,000. Foreign merchant in Liverpool.

Born in Co. Antrim, Ireland, he was the son of Alexander Brown (1764-1834), who spent most of his career in Baltimore, Maryland, where he became a leading importer and a founder of the pioneering B.& O. Railway. Our man was one of the founders of Brown, Shipley & Co. of Liverpool, the largest importer of American cotton in that city, and at one time held one-sixth of the trade between Britain and the USA. He served as a Liberal M.P. from 1846-59 and was created a baronet in 1863. He lived at Richmond Hill, Walton near Liverpool.

24. Henry Vane, 2nd Duke of Cleveland (1788-1864) – left £800,000. Landowner.

The son of Henry Vane, 1st Duke of Cleveland (1766-1842), the millionaire landowner, the 2nd Duke was educated at Christ Church, Oxford, and served as a Tory M.P. from 1812 till 1842, when he succeeded to the dukedom. His main residences were at Raby Castle near Darlington and Cleveland House, St. James's Square, Middlesex. He was succeeded by his brother William, 3rd Duke of Cleveland (1792-1864, left £80,000), who died only eight months later.

25. (John) Frederick Huth (1777-1864) – left £500,000. Merchant banker and merchant in the City of London.

Born in Hanover, Germany, the son of a Lutheran soldier who then became a tailor, Huth was apprenticed to Spanish merchants in Hamburg, and married into the Spanish aristocracy. He lived in Spain and South America before founding Frederick Huth & Co., chiefly timber merchants, and then became a leading merchant banker at South Place, Finsbury Square. He was naturalised in 1819 and served as financial advisor to the Queen of Spain. He lived at 33 Upper Harley Street, Marylebone.

26. William Baird (1796-1864) – left £998,765. Ironmaster in Lanarkshire.

The brother of Alexander Baird (1799-1862, *q.v.*), who left £694,631, and of James Baird (1802-76), who left £1,190,869, Baird's family were among the greatest ironmasters in Scotland, and were also significant coal owners. He was the Senior Partner of the firm, William Baird & Co., and lived at Elie, Rosemount, Fifeshire.

27. Richard Barrow (1787-1865) – left £500,000. Ironmaster and colliery owner in Derbyshire; foreign merchant in the City of London.

Unusually, Richard Barrow was the son of an Anglican clergyman, (Revd.) Richard Barrow, who died at the age of 100 in 1838. He took over the Staveley Ironworks near Chesterfield, Derbyshire from his brother, and greatly expanded it. His firm made most of the ironworks for the 1862 London Exhibition. Barrow was also an extensive colliery owner, and then a foreign merchant in London, trading with Spain and Portugal. He lived at Ringwood Hall near Chesterfield.

28. Thomas Miller (1811-65) – left £600,000. Cotton manufacturer in Preston, Lancashire.

The son of a cotton manufacturer in Preston, Thomas Miller (1767-1840), who left £40,000, our man expanded the business, Horrocks, Miller & Co., and became the largest employer of labour in north Lancashire. He also became a landowner in Lancashire, and donated Miller Park to Preston. He lived at Winkley Square, Preston, and at Singleton, Poulton-le-Fylde, Lancashire.

29. Algernon Percy, 4th Duke of Northumberland (1792-1865) – left £500,000. Landowner.

One of the largest and wealthiest landowners in Britain (see previous section), whose successor in 1883 owned 186,397 acres worth £176,048 p.a., the 4th Duke was the younger son of the 2nd Duke, who left £660,000 in personalty in 1817, and then succeeded his brother, the 3rd Duke, in 1847. The 4th Duke entered the Royal Navy in 1804, serving until 1815 when he was a captain. He had been created Baron Prudhoe in 1814 to enable him to sit in the Lords, and served as First Lord of the Admiralty in 1852. He lived at Northumberland House near Charing Cross, Middlesex, and at Alnwick Castle, Northumberland.

30. Peter Arkwright (1784-1866) – left £800,000. Cotton manufacturing fortune in Derbyshire.

The third son of the millionaire cotton manufacturer Richard Arkwright (1755-1843, *q.v.*), he continued in trade, and was listed in the 1851 Census as a "banker," and in the 1861 Census as a "cotton spinner." He had eight sons, two of whom were Anglican clergymen and seven of whom left over £100,000, and five daughters. He lived at Matlock Castle, Willersley, Derbyshire.

31. Matthias Wolverley Attwood (1808-65) – left £900,000. Banker in the City of London.

The son of Matthias Attwood (1780-1855), a banker in the City of London and an M.P., who left £160,000, he was a successful banker with Spooner, Attwood & Co. of 27 Gracechurch Street (later 69 Lombard Street), City of London. Attwood served as a Tory M.P. from 1837 till 1841. Unmarried, his executor was his uncle Benjamin Attwood (d. 1874), who left £600,000. Our man lived at Dulwich, Surrey.

32. Don Pedro Gonzales de Candamo (1799-1866) – left £800,000. Entrepreneur in Peru.

Known as "the richest man in Peru," how de Candamo became so wealthy is unclear, although probably it was in mining and banking. Little is known of his life or career. His connection with the UK is also unclear, but he probably kept his great wealth in English banks because they were completely secure, unlike banks in Latin America.

33. Thomas Joseph Eyre (1780-1866) – left £850,000. Inherited banking and colliery wealth in Sheffield.

The son of Vincent Eyre (1744-1801), the Principal Agent to the Duke of Norfolk's estates, and then a wealthy banker and colliery owner in Sheffield, our man was a leading Roman Catholic, and also a landowner in Ireland, where he left £500,000 in personalty. It is unclear if he was active in trade or simply reinvested his income. He lived at Pulteney Street, Bath, not in Sheffield.

34. Frederick David Goldsmid (1812-66) – left £800,000. Bullion broker in the City of London.

The fifth son of the millionaire bullion broker Sir Isaac Lyon Goldsmid, 1st Bt. (1778-1859, *q.v.*), our man attended University College London (which his father had helped to found), and was a bullion broker with Mocatta & Goldsmid in the City of London, as well as a large-scale landowner. He was related to many of the wealthy families of the "Anglo-Jewish Cousinhood," and lived at Somerhill near Tonbridge, Kent and at 20 Portman Square, Middlesex.

35. William Henry Goschen (1793-1866) – left £500,000. Merchant or merchant banker in the City of London.

Born to Lutheran parents in Saxony, Germany, he emigrated to London around 1815 and founded Fruhling & Goschen, "merchants" of 12 Austin Friars, City of London. It is unclear whether his firm were import-export merchants or merchant bankers, or both. He was made a Freeman of London in 1863. His son George Joachim Goschen, 1st Viscount Goschen (1831-1807, left £151,568) was a leading late Victorian politician and Chancellor of the Exchequer in 1887-92. Our man lived at Roehampton, Surrey.

36. William Henry Lambton (1793-1866) – left £500,000. Banker in Newcastle-upon-Tyne.

The son of William Henry Lambton (1764-97), an extensive land and colliery owner and M.P. and the brother of Sir John Lambton, 1st Earl of Durham (1792-1840, left £250,000), the famous Governor-General of Canada, our man was educated at Eton and at Trinity College, Cambridge. It was most unusual for someone of his background to become an active and successful banker, which he may have done because he married Henrietta, the daughter of Cuthbert Ellison (d. 1860, left £140,000), a leading banker in Newcastle-upon-Tyne. Our man lived at Biddle Hall, Co. Durham and at 17 Chesham Place, Middlesex.

37. Alexander Cunninghame (1804-66) – left £571,683. Ironmaster and colliery owner in Lanarkshire and Ayrshire.

The son of John Cunninghame (1759-1822), an extensive landowner and colliery owner in Scotland, our man attended Glasgow University, and expanded his family's iron and coal business to become one of the most extensive in Scotland, in partnership with James Merry (1805-77), who left £680,402. He lived at Craigends, Renfrewshire, which had been owned by his family for many generations.

38. Ann Thwaytes (1789-1866) – left £500,000. Inherited wealth from a tea merchant and food importer in the City of London.

Ann Thwaytes inherited £500,000 from her husband William Thwaytes (1749-1834), who left £700,000, *q.v.*, in a true "rags to riches" story. She was the illegitimate daughter of a "Mrs. Hook" of Kingsland, Middlesex and was a housekeeper to her future husband when she married him in 1817; he was sixty-nine, she twenty-eight. An eccentric religious fanatic, she later lived with a physician, John Seth Smith (1793-1877, left £25,000), who was the grandfather of the poet Gerard Manley Hopkins. She lived at Charman Dean near Worthing, Sussex.

39. John George Abbot (1816-67) – left £600,000. An iron and brass founder at Gateshead, Co. Durham.

The son of the wealthy ironmaster of Gateshead John Abbot (1784-1863, left £400,000), who died only four years before him, he took over and expanded his family firm, which produced anchors, chains, cables, steam engines, cranes and the like, probably for the shipping and engineering industries of the north-east. He died at only fifty-one; his widow Catherine nee Adamson (1823-1900), left £657,491. Our man lived at 4 Saville Place, Newcastle-upon-Tyne.

40. Jean-Louis Greffulhe (1774-1867) – left £500,000. Merchant banker in the City of London and elsewhere.

Born in Amsterdam, our man died at ninety-two in Paris. He was a merchant banker (Banque Greffulhe) at Cornhill in the City of London; it had branches at Pall Mall in London, in Paris, and elsewhere. His bank invested heavily in railways and canals. The Greffulhes were apparently Huguenots, not Roman Catholics. In London he lived at Seymour Place in Mayfair.

41. Charles Hardy (1813-67) – left £500,000. Ironmaster at Bradford, Yorkshire.

The son of the wealthy ironmaster John Hardy (1773-1855), who left £500,000 (*q.v.*), our man was educated at Shrewsbury School, and then took over the family's ironworks at Low Moor near Bradford. His brother Gathorne Hardy, 1st Earl of Cranbrook (1814-1906, left £274,099) was a Tory Cabinet minister; another brother, Sir John Hardy, 1st Bt. (1809-99) left £1,036,498. Our man lived at Chilham Castle near Canterbury, Kent, and at Odsal House, Bradford.

42. William Henry Sparrow (1789-1867) – left £500,000. Ironmaster and colliery owner in Staffordshire and Shropshire.

An extensive ironmaster and colliery owner at Penn, Wolverhampton, and at Albrighton near Shrewsbury, William Henry Sparrow was the son of William Sparrow (1764-1834), who was also apparently an ironmaster. Our man was also a landowner in these two counties. He was an Anglican

– one of his executors was an Anglican clergyman – and lived at Penn Court near Wolverhampton and at Albrighton Hall near Shrewsbury.

43. John Ames (1784-1867) – left £500,000. Banker in Bristol.

The son of Levi Ames (1739-1820), a banker in Bristol and its Mayor in 1788 who left £120,000, our man was a director of Cave, Ames & Co., one of Bristol's largest banks, but, it appears, retired around 1826. He was a Unitarian. His brother Lionel Ames (later Lyde, 1775-1855, *q.v.*) left £500,000. Our man lived at Clevelands near Lyme Regis, Devon.

44. Thomas Bridges (1788-1868) – left £600,000. Unclear: probably a London land and property owner.

The son of Robert Bridges (1758-1821), who left £100,000, a gunpowder manufacturer at Ewell, Surrey and landowner in Surrey, our man was apprenticed to a "Citizen and Grocer" of the City of London. How he became so wealthy is unclear, but he probably owned land and property in London and Surrey, and may also have been a gunpowder manufacturer like his father. He lived at Elmer near Fetcham, Surrey, and at 33 St. James's Place, Middlesex.

45. Cristobel De Murrieta (1789-1868) – left £600,000. Merchant and merchant banker in the City of London.

A Spanish and South American merchant (Murrieta & Co.) trading chiefly with South America, and a merchant banker, of 7 Adams Court, Old Broad Street in the City of London. He arrived in London around 1841, and quickly became very wealthy. Much about his previous history is unclear. His brother and partner Francisco Murrieta (1793-1856) left £140,000. Our man lived at 11 Kensington Palace Gardens, Middlesex.

46. Welborne Agar, 2nd Earl of Normanton (1778-1868) – left £831,749. Landowner.

The son of (Rt. Revd.) Charles Agar, 1st Earl of Normanton (1736-1809, left £175,000), who was the Anglican Archbishop of Dublin, as well as an Irish landowner, and a successful bank speculator, our man attended Westminster School; Trinity College, Dublin; and Christ Church, Oxford. He held an Irish peerage, and did not sit in the House of Lords. Normanton was a landowner in Ireland and England; in 1883 his successor owned 42,961 acres worth £48,280 p.a. He lived chiefly in England, at Somerley, Hampshire and at 3 Seamore Place, Middlesex.

47. Edward Marjoribanks (1776-1868) – left £600,000. Banker in The Strand, Middlesex.

The Senior Partner, from 1837 until his death, of Coutts & Co., the famous private bankers at 37 The Strand in central London, Edward Marjoribanks was born in Berwickshire and attended Edinburgh High School and Edinburgh University. He became a Junior Partner in Coutts in 1787, and served as a Partner for over seventy years before his death at ninety-one. His son Dudley Coutts Marjoribanks (1820-94, left £714,861), a brewer and M.P., was created 1st Baron Tweedmouth in 1881. Our man lived at 34 Wimpole Street, Middlesex and at Henley-on-Thames.

48. Peter Pantia Ralli (1837-68) – left £500,000. Merchant in the City of London.

The son of Pantia Stephen Ralli (1793-1865, left £400,000), of the great Greek mercantile and banking family of Ralli Brothers of Finsbury Circus, City of London, our man was born in

London and educated at Eton and at King's College London. His extended Greek Orthodox family, which traded heavily with Russia and the Levant, was among the richest in Europe, and were often regarded as the Rothschilds of the east. Our man died at only thirty-one. He lived at 14 Hyde Park Place, Middlesex.

49. William Cook (1784-1869) – left £600,000. Wholesale warehouseman in the City of London.

The son of a farmer in Norfolk, Cook allegedly came to London with five sovereigns in his pocket and a letter of introduction to a banking firm. He founded a retailing business in 1809, and in 1819, established Cook, Son & Co. at Cheapside and later at St. Paul's Churchyard in the City of London. It became the most successful wholesale firm in London, supplying silk, linen, and woollens to retailers. He lived at Royden Hall, Tunbridge, Kent. His son Sir Francis Cook, 1st Bt. (1817-1901), left £1,600,000.

50. Joseph Crossley (1811-68) – left £700,000. A carpet manufacturer in Halifax, Yorkshire.

The son of Joseph Crossley (1772-1837), a carpet manufacturer in Halifax who left £18,000, he ran the firm with his three brothers. By the 1860s it employed 5,000 to 6,000 workers and was the largest carpet manufacturing firm in the world. He lived at Broomfield in Halifax. His brother Sir Francis Crossley, 1st Bt. (1817-71) left £800,000, and his nephew Sir Saville Crossley (1857-1935, left £192,679) was created 1st Baron Somerleyton in 1916.

51. Robert Gosling (1795-1869) – left £700,000. Banker in Fleet Street, City of London.

The son of William Gosling (1765-1834, q.v.), banker of Fleet Street who left £600,000, our man was educated at Christ Church, Oxford, and became head of the firm Gosling & Sharpe, private bankers at 19 Fleet Street, from 1834 until his death. He lived at 5 Portland Place, Middlesex, and at Botley's Park, Surrey. His son Robert Gosling (1831-95) left £900,599.

52. Richard Grosvenor, 2nd Marquess of Westminster (1795-1869) – left £800,000 in personalty. Land and property owner, chiefly in London.

The owner of the ground-rents of Mayfair, Belgravia, and Pimlico, which were developed during his lifetime into prime upper-class housing, he was the son of Robert Grosvenor, 1st Marquess of Westminster (1767-1845, left £350,000 – see previous section), and was educated at Westminster School and at Christ Church, Oxford. He served as an M.P. in 1818-34. His family became the richest landowners in Britain, and is still worth an estimated £10 billion. He lived at Grosvenor House, Mayfair and at Eaton Hall, Cheshire.

1870-1879

Britain's financial and manufacturing ascendancy continued, although, as in the previous decade, these were increasingly challenged by Germany and the United States. In 1876 Queen Victoria was proclaimed Empress of India by Disraeli's government, symbolic of the importance of the British Empire, both the self-governing dominions and the colonies. The number and scale of wealthy estates increased, as did notions of a later Victorian "plutocracy." As in the previous sections, millionaire estates probated in this decade are set out first, followed by half-millionaire estates. As before, the valuation figures are for personalty, and exclude land.

1. Thomas Brassey (1805-70) – left £3,200,000. Railway and public works contractor.
The wealthiest of the Victorian railway contractors, Thomas Brassey constructed one-third of all the railway mileage in Britain and 5 per cent of the world's railways built during the nineteenth century. He also built the *Great Eastern* steamship and much of the Thames Embankment. The son of a tenant farmer in Cheshire, he lived at 56 Lowndes Square, Belgravia, Middlesex. His son Sir Thomas Brassey (1836-1918, left £134,806), M.P. and Governor of Victoria, Australia, was created 1st Earl Brassey.

2. Baron Nathan de Rothschild (1812-70) – left £1,800,000. Merchant banker in Paris, France.
The head of the French branch of the great merchant bank, he was the son of Nathan Mayer Rothschild (1777-1836, *q.v.*), the millionaire founder of the bank's London branch. Our man also owned the renowned Mouton Vineyards in Bordeaux, now known as Château Mouton-Rothschild.

3. Giles Loder (1786-1871) – left £2,900,000. Russia merchant in the City of London.
The son of a "gentleman" in Wiltshire who left £6,000, worked as an exporter at St. Petersburg, Russia from about 1810, and was then a Russia merchant at 15 Austin Friars, City of London. He also became a substantial landowner. His firm chiefly imported tallow from Russia, but just how he accumulated nearly £3 million is unclear. His grandson Gerard Loder (1861-1936, left £154,574), was a Tory M.P. and was created 1st Baron Wakehurst in 1932. Despite its great wealth and eventual status in the aristocracy, the family remains virtually unknown. He lived at 1 Clarendon Place, Hyde Park Gardens, Middlesex.

4. Sir David Baxter, 1st Bt. (1793-1872) – left £1,098,810. Flax spinner in Dundee.
A partner with his father William Baxter (1766-1854) and brothers in Baxter Brothers, flax spinners of Dundee. His firm introduced power looms into the manufacturing process and became among the largest flax spinners in the world. His business helped to transform Dundee into a major international manufacturing centre. Baxter became well-known for his many philanthropic gifts to Dundee, and was created a baronet in 1863 for his efforts. He lived at Dundee and at Kilmaron, Fifeshire.

5. Thomas Baring (1799-1873) – left £1,500,000. Merchant banker in the City of London.
The head of Baring Brothers, the great merchant bank at 8 Bishopsgate Within, until he retired in 1871. He was also Chairman of Lloyd's of London, 1838-68, and was a director of the Bank of England 1848-67. He was the son of Sir Thomas Baring, 2nd Bt. (1772-1848), and was educated at Winchester. He served as a Tory M.P. from 1835-37 and 1844-77. Baring lived at Norman Court, Hampshire and at 4 Hamilton Place, Middlesex.

6. George Carr Glyn, 1st Baron Wolverton (1797-1873) – left £1,000,000. Banker in the City of London.
The head of Glyn, Halifax, Mills, Currie & Co., of Lombard Street in the City of London. It

specialised in railway finance. He was also the Chairman of the London & North-Western Railway in 1846-52 and a director of other railway companies. The fourth son of Sir Richard Carr Glyn, 1st Bt. (1755-1826), banker and M.P., who left £250,000, our man was educated at Westminster School and served as a Liberal M.P. from 1836 until 1868, when he was created 1st Baron Wolverton. He lived at Stanmore Place, Middlesex, and at Eccleston Street, Belgravia.

7. Francis Wright (1806-73) – left £1,400,000. Ironmaster, colliery owner, and engineering contractor, chiefly in Derbyshire.

The head of the Butterley Ironworks in Derbyshire, one of the largest in Britain, and a colliery owner, Francis Wright was also a manufacturing engineer who built the roof of St. Pancras Station and many other notable works. He was the son of John Wright (1758-1840), a banker and ironmaster in Nottingham. Our man lived at Osmanton Manor near Ashbourne, Derbyshire, supposedly the first building in Britain since Roman times to be centrally heated.

8. Baron Mayer Amschel de Rothschild (1818-74) – left 2,100,000. Merchant banker in the City of London.

A Baron of Austria and the fourth son of Nathan Mayer de Rothschild (1777-1836), the multimillionaire founder of the London branch of the celebrated merchant bank, he spent several terms at Cambridge, and was noted for his fabulous art collection, his successful racehorses, and for hiring Joseph Paxton to build Mentmore, his country mansion in Buckinghamshire. He also lived at 197 Piccadilly, Middlesex.

9. Edward Ryley Langworthy (1796-1874) – left £1,200,000. A cotton manufacturer and merchant in Salford, Lancashire.

One of the only genuine cotton manufacturing millionaires from Manchester (or Salford, adjacent) during the nineteenth century, surprisingly little is known of Edward Langworthy's background. He was the son of a "packer and callendar" in London, and established his cotton manufacturing business in Salford with his brother in 1832. In 1868 he employed 900 workers. He served as a Liberal M.P. in 1857 and was twice Mayor of Salford. Langworthy lived at Victoria Park near Manchester.

10. Joseph Love (1796-1875) – left £1,000,000. Colliery owner in Co. Durham.

The son of Thomas Love (1757-1842), a working miner and then an inspector of mines at South Shields, Northumberland, Love was a genuine self-made millionaire who began as a working miner at the age of eight, and became in turn a shopkeeper, a builder, and a timber merchant, before he opened the Brancepeth Coliery in 1838. A prominent Methodist, he lived at Mt. Buelah near Durham.

11. Sir Anthony Nathan de Rothschild, 1st Bt. (1810-76) – left £1,800,000. Merchant banker in the City of London.

A partner in the great merchant bank at St. Swithin's Lane in the City of London, he was the second son of Nathan Mayer Rothschild (1777-1836), the multimillionaire founder of the British branch of Rothschild's Bank. Our man was educated at universities in Germany and was the first President, from 1870 until his death, of the United Synagogue, the mainstream Anglo-

Orthodox strand, headed by the Chief Rabbi. He lived at 19 Grosvenor Place, Middlesex, and at 107 Piccadilly, Middlesex.

12. James Baird (1802-76) – left £1,190,868. An ironmaster and colliery owner in Lanarkshire.
One of the wealthiest members of the very rich Baird family, ironmasters at Gartsherrie, Lanarkshire, and colliery owners there, James Baird was the fourth son of the farmer Alexander Baird (1765-1823). All of his six sons left estates of £100,000 or more. James Baird served as a Tory M.P. in 1851-57, and gave an estimated £500,000 to the Church of Scotland to teach the Bible in schools. He lived at Auchmedden, Aberdeenshire.

13. David, Viscount De Stern (1807-77) – left £1,000,000. Merchant banker in the City of London.
Born in Frankfurt, he was a member of one of the richest but least known of the great Anglo-Jewish banking families. His brother Herman, Baron De Stern (1815-87) left £3.5 million. Like him, our man was made a Baron of Portugal. He was a Deputy Lieutenant of the City of London, but otherwise had no public role. He lived at 22 Queen's Gate, Hyde Park, Middlesex and in Hove, Sussex.

14. John Pemberton Heywood (1803-77) – left £1,900,000. A banker in Liverpool and in the City of London.
The son of a barrister in Wakefield, Yorkshire, Heywood became a banker (Arthur Heywood, Son & Co.) in Liverpool and then a Partner in Heywood, Kennard & Co., bankers of Lombard Street, City of London. He became one of the richest men in Liverpool, probably the richest banker in that city. A Unitarian, he was prominent in the Liberal Party and was a relative by marriage of William E. Gladstone, who offered him a peerage, which he declined. Heywood lived at Norris Green, West Derby and at 15 Hyde Park gardens, Middlesex.

15. Lionel John Tollemache, 7th Earl of Dysart (1794-1878) – left £1,700,000. Landowner and investor.
Our man inherited his title from his grandmother, the 7th Countess of Dysart (d. 1840, left £140,000). He was educated at Harrow and served as a Tory M.P. in 1827-30. Although he was a substantial landowner (27,190 acres worth £44,500 p.a.), most of his wealth apparently came from astute investments. He was well-known as a miser, hermit, and eccentric, and often used his female servant to invest for him. On one occasion she was sent to a leading railway company and asked if she could invest some money in it. They expected £50 or so, and were astonished when she took out £60,000 in cash to invest. He lived at Buckminster near Grantham and at 34 Norfolk Street, Strand, Middlesex.

16. Sir Francis Henry Goldsmid, 2nd Bt. (1808-78) – left £1,000,000. Bullion broker fortune in the City of London and barrister in London.
He inherited a fortune from his father, Sir Isaac Lyon Goldsmid, 1st Bt. (1778-1859), the millionaire bullion broker and merchant banker, and became a barrister of Lincoln's Inn (being called in 1833) and then a Q.C. When called to the bar he became the first professing Jew allowed to swear on the *Old Testament* alone. He was also a substantial landowner in Brighton and Sussex, owning 6,927

acres worth £30,217 p.a. in that county. He served as a Liberal M.P. from 1860 until his death and was a leader of the Anglo-Jewish community. He lived at St. John's Lodge in Regent's Park, Middlesex and in Brighton.

17. John Penn (1805-78) – left £1,000,000. Marine engineer at Greenwich, Kent.

A large-scale naval engineering contractor (John Penn & Sons) in Greenwich which built 735 engines for steamships, both for the Royal Navy and for merchant ships. He was the son of a marine engineer at Greenwich, John Penn (1770-1843), who left £35,000. Penn's firm introduced many innovations, especially to screw propellers. He was twice President of the Institution of Mechanical Engineers. He lived at The Cedars, Lee, Kent.

18. Richard Thornton West (1813-78) – left £1,000,000. East India merchant in the City of London.

The son of William Ogle West (1781-1853), a merchant trading with the Dutch East Indies who left £120,000, and the nephew of Richard Thornton (d. 1865, q.v.) an East Indies merchant who left the vast sum of £2.8 million, he lived for much of his life in Exeter, but was described as an "east India merchant" in the 1851 and 1861 Censuses. His brother William Thornton West (d. 1870, q.v.) left £600,000. Our man lived at Streatham Hall, Exeter, Devon.

19. Baron Lionel Nathan de Rothschild (1808-79) – left £2,700,000. Merchant banker in the City of London.

The eldest son of Nathan Mayer Rothschild (1777-1836, q.v.), the founder of the British branch of the famous merchant bank, he was a Baron of Austria, but was resident in Britain, where he was the head of Rothschild's Bank at New Court, St. Swithin's Lane, City of London. He was educated at Gottingen University in Germany, where he met Goethe. In 1858 he became the first professing Jew to take his seat in the House of Commons, where he served until 1874. He was President of the Great Synagogue in London. Rothschild lived at 148 Piccadilly – where Benjamin Disraeli lived as the Rothschild's guest for most of the last two years of his life – and at Gunnersbury Park in Acton, Middlesex.

20. John Cavendish-Scott-Bentinck, 5th Duke of Portland (1800-79) – left £1,500,000 in personalty. Landowner.

The son of William, 4th Duke of Portland (1768-1854, q.v.), among the very greatest landowners in Britain (see previous section), he served as an M.P. in 1824-26 but then became renowned as a recluse and an eccentric, building vast underground chambers at his stately home, Welbeck Abbey. In London, he only went out at night, when he was preceded by a lady servant carrying a lantern forty yards ahead of him; he never spoke to anyone unless it was absolutely necessary. He was also alleged to have lived a double life as a London upholsterer named Thomas Druce. He never married. He lived at Harcourt House, Cavendish Square, Middlesex and at Welbeck Abbey, Nottinghamshire.

21. John Remington Mills (1798-1879) – left £1,300,000. A silk manufacturer in the City of London.

From a very obscure but enormously wealthy family of silk manufacturers at Milk Street, Cheapside,

City of London. His father Samuel Mills (1769-1841, *q.v.*) left £500,000. Our man was engaged as a silk manufacturer for most of his career, although almost nothing is known of his business life. A Congregationalist, he served as a Liberal M.P. from 1862-68. His son Joseph Trueman Mills (1836-1924) left no less than £4.1 million. Our man lived at Kingswood Lodge, Tunbridge Wells, Kent.

22. Robert Thompson Crawshay (1817-79) – left £1,200,000. An ironmaster in South Wales.
Known as the "Iron King of Wales," after the death of his brother Richard Crawshay (d. 1859) he became head of the famous firm, located at Cyfarthfa near Merthyr Tydfil. Our man was the son of William Crawshay (1788-1867), who left £2 million. He lived at Cyfarthfa Castle near Merthyr Tydfil and at Caversham Park in Oxfordshire.

23. Don Gregorio De Mier y Feran (1796-1869 – estate probate in the UK in 1870) – left £500,000. Banker in Mexico.
Known as "the Mexican Rothschild," Mier y Feran was a banker in Mexico City who dealt largely in personal loans. He left $6.3 million in Mexico. He died in Mexico City, and was the great-grandfather of Prince Rainier of Monaco.

24. John Brocklehurst (1788-1870) – left £800,000. Silk manufacturer and banker in Macclesfield, Cheshire.
The son of John Brocklehurst (1754-1839), a silk manufacturer in Macclesfield who left £80,000, he was in partnership with two brothers as silk manufacturers there, and was also a banker. He served as a Liberal M.P. from 1832 until 1868, and lived at Hurdsfield House in Macclesfield.

25. Thomas Brocklehurst (1791-1870) – left £600,000. Silk manufacturer and banker in Macclesfield, Cheshire.
The brother of the previous half-millionaire, he was also a silk manufacturer and banker in Macclesfield. He lived at The Fence in that town. A third brother, Henry Brocklehurst (1819-70), who left £120,000, also died in 1870.

26. Robert Rankin (1801-70) – left £500,000. Shipowner and timber merchant in Liverpool.
Born in Mearns, Renfrewshire, he was employed as a cashier in Liverpool, and then went to Newfoundland, where he started a successful timber exporting firm. He returned to Liverpool, where he became head of Rankin, Gilmour & Co., one of the city's largest shipping firms. He lived at Bromborough Hall, Cheshire.

27. Thomas Thornton (1806-70) – left £900,000. An East India merchant in the City of London.
He inherited a fortune from his uncle, the multi-millionaire Richard Thornton (1776-1865, *q.v.*) and was an East India merchant at 61 Moorgate, City of London. His firm, although successful, was wound up after his death and the death of his nephew in the same year. He lived at Brixton Rise, Surrey.

28. William Thornton West (1810-70) – left £600,000. An East India merchant in the City of London.

The nephew of the previous man, he was the son of William Ogle West (1781-1853), an East India merchant who left £120,000, and was involved with his uncle's firm, Thornton & West. He was also engaged in the Baltic trade and in insurance. He lived at Clapham Park, Surrey.

29. George Baird (1810-79) – left £18,458. Ironmaster and colliery owner in Lanarkshire.

Another of the wealthy Baird brothers, who were among the wealthiest industrialists in Scotland. He was also a significant landowner, and lived at Strichen, Aberdeenshire. His son George Alexander Baird (1862-93) was a professional jockey who died in a fistfight in New Orleans, leaving over £500,000.

30. Robert Seymour-Conway, 4th Marquess of Hertford (1800-70) – left £500,000. Landowner.

In 1883 his successor owned 12,239 acres worth £18,392 p.a. in England and Ireland, while the bulk of our man's estate went to his illegitimate son Sir Richard Wallace, Bt. (see the previous section), who owned 72,307 acres worth £85,737 p.a. Our man was the son of Francis, 3rd Marquess of Hertford (1777-1842), and was educated at Exeter College, Oxford. He lived mainly in Paris, and had residences at Ragley Hall, Warwickshire and at Hertford House (now the home of the Wallace Collection) in Manchester Square, Middlesex.

31. Lord William Cavendish Scott Bentinck (1804-70) – left £600,000. Landed family.

The fourth son of the enormously wealthy William, 4th Duke of Portland (1728-1854), who left £980,000 and 183,199 acres of land (see previous section), he was educated at Christ Church, Oxford, and served as a Tory M.P. from 1846 till 1857. His brother was Lord George Bentinck, the ally of Disraeli. How a fourth son became so wealthy is unclear. He lived at Tathwell near Louth, Lincolnshire.

32. Beaumont Hotham, 3rd Baron Hotham (1794-1870) – left £500,000. Landowner.

The grandson and successor of Beaumont, 2nd Baron Hotham (1757-1814), he was educated at Westminster School and at Sandhurst, and was a professional army officer, retiring in 1865 as a general. He also owned 20,352 acres of land worth £19,487 p.a. in Yorkshire. He lived at South Dalton Hall, Yorkshire, and at 46 Grosvenor Street, Middlesex.

33. James Lees (1794-1871) – left £500,000. Cotton manufacturer in Oldham, Lancashire.

The son of John Lees (1759-1828), a cotton manufacturer in Oldham who left £20,000, he developed the business into one of the largest in Britain, and served as Mayor of Oldham in 1852-54. His son Thomas Evans Lees (1829-79) left £600,000. Our man lived at Green Bank, Oldham.

34. John Shaw Leigh (1791-1871) – left £800,000. Solicitor and property developer in Liverpool.

The son of a solicitor in Liverpool, John Shaw Leigh (1752-1823), who left £25,000, our man was educated at Rugby and became a wealthy solicitor and a member of Liverpool's civic elite, serving as Mayor of Liverpool in 1841-2. He was also a property developer and a partner in Allsopp's Brewery. He lived at Luton Hoo Park near Luton, Bedfordshire, where he owned land.

35. Leo Schuster (1791-1871) – left £500,000. Export merchant and merchant banker in the City of London.

Born in Frankfurt, Germany, Leo Schuster emigrated to England around 1808 and founded his firm, Leo Schuster, Brothers & Co., of 90 Cannon Street, City of London around 1820. It mainly exported goods to Germany and other parts of Europe, and had branches in Manchester and elsewhere. He was also a merchant banker. He was originally Jewish, but became a Unitarian; several of his descendants were Anglican clergymen. His grandson Sir Claude Schuster (1869-1956, left £24,897) was created 1st Baron Schuster in 1944. Another descendant was Sir Stephen Spender (1909-95), the poet. Our man lived at 11 Upper Belgrave Street, Middlesex.

36. Benjamin Bacon Williams (1796-1870) – left £600,000. Stockbroker in the City of London.

A wealthy stockbroker at Crown Court, City of London for many years, his background and career are somewhat obscure. He was born in Old Street, Finsbury, the son of William Williams (1767-1833), a merchant and Freeman of the City of London, and lived at Buscot Park, Berkshire and at Maida Hill, Middlesex. In 1817 he was made a Freeman of the City of London, when he was described as a "merchant" of Finsbury Square.

37. (Revd.) James Williams (1813-71) – left £500,000. Inherited silk manufacturing wealth in Norwich and London?

Apparently the illegitimate son of William Grout (1776-1832), a manufacturer of silk mourning gauze of Norwich and London, and a partner in the East London Waterworks Co. and in coal mines. Our man was educated at Christ's College, Cambridge. His mother was probably his father's servant girl, Sarah Williams. He lived at Tring Park, Hertforshire (later owned by the Rothschilds) and at Glevering Hill, Suffolk. Much about his life and career is obscure.

38. William Russell, 8th Duke of Bedford (1809-72) – left £600,000. Land and urban property owner.

The only son of Francis Russell, 7th Duke of Bedford (1788-1861, left £600,000, *q.v.*), he was educated at Eton and at Christ Church, Oxford, and served as a Whig M.P. from 1830 until 1841. He was the owner of a vast amount of rural land (see previous section), and of 248 acres in central London, especially in the Bloomsbury area. Unmarried, he was succeeded by his cousin. He lived at 6 Belgrave Square, Middlesex and at Woburn Abbey, Bedfordshire.

39. Santiago Drake del Castillo (1805-71) – left £600,000. Owner of plantations in Cuba and vineyards in France.

The son of William Drake y Spence (*sic*, 1763-1838), the owner of sugar plantations in Cuba, apparently of English descent, our man also owned vineyards in France. There is no evidence that he ever lived in Britain; presumably he left vast amounts in British banks because they were totally safe, as did other wealthy men in insecure countries.

40. Thomas Dent (1796-1872) – left £500,000. China merchant in Canton and then in the City of London.

The son of a small farmer in Westmorland, Dent spent three terms as Christ's College, Cambridge, and then went to Canton and became a merchant there. In Canton, he became the Sardinian Consul, which enabled him to bypass the monopoly on trade held by the East India Company. He returned to England in c. 1835 and founded Dent Palmer & Co. of 1 King's Arms Yard, Coleman Street in the City of London, one of the most important firms trading with China. He lived at 12 Hyde Park Gardens, Middlesex.

41. William Lowther, 2nd Earl of Lonsdale (1787-1872) – left £700,000. Landowner.
The son of William Lowther, 1st Earl of Lonsdale (1757-1844), who left £200,000 in personalty, he was educated at Harrow and at Trinity College, Cambridge, and served as a Tory M.P. from 1809 until 1841, when he was given a peerage in his father's lifetime and sat in the Lords. He served in three Cabinets. In 1883 his successor owned 68,065 acres worth £71,373 p.a. He lived at Lowther Castle, Westmorland and at 15 Carlton House Terrace, Middlesex.

42. Sir Charles Mills, 1st Bt. (1782-1872) – left £600,000. Banker in the City of London.
The son of a banker and M.P., he was educated at Winchester and then became a partner and later Senior Partner in Glyn Mills & Co., of Lombard Street in the City of London, a major private bank that was heavily involved in railway finance. His son Sir Charles Mills, 2nd Bt. (1830-98), who left £1.5 million, was created 1st Baron Hillingdon in 1886. Our man lived at Hillingdon Court, Uxbridge and at Camelford House, Park Lane, Middlesex.

43. Gurney Pease (1839-72) – left £500,000. Colliery owner and ironmaster, etc. in Darlington.
The son of the wealthy Quaker woollen manufacturer Joseph Pease (1799-1872), who died in the same year as our man and left £350,000, Gurney Pease branched out to coalmining and the iron industry as well as woollen manufacturing before dying at only thirty-three. He was also a Quaker and taught in a Quaker Sunday school. He lived at Walworth Castle, Co. Durham.

44. John Platt (1817-72) – left £800,000. Textile machinery manufacturer in Oldham.
The son of a small woollen manufacturer in Oldham, Lancashire, John Platt expanded the business so that it (Hibbert & Platt) became one of the largest in the world and employed sixty per cent of the workforce in that town. He served as a Liberal M.P. from 1865 until his death and was twice Mayor of Oldham. He lived at Werneth Park, Oldham and in Caernarvonshire.

45. Edward Walker (1803-72) – left £500,000. A solicitor in Lincoln's Inn, Middlesex.
A very wealthy London solicitor who practiced at 8 New Square in Lincoln's Inn. He was born in Chesterfield, Derbyshire, but little information could be learned about his background or career, or how he became so wealthy. He lived at 71 Oxford Terrace, Hyde Park, Middlesex.

46. Solomon Levi Behrens (1788-1873) – left £700,000. Cotton merchant in Manchester.
Born in Waldeck, Germany, the son of Louis Behrens, a textile importer there. he came to England in 1814 and became a cotton merchant in Manchester (Louis Behrens & Sons), with offices in Bradford and Leeds. He was a prominent member of the Jewish community of Manchester. He lived at Alderley Edge, Cheshire.

47. George Crawshay (1794-1873) – left £500,000. Ironmaster in south Wales and iron merchant in London.

The third son of the wealthy ironmaster William Crawshay (1764-1834, left £700,00, *q.v.*), ironmaster of Cyfathfa, our man was chiefly an iron merchant in London, although his business address is unclear. He lived at the Manor House, Colney Hatch, Middlesex.

48. John Robinson McClean (1813-73) – left £600,000. Civil engineer at Great George Street, Westminster.

Born in Belfast, the son of a hardware merchant, J.R. McClean was educated at the Royal Belfast Academical Institution and at Glasgow University. He became a prominent civil engineer who constructed Dover Harbour and was President of the Institution of Civil Engineers in 1864-65. His offices were at Great George Street, Westminster. He was also the sole owner of the South Staffordshire Railway Co., the only British railway to be owned by one man. He lived at 2 Park Street, Westminster.

49. Samuel Moses Samuel (1773-1873) – left £500,000. A Brazil merchant and financier in the City of London.

The son of Moses Samuel (1742-1839), a merchant in London, he became a Brazil merchant in the City of London with his brother, who was created a Baron of Brazil when it was a monarchy. He presumably provided finance to the Brazilian government, as well as engaging in mercantile activities. Although he married a relative of the Rothschilds and was related to many prominent British Jews, very little is known about his career. He lived at 29 Park Crescent, Regent's Park, Middlesex.

50. Benjamin Attwood (1794-1874) – left £600,000. Glass manufacturer in Birmingham.

The son of Matthias Attwood (d. 1836, left £120,000), a wealthy ironmaster and banker in Birmingham, Benjamin Attwood became a glass manufacturer and merchant in Birmingham. Four of his close relatives became M.P.s, including his brother Thomas Attwood (1783-1856), also a well-known theorist of currency. In later life our man lived at Pengelly House, Cheshunt, Hertfordshire.

51. Sampson Copestake (1801-74) – left £600,000. Lace manufacturer and merchant in the City of London.

Born in Nottinghamshire, Copestake's career is rather obscure. He became an extremely successful lace manufacturer and merchant at 5 Bow Churchyard in the City of London. His business partner George Moore (1806-76, left £500,000) was the subject of a biographical essay in Samuel Smiles's *Self-Help*. Our man lived at The Grove, Highbury Road, Middlesex.

52. Joseph Godman (1791-1874) – left £800,000. A brewing fortune in Southwark and a landowner.

Joseph Godman was the son of another Joseph Godman (1763-1840, left £250,000), a partner in Whitbread's Brewery in Southwark and a landowner in Sussex. Our man was educated at Eton. It is unclear if he was active in trade, but in any case he managed to triple the large fortune left by his father. He lived at Park Heath near Godalming, Surrey.

53. William Joynson (1802-74) – left £500,000. Paper manufacturer at St. Mary Cray, Sidcup, Kent.

He began as a journeyman in a paper-mill and worked his way up, taking over the paper-mills of Thomas Barnet in 1828. He introduced many innovations into the industry, such as the printing of watermarks by machine, and was known as the most successful paper manufacturer of his day. He lived at The Rookery near Orpington, Kent.

54. Richard Ovey (1789-1874) – left £500,000. Inherited from a furniture printer in Covent Garden, Middlesex.

The son of Richard Ovey (1756-1834, left £250,000), a furniture printer at 22 Tavistock Street, Covent Garden, whose firm apparently sold high-class furniture to the rich, printed with artistic designs. Our man was apparently a member of the "idle rich," and "did nothing all his life," according to one source. He lived at Henley-on-Thames, Oxfordshire and at 4 Avenue Road, Regent's Park, Middlesex.

55. (Revd.) Richard Thomas Pulteney (1811-74) – left £500,000. Inherited from a landed aristocrat.

Pulteney inherited an alleged £600,000 from his aunt, Henrietta, Countess of Bath (1766-1808), who was created Countess of Bath in her own right and was said to have been the richest spinster in Europe. He was educated at Trinity College, Oxford. Despite his wealth and elite status, he only served as Rector of Ashley, Northamptonshire rather than in a more senior clerical post. He appears to have made no mark on wider society. Pulteney lived at Ashley near Market Harborough, Northamptonshire.

56. Wynne Ellis (1790-1875) – left £500,000. Wholesale silk merchant in the City of London.

Born in Northamptonshire, Wynn Ellis established a haberdashery business at Ludgate in the City of London in 1812, which grew into the largest silk retailer in London. It then evolved from a retailer to a wholesaler in the silk trade. Ellis served as an "advanced Liberal" M.P. between 1831 and 1847, and was a noted art collector, leaving 402 paintings to the National Gallery. He lived at Whitstable in Kent and at 30 Cadogan Place, Middlesex.

57. John Fletcher (1798-1875) – left £800,000. Merchant in Peru and Liverpool.

Born in Elgin, Scotland, the son of William Jack (1767-1829), a nailmaker, he later changed his name to "Fletcher," for unknown reasons. He went with his brother James to Peru, where he made a fortune as a merchant, and then returned to Liverpool before 1841, where the brothers became very wealthy as commission merchants. His brother James Fletcher (1807-85) left £1.4 million. In later life our man lived at Dale Park, Sussex and at 88 Eaton Place, Middlesex.

58. William Gibbs (1790-1875) – left £800,000. Merchant in Peru and in the City of London.

The son of Anthony Gibbs (1756-1815), a merchant in Exeter and in Spain, our man became a merchant in Spain and then went to Peru, where he became very wealthy as an exporter of guano – bird droppings used as fertilizer. He was later a South American merchant at Bishopsgate in the City of London. It is unclear if he had any connection with the previous man, also a wealthy merchant in Peru. Gibbs's firm later became a leading merchant bank. His grandson, nephew, and great-nephew were all given peerages, as Barons Wraxall, Aldenham, and Hunsdon. He lived at 46 Hyde Park Gardens, Middlesex and at Tyntesfield near Bristol. The house there is now a National Trust property.

59. John Hargreaves (c. 1800-74) – left £600,000. Apparently a locomotive and pump manufacturer in Bolton, Lancashire.

The identity of this man has proved unusually difficult to pin down. He was probably the son of John Hargreaves (c. 1779-1860, left £400,000), a "common carrier" of Westhoughton, Lancashire, who then founded an engineering firm at the Soho Ironworks near Bolton, Lancashire; this man was also a colliery owner. His identification is, however, uncertain, because of the number of successful businessmen of the time named John Hargreaves, one of whom was a cotton manufacturer and another a "common carrier," both in Lancashire. Our man lived at Silwood Park, Sunninghill, Berkshire.

60. Henry Blundell Leigh (1823-75) – left £500,000. Inherited from a Liverpool solicitor and property developer.

The son of John Shaw Leigh (1791-1871, left £900,000, *q.v.*), a wealthy Liverpool solicitor and property developer. He was an army officer in early life, and managed to keep the wealth he inherited intact without being active in trade. Leigh lived at Amington Hall near Tamworth, Warwickshire. He was the younger brother of the next man.

61. John Gerard Leigh (1821-75) – left £700,000.

The elder brother of the preceding wealth holder, and even richer, John Gerard Leigh was educated at Eton and at Lincoln College, Oxford. Like his brother, he does not appear to have been active in any trade or profession, and did not live in or near Liverpool. He had residences at Luton Hoo near Bedford and at 138 Piccadilly, Middlesex.

62. Thomas Clement Mundey (c. 1811-75) – left £500,000. A stockbroker in the City of London.

The son of a grocer, George Mundey, our man was born in Guernsey in the Channel Islands. He was admitted to the Stock Exchange in 1846 and thus made a great fortune in less than thirty years; his office was at 13 Angel Court in the City of London. Mundey was also the Chairman of the Van Lead Mines in Ceredigion. He lived at Upper Tooting in Surrey.

63. Peter Ormrod (1795-1875) – left £700,000. A banker and cotton spinner at Bolton, Lancashire.

The son of James Ormrod (d. 1825), a banker in Rochdale, our man was both a banker (Hardcastle, Cross & Co.) and also a cotton spinner (Ormrod & Hardcastle) in Bolton. He was also a significant landowner, owning 5,290 acres worth £7,196 p.a. in Lancashire. He had residences at Halliwell Hall and at Wyersdale Park in Lancashire.

64. Charles Turner (1803-75) – left £500,000. East India merchant and shipowner in Liverpool.

The son of a merchant in Hull, Charles Turner became Chairman of the Pacific Steam Navigation

Co., a director of the Bank of Liverpool, and Chairman of the East India China Association. He served as a Conservative M.P. from 1852 until his death. At the 1868 general election, he managed to defeat William E. Gladstone, who promptly found another seat and became Prime Minister. Our man's widow Anne (1819-1902) left £619,999. Turner lived at Toxteth Park, Liverpool.

65. Anthony Radford Strutt (1791-1875) – left £900,000. Cotton manufacturer at Belper, Derbyshire.

A member of the wealthy Strutt cotton manufacturing family of Belper, he was the son of George Benson Strutt (1796-1841, left £180,000). Our man's brother Edward Strutt (1801-80) was created 1st Baron Belper in 1854, the first active industrialist to receive a peerage. Our man was a Unitarian and a distant relative of Joseph Chamberlain. He lived at Makeney, Derbyshire.

66. William Tarn (1817-75) – left £500,000. Retailer in Southwark.

The son of a farmer, William Tarn opened a drapery shop at Newington Causeway, Southwark, Surrey, which evolved into an early department store, selling a variety of upholstery goods and furniture. His shop was located at Elephant and Castle, and continued to do business until the Second World War. He lived at Chislehurst, Kent.

67. Francis Conyngham, 2nd Marquess Conyngham (1797-1876) – left £500,000. Landowner.

A large landowner in Kent and Ireland (166,710 acres worth £50,076 p.a. in 1883), and a General in the British Army, he was the son of Henry, 1st Marquess Conyngham (1766-1832) and was educated at Eton. He was a Tory M.P. from 1818 until 1832, and then sat in the Lords. He served as Postmaster-General in 1834-5. He also held the post of Lord Chamberlain and, in 1837, he had the duty of informing the Princess Victoria that she was now Queen; he was the first person to address her as "Your Majesty." He lived at Hamilton Place, Middlesex, and at Slane castle, Co. Meath, Ireland.

68. William Perry-Herrick (1794-1876) – left £800,000. Landowner.

Although he was a large-scale landowner who owned 13,747 acres worth £22,325 p.a. in Leicestershire and in Wales, how William Perry-Herrick became so wealthy is unclear. He was educated at Rugby and at University College, Oxford, and was a barrister of Gray's Inn. He lived at Beau Manor Hall near Loughborough, which was used during World War II as "Station Y," where German messages were decrypted and then sent by messenger to Bletchley Park.

69. Charles Lambert (1793-1876) – left £900,000. Copper merchant and copper smelter in the City of London.

Born in Bavaria, the son of a member of the minor French nobility, Charles Lambert went to Peru (as did a number of other wealth holders noted here) and made a fortune there in copper. He then became a copper merchant and copper smelter at Upper Thames Street in the City of London. He also owned property in Chile. He lived at Folkestone, Kent in later life.

70. Charles McGarel (c. 1788-1876) – left £500,000. West India merchant in the City of London and in British Guiana.

The son of a cobbler in Co. Antrim, Ireland, Charles McGarel went at sixteen with his brothers to British Guiana and became a leading merchant and the owner of slave plantations. He returned to London around 1818 and became head of Hall McGarel, West India merchants of 7 Austin Friars, City of London. His wife's brother Sir James Mcgarel-Hogg (1823-90) was created 1st Baron Margheramorne (*sic*) in 1887. Our man lived at 2 Belgrave Square, Middlesex and at Margheramorne, Co. Antrim.

71. George Moore (1806-76) – left £500,000. Lace manufacturer and merchant in the City of London.

The partner of Sampson Copestake (d. 1874, *q.v.*) as a lace manufacturer and merchant at Bow Churchyard in the City of London, George Moore was the son of a small farmer in Cumberland. He was very famous in his day as a "self-made man," and was the subject of a biography by Samuel Smiles. His firm was a wholesale silk merchants business, with a factory at Nottingham. He lived at 14 Kensington Palace Gardens, Middlesex and at Whitehall, Cumberland.

72. Henry Moses (1790-1875) – left £600,000. Woollen merchant and wholesale clothier in the City of London.

Remarkably little is known about the career of Henry Moses, who appears to have been chiefly a wool importer, bringing in wool from Australia and New Zealand, with his office at 14 Cannon Street, St. Paul's, City of London. He was probably also a wholesale clothier. A member of the Anglo-Jewish elite, his six sons and seven daughters later changed their surname to "Beddington." His son Maurice Beddington (d.1898) left £1,030,574. Henry Moses lived at 2 Park Square West, Regent's Park, Middlesex, and in Brighton.

73. Edward Tew (1795-1876) – left £600,000. Banker at Wakefield and Pontefract, Yorkshire.

The son of a banker at Pontefract, Edward Tew expanded the bank, Latham, Tew & Co., with a branch at Wakefield and became very wealthy. It is rather surprising that a banker in two medium-sized towns should have left so much, and he may well have had other interests. He lived at Crofton Hall near Wakefield, West Riding, Yorkshire.

74. George Smith (1803-76) – left £599,130. A shipowner in Glasgow.

The Senior Partner in George Smith & Sons, shipowners of Glasgow and also the Senior Partner in the City Lines, he was the son of George Smith (1777-1867), a draper and later a shipowner. Our man also began as a draper and became a shipowner with father and brother around 1840. Their firm specialised in shipping to India. He lived in Glasgow.

75. William Matthew Coulthurst (1793-1877) – left £600,000. Banker in the Strand, Middlesex.

The Senior Partner of Coutts & Co., the famous private bank at 59 The Strand, he also profited from investing in the growing London suburb of Surbiton. His father, John Coulthurst (1759-1816), was educated at Eton and Cambridge. Our man was educated at Eton, and was a favourite of Baroness Burdett-Coutts, the friend of Charles Dickens. She inherited the bank from her father Thomas Coutts. He lived at Streatham Lodge, Streatham, Surrey.

76. Raphael de Galliera, Duc de Ferrari (1803-76) – left £500,000. A resident of Genoa, Italy

who spent much of his life in Paris, the Duke was the son of a banker.
He began life as a commoner and was made a Duke by the Pope. He was important in the development of French railways, and is said to have left £8 million in France and Italy. Why he left £500,000 in England is unclear.

77. Nathaniel Caine (1808-77) – left £500,000. An iron merchant in Liverpool.

The son of a merchant tailor in Liverpool, Nathaniel Caine became an iron merchant with the firm of Caine & Fallows of 12 Dutton Street, Liverpool. He was also active in the Hallbarrow Mining Co. of Cumberland. Little is known about the details of his career. His son William Sprotson Caine (1842-1903, left £2501) served as an M.P. between 1880 and 1889. Our man lived in Liverpool and in Broughton-in-Furness, Lancashire.

78. Baron Charles Joachim Hambro (1807-77) – left £500,000. Merchant banker in the City of London.

Born in Copenhagen, the son of Baron Joseph Hambro (1780-1848), later a merchant banker in London, who left £300,000, our man moved from Denmark to London in 1832, and became a leading merchant banker at 76 Old Broad Street, City of London. His ancestors were Jewish, but he was baptised as a Lutheran and later as an Anglican. His country house, Milton Abbey, Dorset, was restored by George Gilbert Scott in 1862.

79. John Leschallas (1791-1877) – left £500,000. A builder in Spitalfields, Middlesex.

A little-known speculative builder, whose office was at 10 Bootle Street, Spitalfields, he was the son of John Leschallas (1758-1833), a painter and glazier in Spitalfields. Little is known of his career. He apparently inherited money from his brother William Lewis Leschallas (d. 1853), who left £140,000, a wholesale stationer in the City of London, who committed suicide under the impression that he was going bankrupt.

80. William Peckover (1790-1877) – left £700,000. A banker in Wisbech, Cambridgeshire.

The son of Jonathan Peckover (1754-1833), a banker in Wisbech, Cambridgeshire, and from a prominent and wealthy Quaker family, he was also a wealthy banker in Wisbech, and involved in the economic development of East Anglia. His brother Algernon (d. 1893) left £1.2 million; Algernon's son, also Algernon Peckover (1830-1919, left £901,602) was made 1st Baron Peckover in 1907, the first professing Quaker to be given a peerage.

81. James Merry (1805-77) – left £680,402. A colliery owner and ironmaster, chiefly in Lanarkshire.

A "coal and ironmaster" (1851 Census) with Merry & Cunninghame, whose offices were in Glasgow. Educated at Glasgow University, he was a partner with his brother-in-law Alexander Cunninghame (1804-66, *q.v.*) in mines and works in Lanarkshire and Ayrshire. Merry served briefly as a Liberal M.P. in 1857, and was also known for his string of racehorses, two of which won the Derby. Merry lived in Glasgow and at 68 Eaton Square, Middlesex.

82. Henry William Ferdinand Bolckow (1806-78) – left £800,000. Ironmaster at Middlesebrough, Yorkshire.

The Chairman of Bolckow & Vaughan, large-scale iron and steel manufacturers of Middlesbrough, Bolckow was born in Mecklenburg, Germany, the son of a landowner. He came to Newcastle-upon-Tyne in 1827 and built up an industrial empire from scratch. He served as Liberal M.P. for Middlesbrough from 1868 until his death, and was the first Mayor of that town in 1868-9, despite his German birth. He lived at Marton Hall in Middlesbrough and at 37 Prince's Gate, Middlesex.

83. Richard Durant (1791-1878) – left £600,000. A silk broker in the City of London.

The son of a "fuller" in Exeter, he inherited from his uncle Enosh (*sic*) Durant (1768-1849, left £120,000), a silk broker in London, and built up his firm, Durant & Co., major silk brokers at Copthall Court in the City of London. His nephew founded Strutt & Parker, one of the now leading national estate agents. Our man lived at 24 Park Crescent, Middlesex and at Sharpham, Devon.

84. James Johnstone (1815-78) – left £500,000. Newspaper proprietor in Fleet Street, City of London.

The son of a Messenger of the Court of bankruptcy who left £5,000, he became an accountant in the City of London and, from 1857, an early press baron, owning *The Standard* and the *Morning Herald* newspapers. In 1860 he founded the *Evening Standard,* which still exists. He was a loyal Tory, like many future press lords. Johnstone lived at Hooley House, Coulsdon, Surrey.

85. James Martin (1807-78) – left £500,000. Banker in the City of London.

A partner in Martin's Bank at 68 Lombard Street, City of London, he was the son of John Martin (1774-1832), senior partner in the bank and a Whig M.P. in 1812-32 who left £90,000. Our man was educated at Charterhouse School and was a Liberal M.P. in 1859-65. He lived at Camden House, Chislehurst, Kent.

86. George Wilson (c. 1802-78) – left £500,000. A snuff manufacturer in Sheffield, Yorkshire.

George Wilson inherited a family snuff making firm founded in 1737 which became the largest in Britain. It continued until the 1930s, when it was absorbed by Imperial Tobacco. Wilson was also a heavy investor in shares and a director of the North Midlands Railway. He lived at Tapton Hall, Sheffield.

87. George Frederick Lambton, 2nd Earl of Durham (1828-79) – left £500,000. Land and colliery owner.

The son of George Lambton, 1st Ear of Durham (1792-1840, *q.v.*), and a great landowner in Co. Durham and Northumberland, where he owned lucrative coal mines. Although his father was a major figure in British political and colonial life, our man made little political impact before his death at only fifty-one. He lived at 39 Hill Street, Berkeley Square, Middlesex and at Lambton Castle, Co. Durham.

88. Henry Gardner (1798-1879) – left £600,000. A brewer in Clerkenwell, Middlesex.

An extremely wealthy brewer at 30 St. John's Street, Clerkenwell, Middlesex in partnership with his two brothers; little could be traced about their careers. His brother William Gardner (d. 1863) left £200,000. Our man lived at 1 Westbourne Terrace, Middlesex.

89. Count Urbain Alexandre Greffulhe (d. 1879) – left £500,000. Merchant banker in Paris, France.

The nephew of Jean Greffulhe (d. 1867, left £500,000, *q.v.*), who was a merchant banker in the City of London. His brother Count Charles Greffulhe (d. 1888) left £661,676 in England. Our man lived in Paris and does not appear to have been in business in Britain.

90. Kirkman Daniel Hodgson (1814-79) – left £500,000. East India merchant and merchant banker in the City of London.

The son of John Hodgson (c. 1779-1858, left £500,000), a merchant in the City of London, he was educated at the Charterhouse School and became a partner in Hodgson & Co., chiefly East India merchants in the City. He then became a partner in Baring Brothers, the great merchant bank at 8 Bishopsgate Within in the City of London. He served as a Liberal M.P. in 1857-8 and 1870-78. Hodgson lived at 67 Brook Street, Mayfair and at Ashgrove, Sevenoaks, Kent.

91. Lionel Lawson (1822-79) – left £900,000. Printing ink manufacturer in London and a newspaper proprietor at Fleet Street, City of London.

Born Lionel Levy, the son of Moses Lionel Levy (1765-1830, left £100,000), a "money broker and agent" in the City of London, he established a successful printing ink manufacturing firm, first in France and then in London, and later became part owner of the *Daily Telegraph* newspaper, which of course still exists. His son Sir Edward Levy Lawson (1833-1916, left £267,878) was created 1st Baron Burnham in 1913. Our man lived at 2 Brook Street, Hanover Square, Middlesex.

92. Thomas Evans Lees (1829-79) – left £600,000. Cotton manufacturer in Oldham, Lancashire.

From a very successful family of cotton manufacturers there, the son of James Lees (1794-1871, *q.v.*), who left £500,000. His firm had 150,000 cotton spindles in operation when he died. Unlike many cotton manufacturers, he was a "staunch" Anglican, a keen Tory, and a Lieutenant-Colonel in the Volunteers. He lived at Woodfield, Werneth, Oldham.

93. Thomas Southey (1799-1879) – left £500,000. A wool broker in the City of London.

The son of Thomas Southey (1768-1854), also a wool broker in the City of London, our man headed the family firm at 23 Coleman Street, City of London. His career is rather obscure. He may have had Australian connections, although these could not be traced. His son-in-law was the father of Maurice Hankey, 1st Baron Hankey (1877-1963), the famous British Cabinet Secretary and "man of secrets," whose father was a pastoralist in South Australia. Our man lived at Balmore House, Caversham, Oxfordshire.

94. Edward Joicey (1824-79) – left £700,000. Colliery owner in Cos. Durham and Northumberland.

One of three brothers who became leading colliery owners on Tyneside, he was the son of George Joicey (1780-1848), a colliery agent there. Our man's brother John (d. 1881) left £710,495; our man's nephew Sir James Joicey (1846-1936) was created 1st Baron Joicey in 1906, and left £1,519,718. Our man lived at Whinney House near Gateshead, Co. Durham and at Blenkinsopp Hall, Northumberland.

95. James Hatton (1795-1879) – left £700,000. Iron merchant in Manchester.

Little is known about his life or career, or how he became so wealthy. He was an iron merchant a t 9 Blackfriars Street, Manchester, which employed 85 people in 1861. His firm also manufactured cast iron girders. He was also a director of the Lancashire and Yorkshire Railway and of a local bank. He lived at Richmond House, Higher Broughton near Manchester.

96. Alexander Whitelaw (1823-79) – left £692,307. Ironmaster and colliery owner in Lanarkshire.

A cousin of the very wealthy Baird family of ironmasters and colliery owners, he became Chairman of William Baird & Co., the largest Scottish iron and coal company. Whitelaw became a Tory M.P. from 1874 until his death, and was the great-grandfather of William Whitelaw, 1st Viscount Whitelaw (1919-99), the prominent Conservative politician serving in Cabinet under Edward Heath and Margaret Thatcher. Our man lived at Gartshorne House, Dumbartonshire and at 91 Eaton Square, Middlesex.

1880–1889

The 1880s were a time when the number of great fortunes grew rapidly, although Britain was being challenged by new and rising powers. The Liberal party split in 1886 over the issue of Irish Home Rule, with many conservative Liberals breaking away to form the Liberal Unionist party, which became an ally of the Tories and helped to keep them in power for most of the time until 1905.

1. John Michael Williams (1813-80) – left £1,503,527. Copper smelter in Cornwall and Swansea.

The largest copper smelter in Britain, he was the son of Michael Williams (1785-1858, left £500,000, *q.v.*), a leading copper smelter and banker and an M.P. from 1853 until his death. His firm (Williams, Foster & Co.) was established as early as 1715 by an ancestor. Our man added the Morfa Copper Smelting Works to the firm and served as its Chairman. A Methodist, he was known – probably correctly – as "the richest man in Cornwall," and was also Chairman of the Cornwall Railway Co. He purchased Caerhays Castle near St. Austell, and lived there and at Scorrier House, Cornwall.

2. Thomas Wrigley (1808-80) – left £1,300,000. A paper and cotton manufacturer in Bury, Lancashire.

The son of James Wrigley, a paper manufacturer in Bury, our man inherited the firm when his father died in 1847, and greatly expanded it to become the largest producer of paper in the north of England. He also became a cotton manufacturer and an insurance broker. Baptised as a Congregationalist, he lived at Timberhurst near Bury, where he amassed a valuable art collection, which, after his death, was used to form the Bury Art Museum.

3. Edward Mackenzie (1811-80) – left £1,000,000. Civil engineering and railway contractor.

The son of Alexander Mackenzie (d. 1836), a Scottish-born civil engineer who built canals,

Edward Mackenzie became a partner with his brother William (1794-1858, left £383,500) as major engineering contractors, often in partnership with Thomas Brassey (*q.v.*). Our man was in particular known for building many early railways, both in Britain and in France, where he built the Paris-Rouen line. In Britain he built the important Liverpool & Manchester Railway in 1832-5. He purchased Fawley Court near Henley-on-Thames, Buckinghamshire in 1853, and retired there soon after.

4. Andrew Jardine (1812-81) – left £1,370,977. East India merchant in Hong Kong.

One of the founders of the famous firm of Jardine Matheson, which became one of the largest mercantile houses trading with China and the Far East, Andrew Jardine was the son of a farmer in Dumfriesshire. His firm had been founded by his uncle around 1845. Our man went with his three brothers to the newly-acquired colony of Hong Kong, where they became very wealthy by dealing in tea and other commodities and also, notoriously, in opium. His brother Sir Robert Jardine, 1st. Bt. (1825-1905) was a Liberal M.P. who left £1,114,489. On returning to Britain, Andrew Jardine lived at Lanrick Castle near Stirling.

5. Francis Wise (1797-1881) – left £1,000,095. Distiller in Cork, Ireland.

The proprietor of the North Mall Distillery in Cork and a landowner in Counties Cork and Kerry, Francis Wise apparently inherited from his uncle Francis Wise (1766-1842). Little is known of his career. A Protestant, he left much of his wealth to his nephew Francis Gubbins. Wise lived at Buxton House, Cork and at Anngrove, Co. Cork.

6. Samuel Jones Loyd, 1st Baron Overstone (1796-1883) – left £2,118,804. Banker in the City of London.

One of the wealthiest men in Britain, Lord Overstone was the son of Lewis Loyd (d. 1858), an Anglican clergyman turned banker, who left £800,000. He was educated at Eton and Trinity College, Cambridge, and served as an M.P. 1819-26. He then became a banker with Jones Loyd & Co. in the City of London, and head of the firm from 1844. Very influential and expert on banking, he was given a peerage in 1850. In addition to his personalty, he also owned land costing £3 million to purchase (see previous section). He lived at Overstone Park in Northamptonshire and at 22 New Norfolk Street, Middlesex. His son-in-law Robert Loyd-Lindsay (1832-1901, left £21,621) was created 1st Baron Wantage in 1885.

7. George Wythes (1811-83) – left £1,524,788. Railway and public works contractor.

A self-made public-works contractor (Wythes & Jackson) he was chiefly a large-scale international railway contractor, sometimes working with Thomas Brassey (*q.v.*). His firm built the earliest railways in India and railways in Argentina and South Africa, as well as public works in Britain and elsewhere. In later life he lived at Bickley Park, Kent and at Copt Hall, Essex.

8. Robert McCalmont (1808-83) – left £1,383,577. Merchant banker in Mexico and the City of London.

Born in Ulster, the son of Hugh McCalmont (1765-1838), a wealthy slave owner and sugar merchant, he was a partner in the Mexican finance house William Inglis & Co., before moving to London and founding McCalmont Brothers with his brother Hugh. Located at 3 Crown Court,

Philpot Lane, City of London, it financed the export of cotton and then provided for American finance, becoming one of the major, but now little known, merchant banks in the City. He lived at 87 Eaton Square, Middlesex and at Gatton Park, Surrey. His brother Hugh (1809-87) left £3,121,932 (see below). Our man's wife was the sister of Hugh Cairns, 1st Earl Cairns (1819-85), Lord Chancellor under Disraeli.

9. Thomas Coats (1809-83) – left £1,308,735. Sewing thread manufacturer at Paisley, Renfrewshire.

The son of James Coats (1774-1857), the founder of the firm, he became one of the main proprietors of Coats & Clark, the great sewing thread manufacturers of Paisley. At least four of his close relatives left millionaire estates, with his son, George Coats, 1st Baron Glentanar (d. 1918), leaving £4,353,267. He lived in Paisley.

10. Sir James Walker, 1st Bt. (1803-83) – left £1,134,685. Landowner?

The son of James Walker (1753-1829), a landowner, and educated at Rugby and Trinity College, Oxford, his wealth apparently derived from his landowning, although this is not entirely clear. He owned 6909 acres worth £13,982 p.a. in four counties, and was known as a major landowner in Beverley and Hull.

11. Michael Thomas Bass (1799-1884) – left £1,830,292. Brewer in Burton, Staffordshire.

The son of another Michael Thomas Bass (1760-1827) who founded the famous brewery at Burton-on-Trent, he took over the business in 1827 and greatly expanded it, especially its export trade, making it into the largest brewery in the world. Bass served as a Liberal M.P. from 1848 until 1883 and was a noted philanthropist. He declined a peerage, but his son Sir Michael Bass (1837-1909, left £1,000,000). He was an M.P. from 1865 till 1886, when he was created 1st Baron Burton. Michael Bass's partners in the Gretton and Ratcliff families also became very wealthy. He lived at Rangemore House, Burton, Staffordshire.

12. James Watney (1800-84) – left £1,022,081. Brewer in Pimlico, Middlesex.

Another millionaire brewer from a firm which remains a household name, he was the son of Daniel Watney (1771-1837), a brewer, and became a partner in the Stag Brewery in Pimlico in 1837, which became James Watney & Co. in 1858. He lived at Haling Park, Croydon, and at 32 Prince's Gardens, Middlesex. His son James Watney, M.P. (1832-86) left £1,264,611.

13. William Foster (1821-84) – left £1,279,813. Worsted manufacturer in Bradford, Yorkshire.

The son of John Foster (d. 1879, left £250,000), a worsted manufacturer at Bradford, and the brother of Johnstone Jonas Foster (1827-80, left £700,000, q.v.), his family were the owners of worsted mills at Queensbury near Bradford, the largest worsted factories in the world, including the famous Black Dyke Mills. He lived at Hornby Castle, Lancashire and in Queensbury, Yorkshire.

14. James Fletcher (1807-85) – left £1,394,503. Alpaca wool importer in Liverpool.

Born James Jack in Elgin, and the brother of John Charles Fletcher (1798-1875, left £800,000, q.v.), he and his brother founded a mercantile business in Liverpool which imported alpaca wool from South America; they later also imported llama and vicuna wool from South America. He is known to have visited South America in the 1840s. His two sons both left over £500,000. He lived at Woolton Hill near Liverpool and at Rosehaugh, Ross and Cromarty.

15. James Arthur (1819-85) – left £1,051,103. Clothing wholesaler and manufacturer in Glasgow.

Born in Paisley, the son of a draper, he ran a drapery shop, then became the partner of Hugh Fraser (1815-73), and later founded a major wholesale clothing business (Arthur & Co.) in Glasgow. His firm then became a leading clothing manufacturer, with three factories in Glasgow alone and 700 commercial travellers around Britain and overseas. His wife Jane *nee* Glen (1827-1907) was a campaigner for female education. Their son Sir Matthew Arthur (1852-1928, left £50,181) was created 1st Baron Glenarthur in 1918. Our man lived at Barshaw, Renfrewshire and at Carlung, Ayrshire.

16. William Ward, 1st Earl of Dudley (1817-85) – left £1,026,325. Landowner.

The son of William Ward, 10th Baron Ward (d. 1835), he was educated at Eton and at Christ Church and Trinity College, Oxford. One of the wealthiest landowners in Britain, owning 25,554 acres worth £123,176 p.a. in Worcestershire and Staffordshire, including great coal and other mineral deposits (see previous section), he was created 1st Earl of Dudley in 1860. He served at Lord Lieutenant of Ireland in 1902-05, and as Governor-General of Australia in 1908-11. He lived at Dudley House, Park Lane, Middlesex and at Witley Court near Stourport.

17. James Watney (1832-86) – left £1,264,611. Brewer in Pimlico, Middlesex.

The son of James Watney (1800-84, *q.v.*, above), the millionaire brewer whose brewery was in Pimlico, he died only two years after his father. He served as a Conservative M.P. from 1871 until 1885. His son Vernon James Watney (d. 1928) left £2,058,815. Our man lived at Thorney House, Palace Gate, Kensington, Middlesex.

18. William Hodgson (1803-86) – left £1,072,340. Sugar refining wealth in Whitechapel, Middlesex.

The son of Thomas Hodgson (1760-1841), a sugar refiner in Whitechapel who left £100,000 and the brother of John Hodgson (d. 1882) who left £692,521, he was educated at Wadham College, Oxford, and then became a barrister (called at Lincoln's Inn, 1828). He does not appear to have been in trade, but continued to derive a very high income from the family business. He lived at Gilston Park near Harlow, Hertfordshire and at 24 Sussex Square, Middlesex.

19. Herman, Baron De Stern (1815-87) – left £3,544,978. Merchant banker in the City of London.

Although little-known today, he was one of the very wealthiest and most successful City merchant bankers of his time. Born in Frankfurt, he settled in London in 1844 with his brother, as partners in Stern Brothers, of Angel Court, Throgmorton Street, City of London. It was heavily involved in foreign loans for Portugal, Spain, Italy and other countries. He was a director of the Imperial Bank and of the Bank of Romania. In 1869 he was created a nobleman of Portugal, along with his brother David, Viscount De Stern (d. 1877, *q.v.*). He was a member of the Anglo-Jewish elite and was related by marriage to the Rothschilds, Goldsmids and other leading families. He lived at

4 Hyde Park Gardens, Middlesex.

20. Hugh McCalmont (1809-87) – left £3,121,932. Stockbroker and merchant banker in the City of London.

The even wealthier brother of the millionaire Robert McCalmont (1808-83, *q.v.*), Hugh McCalmont was the son of the Demerara merchant and slave owner Hugh McCalmont (1765-1838), who died in Northern Ireland. Our man was born in Co. Antrim, and formed McCalmont Brothers at Philpot Lane, and later at 122 Cannon Street, in the City of London. It became a leading City financial house, specialising in loans to Mexico and the United States. It made our man one of the very richest financiers in Britain, although today little known. He lived at 9 Grosvenor Place, Hyde Park, Middlesex and at Abbeylands, Co. Antrim, Ireland.

21. Sir Robert Miller, 1st Bt. (1809-87) – left £1,023,390. Russia merchant in St. Petersburg and in London.

Born in Leith, Scotland, the son of the shipowner James Miller (1775-1853) and educated at Edinburgh High School, he was sent to St. Petersburg, Russia by his father to develop a herring export business, and remained there from 1832 until 1854. The firm exported fish, coal, hemp and other products to Russia and opened manufacturing businesses there. He returned to England in the 1850s and directed the firm from London. He served as a Liberal M.P. in 1859-68 and from 1873 until his death and was made a baronet in 1874. He lived at 1 Park Lane, Middlesex and at Manderston, Berwickshire.

22. John Rylands (1801-88) – left £2,574,922. Cotton manufacturer in Manchester.

The son of Joseph Rylands (d. 1847), a cotton manufacturer in St. Helens, Lancashire, he was educated at St. Helens Grammar School and, from 1819, was in partnership with his father and brothers as Rylands & Sons at Manchester. It grew into the largest textile manufacturers in Victorian Britain, employing 15,000 workers in seventeen mills and factories. He was also the owner of dye works and collieries. A prominent Congregationalist, he was a noted philanthropist. His fortune was the largest left by a Manchester businessman in the nineteenth century. He left most of his wealth to his third wife, Enrequetta Rylands (*nee* Tennant, 1843-1908), who herself left £3,448,693. In 1900 she founded the famous John Rylands Library in Manchester, now associated with Manchester University.

23. George Carr Glyn, 2nd Baron Wolverton (1827-87) – left £1,817,726. Banker in the City of London.

The son of George Carr Glyn, 1st Baron Wolverton (1793-1873, left £1,000,000, *q.v.*), he entered the family bank, then known as Glyn, Mills, Currie & Co., of 67 Lombard Street, City of London. He served as a Liberal M.P. from 1857 until 1873, when he succeeded to the peerage, and held ministerial office under Gladstone, including Postmaster-General in 1886. He lived at Iwerne Minster, Dorset.

24. Sir William Pearce, 1st Bt. (1809-88) – left £1,069,670. Shipbuilder in Glasgow.

Born in Kent and trained as a naval architect at Chatham Dockyard, he settled in Glasgow in 1863, heading the Fairfield Shipbuilding Co. and John Elder & Co. at Govan Shipyards. His firms

were noted for their technical innovations. He served as a Conservative M.P. from 1885 until his death. He was created a baronet in 1887. He lived at 10 Park Terrace, Glasgow, at 119 Piccadilly, Middlesex, and at Cardell, Renfrewshire.

25. Sir John Hardy, 1st Bt. (1809-88) – left £1,036,498. Ironmaster at Bradford, Yorkshire.
The son of John Hardy (1773-1855, left £550,000, *q.v.*), who was both an ironmaster and a barrister, as well as a Conservative M.P. He was educated at Oriel College, Oxford, and headed the Low Moor Ironworks in Bradford. He served as a Conservative M.P. in 1859-74, and was created a baronet in 1876. He died after being hit by a carriage late at night in Mayfair while mailing a letter. His brother was Gathorne Hardy, 1st Earl of Cranbrook (1814-1906), a senior Conservative politician who served as Home Secretary and Secretary for War.

26. Samuel Fielden (1816-89) – left £1,170,113. Cotton manufacturer in Todmorden, Lancashire.
A member of the wealthy family of cotton manufacturers in Todmorden near Manchester, he was the son of John Fielden, M.P. (1784-1849), cotton spinner who left £120,000. He was head of the family firm of Fielden & Co. after 1869, and a director of the Lancashire & Yorkshire Railway Co. His son John Ashton Fielden (1859-1942) left £1,406,942. Our man lived at Centre Vale near Todmorden.

27. (Hon.) and (Very Revd.) Augustus Duncombe (1814-80) – left £500,000. Landed wealth and Dean of York.
The fifth son of Charles Duncombe, 1st Baron Feversham (1764-1841, *q.v.*), who left £900,000 in personalty and over 39,000 acres of land in Yorkshire, our man was educated at Worcester College, Oxford, and, after lesser appointments, became Dean of York from 1858 until his death. It is difficult to see how, as a fifth son, he could have become so wealthy, although presumably his clerical income helped. He donated funds to rebuild York Minster. He is listed as having had three residences: Waresley Park, Huntingdonshire; Westerdale in Yorkshire; and 84 Eaton Square, Middlesex.

28. John Easton (1804-80) – left £600,000. A colliery owner near Gateshead, Co. Durham.
A very obscure wealthy colliery owner about whom little can be traced, his mines were at Ryton-on-Tyne and elsewhere on Tyneside. He retired to West Layton Manor at Hutton Magna in North Yorkshire, where his daughter Emma (1841-80) died in mysterious circumstance shortly before his own death. A recent local newspaper account of this matter described her, incorrectly, as his sister; apart from that, almost nothing is known about his life or career. His sister Emily Matilda Easton (1818-1913) left £1,079,780.

29. Johnston Jonas Foster (1827-80) – left £700,000. Worsted manufacturer at Bradford.
From a wealthy family of woollen manufacturers at Bradford, he was the son of John Foster (1798-1879, left £250,000), a worsted manufacturer there, and the brother of William Foster (1821-84), who left £1,279,813, and of Abraham Briggs Foster (1821-1904), who left £501,319. His family owned the Black Dyke Mills, the first (in 1836) to use powered looms, which gave its name to the famous Black Dyke Mills Band.

30. John Messer Knight (1813-80) – left £500,000. Cement manufacturer at North Fleet, Kent.

The son of a chemist in Rochester, Kent, from 1841 he became one of the heads of Knight, Bevan & Sturge, leading cement manufacturers at North Fleet near Gravesend in Kent, which became one of the main centres of cement manufacturing in Britain. Knight was a Quaker. His daughter Elizabeth Knight (1869-1933) has an entry in the *ODNB* as a "doctor and campaigner for women's suffrage."

31. Joseph Mayer Montefiore (1816-80) – left £600,000. Merchant banking and stockbroking wealth in the City of London.

The son of Abraham Montefiore (1788-1824), the brother of the famous Jewish leader and wealthy stockbroker Sir Moses Montefiore (1784-1885, *q.v.*), our man was the daughter of Henrietta *nee* Rothschild (1791-1866, left £400,000), of the celebrated and immensely wealthy family. Our man was a Freeman of the City of London but does not appear to have had a specific occupation as such. He lived at Worth Park near Crawley, Sussex and at Great Stanhope Street, Mayfair.

32. Allan Morrison (1842-80) – left £500,000. Inherited wholesale and retail mercantile and merchant banking wealth in the City of London.

The youngest of the many sons of James Morrison (1789-1857, *q.v.*), the multi-millionaire wholesale and retail merchant and later a merchant banker in the City of London, and an M.P., little could be traced about his career. In the 1871 Census he was living with his unmarried brother Charles Morrison (1817-1909) at 93 Harley Street, Middlesex; Charles was one of the very richest men in Britain, leaving £11 million at his death. He was also a reclusive invalid, as Allan, who died at thirty-eight, may have been. Allan also had a residence at Hall Barn Park near Beaconsfield, Buckinghamshire.

33. Edward Pease (1834-80) – left £500,000. Woollen manufacturer and colliery owner in Darlington, Co. Durham.

From the famous Quaker family of woollen manufacturers at Darlington, Co. Durham, he was the son of Joseph Pease (1799-1872, left £250,000), the first professing Quaker to sit in Parliament, in 1832. Our man was educated at Grove House School at Tottenham, Middlesex, a Quaker school where many wealthy Quakers were educated. He was a woollen manufacturer and also the owner of coal mines near Darlington. He was a committed Quaker, who taught at Quaker Sunday schools. He lived in Darlington.

34. Thomas Philippe De Casa Ariera, Marquess De Casariera (1790-1881) – left £510,605. A Spanish nobleman living in Paris, he left a great sum in England.

Both the sources of his wealth and his connections with Britain are unknown. He was created a peer of Spain in 1834, and was succeeded by his nephew.

35. Edward Hermon (1822-81) – left £585,605. Cotton manufacturer in Preston, Lancashire.

The head of Horrocks, Miller & Co., the leading cotton manufacturing firm in north Lancashire, and also an East India merchant, Edward Heron was Conservative M.P. for Preston from 1868 until his death, and was a noted art collector. In later life he lived at Wyfold Court near Henley-on-Thames and at 13 Berkeley Square, Middlesex. His son Robert Hodge (later Hermon-Hodge, 1851-1937, left £154,522), a long-serving Conservative M.P., he was created 1st Baron Wyfold in 1919.

36. Joseph Jones (1816-80) – left £500,000. Cotton manufacturer and colliery owner in Oldham, Lancashire.

The son of Joseph Jones (1782-1858, left £14,000), a banker in Oldham, Joseph Jones became a leading cotton manufacturer there and also an early colliery owner in the area, as well as having banking interests. Most of his wealth came to his nephew John Jones (1830-88), who left £247,245. In later life Joseph Jones lived at Abberley Hall, Worcestershire.

37. Louis Cohen (1799-1882) – left £625,056. Stockbroker and banker in the City of London.

A member of the Anglo-Jewish "Cousinhood," Louis Cohen was the son of Joseph Cohen (1774-1828), a banker, and was the nephew of Nathan Mayer Rothschild. He became the head of the stockbroking firm of Louis Cohen & Co. in the City of London, and was also involved in finance. He was Warden of the Great Synagogue in London. His son Sir Benjamin Louis Cohen, 1st Bt. (1844-1909, left £385,146) was a Conservative M.P. from 1892 until 1906. Our man lived at 84 Gloucester Place, Portman Square, Middlesex.

38. Nathan James Edward De Rothschild (1844-81) – left £530,934. Merchant banker in Paris, France.

A member of the French branch of the great merchant banking family, he worked for the family bank from 1870 until his death aged only thirty-six. He was a noted book collector. There is no evidence that he ever lived in England.

39. John Hodgson (1805-82) – left £692,521. Sugar refining wealth in Whitechapel.

The son of Thomas Hodgson (c.1760-1841, left £100,000), a sugar refiner in Whitechapel, he was a solicitor. His wealth presumably derived from the sugar refining business, but this is not entirely clear. His brother William Hodgson (d. 1886), a barrister, left £1,072,340. John Hodgson lived at Gilston House, Harlow, Hertfordshire and at 14 Sussex Square, Middlesex.

40. John Joicey (1816-81) – left £710,465. Colliery owner near Gateshead, Co. Durham.

The fourth son of George Joicey, and a member of the wealthy colliery family on Tyneside, he served as a Liberal M.P. from 1880 until his death the following year. His nephew James was created 1st Baron Joicey. John Joicey lived at Newton Hall, Stocksfield-on-Tyne, Northumberland.

41. James MacFarlane (1798-1881) – left £893,489. West India merchant in the City of London.

Born in Perth, Scotland, James Macfarlane became a West India merchant at 1 Gresham Buildings in the City of London and later at 147 Leadenhall Street in the City of London. Almost nothing about his career could be traced. He lived at 35 Gloucester Road, Regent's Park, Middlesex.

42. Samuel Courtauld (1793-1881) – left £700,000. Silk manufacturer at Bocking and Halstead, Essex.

The son of George Courtauld (1761-1823), a silk manufacturer of Huguenot descent in Spitalfield, London, he founded the present firm in 1794 in Pebmarsh, Essex as silk weavers and manufacturers. Its main factories were at Bocking and Halstead, Essex. His firm was notable for introducing steam power, although most of the work was done by women, who comprised 92 per cent of its workforce. Courtauld became a well-known Unitarian and political radical. He lived at Gosfield Hall near Halstead, Essex.

43. Thomas James Agar-Robartes, 1st Baron Robartes (1808-82) – left £596,771. Landowner.

The son of (Hon.) Charles Agar and the grandson of James Agar, 1st Viscount Clifden, he was educated at Harrow and at Christ Church, Oxford, and was a significant landowner in Cornwall, owning 22,234 acres worth £30,730 p.a. there. He probably earned part of his wealth from copper and other minerals there. He served as a Liberal M.P. from 1847 until 1868, and was given a peerage in 1869. He lived at Lanhydrock House, near Truro, Cornwall, and at 1 Dean Street, Park Lane, Middlesex.

44. Thomas Agnew (1827-83) – left £530,257. Art dealer in Manchester.

A member of the well-known firm of art dealers, Agnew & Co., he was the son of Thomas Agnew (1794-1871, left £80,000), who founded the firm in Manchester. It specialised in selling art works to the new rich of Lancashire and Yorkshire. It opened a London branch in 1860, which was headed his brother Sir William Agnew, 1st Bt. (1825-1910), who left £353,593, while Thomas remained in Manchester, where he had other business interests. He lived at Fairhope, Pendleton near Manchester.

45. Maria De Fuentes, Marquesa De Savillano (1817-82) – left £531,204. A Spanish noblewoman who lived in Madrid.

The source of her wealth, and why she left so much in England, are unclear.

46. Sir Samuel Stephens Marling, 1st Bt. (1810-83) – left £627,443. Woollen cloth manufacturer in Stroud, Gloucestershire.

A self-made woollen cloth manufacturer at Stroud, far removed from industrial England, his Ebley Mills employed around 800 persons in 1870. Marling served as Liberal M.P. for Gloucestershire West from 1868 till 1880, and was made a baronet in 1882, shortly before his death. He lived at Stanley Park near Stroud and at 42 St. James's Place, Middlesex.

47. Robert Ormston (1789-1882) – left £888,197. Glass manufacturer at Newcastle-upon-Tyne.

A Quaker at birth, the son of Robert Ormston, a banker in Newcastle-upon-Tyne, he was one of a number of entrepreneurs who became major glass manufacturers on Tyneside, producing, among other things, glass bottles. He died at ninety-three. He lived at 5 Savile Place, Newcastle-upon-Tyne.

48. Sir Henry Meux, 2nd Bt. (1817-83) – left £605,292. Brewer at Tottenham Court Road, Middlesex.

The head of Meux & Co., the great brewery founded by his father Sir Henry Meux, 1st Bt. (1770-

1841, left £300,000), he was educated at Eton and at Christ Church, Oxford. Their brewery was located, implausibly, at 269 Tottenham Court Road in central London. This did not prevent many of his relatives from marrying into the aristocracy surprisingly early. His son, Sir Henry Meux, 3rd Bt. (1856-1900), left £696,823. Our man lived at Theobald's Park, Hertfordshire and at 36 Grosvenor Square, Middlesex.

49. Sir Edward Henry Scott, 5th Bt. (1842-83) – left £917,429. Banking fortune in the City of London and in Marylebone.
His family's bank was founded by Sir Claude Scott, 1st Bt. (1742-1830), an M.P. and grain merchant turned banker. Our man's father Sir Samuel Scott, 2nd Bt. (1772-1843), also an M.P., headed Scott, Dent & Co., bankers of Aldermanbury, City of London and Cavendish Square, Marylebone, and left £700,000 (q.v.). Our man succeeded his brother Sir Edward, 4th Bt. (1840-80), but died only three years later. It is unclear if he was active as a banker. He lived at Sundridge Park, Bromley, Kent.

50. Joseph Shuttleworth (1819-83) – left £554,613. Portable steam engine manufacturer at Lincoln.
The son of a boat builder, in 1842 he established the firm of Clayton & Shuttleworth at Lincoln with his brother-in-law Nathaniel Clayton (1811-90, left £1,365,497). The firm built thousands of portable steam engines, sold all over the world for use in tractors, etc., and also thousands of threshing machines. His son Alfred Shuttleworth (1843-1925) left £1,026,809. During the First World War his firm built the famous Sopwith Camel airplane. He lived in Lincoln.

51. Thomas Jones-Gibb (1821-84) – left £772,118. East India and China merchant in the City of London.
The son of Thomas Augustus Boothby Gibb (1799-1866, left £300,000), an East India and China merchant in London, he was also a merchant trading with the East in the City of London. Little is known about his career. An executor was the merchant and banker Edward Ford Duncanson (1833-99, left £188,325), probably a relative, whose son Thomas Jones Gibb Duncanson (1873-1933) left £533,728. Our man lived at Bredbury, Tunbridge Wells, Kent.

52. Robert Hanbury (1796-84) – left £701,367. Brewer in Brick Lane, east London, Middlesex.
The son of Osgood Hanbury (d. 1852), a banker, our man was born a Quaker but was baptised as an Anglican in 1820. He became the Senior Partner in Truman, Hanbury & Buxton, the well-known brewers of Brick Lane, Middlesex, a firm which still exists (although no longer at Brick Lane). He lived at Poles, Thundridge, Hertfordshire.

53. Thomas Holloway (1800-83) – left £596,335. Patent medicine manufacturer in London.
The famous maker of "Holloway's Pills," probably the first mass marketed patent medicine, meant for indigestion, rampant then as now, he was the son of a baker in Devonport. His early career had its ups and downs, including a spell in debtor's prison. From 1839 he manufactured his "digestive pills" at 244 Strand in central London, and then at New Oxford Street. He spent £20,000 a year on advertising, and employed 100 persons at his death in 1883. He was also a successful financier.

Childless, he left much of his wealth to found Royal Holloway College at Egham Surrey, established for the higher education of women.

54. William Charles Jones (c. 1803-84) – left £875,864. Cotton manufacturer in Manchester.
The son of John Jones (1770-1850), a cotton manufacturer in Tydesley, Lancashire, our man's firm employed 400-450 people in 1871. He lived at The Elms near Warrington, Cheshire and at Hove, Sussex.

55. Eustratios Ralli (1800-84) – left £611,707. Foreign merchant in the City of London.
Born on the Island of Chios, the son of Stephanos Ralli, a merchant in France, he was a member of the great firm of foreign merchants, Ralli Brothers, of 25 Finsbury Circus in the City of London. The Rallis and their Greek relatives were among the wealthiest businessmen in Britain. He also had a branch in Manchester, and was a member of the Baltic Exchange in London. His son Sir Lucas Eustratios Ralli, 1st Bt. (d. 1931) left £2,290,447. Our man lived at 93 Lancaster Gate, Middlesex and at Scio House, Putney Heath, Surrey.

56. Francis James Sumner (1807-84) – left £560,970. Cotton manufacturer in Glossop, Derbyshire.
Born in Foleshill near Coventry, he became a cotton manufacturer in Glossop. His firm employed about one thousand people in 1881, when he was High Sheriff of Derbyshire. According to one report, he was a Roman Catholic, and brought over girl mill hands from Ireland. He lived at East View, High Street, Glossop, and at Park Hill, Little Hayfield, in Stockport, Cheshire.

57. James White (1812-84) – left £904,114. Chemical manufacturer at Rutherglen, Lanarkshire, near Glasgow.
The son of John White (d. 1860), the founder, with his brother, of J.& J. White, chemical manufacturers of Rutherglen near Glasgow, he was a partner in the firm from 1860. The company mainly manufactured bichromate of potash, a substance very injurious to the health; his firm was later criticised for injuring the health of its workers. His son John Campbell White (1843-1908) was created 1st Baron Overtoun (*sic*) in 1893 and left £689,023. Our man lived at Overtown, Dumbartonshire and at Hayfield, Rutherglen. After their deaths the firm was headed by his cousin William James Chrystal (1854-1921), who left £1,139,140.

58. Henry Browne Alexander (1800-85) – left £558,857. Urban property owner in South Kensington, Middlesex.
The owner of the Alexander Estate in London, better known as the Thurloe Estate, which consisted of fifty-four acres in six separate plots in South Kensington, including Alexander and Thurloe Squares. He was a remote relative of John Thurloe (d. 1668), from whom his family inherited the property. It was developed by his father John Alexander (1762-1831) and by our man. Our man gave £80,000 to the National Portrait Gallery to construct its present building. He lived at The Laurels, Barnes, Surrey, not in South Kensington.

59. John Bald (1812-85) – left £564,280. Distiller at Alloa, Scotland and merchant in Liverpool.

159

The owner of the Carsebridge Whisky Distillery in Alloa, which was founded in 1799 by his father John Bald (d. 1844), he also was engaged as a "general merchant" (1851 Census) in Liverpool. The nature of his mercantile activities is unclear. His distillery became part of the Distillers Company in 1877. He lived at Monzie Castle near Crieff, Perthshire, and at Hollenden, near Tunbridge Wells, Kent.

60. Jeremiah Colman (1807-85) – left £551,893. Mustard and starch manufacturer in Norwich and in the City of London.

A member of the family which is still renowned for its mustard, it was located at Norwich from c. 1860 and employed 1100 workers by 1869. The Colmans were leading Baptists, and gave generously to Baptist charities. His firm, curiously, also produced starch. It appears that our man headed the London offices of the firm, at 108 Cannon Street, City of London. His son Sir Jeremiah Colman, 1st Bt. (1859-1942, left £1,832,069) was created a baronet in 1907. Our man lived at Carshalton Park, Surrey.

61. Sir Charles James Freake, 1st Bt. (1814-84) – left £718,575. Architect and builder in London.

A self-taught architect and builder, he was the son of Charles Freake, a coal merchant and publican. He then became a builder in Mayfair and a well-regarded architect, building the facades of houses at Eaton Square, at Exhibition Road, and elsewhere. He often worked in partnership with the distinguished architect George Basevi (1794-1845), Disraeli's cousin. The unfortunately named Freake was created a baronet in 1882, and lived at 21 Cromwell Road, Middlesex, now the French Legation. In his buildings Freake always used straight chimneys, doing away with the need to use the "climbing boys" to clean them.

62. John Straker (1815-85) – left £919,646. Colliery owner and landowner in Tynemouth, etc.

The son of the wealthy colliery owner Joseph Straker (1784-1867), who left £300,000, our man was a major colliery owner on Tyneside and the owner of 12,372 acres worth £12,156 p.a. in Northumberland and Co. Durham. He lived at Stagshaw House, Northumberland.

63. John Kemp-Welch (1810-85) – left £715,144. Soda water manufacturer in Bristol, Derby, and London.

The son of Martin Kemp-Welch (1772-1837), a merchant in Poole, he was originally a wine merchant but bought J. Schweppes & Co. with his partner William Evill in the 1830s, the world-famous manufacturer of aerated water. It had factories in Bristol and Derby and later in London. They introduced aerated lemonade in 1835 – much earlier than many would have guessed – as well as seltzer water, and exported or opened factories around the world, including America and Australia. He lived at Clapham Common, Surrey.

64. Joseph Whitaker (1802-84) – left £640,391. Vineyard owner and exporter of marsala wine in Sicily.

The son of Joseph Whitaker, who settled in Sicily along with another relative, Benjamin Ingham, he became very wealthy as the owner of prime vineyards there and as the exporter of marsala wines. His son Benjamin Ingham Whitaker (d.1922) left £509,842 in the UK. Our man died in Palermo, Sicily. There is a history of his family by Raleigh Trevelyan, *Princes Under the Volcano* (1972).

65. Henry Wigan (1833-85) – left £624,326. Hop merchant in Southwark, Surrey.

Southwark became the centre of the hop trade in the nineteenth century, chiefly providing it to London's many breweries. Our man was regarded as the leading hop merchant in London. Born in Highbury, Islington, the son of John Alfred Wigan, he was also an isinglass merchant. His brother Sir Frederick Wigan, 1st Bt. (1827-1907, left £452,360) was created a baronet in 1898.

66. Dunbar James Douglas, 6th Earl of Selkirk (1809-85) – left £515,097. Landowner and investor in Canada.

The son of Thomas, 5th Earl of Selkirk (1771-1820) and educated at Eton and at Christ Church, Oxford, he served as a Scottish Representative Peer from 1830 until his death. The owner of 22,264 acres worth £21,473 p.a. in Kirkcudbright and Linlithgow, he also benefitted from fortunate investments in the Hudson's Bay Company in Canada. He lived at St. Mary's Isle, Kirkcudbrightshire.

67. Abraham Laverton (1819-86) – left £647,417. Woollen cloth manufacturer at Westbury, Wiltshire.

A woollen cloth manufacturer at Westbury, Wiltshire, near Trowbridge and Warminster, he was born at Tunbridge Wells, the son of William Laverton. He was a J.P. for Wiltshire, but little is known of his career. He lived at Farleigh Castle near Farleigh Hungerford, Somerset.

68. Andrew Low (1813-86) – left £617,415. A cotton merchant in Savannah, Georgia.

Born in Scotland, Andrew Low went to America in 1830 and became a wealthy cotton merchant and slave owner in Savannah, Georgia. Perhaps because of the Civil War, he moved to England, where he lived at Beauchamp Hall, Leamington, Warwickshire. He moved back to Georgia before 1880. His house in Savannah has been preserved and is open to the public. His daughter-in-law Juliet Gordon Low (1860-1927) founded the Girl Scouts of the United States.

69. Alexander Ogilvie (1812-86) – left £747,802. Railway and engineering contractor.

Born in Angus, Scotland and educated at Edinburgh High School, he was apprenticed to a civil engineer, and then became a successful railway and engineering contractor, often working with Thomas Brassey (*q.v.*). Ogilvie worked on the Great Eastern Railway, the London & South Western Railway, and many others, and helped to build the Thames Embankment. According to one obituary, he "executed over £10 million of work," from his office at 4 Great George Street, Westminster. He lived at Sizewell House in Saxmundham, Suffolk and at 28 Fitzroy Square, Middlesex.

70. Edward Gordon Douglas-Pennant, 1st Baron Penrhyn (1800-86) – left £781,880. Landowner and owner of slate quarries.

The son of (Hon.) John Douglas, he inherited the Penrhyn estate in Wales from his wife's father George Hay Dawkins-Pennant (1764-1849, left £600,000, *q.v.*), as well as wealth deriving from

Jamaica plantations. He owned 49,548 acres worth £71,018 p.a. in Caernarvonshire and other counties, including the Penrhyn Quarry, the largest slate quarry in the world. He served as a Conservative M.P. from 1841 until 1866, when he was created 1st Baron Penrhyn. He lived at Penrhyn Castle near Bangor, Caernarvonshire.

71. Charles Hilditch Rickards (1812-86) – left £511,189. Paper manufacturer in Manchester.

Little is known of his background or early career. He became a wealthy paper manufacturer in Manchester, as well as a well-known patron of the arts and of painters. He was a J.P. of Manchester. His estate was first sworn for probate at only £48,098, and then revised sharply upwards. He lived at The Beeches, Old Trafford near Manchester.

72. Zanni Schilizzi (1806-86) – left £502,828. Foreign merchant and banker in Constantinople and the City of London.

Born in the island of Chios, and a member of the wealthy community of Greek merchants and bankers, our man lived in Constantinople. His sons apparently ran the London end of the business at 25 Austin Friars, City of London. His mercantile and banking business also had branches in Manchester and Calcutta.

73. Frederick William Thomas Vernon Wentworth (1796-1885) – left £962,859. Landowner and colliery owner.

Born with the surname of Vernon, his father Frederick William Thomas Vernon, later Wentworth (1748-1814) changed their surname to "Wentworth" when he inherited Wentworth Castle and much landed property from Frederick Wentworth, 3rd Earl of Strafford (1732-99). Our man was educated at Christ Church, Oxford. He owned 22,930 acres worth £20,546 p.a., of which 5,111 acres worth £15,240 p.a. was in the West Riding. Much of his income must have come from collieries. His son Thomas Frederick Charles Vernon Wentworth (1831-1902) left £1,033,766. Our man lived at Wentworth Castle, Yorkshire, at Castle Down House, Hastings, Sussex, and at Connaught Place, Westminster.

74. Colin Campbell (1820-86) – left £715,419. West Indies plantation and mercantile wealth in Glasgow.

Known as Colin Campbell of Colgrain, after the estate purchased by his father, he was the son of Colin Campbell (1782-1863), a planter in British Guiana and a sugar merchant in Glasgow. Our man does not appear to have been in trade, but was a landowner at Colgrain, Perthshire, owning 2,124 acres worth £2,429 p.a. His son William Middleton Campbell (1849-1919, left £711,389) was Governor of the Bank of England in 1907-09. This man's son Colin Campbell (1866-1954), a banker, was created 1st Baron Colgrain in 1946.

75. Robert Donaldson (1828-85) – left £522,338. Iron merchant in Glasgow.

An iron merchant of 5 Prince's Terrace, Dowanhill, Glasgow, he was in business there and died at fifty-seven. Little is known about the details of his career.

76. Robert Campbell (1811-87) – left £617,818. Mercantile and landed fortune in Sydney, Australia and landowner in England.

Known as Robert Tertius Campbell, he was the son of Robert Campbell (1789-1851), who settled in Sydney, New South Wales, and became wealthy as a merchant and landowner. Our man returned to England in the 1850s and bought Buscot Park, Berkshire in 1859, which he ran as a famous experimental farm. It produced crops previously unknown in Britain such as the sugar beet. He briefly served as a Liberal M.P. in 1866. His daughter Florence (1845-78) was married to Charlie Bravo (1845-76), who died of antimony poisoning, a famous case; she was widely believed to have poisoned him. He lived at Buscot Park, Berkshire and in Brighton.

77. Charles Cave (1796-1887) – left £613,901. Banker in the City of London.

Born in Bristol, the son of Stephen Cave (1763-1838), a banker and glass manufacturer, he became a partner in Prescott, Grote, Cave & Co., private bankers of 62 Threadneedle Street, City of London. He lived at 22 Lowndes Street in Chelsea.

78. Octavius Edward Coope (1814-86) – left £542,765. Brewer in Romford, Essex and in Burton, Staffordshire.

The son of John Coope (1766-1845), a sugar refiner in Whitechapel who left £250,000, our man became a partner in the well-known brewers Ind Coope, of Romford, Essex and Burton-on-Trent. He served as a Conservative M.P. in 1847-8, 1868, and 1874 until his death. He lived at 41 Upper Brook Street, Middlesex and at Rochetts and Berechurch Hall, Essex.

79. Joshua Fielden (1827-87) – left £503,599. Cotton manufacturer in Todmorden, Lancashire.

The son of the cotton manufacturer John Fielden (1784-1849), who left £120,000, he was a partner in Fielden Brothers, cotton manufacturers of Todmorden near Manchester. He served as a Conservative M.P. in 1868-80. His brother Thomas Fielden (1790-1869, *q.v.*) left £1,300,000. Our man lived at Stansfield Hall, Halifax and then at Nutfield Priory near Redhill, Surrey.

80. Jesse Haworth (1804-87) – left £593,004. Cotton manufacturer at Bury, Lancashire.

A leading cotton and fustian manufacturer at Bury, little is known of his career. He was born in Bury, the son of James Haworth (d. 1856), a cotton manufacturer there. In 1871 his factories employed about 400 people. He lived at High Bank, Walshaw near Bury, Lancashire.

81. Anna Maria Heywood (1813-87) – left £651,238. The widow of a banker at Liverpool.

The daughter of the wealthy Liverpool banker Hugh Jones (1777-1842), who left £200,000, she became even wealthier by marrying John Pemberton Heywood (1804-77), the richest banker in Liverpool, who left £1,900,000. Most of her wealth came to her husband's nephew Arthur Pemberton Heywood-Lonsdale (d. 1897) who left £1,429,779. She lived at Norris Green, West Derby near Liverpool.

82. Henry Allsopp, 1st Baron Hindlip (1811-87) – left £557,577. Brewer at Burton, Staffordshire.

The son of Samuel Allsopp, the head of a long-established family brewing business in Burton, he developed the firm to become the third largest brewing company in Britain. He served as a Conservative M.P. from 1874-80. He was made a baronet in 1889, and in 1886 joined the

"Beerage," as brewers given peerages were known, as 1st Baron Hindlip. He lived at Hindlip Hall, Worcestershire and at Alsop-en-le-Dale, Worcestershire.

83. Sir Alexander Matheson, 1st Bt. (1805-87) – left £643,760. China merchant and financier in the City of London.

Educated at Edinburgh University, he was the nephew of Sir James Matheson, 1st Bt., one of the founders of Jardine Matheson, the famous China merchants in Hong Kong who dealt in tea and opium. Our man was the senior partner in Matheson & Co., of 3 Lombard Street, City of London, which provided finance to Jardine Matheson's operations in the East. He served as a Liberal M.P. from 1847-84, and was given a baronetcy in 1882. He lived at 38 Hill Street, Berkeley Square, Middlesex and at Ardross Castle in Ross-shire.

84. Mary Ann Morrison (1796-1887) – left £617,364. Widow of a wholesale and retail merchant and merchant banker in the City of London.

The daughter of Joseph Todd, a draper in London, she married his employee James Morrison (1789-18657, *q.v.*), who became a multi-millionaire as a wholesale and retail merchant at Fore Street in the City of London and as a merchant banker there. Most of their children were remarkably wealthy; her eldest son Charles Morrison (1817-1909) left £11 million. She lived at Basildon, Berkshire.

85. James Dyson Perrins (1823-87) – left £664,431. Worcestershire sauce manufacturer at Worcester.

The head of Lea & Perrins, the famous sauce manufacturers, he was the son of William Henry Perrins (1793-1867, left £70,000), who founded the firm with John Wheeley Lea (1791-1871, left £100,000). Our man's son Dyson Perrins (1864-1958, left £817,808) has an entry in the *ODNB* as a "book and porcelain collector." Our man lived at Davenham Bank, Great Malvern, Worcestershire.

86. Charles Waring (1827-87) – left £560,429. Engineering contractor in Westminster.

The son of a small landowner John Waring (1796-1867, left £2,000), he founded Waring Brothers with his two brothers in the 1840s. It was an engineering contractor which built railway structures like viaducts, and also railway lines, in England and also in Europe and South America. Its offices were at 10 Victoria Chambers, Westminster. He lived at 2 Grosvenor Square, Middlesex.

87. Henry Browning (1797-1888) – left £541,216. Probably a wine and spirit broker in the City of London.

Little could be found about the career of Henry Browning, who was described in the 1851 Census as a "merchant," and in the 1861 Census as a "general merchant." He appears to have been a partner in Twiss & Browning, a wine and spirit brokers at 37 Mark Lane in the City of London. He lived at 72 Grosvenor Street, Grosvenor Square, Middlesex.

88. William Isaac Cookson (1812-88) – left £529,571. Colliery owner near Newcastle-upon-Tyne.

The son of Isaac Cookson (1776-1851, left £100,000), a glass manufacturer and colliery owner on Tyneside, he was first associated with the family firm of Cookson & Cuthbert of South Shields, which produced glass and alkali. He was then primarily a large-scale colliery owner, living at Benwell Tower, Northumberland. In later life he lived at Worksop Manor, Worksop, Nottinghamshire.

89. Harvie (*sic*) Morton Farquhar (1816-87) – left £544,684. Banker in Westminster.

The son of Sir Walter Farquhar, 1st Bt. (1738-1819), a Scottish-born physician who became Physician-in-Ordinary to the Prince of Wales and was made a baronet in 1796, he became a Partner in the Herries Farquhar Bank, a private bank at 16 St. James's Street, Westminster, Middlesex. It was taken over in 1893 by Lloyd's Bank. He lived at 11 Belgrave Square, Middlesex.

90. Thomas Jessop (1804-87) – left £663,079. Steel manufacturer in Sheffield.

The son of the steel refiner William Jessop (1772-1846), he became head of the largest steel manufacturers in Sheffield, a city which grew into the steel manufacturing centre of Britain. He served as Mayor of Sheffield in 1863-4. Jessop founded a hospital for women there. He lived at Endcliffe Grange, Sheffield.

91. George William Petter (1824-88) – left £515,481. Printer and publisher in the City of London.

Little is known about his early life apart from the fact that he was born in Barnstaple. From 1855 he became a partner in Cassell, Petter & Galpin of La Belle Sauvage Yard (*sic*), Ludgate Hill in the City of London. In the 1861 Census he was stated to be a "printer, publisher, and manufacturer" of a firm which employed 380 persons. He retired in 1883.

92. William Quilter (1808-88) – left £580,934. Accountant in the City of London.

The best known and most influential accountant of his time, he was the son of a printer, and entered the office of an accountant in 1825. From 1829 he was a partner with John Ball, in Quilter Ball & Co., which grew in importance after auditing failed businesses following the collapse of the "Railway Mania" in 1847. Its offices were at 3 Moorgate Street in the City of London. He was one of the founders of the Institute of Accountants in 1870, and its first President. He lived at 38 Norfolk Street, Park Lane, Middlesex. His son Sir William Cuthbert Quilter, 1st Bt. (1841-1911), an accountant and Conservative M.P., left £1,220,638.

93. Dame Charlotte Anne Scarlett (1805-88) – left £627,739. Colliery wealth in Burnley, Lancashire.

The daughter of John Hargreaves (1774-1834), the leading colliery owner in Burnley, she married (General) Sir James Yorke Scarlett (1799-1871, left £200,000). He was the son of James Scarlett, 1st Baron Abinger (1769-1844), the judge, and led the successful British army charge at Balaklava which took place the day before the "Charge of the Light Brigade" in 1855. She inherited her father's colliery wealth and lived at Bank Hall, Burnley, Lancashire.

94. Daniel Wood (1818-88) – left £613,519. Cotton manufacturer in Glossop, Derbyshire.

The son of the woollen and cotton manufacturer at Glossop John Wood (1784-1854), he and his brother, the next entry, headed Wood Brothers, the largest cotton manufacturers in Glossop. He lived at Moorfield, Whitfield in Glossop, Derbyshire.

95. Samuel Wood (1819-88) – left £629,944. Cotton manufacturer in Glossop, Derbyshire.

The brother of the previous man, who died a few months after him also leaving great wealth, he served as an early Mayor of Glossop in 1874-6. His son Sir Samuel Hill-Wood, 1st Bt. (1872-1949, left £6989), educated at Eton, was a Tory M.P. from 1910 till 1929, and was created a baronet in 1921. He was the Chairman of The Arsenal Football Club in 1921-36 and just after World War Two. Our man lived at Talbot House, Glossop.

96. John Beaumont (1808-89) – left £520,241. A fancy waistcoat manufacturer in Huddersfield, Yorkshire.

A little-known manufacturer of fancy waistcoats in Huddersfield and a director of the North British Railway, he was a partner in the waistcoat business with his brother-in-law George Senior. He left his wealth to his only daughter Sarah Martha Grove-Grady (1831-1925), who left £607,894, who used it to found animal wildlife sanctuaries. Beaumont's home near Huddersfield, Ravens Knowle, is now the Tolson Museum.

97. Joseph Evans (1818-89) – left £674,545. Colliery owner near St. Helens, Lancashire.

The son of Richard Evans (1778-1864), a colliery owner (Richard Evans & Co.) at St. Helens who left £100,000, he continued the firm but did not take part in public life. He lived at Hurst House, Prescot, Lancashire.

98. Charles Cubitt Gooch (1811-89) – left £587,670. Merchant banker in the City of London.

A partner in Junius Spencer Morgan & Co., of 22 Old Broad Street, City of London, which specialised in American finance (J.P. Morgan, the great American banker, was the son of Junius Spencer Morgan, d. 1890, q.v.). Charles Cubitt Gooch was the father of George Peabody Gooch (G.P. Gooch, 1873-1968), the famous historian, who was a Liberal M.P. 1906-10, and of Sir Henry Cubitt Gooch (1871-1959), a Conservative M.P. from 1908-10 who was knighted in 1928. Our man lived at 8 Porchester Gate, Paddington, Middlesex.

99. Sir Daniel Gooch, 1st Bt. (1816-89) – left £669,658. Railway and telegraph cable engineer and railway chairman in London and elsewhere.

Apprenticed to a railway engineer, he became the Superintendant of Locomotive Engineers on the Great Western Railway from 1837 to 1864, and was then Chairman of the Great Western Railway from 1865 until 1889. He was significant in laying the Transatlantic Cable, completed in 1866, which cut the time of communications between Britain and America from a week to a few minutes, and was given a baronetcy in 1866 for this. He also served as a Conservative M.P. from 1865 till 1885. He lived at Clewer Park near Windsor and at Fulthorpe House in Maida Vale. He was not related to the man in the previous entry.

100. Christopher North Graham (1818-89) – left £534,213. Wholesale tea merchant in the City of London, at 190 Fleet Street, and a Freeman of the City of London, although little is known of his background or career.

He lived at Silwood, Tulse Park, Surrey.

101. Count Louis-Charles Greffulhe (1814-88) – left £661,676. Merchant banker in Paris.

A member of a family of French merchant bankers who left large sums in England, like them he had no traceable connections with banking in London or elsewhere in England, and lived and worked in Paris. Why they left these great sums in England is unclear.

102. William Hargreaves (1822-89) – left £586,456. Engineer and iron founder in Bolton, Lancashire.

One of the proprietors of Hick, Hargreaves & Co., engineers and millwrights in Bolton, a firm which built locomotive engines and other engineering components at its Soho Works in Bolton, employing 765 men in 1871, he was the son of John Hargreaves (1780-1860, left £400,000), and the brother of John Hargreaves (1800-74, left £600,000, *q.v.*). There is some uncertainty about how his family had become so wealthy. Our man was in business with his brother-in-law Benjamin Hick. He lived at Moss Bank, Halliwell near Bolton, lancashire.

103. Alexander Leslie-Melville, 10th Earl of Leven and Melville (1817-89) – left £527,064. Banker in the City of London.

The son of John, 9th Earl of Leven and Melville (1786-1876), he was educated at Eton and at Trinity College, Cambridge. His family owned comparatively little land – 8,821 acres worth £3,078 p.a., in Scotland – and he became a Partner in Williams Deacon & Co., a leading bank at 20 Birchin Lane in the City of London. He also served as a Representative Peer for Scotland from 1880 until his death. He was succeeded by his half-brother Ronald, 11th Earl of Leven and Melville (1835-1906), who left £1,300,013. Our man lived at 21 Upper Grosvenor Street, Middlesex and at Glenferness in Scotland.

104. Charles Loyd Norman (1833-89) – left £920,829. Merchant banker in the City of London.

The son of the banker George Warde Norman (1793-1882), who left £126,131, he was educated at Eton and at Trinity College, Cambridge. He was a Partner in Baring Brothers, the great merchant bank at 8 Bishopsgate in the City of London from 1853 till 1889. He had previously been an East India merchant in the City. Norman's first wife was Julia Hay Cameron (1838-73), the daughter of Julia Margaret Cameron (1815-79), the famous photographer. He lived at The Rookery, Bromley, Kent.

105. Louisa Anne Ryland (1814-89) – left £745,973. Ground rent landowner in Birmingham.

She was the daughter of Samuel Ryland (1764-1843, left £120,000), the owner of a wire-drawing business in Birmingham who then invested heavily in undeveloped land there. She inherited his wealth, and became very rich as the city expanded. Unmarried, she gave an estimated £120,000 to charitable causes in Birmingham, to build parks, hospitals, orphanages, and the like. Her wealth came to a relative Charles Alston Smith-Ryland (1859-1914), who was twice Mayor of Birmingham, but left only £52,766. She lived at Barford Hill, Warwickshire.

106. Thomas Andrew Walker (1828-89) – left £982,243. Civil engineering and railway contractor in the City of London and elsewhere.

Another of the great railway and civil engineering contractors of Victorian England, he was the son of a land agent and – like others – was associated with Thomas Brassey (*q.v.*), the great railway builder. Our man built railways in England and Canada (where he lived from 1854 till 1861), and in Russia, Egypt, and the Sudan. He helped to build the Metropolitan District Railway, the East London Railway, and a variety of engineering projects including the Barry Docks and the Manchester Ship Canal. He was noted for his humanitarian attitude towards his navvies. In later life he lived at Mt. Balan, Caerwent, Monmouthshire.

1890-1899

The 1890s saw a sharp increase in the number of large fortunes in Britain, and, from this point on, only millionaire estates will be included in this work. Estates between £500,000 and £1 million are too numerous to survey here. In these years the late Victorian and Edwardian plutocracy was nearing its peak. As will be seen from the fields in which the people here earned their wealth, fortunes came from finance and commerce, from manufacturing and industry, and from landownership; some were made overseas. As will be seen as well, there were many self-made men and foreigners who became wealthy in Britain, as well as many who inherited money, many of whom were being accepted in the British elite, with peerages and baronetcies. This would continue until the First World War and indeed beyond.

1. Junius Spencer Morgan (1813-90) – left £1,842,348. Merchant banker in the City of London and New York.

The American Junius Spencer Morgan was the son of Joseph Morgan (d. 1847) of Connecticut, the founder of the Aetna Insurance Company. From about 1850, Junius Morgan was a major figure in the City of London, living in New York but making frequent trips to England. He took over the London merchant bank of the American George Peabody (1795-1869) and renamed it J.S. Morgan & Co., situated at 22 Old Broad Street in the City of London. It became a major financial house, making loans to governments and companies in Europe, Latin America, and the United States. In addition to his wealth in England, Morgan also left $12.4 million in the US, around £2.6 million, plus a valuable art collection not included in these figures. His son was the celebrated banker J.P. Morgan (John Pierpont Morgan, 1847-1913), who left £1,179,832 in Britain, but lived mainly in New York.

2. Christopher Rice Mansel Talbot (1803-90) – left £1,399,173. Landowner.

The son of the landowner Thomas Mansel Talbot (1747-1813) and educated at Harrow and at Oriel College, Oxford, he was a large landowner, owning 33,920 acres worth £44,057 p.a. in Glamorganshire. He also enjoyed an income from coal and copper on his lands, and was Chairman of the South Wales Railway Company. He is said to have owned £1 million in railway shares at his death. Talbot was also a Liberal M.P. from 1830 until his death sixty years later, when he was the "Father of the House" and the last M.P. to have served in a pre-1832 Parliament. He was offered a peerage by Gladstone in 1869, which he declined. His daughter and heiress, Emily Charlotte Talbot (1840-1918) left £2,000,000. he lived at Magram Park near Aberfan, Glamorganshire.

3. Nathaniel Clayton (1811-90) – left £1,365,497. Portable steam engine manufacturer and engineer at Lincoln.

The son of Nathaniel Clayton (d. 1817), a river packet boat owner, he founded a small iron foundry in Lincoln with his brother-in-law Joseph Shuttleworth. It manufactured portable steam engines, used in farming, and also railway equipment and threshing machines. By 1890 his firm had manufactured no fewer than 26,000 portable steam engines, many of which were exported around the world, and was a leading employer of labour in Lincoln. He served as Mayor of Lincoln in 1856-57. Clayton lived at Eastcliffe House in Lincoln.

4. Sir Richard Wallace, 1st Bt. (1818-90) – left £1,226,353. Inherited landed wealth.
Wallace's life was discussed in an earlier part of this work. He was the illegitimate son of Richard Seymour-Conway, 4th Marquess of Hertford (1800-70, left £500,000, *q.v.*) and inherited much of his great wealth. In 1883 he owned 72,307 acres worth £85,737 p.a. He lived much of his life in Paris, where he built up a great art collection, but returned to England in 1871, and served as a Conservative M.P. from 1873 until 1885. He lived at Hertford House, Manchester Square, Middlesex and at Sudbourne Hall, Wickham Market, Suffolk. He left Hertford House and the great art collection he kept there to the nation; it is now the Wallace Collection. His widow Amelie *nee* Castlenau (1819-97, left £752,473).

5. Christian Allhusen (1806-90) – left £1,126,852. Chemical manufacturer in Newcastle-upon-Tyne.
Born in Kiel, Germany, the son of a merchant, he came to Newcastle-upon-Tyne around 1825 as a grain merchant. In 1840 he purchased a soap works at Gateshead, and then became a major chemical manufacturer at the Newcastle Chemical Works Co. Ltd., which chiefly produced alkali. He was also a director of many local and national companies and banks. He had lived at Elswick Hall, Newcastle-upon-Tyne, but later moved to Stoke Court in Buckinghamshire.

6. William Cavendish, 7th Duke of Devonshire (1808-90) – left £1,782,239. Landowner.
One of the richest landowners in Britain, whose wealthy family was discussed in a previous section, he was the son of (Hon.) William Cavendish (1783-1812, left £150,000), and succeeded as 3rd Earl of Burlington in 1834 and then succeeded his cousin as 7th Duke of Devonshire in 1858. He was educated at Eton and at Trinity College, Cambridge, and served as an M.P. (as "Lord Cavendish") from 1829 until 1834. He owned 198,572 acres worth £180,750 p.a. in Derbyshire and eleven other counties. He played a major role in developing Eastbourne and Barrow-in-Furness, and in opening iron mines. The Duke was the first Chancellor of London University, from 1836 till 1856. He lived at Chatsworth, Derbyshire, at Holker Hall in Lancashire, and at Devonshire House in Piccadilly, Middlesex.

7. William Henry Smith (1825-91) – left £1,773,388. Multiple newsagent, and government minister.
The developer of the renowned firm of W.H. Smith, he was the son of William Henry Smith (1792-1865, left £35,000), a wholesale newsagent. He became head of the firm and opened newsagencies at London railway stations, eventually gaining a monopoly on all of Britain's railways. He also was a pioneer of outdoor advertising and of lending libraries. Many will be surprised that he was also a major political figure, who served as a Conservative M.P. from 1868 until his death. He served, implausibly, as First Lord of the Admiralty from 1877 until 1880, which caused Gilbert and

Sullivan to write their famous song about being "ruler of the Queen's Navee." He rose to become First Lord of the Treasury from 1887 until his death. Shortly after his death his widow Emily *nee* Danvers (1828-1913, left £24,162) was created 1st Viscountess Hambleden in his honour. Smith's son William Frederick Danvers Smith, 2nd Viscount Hambleden (1868-1928) left £2,700,998.

8. Harry George Powlett, 4th Duke of Cleveland (1803-91) – left £1,449,242. Landowner.

The son of William Henry Vane, 1st Duke of Cleveland (1766-1842, left £1,000,000), he succeeded two older brothers to become Duke. His family's great landed holdings were discussed in a previous section. In 1883 he owned 104,194 acres worth £97,398 p.a. in Co. Durham, Shropshire, and elsewhere. He had served in Parliament (as "Lord Harry Vane") from 1841 till 1864, when he succeeded to the title, and later changed his surname to "Powlett." The dukedom became extinct with his death, with much of his property passing to Henry De Vere Vane, 9th Baron Barnard (1854-1918, left £130,000). The Duke lived at Raby Castle, Co. Durham, at Battle Abbey, Sussex, and at Cleveland House, 19 St. James's Square, Middlesex.

9. John Bullough (1837-91) – left £1,228,184. Manufacturer of power looms in Accrington, Lancashire.

The son of James Bullough (1799-1868, left £25,000), a textile machinery manufacturer and inventor in Accrington, John Bullough entered the family firm of Howard & Bullough in Accrington. It became the world's largest manufacturer of power looms and ring spinning frames. It employed over 2,000 workers. He was also an inventor in his industry. His son Sir George Bullough, 1st Bt. (1870-1939) was given a baronetcy in 1916 and left £710,037. Our man lived at The Rhyddings, Oswaldtwistle, Lancashire and at Castle Meggerne in Perthshire.

10. David Barclay Chapman (1799-1891) – left £1,117,877. Banker in the City of London.

From a Quaker banking family- although he was apparently an Anglican at death- he was the son of Abel Chapman (1752-1849), and was a banker and bill discounter with Overend, Gurney, a leading City bank which spectacularly crashed in 1866, causing a recession. Chapman's career after 1866 is unclear, and it cannot be readily traced, although he plainly remained very wealthy. Chapman also has the strange distinction of being mentioned by name in Karl Marx's *Das Capital*, in connection with the Overend, Gurney crash. The father of eleven children with three wives, he lived at Roehampton, Surrey and at 33 Queen's Gate, South Kensington, Middlesex.

11. Henry Arthur Brassey (1840-91) – left £1,099,086. Inherited from a civil engineer and railway builder.

The younger son of Thomas Brassey (1805-70, *q.v.*), the multi-millionaire railway builder and civil engineer, he was educated at Harrow and at University College, Oxford. He does not appear to have had an active profession, and served as a Liberal M.P. from 1868 till 1885. He lived at Preston Hall near Aylesford, Kent and at Bath House, Piccadilly, Middlesex.

12. Frank Clarke Hills (1808-92) – left £1,942,837. Chemical manufacturer at Deptford, Kent.

The son of Thomas Hills (1778-1837), he established a business as a manufacturing chemist, making sulphuric acid, ammonia, and other products at Deptford, Kent, and with a branch at

Greenwich. Hills achieved some fame as a pioneer of steam coaches, an early "horseless carriage" powered by a steam engine, which actually ran along the roads of Kent. In 1861 he lived at Denmark Hill, Lambeth, and in later life at Redleaf, Penshurst, Kent.

13. George Sutherland-Leveson-Gower, 3rd Duke of Sutherland (1828-92) – left £1,275,089. Landowner.

The remarkable wealth of the 1st Duke of Sutherland was discussed in a previous section, as well as how his lands were split between two of his sons. Our man was the son of George, 2nd Duke of Sutherland (1786-1861, left £1,000,000, *q.v.*), and was educated at Eton and at King's College, London. He served as a Liberal M.P., known as the Marquess of Stafford, from 1852 until he succeeded to the dukedom. In 1889 he married his second wife, Mary Blair, only four months after the death of his first wife, and later allegedly disinherited his legal heirs to leave his wealth to her. She served six months in prison as a result for "destroying documents." The 3rd Duke clearly did not disinherit his rightful heirs, since his son Cromartie, 4th Duke of Sutherland (1851-1913) left £1,220,906. The 3rd Duke lived at Dunrobin Castle in Scotland and at the magnificent Stafford House (now Lancaster House, the scene of international conferences) in St. James's, Middlesex.

14. Samuel Henry Thompson (1807-92) – left £1,134,394. Banker in Liverpool.

The son of Samuel Thompson (1767-1836, left £135,000), a banker in Liverpool with Heywood & Co., our man was a banker there with the same firm, then known as Arthur Heywood & Sons. It was sold before his death to the Bank of Liverpool. Our man was a J.P. and D.L., but had little in the way of a public presence, and little is known about his career. He lived at Thingwell Hall, Broad Green near Liverpool.

15. Sir Andrew Barclay Walker, 1st Bt. (1824-93) – left £2,876,782. Brewer in Liverpool.

The son of Peter Walker (1795-1879, left £366,005), who established the well-known brewery in Liverpool, our man was educated at Ayr Academy and at the Liverpool Institution. He became a partner in the firm, Peter Walker & Son, and expanded it, opening branches in Warrington and Burton. Walker served as Mayor of Liverpool in 1873-4 and 1876-7, and was made the first Hon. Freeman of Liverpool in 1890. In 1877 he built the Walker Art Gallery there, and was a great philanthropist of the city. He was knighted in 1877 and made a baronet in 1886. Walker lived at Gateacre Grange near Liverpool and at Osmaston Manor, Derbyshire, which he bought in 1884 for £250,000.

16. Edward Henry Stanley, 15th Earl of Derby (1826-93) – left £1,935,554. Land and colliery owner.

From the great landed Stanley family, he was the son of Edward Smith Stanley, 14th Earl of Derby (1799-1869, left £250,000), three times Conservative Prime Minister. He was educated at Rugby and at Trinity College, Cambridge, and served as a Conservative M.P. (as "Lord Stanley") from 1848-69. He was Foreign Secretary in 1866-8 and 1874-78, when he joined the Liberal party, serving under Gladstone as Colonial Secretary in 1882-5. His family's enormous landed holdings – 68,942 acres worth £163,273, chiefly in Lancashire, where they owned coal mines and urban property – was discussed in a previous section. He was succeeded by his brother Frederick, 16th

Earl of Derby (1841-1908), who left £917,350. Our man lived at Knowsley Hall in Lancashire and at Derby House in St. James's Square, Middlesex.

17. Algernon Peckover (1803-03) – left £1,161,476. Banker in Wisbech, Cambridgeshire.

From a prominent Quaker banking family in East Anglia, he was the son of Jonathan Peckover (d. 1834) a banker in Wisbech, and was educated at Wisbech Grammar School. He joined the Bradford Old Bank and then became a partner in Peckover, Gurney & Co., bankers of Wisbech. He remained a Quaker Elder until his death, not becoming an Anglican. His son Algernon Peckover, 1st Baron Peckover (1830-1919, left £901,601) was given a peerage in 1907. Our man's daughter Priscilla Peckover (1833-1931) was a prominent peace campaigner, with an entry in the *ODNB*. It is strange that a banker outside of London or a major urban area could become a millionaire, and how Peckover became so wealthy is unclear. He lived at Sibald's Holme, Wisbech, Cambridgeshire.

18. Sir Archibald Orr-Ewing, 1st Bt. (1818-93) – left £1,077,235. Calico printer and dyer in the Vale of Leven near Glasgow.

The son of William Ewing (1772-1853), a merchant in Glasgow, he was educated at Glasgow University and became a leading calico printer and turkey red dyer at Levenbank in West Dunbartonshire near Glasgow. It also had an office as 12 Lawrence Lane in the City of London, and was one of the largest dye works in Britain. He served as a Conservative M.P. from 1868 till 1892 and was made a baronet in 1886. He lived in later life at Ballikinrain Castle in Stirling, which he built.

19. Henry Page (1813-94) – left £1,037,698. Maltster and grain merchant at Ware, Hertfordshire.

A maltster and grain merchant in the town of Ware, Hertfordshire, near Hertford, he managed to become a millionaire, presumably by supplying breweries. He was the son of Henry Page (1780-1852). His widow Ann Elizabeth Page (1819-1900) left £947,700. His grandson was Sir Henry Page Croft, 1st Baron Croft (1881-1947), the well-known right-wing M.P. and Under-Secretary for War in 1940-45. Henry Page lived at Fanhams Hall in Ware and at 87 High Street, Ware, now the County Library.

20. Sir Gilbert Greenall, 1st Bt. (1806-94) – left £1,025,742. Brewer in Warrington, Lancashire.

The son of Edward Greenall (1758-1835), a brewer in St. Helens and Warrington, Gilbert Greenall became a partner in Parr, Lyons & Greenall, brewers of Warrington, now Greenall Whitley, the well-known brewers. He served as a Conservative M.P. between 1847 and 1892, and was made a baronet in 1876. His son Sir Gilbert Greenall, 2nd Bt. (1867-1938) was awarded a peerage in 1927 as 1st Baron Daresbury, and left £2,205,999. Our man lived at Walton Hall, Cheshire, near Warrington.

21. Andrew Montagu (1815-95) – left £2,005,000. Landowner.

This great untitled landowner was discussed in a previous section. He was the son of Richard Fountayne Wilson (1783-1847, left £100,000), and changed his name to "Montagu" in 1826 on inheriting a legacy. In 1883 he owned 27,265 acres worth £53,034, of which most was in the West Riding (20,700 acres worth £35,234 p.a.). Most of his wealth apparently derived from collieries and from urban property near Leeds. Montagu was a keen Tory, and paid off Disraeli's debts, charging him a much below market rate in repayments. Montagu lived at Melton Park, Doncaster, and at Ingmanthorpe Hall, Wetherby, Yorkshire.

22.George Henry Strutt (1826-95) – left £1,624,483. Cotton Manufacturer at Belper, Derbyshire.

A descendant of the famous pioneer of the cotton industry Jedidiah Strutt (1726-97) and the son of another Jedidiah Strutt (1785-1854), a cotton manufacturer in Belper who left £140,000, he continued the family business and died a millionaire. He was known for his philanthropy and was High Sheriff of Derbyshire in 1869. His son George Herbert Strutt (1854-1928) left £1,012,940. Our man was a relative of Edward Strutt, 1st Baron Belper (1801-80, left £180,000), in 1856 the first industrialist to receive a peerage. Our man lived at Bridgehill, Belper, Derbyshire.

23. John Peter Robinson (1837-95) – left £1,203,000. Retailer, chiefly in London.

The proprietor of the formerly well-known retail chain of Peter Robinson, he was the son of its founder, Peter Robinson (1804-74, left £350,000), who began in 1833 as the owner of a drapery shop. Our man developed the firm as department stores, centring on its flagship shop on Oxford Street in central London, but with branches around the country. It now exists as the Topshop chain, which branched off from it in the 1960s. Our man lived at Brookleigh, Esher, Surrey.

24. Roger Cunliffe (1824-95) – left £1,118,738. Banker in the City of London.

Born in Blackburn, Lancashire, he was the son of James Cunliffe (1798-1854, left £190,000, a banker with Cunliffe Brooks & Co. at 29 Lombard Street, City of London. Our man was a private banker with Roger Cunliffe, Sons & Co. at 6 Princes Street, Mansion House in the City of London. The nature of its business is unclear. He was the father of Walter Cunliffe, 1st Baron Cunliffe (1855-1920, left £650,000), Governor of the Bank of England 1914-18, during the First World War. Our man lived at 69 Cromwell Road, Middlesex and at Leatherhead, Surrey.

25. Sir Charles Booth, 3rd Bt. (1812-96) – left £1,932,201. Gin distiller at Clerkenwell, Middlesex.

The founder of the famous distillery which produced Booth's Gin was Sir Felix Booth, 1st Bt. (1775-1850, left £250,000), who established its works at Clerkenwell. He also funded various expeditions to the Arctic and received a baronetcy in 1835. The title then passed to our man's elder brother Sir Williamson Booth, 2nd Bt. (1810-77, left £90,000), and then to our man, who was educated at Eton and Christ Church, Oxford, but who was active in heading the distillery at 35 Cow Cross Street, Clerkenwell. He lived at Netherfield near Ware, Hertfordshire.

26. Maurice, Baron de Hirsch (1831-96) – left £1,372,164. Merchant banker in the City of London and in Paris.

He was born in Munich, Bavaria, the son of the banker to the King of Bavaria, who made him a Baron in 1869. Our man was the head of the merchant bank Bischoffscheim & Goldschmidt, with branches in London, Paris, and Brussels. He lived mainly in Paris and died in Brunn, Austria. De Hirsch is best known as a great philanthropist to develop Jewish agricultural settlements in Argentina, the US, and Canada. He was alive when Herzl wrote *Der Judenstaat* in 1895, advocating an independent Jewish state in Palestine, but was apparently not a Zionist. His wife Clara *nee*

Bishoffscheim (1833-99) was also a great philanthropist.

27. Sir Julian Goldsmid, 3rd Bt. (1838-96) – left £1,021,000. Bullion broker and financier in the City of London.

The first holder of this baronetcy was Sir Isaac Lyon Goldsmid, 1st Bt. (1778-1859, *q.v.*), the millionaire bullion broker. Our man was the son of Frederick David Goldsmid (d. 1866, left £400,000), and succeeded his uncle Sir Francis Goldsmid, 2nd Bt. (1808-78, left £1,000,000, *q.v.*). He was educated at University College London, and later served as Vice-Chancellor of London University from 1895 until his death. He was also a practicing barrister (called at Lincoln's Inn, 1864), and a significant financier in the City. He was Chairman of the Submarine Telegraph Co. and other bodies. He served as a Liberal, later Liberal Unionist M.P. in 1866-68, 1870-80, and 1885 until his death, and was Deputy Speaker of the House when he died. He lived at 105 Piccadilly, Middlesex and at Somerhill, Tonbridge, Kent.

28. William Louis Winans (1823-97) – left £2,522,006. Railway contractor in Russia.

Born in New Jersey, the son of the pioneering American railway contactor Ross Winans (1796-1877), he became a railway contractor in Russia, based in St. Petersburg, and was paid a fortune for his work by the Tsar. This was the basis of his wealth. He never returned to the United States, but settled in Britain. According to one account, this was because he became so seasick on his first voyage across the Atlantic that he simply could not face another sea voyage. Winans appears to have had no occupation at all in Britain. He lived at 1 Chichester Terrace, Brighton and at 10 Pembridge Square, Middlesex, and rented an estate in Scotland.

29. James Jenkinson Bibby (1813-97) – left £1,773,533. Shipowner in Liverpool.

The head of the well-known Bibby Steamship Line, which mainly consisted of a merchant fleet trading with the Mediterranean, he was the son of John Bibby (1775-1840), the founder of the line, who was murdered in mysterious circumstances one night in 1840 in Liverpool. The case remains open after over 180 years. Our man then became head of the firm, whose official name was John Bibby & Son. He was also a metal merchant in Liverpool. Bibby was Chairman of the Liverpool Steam Ship Owners Association. His son Frank Bibby (1857-1923) left £1,229,483. Our man lived at Hardwicke Grange in Shropshire.

30. Arthur Pemberton Heywood-Lonsdale (1835-97) – left £1,428,779. Banking fortune in Liverpool.

He was the son of (Revd.) Henry Gylby Lonsdale (d. 1851), and was educated at Eton and at Balliol College, Oxford. He was the grandson of John Pemberton Heywood (1804-77, q.v.) who was the richest banker in Liverpool, and left £1,900,000; his wealth was inherited in large measure from Heywood's widow Anna Maria Heywood (*nee* Jones, 1813-87, *q.v.*), who left £651,238. Heywood-Lonsdale was also a landowner, owning 4049 acres worth £7,048 p.a. in Shropshire and Lancashire. He does not appear to have had any occupation. He had residences at Shavington and Cloverly, Shropshire, and at Garristown, Co. Louth.

31. Sir William Gray (1823-98) – left £1,500,423. Shipbuilder at Hartlepool, Co. Durham.

The son of Matthew Gray, a draper and shipowner in Hartlepool, he became a draper and then went into shipbuilding there. His firm, Denton, Grey & Co., became the largest shipbuilders in the world, producing cargo steamers and early oil tankers. He also owned iron and steel mills. He served as Mayor of Hartlepool in 1861-63 and was knighted in 1890. His son Sir William Cresswell Gray, 1st Bt. (1867-1924, left £417,548) was made a baronet in 1917.

32. Baron Ferdinand James Anselm de Rothschild (1839-98) – left £1,488,129. Merchant banker in the City of London.
The son of Baron Anselm de Rothschild (1803-74), the head of the Austrian branch of the renowned family, he was a partner in its British branch in the City of London. He served as a Liberal, later Liberal Unionist, M.P. from 1885 until his death. He is best known for building the great Rothschild mansion at Waddesdon Manor near Aylesbury, Buckinghamshire, which became the scene of many dinners and parties by the British elite. He was also a major art collector. He lived at 143 Piccadilly, Middlesex and at Waddesdon.

33. Charles Henry Mills, 1st Baron Hillingdon (1830-98) – left £1,479,261. Banker in the City of London.
The son of the wealthy banker Sir Charles Mills, 1st Bt. (1792-1872, left £600,000, *q.v.*), he was educated at Eton and at Christ Church, Oxford, and then joined the family bank, Glyn, Mills & Currie at 67 Lombard Street in the City of London, a private bank, where he became Senior Partner. He also served as a Conservative M.P. between 1865 and **188???**. In 1886 he was created 1st Baron Hillingdon. In 1853 he married into the aristocracy, his wife being Lady Louisa, Lascelles, daughter of the 3rd Earl of Harewood. Their son Charles William Mills, 2nd Baron Hillingdon (1855-1919), left £1,000,000. He lived at Hillingdon House, Uxbridge, Middlesex, and at Camelford House, Park Lane, Middlesex.

34. Edward Davies (1852-98) – left £1,206,311. Colliery owner, etc. in South Wales.
The son of Davies Davies (1818-90), a well-known colliery owner and engineering contractor in south Wales who served as a Liberal M.P. from 1874-80 and left £404,435, he was also a colliery owner before dying at forty-five. His son David Davies, 1st Baron Davies (1880-1944, left £506,445) was a Liberal M.P. from 1906 till 1929 and was given a peerage in 1932. Our man lived at Plasdinam, Llandinam, Montgomeryshire.

35. Richard Ratcliff (1830-98) – left £1,116,190. Brewer in Burton-on-Trent, Staffordshire.
The son of Samuel Ratcliff (1783-1861, left £160,000), one of the founders of what became Bass, Ratcliff & Gretton, the great brewers in Burton, he continued the business and died a millionaire. Ratcliff was a J.P. for Derbyshire and Staffordshire, but otherwise did not participate in public life, and little is known about his career. In later life he lived at Stanford Hall, Nottinghamshire.

36. Charles Wheeley Lea (1827-98) – left £1,100,517. Worcestershire-sauce manufacturer in Worcester.
The son of John Wheeley Lea (d. 1874, left £90,000), one of the founders and proprietors, along with the Perrins family, of the famous brand of Worcestershire sauce, he became a partner in the firm and helped to expand it. Little is known of his life or career. He lived at Parkfield, Hallow, Worcestershire.

37. Frederick Wootton Isaacson (1831-98) – left £1,052,116. Silk importer and retailer in London.

Born in Mildenhall, Suffolk, the son of Frederick Isaacson, he had a diverse and somewhat mysterious career as, first, a silk importer, then as a retailer, the proprietor of "Madam Elise," a millinery shop on Regent Street in central London, and later as an importer from the West Indies. How he became a millionaire from this is unclear, and he may well have had other interests. He may also have been involved in coal mining. He served as Conservative M.P. for Stepney from 1886 until his death. He lived at 18 Upper Grosvenor Street, Middlesex.

38. Maurice Beddington (1821-98) – left £1,030,574. Import /export merchant in London.

The son of Henry Moses (1790-1875, left £600,000, *q.v.*), a woollen merchant, apparently trading with Australia and New Zealand, along with his brothers and sisters he changed his surname to "Beddington." The exact nature of his business is unclear. He was described in the 1871 Census as an "export and import merchant" and in the 1881 Census as a "merchant," but nothing further could be found about his business life. He lived at 91 Lancaster Gate, Hyde Park, Middlesex, and at The Limes, Carshalton, Surrey.

39. George Frederick Muntz (1822-98) – left £1,017,653. Metal manufacturer in Birmingham.

The son of George Frederick Muntz (1794-1857, left £600,000, *q.v.*), a wealthy metal manufacturer in Birmingham and a radical M.P., he continued the family business and served as a J.P. and D.L. for Warwickshire but did not enter politics. His brother Sir Philip Muntz, 1st Bt. (1839-1908, left £60,687), a Conservative M.P. from 1884 until his death, he was made a baronet in 1902. Our man lived at Umberslade, Hockley Heath, Warwickshire.

40. John Gretton (1836-99) – left £2,883,640. Brewer in Burton-on-Trent.

The son of John Gretton (1793-1867, left £80,000), a brewer in Burton-on-Trent, Staffordshire, he became a very wealthy partner in Bass, Ratcliff & Gretton of Burton, one of the largest brewers in Britain. Little is known of his business career, but he was also a maltster in Burton. His son John Gretton, 1st Baron Gretton (1867-1944, left £2,302,973) was a well-known right-wing Conservative M.P. from 1895 until 1943, and was given a peerage in 1944. Our man lived in Moncorvo House, 66 Ennismore Gardens, Middlesex.

41. William Orme Foster (1814-99) – left £2,587,081. Ironmaster in Stourbridge, Worcestershire; also a landowner.

The son of the Stourbridge ironmaster William Foster (1784-1860, left £50,000), he was educated at Shrewsbury School and inherited much of the wealth of his uncle James Foster (d. 1853), ironmaster and M.P., who left £734,000. In 1871 our man was described in the Census as an "ironmaster employing 3000 men and boys." He served as a Liberal M.P. from 1857 until 1868. In 1883, he owned 21,062 acres of land worth £28,426 p.a. in Shropshire and elsewhere. His son William Henry Foster (1846-1924) left £1,250,000. Our man lived at 35 Lowndes Square, Middlesex and at Stourton Court, Worcestershire.

42. Henry Lewis Raphael (1832-99) – left £1,527,842. Merchant banker and stockbroker in the City of London.

From a well-connected Anglo-Jewish family – his mother was a Mocatta, and related to the Rothschilds and other "Cousinhood" families – he was the son of the City of London merchant banker Lewis Raphael (1794-1856, left £100,000), he became a merchant banker and stockbroker with Raphael & Joseph at 25 Throgmorton Street, City of London. His bank specialised in financing American and European firms and in arbitrage, and was one of the most successful of its time in the City. Two of his brothers left millionaire estates. He lived at 31 Rutland Place, Middlesex and at Newmarket in Suffolk.

43. Sir Henry Tate, 1st Bt. (1819-99) – left £1,264,215. Sugar refiner and sugar cube manufacturer in Liverpool and London.

The son of (Revd.) William Tate (1773-1836), a Unitarian minister in Chorley, Lancashire, he was apprenticed at thirteen to his brother, a grocer in Liverpool, and then began a retail and later wholesale grocery business. From 1859 he was a partner in a firm of sugar refiners, which grew enormously when, in 1875, he acquired the patent on the making of sugar cubes. He had factories in Liverpool and later at Silvertown in London. In 1897 he endowed the Tate Gallery as a museum of British art, and was made a baronet in 1898. His sugar cubes and art gallery have guaranteed that he remains a household name. His son Sir William Henry Tate, 2nd Bt. (d. 1921) left £1,072,569. Our man lived at Park Hill, Streatham Common, Surrey.

44. Thomas Henry Ismay (1837-99) – left £1,217,882. Shipbroker and shipowner in Liverpool.

The son of Joseph Ismay, a shipowner and shipbroker at Maryport, Cumberland, he was apprenticed to shipbrokers in Liverpool, and set up his own business as a shipbroker and shipowner in 1858. He then formed the famous White Star Line, which in 1892 owned eighteen steamers, and was also a shipbuilder. His son Joseph Bruce Ismay (1862-1937, left £693,306), Chairman of the White Star Line, became internationally notorious in 1912 when, a passenger on the Line's new ship the *Titanic,* he got into a lifeboat rather than go down with the ship, while 1,500 other passengers and crew drowned. Our man lived at Dawpool, Thurstaston, Cheshire.

45. John Nixon (1815-99) – left £1,115,070. Colliery owner in South Wales.

The son of a tenant farmer, he was apprenticed to a mining agent, and then began exporting Welsh coal to France. Remarkably, in 1860 he succeeded in getting the French navy to adopt Welsh coal. He then opened a colliery in south Wales, later known as Nixon's Navigation Co., and introduced many innovations in the mining of coal. All of his mines appear to have been in south Wales. In later life he lived at 117 Westbourne Terrace, Middlesex, which is virtually next door to Paddington Station, making it easier for him to return to south Wales.

Chapter 4: The Largest Estates Left in the UK, 1900–1949

1900–1909

The first decade of the twentieth century saw the growth of the "Plutocracy" as it is widely imagined, with new wealth-holders accumulating vast fortunes which dwarfed the wealth of the old aristocracy, rich as they still were. The two largest estates of this period were worth £11 million and £8 million, dwarfing anything seen in the past. The following list of millionaires deceased between 1900 and 1909 is in chronological order, with those probated in each year listed in descending order. It includes only millionaire estates, not half-millionaires.

1. Baron Adolphe Charles de Rothschild (1823-1900) – left £2,257,980. Merchant banker in Paris.
The son of Baron Carl Mayer de Rothschild (1788-1857), the head of the Naples branch of the famous merchant bank, which was closed down in 1861, he lived in Paris, where he died, and at Lake Geneva in Switzerland. He appears to have had no direct connection with the London branch of the bank, and why he left such a vast sum in England is unclear.

2. William Richard Sutton (1836-1900) – left £2,137,159. Carrier in London and elsewhere, also a distiller, etc.
The son of Frederick Wilson Sutton (1798-1852), a stationer in the City of London, our man attended the City of London School, and then established the carriers Sutton & Co., which grew into the largest in Britain. It carried goods door-to-door in bulk, using bulk carrying on the railways, and had no fewer than 600 offices in Britain and abroad in 1900. It headquarters was at Golden Lane in the City of London. He was also a property developer in London and the owner of a distillery, Sutton, Carden & Co., in Finsbury. In his will he established the well-known Sutton Dwellings Trust, which built flats for the poor; by 1939 it had constructed 8,000 such houses. He lived at Sunnydene, Sydenham Hill, Kent.

3. Samuel George Smith (1822-1900) – left £1,574,644. Banker in the City of London.
The son of the banker Samuel George Smith (1789-1863, left £500,000, *q.v.*), our man was educated at Rugby and at Trinity College, Cambridge, and became a partner in his family's private bank of Smith, Payne & Smith, of Lombard Street in the City of London. He served as a Conservative M.P. from 1859 till 1880. His Smith relatives received two peerages, as Baron Carrington and Baron Bicester. He lived at 5 Albemarle Street, Middlesex and at Sacombe Park, Ware, Hertfordshire.

4. William George Armstrong, 1st Baron Armstrong (1810-1900) – left £1,400,682.

Engineering and armaments manufacturer at Newcastle-upon-Tyne.

The son of William Armstrong (1778-1857), a corn merchant who served as Mayor of Newcastle-upon-Tyne, he was trained as a solicitor and practiced for eleven years. In the 1840s, and with no engineering training, Armstrong began to design piston engines. In 1847 he set up in business (W.G. Armstrong & Co.) at Elswick in Newcastle-upon-Tyne as the manufacturer of cranes and hydraulic equipment. Later known as Armstrong, Whitworth & Co., it also manufactured military equipment and warships; he is also regarded as the inventor of modern artillery. His mansion at Cragside, Westmorland, was the first house in Britain to be powered by hydroelectricity. He was President of the Institution of Civil Engineers in 1881-2. Armstrong was knighted in 1859 and awarded a peerage in 1887. He had no children, and his title was revived in 1903 for his great-nephew William Watson, 1st Baron Armstrong (1863-1941, left £216,846).

5. Sir William Cunliffe-Brooks, 1st Bt. (1819-1900) – left £1,112,477. Banker in Manchester and in the City of London.

The son of the Manchester cotton manufacturer and banker Samuel Brooks (1793-1864, left £250,000), he was educated at Rugby and at St. John's College, Cambridge, and was then called to the bar at Lincoln's Inn. He then became the Senior Partner in Cunliffe Brooks & Co., bankers of Manchester. It later opened a branch at 81 Lombard Street in the City of London. Cunliffe-Brooks served as a Conservative M.P. between 1869 and 1892, and was awarded a baronetcy in 1886. He lived at Barlow Hall, Chorlton-cum-Hardy, Lancashire, and at Glentanar, Aberdeenshire.

6. John Crichton-Stuart, 3rd Marquess of Bute (1847-1900) – left £1,142,247. Landowner.

One of the wealthiest of landowners (see previous section), much of his income derived not from his Scottish lands but from his holdings in Glamorganshire, especially in Cardiff, which his father had helped to develop. He was the son of John, 2nd Marquess of Bute (1793-1848, left £100,000) and was educated at Harrow and at Christ Church, Oxford. In 1883 he owned 116,668 acres worth £151,135 p.a., of which 21,402 acres worth £100,000 p.a. was in Glamorganshire. At the age of twenty-one he converted to Roman Catholicism, causing a scandal, and is depicted in Disraeli's novel *Lothair*. He was known as an author and rebuilder of stately homes. He lived at Dumfries House, 83 Eccleston Square, Middlesex, and at Mt. Stuart, Rothesay, Isle of Bute.

7. James Craig (1828-1900) – left £1,032,445. Distiller in Belfast.

The head of Dunville & Co., the largest distillers in Belfast. He entered the firm as a clerk, and rose to become its Senior Partner. He is best remembered as the father of James Craig, 1st Viscount Craigavon (1871-1940, left £27,500), Conservative M.P. 1906-27, and the first Prime Minister of Northern Ireland after its Partition, from 1921-40, created a baronet in 1918 and a viscount in 1927. Our man lived at Craigavon in Belfast.

8. Samuel Lewis (1838-1901) – left £2,682,597. Money lender in Mayfair.

The son of an impoverished Jewish immigrant in Birmingham, Lewis worked as a pedlar from the age of thirteen, and was then a travelling jeweller. In 1869 he became a money lender, operating at 17 Cork Street, Mayfair. He lent in large measure to aristocrats, often giving much better terms than the banks, as well as being more discrete and offering larger loans. Engaging and witty, most aristocrats became friendly with him, despite his lowly background. He and his wife Ada

Lewis-Hill (d. 1906, left £1,151,073) are said to have given £3.4 million to charity. He lived at 23 Grosvenor Square, Middlesex. There is a biography of Lewis by Gerry Black, *Lender to the Lords, Giver to the Poor* (1992).

9. Henry Wyndham, 2nd Baron Leconfield (1830-1901) – left £1,861,959. Landowner.

The son of George Wyndham, 1st Baron Leconfield (1787-1869, left £250,000), who had succeeded to the estates of Lord Egremont, in 1883 he owned 109,935 acres worth £88,112 p.a., in Sussex, Yorkshire, Co. Clare, and three other counties (see previous section). He was educated at Eton and at Christ Church, Oxford, and served as a Conservative M.P. from 1854 until 1869, when he succeeded to the peerage. In 1867 he married Lady Constance Primrose, sister of the Earl of Rosebery. Leconfield lived at 9 Chesterfield Gardens, Middlesex and at Petworth in Sussex. His son Charles, 3rd Baron Leconfield (1872-1951) left £2,136,439.

10. Sir Francis Cook, 1st Bt. (1817-1901) – left £1,600,000. Wholesale clothing merchant and clothing manufacturer in the City of London.

The son of the wealthy wholesale linen draper at St. Paul's Churchyard in the City of London William Cook (1784-1869, left £600,000, *q.v.*), he continued as a large-scale wholesale clothing merchant and importer (Cook, Son & Co.) at that address, as well as a clothing manufacturer. In 1864 he was created a Viscount of Portugal (although why is unclear) and in 1886 received a baronetcy. He was a noted art collector, owning paintings by El Greco, Van Eyck, Turner, and Constable among others. His second wife was the sister of Victoria Claffin Woodhill (1838-1927), the well-known campaigner for female suffrage. His son Sir Frederick Lucas Cook, 2nd Bt., M.P. (1844-1920) left £1,082,973. Another son, Wyndham Francis Cook (1860-1905) left £1,203,810. Our man lived at Doughty House, Richmond, Surrey, and at Cintra in Portugal.

11. James Stern (1835-1901) – left £1,114,173. Merchant banker in the City of London.

The son of Julius Jacob Stern (1807-52), a banker in Berlin, he was a member of the enormously wealthy but little-known Stern family, of Stern Brothers, of 6 Angel Court in the City of London. Herman, Baron de Stern (1815-87, left £3.5 million, *q.v.*) was his uncle. Our man was a Partner in the merchant bank. He lived at 25 Princes Gate, Middlesex.

12. Panaghi Athanarius Vagliano (1814-1902) – left £2,888,095. Merchant and shipowner in Greece and in the City of London.

Born on the Greek island of Cephalonia, he and his brothers established Vagliano Brothers, which became a major exporter of grain from Russia via the Black Sea, and a major Greek shipowning concern. He moved to London in 1858, where he was heavily involved in Greek shipping, insurance, and mercantile activities from his office at Old Broad Street in the City of London. Her was one of the very richest of the many wealthy Greek merchants in London. His nephew Alcibiades Vagliano (d. 1924) left £1,700,641. Our man lived at 16 Dawson Place, Bayswater, Middlesex.

13. William Wentworth Fitzwilliam, 6th Earl Fitzwilliam (1815-1902) – left £2,590,271. land and colliery owner.

The son of Charles, 5th Earl Fitzwilliam (1786-1857, left £250,000), he was educated at Eton and Trinity College, Cambridge, and served as a Whig M.P. in 1837-41 and 1846-57, when he succeeded to the peerage. From one of the greatest of landed families, in 1883 he owned 115,743 acres worth £138,801 p.a. (see previous section), chiefly in Yorkshire and Co. Wicklow, which included extensive collieries. His son William, 7th Earl Fitzwilliam (1872-1943) left £1,320,969. He lived at Wentworth House near Rotherham, Yorkshire and at 4 Grosvenor Square, Middlesex.

14. Harry Leslie Blundell McCalmont (1861-1902) – left £2,279,227. Inherited merchant banking wealth from the City of London.

He inherited most of the wealth of the enormously wealthy City of London merchant banker Hugh McCalmont (1809-87, *q.v.*), his uncle, who left £3.1 million. He was the son of the barrister Hugh Barklie Blundell McCalmont (d. 1888, left £44,265), and was educated at Eton. A professional army officer who fought in the Boer War, he served as a Conservative M.P. from 1895 until his death, and was a highly successful racehorse owner. He lived at Cheveley Park, Newmarket, Cambridgeshire, and at 11 St. James's Square, Middlesex.

15. Edwin Salvin Bowlby (1830-1902) – left £1,316,000. Inherited a sugar refining fortune from Whitechapel, Middlesex.

He was the nephew and heir of William Hodgson (1803-86, left £1.1 million), who inherited wealth earned as sugar refiners in Whitechapel. He was educated at Rugby and at St. John's College, Cambridge, and was a barrister of the Inner Temple, although he did not practice. It does not appear that he had any occupation. He lived at Galston Park, Hertfordshire and at 56 Lowndes Square, Middlesex.

16. Stephen Augustus Ralli (1829-1902) – left £1,068,824. Import-export merchant in the City of London.

A member of the great Greek mercantile family of Ralli, he was born in Marseilles, France, the son of Augustus Ralli (1792-1868, left £80,000). He became a Partner in Ralli Brothers of 25 Finsbury Circus and of 5 Fenchurch Street in the City of London, and expanded the firm's trade with the United States, India, and Russia. He lived at 32 Park Lane, Middlesex and in Hove, Sussex.

17. Thomas Frederick Charles Vernon-Wentworth (1831-1902) – left £1,032,755. Land and colliery owner.

The son of the landowner Frederick Vernon-Wentworth (1795-1885, left £962,359, *q.v.*), he was educated at Eton and at Trinity College, Cambridge, and served briefly as an M.P. in 1859. In 1883 he owned 22,930 acres worth £20,546 p.a. in Yorkshire, Suffolk, and other counties. His wealth derived in part from coal mines. He lived at Wentworth Castle near Barnsley, Yorkshire and at 11 Connaught Place, Middlesex.

18. Sir John Blundell Maple, 1st Bt. (1845-1903) – left £2,153,000. Retailer at Tottenham Court Road, Middlesex.

He was the son of John Maple (d. 1900, left £892,503), the founder of the well-known furniture retailer, Maple & Co., on Tottenham Court Road in central London. He was educated at King's College, London, and became head of the firm. Maple served as a Conservative M.P. from 1887 until his death, and was also a member of the London County Council from 1895 until 1901. He was also a successful racehorse owner. He was knighted in 1892 and was made a baronet in 1897.

A noted philanthropist, he paid for the rebuilding of University College Hospital in London. He lived at Childwick Bury, Hertfordshire and at Clarence House, Regent's Park, Middlesex.

19. Samuel Palmer (1820-1903) – left £1,334,830. Biscuit manufacturer at Reading, Berkshire.

One of three Quaker brothers who founded the famous biscuit manufacturers, Huntley & Palmer, of Reading, Berkshire. They developed it into the largest biscuit manufacturers in the world, employing 5,000 workers by the 1890s. His brother George (d. 1897) left £967,554. Our man's son Samuel Ernest Palmer, 1st Baron Palmer (1858-1948, left £1,104,558), was the founder of the Royal College of Music, and was given a peerage in 1933. Another son, Charles Herbert Palmer (1860-1937) left £1,335,840. Our man lived at Northcourt, Hampstead, Middlesex.

20. Edward Louis Raphael (1831-1903) – left £1,127,849. Merchant banker in the City of London.

The son of Louis Raphael (d. 1856, left £100,000), he was the brother of the millionaire Henry Lewis Raphael (1832-1899, *q.v.*), whose merchant bank was at Throgmorton Street in the City of London. Our man lived at 4 Connaught Place, Hyde Park, Middlesex.

21. Sir Joseph Sebag-Montefiore (1822-1903) – left £1,019,849. Stockbroker in the City of London.

The son of Solomon Sebag (d. 1831) and the nephew of the famous Sir Moses Montefiore (1784-1885), he established the stockbroking firm of Joseph Sebag & Co., of 14 Throgmorton Street, City of London. He was a notable figure in the Anglo-Jewish community, especially as President of the Council of Spanish and Portuguese Jews, and was knighted in 1896. He lived at East Cliff Lodge, Ramsgate, Kent and at 4 Hyde Park Gardens, Middlesex.

22. Alexandra Ralli (1842-1903) – left £1,012,171. Mercantile fortune from the City of London.

She was the widow of Peter Pantia Ralli (1837-68, left £500,000, *q.v.*), of the great Greek merchant family based in the City of London, who were import-export merchants. She is not known to have taken part in any public matters. She lived at 5 Hyde Park Place, Middlesex. Her son Peter Ralli (1868-1835) left £1,330,658.

23. Edward Brook (1825-1904) – left £2,181,318. Silk and sewing thread manufacturer at Meltham near Huddersfield, Yorkshire.

The son of the cotton manufacturer Jonas Brook (1775-1836), who established the silk and sewing thread manufacturers at the Meltham Mills near Huddersfield, he succeeded his cousin Charles Brook (1814-72, left £250,000) as Senior Partner in the firm, Jonas Brook & Brothers. The firm employed over 1,000 people by the late nineteenth century. He lived at Hoddom Castle, Dumfriesshire, which he purchased for £225,000, and at Southport, Lancashire.

24. Baron Horaz (*sic*) von Landau (1824-1903) – left £1,485,950. Merchant banker in Paris and Florence, Italy.

Born in Odessa, the son of Leon Rafael Landau (c. 1797-1882), a banker at Budapest, von Landau worked for the Rothschilds before becoming a merchant banker in France and at Florence, Italy, where he lived after 1866. He died in Budapest. He was a well-known collector of rare books and manuscripts. As with some other foreign bankers, he had no apparent connections with Britain, and why he left a vast sum in the UK is unclear.

25. George William Duff Assheton-Smith (1848-1904) – left £1,485,112. Landowner and slate quarry owner in Caernarvonshire.

The son of Robert George Duff (1819-90, left £204,846), he was educated at Eton and Christ Church, Oxford. He added "Assheton-Smith" to his name in 1859 when he inherited the Vaynol estate near Bangor from Matilda (d. 1859, left £200,000), the widow of his great uncle Thomas Assheton-Smith (d. 1858, left £200,000). It included one of the most lucrative slate quarry mining areas in Britain. In 1883 he owned 34,482 acres worth £43,022 p.a., nearly all in Caernarvonshire. His mines experienced a major strike in 1885-6. He lived at Vaynol, Carnarvonshire.

26. Spencer Charrington (1818-1904) – left £1,255,000. Brewer in Mile End, Middlesex.

The Senior Partner in the Anchor Brewery in Mile End, Middlesex, in London's East End, he was the son of Nicholas Charrington (1771-1827), already a wealthy brewer, as our man was educated at Eton. He became Senior Partner in the brewery following the death of his brother Edward Charrington (d. 1888, left £386,082). Our man served as a Conservative M.P. from 1885 until his death. At the time of his death aged eighty-six, he was the oldest serving Member of the House of Commons. Charrington's beer is still a household name. He lived at 19 Carlton House Terrace, Middlesex, and at Hunsdon House near Ware, Hertfordshire.

27. John Pennington Thomasson (1841-1904) – left £1,161,792. Cotton manufacturer in Bolton.

From a Quaker family but later an Anglican, he was the son of Thomas Thomasson (1808-76, left £25,000), a cotton manufacturer in Bolton who was also a well-known radical who financed the Anti-Corn Law League and has an entry in the *ODNB*. Our man was educated at University College School in London, and became head of the family cotton firm of John Thomasson & Son in Bolton, which employed 650 hands by the 1850s. He served as a Liberal M.P. from 1880 till 1885. His son Franklin Thomasson (1873-1941, left £223,209) was the proprietor of *The Tribune* newspaper and a Liberal M.P. in 1906-10. Our man lived at "Woodside" in Bolton, Lancashire.

28. Edmund Denison-Beckett, 1st Baron Grimthorpe (1816-1905) – left £2,126,324. Inherited money from railway promotion in Doncaster and from banking in Leeds; also a barrister.

The son of Sir Edmund Beckett, 4th Bt. (1784-1874, left £350,000), a railway promoter who was known as the "richest man in Doncaster," and the brother of William Beckett (1826-1890, left £460,426), of a Leeds bank, of which he probably inherited a share, he was educated at Eton and at Trinity College, Cambridge, and was a barrister of Lincoln's Inn (called 1841) and a Q.C. from 1854. He was a noted ecclesiastical controversialist, and Chancellor of the Diocese of York, and also a well-known amateur horologist who was responsible for designing the chimes of Big Ben. He was given a peerage in 1886. He lived at "Blatchwood," St. Albans, Hertfordshire and at 33 Queen Anne Street, Middlesex.

29. Francis Thomas de Grey, 7th Earl Cowper (1834-1905) – left £1,117,914. Landowner.

The son of Frederick, 6th Earl Cowper (1806-56, he also inherited much wealth from his maternal grandfather Thomas, 2nd Earl De Grey (1781-1859, left £100,000. Our man's paternal grandmother was the sister of Lord Melbourne the Prime Minister. Our man was educated at Harrow and at Christ Church, Oxford. In 1883 he owned 37,869 acres worth £60,392 p.a., in Hertfordshire, Bedfordshire, and nine other counties. He served as Lord Lieutenant of Ireland from 1880-82. He lived at Panshanger, Hertford, where "the Souls" group often met, and at 4 St. James's Square, Middlesex.

30. Wyndham Francis Cook (1860-1905) – left £1,203,810. Wholesale clothing warehouseman and manufacturer in the City of London.

The younger son of Sir Francis Cook, 1st Bt. (1817-1901, left £1,600,000, *q.v.*), he was educated at Harrow before becoming a Partner in the firm at St. Paul's Churchyard in the City of London, before dying at forty-four. He lived at 69 Cadogan Square, Middlesex.

31. Sir Robert Jardine, 1st Bt. (1825-1905) – left £1,114,489. China merchant in Hong Kong.

The son of a farmer in Scotland and educated at Merchiston Castle School, Edinburgh, he worked in a bank in London before going with his brothers to Hong Kong in 1845, where he became the head of Jardine Matheson, the famous export merchants. He dealt mainly in tea. Returning to England, he served as a Liberal, later Liberal Unionist, M.P. from 1865 until 1892. He was created a baronet in 1885. His son Sir Robert William Jardine, 2nd Bt. (1868-1927) left £1,547,203. Our man lived at Carrick Castle, Argyllshire, and at 24 St. James's Square, Middlesex.

32. Francis Edward Fox-Strangways, 5th Earl of Ilchester (1847-1905) – left £1,009,000. Land and urban property owner.

The son of (Hon.) (Revd.) John Fox-Strangways (d. 1859, left £18,000), he succeeded his uncle William, 4th Earl of Ilchester (d. 1865, left £70,000). He was educated at Eton and at Christ Church, Oxford. In 1883 he owned 32,849 acres worth £43,452 p.a. in Dorset and Somerset, and also owned fifty-four acres around Holland House in west London, much of which was not developed until his time. His son Giles, 6th Earl of Ilchester (1874-1959, left £195,240), was an historian of note. Our man lived at Holland House, Middlesex and at Melbury House, Dorchester, Dorset.

33. Alfred Beit (1853-1906) – left £8,049,886. Diamond and gold magnate and financier in South Africa.

One of the richest of the "Randlords" who became wealthy by owning diamond and gold mines in South Africa, he was born in Hamburg, the son of a merchant, and was apprenticed to a diamond firm in Amsterdam. Beit went to the Kimberleys in 1875 and befriended other "Randlords" including Cecil Rhodes and Sir Julius Wernher. Beit and Wernher gained control of the diamond mines there. He also opened gold mines, and was a major financier. He settled in England in 1888, where he lived at Aldford House on Park Lane and at Tewin Water near Welwyn, Hertfordshire. He was a noted philanthropist, establishing the Beit Professorship of British Commonwealth History at Oxford and supporting many charities. Unmarried, his heir was his brother Sir Otto Beit, 1st Bt. (1865-1930), who left £3,784,343.

34. Sir Charles Tennant, 1st Bt. (1823-1906) – left £3,151,975. Chemical manufacturer in Glasgow.

Probably the richest Scotsman of his time, he was the son of John Tennant (1796-1878, left £75,723), a chemical manufacturer at St. Rollox near Glasgow. He entered the firm in 1843, developing it, the United Alkali Company, into the largest producer of alkali and other chemicals in Europe. He was also Chairman of the Union Bank of Scotland and the head of a merchant bank, C. Tennant & Sons, in the City of London. Tennant served as a Liberal M.P. from 1879 till 1886, and was created a baronet in 1885. His eldest son, Sir Edward Tennant, 2nd Bt. (1858-1920, left £819,480) was created 1st Baron Glenconner in 1911. Our man's daughter, the famous Margot (1864-1945) was the second wife of H.H. Asquith the Prime Minister. Another daughter, Katherine Tennant (1903-94), was created Baroness Elliot of Harewood in 1958. Born when he was seventy-nine, she was one of the first women to be given a life peerage. Sir Charles lived at 40 Grosvenor Square, Middlesex and at The Glen, Peeblesshire.

35. Thomas Valentine Smith (1825-1906) – left £1,931,997. Brewer and distiller in Bow, east London.

The son of Octavius Henry Smith (1797-1871, left £300,000), the wealthy proprietor of the Thames Bank Distillery, he became a millionaire brewer as the head of Smith, Garrett & Co. of 246 Bow Road, Bow in east London. He was also a distiller and a landowner in Scotland. He became a Freeman of the City of London in 1867. Smith lived at 111 Grosvenor Road, Middlesex. His grandson Gerard Henry Craig-Sellar (1871-1929, *q.v.*) left £1,729,161.

36. Vyell Edward Walker (1837-1906) – left £1,598,177. Brewer in Limehouse, Middlesex.

The son of Isaac Walker (1794-1853, left £200,000), a brewer (Taylor, Walker & Co.) at Limehouse, who lived at Southgate, Middlesex, he was educated at Harrow and was one of five brothers who were famous cricketers. He was regarded as the best one, and, indeed, was seen as arguably the best cricketer in England; his entry in the *ODNB* describes him as a "cricketer." In 1864 he helped to found the Middlesex Cricket Club. His family had originally been Quakers but became Anglicans. His brewery remained at Limehouse into the twentieth century. He lived at Arnos Grove, Southgate, Middlesex.

37. Johann Carl Ludwig Loeffler (1832-1906) – left £1,505,004. Engineer in Woolwich and Italy.

Born in Nordhausen, Germany, he became an engineer with Siemens Brothers, whose British branch was at Woolwich. He became its manager, and was connected with its electrical engineering works and submarine cables, and also helped to lay the New York-Paris telegraph cable in 1876. He also invested heavily in mines in Western Australia. After 1888 he lived in Tirol in Italy, where he died.

38. George Herring (c. 1833-1906) – left £1,356,398. Financier in the City of London.

A remarkable self-made man, he allegedly began as a carver in a boiled beef shop on Ludgate Hill in the City of London. He then became a leading turf commission agent, and later began a business partnership with the millionaire Henry Louis Bischoffsheim (1829-1908, *q.v.*) as a financier in the City of London. He was known for his strict integrity. He achieved some fame as an important witness against William Palmer in the famous Rugeley poisoning case in 1856. Herring was important enough to have an entry in the *ODNB*. He lived at 1 Hamilton Place, Middlesex and at Putteridge Park, Luton.

39. Gilliat Hatfeild (*sic*- not Hatfield) (1834-1906) – left £1,342,197. Snuff and tobacco manufacturer in the City of London.

The son of the wealthy tobacco manufacturer Alexander Hatfeild (d.1865), who left £180,000, he became the head of James Taddy & Co., of 45 Minories in the City of London, one of the largest snuff makers in Britain, and also a leading manufacturer of tobacco. Little is known about his career. He lived at Morden Hall, Morden, Surrey, now a park. His son Gilliat Edward Hatfeild (1864-1941) left £1,237,222.

40. Edward Steinkopff (1841-1906) – left £1,247,023. Bottled water manufacturer and newspaper proprietor in London.

Born in Frankfurt, Steinkopff went to Glasgow where he worked as in a chemical plant and then became a commission agent there. From the 1860s he became the chief British proprietor of the Apollinaris Sparkling Water Company, which imported this popular mineral water from Germany. Its offices were at Stratford Place off Oxford Street, and its warehouse was at St. Katherine's Dock in east London. With George Smith, he was also the proprietor of the *St. James's Gazette* newspaper between 1888 and 1903. His only child, Mary Margaret (1862-1933, left £185,996) married James Steward-Mackenzie, 1st Baron Seaforth. Our man lived at 47 Berkeley Square, Middlesex and at Lyndhurst, Sussex.

41. Ronald Ruthven Leslie-Melville, 11th Earl of Leven and 10th Earl of Melville (1835-1906) – left £1,300,013. Banker in the City of London.

The son of John, 9th Earl of Leven and 8th Earl of Melville (1817-89, left £527,064, *q.v.*), who was a banker in the City of London and only a relatively small landowner, our man was educated at Eton and Christ Church, Oxford, and succeeded his half-brother in the peerage. He served as a Scottish Representative Peer from 1892 until his death and was a Director of the Bank of England from 1888 until 1894. He lived at Roehampton House, Roehampton, Surrey and at Glenferness House, Morayshire.

42. Ada Hannah Lewis-Hill (c. 1846-1906) – left 1,151,073. The widow of a money-lender in Mayfair.

The widow and heir of Samuel Lewis (1838-1901, *q.v.*), the millionaire money-lender of 17 Cork Street, Mayfair, like him she was noted for her philanthropy. In 1904 she remarried a William James Montagu Lewis Hill (1883-1970), thirty-seven years her junior, who did not die until 1970, when he was living in France and left £12,919 in England. She had residences at 16 Grosvenor Square, Middlesex and at "Woodside," Maidenhead, Berkshire.

43. George Charles Raphael (1837-1906) – left 1,103,247. Merchant banker of the City of London.

The third brother to leave a millionaire estate, after Henry Lewis Raphael (1832-99, *q.v.*) and Edward Louis Raphael (1831-1903, *q.v.*), he was a merchant banker – described in the 1871 and

1891 Censuses as a "foreign banker" at Throgmorton Street in the City of London. He lived at 37 Portland Place, Middlesex and at Castle Hill, Englefield Green, Surrey.

44. William Sturdy (1832-1906) – left £1,023,893. Stockbroker in the City of London.
The son of Daniel Sturdy (c. 1793-1873, left £60,000), a corn factor and oatmeal manufacturer at Blackfriars, he was born in Brixton and became a stockbroker at 3 Copthall Court, Throgmorton Street, in the City of London. Little is known about his career or business. In the 1851 Census he was described as a "stockbroker's clerk," and in later Censuses as a "Member of the Stock Exchange." He lived at Paxhill Park, Lindfield, Surrey.

45. Wentworth Blackett Beaumont, 1st Baron Allendale (1829-1907) – left £3,234,807. Land and colliery owner.
The son of Thomas Wentworth Beaumont, M.P. (1792-1848, left £335,000), he was educated at Harrow and St. John's College, Cambridge. He served as an M.P. from 1852 until 1892, and was one of the few great landowners to remain in the Liberal party after 1886. (See previous section.) In 1883 he owned 24,098 acres worth £34,670 p.a., chiefly in Northumberland, the West Riding, and Co. Durham, which included many coal mines. He was awarded a peerage in 1906. He lived at Allanheads, Allandale, Northumberland and at 144 Piccadilly Terrace, Middlesex. The value of his estate, which included only his personalty, was one of the highest ever left in the UK by a landowner. His son Wentworth, 2nd Baron and 1st Viscount Allandale (1860-1923) left £3,269,000.

46. Stewart Clark (1830-1907) – left £1,947,282. Sewing thread manufacturer in Paisley.
A Partner in the famous firm of Coats & Clark Sewing Thread of Paisley near Glasgow, one of the most successful businesses in Britain, he was the son of John Clark (1792-1864), sewing thread manufacturer of Paisley. Our man was educated at Paisley Grammar School and at Glasgow University, and served as a Liberal M.P. from 1884-85. He lived at Kilnside, Paisley. His son Sir John Stewart-Clark, 1st Bt. (1864-1924) left £1.5 million.

47. William Whiteley (1831-1907) – left £1,453,825. Department store proprietor in Bayswater, London.
Arguably the first proprietor of a department store in the modern sense, Whiteley was the son of a corn merchant in Yorkshire. He was apprenticed to a draper in Wakefield, and allegedly came to London with £10. He is said to have had the idea for a department store at the Great Exhibition of 1851. From 1863 he opened, and progressively enlarged, a department store at 31-55 Westbourne Grove in Bayswater, and was known as "the Universal Provider." On 26 January 1907 he was shot and killed by a man claiming (quite possibly correctly) to be his illegitimate son. Whiteley lived at 31 Porchester Terrace, Hyde Park, Middlesex.

48. Thomas Francis Blackwell (1838-1907) – left £1,028,000. Condiments manufacturer in London.
Crosse & Blackwell, the famous manufacturers of condiments and food sauces, was founded by our man's father Thomas Blackwell (1804-79, left £160,000). It was further developed by our man, who was described in the 1881 Census as a "preserved provision manufacturer, employing

654 men and boys and 552 women." The firm had its offices at 10-11 Soho Square, with factories on Charing Cross Road and Caledonian Road in London. He lived at The Cedars, Harrow Weald, Middlesex.

49. Enriquetta Augustina Rylands (1843-1908) – left £3,448,693. Widow of a millionaire cotton manufacturer in Manchester.

She was born in Havana, Cuba, the daughter of Stephen Cattley Tennant (1800-48), an English merchant there, and a Cuban mother, and was a Roman Catholic in her youth, although she later became a Congregationalist. In 1875 she married the multi-millionaire Manchester cotton manufacturer John Rylands (1801-88, q.v.), and inherited most of his vast wealth, making her probably the wealthiest woman in her own right in Britain. She was a noted philanthropist, and is best known for founding, in 1899, the famous John Rylands Library in Manchester. She lived at Longford Hall, Stretford, Manchester and at 67 Queen's Gate, Middlesex.

50. John Stefanovitch Schilizzi (1840-1908) – left £2,088,895. Merchant and foreign banker in the City of London.

From another of the great Greek mercantile and financial families based in London, he was the son of Zanni Schilizzi (1806-86, left £502,828, q.v.). Our man was born in Constantinople and was naturalised in 1871 and was both a merchant and "foreign banker" (1881 Census) at 25 Austin Friars in the City of London. He lived at 31Cromwell Road, South Kensington, and at Redcourt, Haslemere, Surrey.

51. Henri Louis Bischoffsheim (1829-1908) – left £1,622,332. Merchant banker and financier in the City of London.

Born in Amsterdam, the son of the banker Raphael Bischoffsheim (1800-73), a relative of Maurice, Baron de Hirsch (q.v.), he settled in London to serve in the bank's British branch. His firm, Bischoffsheim & Goldschmidt, was a merchant bank at 31 Throgmorton Street, City of London. He was noted for his philanthropy. His daughter and only child Ellen (1857-1933) married William Cuffe, 4th Earl of Desart (1845-98) an Irish peer. She became an authority on Gaelic literature and, most implausibly, in 1922 was appointed the first female member of the Senate of the Irish Free State. Our man lived at Bath House, 82 Piccadilly, Middlesex.

52. Spencer Compton Cavendish, 8th Duke of Devonshire (1833-1908) – left £1,164,961. Landowner.

One of the best known and most important political figures of his time, and known by his courtesy title of the Marquess of Hartington until he succeeded to the dukedom, he was the son of William, 7th Duke (1808-91, left £1,782,239, q.v.) and was educated at Trinity College, Cambridge. He served as an M.P. from 1857 until 1891, and held Cabinet posts, such as Secretary for India from 1880-2 and Lord President of the Council, 1895-1903. He was one of the leading figures in the Liberal Unionist split from Gladstone in 1886, and declined appointment as Prime Minister three times. In 1883 he owned 198,572 acres worth £180,750 p.a., and was one of the wealthiest of landowners (see previous section). His residences included Chatsworth at Bakewell, Derbyshire, Hardwick Hall at Chesterfield, and Devonshire House at 78 Piccadilly, Middlesex.

53. Frederick Arthur Stanley, 16th Earl of Derby (1841-1908) – left £1,101,000. Landowner.
The younger son of Edward Stanley, 14th Earl of Derby (1799-1869, left £250,000), three times Prime Minister, he was educated at Eton and served as a Conservative M.P. from 1865 until 1886, when he was given a peerage as Baron Stanley of Preston. In 1893 he succeeded his older brother Edward, 15th Earl of Derby (1826-93, left £1,935,554, *q.v.*). Our man served as Secretary of State for War from 1878 till 1880 and was Governor-General of Canada from 1888 to 1893, when he donated the famous Stanley Cup for ice hockey. He was one of the wealthiest of landowners, in 1883 owning 68,942 acres worth £163,273 p.a., which included valuable coal mines in Lancashire (see previous section). His son Edward, 17th Earl of Derby (1865-1948) left £3,217,839. Our man's residences included Knowsley at Prescot, Lancashire and Derby House, Stratford Place, Middlesex.

54. James Marke Wood (1841-1908) – left £1,041,614. West India merchant and shipowner in Liverpool.
The son of the wealthy Liverpool merchant James Marke Wood (1809-79, left £200,000), our man was described in the 1861 and 1871 Censuses as a "West India merchant." He was later a shipowner, operating from the Commercial Building, 17 Water Street, Liverpool, but the details of his career are unclear. He lived at The Towers, Ullet Road, Liverpool.

55. William Todd Lithgow (1854-1908) – left £1,000,237. Shipbuilder at Port Glasgow.
The son of a cotton salesman, from 1874 he was a Partner in a firm of shipbuilders at Port Glasgow, up the Clyde from Glasgow. He became sole proprietor of the firm in the 1880s. It built merchant ships, many of which still had masts as well as steam engines until the 1890s or later. His firm continued after his death, and in 1950s were said to be the largest private shipbuilders in the world. He lived at Drums, Langbank near Glasgow. His son Henry Lithgow (1886-1948) left £1,960,035; he was in partnership in the firm with his brother Sir James Lithgow, 1st Bt. (1883-1952), awarded a baronetcy in 1923, who left £436,961.

56. Michael Arthur Bass, 1st Baron Burton (1837-1908) – left £1,000,000. Brewer at Burton-on-Trent, Staffordshire.
The son of the millionaire brewer at Burton Michael Thomas Bass (1799-1884, *q.v.*), he was educated at Harrow and at Trinity College, Cambridge, and served as a Liberal M.P. from 1865 till 1885. A Partner in Bass & Co., the famous brewery, in 1886 he joined the "Beerage," as it became known, when he was created 1st Baron Burton. He had no sons, and, most unusually, in 1897 he received a second peerage with a special remainder to his daughter and then to her male offspring. His daughter Nellie Lisa Bass, later Bruce-Baillie and then Mells (1873-1962, left £215,230) thus succeeding as the 2nd Baroness Burton. He lived at Rangemore, Burton, Staffordshire, and at Chesterfield House, Mayfair.

57. Charles Morrison (1817-1909) – left £10,939,298. Merchant banker in the City of London.
The eldest son of the multi-millionaire wholesale and retail merchant at Fore Street in the City of London, James Morrison (1789-1857, *q.v.*), Charles Morrison attended Edinburgh University and Trinity College, Cambridge, but, because of ill health, did not graduate. He worked at the City merchant bank established by his father, Morrison, Sons & Co., and was then an independent

merchant banker, specialising in South American finance, at 53 Coleman Street, City of London. Despite chronic cystitis – which may be why he lived at 93 Harley Street – he survived to be ninety-two, and managed to accumulate probably the greatest business fortune ever seen in Britain up to that time. His estate was the first ever probated as worth more than £10 million. Many of his relatives were also very rich, including his sister, Number 59 below. He was also a major landowner in Scotland (see previous section). His country residence was at Basildon Park, Berkshire.

58. Sir Frederick Wills, 1st Bt. (1838-1909) – left £2,918,115. Tobacco manufacturer in Bristol.

A member of the extraordinarily wealthy Wills family of W.D. & H.O. Wills, of Bristol, later a component of Imperial Tobacco, Sir Frederick Wills was the son of Henry Overton Wills II (1800-71, left £50,000), a tobacco manufacturer in Bristol. He was educated at Amersham School. His family were Congregationalists. Wills served as a Liberal Unionist M.P. from 1900-06; he had received a baronetcy in 1897 for his charitable donations. Two of his brothers, also Partners in the family tobacco firm, were millionaires, as were other relatives. His son Sir Gilbert Wills, 2nd Bt., M.P. (1880-1956) was created 1st Baron Dulverton in 1929, and left £4,268,271; his daughter Kathleen Rees-Mogg (1884-1949) left £1,787,398. Our man lived at Manor Heath, Bournemouth and at 9 Kensington Palace Gardens, Middlesex.

59. Sir Donald Currie (1825-1909) – left £2,432,810. Shipowner based in the City of London.

The well-known shipowner Sir Donald Currie was born in Greenock, the son of a barber. The family moved to Belfast, where he attended the Royal Belfast Academical Institution. In 1844 he joined Cunard, where he established branches abroad. He returned to Liverpool in 1854, and established the "Castle" line of ships, later known as Union-Castle. It owned forty-seven ships by the 1890s. Its headquarters was at 3 & 4 Fenchurch Street in the City of London. Currie served as a Liberal, later Liberal Unionist, M.P. from 1880 till 1900, and was knighted in 1906. He lived at Garth and Glenlyon in Perthshire and at 4 Hyde Park Gardens, Middlesex.

60. Ellen Morrison (1834-1909) – left £2,008,228. Inherited from a wholesale-retail merchant in the City of London.

Ellen Morrison was the daughter of James Morrison (1789-1857, q.v.), the multi-millionaire proprietor of the Fore Street Warehouse in the City of London, and inherited part of his vast fortune. She lived quietly at Basildon Park, Berkshire, and apparently spent little of her considerable income.

61. George Salting (1835-1909) – left £1,256,669. Inherited Australian mercantile and pastoralist wealth.

Born in Sydney, New South Wales, he was the son of the Danish-born Severin Kanute Salting (1805-65), who became a successful merchant, banker, and pastoralist there, leaving £90,000 in England and £85,000 in New South Wales. George Salting was sent to England to be educated at Eton, and then returned to the newly-founded Sydney University, before settling permanently in London, at 87 St. James's Street, Middlesex. He apparently did not have any occupation, living as a *rentier*, although how he became so wealthy is unclear. He assembled one of the great art collections of his time, specialising in Chinese porcelains and Old Master paintings, which was donated after his death as the "Salting Bequest" to the National Gallery and the Victoria & Albert Museum. His brother William Severin Salting (1837-1905) left £991,324; his brother's widow Millicent Emily Salting (1848-1924, *q.v.*) left £1,868,185.

62. Ludwig Mond (1839-1909) – left £1,422,000. Chemical manufacturer as Winnington, Cheshire.
Born in Kassel, Germany, the son of Meyer Mond, he was educated at two German universities. After working in factories in Germany, he emigrated to Widnes in Cheshire in 1862 as a chemical manufacturer, forming a partnership with another German immigrant, John Brunner, as Brunner, Mond, which later became one of the components of ICI. The firm mainly produced soda ash, and later nickel alloys. His son Sir Alfred Mond, 1st Bt. (1868-1930, left £1,044,000) was given a baronetcy in 1910 and in 1928 was created 1st Baron Melchett. In later years Ludwig Mond lived at The Poplars, 20 Avenue Road, Regent's Park, Middlesex.

1910–1919

This decade marked the apogee of the Edwardian and post-Edwardian plutocracy, just before the catastrophe of the First World War. As will be seen, many millionaires were given baronetcies-hereditary knighthoods- and peerages; their number made a significant impact on the nature of the titled upper classes; this also demonstrated the flexibility of the British upper classes and their willingness to become open to new men and new wealth. The First World War changed a great deal, killing off heirs and male relatives, and diminishing the number and size of millionaire fortunes, at least temporarily. About 20 per cent of the graduates of the great public schools such as Eton, Harrow, and Rugby who fought in the War were killed- although only two millionaires on this list were killed in the Great War. The War also disrupted the free flow of capital and the City of London's role as the world's financial centre, which now passed to New York, although the City of London remained of the greatest importance. Much higher rates of taxation became permanent. Before 1914, the highest marginal rate of income tax in the UK was 10 per cent. From 1914 on, it never fell below 40 per cent, even under Tory governments.

1. Sir Edward Payson Wills, 1st Bt. (1834-1910) – left £2,633,477. Tobacco manufacturer in Bristol.
Another son of Henry Overton Wills II (1800-71, left £50,000), one of the founders of W.D. & H.O. Wills of Bristol, later the major part of Imperial Tobacco, the largest tobacco manufacturers in Britain, he was, like many of his relatives, a multi-millionaire. He was a Partner in the family firm, and was created a baronet in 1904. His son Sir Edward Channing Wills, 2nd Bt. (1861-1921) left £947,754. Our man lived at "Hazlewood," Stoke Bishop, Bristol and at Clapton Manor, Somerset.

2. Baron Sir John Henry William Schroder, 1st Bt. (1825-1910) – left £2,079,611. Merchant banker and merchant in the City of London.
The son of Baron John Henry von Schroder (1784-1883), a merchant banker in Hamburg, where he was born, who established a London branch of his firm in 1818. Our man came to London in 1841, establishing his merchant bank, J. Henry Schroder of 145 Leadenhall Street, City of London,

as an important financial institution. It dealt in international finance, such as a lucrative loan to the Confederate States of America during the Civil War. His firm also engaged as merchants in trading with Russia and elsewhere. He was naturalised in the UK in 1864 and made a baronet in 1892. He donated to Lutheran and other charities. His nephew and heir, Baron Bruno Schroder (1867-1940), left £502,503. Our man lived at The Dell near Windsor.

3. Sir Walter Scott, 1st Bt. (1826-1910) – left £1,424,130. Colliery owner, civil engineer, and publisher in Newcastle-upon-Tyne and elsewhere.

The son of an innkeeper and farmer in Cumberland, he was apprenticed to a mason at fourteen and then had a highly unusual career. He became a railway contractor in 1849 and had a long career (Walter Scott & Middleton Ltd.) building railways and docks, including London's first underground railway in 1890. He was also an extensive colliery owner and, bizarrely, became a publisher of note, without any previous connection to the literary world. He took over a publisher in Newcastle-upon-Tyne in lieu of payment, and his Walter Scott Publishing Co. published works by Shaw and Yeats, and the first English translation of Ibsen. His son Sir John Scott, 2nd Bt. (1854-1922) left £582,166. Our man lived at Beauclerc House, Northumberland and at Bentinck House, Newcastle-upon-Tyne.

4. Sir William Agnew, 1st Bt. (1825-1910) – left £1,353,592. Art dealer at Bond Street, Mayfair and in Manchester.

The son of the founder of the well-known art dealers, Thomas Agnew (1794-1871, left £80,000) of Manchester, our man was a Partner in the firm from 1850 and established its London branch, first at Waterloo Place and then at 39 Old Bond Street. It became probably the leading firm of art dealers, selling to the rich. He was also Chairman of Bradbury & Agnew, the publishers of *Punch*. He served as a Liberal M.P. from 1880 until 1886 and was given a baronetcy in 1895. His son Sir George Agnew, 2nd Bt. (1852-1941) left £323,417. Our man lived at 11 Great Stanhope Street, Mayfair.

5. Charles Butler (1821-1910) – left £1,148,356. Probably an insurance company director in Liverpool.

Very little is known about the career of Charles Butler. He was known to be a director of the Royal Insurance Company, which was located in Liverpool, but all other aspects of his business career are unclear. He was born in Finchley, the son of John Laforey Butler (d. 1848), of H. & I. Johnstone, merchants and bankers of Bush Lane in the City of London. Our mans was a J.P. and D.L. of Hertfordshire and its High Sheriff in 1879, and was a noted collector of art works and rare books. His brother, (Revd.) William John Butler (1818-94, left £15,742), was Dean of Lincoln. Our man's son Hubert Lavie Butler (1858-1937), who was educated at Eton and Cambridge, was also a millionaire, leaving £1,023,908. There is no evidence that our man lived in Liverpool; his addresses in later life were Warren Wood, Hatfield, Hertfordshire and 3 Connaught Place, Hyde Park, Middlesex. Warren Wood was given as his address when his son was at Cambridge in the late 1870s.

6. Henry Silver (1828-1910) – left £1,197,867. His source of wealth is unclear.

A very mysterious case. Silver achieved some fame as a "comic journalist," but nothing whatever could be traced about how he became a millionaire. He was the son of Thomas Temple Silver (1778-1855), an ironmonger in Woodbridge, Suffolk, where his son was born. In 1866 he married a French woman, Blanche Renouf (1844-1907). In the 1851 Census he was described as a "law student" and in the 1861 Census as a "merchant, clerk, and public writer," a visitor at a house in Croydon. In later life he lived at 6 Princes Gardens, Middlesex. His great wealth apparently came as a surprise to his friends when his probated estate was made public.

7. John Foster (1833-1910) – left £1,052,000. Worsted manufacturer in Bradford.

A member of the wealthy Foster family who were worsted (and alpaca and mohair) manufacturers at the Black Dyke Mills near Bradford, he was the son of John Foster (1798-1879, left £250,000), worsted manufacturer who later lived at Hornby Castle in Yorkshire. His brother William Foster (1821-84, *q.v.*) left £1,280,000. Our man was Chairman of the family firm, John Foster & son, and lived at Eyton, Cleveland, Yorkshire and at Coombe Park, Whitchurch, Oxfordshire.

8. John Poyntz Spencer, 5th Earl Spencer (1835-1910) – left £1,140,000. Landowner.

The son of (Rear Admiral) Frederick, 4th Earl Spencer (1788-1857, left £250,000) and educated at Harrow and at Trinity College, Cambridge, he served briefly as an M.P. in 1857, when he succeeded to the title. He was a significant political figure, who remained in the Liberal party after the 1886 split, and was Lord President of the Council 1880-83 and 1886, Lord Lieutenant of Ireland in 1882-5, and First Lord of the Admiralty in 1892-5. In 1883 he owned 27,185 acres worth £46,784 p.a., chiefly in Northamptonshire, where his country house, Althorp, was located. His brother and successor Charles, 6th Earl Spencer (1857-1922) left £1,197,827. He was an ancestor of Diana, Princess of Wales.

9. Sir Alfred Hickman, 1s t Bt. (1830-1910) – left £1,000,000. Ironmaster and steel manufacturer in Staffordshire; also a colliery owner, etc. there.

The son of George Rushbury Hickman (1795-1854), an ironmaster and colliery owner of Tipton, Staffordshire, He was educated at the King Edward VI School in Birmingham, and joined his father's firm and manufactured pig iron at Bilston, Staffordshire. From 1864 he was a leading steel manufacturer there, who introduced many innovations, and also a colliery owner. He was also the Chairman of Tarmac Ltd., which produced macadamised tar for roads. He served as a Conservative M.P. from 1885-6 and 1892-1906, and was created a baronet in 1903. His grandson and successor, Sir Alfred Hickman, 2nd Bt. (1885-1947), left £19,027. Our man lived at Wightwick near Wolverhampton, Staffordshire and at 22 Kensington Palace Gardens, Middlesex.

10. Henry Overton Wills (1828-1911) – left £5,214,356. Tobacco manufacturer in Bristol.

One of eighteen children of Henry Overton Wills II(1800-71, left £50,000), tobacco manufacturer in Bristol, he and his family grew enormously wealthy with the growth of cigarette smoking and the creation of Imperial Tobacco, of which his firm, W.D. & W.O. Wills, was a major component. The dire and deadly effects of cigarette smoking were, of course, not fully known until many decades later. He was a director of his family firm from 1846 till 1880. He is best known for funding the establishment of Bristol University in 1909, shortly before his death, and serving as its first Chancellor. He lived at Kelston Knoll near Bath, Somerset. He was one of the wealthiest member of his family of multi-millionaires; three of his sons left over £20 million among them.

11. William Henry Wills, 1st Baron Winterstoke (1830-1911) – left £2,465,503. Tobacco manufacturer in Bristol.

Another very wealthy member of the tobacco dynasty, he was the son of William Day Wills (d. 1865, left £50,000), tobacco manufacturer of Bristol. He was educated at the Mill Hill School, a public school for Non-conformists; he was prominent in defending the Non-conformist Protestant churches. He became the first Chairman of Imperial Tobacco when it was formed, and served as a Liberal M.P. from 1880-85 and 1895 till 1900. He was given a peerage in 1906. A notable philanthropist in Bristol, he presented the Bristol Art Gallery to the city. He lived at Coombe Lodge, Blagdon-on-Thames, Sussex, and at 25 Hyde Park gardens, Middlesex.

12. Walter Savill (1837-1911) – left £1,631,417. Shipowner based in the City of London.

The son of Jonathan Savill (d. 1846), a builder in Chigwell, Essex, he was employed with a firm of shipbrokers in London and then was the co-founder of the well-known Shaw Savill Line of ships, which was especially prominent in the trade to New Zealand. Its offices were at 14 Billiter Street in the City of London. He lived at The Finches, Lindfield, Sussex.

13. Anton Dunkels (1846-1911) – left £1,588,593. Diamond merchant at Hatton Garden, Middlesex and in the City of London.

Born Anton Dunkelsbuhler in Furth, Germany, little is known of his career in Britain, although it is known that he went to South Africa in 1876 and was connected with the Oppenheimers and other prominent families engaged in the diamond trade there. In London his offices were at 97 Hatton Gardens near the City of London, and at 1 St. Andrews Street in the City of London. He lived at 9 Hyde Park Gardens, Middlesex.

14. Charles Joseph Sofer-Whitburn (1836-1911) – left £1,481,220. Banker in the City of London.

Little is known of the career of Charles Sofer-Whitburn, who was Senior Partner of Reeves, Whitburn & Co., bankers of 18-20 St. Clement House, Clement Lane, City of London. He was born in Kennington, Surrey, the son of Charles Whitburn (d. 1849), of whom little is also known. According to his baptismal record at St. Mark Church, Kennington, his name at birth was Charles Joseph Sofa (sic) Whitburn, without a hyphen. A patron of two livings in the Anglican Church, he lived at 16 Ennismore Gardens, Middlesex and at Addington Park, Maidstone, Kent.

15. Sir William Cuthbert Quilter, 1st Bt. (1841-1911) – left £1,220,639. Stockbroker in the City of London.

The son of William Quilter (1808-88, left £580,934, *q.v.*), the important City of London accountant and first President of the Institute of Accountants, he joined his father's firm, and then became a stockbroker with Quilter, Balfour & Co., of 14 King's Arms Yard, City of London. He was also the founder of the National Telephone Company in 1881. Quilter served as a Liberal, later Liberal Unionist M.P. from 1885 until 1906. He was made a baronet in 1897; he was also, like other rich businessmen of his time, a noted art collector, whose collection was sold at Christie's in 1909 for £87,780, a great sum at the time. His son Sir William Quilter, 2nd Bt. (1873-1952), a Liberal M.P., left £319,917. Another son was Roger Quilter (1877-1953), a well-known composer. Our man lived at Bawdsey Manor, Suffolk and at 28 South Street, Park Lane, Mayfair. His Mayfair house later became the childhood home of Sir Alec Douglas-Home, the future Prime Minister, and still later the home of the novelist Barbara Cartland.

16. Samuel Montagu, 1st Baron Swaythling (1832-1911) – left £1,150,000. Merchant banker in the City of London.

Born Montagu Samuel – he reversed his names in 1894 – in Liverpool, the son of Louis Samuel (1794-1859, left £12,000), a jeweller, he worked as a money-changer in London for a relative and, in 1852, started his own firm, Montagu & Samuel, of 60 Old Broad Street, City of London. It was especially active in the silver market. Montagu made a point of signing literally every cheque and letter issued by the firm. He served as a Liberal M.P. from 1885 till 1900. He was made a baronet in 1894 and received a peerage in 1907. An Orthodox Jew, he was very prominent in the Anglo-Jewish community, and was one of the founders of the very Orthodox Federation of Synagogues. His son Edwin Montagu, M.P. (1879-1924) was Secretary of State for India from 1917-22 and is regarded as significant in putting India on the road to self-government. Our man's son Louis, 2nd Baron Swaythling (1869-1927) left £452,500. Our man lived at South Stoneham House, Hampshire and at 12 Kensington Palace Gardens, Middlesex.

17. Sir John Aird, 1st Bt. (1833-1911) – left £1,057,859. Engineering contractor, based in Westminster.

The son of John Aird (1800-76, left £140,000), a Scottish-born engineering contractor in London, he joined his father's firm, John Aird & Sons, and over the years built a remarkable range of structures, both in Britain and abroad, including gas works, waterworks, railways, as well as the Royal Albert and Tilbury Docks and the Aswan Dam in Egypt. His offices were at 37 Great George Street, Westminster and at Belvedere Road, Lambeth, Surrey. In 1874 his firm employed 30,000 workers. He served as a Conservative M.P. from 1887 until 1906, and was made a baronet in 1901. His son Sir John Aird, 2nd Bt. (1861-1934) left £466,501. Our man lived at 13 Hyde Park Terrace, Middlesex.

18. James Kitson, 1st Baron Airedale (1835-1911) – left £1,000,000. Locomotive manufacturer in Leeds.

The son of James Kitson (1807-85), a locomotive manufacturer at Leeds, who left only £100, he was educated at University College London, and became an ironmaster near Leeds before taking over the Airedale Foundry in Leeds, which built the extraordinary total of 6000 locomotives and employed 2000 people in 1911. He was also a director of the London & Midland Bank and other companies. He was very active in government in Leeds, serving as its first Lord Mayor in 1896-7 and as a Liberal M.P. from 1892 till 1907. He was awarded a baronetcy in 1886 and a peerage in 1907. He was a prominent Unitarian. Airedale lived at Gledhow in Leeds.

19. Sir Julius Charles Wernher, 1st Bt.(1850-1912) – left £10,044,301. Diamond magnate and company director in South Africa and London.

Probably the very richest of the "Randlords," and one of the richest men in Britain, he was born in Darmstadt, the son of Frederick Wernher, a well-known railway contractor in Frankfurt. Unlike many of the South African magnates, he was an "Aryan" Lutheran, although his second wife was of Jewish descent. After serving in the Franco-Prussian War, he came to London in 1882 and was then sent by the diamond dealer Jules Porges to the Kimberleys in South Africa to buy diamonds.

He then became a partner with Alfred Beit (*q.v.*) in Wernher Beit, a great diamond firm; they also owned many other companies in South Africa. He then lived in London, directing his holdings in collaboration with Beit. Wernher was naturalised and was given a baronetcy in 1905. Much of his wealth came to his widow, Alice *nee* Mankiewicz, later Baroness Ludlow (1862-1945), who left £2,829,969. Wernher lived at Bath House, 82 Piccadilly, Middlesex and at Luton Hoo, Bedfordshire.

20. James Coats (1841-1912) – left £1,923,264. Sewing thread manufacturer in Paisley, Renfrewshire.

Another of the extremely wealthy Coats family of J. & P. Coats Sewing Thread (later Coats & Clark) of Paisley, he was the son of Sir Thomas Coats (1809-83, *q.v.*) who left £1,308,725. Almost nothing is known of his life, and he was described in one source as a "recluse." He is known for establishing 4000 small libraries throughout Scotland. Two of his brothers were multi-millionaires, including George Coats, 1st Baron Glentanar (1840-1918), who left £4,383,267. Our man lived at Ferguslie near Paisley.

21. Christopher Furness, 1st Baron Furness (1852-1912) – left £1,844,305. Shipowner and shipbuilder at West Hartlepool, Co. Durham.

The son of John Furness (1808-85, left £460), a provision merchant in Hartlepool, he took over the firm and made a fortune importing grain during the Franco-Prussian War. He then became a shipowner, as Christopher Furness & Co., and a shipbuilder, as Furness Withy & Co., both based in West Hartlepool. Furness also owned collieries, steel mills, and other concerns in that area. He built Britain's first motor powered ships, and owned about one million tons of shipping at his death. He served as a Liberal M.P. in 1891-95 and 1900-10. he was knighted in 1895. Furness was a "radical Liberal," and is on record as opposing the hereditary basis of the House of Lords. This did not prevent him, however, from accepting a peerage in 1910. His son, Marmaduke, 2nd Baron Furness (1883-1940), was created 1st Viscount Furness in 1918 and left £3,681,955. Our man lived at Grantley Hall near Ripon, Yorkshire and at 23 Upper Brook Street, Middlesex.

22. Sydney James Stern, 1st Baron Wandsworth (1845-1912) – left £1,555,985. Merchant banker in the City of London.

A member of the very wealthy family of Stern, merchant bankers, he was the son of the millionaire David, Viscount de Stern (1807-77, *q.v.*). His mother was the niece of Sir Moses Montefiore, the great Jewish communal leader. Our man was educated at Magdalene College, Cambridge. He became head of Stern Brothers, the family merchant bank at 6 Angel Court, City of London. Stern served as a Liberal M.P. from 1891-95. In 1895, after he "generously subscribed to party funds," he was given a peerage. He lived at 10 Great Stanhope Street, Middlesex and at Hengrove Hall, Bury St. Edmonds, Suffolk.

23. Don José Garvey y Capdepon (d. 1912) – left £1,398,944. Vineyard owner in Spain.

His father, Patrick Garvey (d. 1872) was an Irishman who moved to Spain and developed the trade in jerez wines; his mother Maria de los Angelese Capdepon y Lacoste (1806-70) came from the Spanish upper classes. His wealth came from producing jerez wine and exporting it to Britain and elsewhere. His only address in the probate calendars was in Spain; there is no evidence that he ever lived in Britain.

24. Archibald Coats (1840-1912) – left £1,504,253. Sewing thread manufacturer at Paisley, Renfrewshire.

The son of Sir Peter Coats (1808-90, left £123,457), he was a member of the great sewing thread manufacturers in Paisley. He became Chairman of J. & P. Coats, and became known as "the Napoleon of the thread trade," expanding its exports to the United States and other overseas areas. He lived at Woodside, Paisley. His son William Hodge Coats (1866-1912) left £1,394,427.

25. Sir William Dunn, 1st Bt. (1833-1912) – left £1,123,000. Bankers and merchants in the City of London and in South Africa.

The son of a shopkeeper in Paisley, Renfrewshire, he went to South Africa in 1852 and established the mercantile firm of Mackie, Dunn & Co. of Port Elizabeth and Durban, and, in London, was Senior Partner of William Dunn & Co., bankers of Broad Street Avenue, City of London. He was Consul General for the Orange Free State in the UK in 1896-99, and served as a Liberal M.P. from 1891 till 1906. Dunn was created a baronet in 1895. In his will, he established the Sir William Dunn Institutes at Oxford and Cambridge, where ten Nobel Prize winners have worked. He lived at 34 Phillimore Gardens, Kensington, Middlesex and at "The Retreat," Lakenheath, Suffolk.

26. William Donaldson Cruddas (1831-1912) – left £1,041,320. Manufacturing engineer at Newcastle-upon-Tyne.

The son of the wealthy manufacturing engineer in Newcastle-upon-Tyne George Cruddas (d. 1879, left £400,000), he became financial director of the great engineering firm W.G. Armstrong & Co., and was described as a "manufacturing engineer" in the 1881 and 1891 Censuses. He was also Chairman of the Newcastle & Gateshead Water Co. Cruddas served as a Conservative M.P. from 1895 till 1900, and was a noted philanthropist of Newcastle-upon-Tyne.

27. Alexander William George Duff, 1st Duke of Fife (1849-1912) – left £1,000,000. Landowner and husband of Princess Louise.

The son of James Duff, 5th Earl of Fife (1814-79) and educated at Eton, he served as a Liberal M.P. from 1874-79, when he succeeded to the peerage. He was Captain Gentlemen at Arms from 1880-81. In 1889 he married Princess Louise, the eldest daughter of the Prince of Wales, later King Edward VII, and was immediately created 1st Duke of Fife. In 1883 he owned 249,220 acres worth £72,563 p.a. in Aberdeenshire and Banffshire. He served Lord Lieutenant of the County of London from 1900 until 1912. He lived at 15 Portman Square, Middlesex and at Mar Lodge, Aberdeenshire. His title came by special remainder to his daughter Princess Alexandra, 2nd Duchess of Fife (1891-1959). The Duke of Fife is the only member of the Royal Family in this work.

28. William Graham Vivian (1827-1912) – left £1,000,000, Copper and colliery mine owner in south Wales.

The son of John Henry Vivian, M.P. (d. 1855, left £200,000) of Stapleton near Swansea, a leading copper smelter in south Wales, he was educated at Eton, and was described in the 1871 Census as the "part owner of copper mines and other mines and coal mines." He was a J.P. and D.L. in Glamorganshire but was never in politics, unlike his brother Sir Henry Hussey Vivian, 1st Bt., 1st Baron Swansea (1821-94, left £163,707), a Liberal M.P. from 1852 until 1893, when he was given a peerage. Our man lived at Clyne Castle, Glamorganshire and at 7 Belgrave Square, Middlesex.

29. Peter Coats (1842-1913) – left £2,562,089. Sewing thread manufacturer at Paisley, Renfrewshire.

Another member of the very wealthy Coats family, he was the son of Sir Peter Coats (1808-90, left £123,851), one of the founders of the firm, he was described in the 1881 and 1891 Censuses as a "thread manufacturer." Very little is known of his career. He was unmarried. He lived at 5 Garthland Place, Paisley and at Whitney Court, Whitney-on-Wye, Herefordshire.

30. William Weir (c. 1834-1913) – left £2,219,708. Ironmaster and colliery owner in Lanarkshire.

Comparatively little is known of the life or career of this multi-millionaire. He was the son of John Weir of Dumbarton. His mother, Janet, was the daughter of Alexander Baird of Gartsherrie, and was the widow of Alexander Whitelaw. Our man was a Partner in Baird & Co., the great iron and coal firm in Lanarkshire, and was a J.P. and D.L in Ayrshire. His executors were two members of the Whitelaw family. He lived at Kildoan near Girvan, Ayrshire and at 168 West George Street, Glasgow, which may have been his business address.

31. Sir James Coats, 1st Bt. (1834-1913) – left £1,902,037. Sewing thread manufacturer in Paisley, Renfrewshire.

The brother of Peter Coats (above), he was made a baronet in 1895. He was a director of J. & P. Coats; his first wife Sarah (d. 1887) was the daughter of John Winthrop Auchincloss of New York, a member of a wealthy "Society" family in America. He lived at Auchendrane, Ayrshire.

32. William McEwan (1827-1913) – left £1,536,460. Brewer in Edinburgh.

The son of John McEwan (d. 1832), a shipowner in Alloa, he was educated at Alloa Academy, and worked for firms of merchants before being apprenticed to brewers in Edinburgh from 1851 till 1856. He then established his own brewery, William McEwan & Co., in Edinburgh. He was helped by the fact that his sister Janet married a member of the Younger family, who had owned a brewery in Alloa and later became wealthy brewers in our man's firm. His firm expanded in both Scotland and overseas, with McEwan's Export Ale. He served as a Liberal M.P. from 1886 till 1900. His daughter, Dame Margaret Greville (1863-1942, left £1,623,192) was a notorious Society figure, and has an entry in the *ODNB* as a "socialite and friend of Royalty." Our man lived at 25 Palmerston Place, Edinburgh and at 16 Charles Street, Berkeley Square, Mayfair.

33. Joseph Storrs Fry (1826-1913) – left £1,333,526. Chocolate and cocoa manufacturer in Bristol.

The head of the well-known chocolate firm which was founded by his great-grandfather Joseph Fry (1728-87), he was the son of Joseph Fry (1795-1879, left £30,000), a chocolate manufacturer in Bristol. Our man briefly attended Balliol College, Oxford and trained as an accountant, and then became head of the firm. He introduced many innovations, such as eating chocolate- it was previously only sold in powder form- and became a leading national brand, based in Bristol, which employed 1500 employees in 1896. It also faced increasing challenges from rivals like Cadbury. Fry came from a devout Quaker family; he served for many years as the Clerk to the London Yearly

Meeting of the Society of Friends. His brother Sir Edward Fry (1827-1918, left £119,052) was a Lord Justice of Appeal in 1877-83 and a Lord of Appeal in 1883-92, and was the father of Roger Fry (1866-1934), the famous art critic. Our man's grandson, Roderick James Fry (1864-1945) left £1,061,450. Our man's addresses were 16 Upper Belgrave Road, Bristol and at Union Street, Bristol.

34. Anthony Nicholas Brady (1841-1913) – left £1,332,994. Entrepreneur in the United States.
Born in France, he was a wealthy businessman in America, especially in the financing of public transport, in tobacco, and as a stockbroker. A Roman Catholic, he was regarded as one of the one hundred richest Americans. He died on a business trip to London, and left a millionaire estate in England. If he had direct business interests in the UK, these are unclear. It seems unlikely that he ever lived in the UK.

35. Cromartie Sutherland-Leveson-Gower, 4th Duke of Sutherland (1851-1913) – left £1,220,906. Landowner.
The great wealth of the Dukes of Sutherland were examined in a previous section. Our man was the son of George, 3rd Duke of Sutherland (1828-1892, left £1,275,089, *q.v.*), and was educated at Eton. He was a professional army officer, and served in the House of Commons (as Lord Stafford) as a Liberal M.P. from 1874 to 1886. He was later a Conservative. In 1883 he owned 1,358,545 acres worth £141,667, mainly in Sutherlandshire. He lived at Sutherland House (now Lancaster House) in St. James's, Middlesex, and at Dunrobin Castle in Sutherlandshire.

36. George John Fenwick (1821-1913) – left £1,186,845. A banker at Newcastle-upon-Tyne and a brewer at Chester-le-Street, Co. Durham.
The son of Thomas Fenwick (1772-1852), a banker at Newcastle-upon-Tyne, he became the Senior Partner in Lambton's Bank in Newcastle-upon-Tyne, and the principal proprietor of Fenwick's Brewery at Chester-le-Street, Co. Durham. In the 1871 Census he was recorded as living at 88 Harley Street in Marylebone and was a "banker, brewer, and landowner." In the 1891 Census he was recorded as a "banker." Fenwick donated to the Anglican church. In later years he lived at Crag Head, Bournemouth.

37. Emily Matilda Easton (1818-1913) – left £1,079,780. Inherited colliery wealth in Co. Durham.
Born in Gateshead, she was the unmarried sister of John Easton (1804-80), a colliery owner who left £600,000 (*q.v.*). She lived by herself at Nest House, Felling, Co. Durham and at Layton Manor, Yorkshire, dying at ninety-five. She was a philanthropist of charities for elderly unmarried women and for education in the north-east.

38. William Henry Walter Montagu-Douglas-Scott, 6th Duke of Buccleuch and Queensberry (1831-1914) – left £1,159,442. Land and mine owner.
One of the greatest of landed aristocrats, in 1883 he owned 460,108 acres worth £217,163 p.a. in Dumfriesshire, Roxburghshire, Northamptonshire, and many other counties (see previous section). He was the son of Walter, 5th Duke of Buccleuch (1806-84, left £475,000), and was educated at Eton and Christ Church, Oxford. As the "Earl of Dalkeith," he served as a Conservative M.P. in 1853-68 and 1874-80, when he was defeated in the General Election of that

year. His opponents circulated a pamphlet, "The Political Achievements of the Earl of Dalkeith," which consisted of thirty-two blank pages. His son, John, 7th Duke of Buccleuch (1864-1935) left £1,125,987, and was the father of Princess Alice, Duchess of Gloucester (1901-2005). Our man had many residences, including Dalkeith House, Dalkeith House, Midlothian, and Montagu House, Whitehall, Middlesex.

39. Louis Edward Raphael (1857-1914) – left £1,000,000. Merchant banking fortune in the City of London and a barrister in London.

The only son of Edward Louis Raphael (1830-1903, left £1,127,723, *q.v.*) of the merchant banking firm at Throgmorton Street, City of London, he was educated at University College School and at Trinity Hall, Cambridge, and was then called to the bar at Lincoln's Inn in 1880. He was a practicing barrister, an Equity Draughtsman and Conveyancer. His role in the family merchant bank is unclear. He was unmarried and lived at 4 Connaught Place, Hyde Park, Middlesex. His sister Jeanette married into the wealthy Sassoon family.

40. Nathan Mayer Rothschild, 1st Baron Rothschild (1840-1915) – left £2,500,000. Merchant banker in the City of London.

The son of Baron Lionel de Rothschild (1809-79, left £2,700,000, *q.v.*), the head of the British branch of the illustrious merchant bank at New Court, St. Swithin's Lane, City of London, he was educated at Trinity College, Cambridge, and served as a Liberal M.P. from 1865 till 1885. In that year, he was awarded a peerage, the first given to a professing Jew. He was later a supporter of the Liberal Unionists. As head of the merchant bank, he expanded its range of operations to include South Africa, and was a friend of Cecil Rhodes, and helped to establish the Rhodes Scholarships. His widow, Emma Louisa Rothschild (1844-1935) left £1,150,972. Their son Lionel, 2nd Baron Rothschild (1868-1937) left £129,096; another son, Nathaniel Charles Rothschild (1877-1923) left £2,250,000. Our man lived at 148 Piccadilly and at Tring, Hertfordshire.

41. James Crossley Eno (1828-1915) – left £1,611,607. Patent medicine manufacturer at Newcastle-upon-Tyne and at New Cross, Surrey.

The creator of "Eno's Fruit Salts" was born in Newcastle-upon-Tyne, the son of a shopkeeper. After working as a chemist's dispenser, a dentist, and the salesman of a hair restorer, in the 1850s he created a sodium bicarbonate mixture as a cure for stomach discomforts. It was known from 1873 as "Eno's Fruit Salts." He spent £15,000 a year on advertising, and moved to a new factory on Pomeroy Street, New Cross, Surrey in the 1880s. His granddaughter was, implausibly, Dame Isobel Cripps (d. 1979, left £354,973), the wife of Sir Stafford Cripps, whose taxation policies when Chancellor of the Exchequer in the Attlee government must, for the wealthy, have increased sales for Eno's product. In later life Eno lived at Wood Hall, Dulwich, Surrey.

42. Alexander Edward Thistlethwayte (1854-1915) – left £1,490,440. Landowner.

The son of the landowner Thomas Thistlethwayte (1809-1900, left £223,023), a landowner in Hampshire, he was educated at Eton and Christ Church, Oxford. In 1883 he owned 8084 acres worth £9929 p.a., all in Hampshire; how he became a millionaire is unclear. It is possible that he owned urban ground rents. He lived at Southwick Park in Fareham, Hampshire.

43. Arthur Keen (1835-1915) – left £1,000,000. Nuts and bolt manufacturer and ironmaster in Birmingham and elsewhere; the creator of GKN.

The son of an innkeeper in Cheshire who left £450, Arthur Keen was a railway clerk at Smethwick, and then established Watkins & Keen, which used a new nut making machine to manufacture nuts and bolts. The firm grew enormously; he had one thousand employees by 1880. He then established Guest Keen, which took over the famous Dowlais iron and steel works in south Wales, and in 1902 formed Guest Keen & Nettlefolds (GKN), one of the largest iron and steel manufacturers in Britain. It then took over the Crawshay's ironworks at Cyfarthfa. Keen was also a bank director and a major figure in Birmingham's economic life. He was a keen supporter of Joseph Chamberlain's tariff reform proposals. Keen lived at Sandyford, Augustus Road, Edgbaston, Birmingham.

44. Hubert George de Burgh Canning, 2nd Marquess of Clanricarde (1832-1916) – left £2,500,000. Landowner.

The son of Ulick, 1st Marquess of Clanricarde (1802-74, left £200,000), a landowner in Ireland and Harriet (d. 1876), daughter of George Canning the Prime Minister, he was educated at Harrow and served as a Liberal M.P. from 1867 till 1871. He served in the diplomatic corps. In 1883 he owned 58,826 acres worth à24,358 p.a. in Co. Galway; how he amassed £2.5 million is unclear. As a landowner, he had a dreadful reputation as the "worst" Irish landlord, notorious for evicting tenants, and he also became a confirmed miser, being forced to leave the Albany in London for refusing to pay an increase in rent. Unmarried, his minor titles passed to the Marquess of Sligo. He lived at 13 Hanover Square, Middlesex and at Portumna castle, Galway.

45. Sir Sigmund Neumann (1857-1916) – left £2,228,000. Diamond and gold magnate in South Africa and merchant banker in the City of London.

Another very wealthy "Randlord," he was born in Bavaria to Jewish parents and went to South Africa as a diamond buyer for a German firm. There, he founded his own firm, S. Neumann & Co., which became a leading diamond producer, pioneering deep shaft mining. He also developed profitable sidelines in gold, coal, and finance. He returned to London, where he became a merchant banker at 241-258 Salisbury House, London Wall, City of London. He lived at 146 Piccadilly and at Cecil Lodge in Newmarket, Cambridgeshire. He was made a baronet in 1912. His son Sir Cecil (1891-1955, left £101,518) changed his surname to "Newman."

46. Sir Charles Cayzer, 1st Bt. (1843-1916) – left £1,946,677. Shipowner in Glasgow and elsewhere.

The son of a schoolmaster in Devonshire, he went to Bombay as a clerk, and founded a firm of shipowners trading between Scotland and India. This developed into the leading firm of Cayzer, Irvine & Co., of Glasgow, and also of Liverpool and London, which traded as merchant ships with India; he also headed the Clan Lines, which mainly traded with South Africa. Cayzer served as a Conservative M.P. from 1892 till 1906, and was made a knight in 1897 and created a baronet in 1904. His son Sir Charles William Cayzer, 2nd Bt. (1869-1917), who died shortly after him, left £2,204,114. Another son, Herbert Cayzer, M.P. (1881-1958, left £636,924) was created 1st Baron Rotherwick in 1939. Our man's addresses were given as St. Lawrence Hall, Isle of Wight, at Gartmore, Perthshire, and at 109 Hope Street, Glasgow, almost certainly his offices.

47. Sir Joseph Beecham, 1st Bt. (1848-1916) – left £1,479,447. Patent medicine manufacturer at St. Helens, Lancashire.

Born in Wigan, the son of Thomas Beecham (1820-1907, left £86,680), the founder of Beecham's Pills, he worked for his father, and greatly enlarged his firm through extensive and clever advertising. He was said to have spent £109,000 in one year on advertising in the print media and on billboards, using such slogans as "Beecham's Pills are worth a guinea a box." He sold 250 million pills in 1890 and 366 million in 1915, and was the largest patent medicine manufacturer in Britain, operating from a factory at St. Helens near Liverpool. Beecham served three times as Mayor of St. Helens. He was knighted in 1912 and made a baronet in 1914. His son and successor was the famous conductor Sir Thomas Beecham, 2nd Bt. (1879-1961, left £10,802). Our man lived in St. Helens and at 9 Arkwright Road, Hampstead, Middlesex.

48. Thomas Fenwick Harrison (1852-1916) – left £1,438,353. Shipowner in Liverpool.

The proprietor of the Harrison Line (later the Harrison-Rennie Line) of Liverpool, he was the son of Thomas Harrison (1815-88, left £271,512), the founder of the shipping line in 1853 with his brother James (d. 1891). It originally imported brandy from France, but expanded under our man as a merchant shipping firm to Latin America, India, and elsewhere. Our man was educated at Rugby. In later life he lived at King's Walden, Hitchin, Hertfordshire, and was High Sheriff of this county in 1905.

49. John Allan Rolls, 2nd Baron Llangattock (1870-1916) – left £1,110,000. Landowner in Wales and urban property owner in London.

He was the son of John Allan Rolls (1837-1912), a Conservative M.P. who was given a peerage in 1892 as 1st Baron Llangattock, one of the last peerages awarded to a landowner of long lineage. In 1883 he owned only 4082 acres worth £3710 p.a. in Monmouthshire, but the family wealth was derived from their ownership of valuable property in Southwark in London, and they had a magnificent mansion, The Hendre, in Monmouthshire. Our man was educated at Eton and Christ Church, Oxford, and was a barrister of the Inner Temple. He served as Mayor of Monmouth in 1907-08. A captain in the Army, he was killed at the Battle of the Somme in 1916. The most famous member of his family was his younger brother (Hon.) Charles Stewart Rolls (1877-1910, left £30,936), who was killed in an early air crash, who, with Henry Royce (1863-1933), were the co-founders of Rolls-Royce.

50. Sir Charles Holcroft, 1st Bt. (1843-1917) – left £1,599,678. Colliery owner in Staffordshire.

The son of Thomas Holcroft (1795-1865), a cement manufacturer at Bilston, Staffordshire, he began at the Horsley Engineering Works at Tipton, Staffordshire in 1848, and later founded, with his brother James and others, the colliery firm of Hall, Holcroft & Pearson, which began the workings at Cannock Chase in that county. He and his brother were notable collectors of fossils, and he helped to found Birmingham University. His main heir was his nephew Sir George Holcroft, 1st Bt. (1856-1951, left £1,176,313), who was awarded a new baronetcy in 1921. Our man lived at The Shrubbery, Kingswinford, Staffordshire.

51. Baron Leopold De Rothschild (1845-1917) – left £1,500,000. Merchant banker in the City of London.

The son of Lionel De Rothschild (1808-79, left £2,700,000, *q.v.*), of the London branch of the famous merchant bank, he was educated at King's College School and at Trinity College, Cambridge. He became head of the London branch of the firm, at New Court, St. Swithin's Lane, City of London, in 1874. Rothschild, a Baron of Austria, was Vice-President of the Anglo-Jewish Association and a notable racehorse owner. The Prince of Wales, a close friend, attended his wedding. He lived at Gunnersbury Park, Middlesex and at Ascott, Leighton Buzzard, Bedfordshire.

51. Sir Thomas Bland Royden, 1st Bt. (1831-1917) – left £1,274,411. Shipbuilder and shipowner at Liverpool.

The son of Thomas Royden (d. 1868, left £35,000), a shipowner at Liverpool, he was educated at Liverpool College. He was described in the 1871 Census and other sources as a "shipbuilder," but was later a shipowner, the head of Thomas Royden & Sons. He was also Deputy Chairman of Cunard Lines and of a number of railways. Royden served as a Conservative M.P. from 1885 till 1892, and was Mayor of Liverpool in 1878-79. He received a baronetcy in 1905. His son Thomas Royden, 1st Baron Royden, M.P. (1871-1950, left £746,394) was given a peerage in 1944. Our man's daughter Maude Royden (1876-1956) was a well-known feminist. Our man lived at Frankby Hall, Cheshire.

53. Philip Henry Vaughan (1829-1917) – left £1,259,000. Brewer in Bristol.

The son of Philip Vaughan (1799-1864, left £140,000), a copper merchant and Alderman in Bristol, he became head of Bristol Brewery Vaughan & Co., the largest brewery in the Bristol area. Little could be found about his career. He lived at Redland Hill House, Bristol.

54. Seth Taylor (1827-1917) – left £1,158,213. Grain miller in London and head of two Exchanges in the City of London.

The son of a miller and baker in Rickmansworth, Hertfordshire, he became the head of the Waterloo Flour Mills at Waterloo Bridge, on the Surrey side of the Thames, the largest grain millers in the world, and was also Chairman of both the Baltic Exchange and the Corn Exchange in the City of London. He lived at Granard, Putney Park lane, Surrey.

55. Samuel Cunliffe-Lister, 2nd Baron Masham (1857-1917) – left £1,016,150. Woollen and worsted manufacturer in Bradford.

The son of Samuel Cunliffe-Lister, 1st Baron Masham (1815-1906, left £648,558), a famous inventor of wool combing machinery and a leading woollen and worsted manufacturer at Manningham near Bradford, he was educated at Harrow and at St. John's College, Oxford. He took over the family firm, Lister & Co., when his father retired. He lived at Swinton Park, Masham, Yorkshire. He died at fifty-nine, and was succeeded by his brother John, 3rd Baron Masham (1867-1924, left £1,557,606). The title became extinct with his death, but the family's property, including Swinton Park, was eventually inherited by t he husband of the first Baron's granddaughter Mary, the Conservative Cabinet minister Philip Lloyd-Graeme (1884-1972, left £454,430), who changed his surname to "Cunliffe-Lister," and was made 1st Viscount Swinton in 1935 and 1st Earl of Swinton in 1955.

56. Francis Reckitt (1827-1917) – left £1,007,166. Starch manufacturer at Hull, Yorkshire.

From a Quaker family, he was one of three sons of Isaac Reckitt (1792-1862, left £14,000), the founder of the starch manufacturers. Our man ran the firm with his brothers, developing it into one of the best known producers of consumer goods in Britain. Reckitt & Sons, as it was known, was probably the largest employer of labour in Hull, with a workforce of 5300 in 1913. Our man's brother Sir James Reckitt, 1st Bt. (1833-1924, left £467,152) received a baronetcy in 1894. After the First World War, the firm merged to become Reckitt & Colman, enlarging the range of its products- for instance, it introduced Dettol in 1932. In later life our man lived at Butler's Court, Beaconsfield, Buckinghamshire.

57. George Coats, 1st Baron Glentanar (1849-1918) – left £4,353,267. Sewing thread manufacturer at Paisley, Renfrewshire.

Yet another enormously wealthy member of the Coats family, and the first to be given a peerage, George Coats was the son of Thomas Coats (1809-83, *q.v.*), the millionaire head of the sewing thread firm in Paisley, he was a member of the Scottish Episcopal Church and was a J.P. of Ayrshire. Coats was awarded a peerage in 1916. He lived at Glentanar, Aberdeenshire, at Belleisle, Ayrshire, and at 11 Hill Street, Berkeley Square, Middlesex.

58. Alfred Charles De Rothschild (1842-1918) – left £2,494,000. Merchant banker in the City of London.

The son of Baron (of Austria) Lionel Nathan De Rothschild (1808-79, left £2,700,000, *q.v.*), who became head of the London branch of the merchant bank at New Court, St. Swithin's Lane, City of London, he was the brother of Nathan, 1st Baron Rothschild (1840-1915, left £2,500,000, *q.v.*), and was also Consul-General for Austria. The First World War greatly affected their international financial links, and made xenophobes call their loyalty to Britain into question. Alfred De Rothschild lived at 1 Seamore Place, Middlesex, and at Halton, near Tring, Buckinghamshire.

59. Emily Charlotte Talbot (1840-1918) – left £2,000,000. Landowner.

The daughter and heiress of Christopher Rice Mansel Talbot (1803-90, left £1,399,173, *q.v.*), and a large landowner in south Wales, she was a notable benefactor of the poor in her area, and ran a colliery which lost £90,000 over ten years in order to keep 500 workers in employment. She helped to develop Port Talbot, and was a notable church builder in south Wales. She lived at Magram Park and at Penrice Castle in Glamorganshire and at 3 Cavendish Square, Middlesex.

60. Asher Wertheimer (1844-1918) – left £1,542,000. Art dealer on Bond Street, Middlesex.

The son of the German-born art dealer on Bond Street Samson Wertheimer (1811-92, left £382,810), he was born in London and further developed the firm as a major source of art works for the very rich. Many of the works he sold were purchased from impoverished European aristocrats. His salesroom was at 182 Bond Street; his rivals in the field included the Duveens and Agnews. Wertheimer is remembered for a highly idiosyncratic portrait of him by John Singer Sargent. The executors of his will were two members of the Rothschild family. He lived at 8 Connaught Place, Hyde Park, Middlesex.

61. William Barwick Crigoe-Colmore (1860-1918) – left £1,147,926. Urban property owner in Birmingham.

Little known outside of Birmingham, his family owned the Colmore estate, which included much of the area in central Birmingham that was developed during the nineteenth century into one of Britain's leading urban areas. He was the son of Colmore Frind (*sic*) Crigoe-Colmore (1827-71, left £40,000) of Moor End, Charlton Kings, Gloucestershire; he avoided public life and little is known about his career. He lived at Moor End and at 14 Cadogan Place, Middlesex.

62. Albert Octavius Worthington (1844-1918) – left £1,356,975. Brewer in Burton-on-Trent, Staffordshire.

The head of another famous brewery located in Burton, he was the son of William Worthington (1797-1871, left £60,000), a brewer in the firm founded by his grandfather. Our man was educated at Repton School. In 1889, his firm occupied an eleven-acre site in Burton. In 1927 it merged with Bass, but still produced its own brands of beer. His son William Worthington Worthington (*sic*, 1871-1949) left £1,539,007. Our man lived at Maple Hayes near Lichfield, Staffordshire.

63. David Alfred Thomas, 1st Viscount Rhondda (1856-1918) – left £1,169,000. Colliery owner and coal shipper in south Wales.

The son of Samuel Thomas (1800-79, left £200,000), a wealthy colliery owner in south Wales, he was educated at Manila Hall, Clifton, Bristol, and at Gonville & Caius College, Cambridge. He then became head of the family firm and Senior Partner in Thomas & Daven, coal shippers of Cardiff. He developed the Cambrian collieries. Thomas served as a Liberal M.P. from 1888 until 1910, and was made a Baron in 1916 and a Viscount in 1918. During the First World War he served as President of the Local Government Board in 1916-17 and as Food Controller in 1917-18. In 1915, he and his daughter survived the sinking of the *Lusitania*. By special remainder, his title passed to his only daughter, Margaret, 2nd Viscountess Rhondda (1883-1958, left £85,458), a well-known figure as the Editor of the magazine *Time and Tide* and a well-know feminist. Lord Rhondda lived at Llanwern, Monmouthshire and at 122 Ashley Gardens, Middlesex.

64. Duncan Mackinnon (1844-1918) – left £1,136,805. Shipowner in Glasgow and in the City of London.

The nephew of Sir William Mackinnon (1823-93, left £560,563), the head of the British India Steam Navigation Company and of Mackinnon Mackenzie, shipowners, our man took over these companies from him. The firms were based in Glasgow and later at 23 Great Winchester Street and at Winchester House, Old Broad Street, City of London, and carried goods and passengers throughout the British Empire. He retired in 1913. He lived at Loup and Balinakill, Argyllshire and at 16 Hyde Parks Square, Middlesex. His entry in the Scottish probate calendar describes him as a "sometime merchant in London, Calcutta, and Bombay."

65. Henry George Percy, 7th Duke of Northumberland (1846-1918) – left £1,169,000. Landowner.

The son of Algernon, 6th Duke of Northumberland (1810-99, left £90,889), he was educated at Christ Church, Oxford. He served as a Conservative M.P. (under the name of "Earl Percy") from 1868 until 1885, and was an important figure in the Conservative party's national organisation. In 1887, he was called to the House of Lords as Lord Lovaine, a minor title held by his family. In 1883 he owned 186,397 acres worth £176,048 p.a. (see previous section). His main residences were at

Alnwick Castle, Northumberland and at 2 Grosvenor Place, Middlesex. His son and heir Alan, 8th Duke of Northumberland (1880-1930) left £2,510,000.

66. Sir Ernest Frederick Schiff (1840-1918) – left £1,656,000. Stockbroker and colonial merchant in the City of London.

Born in Trieste, then a part of Austria, he came to England as a young man and was naturalised in 1875. With his two brothers he founded the stockbroking firm of A.G. Schiff & Co., of Warnford Court, Throgmorton Street, City of London, and was later also a colonial merchant at that address. His brother Alfred (d. 1908) left £576,769. During the First World War, he faced considerable hostility as an "Austrian," although he had been naturalised forty-five years earlier. He was the uncle of the novelist Sydney Schiff (1868-1944), who wrote under the pseudonym "Stephen Hudson." Our man lived at 19 Seymour Street, Portman Square, Middlesex.

67. Thomas Holt Hutchison (1861-1918) – left £1,023,812. Shipowner in Glasgow.

A shipowner in Glasgow, he was a Town Councillor of Glasgow and a Baillie of the City in 1916-17. The son of Peter Adam Hutchison (1834-99), our man lived at 16 Crown Terrace, Glasgow. His son Sir James Hutchison, 1st Bt. (1893-1979) was a Conservative M.P. from 1945 till 1959 and was awarded a baronetcy in 1956.

68. Sir Richard Vincent Sutton, 6th Bt. (1891-1918) – left £1,000,000. Land and urban property owner in London.

Born posthumously to Sir Richard Francis Sutton, 5th Bt. (1853-91, left £149,340), and educated at Eton, he was an army officer and died of wounds received in 1914 just after the end of the War in November 1918. He and Lord Llangattock (see above) were the only millionaires who were killed in the First World War. In 1883 his father owned 9340 acres worth £15,500 p.a. in Berkshire and other counties, but their wealth derived largely from owning twenty-one acres in the West End of London. His successor was his uncle Sir Arthur Edward Sutton, 7th Bt. (1857-1948, left £7470). Our man lived at Benham Park, Benham Valence, Berkshire.

69. James Cleland Burns,3rd Baron Inverclyde (1864-1919) – left £2,017,798. Shipowner in Glasgow.

The younger son of John Burns, 1st Baron Inverclyde (1829-1901, left £886,768), a prominent shipowner in Glasgow, he was educated at Repton School and succeeded his elder brother George, 2nd Baron Inverclyde (1861-1905, left £295,437). Our man was the head of G. & J. Burns, shipowners, and also of Cunard Lines. He was Chairman of the Glasgow Shipowners Association, and Deputy Chairman of the Clydesdale Bank. He lived at Castle Wemyss, Renfrewshire and at 10 Berkeley Square, Middlesex.

70. Herbert Stern, 1st Baron Michelham (1851-1919) – left £2,000,000. Merchant banker in the City of London.

The only son of Herman, Baron De Stern (1815-87), who left £3,544,978 (q.v.), the extremely wealthy head of the merchant bank Stern Brothers in the City of London, and a cousin of Lord Wandsworth (q.v.), he was an Alderman of the London County Council from 1907, and created a baronet in 1905 and a peer later the same year. He lived at Strawberry Hill, Twickenham; Hellingly,

Sussex, and at 26 Princes Gate, Middlesex.

71. Rowland Winn, 2nd Baron St. Oswald (1857-1919) – left £1,394,141. Landowner and mineral owner.
The son of Rowland Winn, M.P. (1820-93, left £84,312), a landowner who was made 1st Baron St. Oswald in 1885, he was educated at Eton. In 1883 Rowland Win owned 7983 acres worth £18,587 p.a. in Lincolnshire and the West Riding, but the family became very wealthy by developing ironstone ore fields in north Lincolnshire, and by making Scunthorpe into a major iron producing centre. Our man served as a Conservative M.P. from 1885 until 1892, and was a captain in the Coldstream Guards. He lived at Nutsell Priory near Wakefield, Yorkshire and at 11 Grosvenor Gardens, Middlesex.

72. Sir Walpole Lloyd Greenwell, 1st Bt. (1847-1919) – left £1,400,000. Stockbroker in the City of London and a cattle and horse breeder.
The son of Walpole Eyre Greenwell (d. 1897, left £10,297), a solicitor in Marylebone, in 1868 he founded what became a leading firm of stockbrokers in the City of London, W. Greenwell & Co. of 2 Finch Lane, City of London. He also developed a second career as one of the leading breeders of cattle and horses. Greenwell was awarded a baronetcy in 1906. His son Sir Bernard Greenwell, 2nd Bt. (1874-1939) left £1,250,974. Our man lived at Marden Park, Woldingham, Surrey and at 17 Portman Square, Middlesex.

73. George Barbour (1841-1919) – left £1,311,254. Cotton merchant fortune in Manchester.
The son of Robert Barbour (1797-1885, left £472,268), a Scotsman who came to Manchester in 1815 and helped to establish a leading firm of cotton merchants and exporters, Barbour & Brothers, he was educated at Harrow and at Trinity College, Cambridge. He was also a barrister of the Inner Temple (called 1865) but did not practice. It does not appear that he was active in trade but lived as a wealthy rentier at Bolesworth Castle near Chester. He was a J.P. and D.L. of Cheshire and its High Sheriff in 1890.His family remained very wealthy. His son Robert Barbour (1876-1928), left £1,124,764 when he was killed falling from a horse.

74. Charles William Mills, 2nd Baron Hillingdon (1855-1919) – left £1,000,000. Banker in the City of London.
The son of Charles Henry Mills, 1st Baron Hillingdon (1830-98, left £1,479,381), Senior Partner in the leading private bank Glyn Mills & Currie of 67 Lombard Street, City of London, our man was educated at Eton and at Magdalen College, Oxford. He became Senior Partner in the family bank, and served as a Conservative M.P. from 1885 until 1892. He lived at Hillingdon, Middlesex and at 6 Park Place, Mayfair, Middlesex.

1920-1929

The aftermath of the First World War produced something of a brief decline in the number of millionaire estates, but then followed by a great increase during the relatively boom conditions of the later 1920s- although, in Britain, unemployment never declined below 10 per cent of the work force, and then rose alarmingly in the wake of the Wall Street Crash of 1929. There were fewer merchant bankers and international financiers among the very rich, and many City figures bemoaned the transfer of much of the City's great influence to Wall Street in New York. But there were more manufacturers of consumer goods and household products, as a more modern economy was emerging in the UK.

1. George Courtauld (1830-1920) – left £2,146,695. Silk manufacturer at Bocking, Essex and rayon manufacturer in Coventry.
A member of the famous silk manufacturing family, he was the son of George Courtauld (1802-61, left £120,000), one of the early heads of the firm, who are said to have begun by manufacturing mourning crape. From 1904, the firm developed and produced rayon at a new plant in Coventry. The family was of French Huguenot descent; its works were at Bocking, Essex. George Courtauld was educated at University College, London, and served as a Liberal M.P. from 1878 till 1885. A relative, Samuel Courtauld (1876-1947, left £1,030,126), founded the Courtauld Gallery in London. Our man lived at Cuthedge, Crosfield, Essex and at 39 St. James's Place, Middlesex.

2. Howard Morley (1846-1920) – left £1,539,430. Hosiery manufacturer in the City of London.
The son of the well-known woollen manufacturer and radical politician Samuel Morley, M.P. (1809-86, left £462,474), he became one of the heads of the family's hosiery manufacturing firm at 18 Wood Street, Cheapside, in the City of London. His brother Samuel Hope Morley, 1st Baron Hollenden (1845-1929, left £1,541,654) was a hosiery manufacturer and Governor of the Bank of England, and was given a peerage in 1929. The family were Congregationalists. Our man lived at 47 Grosvenor Square, Middlesex.

3. Sir Joshua Kelley Waddilove (1841-1920) – left £1,250,000. Head of a credit agency centred in Bradford, Yorkshire.
The son of an innkeeper, he was born in Bradford and began as an insurance agent. He then founded a credit agency for the working classes, which allowed them to buy credits and pay for them over time. Known as the Provident Clothing & Supply Co. Ltd., it was centred in Bradford and had 115 branches and 5,000 agents around the UK. It still exists, as Provident Financial PLC. Waddilove was a Methodist, and was knighted in 1919. In later life he lived at The Elms, Spaniards Road, Hampstead, Middlesex.

4. Sir Frederick Lucas Cook, 2nd Bt. (1844-1920) – left £1,082,973. Wholesale clothing merchant and manufacturer in the City of London.
The elder son of the millionaire Sir Francis Cook, 1st Bt. (1816-1901, left £1,600,000, *q.v.*), the proprietor of Cook, Son & Co., a wholesale clothing and clothing manufacturing firm at St. Paul's Churchyard in the City of London, he was educated at Harrow. With his brother Wyndham Francis Cook (1860-1905, left £1,203,810, *q.v.*) he continued the firm. He served as a Conservative M.P. from 1895 until 1906. His son Sir Herbert Frederick Cook, 3rd Bt. (1868-1939) left £671,634. Our man lived at 24 Hyde Park Gardens, Middlesex and at Doughty House, Richmond, Surrey.

5. Charles Combe (1836-1920) – left £1,067,264. Brewer at Long Acre, central London.

From a brewing family, he became head of the family firm, known as Combe & Delafield, after 1858. He had previously been an army officer with the 23rd Bombay Cavalry, and had participated in the suppression of the Indian Mutiny in 1857. The brewery was located at Castle Street, off Long Acre, in Covent Garden. It became one of the largest in Britain, and was known as Combe & Co. from 1866, and, from 1898, became a component of Watney, Combe & Reid. Our man's son Charles Harvey Combe, M.P. (1863-1935) left £724,657. Our man lived at Pains Hill, Surrey and at Cobham Park, Surrey.

6. Sir Ernest Joseph Cassel (1852-1921) – left £7,333,411. Merchant banker in the City of London.

One of the richest and most famous City merchant bankers, like many others he was born in Germany, in Cologne. His father, Jacob Cassel, was a small banker. Our man allegedly arrived penniless in Liverpool in 1869, became a banker in Paris, and then worked for Bischoffsheim & Goldschmidt, a leading merchant bank at 31 Throgmorton Street in the City of London, eventually becoming one of the heads of the firm. Cassel then operated as an independent financier, and finally worked for S. Japhet, another merchant bank, at the same address. Highly competent and with an ability for continuous hard work, he became one of the richest men in Britain. He became a close friend of King Edward VII (whom he closely resembled in appearance) – so much so, that he became known as "Windsor Cassel," for his frequent visits with the King. Born to Jewish parents, he became a Roman Catholic to please his wife. He is also well-known as the grandfather of Edwina Ashley, Countess of Mountbatten (1901-60, left £589,901), the wife of Lord Louis Mountbatten (1900-79, left £2,196,949), the last Viceroy of India; Cassel thus posthumously joined the Royal Family. He lived at Brook House, Park Lane, Middlesex and Compton Verney, Warwickshire.

7. Walter Morrison (1836-1921) – left £2,000,000. Merchant banker and financier in the City of London.

Another son of the multi-millionaire warehouseman and merchant banker in the City of London James Morrison (1789-1857, q.v.), and the brother of Charles Morrison (1817-1909, q.v.), who left nearly £11 million, he was educated at Eton and at Balliol College, Oxford, where he graduated with a First. He was an independent financier and merchant banker at 53 Coleman Street in the City of London, and was Chairman of the British Aluminium Company. Morrison served as a Liberal, later Liberal Unionist M.P. in 1861-74 and 1886-1900. He was also a large landowner in Yorkshire, from a family which had become large-scale landowners (see previous section). He lived at 77 Cromwell Road, Middlesex and at Malham Tarn near Settle, Yorkshire.

8. Henry Greenwood Tetley (1852-1921) – left £1,917,819. Rayon and silk manufacturer in Coventry and in Bocking, Essex.

The son of Samuel Tetley (1808-91, left £4,782), a stuff-merchant in Leeds, he joined Samuel Courtauld & Co., and eventually became its effective head. The firm was in entrepreneurial decline as silk manufacturers. He reoriented it to become manufacturers of rayon, the first artificial fabric widely made, buying the patent on rayon in 1904 and opening a new factory in Coventry to produce rayon goods. His strategy paid off, and he became a millionaire. Tetley has three children with his wife and six more with a long-term mistress. He lived at 17 Avenue Road, Regent's Park, Middlesex.

9. George Stephen, 1st Baron Mount Stephen (1829-1921) – left £1,414,319. Railway magnate and banker in Canada.

The son of a carpenter in Banffshire, he left school at fourteen and was apprenticed to a draper in London. He migrated to Canada in 1850 and became a wool purchaser. He eventually became President of the Bank of Montreal, and then the President of the Canadian Pacific Railway, which was completed in 1885. He worked in collaboration with his cousin, the Scottish born Donald Alexander Smith, later 1st Baron Strathcona and Mount Royal (1820-1914, left £421,655). Stephen returned permanently to Britain in 1888, and was created a baronet in 1886, before his permanent return, and a peer in 1891, the first Canadian to be awarded a peerage. In England, he lived at 17 Carlton House Terrace, Middlesex and at Brocket Hall, Hatfield, Hertfordshire.

10. Adelbert Wellington Brownlow-Cust, 3rd Earl Brownlow (1844-1921) – left £1,295,984. Landowner.

The younger son of John Cust, 1st Earl Brownlow (1779-1853), he was educated at Eton and succeeded his older brother John, 2nd Earl Brownlow (1842-67, left £160,000). He served briefly as a Conservative M.P. in 1866-67 before succeeding to the title, and was Paymaster-General from 1887-89, as well as Lord Lieutenant of Lincolnshire. In 1883 he owned 58,335 acres worth £86,426 p.a. Hes was succeeded by his cousin Adelbert Cust, 4th Earl Brownlow (1867-1927, left £746,047). Our man lived at 8 Carlton House Terrace, Middlesex and at Belton House, Grantham, Lincolnshire.

11. Henry Radcliffe (1857-1921) – left £1,250,000. Shipowner in Cardiff.

The son of Rees Radcliffe (d. 1906), a hay merchant in Cardiff who left £1130, he became a leading shipowner in Cardiff in the firm of Evan Thomas, Radcliffe & Co, which mainly carried Welsh steam coal. He was also involved in developing iron mines and local railways in south Wales. He was succeeded in his shipping firm by his brother Daniel (d. 1933, left £255,488). Henry Radcliffe lived at Druidstone, St. Mellons, Monmouthshire.

12. William James Chrystal (1855-1921) – left £1,141,969. Chemical manufacturer in Rutherglen near Glasgow.

The son of Robert Alexander Chrystal (1815-1908, left £84,642), an insurance broker in Glasgow and of Jean, the daughter of John White Sr., the founder of the major chemical manufacturer J. & J. White of Rutherglen, he was educated at Glasgow Academy and at Glasgow University. He joined his relatives' firm as an expert chemist. The company was headed by his great-uncle James White (1812-84, left £904,114, *q.v.*), and then by James's son John Campbell White, 1st Baron Overtoun (1843-1908, left £689,023). Chrystal was an innovating chemist who served as technical advisor to the firm, which produced bichromate of potash and other chemicals. He lived at Auchendennan, Dumbartonshire on Loch Lomond; his address was also given as 7 West George Street, Glasgow, which was probably the firm's business address.

13. James Smith Park (1854-1921) – left £1,081,187. Shipowner and insurance broker in Glasgow and London.

The son of Robert Ballantyne Park (d. 1875), a manufacturer who left £439, he was educated at Glasgow University and became the proprietor of the well-known "Allan" Line of steamships and also of the Park Steamship Company, both based in Glasgow. He was also a Lloyd's underwriter, probably in London, and was a colonel in the Volunteers. He lived at 20 Park Terrace, Glasgow and at Auchankyle, Ayrshire.

14. Sir William Henry Tate, 2nd Bt. (1842-1921) – left £1,072,569. Sugar manufacturer in Liverpool and in Silvertown, east London.
The son and successor of Sir Henry Tate, 1st Bt. (1819-99, left £1,264,215, *q.v.*), the head of Tate & Lyle, the famous sugar firm, of Liverpool and Silvertown, West Ham, in east London. Little is known about his career. The family were Unitarians. He lived at Highfield, Woolton, Liverpool, and at Bodrhyddan, Flintshire. His son Sir Ernest Tate, 3rd Bt. (1867-1939) left £1,467,736.

15. Alfred Charles Harmsworth, 1st Viscount Northcliffe (1865-1922) – left £5,248,973. Newspaper owner in Fleet Street, City of London.
Probably the greatest British "Presslord," Lord Northcliffe was born in Dublin, the son of a failed barrister, Arthur Harmsworth (1837-89), whose estate is unlisted in the probate records. He was educated at Henley House School in Kilburn, and became a freelance journalist. With his brother he established a successful magazine, *Answers*, and, in 1896, established the *Daily Mail*, the first popular newspaper in a recognizably modern style. He then began the *Sunday Dispatch* in 1903, and, in 1908, took over the *Times* and the *Sunday Times*. By 1914 he owned newspapers with 40 per cent of the total circulation of newspapers in Britain. A fierce anti-German even before the War, he helped to bring down H.H.Asquith as Prime Minister in 1915 and was placed in charge of government propaganda during the First World War. Two of his brothers became peers, including Harold Harmsworth, 1st Viscount Rothermere (1868-1940, left £335,308), and two others became baronets, including Sir Hildebrand Harmsworth, 1st Bt. (1871-1929), who left £1,384,918. Northcliffe lived at 1 Carlton Gardens, Middlesex.

16. Alice Charlotte De Rothschild (1847-1922) – left £3,062,000. Merchant banking fortune made in Frankfurt, Vienna, and the City of London.
The daughter of Anselm von Rothschild (1803-74), of the Frankfurt and Vienna branches of the great merchant bank, who left £90,000 in England, she inherited Waddesdon Manor and a fortune from her brother Baron Ferdinand De Rothschild (1839-98, left £1,488,129, *q.v.*). Unmarried, she was known for her outstanding gardens in her French mansion and for her art collection, which became the Waddesdon Bequest to the British Museum. She lived at 142 Piccadilly, Middlesex and at Waddesdon Manor, Buckinghamshire.

17. Henry Herbert Wills (1856-1922) – left £2,750,000. Tobacco manufacturer in Bristol.
A member of the immensely wealthy cigarette manufacturing family which owned most of Imperial Tobacco, he was the son of Henry Overton Wills III (1828-1911, *q.v.*), who left £5,214,356, and was educated at Clifton College. He was a director of Imperial Tobacco, based in Bristol, and was a notable philanthropist, building Wills Hall at Bristol University. He served as High Sheriff of Somerset in 1910-11. His brother Sir George Alfred Wills, 1st Bt. (1854-1928, *q.v.*) left no less than £10,000,000. Our man lived at Barley Wood, Wrington, Somerset.

18. Sir Thomas Isaac Birkin, 1st Bt. (1831-1922) – left £2,144,804. Lace manufacturer in Nottingham.

The son of the Nottingham lace manufacturer Richard Birkin (1805-70, left £35,000), he greatly expanded the firm, so that Nottingham became the lace manufacturing centre of the world. He had two separate firms there, Birkin & Co. (Fancy Lace) and T.I. Birkin & Co. (Lace Curtains). He was made a baronet in 1905, and was High Sheriff of Nottinghamshire in 1892. Several of his relatives are well-known: his grandson Sir Henry "Tim" Birkin (1896-1933, left £6439) was a "Bentley Boy," from a set of racing car enthusiasts and playboys who were nationally known during the 1920s; he died aged thirty-six from an arm injury while racing, and from malaria. Our man's granddaughter was Freda Dudley White (1894-1983), the mistress of the Prince of Wales (later Edward VIII) from about 1918 till 1929; our man's great-grandaughter is Jane Birkin (b. 1946), the actress. Our man lived at Ruddiington Grange, Nottinghamshire.

19. Sir Thomas Glen Gen-Coats, 1st Bt. (1846-1922) – left £1,708,696. Sewing thread manufacturer in Paisley, Renfrewshire.

Another very wealthy member of the family who owned J. & P. Coats Sewing Thread, later Coats & Clark, of Paisley, his surname at birth was Coats: he added "Glen-" in 1894. He was educated at Queenwood College, Hampshire, an experimental school founded by Quakers with an emphasis on science. He served as a Liberal M.P. from 1906-10, and had been made a baronet in 1894. A director of the family firm, he was Lord Lieutenant of Renfrewshire from 1908. He lived at Ferguslie Park near Paisley and at 29 Belgrave Square, Middlesex.

20. Joseph Constantine (1856-1922) – left £1,563,195. Shipowner at Middlesbrough, North Yorkshire.

He was born in Denmark to British subjects, and set up the shipowners Constantine & Pickering of Middlesbrough, which mainly operated in the North Sea area as merchant shippers. Little is known of his career. An ardent Methodist, he served as High Sheriff of Yorkshire in 1916-17. In 1916 he gave the funds to establish what is now Teesside University.

21. Sir Alexander Hargreaves Brown, 1st B t. (1844-1922) – left £1,408,309. Merchant banker in the City of London.

The son of Alexander Brown (d. 1849) of Beilby Grange, Yorkshire and the grandson of Sir William Brown, 1st Bt, M.P. (1784-1864, left £900,000, q.v.), the founder of Brown Shipley, which was at first a cotton importing firm based in Liverpool. From the 1860s it became a leading merchant bank, at Founders' Court, Lothbury, in the City of London. Our man became its head. He was also a Liberal, later Liberal Unionist M.P. from 1884 till 1906, and was made a baronet in 1903. He lived at Broome Hall, Holmwood, Surrey and at 16 Grosvenor gardens, Middlesex.

22. Charles Thomas Milburn (1860-1922) – left £1,304,740. Shipowner at Newcastle-upon-Tyne and in the City of London.

The son of William Milburn (1826-1903, left £247,929), a shipowner, like his son, at Newcastle-upon-Tyne and in London, he became head of William Milburn & Co., of Newcastle and of 130 Fenchurch Street, City of London. Our man was also a director of the London Joint Stock bank. His brother, Sir John Davison Milburn, 1st Bt. (1851-1907), a colliery owner and shipowner, left £391,340. Our man lived at Compton Manor, King's Somborne, Hampshire and at 2 Park Place, Middlesex.

23. Daniel Coats (1844-1922) – left £1,234,578. Sewing thread manufacturer at Paisley, Renfrewshire.

The fifth and last surviving son of Sir Peter Coats (1808-90, left £123,457), sewing thread manufacturer at Paisley, he was unmarried. Many of his close relatives were also millionaires, such as his brother Sir James Coats, 1st Bt. (1834-1913, *q.v.*), who left £1,902,037. Daniel Coats lived at 5 Garthland Place, Paisley and at Brockwood Park, Alresford, Hampshire.

24. Charles Robert Spencer, 6th Earl Spencer (1857-1922) – left £1,197,827. Landowner.

The son of Frederick, 4th Earl Spencer (1788-1857, left £250,000), he was educated at Harrow and at Trinity College, Cambridge, and succeeded his older half-brother John, 5th Earl Spencer (1835-1910, left £1,140,000, *q.v.*). Our man served as a Liberal M.P. in 1880-95 and 1900-05, when he was created Viscount Althorp in his own right. He served as a Liberal Whip from 1900-05 and as Lord Chamberlain of the Household, 1905-12. He lived at Althorp House, Northamptonshire and at Spencer House, St. James's Place, Middlesex.

25. Alexander Miller (1837-1922) – left £1,219,112. West Africa merchant in Glasgow and in the City of London.

Born in Glasgow, the son of James Miller (d. 1850), a straw-hat manufacturer there, he established Alexander Miller & Brothers in 1868 with his brother George. It was part of the Royal Niger Company, of which he was Managing Director, which operated mainly in northern Nigeria, and imported palm oil, which was used in machinery as a lubricant. It also traded in the Gold Coast. It was later known as the African & Eastern Trade Corporation. Originally based in Glasgow, it moved to Warnford Court in the City of London. He lived at Stoatley Hall, Haslemere, Hampshire.

26. Louis Samuel Cohen (1846-1922) – left £1,192,701. Department store owner in Liverpool.

Born in Maitland, New South Wales, the son of Samuel Cohen (1812-61), who came to Sydney in 1834 and established a firm of wholesale merchants, our man returned to England, where he established Lewis's Ltd., the largest department store in that city. He served as Lord Mayor of Liverpool in 1899-1900. His brother, George Judah Cohen (1842-1937, left £510,910), was a major banker and Jewish communal leader in Sydney. Our man's son Harold Leopold Cohen (1873-1936) left £1,285,499; another son, Rex David Cohen (1876-1928) left £1,218,287; a third son, Stanley Samuel Gilbert Cohen (1880-1944) left £1,206,679. A fourth son, Sir Jack Benn Brunel Cohen (1886-1965, left £25,768), was a Conservative M.P. despite losing both legs in the First World War. Our man lived at The Priory, St. Michael's Hamlet, Liverpool.

27. Sir Prince (*sic*) Smith, 1st Bt. (1840-1822) – left £1,181,706. Worsted machinery manufacturer at Keighley, Yorkshire.

The son of Prince Smith (1819-90, left £305,540), a successful textile machinery manufacturer in Keighley, Yorkshire, our man was educated at Wesley College, Sheffield, and became head of the family business, which made precision parts for worsted spinning machinery. It became one of the largest machinery manufacturers in Yorkshire, employing 1800 people at the time of his death. He was made a baronet in 1911. His son Sir Prince Prince-Smith, 2nd Bt. (1869-1940) left £173,662. Our man lived at Hillbrook, Keighley, Yorkshire and at Southburn near Driffield, Yorkshire.

28. Sir William Pickles Hartley (1846-1922) – left £1,099,936. Jam manufacturer at Aintree, Lancashire and at Bermondsey, London.

The son of a tinsmith in Colne, Lancashire, he was educated at Colne Grammar School. He began his business in 1871 when he started to make his own jam. This proved so popular that he opened a factory to make jam, first at Bootle, Lancashire, then at Southport, and finally at Aintree in the outskirts of Liverpool, where his business remained for many years. He later opened another factory at Bermondsey in London. He was a lifelong member of the Primitive Methodists, and one of its best-known lay leaders, who treated his workmen exceptionally well and was noted for his philanthropy. Hartley was knighted in 1908. His daughter Christiana Hartley (1872-1948, left £198,251), in 1922 was the first woman Mayor of Southport. Our man lived at 11 Oxford Road, Birkdale, Lancashire.

29. George Cadbury (1839-1922) – left £1,071,092. Cocoa and confectionery manufacturer at Bournville near Birmingham and newspaper publisher in London and elsewhere.

The son of John Cadbury (1801-89, left £43,773), a chocolate and cocoa manufacturer at Birmingham, he was educated at Lean's Quaker School at Edgbaston. With his brother Richard (d. 1899, left £42,817), he greatly enlarged the family firm, introducing many new products and opening a larger factory at Bournville near Birmingham, which employed 8,600 persons by the 1900s. From a well-known Quaker family, he also established a model village for his workers, who enjoyed many amenities. An ardent Liberal and opponent of the Boer War, he bought the *Daily News* newspaper in London and other newspapers in Birmingham to espouse his views. He lived at The Manor House, Northfield near Birmingham.

30. Joseph Watson, 1st Baron Manton (1873-1922) – left £1,000,000. Soap manufacturer in Leeds.

The son of a soap manufacturer in Leeds, he was educated at Repton School and at Clare College, Cambridge. He joined the family firm, Joseph Watson & Sons, soap manufacturers of Leeds, and greatly expanded it into the second largest soap makers in England, although an attempt to establish a "Soap Trust" with Lord Leverhulme, the largest manufacturer of soap, came to nothing. During the First World War, he was successfully in charge of shell production in Leeds and Yorkshire. In 1922 he purchased the Compton Verney estate in Warwickshire from Lord Willoughby de Broke, and was created a peer shortly afterward, but a few months later died of a heart attack while hunting, aged forty-nine. One of his younger sons was the step-grandfather of David Cameron, the Conservative Prime Minister. Watson was widely accused of having bought his peerage from Lloyd George for £50,000, although, even if true, he was certainly not alone in this.

31. Maurice Marcus (1844-1923) – left £3,145,751. Diamond merchant and banker in South Africa and Redhill, Surrey.

The son of Lewis Marcus (1818-84, left £21,395), a merchant of Fenchurch Street in the City of London, he went to South Africa from 1863 till 1870, where he became the partner of Sir Joseph Robinson as a "Randlord" and diamond merchant. He returned to London and was Chairman of the British Bank of South Africa at 10 Clement's Lane, Lombard Street, City of London and was also a diamond merchant at Holborn Viaduct. He spent the rest of his life as an independent financier, operating from his home in Redhill, Surrey. Unmarried, his enormous wealth was unknown even to his relatives. His wealth "was an absolute secret…he is said to have done his own bookkeeping to prevent knowledge of his fortune." (Jewish Telegraphic Agency, 26 November 1923), and was said by the *Guardian* (23 November 1923) to be "the biggest surprise of its kind since the death of Charles Morrison" in 1909 – he (*q.v.*) left nearly £11 million. Marcus's residuary legatees were his five nieces. He lived at High Trees, Redhill, Surrey.

32. (Hon.) Nathaniel Charles De Rothschild (1877-1923) – left £2,250,000. Merchant banker in the City of London.

The younger son of Nathan Mayer De Rothschild, 1st Baron Rothschild (1840-1915, left £2,500,000, *q.v.*), merchant banker in the City of London, he was educated at Harrow and at Trinity College, Cambridge. His mother, Emma Louisa Rothschild (1844-1935, *q.v.*) left £1,150,972. He worked successfully for the famous family merchant bank, but is best known as a naturalist. He was probably the greatest expert on fleas, and especially on their negative effects as parasites, and was the first to identify the rat-flea as the carrier of the plague and other diseases. He was also an important supporter of the Nature Reserve movement. He became clinically depressed through contracting encephalitis and committed suicide at forty-six. His children included the distinguished naturalist Dame Miriam Rothschild (1908-2005) and Sir Victor Rothschild, 3rd Baron Rothschild (1910-90, left £506,712), Director-General of the Central Policy Review Staff in 1971-74. Our man lived at Ashton Wold, Oundle, Northamptonshire.

33. Wentworth Canning Blackett Beaumont, 1st Viscount Allendale (1860-1923) – left £2,006,770. Land and mineral owner.

The son of Wentworth, 1st Baron Allendale (1829-1907, left £3.2 million), our man was educated at Eton and at Trinity College, Cambridge. In 1883 his father owned 24,096 acres worth £34,670 p.a., mainly in Northumberland and the West Riding, which included collieries. Our man served as a Liberal M.P. from 1895 until 1907, when he succeeded to the peerage. He was one of the few great landowners to support the Liberal party in the Edwardian period; he held the posts of Captain, Yeoman of the Guards (i.e., Liberal Chief Whip in the Lords) 1907-11, and was a Lord-in-Waiting from 1911-16. In 1911 he was elevated in the peerage to become 1st Viscount Allendale. He lived at Allendale, Hexham, Northumberland and at 25 St. James's Place, Middlesex.

34. Frank Bibby (1857-1923) – left £1,229,483. Shipowner in Liverpool.

The son of the millionaire shipowner James Jenkinson Bibby (1813-97, left £1,773,533, *q.v.*), head of the Bibby Lines in Liverpool, he was educated at Eton, and continued in the family business. He lived at Hardwicke Grange near Shrewsbury, and served as High Sheriff of Shropshire in 1900-01. His son Frank Brian Frederick Bibby (1893-1929) left £1,083,073. Our man also had a residence at 39 Hill Street, Berkeley Square, Middlesex.

35. Charles Beasley (1842-1923) – left £1,203,000. Brewer in Plumstead, Kent.

The son of Frederick Beasley (1809-88, left £45,398), a wine merchant in Marylebone, Charles Beasley became head of the North Kent Brewery in Plumstead, Kent in 1878, as Mitchell & Beasley, and became its sole owner in 1887. It was the last independent brewery in London when it was taken over by Courage in 1963. Our man's son Charles Gerald Beasley (1878-1947) left

£478,745. Our man lived at The Cottage, Abbey Wood, Kent.

36. George Herbert Child Villiers, 8th Earl of Jersey (1873-1923) – left £1,170,000. Banker in the City of London and landowner.

The son of Victor, 7th Earl of Jersey (1845-1915, left £789,970), the principal proprietor of Child's Bank, a private bank at 1 Fleet Street in the City of London, the oldest bank in Britain, and a considerable landowner. In 1883 he owned 19,389 acres worth £34,599 p.a., in Glamorganshire and other counties. The Bank was founded by an ancestor. Our man was educated at Eton and at New College, Oxford, and served as a Conservative Lord-in-Waiting in 1919. Our man sold the family's share in Child's Bank to Glyn Mills & Co. in 1923, just before his death. He lived at Middleton Park, Bicester, Oxfordshire.

37. Francis Burdett Thomas Nevill Money-Coutts, 5th Baron Latymer (1852-1923) – left £1,038,972. Inherited banking wealth on The Strand, Westminster.

A very unusual career: he was the son of (Revd.) James Drummond Money (d. 1875, left £6,000), an Anglican clergyman, and of Clara (d. 1849), daughter of the wealthy banker Francis Burdett (1770-1844). He was educated at Eton and at Trinity College, Cambridge, and was both a barrister (called at the Inner Temple, 1879) and a solicitor. After a protracted lawsuit, he became the sole beneficiary of Baroness Burdett-Coutts (*q.v.*) after her death in 1906, who had inherited much of Coutts's Bank. After another protracted lawsuit, he was declared to be the 5th Baron Latymer, a title which was called out of abeyance in 1913 after *336* years. He was never a Partner in the Bank, but spent his time as a writer under the name "Mountjoy," who edited the poet laureate Tennyson's collected works in twenty-seven volumes, and was the author of opera libretti. His family owned no land listed in Bateman. He lived at 15 Hanover Square, Mayfair.

38. Sir Charles James Jackson (1849-1923) – left £1,023,000. Urban property wealth in Cardiff and a newspaper proprietor in Fleet Street, City of London.

The son of James Edwin Jackson (d. 1892, left £7002), a building contractor in Cardiff who owned much urban land there, he became a barrister (called at the Middle Temple in 1888) on the south Wales circuit, and then, through a relative, became a director of the *Western Mail* newspaper in 1893 and the Chairman of the *News of the World* Fleet Street newspaper from 1902 until his death. After 1901 he lived in London, and amassed an important silver collection. He was also important in founding the National Museum of Wales, located in Cardiff. He was knighted in 1919. His son Derek Jackson (1906-82, left £186,506), Professor of Spectroscopy at Oxford, was married six times and has been the subject of biographical interest. Our man lived at 6 Ennismore Gardens, Westminster.

39. Joseph Trueman Mills (1836-1924) – left £4,104,000. Inherited a silk manufacturing fortune in the City of London.

The son of John Remington Mills, M.P. (1798-1879, *q.v.*), a silk manufacturer at Milk Street, Cheapside, City of London, of whose career little is known, who left £1,300,000. As with his father remarkably little can be traced about a man who left over £4 million. He was a Congregationalist at birth, and was a significant landowner, in 1883 owning 13,800 acres worth £17,991 p.a. in several counties. Mills served as High Sheriff of Leicestershire in 1880-81, and in the 1911 Census was described as a "railway director." His son Henry Trueman Mills (1860-1933) left £2,089,677. In later life our man lived at Stockgrove near Leighton Buzzard, Buckinghamshire.

40. Sir (Emil Hugo Oscar) Robert Ropner, 1st Bt. (1838-1924) – left £3,615,128. Shipowner at Hartlepool and shipbuilder at Stockton-on-Tees, Co. Durham.
Born in Magdeburg, Prussia, the son of Johann Heinrich Ropner and educated in Germany, he came to Hartlepool, where he worked for a coal exporting firm, and then opened the Ropner Shipping Company, and then became a major shipbuilder at Stockton-on-Tees, Co. Durham. He was an important figure in the life of the town, serving as its Mayor in 1892-93 and as its Conservative M.P. from 1900 to 1910. Ropner received a knighthood in 1902, and was made a baronet in 1904. His son Sir John Ropner, 2nd Bt. (1869-1936) left £799,203. Sir Robert lived at Preston Hall near Stockton-on-Tees.

41. Brenton Halliburton Collins (1828-1924) – left £1,975,494. Inherited a banking and shipping fortune made in Halifax, Nova Scotia.
Born in Halifax, Nova Scotia, he was the son of Enos Collins (1774-1871), the head of the Halifax Bank and a shipowner, who was regarded as the richest man in Canada when he died, leaving an estimated $6 million. Our man was educated at Wadham College, Oxford, matriculating in 1849 aged twenty, but returned to Canada and then re-emigrated to England by the 1890s. In 1871 he had been living in Halifax, Nova Scotia, and was described in the Canadian Census as a "banker." In Britain, he was recorded as "living on his own means," and appears not to have had a profession. His son Carteret Collins (1865-1941), a London barrister educated at Oxford, left £592,562. Our man lived at Dunorlan, Tunbridge Wells, Kent.

42. Millicent Emily Salting (1848-1924) – left £1,868,185. The widow of a man who inherited wealth from a merchant and pastoralist in New South Wales.
The daughter of (Ven.) Robert William Browne (1810-95, left £32,186), Archdeacon of Bath, she married William Severin Salting (1837-1905, left £991,324), the son of a wealthy merchant and pastoralist in New South Wales, a barrister who lived in London. Her husband's brother, George Salting (1835-1908, *q.v.*) left £1,256,669, and is known for the "Salting Bequest" he left to the National Gallery in London. Our lady was also a noted collector of porcelain. She lived at 49 Berkeley square, Middlesex.

43. Alcibiades Vagliano (c. 1849-1924) – left £1,700,641. Foreign merchant and shipowner in the City of London.
The nephew of the multi-millionaire Panaghi Vagliano (1814-1902, left £2,888,095), a Greek-born merchant and shipowner in the City of London, he was born in Russia but lived in London, where he was a merchant and shipowner at Winchester House, Old Broad Street, City of London. In the 1871 Census he was described as a "foreign coal merchant." He lived at 28 Hill Street, Berkeley Square, Middlesex.

44. John Reddihaugh (1841-1924) – left £1,653,305. Woollen merchant and manufacturer in Bradford.
Little could be traced about the career of John Reddihaugh. He was the son of Jonathan Reddihaugh

(or Reddehaugh, 1814-55) of Baildon near Bradford. The exact nature of his business is somewhat unclear, but it involved mercantile dealings in wool in Bradford as well as top manufacturing from wool. He was apparently a self-made man, and born in meagre circumstances. His firm became a limited liability company in 1919. Its premises were at Horton Lane, Bradford. His son Frank Reddihaugh (1871-1938) left £1,176,814. Our man lived at Beech Mount, Basildon, Yorkshire.

45. John Cunliffe-Lister, 3rd Baron Masham (1867-1924) – left £1,557,606. Woollen and worsted manufacturer in Bradford.

The younger son of Samuel Cunliffe-Lister, 1st Baron Masham (1815-1906, left £648,558), a major woollen and worsted manufacturer in Bradford, he was educated at Radley College, and succeeded his elder brother Samuel Cunliffe-Lister, 2nd Baron Masham (1857-1917, *q.v.*), who left £1,016,150. Our man lived at Swinton Manor, near Ripon in Yorkshire, the family's country house.

46. Sir John Stewart-Clark, 1st Bt. (1864-1924) – left £1,522,992. Sewing thread manufacturer in Paisley.

From the sewing thread family in Paisley who eventually became half of Coats & Clark, he was the son of Stewart Clark (1830-1907, *q.v.*), sewing thread manufacturer in Paisley who left £1,947,282, he was educated at Merchiston Castle School and at Jesus College, Cambridge before becoming a director of the family firm. He added "Stewart-" to his surname in 1909. He was created a baronet in 1918, and lived at Dundas Castle, South Queensferry, West Lothian.

47. Sydney Larnach (1855-1924) – left £1,317,219. Inherited a banking fortune made in Sydney, New South Wales.

The son of Donald Larnach (1817-96, left £885,468), who migrated to Sydney and became wealthy as the Managing Director of the Bank of New South Wales. Donald Larnach came to London in 1879, where he became a director of the London Joint Stock Bank. Little is known about the career of Sydney Larnach, who was described in the 1881 Census as having "no profession," and in the 1901 Census as "living on own means." He was apparently a rentier, but the details could not be traced. He lived at Yew Lodge, East Grinstead, Sussex.

48. William Henry Foster (1846-1924) – left £1,250,000. Ironmastery fortune at Stourbridge, Shropshire; also a colliery owner and landowner.

The son of the multi-millionaire ironmaster in Stourbridge, Shropshire William Orme Foster (1814-99, left £2,387,081, *q.v.*) he was educated at Eton and Christ Church, Oxford. Apart from inheriting his father's ironworks, he was also a colliery owner (John Bradley & Co.) in Shropshire and Staffordshire, and a considerable landowner, especially in Shropshire – in 1883 his father owned 21,062 acres worth £28,426 p.a.. He served as a Liberal, later Conservative M.P. from 1870 until 1885. He lived at Apley Park, Bridgnorth, Shropshire and at 6 Belgrave Square, Middlesex.

49. Robert Millington Knowles (1843-1924) – left £1,084,704. Colliery owner in Nottinghamshire and Lancashire.

The son of James Knowles (1812-86, left £184,493), a colliery owner in Bolton, Lancashire, where he was born, he was educated at University College London, and was a director of colliery companies in Nottinghamshire and Lancashire; in the 1871 Census he was described as a "coal proprietor." He served as High Sheriff of Nottinghamshire in 1885. Knowles lived at Colston Bassett Hall, Bingham, Nottinghamshire.

50. Sir William Ernest Cain, 1st Bt. (1864-1924) – left £1,079,781. Brewer and distiller in Liverpool.

The son of Robert Cain (1826-1907, left £411,457), a wealthy Irish-born brewer in Liverpool, he was educated at Winwick Priory School and joined the family firm of Robert Cain & Sons (later Walker Cain), brewers of Liverpool. They were also distillers. He was awarded a knighthood in 1917 and a baronetcy in 1920. His son and successor, Sir Ernest Cain, 2nd Bt. (1891-1969) left £801,993. Our man's brother Sir Charles Nall-Cain, 1st Bt. (1866-1934), Joint Managing Director with him in the firm, was made a baronet in 1921 and, in 1933, given a peerage as 1st Baron Brocket. he left £413,707. Sir William Cain lived at Wargrave Manor, Wargrave, Berkshire and at 31 Croxeth Road, Liverpool.

51. William Dickson Winterbottom (1858-1924) – left £1,063,851. Book cloth manufacturer at Dukinfield near Manchester.

William Winterbottom was the son of Archibald Dickson Winterbottom (1814-84, left £129,909), a cotton manufacturer and later a book cloth manufacturer in Manchester. From a prominent Unitarian family, he was educated at Brighton College, and took over and enlarged the family business, the Winterbottom Book Cloth Co., whose works were in Dukinfield near Manchester. He was also a plaster manufacturer. His partner was his brother George Harold Winterbottom (1861-1934), who left £1,012,972. In later life he was a country gentleman at Aston Hall, Derbyshire.

52. Sir Edward Hulton, 1st Bt. (1869-1925) – left £3,795,125. Newspaper proprietor in Manchester and Fleet Street, City of London.

The son of a wealthy Manchester newspaper proprietor, Edward Hulton (1838-1904, left £558,904), he was educated at St. Bede's Commercial College in Manchester. Hulton was one of the few Roman Catholic newspaper proprietors, and gave to Catholic charities. His father had founded the *Manchester Evening Chronicle*, which had the highest circulation of any newspaper outside of London. Around 1900, Sir Edward moved to London and founded the *Daily Dispatch* in 1900 and the *Daily Sketch* in 1909, as well as the *Sunday Herald* in 1915. Most of his papers were tabloids, which made heavy use of photographs and emphasised "celebrities" and sport. Unlike most "Presslords," Hulton did not seek political influence or office. He was also a notable racehorse owner and the Chairman of the Manchester City Football Club. He was created a baronet in 1921. He lived at 20 Upper Brook Street, Mayfair and at Downside, Leatherhead, Surrey. His son, Sir Edward George Hulton (1906-88, left £1,141,214), was born before his parents married, and could not inherit his baronetcy. He was a notable magazine proprietor, and was knighted in 1957. Our man's sister Dame Margaret Strickland (1878-1950) left £2,066,264.

53. Sir Everard Alexander Hambro, 1st Bt. (1842-1925) – left £2,323,711. Merchant banker in the City of London.

He was the son of Baron Carl Joachim Hambro (1807-77, left £500,000, *q.v.*), an important Danish-born merchant banker in the City. The family had originally been Jewish, but became Lutherans and then Anglicans. Our man was born in London and educated at Trinity College,

Cambridge. He joined his father's bank, C.J. Hambro & Son, in 1864, become a Partner in 1869 and Senior Partner in 1877. He developed the bank, whose offices were at 123 Old Broad Street, into one of the most important finance houses in Britain. He was especially active in North and South American loans, and in the finance of Italy. From 1879 till 1925 he was a Director of the Bank of England. Hambro was given a knighthood in 1908. He lived at Hayes Place, Kent and at Milton Abbey, Dorset.

54. William Hesketh Lever, 1st Viscount Leverhulme (1851-1925) – left £1,625,409. Soap and household products manufacturer at Port Sunlight, Cheshire.

One of the most famous manufacturers of his time, William Hesketh Lever was the son of James Lever (1809-97, left £58,452), a wholesale and retail grocer in Bolton, Lancashire. He was educated at the Bolton Church Institute, and was a lifelong Congregationalist. He worked for his father from 1867, becoming a junior partner in the firm from 1872, and its effective head. He reoriented the firm as manufacturers of soap and other household products, his soap being made from vegetable oil rather than from animal fat as most were, and sold his products nationally via heavy advertising. With his brother James he renamed the firm "Lever Brothers," as it is still often known, although in 1930 it became "Unilever," which today is probably the largest multinational firm making and selling consumer goods in the world. Originally based in Warrington, he built a new factory town to make his products, Port Sunlight in Cheshire near Liverpool. Lever served as a Liberal M.P. from 1906 till 1910, and was High Sheriff of Lancashire in 1917-18. He was made a baronet in 1911, and then ennobled as 1st Baron Leverhulme (derived from the surname of his father, Lever, and of his mother, Hulme), and was elevated as 1st Viscount Leverhulme in 1922. His son William, 2nd Viscount Leverhulme (1888-1949) left £2,372,039. Our man had residences, among other places, at Lewis Castle on the Isle of Lewis and at The Hill, North End, Hampstead Heath, Middlesex.

55. (James) Warley Pickering (1868-1925) – left £1,495,491. Shipowner at Middlesbrough, Yorkshire.

The son of Warley Pickering (1828-80, left £14,000), a grocer who was described in the 1871 Census as a "merchant and importer of wines and spirits [and a] ship's biscuit manufacturer" in Middlesbrough, he was successively a "ship's chandler and wine and spirit merchant" (1881 Census), a "shipowner" (1891 Census), and a "steamship owner and director of limited companies." As a shipowner, he was a partner with the millionaire Middlesbrough shipowner Joseph Constantine (1856-1922, q.v.) in a firm of cargo ships, mainly in the North Sea. He was also involved in investments overseas. He discarded his forename at birth, James, and was usually known as Warley Pickering. His son, another Warley Pickering (1882-1932) left £416,995. Our man lived at Hutton Hall, Guisborough, Yorkshire.

56. Joshua Hirst Wheatley (1854-1925) – left £1,379,491. Woollen manufacturer at Mirfield, Yorkshire and South American merchant.

The son of Joshua Hirst Wheatley (1802-76, left £300,000), a woollen manufacturer at Mirfield near Dewsbury, Yorkshire he was educated at Harrow and at Wadham College, Oxford, and took over his father's business. In the 1881 Census he was described as a "woollen cloth manufacturer employing 150 hands." In the 1891 Census, however, he was described as a "South American merchant." It is unclear of what his activities as a South American merchant consisted, although he may have traded in alpaca and other South American woollen products. It is also unclear where his offices were at that stage of his career. In the Censuses of 1901 and 1911 he was described as a "retired South American merchant." His son Charles Joshua Hirst Wheatley (1888-1943) left £1,026,303. Our man lived at Berkswell Hall, Berkswell near Coventry, Warwickshire.

57. Alfred Shuttleworth (1843-1925) – left £1,020,809. Portable steam engine manufacturer at Lincoln.

The son of Joseph Shuttleworth (1819-83, left £554,613, *q.v.*), the proprietor of Clayton & Shuttleworth, the world's largest producer of portable steam engines, he was educated at Rugby. After the death of his father, he became Managing Director of the firm. He served as High Sheriff of Lincolnshire in 1889-90. In 1929, after his death, the firm went bankrupt, and was taken over by a rival company. He lived at Eastgate House, Lincoln.

58. William Allan Coats (1853-1926) – left £4,019,540. Sewing thread manufacturer in Paisley.

Another of the immensely wealthy members of the Paisley sewing thread family. He was the son of Thomas Coats (1809-83, left £1,308,735, *q.v.*), of the firm, and was the brother of other millionaires such as Sir Thomas Glen-Coats, 1st Bt. (1846-1922, *q.v.*). He lived at Ferguslie House, Paisley and Dalskairth, Dumfriesshire.

59. Margaret Hamilton-Fellowes (1874-1926) – left £1,974,129. Tobacco manufacturing fortune in Bristol.

The daughter of Sir Frederick Wills, 1st Bt. (1838-1909, left £2,918,115, *q.v.*), tobacco manufacturer (W.D. & H.O. Wills, later Imperial Tobacco), in Bristol, one of the very wealthiest families in Britain. In 1903 she married (Major) Ernest Gaddesden Fellows (*sic*- not Fellowes, 1875-1948, left only £540), born in Canada, whom she divorced in 1911. She went by the name of Hamilton-Fellowes, "Hamilton" being her mother's maiden name. She died at the age of fifty-two. She lived at Tangley Park, Worplesdon, Surrey and at The Old Guard House, Margarets-at-Cliffe, Kent.

60. Windham Thomas Windham-Quin, 4th Earl of Dunraven and Mt. Earl (1845-1926) – left £1,962,971. Landowner.

The son of Edwin, 3rd Earl of Dunraven and Mt. Earl (1812-71, left £100,000), he was educated at Christ Church, Oxford. In 1883 he owned 39,755 acres worth £35,478 p.a. in Glamorganshire and Ireland. In his youth, he became a Roman Catholic. From 1871 he sat in the House of Lords under his UK title, Baron Kenry, and was Under-Secretary for the Colonies (Conservative) in 1885-6 and 1886-7. After a colourful life, which included being a war correspondent for the *Daily Telegraph*, living as a rancher on the American frontier, and competing twice as a yachtsman for the America's Cup, he became an influential figure for peace in Ireland, helping to pass the Land Act of 1903 leading to the compulsory purchase by Irish tenants of holdings by landowners. In 1922 he was appointed to serve in the initial Senate of the Irish Free State. He lived at Adare, Co. Limerick and at 22 Norfolk Street, Park Lane, Mayfair.

61. John Scott, 3rd Earl of Eldon (1845-1926) – left £1,390,374. Landowner and legal fortune.

The descendant of John Scott, 1st Earl of Eldon (1751-1838, left £700,000, *q.v.*), Lord Chancellor for nearly forty years, he was the son of John, 2nd Earl of Eldon (1805-54, left £120,000), and was educated at Eton and at Christ Church, Oxford. He was primarily a landowner. In 1883 he owned 25,761 acres worth £28,457 p.a. on Co. Durham, Dorset, etc. He played no public role beyond being a J.P. and D.L. for Gloucestershire and serving on its County Council. He lived at Encomb, Dorset and at 43 Portman Square, Middlesex.

62. Edward Cecil Guinness, 1st Earl of Iveagh (1847-1927) – left £12,486,147. Brewer in Dublin.

Among the five or six richest men in the UK, Edward Guinness was the son of Sir Benjamin Lee Guinness, 1st Bt. (1798-1868, left £1,160,000, *q.v.*), head of the great brewery in Dublin and regarded as the richest man in Ireland. He entered his father's brewery at fifteen, but managed to graduate from Trinity College, Dublin. A Protestant, he was well-regarded as a philanthropist by all religions, and served as Chancellor of Dublin University from 1908. Under his control Guinness in Dublin grew to be the second largest brewery concern in the world, and he became astronomically wealthy, with an estimated income of £650,000 p.a. in 1910. He was made a baronet in 1885, and a baron in 1891, and was then promoted to a viscount in 1905 and to an earl in 1919, the only member of the "Beerage" to attain that rank. Shortly before his death he gave Kenwood House in Hampstead, with its great art collection, to the Nation. His brother Arthur Guinness (1840-1915, left £495,638) was created 1st Baron Ardilaun in 1880. Iveagh's younger son Walter Guinness (1880-1944, left £2,000,000) was created 1st Baron Moyne in 1932. Lord Iveagh had residences at Elveden Hall near Thetford, Suffolk, at 43 St. Stephen's Green in Dublin; and at 5 Grosvenor Place, Middlesex. His probated estate was the largest ever left in the UK up to that point.

63. Frederick Noel Hamilton Wills (1887-1927) – left £5,053,361. Tobacco manufacturer in Bristol.

Another director of W.D. & H.O. Wills, the tobacco manufacturers of Bristol and of Imperial Tobacco, he was the son of Sir Frederick Wills, 1st Bt., M.P. (1838-1909, left £2,918,115, *q.v.*), of the great tobacco manufacturers, and was educated at Clifton College and at Magdalen College, Oxford. He died at only forty. He lived at Miserden Park, Cirencester, Gloucestershire, at Holme Lacy, Herefordshire, and at Invergarry, Inverness-shire. His son Michael Desmond Hamilton Wills (1915-43) left £1,579,947.

64. Marcus Samuel, 1st Viscount Bearsted (1853-1927) – left £4,000,000. Petroleum company head in the City of London.

Born in Whitechapel, he was the son of another Marcus Samuel (d. 1870, left £14,000), described as an "East Indian merchant" in the 1861 Census, but actually the proprietor of a shell and curio shop in the East End. His son began in the same business, and, on a business trip to Japan, became involved as an oil shipper by sea. He secured the right to send his oil ships through the Suez Canal, thus undercutting the Rockefeller petrol interests. In 1897 he established Shell Transport and Trading, named for his former business in the East End. In 1906, after losing a trade war with the Royal Dutch Petroleum Company headed by Henry Deterding, the two firms merged as Royal Dutch-Shell. Its London offices were at Shell House, Bishopsgate Street Within, City of London. The firm of course still exists, and is today the fourth largest company of any kind in the world. Its symbol, on hundreds of petrol stations, of a seashell, derives from Samuel's East End business. He was also active in the municipal affairs of the City of London, serving as Lord Mayor in 1902-03, and helping to formulate the plans for the Port of London Authority. He was made a knight in 1898 and a baronet in 1903. In 1921 he was given a peerage as 1st Baron Bearsted, and was advanced to a viscountcy in 1925. His wife Fanny, who died one day before him in 1927, left £424,713. His brother Samuel Samuel (*sic*, 1855-1934), a merchant banker and Conservative M.P., left £1,516,903. Our man's son Walter, 2nd Viscount Bearsted (1882-1948) left £863,573. Our man lived at 3 Hamilton Place, Park Lane, Mayfair and at The Mote, Maidstone, Kent.

65. Weetman Dickinson Pearson, 1st Viscount Cowdray (1856-1927) – left £4,000,000. Engineering contractor based in the City of London and oil proprietor in Mexico.

The son of George Pearson (d. 1899, left £215,872), of the engineering firm of S. Pearson & Son, of Bradford, founded by our man's grandfather, he was educated at Pannal College, Harrogate to sixteen, and then apprenticed to his father. The firm made bricks, tiles, and piping. He soon became the effective head of the firm, greatly expanding its scope as extraordinarily successful engineering contractors. It built the docks in Milford Haven and elsewhere and, most remarkably, built the railway tunnels under the Hudson River linking Manhattan with New Jersey, tunnels which did not exist before 1910. His firm also constructed the Blackwall Tunnel in London. Its offices were at 10 Victoria Street, Westminster. He then began a second career as the owner of most of the petroleum in Mexico. By 1914 he owned 60% of its petrol when it was the third largest oil producing nation. He served as a Liberal M.P. from 1895 till 1910 (and was known as "the M.P. for Mexico" for his frequent trips there), and served as President of the Air Board. He was awarded a baronetcy in 1894, and was given a peerage, as 1st Baron Cowdray in 1910, and became 1st Viscount Cowdray in 1917. His son Weetman, 2nd Viscount Cowdray (1882-1933) left £457,416. His grandson, John, 3rd Viscount Cowdray (1910-95), who was regarded as one of the richest men in Britain, left £59,736,059. Our man lived at Cowdray Castle, Midhurst, Sussex and at 10 Carlton House Terrace, Middlesex.

66. Edith Anne Hamilton Douglas-Hamilton (*nee* Wills, 1871-1927) – left £1,755,795. Tobacco manufacturer fortune in Bristol.

Yet another member of the Wills tobacco family, she was the daughter of Sir Frederick Wills, 1st Bt. (1838-1909, left £2,918,115) and the sister of Margaret Hamilton-Fellowes (1874-1926, *q.v.*) above. She was also closely related to many other millionaires of this family noted in this work. In 1901 she married Percy Seymour Douglas-Hamilton, a Cambridge graduate who was born in Sydney, New South Wales in 1875 and died in South Africa in 1940. She lived at 6 Queen's Gate Gardens, Middlesex.

67. Sir Robert William Buchanan Jardine, 2nd Bt. (1868-1927) – left £1,547,203. China merchant fortune in Hong Kong.

The son of Sir Robert Jardine, 1st Bt., M.P. (1825-1905, left £1,114,489, *q.v.*), the head of Jardine Matheson, the great firm of China merchants, based in Hong Kong, he was educated at Eton and at Magdalene College, Cambridge. His mother was the daughter of the head of Clan Buchanan, and his children changed their surnames to "Buchanan-Jardine." An officer in the Volunteers and a racehorse owner, he does not appear to have had a business or professional career. He lived at

Castlemilk, Lockerbie, Dumfries-shire and at 24 St. James's Place, Middlesex.

68. William Fox Tibbitts (1842-1927) – left £1,533,949. Urban property owner in Sheffield.

The occupation of his father, James Tibbitts of Sheffield, could not be traced. Our man was educated at Sheffield Collegiate School and became a solicitor in Sheffield. A loner, eccentric, and miser, he was unmarried and, according to one local newspaper account, "bought block after block of property at Upperthorpe [in Sheffield] and ultimately all that district fell into his hands." He also owned property at Skegness and in London. Tibbitts lived at 97 Meadow Street, Sheffield, in a slum area of the city, dying at eighty-five. His wealth came to his niece Henrietta Sarah Fisher (d. 1950), who left £1,491,899.

69. James Deuchar (1849-1927) – left £1,331,716. Brewer in Newcastle-upon-Tyne.

Born in Forfar, the son of a farmer, as a youth he moved to Newcastle-upon-Tyne with his three brothers. In 1868 he began as a wine and spirit merchant there, and became a brewer in Newcastle in 1870. His firm, James Deuchar Ltd. became one of the largest in the area, with branches in the north-west. At the time of his death he owned 150 public houses as well as other smaller breweries. His son and successor, James William Deuchar (1882-1961) left £223,096. Our man lived at Middleton near Wooler, Northumberland and at 7 Eldon Square, Newcastle-upon-Tyne.

70. Henry Charles Keith Petty-Fitzmaurice, 5th Marquess of Lansdowne (1845-1927) – left £1,278,501. Landowner.

One of the most distinguished political figures of his time, he was the son of Henry, 4th Marquess of Lansdowne (1816-66, left £80,000) and was educated at Eton and at Balliol College, Oxford. In 1883 he owned 142,916 acres worth £62,025 p.a., chiefly in Wiltshire and in Ireland. Under Gladstone, he served as Secretary of State for War from 1872-74, and was then Governor-General of Canada 1883-88, and Viceroy of India 1888-94. He then joined the Liberal Unionists, serving in a Conservative government as Foreign Minister 1900-05 and as Leader of the Unionist peers from 1905. In 1915-16 he was back in Asquith's wartime Cabinet as Minister Without Portfolio, 1915-16. In 1917, appalled by the continuing slaughter, he published in the press the famous "Lansdowne Letter" recommending a negotiated settlement to end the War. He lived at Bowood, Calne, Wiltshire and at 54 Berkeley Square, Middlesex. His son Henry, 6th Marquess of Lansdowne (1872-1936) left £1,404,132.

71. Emma Grace Marryat (*nee* Caird, 1849-1927) – left £1,197,505. Jute manufacturing fortune in Dundee.

The daughter of Edward Caird (1805-89, left £58,953), the founder of Caird (Dundee) Ltd., the leading jute manufacturers in Britain, she was the sister of Sir James Key Caird, 1st. Bt. (1837-1916, left £759,989), who greatly expanded the firm. In 1892 she married (Col.) Herbert Charles Marryat (1844-1917, left £518) of Belmont Castle, Meigle. She was her brother's executor and closest surviving relative, and continued his philanthropic work for Dundee. She lived at 8 Roseangle, Dundee.

72. Sir Alfred Seale Haslam (1844-1927) – left £1,064,394. Refrigeration equipment manufacturer at Derby.

The son of William Haslam (d. 1878, left £3,000), a small ironmaster at Derby, he was apprenticed to the Midland Railway and then became an hydraulic engineer with the W.G. Armstrong Co. In 1871 he began Haslam Engineering in Derby, which became probably the leading pioneer of refrigeration equipment in Britain. Haslam saw that the refrigeration of foods when they were imported from overseas would fundamentally change Britain's eating habits. In 1881 he brought the first consignment of frozen meat from Australia, to great publicity. He later developed other types of refrigeration equipment. Haslam served as Mayor of Derby in 1890-91 and as a Liberal Unionist M.P. from 1900 till 1906. He was knighted in 1891. He lived at Breadsall near Derby.

73. Sir George Alfred Wills, 1st Bt. (1854-1928) – left £10,000,000. Tobacco manufacturer at Bristol.

The very richest of the many very wealthy members of the Wills tobacco family, he was the son of Henry Overton Wills (1828-1911, left £5,214,756, *q.v.*), one of the founders of the immensely wealthy Bristol family's fortune. He was educated at Mill Hill School, a public school for Nonconformists like his family, and became a factory manager at 1875, a partner in 1882, and Chairman of Imperial Tobacco from 1911-24. He introduced the cigarette-making machine in 1888, which was used to make "Woodbines" cigarettes, the firm's most popular product, in its enlarged factory near Bristol. Sir George was the main founder and first Chancellor of Bristol University, to which he made generous gifts. His was given a baronetcy in 1923. His son Sir George Vernon Proctor Wills, 2nd Bt. (1887-1931) left £1,100,000. Our man's probated estate of £10 million was one of the largest left in Britain before the Second World War. He lived at Burwalls, Leigh Woods, Long Ashton, Somerset and at Coombe Lodge, Blagdon, Somerset.

74. Davison Alexander Dalziel, 1st Baron Dalziel of Wooler (1854-1928) – left £2,274,219. Newspaper owner at Fleet Street, London and transport magnate in London.

The son of Davison Octavian Dalziel (1825-75, left £20,000), a wholesale merchant in London, he migrated to Sydney in the early 1870s and worked as a journalist. After some years there and in America, he returned to England in 1890 and founded Dalziel's News Agency, and then became a newspaper owner on Fleet Street, owning *The Standard, The Evening Standard* (which still exists), and *The Pall Mall Gazette*. In 1906 Dalziel had founded the General Motor Cab Company, which introduced motor taxis in London, and served as its Chairman from 1907. After selling his newspapers in 1916, he became more involved in transport, as Chairman of the Pullman Car Company and of the International Sleeping Car Company. Dalziel served as a Conservative M.P. from 1910 until 1927. He was made a baronet in 1919 and was given a peerage in 1927. He lived at 18 Grosvenor Place, Westminster.

75. James Walker Oxley (1834-1928) – left £2,774,541. Banker of Leeds.

The son of Henry Walker (1803-90, left £420,286), a banker of Leeds and Mayor of Leeds in 1872-3, he was a wealthy banker of Leeds, a Partner in the Leeds bank of William Williams, Brown & Co., and a director of the Midland Railway and other companies. He may have been the richest man in Leeds at the time of his death, but is surprisingly obscure. He was known as a major art collector and benefactor of Leeds University and of the Leeds Art Gallery. His son Henry Oxley (1869-1948) left £1,543,533. Our man lived at Spenfield, Weetwood, Leeds.

76. (William) Frederick Danvers Smith, 2nd Viscount Hambleden (1868-1928) – left £2,700,998. Multiple bookstall retailer based in London.

The son of William Henry Smith (W.H. Smith 1825-91, left £1,773,388, *q.v.*), the founder of the famous chain of railway and other bookstalls and an important Cabinet minister and political figure, he was educated at Eton and at New College, Oxford. He served as a Conservative M.P. from 1891 until 1910, inheriting his father's London seat when he died. In 1913 he succeeded his mother as 2nd Viscount Hambleden- she had been given a viscountcy in her own right shortly after her husband's death. Known as "Freddy" Smith, he is best known politically as, in 1906, he assumed that he was the "Mr. Frederick Smith" being asked to speak in the Commons by the Speaker. As he rose and began his speech, the Speaker indicated that he actually meant F.E. Smith (Frederick Edwin Smith, later 1st Earl of Birkenhead), who then gave what was probably the most famous Maiden Speech in the history of Parliament, and he was forced to sit down. Hambleden was an excellent head of W.H. Smith, and began its national chain of high street bookshops when it lost its monopoly on operating at train stations. He was also a major figure in the reform of voluntary hospitals, and one of the founders of King's College Hospital in London. He lived at Greenlands, Henley-on-Thames, Oxfordshire. His son and heir, William Henry Smith, 3rd Viscount Hambleden (1903-48, *q.v.*) left £3,088,066.

77. Vernon James Watney (1860-1928) – left £2,058,815. Brewer in Pimlico, London.

The son of James Watney M.P. (1832-86, left £1,264,611), head of the famous brewery in Pimlico, he was educated at Eton and New College, Oxford. He married into the old aristocracy, his wife, whom he married in 1891, being Lady Margaret Wallop, daughter of the 5th Earl of Portsmouth. He served as High Sheriff of Oxfordshire in 1908-9. Watney lived at 11 Berkeley Square, Mayfair and at Cornbury Park near Charlbury, Oxfordshire.

78. Alfred Farquhar (1852-1928) – left £1,667,682. Banker in St. James's, Middlesex.

The son of Harvie Morton Farquhar (1816-87, left £544,684, *q.v.*), banker with Herries Farquhar Bank at 16 St. James's Street, Middlesex, a long-existing private bank catering for the rich, he was educated at Eton. He then joined the family bank, which became part of Lloyd's in 1893 but continued to operate from its old address. He lived at 11 Belgrave Square, Middlesex.

79. John George Lambton, 3rd Earl of Durham (1855-1928) – left £1,543, 689. Landowner.

The son of George, 2nd Earl of Durham (1828-79, left £500,000, *q.v.*), he was educated at Eton. In 1883 he owned 30,471 acres worth £71,671 p.a., mainly in Co. Durham. He was Lord Lieutenant of Co. Durham and Chancellor of Durham University from 1919-28. In 1882 he married Ethel (d. 1931, left £3,133), daughter of Henry Milner. She was committed for many years to a mental institution. Under the laws of the time, the Earl was unable to divorce her, and had an illegitimate son, John H.R. Rudge, with his mistress. Without a legitimate son, the earldom passed to his younger twin brother, Frederick, 4th Earl of Durham (1855-1929, left £1,106,897). The 3rd Earl lived at Lambton Castle, Co. Durham and at 39 Grosvenor Square, Mayfair.

80. Edwin Pope (1845-1928) – left £1,533,929. Brewer in Dorchester, Dorset.

The son of John Allen Pope (1802-75, left £50,000) a large farmer in Dorset who died in Bath, he was born in Clifton, Somerset and with his brother Alfred (d. 1934, left £292,575) he bought the Eldridge Brewery in Dorchester and renamed it Eldridge, Pope & Co. It produced Dorchester Ales. He lived at Mentone Lodge, Dorchester.

81. (Hugh) Frederick Gretton (1869-1928) – left £1,474,058. Brewer in Burton, Staffordshire.

The son of the multi-millionaire Burton brewer John Gretton (1836-99, left £2,883,640, *q.v.*), he was a Captain in the Imperial Yeomanry. Little could be learned about his career. Gretton was the brother of John Gretton, 1st Baron Gretton, M.P. (1867-1944, left £2,302,973), a well-known "diehard" Conservative politician, who was awarded a peerage in 1944. Our man lived at Egglinton Hall, Derbyshire and at Sudbury Hall, Derbyshire.

82. John Nairn (1853-1928) – left £1,411,860. Linoleum manufacturer in Kirkcaldy, Fifeshire.

The son of Michael Nairn (1804-58), the founder of the well-known firm of linoleum and floorcloth manufacturers at Kirkcaldy, he was the brother of Sir Michael Barker Nairn, 1st Bt. (1858-1915, left £881,973), who greatly expanded it into a firm known around the world. Our man was a Partner in the company. Its management was also unusual in that their mother, Catherine Ingram Nairn (1814-91, left £79,519), the widow of its founder, was a Partner in the firm for fifteen years after her husband's death. Our man lived at Forth, Park, Kirkcaldy.

83. Henry Pelham Archibald Douglas Pelham-Clinton, 7th Duke of Newcastle (1864-1928) – left £1,407,000. Landowner.

The son of Henry, 6th Duke of Newcastle (1834-79), who left only £1,500 because of huge gambling debts. His father managed to marry Henrietta Hope, the heiress of the wealthy banker Henry Thomas Hope and owner of the Hope Diamond. The Duke's father-in-law agreed to settle his debts and pay a substantial dowry, but the Duke was unable to touch the capital. Our man was educated at Eton and Magdalen College, Oxford. In 1883 he owned 35,547 acres worth £74,547 p.a., chiefly in Nottinghamshire (see previous chapter). In poor health and an Anglo-Catholic, he played little role in politics, but rebuilt his country house, Clumber Park, in an admired way. He was succeeded by his brother Francis, 8th Duke of Newcastle (1866-1941, left £9,615). Our man lived at Clumber Park, Worksop, Nottinghamshire and at Forest Farm, Windsor Forest.

84. William Hodge Coats (1866-1928) – left £1,394,427. Sewing thread manufacturer at Paisley, Renfrewshire.

Another millionaire member of the Paisley sewing thread family, he was the son of Archibald Coats (1840-1912, left £1,504,252, *q.v.)*, the Chairman of the company. Our man stayed out of the public eye, but was known as a benefactor of Paisley. He lived at 50 Bothwell Street, Glasgow and at Woodside, Paisley.

85. Stephen Cliff (1852-1928) – left £1,326,901. Steel manufacturer and colliery proprietor in Leeds.

The son of Joseph Cliff, a fireclay manufacturer in Leeds, he was described in the 1881 Census as a "tube and brick manufacturer" in Leeds. Twenty years later, the 1901 Census recorded him as a "iron and steel manufacturer and colliery owner." He was Chairman of the Micklefield Coal and Iron Co. Ltd. and a director of the Frodingham Iron & Steel Co. Ltd. He lived at Western Flatts, Wortley, Leeds and at Crayke Manor, Easingwold, Yorkshire.

86. Rex (*sic*) David Cohen (1876-1928) – left £1,218,287. Department store owner in Liverpool.

The son of Lewis Samuel Cohen (1846-1923, left £1,192,701, *q.v.*), Chairman of Lewis's Ltd., the largest department store in Liverpool, our man became its Joint Managing Director before dying at fifty-two. At the time of his death he was living at Condover Hall near Shrewsbury, Shropshire. His son Sir Rex Arthur Louis Cohen (1906-88, left £2,318,608) was the Chairman of the NAAFI (the Navy, Army, and Air Force Institutes) and was knighted in 1964.

87. John James Sainsbury (1844-1928) – left £1,158,615. Grocery chain proprietor, based in Blackfriars, London.

The founder of the famous chain of grocery shops and supermarkets, he was born in Lambeth, the son of John Sainsbury (1809-63), an ornament and picture frame manufacturer. After beginning as a shop assistant to a grocer, together with his wife Mary Ann he opened his first shop at 173 Drury Lane near Covent Garden. By the 1880s he had opened several shops, which emphasised high quality, good hygiene, and low prices. His shops were increasingly aimed at middle class patrons. Owned exclusively by Sainsbury and his family, it became a limited firm in 1922. Its headquarters were at Stamford House, Stamford Street, Blackfriars. Our man's grandson, Alan John Sainsbury, Baron Sainsbury (1902-98, left £9,113,876), a supporter of the Labour Party, was given a life peerage in 1962. Our man lived at Bishopsfield, Broadlands Road, Highgate, Middlesex.

88. Robert Barbour (1876-1928) – left £1,124,764. Cotton merchant fortune, earned in Manchester.

The son of George Barbour (1841-1919, left £1,311,254, *q.v.*), whose ancestors made a fortune as cotton merchants in Manchester, he was educated at Harrow and Trinity College, Cambridge, was a major in the Yeomanry, and served as High Sheriff of Cheshire in 1925-6, but does not appear to have been active in trade. He was killed at fifty-two by falling from a horse. He lived at Bolesworth Castle, Tattenhall near Chester.

89. Henry Seymour Berry, 1st Baron Buckland (1877-1928) – left £1,116,448. Colliery proprietor and heavy industry industrialist in south Wales.

Buckland's was an unusual career. He was born in Merthyr Tydfil in south Wales, the son of John Mathias Berry (d. 1917, left £23,842), an estate agent there. Our man was a pupil teacher and then an estate agent. The next phase of his career is opaque, but during the First World War he emerged as a considerable colliery owner, and was known as a protégé of Lord Rhondda (1856-191, *q.v.*), and took control of many collieries during the First World War. In the 1920s Buckland sat on the boards of sixty companies and was the Chairman of GKN, by then a steel and engineering firm. He was given a peerage in 1926, as 1st Baron Buckland. He died at fifty-one from dashing his head on a telegraph pole when a horse which he was riding bolted. He lived at Bwlch, Breconshire. More remarkably still, two of his brothers also became peers, despite having no family connections with the rich or well-born, William Ewart Berry, 1st Viscount Camrose (1879-1954, left £1,480,686), made a baron in 1929 and a viscount in 1941, and James Gomer Berry, 1st Viscount Kemsley (1883-1968, left £310,153), made a baronet in 1928, a baron in 1936, and a viscount in 1945. Both were major newspaper proprietors, with Camrose and his descendants owning the *Daily Telegraph*.

90. George Herbert Strutt (1854-1928) – left £1,012,940. Cotton manufacturing fortune in Belper, Derbyshire.

From one of the pioneering families of the Industrial Revolution, he was the son of George Henry Strutt (1826-95, left £1,624,483, *q.v.*), a descendant of Jedediah Strutt, the famous early cotton manufacturer. He was educated at Harrow and Magdalene College, Oxford, and served as High Sheriff of Derbyshire in 1903-04. He lived at Mackenzie House, Belper and at Bridgehill, Belper, both in Derbyshire.

91. Bernhard Baron (1850-1929) – left £4,944,820. Tobacco manufacturer in London.

Born in Brest-Litovsk, Russia to Jewish parents, he migrated to New York in 1867 and, after working in a cigarette factory, patented a cigarette making machine. From 1890-95 he was Managing Director of the National Cigarette Tobacco Company of New York. In 1895 he settled in London and manufactured cigarettes at St. James' Place, Aldgate, City of London as well as heading the Baron Cigarette Machine Co. In 1903 Baron became director of Carreras Ltd., a well-known cigarette makers, and, in 1904, its Managing Director. The firm made Black Cats, a popular brand. Like the Wills family of Imperial Tobacco, Baron became one of the richest men in Britain through the sale of a commodity now known to be deadly. In 1920 he opened an enlarged factory, the Arcadia Works, City Road, London, and, in 1928, an even larger factory – known locally as 'The Black Cat Factory' – at Mornington Crescent, Middlesex. Baron was a great philanthropist, who gave away an estimated £2 million to good causes, and, despite his wealth, was a supporter of the Labour party. His son Sir Louis Baron, 1st Bt. (1876-1934, left £652,102), was created a baronet in 1930.

92. John Alexander Dewar, 1st Baron Forteviot (1856-1929) – left £4,405,348. Whisky distiller in Perth.

The son of John Dewar (1806-80, left £34,797), who founded the well-known firm of distillers, John Dewar & Sons Ltd., of Perth, he was educated at Perth Academy and, with his brother and partner Thomas Robert Dewar, greatly expanded the firm so that it became internationally known; the brothers became astronomically wealthy. The firm became part of Distillers Ltd., the great whisky combine, in 1925. Dewar served as a Liberal M.P. from 1900-06, but was increasingly out of sympathy with the party's pro-Temperance elements. He was served as Lord Provost of Perth from 1893-99. He was made a baronet in 1907 and 1st Baron Forteviot in 1916, a title he took from the location of his country estate. His brother, Thomas Robert Dewar, 1st Baron Dewar (1864-1930, *q.v.*), was even wealthier than he was, leaving £5 million. Forteviot lived at Dupplin Castle, Perthshire.

93. John Baring, 2nd Baron Revelstoke (1863-1929) – left £2,558,779. Merchant banker in the City of London.

The son of Edward Baring, 1st Baron Revelstoke (1828-97), head of the great merchant bank at 8 Bishopsgate Within, City of London, he was educated at Eton and at Trinity College, Cambridge. He became a Partner in the bank in 1890 and its Senior Partner in 1901. He had to deal in 1890 with the great Baring Brothers crisis, which almost brought about a crisis throughout the City of London, caused by his father's incompetent handling of a huge loan to the Buenos Aires Water Supply Company. (As a result, his father left only £36,879, the Baring equivalent of living in a tent on Skid Row.) Our man became Senior Partner in Baring Bros. in 1901, and restored the family's wealth, having raised his own income to over £100,000 a year by 1909. He served as a Director of the Bank of England from 1898 until his death, and was Lord-Lieutenant of Middlesex from 1926 until his death. He was knighted in 1911. Unmarried, he was succeeded by his brother Cecil, 3rd Baron Revelstoke (1864-1934, left £406,773). Our man lived at 3 Carlton House Terrace, Middlesex and at Firbank, Market Harborough, Leicestershire.

94. Evan Evans-Bevan (1853-1929) – left £2,127,857. Brewer and colliery owner in Neath, Glamorganshire.

The proprietor of the Vale of Neath Brewery which was established by a relative, David Evans, in 1846, and was then acquired by another relative, David Evans (1794-1871, left £60,000) in 1850, little is known of his early life. He also owned the Swansea Vale Brewery and was a significant colliery owner in the area. He served several times as Mayor of Neath. He lived at Cadoxton House, Cadoxton-juxta-Neath, Glamorganshire. His son Sir David Martyn Evans-Bevan, 1st Bt. (1902-73), who lived for taxation purposes in Jersey, left £18,723 in the UK. He was created a baronet in 1958.

95. Archibald Primrose, 5th Earl of Rosebery (1847-1929) – left £1,641,706. Landowner; may have inherited a merchant banking fortune from his wife.

Prime Minister at age forty-seven, but holding this office for less than two years and declining all further Cabinet posts, the 5th Earl of Rosebery was one of the great enigmas of late Victorian politics. He was the son of Archibald, Lord Dalmeny (d. 1851), and succeeded his grandfather Archibald, 4th Earl of Rosebery in 1868. He was educated at Eton and Christ Church, Oxford, and served under Gladstone as Foreign Secretary in 1886 and 1892-4 and as Liberal Prime Minister in 1894-5. In 1883 he owned 32,411 acres worth £36,479 p.a. in Midlothian and six other counties. In 1878 he married Hannah (d. 1890, left £764,833), daughter of Baron Meyer Amschel De Rothschild, of the great merchant banking family. In 1911, he was created 1st Earl of Midlothian in the UK peerage – the Rosebery earldom was a Scottish peerage. He also served as Chancellor of London University. His son, (Albert) Harry, 6th Earl of Rosebery (1882-1974), left £9,941,699. Our man's many residences included Dalmeny House, Edinburgh and 38 Berkeley Square, Middlesex.

96. Gerard Henry Craig-Sellar (1871-1929) – left £1,729,161. Inherited brewery and distillery fortune in east London.

Gerard Craig-Sellar was the son of Alexander Craig Sellar (1835-1890, left £11,597), a Scottish barrister and Liberal, later Liberal Unionist M.P. 1882 until his death, who married Gertrude Smith (d. 1929, left £350,186), the sister of Thomas Valentine Smith (1825-1906, left £1,931,997, *q.v.*). She inherited much of his property. He was a brewer and distiller, the head of Smith Garrett & Co. of 246 Bow Road in east London. Our man was educated at Eton and Balliol College, Oxford, and was called to the bar in 1896 at Inner Temple. He does not appear to have played a direct role in business life but served for some years as Clerk of the Councils in the Transvaal Colony. He lived at 18 Prince's Gate, Middlesex and at Ardtornish, Argyllshire.

97. Samuel Hope Morley, 1st Baron Hollenden (1845-1929) – left £1,541,654. Hosiery manufacturer in Nottingham and banker in the City of London.

The son of Samuel Morley, M.P. (1809-90, left £165,328), the head of I. & R. Morley, hosiery manufacturers of Nottingham, he was educated at Trinity College, Cambridge. He became Senior Partner in his family's firm, and also served as a Director of the Bank of England from 1903-05. He served as High Sheriff of London County in 1893-4, and was awarded a peerage, as 1st Baron Hollenden, in 1912. He lived at 2 Grosvenor Square, Middlesex. His son Geoffrey, 2nd Baron Hollenden (1885-1977) left £666,107.

98. Sir Hildebrand Aubrey Harmsworth, 1st Bt. (1872-1929) – left £1,384,918. Newspaper proprietor in Fleet Street, City of London, etc.
The brother of Viscount Northcliffe (1865-1922, *q.v.*), who left over £5 million, of Viscount Rothermere, and of other members of this family of Presslords, he was educated at Merton College, Oxford, but did not graduate. From 1908-11 he owned *The Globe* newspaper, but must have derived his wealth from other sources or from a family trust. In 1922 he received a baronetcy from the Lloyd George government, for which he almost certainly paid. He was regarded as the least able of the Harmsworth brothers; when his baronetcy was announced, he allegedly received a telegram sent by his relatives which said, "At last, a grateful nation has given you your due reward." He lived at 3 Adelaide Crescent, Hove, Sussex. He died at age fifty-seven of cirrhosis of the liver.

99. James Fleming Fyfe-Jamieson (1866-1929) – left £1,332,434. Colliery owner, etc. in Scotland.
The son of James Fyfe Jamieson (1816-79), a "retired merchant" (1871 Census) who lived at Queen's Gate in South Kensington who left £90,000, he was born in Torquay and educated at Harrow and at Trinity College, Cambridge, where he was a close friend of Stanley Baldwin, the future Prime Minister. Fyfe-Jamieson's wealth was mainly derived from collieries in Scotland, and he was known to have been involved in iron, shipping, and other interests, but much of his career is obscure. He lived at Ruthven, Meigle, Perthshire.

100. Frank Brian Frederick Bibby (1893-1929) – left £1,082,073. Shipowner in Liverpool.
The son of the Liverpool shipowner Frank Bibby (1857-1923, left £1,229,483, *q.v.*), he was educated at Christ Church, Oxford. He was an officer in the 1st Life Guards, retiring as a major, having served in the First World War. He was described in a number of passenger lists from the 1920s as a "shipowner," but his connection with the family shipping firm is unclear. He died at only thirty-six. Bibby lived at Sansaw, Shrewsbury and at 31 Charles Street, Mayfair.

101. Frederick William Lambton, 4th Earl of Durham (1855-1929) – left £1,106,897. Landowner.
He succeeded his older twin brother John, 3rd Earl of Durham (*q.v.*), who had died the previous year. Frederick was educated at Eton and served in the Coldstream Guards. He served as a Liberal M.P. from 1880-85 (as (Hon.) Frederick Lambton) and then as a Liberal Unionist M.P. from 1900-10. Prior to succeeding, he lived at Fenton House, Northumberland. He was succeeded by his son John, 5th Earl of Durham (1884-1970), who left £669,445.

102. James Francis Mason (1861-1929) – left £1,118,449. Proprietor of copper mines in Portugal.

The son of James Mason (1825-1903, left £869,853) who, with his brother-in-law Sir Francis Tress Barry, 1st Bt., M.P. (1825-1907, left £640,271) made a fortune in the firm Mason & Barry, which owned a lucrative copper mine in southern Portugal that had begun operations in 1859. Our man was born in Portugal and educated at Eton, and became the head of Mason & Barry. He was a Captain in the Hussars, and served as a Conservative M.P. from 1905-18 in succession to his uncle. In 1895 he married into the aristocracy, to Lady Evelyn, daughter of the 25th Earl of Crawford. He was also a director of Dorman Long, the steel manufacturers, and of other companies. He lived at Eynsham Hall, Witney, Oxfordshire and at 18 Brunton Street, Mayfair.

103. William Brocklehurst Brocklehurst (sic, 1851-1929) – left £1,072,885. Silk manufacturer at Macclesfield, Cheshire.

The son of William Coare Brocklehurst, M.P. (1818-1900, left £517,241), a leading silk manufacturer at Macclesfield, he was educated at Cheltenham College and at Magdalen College, Oxford, and was a Colonel in the Yeomanry. He became the head of the family firm, Brocklehurst & Sons, and served as a Liberal M.P. from 1906-18. He lived at Butley Hall, Prestbury near Macclesfield.

1930-1939

The 1930s were, of course, the decade of the Great Depression. It had an effect on the nature of wealthholding in Britain, decreasing the number of millionaires compared with the 1920s, and reducing the number of international bankers and traditional great landowners. Its consequences, however, should not be exaggerated. The largest individual estate left prior to the 1970s, the £36.7 million left by the shipowner and financier Sir John Ellerman, was left in 1933, as were other very large estates, although more at the beginning of the decade than at its end. The introduction of tariffs around Britain and its Empire in 1931-32 had a strongly positive effect upon the British economy, as did rearmament after the rise of Hitler. Britain continued its move to a more modern-looking society of home and automobile owners and purchasers of mass consumer items, which would resume after the Second World War.

1. James Williamson, 1st Baron Ashton (1842-1930) – left £10,501,196. Linoleum manufacturer in Lancaster.

"The Linoleum King," as he was known, was the son of James Williamson (d. 1879, left £80,000), an oil cloth manufacturer in Lancaster. He was educated at the Royal Grammar School, Lancaster, and entered his father's firm around 1860. By 1875 he was in control of the firm, and pioneered the mass production of cheap linoleum and floor coverings, sold throughout Britain and widely exported. His factory in Lancaster employed 4,000 people, and was probably the largest employer of labour in that part of Lancashire. An eccentric recluse in later life, he built the striking Ashton Memorial Building in Lancaster in honour of his wife. Earlier, he had served as a Liberal M.P. from 1886 till 1895, and was High Sheriff of Lancashire in 1885-6. He was created 1st Baron Ashton in 1895. He lived at Ashton Hall near Lancaster and at Alford House, Prince's Gate, Middlesex. His fortune of over £10 million was one of the half dozen largest estates left in Britain up to that time. His daughter Eleanor (1871-1949) married William Robert Peel, 1st Earl Peel (1867-1937); she left £4,274,902.

2. Thomas Robert Dewar, 1st Baron Dewar (1864-1930) – left £5,000,000. Whisky distiller in Perth.
The son of John Dewar (1806-80, left £34,797), the founder of the great distillers John Dewar & Sons, and the younger brother of John Alexander Dewar, 1st Baron Forteviot (1856-1929, *q.v.*), who left £4,405,348, he joined the family firm and became its Managing Director, as well as a director of the Distillers Company, which was formed by the merger of Scotland's largest distilleries. Much of his life was spent in London, where he was a member of the London County Council from 1892 to 1895 and Sheriff of the City of London in 1897-98. He also served as a Conservative M.P. from 1900-06. He received a knighthood in 1902 and was created 1st Baron Dewar in 1991. He lived at 26 Savoy Court, Middlesex and at Homestall, East Grinstead, Sussex.

3. Sir Otto John Beit, 1st Bt. (1865-1930) – left £3,784,343. Financier in the City of London and diamond magnate and stockbroker in South Africa.
The brother of the multi-millionaire Alfred Beit (1853-1906, left £8,049,986, *q.v.*). They were born to Sephardic Jewish parents in Hamburg, the sons of a silk merchant; he came to London in 1880. He then went to South Africa, and became associated with his brother's firm, Wernher Beit of Johannesburg, and was a member of the Johannesburg Stock Exchange. In 1896 he returned permanently to London, where he was a director of the British South Africa Company and headed their many financial interests from his offices at 1 London Wall, City of London. He also accumulated a great art collection, as did many other millionaires of the time. It became the victim of a great art robbery by the IRA in 1974 at the Irish home of his son Sir Alfred Lane Beit, 2nd Bt. (1903-94), an Old Etonian who served as a Conservative M.P. from 1931 till 1945, but then lived in a mansion in Ireland. Otto Beit was made a knight in 1920 and was given a baronetcy in 1924, He spent his last decades administering the Beit Trust, which funded many projects in southern Africa and medical research in Britain. He lived at 49 Belgrave Square, Belgravia and at Tewin Water, Welwyn, Hertfordshire.

4. Andrew Coats (1862-1930) – left £2,812,908. Sewing thread manufacturer in Paisley, Renfrewshire.
Another son of Thomas Coats (1809-83, left £1,308,735, *q.v.*), one of the founders of the great sewing thread manufacturing firm in Paisley; his two brothers also left millionaire estates. He was a major in the Yeomanry and served in the Boer War. He lived at Castle Toward, Dunoon, Argyllshire.

5. Alan Ian Percy, 8th Duke of Northumberland (1880-1930) – left £2,510,000. Landowner.
The son of Henry, 7th Duke of Northumberland (1846-1918, left £1,160,000, *q.v.*), he served in the Grenadier Guards in the Boer War and the First World War. He was Lord Lieutenant of Northumberland, but otherwise held no political offices, although he was a strong supporter of right-wing causes. His many residences included 17 Prince's Gate, Westminster, Alnwick Castle, Northumberland, and Albury Park, Guildford, Surrey. His son Henry, 9th Duke of Northumberland (1912-40) left £1,802,089.

6. Sir William George Watson, 1st Bt. (1861-1930) – left £2,020,312. Dairy products and food multiple retailer, based in Manchester and then Southall, Middlesex.

The son of William Watson (1828-1912, left £9790), a tenant farmer in Warwickshire, Watson was apprenticed to a Birmingham provision merchant and, with a relative, in 1887 founded the Danish Dairy Company, later known as the Maypole Dairy Company. Based in Manchester, it sold high quality Danish butter, and later, Danish bacon. It moved to a larger factory at Southall, Middlesex. The firm had sixty branches by 1895, but greatly expanded, and had no fewer than 844 branches in 1914. The firm suffered by import restrictions during the First World War. Watson retired in 1924. He was created a baronet in 1912, and served as High Sheriff of Berkshire in 1917-18 and 1920-21. His son Victor William (Peter) Watson (1908-56, left £121,017) was one of the founders of the Institute of Contemporary Arts. During the 1930s, he funded *Horizon* magazine. He was found dead in his bath; there has been speculation that he was murdered by his male lover, who inherited the bulk of his estate. Our man lived at Sulhamstead House near Reading, Berkshire.

7. Edward Allen Brotherton, 1st Baron Brotherton (1856-1930) – left £1,780,485. Chemical manufacturer at Wakefield, Yorkshire.
The son of Theophilus Brotherton (1823-79), a yarn agent in Manchester, he left school at fifteen and took night classes in chemistry at Owens College, Manchester. He was employed in a chemical works at nineteen, and became a partner in a Wakefield chemical firm in 1878, later known as Brotherton & Co. It produced ammonium sulphate, and later, coal tar and TNT. It became the main supplier of these substances to Brunner Mond and grew into what was regarded as the largest privately owned chemical works in Britain. He is best remembered for endowing the Brotherton Library at Leeds University, and was probably the greatest donor to that new university. He served as Conservative M.P. for Wakefield in 1902-10 and 1918-22. Brotherton was created a baronet in 1918 and given a peerage, as 1st Baron Brotherton, in 1929. He lived at The Hall, Roundhay, Leeds.

8. Osbert Cecil Molyneux, 6th Earl of Sefton (1871-1930) – left £1,758,376. Landowner.
The younger son of William, 4th Earl of Sefton (1835-97, left £273,937), he succeeded his elder brother Charles, 5th Earl of Sefton (1867-1901, left £91,113). The 6th Earl's education is not given in any source. In 1883 his father owned 20,250 acres worth £43,000 p.a., all in Lancashire, including valuable land in and near Liverpool. Our man served as Master of the Horse from 1905-07 in the Liberal government. His son Hugh, 7th Earl of Sefton (1898-1972) left £5,242,848. The 6th Earl lived at Croxteth Hall, Liverpool, and at 13 Charles Street, Berkeley Square, Middlesex.

9. Sir Friedrich [Frederick] Gustav Jonathan Eckstein, 1st Bt. (1857-1930) – left £1,381,000. Gold and diamond magnate in South Africa and financier in the City of London.
Born in Stuttgart, Germany, the son of (Revd.) Carl Eckstein, apparently a Lutheran minister, and educated at Stuttgart Gymnasium, he went to Johannesburg, South Africa and became a partner in Wernher, Beit & Co., which developed South Africa's diamond and gold mining wealth. He later was a financier at 1 London Wall Buildings, City of London, where he was Chairman of the Sudan Plantations Syndicate. He received a baronetcy in 1929. Eckstein was buried in an Anglican churchyard in Uckfield, Sussex. He lived at 3 Whitehall Court, Middlesex and at Oldlands Hall, Uckfield, Sussex.

10. Francis Charles Le Marchant (1844-1930) – left £1,096,417. Merchant banker in the City of London.

The younger son of Sir Denis Le Marchant, 1st Bt. (1795-1874, left £9,000), barrister, M.P., Chief Clerk of the House of Commons from 1871, and Member of the Council of India. Francis Le Marchant was educated at Eton and at Balliol College, Oxford, and became Senior Partner in the merchant bank H.S. Lefevre & Co., of 16 Bishopsgate Street Within, City of London. He was also a director of the National Provincial Bank. Le Marchant was a Member of the Council of India, 1896-1906. He lived at 2 West Eaton Place, Belgravia.

11. Sir John Ritchie Findlay, 1st Bt. (1860-1930) – left £1,083,310. Newspaper proprietor in Edinburgh.
The son of John Ritchie Findlay (1824-98, left £299,332), the proprietor and Editor of *The Scotsman* newspaper, produced in Edinburgh. He was educated at Harrow and at Balliol College, Oxford, and inherited the ownership of the newspaper on his father's death. He held numerous educational and cultural positions in Scotland, such as serving on the Board of the National Gallery of Scotland, founded in large part by his father. He was made a knight in 1917 and a baronet in 1925, and was Lord Lieutenant of Banffshire from 1928 until his death. His son Sir Edmund Findlay, 2nd Bt. (1902-62) was a Conservative M.P. from 1935 to 1945. Our man lived at 3 Rothesay Terrace, Edinburgh and at Aberlour House, Banffshire.

12. Ellis Carr (1852-1930) – left £1,051,208. Biscuit manufacturer at Bermondsey, London.
The son of John Carr (1824-1912, left £171,729), a biscuit manufacturer in Carlisle, after an apprenticeship in the industry he joined his brother Arthur Carr (1855-1947, left £630,206) in Peak Frean, the biscuit manufacturing firm in London founded in 1857. He became a Partner in the firm in 1875, which had opened an enormous factory to produce its biscuits in Bermondsey. The firm prospered through producing new products and via heavy advertising. In 1921 it merged with its rival Huntley & Palmer, to form Associated Biscuit Manufacturers Ltd. Ellis Carr appears to have operated behind the scenes; his more dynamic brother has an entry in the *ODNB* which mentions Ellis only in passing. Originally Quakers, by the 1890s they had become Anglicans. Ellis Carr lived at "Yewbarrow," 8 Broadwater Down, Tunbridge Wells, Kent.

13. Alfred Mond, 1st Baron Melchett (1868-1930) – left £1,029,694. Chemical manufacturer in Winnington, Cheshire and elsewhere.
The son of Ludwig Mond (1839-1909, left £1,422,000, *q.v.*), the chemical manufacturer and co-founder of Brunner Mond, he was educated at Cheltenham College, at St. John's College, Cambridge, and at Edinburgh University, and then became a barrister of the Inner Temple (called 1894). He joined the family firm, becoming its Managing Director, as well as head of the Mond Nickel Company, and a company director of many enterprises. Mond was also a leading figure in the establishment of ICI (Imperial Chemical Industries), which remained one of the most important companies in Britain. He served as a Liberal M.P. in 1906-23 and 1924-28, and held Cabinet office as First Commissioner of Works 1916-21 and Minister of Health in 1921-22. He was known for his attempts to bring capital and labour together, and was an important figure in trying to avert the Coal Strike of 1926. He was also a major early backer of the Zionist movement. In the 1920s he joined the Conservative party. He was created a baronet in 1910 and a peer, as 1st Baron Melchett, in 1928. He lived at Melchet (*sic*) Court, Romsey, Hampshire and at 35 Lowndes Square, Belgravia.

14. Sir Lucas Eustratios Ralli, 1st Bt. (1846-1931) – left £2,290,447. East India merchant in the City of London.

The Senior Partner in Ralli Brothers, the great Greek firm of East India merchants at 25 Finsbury Circus, City of London, he was the son of Eustratio Ralli (1800-84, left £611,707, *q.v.*), East India merchant of Ralli Brothers. Sir Lucas was educated at Harrow and at Trinity College, Cambridge, and joined the family firm in 1879. He was a Governor of the London Hospital, and was made a baronet in 1912. His son Sir Eustratio Ralli, 2nd Bt. (1876-1964) left £237,721. Sir Lucas lived at 2 Park Street, Grosvenor Square, Middlesex.

15. Hugh Morrison (1868-1931) – left £1,856,418. Merchant banking and retail/wholesale fortune in the City of London and landowner.

The grandson of James Morrison (1789-1857, *q.v.*), the great multi-millionaire warehouseman at Fore Street, City of London, and then a merchant banker, and the son of Alfred Morrison (1821-97, left £869,175), a famous art and autograph collector, he also inherited substantial sums and land from his other wealthy relatives, including his uncle Charles Morrison (1817-1909, *q.v.*) who left £11 million. Hugh Morrison was educated at Eton and at Trinity College, Cambridge, and, in 1892, married Lady Mary Leveson-Gower, daughter of the 3rd Earl Granville. He served as a Conservative M.P. in 1918-23 and 1924-31, and was High Sheriff of Wiltshire. His son John Granville Morrison, 1st Baron Margadale (1906-96), was a Conservative M.P. from 1942-64 and Chairman of the "1922" Committee from 1955 to 1964, and in 1965 was awarded one of the last hereditary peerages. Hugh Morrison lived at 9 Halkin Street, Belgravia; Fonthill, Tisbury, Wiltshire, and at Islay House, Islay, Scotland. The lands managed by his family had their offices at 32 Coleman Street, City of London.

16. Thomas Lunham Boyd (1849-1931) – left £1,528,498. Provision merchant in Southwark, etc.

The son of Robert Andrew Boyd (1814-69, left £90,000), a sugar refiner in Walthamstow, little is known of his career. Born in Cork, Ireland, in the 1881 and 1901 Censuses he was described as a "provision merchant" who lived at Hadlow near Tonbridge, Kent. In the 1920s he was a "provision merchant" at the New Hibernia Chambers, 4 Borough High Street, Southwark. In later life he lived at the Villa Lieta, San Remo, Italy. He may have been connected with Boyd Brothers, provision merchants of Liverpool. He was probably engaged in meat imports and exports, but this is not entirely clear.

17. Montague Stanley Napier (1870-1931) – left £1,243,578. Automobile and aircraft engine manufacturer in Acton, Middlesex.

The son of James Murdoch Napier (d. 1895, left £14,040), a manufacturer of printing machinery for newspapers and of coin weighing machines, of Lambeth, trading as D. Napier & Son, he took over the company when his father died and became one of the most important early British makers of motor engines and a pioneer of auto racing. He then developed aircraft engines, especially the successful Lion engine used in British planes in the First World War. His firm, whose works were in Acton, Middlesex and whose showrooms were in Regent Street, employed 1,600 men in 1927. Described by one historian as "very secretive by nature," and chronically ill in later life, from 1915 he lived in the south of France, dying at Villa des Cistes, Cannes.

18. Sir Charles Algernon Parsons (1854-1931), left £1,214,000. Turbine engine manufacturer and optical works proprietor in Newcastle-upon-Tyne.

The inventor of the compound steam turbine engine, as well as an innovator in other types of engineering and in optical works, Sir Charles Parsons was born in London, the fourth son of William Parsons, third Earl of Rosse (1830-67), an Irish peer and also a famous astronomer. Our man was educated at home, at Trinity College, Dublin, and at Cambridge, and worked for W.G. Armstrong, the great engineering firm of Newcastle-upon-Tyne. In 1889 he founded C.A. Parsons & Co., in that city to produce steam turbine engines for ships, especially naval ships, whose design he pioneered. Parsons became one of the best known British inventors of his day. He was knighted in 1911 and was awarded the Order of Merit (O.M.) in 1927. In London he lived at 1 Upper Brook Street, Mayfair.

19. Sir Joseph Hood, 1st Bt. (1863-1931) – left £1,200,650. Tobacco manufacturer in Bristol.

Born in Ashby-de-la-Zouche, Leicestershire and educated at the Grammar School there, in 1890 he became a solicitor in Liverpool. He then acted as solicitor to British-American Tobacco and to Imperial Tobacco, becoming the Deputy-Chairman of British-American Tobacco until he retired in 1921. He served as Mayor of Wimbledon, Surrey in 1910-11, and as a Conservative M.P. from 1918-24. During the First World War he was Assistant Controller of the Ministry of Information in 1918. He lived at Greycourt, Wimbledon Common and at "Ivanhoe," Frinton-on-Sea, Essex. His son, Sir Harold Hood, 2nd Bt, (1916-2005), was an important figure in the British Roman Catholic press.

20. John Henry Keene (1864-1931) – left £1,144,202. Insurance company proprietor of High Holborn, London.

The Secretary (1892-1914) and a Director (1914-31) of the Pearl Insurance Company, whose headquarters at 252 High Holborn is now a luxury hotel, he was the son of John Keene (1823-92), one of the founders of the company, who lived in New Cross, Kent, and left only £370. Pearl Insurance began in order to provide cheap insurance in the East End and environs, and then expanded. Little is known of the details of our man's career. He was childless, and left his entire estate to his wife, Lavinia *nee* Stevens (1863-1949), who left £1,347,910 at her death, of which an incredible £937,663 went to pay the astronomical rates of death duties in place at the time, 70 per cent of what she left. Both were notable philanthropists of Chelmsford, where they lived at Carlton House, Galleywood.

21. Sir George Vernon Proctor Wills, 2nd Bt. (1887-1931) – left £1,100,000. Tobacco manufacturer in Bristol.

The son of Sir George A. Wills, 1st Bt. (1854-1928) of Imperial Tobacco in Bristol, who left £10 million, he was educated at Sherborne School and served as a Director in the family firm. He held the baronetcy for only three years, dying at the age of forty-four. During the First World War he was an Administrative Officer of the Gloucestershire Royal Field Artillery, and was later President of the Bristol General Hospital. He lived at Coombe Lodge, Blagdon, Somerset and at Langford Court, Langford, Somerset.

22. Frank Henry Cook (1862-1931) – left £1,054,719. Travel agency head in London.

One of three sons of John Mason Cook (1834-99, left £622,534), head of the famous travel agency, Thomas Cook & Sons, he became its head. For many years its headquarters were on Fleet Street in the City of London; it had dozens of branches throughout the UK and around the world. He was a D.L. of the City of London and lived in later life at Barnett Hill, Wonersh, Surrey. He married an American, Beatrice Elliott Lindell (d. 1953), who left £222,428. They had one child, Frances Beatrice Cook (1897-1991), who left £6,610,852.

23. Solomon Barnato Joel (1865-1931) – left £1,000,000. Diamond mine proprietor and financier in South Africa and in the City of London.

The son of Joel Joel (*sic*, d. 1893, left £1852), a cigar manufacturer in Spitalfields, London, and the nephew of the famous Barnett Isaacs Barnato, known as Barney Barnato (1852-97, left £963,865), the South African diamond "Randlord" who committed suicide by jumping off of a ship, he was educated at the Jews' Free School in Spitalfields. He went to Kimberley in South Africa in the 1880s, and became wealthy as a director, from 1901-31, of Barnato Brothers and of De Beers Consolidated Diamond Mines. In South Africa he was President of the Johannesburg Stock Exchange. Back in London, he was connected with investments in many companies from his offices at 10/11 Austin Friars in the City of London, and was known as a major owner of successful racehorses. He lived at 2 Great Stanhope Street in Mayfair. His brother Isaac [Jack] Barnato Joel (1862-1940) left £3,634,496; his son Dudley Jack Barnato Joel (1904-41) left £1,071,318; his daughter Eileen Daphne Solvia Rogerson (1907-74) left £2,874,078.

24. Sir John Reeves Ellerman, 1st Bt. (1862-1933) – left £36,684,995. Shipowner, financier, and London property owner in the City of London.

The King. Sir John Ellerman left nearly £37 million, almost three times as much as the *second* largest estate prior to the 1970s. The son of a German-born Lutheran corn merchant in Hull, Johann Hermann Ellerman (d. 1871), who left £6,000, and his wife Anne Reeves, the daughter of a solicitor, Ellerman was apprenticed to a Birmingham accountant and joined the leading London firm of accountants, Quilter, Ball & Co., but then became an independent accountant at 12 Moorgate Street in the City of London. He had no connections with shipping until he was twenty-nine, but nevertheless became, over the next twenty years, the largest shipowner in Britain, buying up old, good firms that were in entrepreneurial decline and greatly improving them as components of the Ellerman Lines. He then branched out in owning collieries, breweries, and newspapers, including a string of Fleet Street papers. He was, for instance, the third largest shareholder in *The Times* when it was bought by Lord Northcliffe, but his role was characteristically shrouded in secrecy. He then became probably one of the half-dozen largest owners of prime London real estate (see previous section). Secrecy was a continuing hallmark of his life. He was given a baronetcy in 1905 and, implausibly, made a Companion of Honour (C.H.) in 1921. He lived a t 1 South Audley Street, Mayfair and at a house at 2 Duke's Drive, Eastbourne, Sussex, but owned no rural property. His daughter Annie Winifred Ellerman (1894-1983, left £462,020), the lesbian companion of the American-born poet "H.D." (Hilda Doolittle) was a significant writer and also an important literary magazine publisher in Paris in the 1920s. His son, Sir John Reeves Ellerman, 2nd Bt. (1909-73) left £53.2 million, the largest estate in nominal value left in Britain up to that time.

25. Henry Trueman Mills (1860-1933) – left £2,989,637. Silk manufacturing fortune in the City of London.

The son of Joseph Trueman Mills (1836-1924, left £4,104,000), of Stockgrove, Buckinghamshire, his wealth originated in a silk manufacturing fortune founded in Milk Street, Cheapside, City of London in the early nineteenth century. Remarkably little is known of how the family became so rich, or much else about them. Our man was born at Bosworth, Leicestershire and lived at Langton Hall, West Langton, Leicestershire; he served as High Sheriff of Leicestershire in 1915-16. He was apparently not in trade, but lived as a member of the landed gentry. He also had a residence at 8 Wilton Crescent, Middlesex.

26. Robert Fleming (1845-1933) – left £2,174,804. Merchant banker in Dundee and in the City of London.

The son of an overseer in a linen and jute mill in Dundee, Robert Fleming was educated at Dundee High School to age thirteen, worked as a clerk, and then founded the Scottish American Investment Trust, based in Dundee, the first investment trust, which specialised in financing American railways. Fleming became a widely respected expert in this field, crossing the Atlantic 128 times. In 1890 he moved his main office to London, as Robert Fleming & Co., of 8 Crosby Square, City of London, which became one of the most important investment firms of its time. He served as High Sheriff of Oxfordshire in 1909-10. His brother Sir John Fleming (1847-1925) served as a Liberal M.P. in 1917-18. Robert Fleming was the grandfather of Ian Fleming (1908-64, left £323,797), the creator of James Bond, and of the writer and explorer (Robert) Peter Fleming (1907-71, left £439,628). Robert Fleming lived at 27 Grosvenor Square, Middlesex and at Joyce Grove, Nettlebed, Oxfordshire.

27. Gerald Oakley Cadogan, 6th Earl Cadogan (1869-1933) – left £2,000,000. Urban property owner in London.

The owner of the Cadogan Estate in central London, which includes Sloane Square and King's Road, Chelsea (see previous section), he was the son of George, 5th Earl Cadogan (1840-1915, left £354,207) and of Lady Beatrix, the daughter of William, 2nd Earl of Craven. He was educated at Eton, and was a long-serving Army officer, serving in the Boer War. He was also Chairman of the British Olympic Council. His family owned little or no rural land, although he served as High Sheriff of Suffolk in 1919-20. He was succeeded by his son, William, 7th Earl Cadogan (1914-97). Our man lived at 46 Grosvenor Square, Middlesex and at Culford Hall, Bury St. Edmunds, Suffolk. The Cadogan Estate in London is now regarded as the second largest in the capital after the Grosvenor Estate and must today be worth billions.

28. Frederick Gulov (*sic*) Salvesen (1855-1933) – left £1,256,744. Shipowner in Leith near Edinburgh.

The son of the Norwegian-born Christian Fredrik (*sic*) Salvesen (1827-1911, left £209,384), a shipowner and whaling entrepreneur of Leith, he was educated in Germany and then joined his father's firm. Little is known of his career; in the 1911 Census he was described as a "shipowner and shipbroker." He was the brother of Edward Theodore Salvesen (1857-1942), a Liberal Unionist M.P. 1900-05 and then a Judge of the Court of Sessions in Scotland, 1905-22. Our man's nephew Harold Keith Salvesen (1897-1970) left £4,116,000. Our man lived at 21 Buckingham

Terrace, Edinburgh.

29. David Guthrie Dunn (1907-33) – left £1,224,092. Inherited a tobacco fortune in Glasgow.

David Guthrie Dunn was only twenty-six when he was lost overboard on his yacht *Southern Cross* in heavy seas between Cape Town and St. Helena. He was the son of John Smith Macpherson Dunn (d. 1923, left £75,696), a member of the tobacco manufacturing firm of F. & J. Smith of Glasgow, which had become part of Imperial Tobacco. He was educated at Cambridge University, and set out in his yacht with two companions from the Clyde in 1930, arriving in Brisbane, Australia a year later, in 1931. In June 1932 they set out again, but he was swept overboard. His two companions survived and piloted the boat to St. Helena. Unmarried, Dunn lived at Knock Castle, Largs, Ayrshire.

30. Charles Henry Garton (1859-1934) – left £2,867,383. Brewery sugar manufacturer at Battersea, Southwark.

The son of William Garton (1832-1905, left £540,457), who established a brewery sugar plant at Southampton, and, in the 1880s, moved it to an enormous factory at Southampton Wharf, Battersea. It chiefly manufactured sugar for London's many breweries, but also made other forms of sugar products. He ran the company, Garton and Sons, with his brother, the next entry. He lived at Banstead Wood, Surrey.

31. Sir Richard Charles Garton (1857-1934) – left £2,641,365. Brewery sugar manufacturer at Battersea and brewery executive in London.

The brother of Charles Henry Garton (see previous entry), he was educated at Owens College, Manchester and at Marburg University in Germany, and became head of the family firm. He was also Deputy Chairman of Watney, Combe & Reid, the great brewers. He was knighted in 1908, and was High Sheriff of Surrey in 1913. He lived at Lythe Hall, Haslemere, Surrey.

32. Courtenay Charles Evan Morgan, 1st Viscount and 3rd Baron Tredegar (1867-1934) – left £2,369,686. Land and mineral owner.

The grandson of Charles Morgan, 1st Baron Tredegar (1792-1875, left £200,000) and the son of (Hon.) Frederick Courtenay Morgan (d. 1909, left £15,802), he succeeded his uncle Godfrey, 2nd Baron Tredegar (d. 1913, left £446,278). He was educated at Eton, and was a Lieutenant-Colonel in the Army, serving in the Boer War and the First World War. In 1883 his predecessor owned 39,157 acres worth £60,000 p.a., including collieries in Monmouthshire and Glamorganshire. He later commanded the Royal Yacht *Liberty*. His son, the eccentric Evan, 2nd Viscount Tredegar (1893-1949) left £1,719,137. Our man's only daughter, (Hon.) Gwyneth Morgan (1895-1924, left £5,063), died in mysterious circumstances, her body being found floating in the Thames, apparently murdered. Our man lived at Tredegar House, Newport, Monmouthshire and at Honeywood House, Dorking, Surrey.

33. Hudson Ewbanke Kearley, 1st Viscount Devonport (1865-1934) – left £1,897,819. Grocery chain retailer, based in the City of London.

Born in Uxbridge, Middlesex, the son of George Ewbanke Kearley (1814-76, left £4,000), a building contractor who died when his son was eleven, he had no schooling past the age of fifteen, and then joined Tetley & Co., tea merchants. In 1876 he formed Kearley & Tonge, wholesale tea merchants, and then began a major chain of food retailers, International Store, its first branch opening at Brentford in 1878. By 1890 it had 200 branches throughout Britain; its headquarters was at 9 Mitre Square, City of London. Kearley served as a Liberal M.P. from 1892 till 1910 and was Parliamentary Secretary to the Board of Trade, 1905-08; in 1916-17 he was Food Controller. From 1909 until 1925 he was Chairman of the Port of London Authority, and is known for suppressing the major Dock Strike of 1912. He was made a baronet in 1908, and was then made 1st Baron Devonport in 1910 and a Viscount in 1917. He lived at Wittington, Buckinghamshire; 41 Grosvenor Place, Middlesex; and at Kinloch, Dunkeld, Perthshire. His son Gerald, 2nd Viscount Devonport (1890-1973) left £568,000.

34. George Allardice Riddell, 1st Baron Riddell (1865-1934) – left £1,838,902. Newspaper proprietor in the City of London.

Born in Brixton, the son of a photographer, He was a clerk to a solicitor and then studied to become a solicitor, finishing first in England in the examinations when he qualified. In 1891 he became legal consultant to the *News of the World* Sunday newspaper, and gained control of the paper in 1903. It specialised in reporting on crimes, divorces, and scandals, and became enormously popular. The newspaper operated from 8 Bouverie Street, City of London, just off Fleet Street. He also gained control of *Country Life* and other more respectable publications. He served as Chairman of the Newspapers' Association and was President of the Advertising Association in 1928-30. Riddell became a close friend and confidante of David Lloyd George. He was given a knighthood in 1909, made a baronet in 1918 and a peer, as 1st Baron Riddell, in 1920. The King was reluctant to award Riddell the peerage recommended by Lloyd George, as Riddell had been the guilty party in his divorce from his first wife; he was one of the first men awarded a peerage despite being the respondent in a divorce. Riddell was the author of a politically important diary, used by historians. He lived at Walton Heath House, Banstead, Surrey, and at 20 Queen Anne's Gate, Westminster.

35. Samuel Samuel (*sic*) (1855-1934) – left £1,676,903. Merchant banker and petrol company director in the City of London.

The brother of Marcus Samuel, 1st Viscount Bearsted (1853-1927, left £4,000,000, *q.v.*), the founder of Shell Transport and Trading, and the son of Marcus Samuel (d. 1870, left £14,000), a shell and curio shop proprietor in the East End, Samuel Samuel was an associate of his brother in founding what is now Royal Dutch-Shell, but also founded the merchant bank M. Samuel & Co., of 26-27 Bishopsgate, City of London, which later became Hill Samuel. He served as a Conservative M.P. from 1913 until his death. Unmarried, he lived at 1 Berkeley House, Hay Hill, Berkeley Square, Mayfair.

36. John Anstruther Berners (1869-1934) – left £1,180,100. Landowner, probably with other interests.

Born in London, the son of Charles Hugh Berners (1842-1919, left £214,045), he was educated at Eton and Sandhurst, and was known as a First-Class Cricketer. In 1883 his father owned 4,815 acres worth £6,808 p.a., in Suffolk, and, to accumulate over £1 million, our man must have had other interests. It is possible that he owned urban property in London, e.g., at Berners Street in

Fitzrovia. His eldest son, Geoffrey Hugh Berners (1893-1972) left £179,556. Our man lived at Woolverstone Park, Ipswich, Suffolk.

37. Washington Merritt Grant Singer (1866-1934) – left £1,096,019. Inherited a sewing machine fortune in America and at Clydebank near Glasgow.

The son of the famous American inventor Isaac Singer (1811-75), who founded the Singer Sewing Machine Co. and left $13 million (including £200,000 in England), he was born in Yonkers, New York. He was one of twenty-four children who were the offspring of his father and his wife or (at least) four mistresses. He grew up at Oldway House, Paignton, Devon, and became a noted racehorse owner and a donor to what is now Exeter University. His brother Sir (Adam) Mortimer Singer (1863-1929) left £462,225. Our man lived at Norman Court, Hampshire, and at 42 Charles Street, Berkeley Square, Mayfair.

38. Sir Heath Harrison, 1st Bt. (1857-1934) – left £1,023,434. Shipowner in Liverpool.

The head of T. & J. Harrison, shipowners of Liverpool, he was the son of James Harrison (d. 1891, left £67,102), a shipowner of Wallasey, Cheshire and Dornden, Kent. Sir Heath was educated at Malvern College and BNC, Oxford, and was Captain of the Cricket XI at Oxford. In 1914, his firm owned fifty-five ships. In later life he lived at Le Court, Greatham, Liss, Hampshire, and was a member of the Hampshire County Council from 1901-27, and High Sheriff of Hampshire in 1916-17.

39. Alexander Henderson, 1st Baron Faringdon (1850-1934) – left £1,021,696. Stockbroker and financier in the City of London.

The son of George Henderson (d. 1889, left £2839), a printer of Ealing, he became a clerk at seventeen, was then articled to Deloitte, the City of London accountants, and in 1873 formed Greenwood & Co., stockbrokers at 28 Austin Friars, City of London, with his brother Henry (1862-1931, left £423,327). It was especially active in South American finance. Henderson helped to finance the Manchester Ship Canal, of which he was a director from 1890-97. He was also Chairman of the Great Central Railway (now Chiltern Trains), the last main line railway constructed into London, and helped in the formation of Imperial Tobacco. He later ran the Witan Investment Trust. He served as a Conservative M.P. in 1898-1906 and 1913-16, and was an important advocate of enacting Empire tariffs. Henderson was created 1st Baron Faringdon in 1916 and was made a Companion of Honour (C.H.) in 1917. He lived on an estate at Buscot Park, Faringdon, Oxfordshire and at 18 Arlington Street, Westminster. His grandson and successor Gavin Henderson, 2nd Baron Faringdon (1902-77, left £282,365) went to the other extreme, becoming a left-wing Labour peer. In 1937 the son met Stalin in Moscow, and in 1960-61 was Chairman of the Fabian Society.

40. Arthur Gilstrap Soames (1854-1934) – left £1,021,000. Brewer and maltster in Newark, Nottinghamshire.

The son of Arthur Soames (1817-94, left £161,530), a maltster in Newark, Nottinghamshire, he was educated at Eton and married Agnes (1865-1964), the daughter of Sir Robert Peel, 3rd Bt. He became head of Hole & Co., brewers and maltsters of Newark. He also served as High Sheriff of Lincolnshire in 1923-4. His grandson was Arthur Soames, Baron Soames (1920-87, left £2,218,825), the well-known Conservative political figure who served as Ambassador to

France 1966-73 and as Governor of Southern Rhodesia 1979-80. Our man lived at Sheffield Park, Uckfield, Sussex.

41. George Harold Winterbottom (1861-1934) – left £1,012,972. Book cloth manufacturer in Dukinfield near Manchester.

The brother of William Dickson Winterbottom (1858-1924, left £1,063,851, *q.v.*), book cloth manufacturer at Dukinfield near Manchester, he was educated at Brighton College in Sussex, and was Chairman of the family firm. He served as High Sheriff of Northamptonshire in 1906-7. He lived at Horton House, Horton, Northamptonshire.

42. James Buchanan, 1st Baron Woolavington (1849-1935) – left £7,150,000. Whisky distiller in the City of London.

Born in Ontario, but raised in Scotland, the son of Alexander Buchanan (d. 1863), quarry manager for Charles Tennant & Co., he became an office boy at fourteen at a salary of £10 p.a. He then started a business as a grain merchant in Glasgow with his brother William. In 1879 he moved to London as an agent for a Scottish whisky firm, and began his own whisky blending company in 1884, James Buchanan & Co., whose premises, the Black Swan Distillery, were at 26 Holborn, City of London, with another distillery in Scotland. By 1909 it was the largest whisky distiller in Britain, making "Black and White" brand whisky. His firm merged with Dewars in 1919, and became part of the Distillers group in 1925. He lived in Sussex, and was its High Sheriff in 1910. Buchanan was created a baronet in 1920, and was given a peerage, as 1st Baron Woolavington, in 1922. He was a notable philanthropist, and also twice won the Derby. He lived at Lavington Park, Petworth, Sussex and at 25 Berkeley Square, Mayfair. His £7.2 million estate was one of the largest of its time.

43. Arthur Stanley Wills (1863-1935) – left £3,499,777. Tobacco manufacturer in Bristol.

Yet another member of the enormously wealthy Wills family of Bristol, he was the youngest son of Henry Overton Wills II (1828-1911, left £5,214,356, *q.v.*), and was educated at Clifton College and at Trinity College Cambridge. In 1886 he was called to the bar at the Middle Temple, and practiced as an Equity Draughtsman and Conveyancer. He was a director of W.D. & H.O. Wills, the family tobacco firm. In later years he lived at Eshton Hall, Gargrave, Skipton, Yorkshire.

44. John Henry Scribbans (1877-1935) – left £2,602,411. Cake manufacturer in Birmingham.

The son of Thomas Scribbans (1843-1904), who founded the Scribbans Bakery in Birmingham and left £2,586, he was said to have "started out as a baker's boy," and apparently greatly expanded the firm. In the 1911 Census he was described as a "cake manufacturer." Little is known of his firm, Scribbans-Kemp, whose main bakery was in Smethwick. He lived in Sutton Coldfield, and, later, at Little Aston Hall, Little Aston, Staffordshire. He had commissioned a seaside mansion in the modern style, Villa Marine in Llandudno, Wales, when he died. To have accumulated £2.6 million by the age of fifty-eight, Scribbans was likely to have had other interests, but these could not be traced.

45. William John Manners Tollemache, 8th Earl of Dysart (1859-1935) – left £2,104,312. Landowner.

He was the son of William, Lord Huntingtower (d. 1872), a notorious spendthrift who left only £300, and succeeded his grandfather Lionel, 7th Earl of Dysart (1794-1878, *q.v.*) who left £1,700,000 in personalty. How he made this colossal fortune is unclear, as his landed holdings were not as great as those of many other aristocrats – in 1883, 27,190 acres worth £44,500 p.a. Because of his father's notoriety, his holdings were held in trust for twenty-one years. Partially sighted, and later blind, the 8th Earl did not attend a public school or university, but he did serve as Lord Lieutenant of Rutland, 1881-1906. He also had cultural interests, and was President of the London Wagner Society. He was unmarried, and his earldom ended with him, his wealth and minor titles passing to distant relatives. Dysart lived at Buckminster Hall, Grantham, Lincolnshire and at Ham House, Petersham, Surrey.

46. James Herbert Benyon (1849-1935) – left £1,586,969. Land and possible urban property owner.

The son of James Fellowes (d. 1889, left £264,882) of Kingston House, Dorsetshire, he inherited the property of his uncle Richard Benyon, M.P. (1811-97, left £722,809) of Englefield House near Reading, and changed his name to "Benyon." Significant untitled landowners, in 1883 they owned 16,007 acres worth £20,004 p.a., chiefly in Berkshire. The family may also have owned London property. Our man was educated at Eton and at Magdalene College, Cambridge, and was a barrister of the Inner Temple (called 1875). He served as Lord Lieutenant of Berkshire and as Chairman of the Berkshire County Council, and a High Sheriff of Dorset in 1892-3. He was also the first Chancellor of Reading University, from 1926. His son Sir Henry Arthur Benyon, 1st Bt. (1884-1959, left £997,588) was awarded a baronetcy in 1958, just before his death. Our man lived at Englefield House, Englefield near Reading, and at 35 Pont Street, Belgravia.

47. Peter Ralli (1868-1935) – left £1,330,658. Foreign merchant fortune in the City of London.

From the great Greek mercantile family, Ralli Brother, of Finsbury Circus, City of London. He was the son of Peter Pandia Ralli (1837-68, left £500,000, *q.v.*) and of Alexandra Ralli (1841-1903, left £1,011,942, *q.v.*), and was educated at Eton and at Trinity College, Cambridge. He apparently retired as a Partner in Ralli Brothers in 1895 at the age of twenty-seven, and bred racehorses thereafter. He lived at 11 Hyde Park Gardens, Middlesex.

48. Geoffrey Russell Rees Colman (1892-1935) – left £1,268,597. Mustard manufacturer in Norwich.

From the famous Colman mustard family of Norwich, he was the son of Russell James Colman (1861-1946, left £1,034,880), and attended Eton and Christ Church, Oxford. He became a well-known First-Class cricketer. In the First World War, he became a captain and was severely wounded. He died at forty-three from the long-term effects of his wounds eighteen years after the Armistice, and eleven years before his father, having been a director of the family firm. He lived at Framingham Chase, Norwich. His son Sir Timothy Colman, K.G. (b. 1929), a well-known yachtsman, was Lord Lieutenant of Norfolk, and was made a Knight of the Garter by the Queen in 1996.

49. Emma Louisa, Baroness Rothschild (1844-1935) – left £1,150,972. Merchant banking fortune in the City of London.

Born in Frankfurt, the daughter of Mayer Carl von Rothschild (1828-86) of the Frankfurt branch of the celebrated family, in 1867 she married Nathan Mayer Rothschild, 1st Baron Rothschild (1840-1915, left £2,500,0000, *q.v.*), the first professing Jew to receive a peerage, and lived at Tring Park, Hertfordshire, one of the Rothschild stately homes. She was the mother of Lionel Walter Rothschild, 2nd Baron Rothschild (1868-1937, left £129,096), and of Charles Nathan De Rothschild (1877-1923, left £2,250,000, *q.v.*).

50. John Charles Montagu-Douglas-Scott, 7th Duke of Buccleuch and Queensberry (1864-1935) – left £1,125,987. Landowner and mineral owner.

The son of William, 6th Duke of Buccleuch (1831-1914, left £1,159,442, *q.v.*), he was educated at Christ Church, Oxford, and served in the Royal Navy. One of the wealthiest landed aristocrats (see previous section), in 1883 his predecessor owned 468,108 acres worth £217,183 p.a. in many counties. He served as a Conservative M.P. from 1895 till 1905, and later sat in the Lords as Earl of Doncaster. He was succeeded by his son Walter, 8th Duke of Buccleuch (1894-1973). His daughter was Princess Alice, Duchess of Gloucester (1901-2004), who was married to Prince Henry, Duke of Gloucester (1900-74). Our man's chief residence was at Dalkeith House, Dalkeith.

51. Sir George Smith Clark, 1st Bt. (1861-1935) – left £1,036,684. Shipbuilder in Belfast.

The son of James Clark (d. 1910, left £324,843), of the sewing thread manufacturing family in Paisley, he was educated at Merchiston Castle School, and then apprenticed to Harland & Wolff, the famous shipbuilders in Belfast. He then founded his own firm, Workman, Clark & Co., shipbuilders of Belfast, which became the fourth largest shipbuilding firm in the UK, serving as its Managing Director. He was also the director of a linen manufacturing company in Belfast owned by his father-in-law, and a director of the Bank of Ireland. Clark served as a Conservative M.P. in 1907-10 and, after Partition, was a Member of the Senate of Northern Ireland from 1925 until his death. Clark was created a baronet in 1917. His shipbuilding firm declined drastically after the First World War, although he was still very wealthy. He lived at "Dunlambert," Fort William Park, Belfast.

52. Sir Henry Solomon Wellcome (1853-1936) – left £3,014,473. Manufacturing chemist in London.

Born in a log cabin in northern Wisconsin, the son of a poor Adventist minister, he left school at fourteen but later graduated from the Philadelphia College of Pharmacy. In 1880 he came to London, where he formed a partnership with the American Silas Burroughs as Burroughs Wellcome & Co., with a factory at Wandsworth and its headquarters at Snow Hill Buildings, Holborn Viaduct, City of London. It manufactured high quality mass-produced pharmaceutical products. Wellcome, who was a gift for advertising, coined the words "tabloid" to describe easily swallowed pills; it later became the term for light-weight newspapers. Wellcome and Burroughs fell out in the 1890s, with Wellcome eventually gaining control of the firm. In 1924 he established the famous Wellcome Foundation on Euston Road, London, which was the first body to mass produce insulin. In 1901 he contracted a disastrous marriage with Syrie (1879-1955, left £3,643), daughter of the famous Dr. Thomas Barnardo. While married to Wellcome, she had an illegitimate daughter with Somerset Maugham, the novelist, who was bisexual. Leaving him, she then had a career as a pioneering female interior decorator. Wellcome was knighted in 1932. He lived at 6

Gloucester Gate, Regent's Park, Middlesex.

53. Henry William Edward Fitzmaurice, 6th Marquess of Lansdowne (1872-1936) – left £1,562,632. Landowner.

The son of Henry, 5th Marquess of Lansdowne (1845-1927, left £1,278,501, *q.v.*), Viceroy of India 1888-94, he was educated at Eton and at Balliol College, Oxford. He served as an army officer in the Boer War and in the First World War. As the Earl of Kerry (his courtesy title), he was a Conservative M.P. from 1908-18, and was a member of the London County Council, 1907-10, and of the Wiltshire County Council from 1919. As well, he served as a Member of the Senate of the Irish Free State from 1922 till 1929. In 1883, his father owned 142,916 acres worth £62,025 p.a. in England and Ireland. Our man lived at Bowood Castle, Wiltshire and at 20 Mansfield Street, Marylebone.

54. Dame Fanny Lucy Houston (1857-1936) – left £1,528,084. Inherited from a Liverpool shipowner.

She has an entry in the *ODNB* which defines her as an "adventuress." The daughter of Thomas Radmall, a "boxmaker" in Kennington, she was a child actress in Paris. Very beautiful, in 1873 she eloped with the married brewer Henry Gretton (d. 1882), and then married, in succession, in 1883 Sir Theodore Brinckman, 3rd Bt, whom she divorced; in 1901 George, 9th Baron Byron (d. 1917); and, finally in 1924, Sir Robert Paterson Houston, 1st Bt. (1853-1926), a right-wing Conservative M.P. from 1892 till 1924, and a shipowner, the head of the Houston Line of Liverpool, reputed to be worth £7 million. He and his new wife lived as tax exiles in Jersey; he left only £6,843 in England. She inherited much of his wealth, and voluntarily agreed to pay HM Treasury £1.6 million in death duties, suggesting that he was probably worth about £4 million at his death. In 1917 she was made a Dame of the British Empire (DBE) for her charitable donations. In 1931 she donated £100,000 for the Schneider Trophy for a race in a seaplane. She was a supporter of Mussolini and in her *ODNB* entry was stated to be a "nudist." She lived at Beaufield, St. Saviour's, Jersey.

55. James Joicey, 1st Baron Joicey (1846-1936) – left £1,519,718. Colliery owner and entrepreneur in Newcastle-upon-Tyne.

The son of George Joicey (d. 1855), a mechanical engineer, he was educated at the Gainford School in Darlington, and joined the family firm of colliery owners, James Joicey & Co., headed by his uncle. He became head of the firm in 1881, and expanded it to become the largest colliery owners in the north-east, renamed the Lambton, Hetton & Joicey Collieries. He also owned three newspapers in the north-east, held other directorships, and was President of the Newcastle-upon-Tyne Chamber of Commerce. Joicey served as a Liberal M.P. from 1885 until 1906, when he was created 1st Baron Joicey; he had been made a baronet in 1893. Originally an "advanced" Liberal, after 1931 he became a right-wing Tory, and expressed admiration for Mussolini. He was succeeded by his son James, 2nd Baron Joicey (1880-1940), who left £925,936. Our man lived at Ford Castle, Northumberland.

56. Harold Leopold Cohen (1873-1936) – left £1,285,499. Department store owner in Liverpool.

The son of Louis Samuel Cohen (1845-1922, left £1,192,701, *q.v.*), the Sydney, New South Wales owner of Lewis's Ltd., the largest department store in Liverpool, and the brother of Rex David Cohen (1876-1928, left £1,218,287, *q.v.*), he became the Chairman of the family store. He is best known for his gift of £100,000, an enormous sum at the time, to Liverpool University, which he gave very shortly before his death. In later life he lived at 5 Palace Green, Kensington, at 40 Ranelagh Street, Liverpool, and in Dunstable, Hertfordshire.

57. Charles Edward Nicholas Charrington (1859-1936) – left £1,195,294. Brewer in Mile End, east London.
The son of Charles Charrington (1809-77, left £180,000), one of the heads of the famous brewery at Mile End in east London, he was educated at Christ Church, Oxford, and became a Partner in the family brewery. In 1889 he married Monica Lilly de la Pasteur of the French nobility, but divorced her for committing adultery with Sir George Bullough, 1st Bt., whom she subsequently married. In 1915, Charrington married Elaine Taylor. He lived at Broadoaks, West Byfleet, Surrey.

58. Annie Lucy Watson (1862-1936) – left £1,005,694. Inherited a carrying company fortune in the City of London.
She was the daughter of Thomas Watson (1838-1910, left £652,445), the partner with William Richard Sutton (1836-1900, left £2,137,159, *q.v.*) in Sutton & Co., the largest door-to-door carrying company in Britain, whose premises were at 22 Golden Lane, Barbican, City of London. According to a brief obituary, she was a director of Sutton & Co. She lived at 14 Avenue Road, Regent's Park, Middlesex.

59. Walter Runciman, 1st Baron Runciman (1847-1937) – left £2,406,854. Shipowner in Newcastle-upon-Tyne.
The son of Walter Runciman, who was in the Coastguard service in Northumberland, he ran away to sea at 12 and later obtained a Master Mariner's Certificate. From 1885 he was a shipowner at South Shields and later at Newcastle-upon-Tyne, heading the Moor Line, later known as Walter Runciman & Co. It also had a London office. It owned twenty-three steamers by 1924. He served as a Liberal M.P. from 1914-18, but was later a Conservative. Runciman was President of the Chamber of Shipping of the UK 1910-11. He was created a baronet in 1906 and 1st Baron Runciman in 1933. He was a lifelong Methodist lay preacher. He lived at Ferwood House, Clayton, Road, Newcastle-upon-Tyne. His son Walter Runciman, 1st Viscount Runciman of Doxford (1870-1949, left £1,038,335) was a prominent Liberal Cabinet minister. Our man's grandson Sir Steven Runciman (1903-2000, left £7,214,845) was a famous historian of the Byzantine Empire.

60. Frederick Scrutton (1859-1937) – left £1,856,658. Stevedore company and insurance broker in the City of London.
The son of a shipowner in the City of London, Thomas Urquhart Scrutton (1828-86, left £5,154), he began as a clerk in his father's firm and became its head. Scrutton & Co. of 16 Fenchurch Avenue, City of London, had two separate arms, one a ship's dischargers, stevedores, and cargo superintendant component, the other a ship and insurance brokers and West India merchants of the same address. He was the brother of Sir Thomas Edward Scrutton (1856-1934, left £105,180), a well-known Judge on the King's Bench and later of the Court of Appeal. Our man lived at

Woopits, Nutfield, Surrey.

61. Charles Willis Harrison (1855-1937) – left £1,644,237. A shipowner in the City of London.

Very little could be learned about the background of this London-based shipowner. He was born in Brixton, Surrey, the son of John Harrison (1814-66) of Kennington, of whom little could be learned. In 1888 our man formed T. & J. Harrison with his brother John. The firm, at 66 Mark Lane in the City of London, was engaged as shipowners, coal exporters, and coaling agents. Our man was apparently very wealthy by the early 1920s, since in that year he formed a family trust which became the subject of an extended lawsuit. He lived in Hampstead and later at 49 Cadogan Place, Belgravia.

62. Mary Woodgate Wharrie (1847-1937) – left £1,509,332. Inherited from her father, a prominent insurance broker in London.

The daughter of Sir Henry Harben (1828-1917, left £383,335), who was a director and later Chairman of the Prudential Mutual Assurance Co., of Holborn Bars, Middlesex, adjacent to the City of London, the famous insurance firm. He was a cousin of Joseph Chamberlain, the political leader, and is regarded as one of the major figures in originating the modern insurance industry. In 1899 she married Thomas Wharrie (1828-1917, left £276,931), a civil engineer. She lived at Wharnham Lodge, Wharnham, Sussex and at 10 Eaton Avenue, Hampstead, Middlesex.

63. William Edward Harrison (1875-1937) – left £1,403,070. Colliery owner in Staffordshire.

The son of William Bealey Harrison (d. 1912, left £200,821), a colliery owner of Walsall and Aldershawe, Staffordshire, he was educated at Eton and Oriel College, Oxford, he was (like his father) a well-known cricketer. Harrison was a member of the Staffordshire County Council and its Chairman from 1927-37, and was High Sheriff of Staffordshire in 1927-28. He lived at Wychnor Park, Burton-on-Trent, Staffordshire.

64. Charles Herbert Palmer (1860-1937) – left £1,335,840. Biscuit manufacturer at Reading.

The son of Samuel Palmer (1820-1903, left £1,334,830, *q.v.*), one of the founders of Huntley & Palmer, the famous biscuit manufacturing firm at Reading, he was a director of the firm, with other members of his family. Although his family were prominent Quakers, he was an Anglican. His brother was Ernest Palmer, 1st Baron Palmer (1858-1948, left £1,014,558). His son was Sir Charles Eric Palmer (1883-1948), who was educated at Harrow and Oxford, and was Chairman of Huntley & Palmer, left £550,571. He was knighted in 1946. Our man lived at Bozedown House, Whitchurch, Oxfordshire.

65. George Edward Henderson (1844-1937) – left £1,327,413. Utilities owner and timber merchant in Newcastle-upon-Tyne.

The son of the Newcastle shipowner Thomas Hood Henderson (d. 1897, left £131,534), little is known of his career. He was described in the 1871 Census as a "timber merchant" and in later sources as a utilities owner in Northumberland. He may also have been a jute merchant, as his executor Thomas Hood Henderson Walker was described as a "jute merchant" in our man's entry in the probate calendars. He received little publicity in his lifetime, and lacks entries in standard reference works. He was known as a philanthropist of what is now Newcastle University and of the city's local art galleries, before dying at the age of ninety-three. He lived at 16 Framlington Place, Newcastle-upon-Tyne.

66. Sir Albert Levy (1864-1937) – left £1,134,867. Tobacco manufacturer in the City of London.

Born in Germany, the son of Moses David Levy (1819-94), he was the founder and Managing Director of the Ardath Tobacco Company, of 62 Leadenhall Street, City of London, which manufactured the popular "State Express 555" brand of cigarettes. It was later taken over by Imperial Tobacco. He was a famous philanthropist, who gave away £400,000 to hospitals and dental clinics, and was knighted in 1929. Levy lived at Westbrook House, Elstead, Surrey and Devonshire House, Piccadilly, Middlesex.

67. Sir Alexander Grant, 1st Bt. (1864-1937) – left £1,039,976. Biscuit manufacturer in Edinburgh and at Harlesden, Middlesex.

The son of Peter Grant (1838-82), a guard on the Highland Railway, he was born in Forres, Morayshire, and educated at the Forres Academy. He became an assistant to Robert McVitie, biscuit manufacturer in Edinburgh, eventually rising to General Manager. He eventually became Chairman and Managing Director of McVitie & Price Ltd., as the firm was known. He opened an enormous factory to produce its biscuits in Harlesden, Middlesex, and another branch in Manchester. He became a noted philanthropist, giving away an estimated £750,000, especially to the National Library of Scotland. Grant became friendly with J. Ramsay Macdonald, the first Labour Prime Minister, who was also from Forres, and, although not a Labour supporter, Grant paid Macdonald's living expenses as Prime Minister in 1924. He was made a baronet in the same year, giving rise to much criticism. He lived at Moray House, Hampstead and at 15 Hermitage Drive, Edinburgh. His son and successor Sir Robert McVitie Grant, 2nd Bt. (1894-1947) left £1,033,000.

68. Sir (William) Gervase Beckett, 1st Bt. (1866-1937) – left £1,034,163. Banker in Leeds and in the City of London and newspaper proprietor in Leeds.

The son of William Beckett, M.P. (1826-90, left £460,426), a leading banker in Leeds who died when he fell under a train, he was educated at Eton, and became a Partner in Beckett & Co., bankers of Leeds. The bank was taken over by the Westminster Bank, and he became a director of the bank. Beckett was also the proprietor of the *Yorkshire Post*. He served as a Conservative M.P. from 1906-22 and 1923-29, and was created a baronet in 1921. His elder brother Ernest (1856-1917, left £33,578) inherited the title of 2nd Baron Grimthorpe. Another brother, Rupert Evelyn Beckett (1870-1955), Chairman of the Westminster Bank, left £1,202,345. Our man's daughter Beatrice (1905-57), was the first wife of Sir Anthony Eden, later Prime Minister, from whom she was divorced. Our man lived at Kirkdale Manor, Newton, Yorkshire and at 37 Green Street, Park Lane, Mayfair.

69. Hubert Lavie Butler (1858-1937) – left £1,023,908. Probably an insurance fortune made in Liverpool, but unclear.

The son of Charles Butler, J.P., D.L. (1821-1910, left £1,148,356, *q.v.*), whose wealth was probably made as an insurance broker in Liverpool, although this is unclear, he was educated at Eton and Trinity College, Cambridge, was a captain in the Army, and served as High Sheriff of Hertfordshire in 1918-19. A noted cricketer, as a military officer he was said to have introduced cricket to the West Indies. The source of his wealth, apart from inheritance from his father, is unclear, and no business occupation or profession could be identified for him. He lived at Warren Wood, Hatfield, Hertfordshire and at 3 Connaught Place, Hyde Park, Middlesex.

70. Sir George Jefford Fowler (1858-1937) – left £1,021,696. Solicitor in Bloomsbury and insurance company director in the City of London.
The son of Charles Walter Fowler, who was described on his son's baptismal record as a "colonial merchant" and on his son's marriage license in 1886 as a "solicitor," probably of Exeter; he may have been the man of this name who died at Teignmouth, Devon in 1873 leaving £5,000. Little is known of our man's background; he was educated "privately" and admitted a solicitor in 1879. He rose to become the Senior Partner of Fowler, Legg & Co., solicitors of 13 Bedford Row, W.C.1, and was also a director of the Eagle Star Insurance Co. of 1 Threadneedle Street, City of London, as well as Chairman of the London & Egyptian Properties Company Ltd. He was knighted in 1920 for serving as the Chief Magistrate for Kingston-upon-Hull for thirty years. He lived at The South House, Hyde Park Street, Middlesex.

71. Edward Montagu Cavendish Stanley, Lord Stanley (1894-1938) – left £2,209,864. Landed fortune.
The eldest son of Edward, 17th Earl of Derby (1865-1948, left £3,217,839), he was educated at Eton and Magdalen College, Oxford. He was the heir to one of the greatest landed fortunes (see previous section). He was a captain in the Grenadier Guards, and was wounded in the First World War. He served as a Conservative M.P. from 1917 until his death, and was Deputy Chairman of the Conservative Party in 1927-29. Lord Stanley, as he was known, served in a number of junior ministerial posts from 1924 until 1938, and was briefly Dominions Secretary, with a seat in the Cabinet, in 1938, when he died of cancer at the age of forty-four. He served in the Cabinet at the same time as his brother Oliver Stanley (1896-1950, left £149,113), one of the few times that two brothers sat in the same Cabinet in recent times. His son, Edward, 18th Earl of Derby (1918-94), left £48,630,312, showing that the high rates of taxation in most of his lifetime had not impoverished the old aristocracy. Lord Stanley lived at 43 Belgrave Square, Belgravia, and at Holwood Keston, Kent.

72. Gilbert Greenall, 1st Baron Daresbury (1867-1938) – left £2,205,999. Brewer in Warrington, Cheshire and landowner.
The son of Sir Gilbert Greenall, 1st Bt. (1809-94, left £1,025,742, *q.v.*), a millionaire brewer at Warrington, Cheshire, he was educated at Eton and became head of the firm. He served as High Sheriff of Cheshire in 1907-8, and was a Director of the Royal Agricultural Society from 1906-30 and its President in 1910 and 1925. Greenall was created 1st Baron Daresbury in 1927. He lived at Walton Hall, Warrington, and at Arlington House, St. James's, Middlesex.

73. John Smith (1868-1938) – left £1,439,000. Tobacco manufacturer in Glasgow.
A partner in the Glasgow cigarette and tobacco manufacturers F. & J. Smith, which was founded

by his father John Smith (1831-78, left £16,372) and John's brother Finlay Smith (d. 1911, left £552,414). The firm became a component of Imperial Tobacco in 1901. Little could be found about our man's career, and his name did not make tracing him any easier. He lived at Giffnock, Renfrewshire.

74. William Henry Anthony Wharton (1859-1938) – left £1,169,685, Land and mineral owner in North Yorkshire.

Wharton apparently owed his wealth to the mining of iron stone on his land in North Yorkshire. In 1883 his father John Thomas Wharton (1809-1900, left £160,228) owned 10,647 acres worth £7,659 p.a. in North Yorkshire. He also owned collieries. Our man was educated at Eton and Magdalene College, Cambridge, and was said to also own utilities in the north-east, but these could not be traced. He lived at Skelton Castle, Skelton-in-Cleveland, Yorkshire and at 98 Eaton Square, Belgravia.

75.Frank Reddihaugh (1871-1938) – left £1,176,814. Woollen manufacturer and merchant in Bradford.

The son of John Reddihaugh (1841-1924, left £1,653,305, q.v.), a woollen merchant and manufacturer in Bradford, he was educated at Bradford Grammar School and became Chairman of the family firm, John Reddihaugh Ltd. He was a Methodist, but little is known of his career. He lived at Kirkfield, Baildon, Yorkshire.

76. William Molyneux Molyneux-Cohan (1879-1938) – left £1,055,000. Shipowner in Liverpool.

Although the *Daily Mail Year Book* for 1939 stated that he left £1,055,000, his entry in the probate calendar records him as having left £471,921. The higher figure may well be that of a later valuation figure written in by hand in the probate calendars, but not included in the online edition of the calendars available on ancestry.co.uk. This should be kept in mind. Born in Liverpool, he was the son of Edward Asher Cohan (1849-1916, left £689,665), a wealthy shipowner and shipbroker in Liverpool, and took over the family business. He is not listed in any standard biographical source, and little could be found about him. His mother was Martha Alice Molyneux (1852-1933). Despite his father's Jewish sounding name, he was baptised and buried as an Anglican. He lived at 10 Aigburth Drive, Liverpool. Another address given for him was 26 Chapel Street, Liverpool, almost certainly his business address.

77. Sir Philip Albert Gustave Sassoon, 3rd Bt. (1888-1939) – left £1,946,893. Foreign merchant and merchant banking fortune in the City of London and Paris.

The son of Sir Edward Albert Sassoon, 3rd Bt., M.P. (1856-1912, left £758,854) of the famous Sephardic family of foreign merchants, David Sassoon & Co., of 12 Leadenhall Street, City of London. His mother was Aline (d.1909, left £240,973), the daughter of Baron Gustave de Rothschild, of the French branch of the renowned merchant bank. He was educated at Eton and at Christ Church, Oxford, and became Chairman of David Sassoon & Co. He served as a Conservative M.P. from 1912, when he was twenty-four, until his death, and held ministerial office as Under-Secretary for Air, 1924-29 and 1931-37, and Cabinet office as First Commissioner of Works, 1937-1940. Despite his studied effeminacy – he was a well-known homosexual – he became

Private Secretary to Sir Douglas Haig, the British Commander-in-Chief, from December 1915 until November 1918, and then was made the chief spokesman in the Commons for the Royal Air Force, which he did a great deal to strengthen. He was also known for his artistic decoration of Port Lympne near Hythe, Kent, one of his country houses. He died at fifty of influenza. His sister Sybil (1894-1989, left £12,451,097) was married to George, 5th Marquess of Cholmondeley (1883-1968, left £270,236). The poet Siegfried Sassoon (1886-1967, left £97,128) was his cousin. Sir Philip's other residences included 45 Park Lane, Mayfair, and Trent Park, Middlesex.

78. Sir Ernest William Tate, 3rd Bt. (1867-1939) – left £1,467,736. Sugar refiner in Liverpool and London.
The son of Sir William Henry Tate, 2nd Bt. (1842-1921, left £1,072,569, *q.v.*) and the grandson of Sir Henry Tate, 1st Bt. (1819-99, left £1,264,215), sugar cube manufacturers of what is now Tate & Lyle, of Liverpool and Silvertown, east London. He does not appear to have had much of a role in business life apart from his connection with the family firm. The first baronet established what is now the Tate Gallery in London. Our man was a Major in the Lancashire Volunteers and High Sheriff of Denbighshire in 1919-20. He lived at Galltfaenan, Trefnant, Denbighshire. His son Sir Henry Tate, 4th Bt. (1902-94) left £1,664,414.

79. Thomas Ruding Davey (1871-1939) – left £1,291,325. Tobacco manufacturer in Bristol.
The son of Thomas Davey (1833-1902, left £341,736), a tobacco manufacturer of the firm of Franklyn Davey of Bristol. It became part of Imperial Tobacco in 1901. Our man was a director of Imperial Tobacco, and of other local firms in Bristol, but little is known of his career. He lived at Wraxall Court, Wraxall, Somerset.

80. David William Traill Cargill (1872-1939) – left £1,285,000. Petroleum company director in Glasgow.
The son of David Sime Cargill (1827-1904, left £929,191, an East India merchant who founded the Burmah Oil Co., and the brother of Sir John Traill Cargill, 1st Bt. (1867-1954, left £296,766), he was a Director of Burmah Oil, which had its headquarters in Glasgow, and of its subsidiary company Anglo-Persian Oil. He was also a member of Lloyd's of London insurance, representing the insurance company Milne & Co. of Glasgow. Burmah Oil supplied petroleum to Royal Navy vessels. After his death, his trustees endowed the David Cargill Chair of Geriatric Medicine at Glasgow University. He lived at Stanmore, Lanarkshire and at 3 Regent's Park Terrace, Middlesex.

81. Sir Howell Jones Williams (1859-1939) – left £1,292,143. Building contractor in London.
The son of Richard Williams, a Welsh-born dairyman in Faringdon, London, he became a building contractor in south-east London, with offices at 13-18 Bermondsey Road SE and at 1-10 Magdalen Street, London Bridge SE. He served as a Progressive member of the London County Council from 1894 till 1925, and was Deputy Chairman of the LCC in 1921-22. He was knighted in 1921. Williams was also High Sheriff of Merionethshire in 1917-18. He lived at 263 Camden Road, Islington.

82. Sir Bernard Eyre Greenwell, 2nd Bt. (1874-1939) – left £1,250,974. Stockbroker and company director in the City of London and cattle breeder.

The son of Sir Walpole Greenwell, 1st Bt. (1847-1919, left £1,400,000, *q.v.*), a leading stockbroker in the City of London and a significant cattle breeder, he was educated at Harrow and at Trinity College, Cambridge. He served as an officer in the Boer War, and was Senior Partner in his family stockbroking firm, W. Greenwell & Co. Greenwell was also Chairman of the London Electric Supply Co., the largest supplier of electricity in the UK He lived at Marden Park, Godstone, Surrey and at 97 Eaton Square in Belgravia.

83. Cuthbert Eden Heath (1859-1939) – left £1,031,061. Insurance broker in the City of London.

One of the most important innovators in the history of British insurance, Cuthbert E. Heath was the son of (Rear-Admiral) Sir Leopold Heath (1817-1907, left £50,066). Partially deaf, he was educated at Brighton College and joined the insurance company Henry Head & Co. as a junior clerk. In 1880 he joined a Lloyd's of London syndicate, and produced fundamental changes in how it operated. It had been exclusively concerned with marine insurance; he introduced it as a venue for fire insurance, jewellery insurance, trade credit insurance, and many other innovations which became accepted. He also made Lloyd's introduce the individual annual compulsory audits of its members. As well, he established his own insurance company, C.E. Heath & Co., of 7 Gracechurch Street, City of London. He was said to have had an income of £60,000 p.a. Heath served as High Sheriff of Surrey in 1925-26. He lived at Anstie Grange, The Holmwood, Dorking, Surrey.

1940-1949

The 1940s were the decade of the Second World War and then of the "Austerity" period headed by the Attlee Labour government of 1945-1951. Rates of taxation, and especially of death duties on large estates, reached what would previously have been considered as unimaginably high levels, in order to pay for the enormous costs of the War and then for both the Welfare State initiated by Labour and for the Cold War against the Soviet Union then emerging. Most of the gross valuation figures set out here were reduced to fractions of their initial worth after the payment of death duties. Nevertheless, eighty-five millionaire estates were left for probate in this decade, by both landowners and businessmen who inherited great wealth and by self-made men. Their considerable variety is evident here. It might be noted that four of these millionaires were killed on active duty in the Second World War, compared with only two during the First World War, despite its much higher casualty rate. This could simply be through bad luck, or it might suggest that their fathers made over a larger share of their wealth to their sons in their own lifetime than before, to avoid death duties, unsuccessfully, as it turned out.

1. Marmaduke Furness, 1st Viscount Furness (1883-1940) – left £3,681,955. Shipbuilder and ironmaster in Stockton-on-Tees and Co. Durham.

The son of Christopher Furness, 1st Baron Furness (1852-1912, left £1,844,305, *q.v.*), Chairman of Furness Withy Shipbuilders in West Hartlepool, Co. Durham, he became Chairman of the Furness Shipbuilding Co. in Stockton-on-Tees, Co. Durham, and of the South Durham Steel & Iron Co., of the Weardale Steel, Coal & Coke Co., and of other industrial companies in the north-east. Married three times, his second wife was Thelma Converse (1904-70), known as Thelma

Viscountess Furness, the daughter of Harry Morgan Sr., an American diplomat; she was the mistress of Edward, Prince of Wales before Wallis Simpson and of Aly Khan. Our man's son William, 2nd Viscount Furness (1929-95, left £481,427), was a well-known theatrical producer. Our man lived at Borrough Court, Melton Mowbray, Leicestershire, at Nidd Hall, Ripley, Yorkshire, and at 60 St. James's Street, Middlesex.

2. Isaac [Jack] Barnato Joel (1862-1940) – left £3,634,496. Diamond merchant and financier in South Africa and in the City of London.

The brother of Solomon Barnato Joel (1865-1931, left £1,000,000, *q.v.*) and the nephew of Barney Barnato, the famous South African "Randlord," he was born in Spitalfields, the son of Joel Joel (*sic*, d. 1893, left £1,852), a cigar manufacturer, and, like his brother, was a diamond magnate in South Africa and then Chairman of Barnato Brothers, diamond merchants and financiers of 10-11 Austin Friars, City of London. Like his brother, he was a famous racehorse owner in England who won the 1921 Derby and many other famous races. He lived at Childwick Bury near St. Albans, Hertfordshire and at 34 Grosvenor Square, Mayfair.

3. Herbrand Arthur Russell, 11th Duke of Bedford (1858-1940) – left £4,651,371. Land and London property owner.

The owner of the ground rents of much of the Bloomsbury and other areas of central London, and a great landowner in Bedfordshire and many other counties (see previous section), he was the son of Francis, 9th Duke of Bedford (1819-91, left £230,970), and succeeded his elder brother George, 10th Duke of Bedford (1852-93, left £335,603). He was educated at home and at Balliol College, Oxford, and was an officer in the Grenadier Guards, serving in the Egyptian campaign in 1882, and later was Aide-de-Camp to the Viceroy of India, 1884-88. He declined all Westminster government posts, but was Lord Lieutenant of Middlesex, 1898-1926; Chairman of the Bedfordshire County Council, 1895-1928; and was the first Mayor of Holborn, 1900-01. The Duke was a noted naturalist, the President of the Zoological Society of London, and one of the founders of the Whipsnade Zoo in 1931. He was also the President of the Crematorium Society of Great Britain, 1921-40. Of the estate left for probate, £3,239,130 was settled land rather than personalty. His wife Dame Mary (*née* Tribe, 1865-1937, left £365,584), known as the "Flying Duchess," was a pioneering woman aviatrix, who flew with her co-pilot to India and South Africa in 1928 and 1930, the longest flights ever made at that time. She died in an air crash off the east coast of England. The Duke's primary residence was Woburn Abbey, Bedfordshire. His son Hastings, 12th Duke of Bedford (1888-1953), with whom he quarrelled and did not meet for twenty years, left £5,792,253.

4. Sir George Alexander Cooper, 1st Bt. (1856-1940) – left £3,001,021. Inherited a fortune made in Chicago real estate and American railways.

The son of Alexander Cooper (1817-87, left £12,093), a solicitor in Elgin, Scotland, he also became a solicitor and an officer in the Seaforth Highlanders. In 1887 he married Mary (1858-1948), the daughter of George S. Smith of Evanston, Illinois. In 1899 he inherited $22 million – about £4.4 million – from his wife's cousin, George "Chicago" Smith (1808-99), a Scotsman who had gone to American and made a fortune in Chicago real estate and in investments in railways and other businesses in the American Midwest. "Chicago" Smith then returned to England, where he lived for thirty years in two rooms he rented at the Reform Club on Pall Mall; almost no one there knew of his vast wealth – he left £59,435 in England but at least $44 million- at least £8.8 million- in America, and was one of the richest men in the UK. Sir George Cooper was an Alderman of the Hampshire County Council, and High Sheriff of Hampshire in 1908-9, and was also a J.P. and D.L. of Elginshire. He was given a baronetcy in 1905. He lived at Hursley Park, Winchester, Hampshire, at 26 Grosvenor Square, Mayfair, and at The College, Elgin.

5. Sir William Julien Courtauld, 1ˢᵗ Bt. (1870-1940) – left £1,839,353. Silk manufacturer at Bocking, Essex and rayon manufacturer at Coventry.

From the famous family of silk and later rayon manufacturers, he was the son of Sydney Courtauld (1840-99, left £87,885), silk manufacturer, and was educated at Rugby and at Trinity College, Cambridge. In 1913 he married his cousin Constance (d. 1954, left £268,081), daughter of George Courtauld, M.P. (1830-1920, left £2,146,695, *q.v.*). Our man served as the Deputy-Chairman and Chairman of the Essex Quarter Sessions, 1921-36, and was High Sheriff of Essex in 1920-21. He received a baronetcy in 1939, shortly before his death. The family were originally Unitarians. His brother Samuel Courtauld (1876-1947, left £1,030,126) founded the Courtauld Gallery in London. Our man lived at Penny Pot, Halstead, Essex.

6. Henry George Alan Percy, 9ᵗʰ Duke of Northumberland (1912-40) – left £1,802,089. Landowner.

From an enormously wealthy landed family – in 1883 his forebear owned 186,347 acres worth £176,048 p.a., chiefly in Northumberland (see previous section) – he was the son of Alan, 8ᵗʰ Duke of Northumberland (1880-1930, left £2,510,000, *q.v.*), and was educated at Eton. He served as a junior minister in 1935-6. A lieutenant in the Army, in 1940 he was killed in Belgium during the retreat to Dunkirk. He was succeeded by his brother Hugh, 10ᵗʰ Duke of Northumberland (1914-88), who left £17,291,957. Our man lived at Alnwick Castle, Northumberland, and at 5 Westminster Gardens, Middlesex.

7. Conrad Penrose Fry (1865-1940) – left £1,253,741. Chocolate and cocoa manufacturer in Bristol.

From the Quaker chocolate and cocoa family in Bristol, he was the son of Francis James Fry (1835-1918, left £500,000), an Alderman of Bristol and head of J.S. Fry & Sons, the family firm. Our man was a director of J.S. Fry & Sons for many years, but little is known of his career. His brother Sir Theodore Fry, 1ˢᵗ Bt. (1836-1912, left £40,899) was a Liberal M.P. from 1880 till 1895 and was given a baronetcy in 1894. Our man lived at 11 Upper Belgrave Road, Clifton, Bristol and at Belcombe Lodge, Weston-Super-Mare.

8. Archibald Inglis Crawford (1869-1940) – left £1,016,000. Biscuit manufacturer in Liverpool.

The son of William Crawford (1817-89, left £8170), a biscuit manufacturer in Leith, Scotland, of a family firm established in 1813, he joined the firm. In 1897, with his brother James Shields Russell Crawford (1863-1927), who later settled in Sydney, Australia, he established a biscuit factory in Liverpool, which expanded enormously and eventually employed 3000 workers. The firm merged with McVities in 1960, when it was headed by our man's son Sir Douglas Inglis Crawford (1904-

81, left £287,414), who was given a knighthood in 1964. Our man lived at Fernlea, Mossley Hill Road North, Liverpool.

9. Walter Melville Wills (1861-1941) – left £4,432,981. Tobacco manufacturer in Bristol.

The fifth son of Henry Overton Wills (1828-1911, left £5,214,356, *q.v.*), of W.D. & H.O. Wills, tobacco manufacturers of Bristol, one of the richest families in Britain, he joined the family firm in 1887 and became its Joint Managing Director with two of his brothers. He continued in that role after the firm became part of Imperial Tobacco in 1901, retiring in 1912. He gave away over £500,000, especially to the Bristol Homeopathy Hospital. His wife Louisa (d. 1936) left £221,096; their son Walter Douglas Melville Wills (1887-1973) left £404,955. Our man lived at Bracken Hill, Leigh Woods, Long Aston, Somerset.

10. Sir John Priestman, 1st Bt. (1855-1941) – left £1,504,774. Shipbuilder and shipowner in Sunderland.

The son of Robert Priestman (1824-67), a baker in Bishops Auckland whose estate is unlisted in the probate records, he was apprenticed at fourteen to a shipbuilder, became Chief Draughtsman to another shipbuilder, and then founded John Priestman & Co., shipbuilders of Sunderland, of which he was the sole proprietor. He was also an extensive shipowner. He was made a Freeman of Sunderland, and was given a knighthood in 1923 and a baronetcy in 1934. He gave away an estimated £500,000, especially to build Anglican churches. He lived at Cliffside, Roker, Sunderland.

11. Sir Walter Herbert Cockerline (1856-1941) – left £1,496,706. Shipowner in Hull.

The son of John Cockerline (d. 1905, left £203), a butcher in Hull, he became a clerk to a shipowner and then an extensive shipowner in Hull, although little is known of his career. He served as High Sheriff of Hull and was knighted in 1922. In 1928, he was committed for trial for a long list of alleged taxation wrongdoings, including income tax evasion from 1918 until 1925, failing to pay Excess Profits Tax, and presenting false accounts to the Inland Revenue from 1910-15. The surviving record states that "the Bill [of Indictments] was ignored by the Grand Jury," and was not proceeded with. If he had been convicted of the charges, his knighthood would have been revoked. Cockerline lived at Hartford House, Filey Road, Scarborough, Yorkshire and in Hull.

12. Gilliat Edward Hatfeild (*sic*- not Hatfield) (1864-1941) – left £1,237,222. Snuff and tobacco manufacturer in the City of London.

The son of the millionaire snuff and tobacco manufacturer Gilliat Hatfeild (1834-1906, left £1,342,197, *q.v.*), he was educated at Harrow and at Oxford University (Non-collegiate). He then succeeded his father as the head of James Taddy & Co., the largest snuff manufacturer in the UK, of 45 Minories, City of London; it also manufactured other tobacco products. After the First World War, he withdrew from business life and, unmarried, lived as a recluse at Morden Hall, Surrey in south London, which is now a National Trust property and park.

13. Dudley Jack Barnato Joel (1904-41) – left £1,071,318. Diamond merchant in the City of London.

The son of Solomon Barnato Joel (1865-1931, left £1,000,000, *q.v.*), of the South African/ London diamond merchant family of Joel and Barnato, he was educated at Repton School and at King's College, Cambridge, and joined the family diamond firm of Barnato Brothers of 10/11 Austin Friars, City of London. Like other members of his family, he was a noted racehorse owner. Joel served as a Conservative M.P. from 1931 until his death. In 1939, although he was thirty-five, he joined the Royal Navy Volunteer Reserve (RNVR) as a lieutenant. In 1941 he was killed when the merchant ship on which he was travelling was bombed by a German aircraft off the coast of Cornwall. He lived at 74 Brook Street, Mayfair and at Moulton Paddocks, Newmarket, Suffolk.

14. William James Tatem, 1ˢᵗ Baron Glanely (1868-1942) – left £2,067,617. Shipowner in Cardiff.

The son of Thomas Tatem (d. 1868), left £300, a "master mariner" of Appledore, Devon who died when he was an infant, he worked at a shipping office in Cardiff and then became a leading shipowner there, as Chairman of W.J. Tatem Ltd., and of the Tatem Steam Navigation Co. He was also a director of many other companies, including the Great Western Railway. He was High Sheriff of Glamorganshire in 1911-12 and was the President of the University College of South Wales (later Cardiff University) in 1920-25 and 1934-42. Tatem was made a baronet in 1916 and was created 1ˢᵗ Baron Glanely in 1918. In the 1930s, he was a strong supporter of the Spanish Republic during the Spanish Civil War, and was a noted racehorse owner. He died in an air raid on Weston-super-Mare. He lived at The Court, St. Fagan's, Cardiff and at 12 Hill Street, Mayfair.

15. Sir Jeremiah Colman, 1st Bt. (1859-1943) – left £1,832,069. Mustard manufacturer in Norwich.

The Chairman, from 1896, of J. & J. Colman, the famous mustard manufacturers in Norwich, he was the son of Jeremiah Colman (1807-85, left £551,893, *q.v.*) of the firm, and was educated at King's College School and at St. John's College, Cambridge. He was also the Chairman of the Union Assurance Co. and of other concerns. In 1909, J. & J. Colman employed 2300 workers. The family were Baptists. He served as High Sheriff of Surrey in 1893-4, and was made a baronet in 1907. He was a noted orchardist. His son, Sir Jeremiah Colman, 2ⁿᵈ Bt. (1886-1961) left £2,130,521. Our man lived at Gatton Park, Reigate, Surrey.

16. Sir Charles Hyde, 1ˢᵗ Bt. (1876-1942) – left £1,666,746. Newspaper proprietor in Birmingham.

Educated at Clifton College and at Exeter College, Oxford, he was the son of George Edwin Hyde (d. 1914, left £2356), a surgeon, who was married to Mary, Daughter of John Frederick Feeney (d. 1869, left £45,000), founder of the *Birmingham Post*. Ownership of the newspaper, which had the largest circulation of any in the Midlands, then passed to Mary's brother John Feeney (d. 1905), who left £928,223, and then to our man, who became its proprietor in 1905. The newspaper had its offices at 38 New Street, Birmingham. Hyde served as High Sheriff of Warwickshire in 1933-34, and was made a baronet in 1922. He was a notable donor to Birmingham University. Hyde lived at The Moat, Berkswell, Warwickshire.

17. (Hon.) Dame Margaret Helen Greville (1863-1942) – left £1,623,192. Inherited a brewing fortune in Edinburgh.

The illegitimate daughter of William McEwen, M.P. (1827-1913, left £1,526,460, *q.v.*), the millionaire brewer in Edinburgh, and his cook and mistress Helen Anderson, whom he married in

1885 when she was twenty-one, she inherited almost all of his wealth. In 1891 she married (Hon.) Ronald Fulke Greville (1864-1908, left £12,962), a Conservative M.P. from 1896 till 1906, the son of William, 2nd Baron Greville. He died of cancer in 1908. For the rest of her life she was a wealthy Society hostess, generally at her stately home, Polesden Lacey near Dorking, Surrey. She was widely regarded as an engaging but venomous *nouveau riche* obnoxio – Rudyard Kipling described her as "a slug." She was also known for her jewellery collection, which included Marie Antoinette's diamond necklace, which she left in her will to Queen Elizabeth, later the Queen Mother. She also had a residence at 16 Charles Street, Berkeley Square, but lived in later life at the Dorchester Hotel, where she died.

18. Joseph Cowen (1857-1942) – left £1,989,624. Firebrick manufacturer and newspaper proprietor in Newcastle-upon-Tyne.

The son of Joseph Cowen (1831-1900, left £501,928), a Liberal M.P. 1873-86, a firebrick manufacturer and proprietor of the *Newcastle Chronicle* newspaper, he followed his father in these fields, and was also an extensive colliery owner. His grandfather was Sir Joseph Cowen (1800-73, left £92,800), a firebrick manufacturer and colliery owner. Little is known of our man's career. Unmarried, he lived at Stella Hall, Blaydon, Co. Durham with his unmarried sister Jane Cowen (1856-1948), who left £1,991,262.

19. Sir Kenneth Skelton Anderson, 1st Bt. (1866-1942) – left £1,467,000. Shipowner in the City of London and elsewhere.

The son of James Anderson (d. 1897, left £133,856), a shipowner who lived in Hampstead, he was educated at Harrow and at New College, Oxford. He became Chairman of the Orient Steam Navigation Co., and a director of Anderson, Green & Co., shipowners, and of the Equitable Assurance Co. His business offices were at 5 Fenchurch Street, City of London. Anderson served as President of the Chamber of Shipping of the UK in 1915. He was knighted in 1909, and given a baronetcy in 1919. Anderson lived at Stamford House, Wimbledon Common and at The Yair, Galashields, Selkirkshire.

20. John Ashton Fielden (1859-1942) – left £1,406,942. Cotton manufacturing fortune in Todmorden near Manchester.

The only son of Samuel Fielden (1816-89) – left £1,170,113, *q.v.*) of the wealthy cotton manufacturing family of Todmorden, near Manchester, he was educated at Harrow and at Jesus College, Cambridge. He disliked Todmorden and never visited it after 1910. In 1902 he purchased Holmewood Hall near Peterborough and 6400 acres of land, and lived there, unmarried, as a virtual recluse, although he did serve as High Sheriff of Cambridge and Huntingdon in 1908-9, and did hunt and shoot. In 1940 he gave £50,000 to HM Treasury to buy Spitfire aeroplanes and ambulances.

21. Stanley Bourne (1876-1942) – left £1,025,105. Cotton doubler and manufacturer in Nottingham.

The son of Samuel Bourne (1835-1912, left £52,017), a "cotton doubler" in Nottingham, he joined his father's trade, but later became Deputy Chairman of Courtaulds, the great silk and rayon manufacturer whose works were centred in Bocking, Essex and in Coventry. Our man appears to have lived in Nottingham throughout his life, although he apparently became wealthy as a senior executive of Courtaulds. He served as High Sheriff of Nottinghamshire in 1927-28. Bourne lived at Epperstone, Nottinghamshire.

22. Sir Henry Edouard Strakosch (1871-1943) – left £3,008,643. Financier in the City of London.

Born in Vienna to Jewish parents, the son of Edward Strakosch, a sugar manufacturer, he came to the City of London in 1891 and worked for the Anglo-Austrian Bank of South Africa. From 1902 until his death, he was managing Director and Chairman of the Union Corporation, which controlled many of South Africa's gold mines and investment. He did this from London, visiting South Africa only twice after 1901. Unconnected with the colourful "Randlords," he played a major behind-the-scenes role as a financial advisor to the South African and British governments, and was an advisor to Montagu Norman, Governor of the Bank of England. Strakosch represented South Africa at the League of Nations in the 1920s, and was a member of the Council of India from 1930-37. Remarkably, he was also Chairman of *The Economist* magazine from 1919 till 1943. He operated from the Union Corporation's headquarters at 95 Gresham Street, City of London. He is probably most famous, however, for paying the private debts of Winston Churchill in 1938 and 1940, allowing him to keep his country house at Chartwell. He left Churchill £20,000 in his will. Strakosch was knighted in 1921, and received higher orders of knighthood in 1924 and 1927. He lived at 45 Chester Square, Middlesex and at Heatherside, Walton-on-the-Hill, Surrey.

23. Ivor Miles Windsor-Clive, 15th Baron Windsor and 2nd Earl of Plymouth (1889-1943) – left £1,824,360. Landowner.

The son of Robert Windsor-Clive, 14th Baron Windsor and 1st Earl of Plymouth (1857-1923, left £870,102), a landowner who in 1883 owned 37,454 acres worth £63,778 p.a. in Glamorganshire, Shropshire, and other counties, who served as First Commissioner of Works 1902-05 and was Chairman of the National Trust, he was educated at Eton and at Trinity College, Cambridge. He served as a Conservative M.P. in 1922-23 (as Lord Windsor), and then succeeded to the title. He held junior ministerial posts in 1925-29 and 1931-39, and was Parliamentary Under-Secretary for Foreign Affairs, 1936-39. He was also Lord Lieutenant of Glamorganshire. His entry in *Who's Who* stated that he owned 30,500 acres. His son Other (*sic*), 3rd Earl of Plymouth (1923-2018) succeeded to the title. Our man lived at St. Fagan's Caste, Cardiff and at Howell Grange, Redditch.

24. Michael Desmond Hamilton Wills (1915-43) – left £1,579,947. Tobacco fortune in Bristol.

Another member of the very wealthy Wills tobacco family, he was the son of Frederick Noel Hamilton Wills (1887-1927), of W.D. & H.O. Wills, who left £5,053,361 (*q.v.*). He was educated at Clifton College and at Magdalen College, Oxford. He was a Captain in the Coldstream Guards, and awarded an M.C, in 1941. In 1943 he was killed on active service in Tunisia. Wills lived at Miserden Park, Cirencester, Gloucestershire.

25. William Charles de Meuron Wentworth-Fitzwilliam, 7th Earl Fitzwilliam (1872-1943) – left £1,326,969. Land and mineral owner.

The son of William, Viscount Milton (1839-77), he succeeded his grandfather William, 6th Earl

Fitzwilliam (1815-1902, left £2,590,271, *q.v.*). The Fitzwilliams were among the very richest landowners (see previous chapter). In 1883 Lord Fitzwilliam owned 115,743 acres worth £138,801 p.a., in Yorkshire, Co. Wicklow, and other counties, which included extensive coal deposits. He was educated at Eton and Trinity College, Cambridge, and served as a Liberal Unionist M.P. from 1895 till 1902, when he succeeded to the peerage. He was also Mayor of Sheffield in 1910-11. He served as ADC to the Marquess of Lansdowne in India, 1892-93, was a Lieutenant-Colonel serving in the Boer War and in the First World War, and was mentioned in despatches in both wars. He lived at Wentworth Woodhouse, Rotherham, Yorkshire.

26. Charles Joshua Hirst Wheatley (1888-1943) – left £1,026,307. Woollen manufacturing fortune made in Mirfield, Yorkshire.

The son of Joshua Hirst Wheatley (1854-1925, left £1,379,491, *q.v.*), a woollen manufacturer in Mirfield near Dewsbury, Yorkshire, he was educated at Eton and Magdalen College, Oxford. He does not appear to have had any direct connection with business life, living at Berkswell Hall, Solihull, Warwickshire, which he inherited from his father. Our man was a J.P. and D.L. of Warwickshire. His widow Christobel (1898-1987) left £125,731.

27. Philip Ernest Hill (1872-1944) – left £3,008,328. Property developer and company financier in London.

Born in Torquay, the son of Philip Hill (1839-1922, left £444), a cab proprietor, and educated at the Taunton Independent College, he was employed at sixteen as an estate agent. In 1912 he moved to London, and established an estate agency at 42 Albermarle Street, Mayfair. In 1914, he bought out the Covent Garden estate from the Beecham Pills Company, which had acquired it from the Duke of Bedford. Over the next thirty years he acquired a remarkable range of major companies, from pharmaceuticals and patent medicine firms like Timothy White, to insurance companies such as Eagle Star Insurance to what became the merchant bank Hill Samuel. He also established the Beecham Research Laboratories to patent new drugs. He also owned the Odeon Cinema Chain and the Royal Opera House, Covent Garden. Hill was married four times, twice to the divorced wives of hereditary aristocrats. His main business offices were at 15-17 King Street, St. James's. Hill lived at Windlesham Moor, Windlesham, Surrey and at 68 Brook Street, Mayfair.

28. Dr. Henry Dreyfus (1882-1944) – left £2,499,492. Celanese manufacturer in Derby and in London.

Born in Switzerland to Jewish parents, Henry Dreyfus received a Ph.D. from Basel University. With his bother Camille (d. 1956 in New York, left £433,616 in England) and another silk manufacturer, he established a firm to manufacture cellulose acetate by a new process, which was used to make films and, in particular, aircraft paint. In 1916 he went to Britain with his brother and established the British Cellulose and Chemical Manufacturing Co. Ltd., with works at Derby, to manufacture the chemical in wartime. In 1920 he began to make rayon by the cellulose process, which he termed "celanese," which like "rayon," became part of the language. He was Chairman and Managing Director of the firm, British Celanese, whose products were used, in particular, in making women's underwear. Its corporate headquarters was at Celanese House, Hanover Square, Mayfair. Dreyfus was engaged in a long and unproductive series of lawsuits against Courtauld for patent infringement. There are mixed views of his ability as an entrepreneur, but he died as one of the richest men in England. He lived in a permanent suite at the Hyde Park Hotel in Knightsbridge.

29. Ernest John Manners (1877-1944) – left £2,160,492. Brewer in Burton-on-Trent.
The son of William Posnett Manners (1847-1915, left £533,778), Managing Director and Deputy Chairman of Worthington & Co., brewers of Burton-on-Trent, he joined the firm and was a director of Worthington & Co., and of Bass, Ratcliff & Gretton Ltd., also of Burton-on-Trent. He served as High Sheriff of Derbyshire in 1943-44. Manners lived at The Old Hall, Nettleseale, Derbyshire.

30. William Edward Guinness, 1ˢᵗ Baron Moyne (1880-1944) – left £2,000,000. Brewer in Dublin.
The son of Sir Edward Guinness, 1ˢᵗ Earl of Iveagh (1847-1927, left £12,486,147, *q.v.*), head of Guinness Breweries in Dublin and one of the very richest men in the UK, he was educated at Eton. He served as an officer in the Boer War, in which he was wounded, and as a Lieutenant-Colonel in the First World War (DSO, despatches). He served as a Conservative M.P. from 1907 till 1931, and was created 1ˢᵗ Baron Moyne in 1932. Guinness, who was a distinguished amateur naturalist, held junior ministerial posts in the early 1920s, and then served in the Cabinet as Minister for Agriculture and Fisheries, 1925-29, and as Colonial Secretary and Leader of the House of Lords in 1941-42. He was also a director of Guinness Breweries. From 1942 until his death he was Deputy Minister of State at Cairo, and Minister Resident at Cairo in 1944. Regarded by Zionists as excessively pro-Arab and even anti-semitic, he was assassinated in Cairo in 1944 by Zionist extremists of the "Stern Gang," a highly counter-productive event which was condemned by all, including Winston Churchill, a close friend. He lived at 10 Grosvenor Place, Belgravia.

31. Lawrence Hignett (1866-1944) – left £1,883,560. Tobacco manufacturer in Liverpool.
The son of John Hignett (1831-98, left £424,658), tobacco manufacturer of Hignett Brothers & Co., of Liverpool, he joined the family firm, which became part of Imperial Tobacco in 1930. Little is known about his business career. In the 1901 and 1911 Censuses, he lived in West Derby, Lancashire. In 1891 he married Lottie (1871-1963), the daughter of W.L. Hundall; she left £361,541. In later life our man lived at 25 Berkeley Square, Mayfair, and at Hook End Farm, Checkendon, Oxfordshire.

32. John Francis Granville Scrope Egerton, 4ᵗʰ Earl of Ellesemere (1872-1944) – left £1,683,895. Landowner.
A descendant of the fabulously wealthy 1ˢᵗ Duke of Sutherland (*q.v.*, and see the previous section), he was the son of Francis, 3ʳᵈ Earl of Ellesmere (1847-1914, left £250,000), and was educated at Eton. He served as a Captain in the Boer War. In his entry in *Who's Who,* he stated that he "owns about 13,300 acres." This was also the acreage owned by his forebear in 1883, who owned 13,222 acres worth £71,290 p.a., mainly in Lancashire, and which included extensive collieries. He was succeeded by his son John, 5ᵗʰ Earl of Ellesmere (1915-2000), who also succeeded as the 6ᵗʰ Duke of Sutherland. Our man lived at Bridgewater House, 14 Cleveland Row, St. James's, Middlesex; at Stretchworth Park, Newmarket, Cambridgeshire; and at Mertoun, St. Boswell's, Scotland.

33. Alfred Mildmay (1871-1944) – left £1,551,460. Merchant banker in the City of London.

The son of Henry Bingham Mildmay (1828-1905, left £569,315), Senior Partner in Baring Brothers, the great merchant bank of 33 Bishopsgate, City of London; our man's mother was a Baring. He was educated at Eton and at Trinity College, Cambridge, and was a director of Baring Brothers from 1897 till 1940, and its Senior Partner. His brother Francis Bingham Mildmay, 1st Baron Mildmay of Flete (1861-1947, left £546,031) was a Liberal, later Liberal Unionist M.P. from 1886 till 1922, and was given a peerage in 1922. This man's son, Anthony, 2nd Baron Mildmay of Flete (1909-50, left £1,173,629) has an entry in the *ODNB* as a "jockey". Our man lived at 28 Portman Square, Marylebone and at Mothercombe House, Holbeton, Devon.

34. William Dudgeon Graham Menzies (1851-1944) – left £1,447,000. Distillery fortune in Edinburgh.

The son of Graham Menzies (d. 1880, left £432,824), head of the Caledonian Distillery in Edinburgh, he was educated at Rugby. The details of his business career are scarce, but he was a director of the family distillery, and was a J.P. for Perthshire. His brother Robert Stewart Menzies (1856-89, left £101,167), was a Liberal M.P. 1885-89. Our man lived at 6 Hereford Gardens, Park Lane, Mayfair and at Hallyburton House near Coupar, Angus.

35. Peter Yates (1854-1944) – left £1,248,132. Proprietor of a chain of wine bars and pubs centred in Manchester.

The son of Simon Yates (1821-60, left £450), an innkeeper in Preston, Lancashire, in 1884 he and his brother, also Simon Yates, founded the chain of Yates's Wine Lodges (as they were then known), the first opened in Oldham. Our man had visited Spain to learn about wine. His chain, which currently has seventy wine bars, was one of the first to serve wine as its main commodity, rather than beer or spirits, and was always considered a cut above over pub chains. The headquarters of his firm was at 54 Carnarvon Street, Manchester. The motto adopted by his chain was "Moderation is true temperance." He lived at Ribblesdale House, Preston, Lancashire.

36. Stanley Samuel Gilbert Cohen (1880-1944) – left £1,206,679. Retail merchant in Liverpool.

The son of Louis Samuel Cohen (1846-1922, left £1,192,701, *q.v.*), head of Lewis's Ltd., the largest department store in Liverpool, he was educated at Cheltenham College, and was a director of Lewis's Ltd. He also had business interests in London, of which he was made a Freeman of the City of London in 1926, giving his business address as 9 Basinghall Street in the City. Two of his brothers also left millionaire estates. He served as a Lieutenant-Colonel during the First World War and saw action in France. For most of his life he lived at Toxteth Park in Liverpool. In later life he lived at Chester House, Belgrave Square, Belgravia and at Old House, Coolham, Sussex.

37. James Hawley Gilbert Feilden (*sic* – not Fielden, 1876-1944) – left £1,170,361. Urban property owner in Lancashire.

His family wealth was apparently derived from owning the ground rents of Blackburn, Darwen, and other areas in Lancashire, which the family acquired in the eighteenth century. In 1883 his father owned 2311 acres worth £7,314 p.a. in Lancashire. Several of his relatives were engaged as cotton manufacturers in Blackburn, but there is no evidence that his wealth derived from cotton. His grandfather, Joseph Feilden (1792-1870, left £100,000) was M.P. for Blackburn 1865-69. His father (Lt. Gen.) James Randle Joseph Feilden (1824-95, left £158,291) was a Conservative M.P. from 1880 until his death. Our man was educated at Eton and was a Major in the Army. He lived at Witton Park, Blackburn and at 12 Porchester Court, Sloane Street, Middlesex.

38. Arthur Thomas Loyd (1862-1944) – left £1,157,484. Inherited a banking fortune in the City in London.
The son of (Revd.) Lewis Haig Loyd (d. 1905, left £40,948), a relative of Samuel Jones Loyd, 1st Baron Overstone (1796-1883, left £2,118,804, plus £3 million worth of land, *q.v.*), probably the richest banker in the City of London, our man inherited the property of his daughter and only child, Harriet Loyd-Lindsay, Baroness Wantage (1837-1920, left £768,587), his father's second cousin. Our man was educated at Eton and at Hertford College, Oxford, and served as a Conservative M.P. from 1921-23. He was High Sheriff of Berkshire in 1927-28, Lord Lieutenant of Berkshire in 1935-36, and a member of the Berkshire County Council from 1938-44. In early life he was in the Egyptian Public Service, and was Chairman of the Governors of Abingdon School. He lived at Lockinge House, Wantage, Berkshire, which he inherited from Lady Wantage.

39. Charles Henry Petty-Fitzmaurice, 7th Marquess of Lansdowne (1917-44) – left £1,023,793. Landowner.
The son of Henry, 6th Marquess of Lansdowne (1872-1936, left £1,404,132, *q.v.*), he was educated at Eton and at Balliol College, Oxford. In 1883 his forebear owned 142,916 acres worth £62,025 p.a. (See previous section.) Our man served in the Second World War as a Captain in the Royal Wiltshire Yeomanry. He was held as a Prisoner of War, and died of wounds in the Italian campaign at the age of twenty-seven. Unmarried, the Marquessate passed to his cousin George, 8th Marquess of Lansdowne (1912-99), and his Scottish title to his sister Katherine (1912-95), who became the 12th Baroness Nairne. Our man lived at Bowood Castle, Wiltshire.

40. Sir Julien Cahn, 1st Bt. (1882-1944) – left £1,014,996. Furniture hire-purchase retailer centred in Nottingham.
The son of Albert Cahn (1856-1921, left £260,398), a German-born immigrant who established the Nottingham Furnishing Company, he became head of the firm and, based in Nottingham, developed two nation-wide hire purchase furniture chains, Jays Ltd. and Campbells Ltd. The two chains had 300 shops throughout the UK when Cahn sold them to Great Universal Stores in 1943, shortly before his death. Cahn was a noted cricketer and organiser of private and successful cricketing clubs, and a significant philanthropist. He was given a knighthood in 1929 and a baronetcy in 1934. It is said that he was given his knighthood for donating £30,000 to the Conservative party in order to get Maundy Gregory to agree to remain abroad – Gregory was the "bagman" who, when Lloyd George was the head of a Coalition government, collected payments from wealthy men in exchange for receiving peerages and knighthoods. Cahn was also a Master of the Foxhounds for three separate hunts from 1928 till 1939, one of the few Jewish MFHs. Cahn lived at Stanford Hall, Nottinghamshire.

41. Alice Sedwick *née* Mankiewicz, later Lady Wernher, and then Baroness Ludlow (1862-1945) – left £2,828,969. Widow of a multi-millionaire "Randlord" and of a landowner who was descended from a West India merchant and landowner.

She was the daughter of Jacob James Mankiewicz (1830-79, left £70,000), a German-born merchant at 6 Mincing Lane, City of London, who lived at 15A Pembridge Square, Bayswater, and his English-born wife, Ada Susan *née* Pigott. She married first, in 1888, Sir Julius Wernher, 1st Bt. (1850-1912), the great German-born "Randlord" in South Africa and financier in London, who left £10,044,301 (*q.v.*). She married secondly, in 1919, Henry Ludlow Lopes, 2nd Baron Ludlow (1865-1922, left £100,745), a descendant of Sir Manasseh Lopes, 1st Bt. (1755-1831, left £160,000), West India merchant and landowner. She inherited much of Wernher's property and was noted for her charitable bequests. Her two sons succeeded to the baronetcy: Sir Derrick Julius Wernher, 2nd Bt. (1889-1948, left £37,023) and (Major-General) Sir Harold Wernher, 3rd Bt. (1893-1973, left £2,774,267), an important military leader of the D-Day invasion. Lady Ludlow lived at Bath House, Piccadilly and at Luton Hoo, Bedfordshire.

42. Charles Heman (*sic*) Hubbard (1886-1945) – left £1,888,813. Chain store (Woolworths) executive, centred in London.

Hubbard was born in Carthage, New York, the son of Armand Hubbard (1845-1917), a local farmer. Our man joined the American multiple retail chain of F.W. Woolworth, which had been founded in 1878 in Utica, New York. In 1909 he was sent to England to establish the chain in the UK, which he did successfully. In 1915 Woolworths had forty-four stores in the UK. During the interwar period it became a household name throughout the country. There are very few details of Hubbard's life in the UK. He retired to Lebouchere Beach, New Providence, Bahamas, where he died, leaving n early £1.9 million in the UK.

43. John Powys, 4th Baron Lilford (1863-1945) – left £1,333,797. Landowner.

The son of John Thomas Powys, 3rd Baron Lilford (1833-96, left £53,278), who has an entry in the *ODNB* as an "ornothologist," and was a leading British naturalist, he was educated at Harrow and at BNC, Oxford. In 1883 his father owned 15,559 acres worth £26,398 p.a. in Northamptonshire and Lancashire. Our man's entry in *Who's Who* stated that he "owns about 15,600 acres." One of his residences was at Bank Hall, Preston, Lancashire, suggesting that much of his wealth derived from urban property or collieries there. His main residence was at Lilford Hall, Oundle, Northamptonshire. Apart from being a D.L. of Northamptonshire, he appears to have had little involvement in public life, but was a noted breeder of shorthorn cattle. He was succeeded by a relative, Stephen Powys, 6th Baron Lilford (1869-1949), who left £1,101,037.

44. Sir Connop Thirwall Robert Guthrie, 1st Bt. (1881-1945) – left £1,186,916. Financier in London.

One of the most mysterious of wealth holders. No reference book lists his parentage or the specifics of his education, and all say that he was born in 1882. The facts are as follows: his name at birth was Connop Robert Schmitz. He was born in the July-September quarter of 1881 (not 1882) in Carmarthenshire, probably at Langhorne, on the south coast of that county. His precise date of birth was probably 6 July 1881. His father was Connop Leonhard Schmitz (1841-1906, left £44), who was born in Islington, and was described in the 1891 Census as an "accountant" in Twickenham, but in a previous listing as a "wine merchant" in Glasgow (1868). His mother, Mary *née* Guthrie (1854-1934) left £336. The only clue as to his education was given in *Kelly's Handbook* for 1923, in which his entry states that he was educated "at Gillingham". He served in the First World War as a Captain in the Grenadier Guards, and was wounded. He served as Special Representative of the Ministry of Shipping in the USA, 1916-19. Because of this, he was described in some sources as a shipowner, but no evidence could be found that he was ever engaged in shipping. In 1913, he was married at St. George's Hanover Square to Mary (1893-1963, left £36,635), the daughter of Sir Malcolm McEacharn. He stated on his marriage licence that his name was Connop Thirwall Robert Schmitz Guthrie, and that he was a "merchant" of 12 Hanover Street (in Mayfair).

How he made his money is also unclear, but most of it probably came as Chairman from 1928-39 of the North Central Wagon Co. of Rotherham, which he transformed into a major hire-purchase firm for buying motor vehicles, at a time when the ownership of automobiles was increasing dramatically. He was also Chairman of the City Central Trust Ltd., and a director of Prudential Assurance and was very important in the development of colour film and in funding the British cinema, including the films of Alexander Korda. Despite being born in Wales and adopting a Scottish surname, his entire business career appears to have been in London, where he lived at 33 Charles Street, Berkeley Square, Mayfair. He was made a knight in 1918 and a baronet in 1936, although the reasons for these awards are unclear, as are many other aspects of his career. He probably dropped "Schmitz" as his surname because of anti-German prejudice, but again this is unclear. He also had a residence at Brent Eleigh Hall, Lavenham, Suffolk. His son Sir Giles Guthrie, 2nd Bt. (1916-79- he died in Jersey) was Chairman of BOAC in 1964-68 and has an entry in the *ODNB* as an "airline administrator".

45. Douglas Crossman (1870-1945) – left £1,139,941. Brewer in London and Burton-on-Trent.

The son of Alexander Crossman (1842-1916, left £512,721), brewer of the firm of Mann, Crossman & Paulin of Burton-on-Trent, Staffordshire and of The Albion Brewery, Whitechapel Road, Mile End, Stepney, he was educated at Charterhouse (Captain of the Cricket XI) and at Oriel College, Oxford. He began as a brewer in Burton-on-Trent, and then headed the Albion Brewery in Mile End. He was a J.P. for Essex and Huntingdonshire, and lived at Cokenach, Royston, Hertfordshire.

46. Jeremiah Inns (1878-1945) – left £1,080,983. Hay and straw and gravel merchant in Stevenage, Hertfordshire.

He was the son of John Inns (1853-1922, left £457,632), who was illiterate but developed the largest hay and straw merchant's business in the UK, taking hay and straw from the farmers of Hertfordshire to London to be sold. His firm had 300 employees when he died. Our man further developed the firm with his brother, and was also a gravel and ballast merchant in Stevenage and a company director. He lived at Springfield, High Street, Stevenage, Hertfordshire.

47. Roderick James Fry (1864-1945) – left £1,061,450. Chocolate and sweets manufacturer in Bristol.

From the famous Quaker chocolate and sweets making family, J.S. Fry & Sons, which, in 1847, invented the chocolate bar, he was the son of Francis James Fry (1835-1918, left £500,000), the head of the firm. Their firm was the largest employer of labour in Bristol, where their factory was located. Our man's grandfather Joseph Storrs Fry (1826-1913, *q.v.*) left £1,333,526. The family probably ceased being members of the Society of Friends by the First World War- our man's son Cecil Roderick Fry (1890-1952, left £190,920) was educated at Harrow and Cambridge, which Quakers would still have been reluctant to attend. Our man lived at The Priory, Abbots Leigh, Somerset.

48. William Johnston Yapp (1861-1946) – left £4,501,438. Tobacco manufacturer in London.
The son of George Yapp (1794-1874, left £10,000), a bootmaker of Chelsea in London, he was described on his marriage license of 1889 as a "bootmaker" of 200 Sloane Street, Chelsea. In 1896, he then acquired the Carreras tobacco company and developed it into the second largest tobacco firm in England. He did this in conjunction with Bernhard Baron (1850-1929, *q.v.*) and John Crowle (1841-1906, left £448,696). It had a cigarette factory at City Road; they opened another one at Mornington Crescent in Camden which was the largest tobacco factory in the world; it was air conditioned and had an onsite medical centre. Like Baron, he became a multi-millionaire and, like him, is virtually unknown. In his will he mainly left legacies to many charities, including £15,000 to the Greenwich Observatory to build a new telescope. Yapp lived at Beech Hurst, Hayward's Heath, Sussex and at Boughton Colemers, Matfield, Tunbridge Wells, Kent.

49. Sir Archibald Moir Park Lyle, 2nd Bt. (1884-1946) – left £1,678,000. Shipowner in Glasgow.
The son of Sir Alexander Park Lyle, 1st Bt. (1849-1933), Chairman of the Lyle Shipping Co. of Glasgow, who left £525,602, he was educated at Fettes College and at Trinity College, Oxford, and succeeded his father as head of the firm. He was also related to the sugar manufacturers of Tate & Lyle. He was a noted athlete, a First Class cricketer and track runner, and served as a Lieutenant-Colonel in the First World War, receiving an M.C. His shipping company consisted mainly of tramp steamers. His son was killed in the Second World War, and he was succeeded by his grandson Sir Gavin Lyle, 3rd Bt. (b. 1941). Our man lived at Glendelvine, Murthly, Perthshire.

50. Frank Parkinson (1887-1946) – left £1,487,286. Electrical engineering goods manufacturer in Leeds, and later Chelmsford and London.
The son of Joseph Parkinson (1862-1902, left £4081), a stonemason and later quarry owner, he was born at Guiseley, Leeds, and attended Guiseley Wesleyan Day School, the Guiseley Mechanics' Institute, and Leeds University: he later became a major benefactor of this university. Apprenticed at fourteen and a works manager at nineteen, he began F. Parkinson & Co., an electrical power engineering firm with his brother Albert. In 1927 he merged with Crompton & Co. of Chelmsford to become Crompton Parkinson, probably the best-known British firm of manufacturing electrical engineers. It had factories at Guiseley and at Chelmsford, and had a major London presence at Bush House, Aldwych and at Electra House, Victoria Embankment. His firm took over many smaller firms. Parkinson lived at a new house he built at Charters, Sunninghill, Berkshire, which was air conditioned and was the first residence in the UK to have an electric dishwasher.

51. (Hon.) Mrs. Esmé Smyth (1863-1946) – left £1,401,089. Landowner.
Born Esmé Edwards, she was the daughter of Sir John Henry Greville Upton Smyth, 1st Bt. (1836-1901, left £412,071) of Ashton Court, Somerset. In 1883 he owned 14,974 acres worth £30,386 p.a. in Somerset and Gloucestershire. Her mother was Lady Emily Frances Way, later

Edwards (1835-1914, left £974,071). Lady Emily was married to her first husband when she gave birth to Esmé, who was given his surname, Edwards, despite Smyth being her father. In 1891 Esmé married her cousin, (Hon.) Gilbert Neville Smyth (1864-1940, left £3184), son of the 5th Baron Boston. They had one daughter, Esmé Frances Sylvia Smyth, later Cavendish (1901-59, left £21,470). Our lady inherited the extraordinarily imposing Somerset mansion Ashton Court, now owned by the Bristol Corporation. The millionaire estate she left was most unusual at the time and was far more than the land owned by her father would suggest. She must have had other sources of inheritance, for instance from the very large sum left by her mother, or income from other investments which could not be traced.

52. Thomas Evelyn Scott-Ellis, 8th Baron Howard de Walden (1880-1946) – left £1,248,490. Urban property and landowner.

The son of Frederick, 7th Baron Howard de Walden (1830-99, left £74,233) and Blanche *née* Holden (later Baroness Ludlow, d. 1911, left £10,252), he was educated at Eton and Sandhurst, and was an army officer, serving in the Boer War and then in the First World War, retiring as a Colonel. He inherited his family's great urban properties in London, inherited by his grandmother from the Duke of Portland, as well as rural properties in Wales and Scotland. In 1914 he sold sixty acres he owned near Regent's Park for £500,000 – if his family had retained this property, they would now be worth billions – and, in 1924, sold forty acres north of Oxford Circus for an undisclosed sum. He still retained London properties in Marylebone and St. John's Wood. A very colourful and accomplished figure, he was a noted sportsman and racehorse owner, an historian who funded *The Complete Peerage*, an author of operas, and a naturalist. He was also involved in a lengthy, high profile libel case against John Lewis, the department store owner. he has an entry in the *ODNB*, unusual for a recent landed aristocrat who played no political role. He married Margharita, daughter of Charles Van Raalte (d. 1908, left £380,332); their daughter Priscilla Scott-Ellis (1916-83) has an entry in the *ODNB* as a "diarist". Lord Howard de Walden lived at Chirk Castle, Denbighshire and, in later years, at 1A and 2 Cadogan Lane, Belgravia.

53. Ernest Leopold Payton (1877-1946) – left £1,103,736. Automobile manufacturer and company director in Birmingham.

The Chairman (from 1941) and previously Deputy Chairman and Financial Director of Austin Motors Ltd., and the Chairman and director of other companies in the Midlands, he was the son of Francis William Payton (1847-1907), a "jeweller employing 17 men" in Birmingham, according to the 1881 Census. Our man was educated at the King Edward Grammar School in Birmingham, and in the 1911 Census was described as the "Managing Director, leather goods manufacturers; director, chemical companies and others." He became Financial Director of Austin Motors in 1922, and then Deputy Chairman, and succeeded Lord Austin (Sir Herbert Austin, 1st Baron Austin, 1866-1941, left £509,712) as Chairman in 1941. Payton lived at Cranford, Cotton Lawe, Moseley, Birmingham.

54. Frank Wallis (1866-1946) – left £1,096,403. Mohair and alpaca manufacturer in Bradford.

The son of Alfred Wallis (1820-1913, left £448,243) of Bradford, regarded as the most successful manufacturer of mohair and alpaca in England, he was educated in part in Germany, and took over his father's firm, which operated under several names, including Benn & Co., of Oak Mills,

Clayton, Bradford. He continued in business until the Second World War, when he closed and sold his factory. A lifelong bachelor, he lived with his unmarried sister Lillie Constance Wallis (1872-1959), who left £347,141.

55. Gaspard Oliver Farrer (1860-1946) – left £1,072,371. Merchant banker in the City of London.

The son of Sir William James Farrer (1822-1911, left £366,476), a solicitor of Lincoln's Inn Square and of 18 Upper Brook Street, Mayfair, and the nephew of Thomas Henry Farrer, 1st Baron Farrer (1819-99), Permanent Undersecretary of the Board of Trade, who has an entry in the *ODNB*, he was educated at Eton and at Balliol College, Oxford, and became a merchant banker in the City of London as a Partner of L.S. Lefevre & Co., and then from 1902 until 1925 as a Partner with Baring Brothers, the great merchant bank at 8 Bishopsgate. He lived at 7 St. James's Square, Westminster and at The salutation, Sandwich, Kent.

56. Russell James Colman (1861-1946) – left £1,034,880. Mustard manufacturer in Norwich.

The son of Jeremiah James Colman (1830-98), head of the famous mustard manufacturing firm of J. & J. Colman of Norwich, and Liberal M.P., who left £687,024, he was educated privately and in Germany and Switzerland. The family were Baptists and prominent supporters of Non-conformist causes. Apart from mustard the firm also produced, strangely, starch; in 1938 it merged with another starch making competitor to become Reckitt & Colman, still a household name in the UK. He served as High Sheriff of Norfolk in 1904-5 and was an Alderman of the Norfolk County Council. Colman lived at Crown Point, Norwich. He was the father of Geoffrey Russell Rees Colman (1892-1935, left £1,268,597, *q.v.*), who died of the effects of wounds he received during the First World War, eleven years before his father.

57. Charles Harry St. John Hornby (1867-1946) – left £1,005,725. Partner in a multiple retail chain (W.H. Smith), centred in London, but with outlets throughout the UK.

The son of (Revd.) Charles Edward Hornby (d. 1918, left £69,822), an Anglican clergyman, he was educated at Harrow and at New College, Oxford, and was also a barrister (called 1892). At Oxford he became friendly with William, 3rd Viscount Hambleden, the heir to the multiple bookstall and bookstore chain, W.H. Smith, who asked Hornby to join the firm, which he did in 1893, becoming a Partner the following year. Hornby gradually became the most important executive in the firm, and oversaw its transformation from chiefly owning news-stalls at railway stations to owning a nationwide chain of High Street newspaper, book, and stationery shops. This change was largely the result of Britain's railways demanding ever increasing rentals from W.H. Smith. Hornby was also the founder of Ashenden Press, an important private press, and was High Sheriff of the County of London in 1906-7. He was married to Cicely, the daughter of Charles Barclay, a director of the National Provincial Bank. In later years, Hornby lived at Chantmarle, Cattistock, Dorchester, Devon.

58. John Gretton, 1st Baron Gretton (1867-1947) – left £2,301,973. Brewer at Burton-on-Trent.

The son of John Gretton (1833-99, *q.v.*) of Bladon House, Burton-on-Trent, who was a director of Bass, Ratcliff & Gretton, the largest brewery in the UK, and who left £2,883,640, he was educated at Harrow. In 1900 he married (Hon.) Maud (d. 1934), daughter of the 4th Baron Verney.

He began working in the family brewery at the age of twenty, becoming a director in 1893, and then serving as Chairman of Bass, Ratcliff & Gretton from 1909 until 1945. During that time, average dividends per share in the firm were usually in the range of 20-30 per cent, but it also failed to respond successfully to increasing competition, although it did merge with a rival firm, Worthington. Gretton is best known as a long serving Conservative M.P. from 1895 until 1906 and then from 1907 until 1943. He received a peerage, as 1st Baron Gretton, in 1944. He was well known as an archetypal right-wing "diehard" M.P. of the old school, and worked with Winston Churchill in 1931-35 to oppose the Government of India Bill. He was also Chairman of the National Union of Conservative and Unionist Associations from 1920-29. He was also a Colonel in the Volunteers, and was often known as "Colonel Gretton." He lived at Stapleford Park, Melton Mowbray, Leicestershire and at 35 Belgrave Square, Belgravia.

59. Godfrey Walter Phillimore, 2nd Baron Phillimore (1879-1947) – left £2,113,155. Inherited urban land in London and a legal fortune.

The son of Walter Phillimore, 1st Baron Phillimore (1845-1929, left £652,392), Justice of the Queen's Bench 1897-1913 and Lord Justice of Appeal 1913-16, and President of the English Church Union, he was educated at Christ Church, Oxford. He was his father's third son, and outlived his two elder brothers. During the First World War, he served as a Captain in the Highland Light Infantry and was wounded and captured by the Germans, spending time as a POW; he later wrote a book about his experiences. He was awarded an MC. No reference work states his occupation, and it appears that he lived by his inheritance. It is interesting to note that of his substantial probate valuation, £982,610 was in settled land. As no one of his name is listed in Bateman, this is probably a reference to the Phillimore estate in Kensington, which the family owned. He lived at Coppice Hall, Henley-on-Thames, Oxfordshire, and died in South Africa. His son Robert, 3rd Baron Phillimore (1939-90) left £768,002.

60. Sir Hugo von Reitzenstein Cunliffe-Owen, 1st Bt. (1870-1947) – left £1,353,745. Tobacco manufacturer in Bristol and company director in London.

The son of Sir Francis Cunliffe-Owen (1828-94, left £4833), Director of the Victoria & Albert Museum in Kensington, he was educated at Brighton College and was apprenticed to Sir John Wolfe Barry as a civil engineer. His sister had, in 1886, married Henry Herbert Wills of W.D. & H.O. Wills, the great tobacco manufacturing firm of Bristol, later the main component of Imperial Tobacco, and a member of a family which specialised in producing millionaires. As a result, he became an executive of the firm. The Wills family formed British-American Tobacco, in order to end a destructive trade war with American cigarette manufacturers. Our man was appointed its Secretary and a director, and later served as its Chairman from 1923-45. From 1927, he took over several American tobacco firms. He was also a director of the Midland Bank and other companies, although an aircraft manufacturing firm he established, Cunliffe-Owen Aircraft, foundered after the Second World War. In 1920 he had been created a baronet, for providing intelligence information about China, which he knew well. He was also a successful racehorse owner, and left half of his estate to his common law wife. He lived at 3 Whitehall Court on the Thames, and at Sunninghill Park, Berkshire.

61. Hermann Marx (1881-1947) – left £1,262,493. Merchant banker and stockbroker in the

City of London.

Little is known of the background of Hermann Marx, who was born in Elberfield, Germany. In the 1901 Census he was described as a "bank clerk," a boarder at 6 Lanark Villas, Maida Vale. In the 1911 Census he was described as a "stockbroker" of 8 Thornton Avenue, Streatham. At that time, he was working for Nelke, Phillips & Co., stockbrokers of 4 Moorgate Street and of Warnford Court in the City of London. From 1921 until 1944, when he retired, he was a Partner in Cull & Co., a newly formed merchant bank at 11 Throgmorton Street in the City of London, which specialised in corporate finance advice. It was sold to Morgan Grenfell in 1944. His German-born wife, Lisbeth (1885-1954) left £113,998, and his son Robert Ian Marx (d. 1975), a stockbroker, left £280,903. In later life Marx lived at Fairmile Lea, Cobham, Surrey; he had a singularly inappropriate surname for a City millionaire.

62. Henry Stanford Mountain (1865-1947) – left £1,122,646. Insurance broker in the City of London.

The son of Stanford Henry Mountain (1833-92, left £18,654), a hop merchant in London, he was the brother of Sir Edward Mortimer Mountain, 1st Bt. (1872-1948, left £593,824), the founder and head of Eagle Star Insurance. Little is known of our man's career, but, with his brother, he established Hawley, Mountain & Co., and later the British Dominions Marine Insurance Co., which became famous as the only insurance broker which, in 1912, declined to insure the *Titanic*. It appears that our man was also connected with Eagle Star Insurance, which insured a wide range of risks beyond shipping, from its headquarters at 1 Threadneedle Street in the City of London. Our man bought the properties in the village of Groombridge, Kent and restored them; he lived at Groombridge Place there and at 124 Knightsbridge, Middlesex. His son Stanford Walton Mountain (1892-1984) left £3,499,434.

63. Sir William Alfred Churchman, 1st Bt. (1863-1947) – left £1,102,720. Tobacco manufacturer in Ipswich.

The son of Henry Charles Churchman (d. 1888, left £54,999), head of an old-established firm of tobacco manufacturers in Ipswich, he was educated at the Ipswich School. His brother was Sir Arthur Churchman, 1st Bt., M.P. (1867-1949, left £1,361,076), who was created 1st Baron Woodbridge in 1932. With his brother he greatly enlarged the family firm, renamed W.A. & A.C. Churchman, of which he was a Partner from 1888 till 1902. It then became a component of Imperial Tobacco. Churchman was a director of Imperial Tobacco and was Vice-Chairman of British-American Tobacco, formed to end an international trade war in cigarettes. He served as Mayor of Ipswich in 1899-1900. A long-serving officer in the Volunteers, during the First World War he was a Lieutenant-Colonel commanding a Suffolk regiment until 1917, when he became Director of the Nitrate Explosives Department of the Ministry of Munitions. He was knighted in 1920 and made a baronet in 1938. Churchman lived at The Lodge, Melton, Woodbridge, Suffolk and at 1 Prince's Row, Buckingham Palace Row, Middlesex.

64. Sir Robert McVitie Grant, 2nd Bt. (1894-1947) – left £1,033,000. Biscuit manufacturer at Edinburgh and at Harlesden, Middlesex.

The son of Sir Alexander Grant, 1st Bt. (1864-1937, *q.v.*), the head of the biscuit manufacturers McVitie & Price, who left £1,039,976, he was educated at George Watson's College, Edinburgh and succeeded his father as Chairman of McVitie & Price. He lived at Glenoriston, 15 Heritage Drive, Edinburgh.

65. Samuel Courtauld (1876-1947) – left £1,030,126. Rayon and silk manufacturer at Bocking, Essex and elsewhere.
The son of Sydney Courtauld (d. 1899, left £87,885), a silk manufacturer of the famous firm whose works were in Bocking, Essex, he was educated at Rugby, and studied textile production in Germany and France. The firm was founded by his great-uncle Samuel Courtauld (1793-1881, left £700,000, *q.v.*). The family was of Huguenot descent. He joined the family firm in 1898. In 1901 he was made Manager of the firm's weaving mills at Halstead, Essex and from 1908 was General Manager of all of its textile mills. He became a director of the firm in 1915, Joint Managing Director in 1915, and Chairman from 1921-46. He was noted for his conservative management style, although he oversaw the great popularity of rayon, which it pioneered. Courtauld is best known as one of the great art collectors of modern Britain. His superb collection of French Impressionists became the basis of the Courtauld Gallery and Institute of Art, now at Somerset House on the Strand, one of the premier art museums in London. Courtauld declined a peerage in 1937. He was also a Trustee of the Tate Gallery and of the National Gallery. His daughter Sydney (*sic*) was married to the Conservative M.P. R.A. Butler, Chancellor of the Exchequer 1951-55. Courtauld lived at 12 North Audley Street, Mayfair.

66. Gerald Berkeley Portman, 7th Viscount Portman (1875-1948) – left £4,493,306. Urban property and landowner.
The owner of very valuable urban property in the West End of London (see previous section), and, in 1883, of 33,891 acres worth £45,972 p.a. in Somerset and other counties, he was the sixth son of William Henry Portman, 2nd Viscount Portman (1829-1919, left £816,650). He was educated at Eton and at Sandhurst, was an ADC to the Viceroy of India from 1901, and served in the First World War as a Captain in the Hussars. Most remarkably (and unfortunately), he unexpectedly succeeded to the title after three of his elder brothers, and the son of one of them, all briefly succeeded to the title and then died: Henry, 3rd Viscount Portman (1860-1923, left £615,088); Claud, 4th Viscount Portman (1864-1929, left £466,805); Edward, 5th Viscount Portman (1898-1942, left £465,075); and Seymour, 6th Viscount Portman (1868-1946, left £135,023). As the enormous estate he left shows, despite many rounds of death duties and other increased costs, there was still plenty left in the kitty. He was succeeded by his son Gerald, 8th Viscount Portman (1803-67), who left £1,308,166. Our man lived at The Manor, Healing, Lincolnshire.

67. Edward George Villiers Stanley, 17th Earl of Derby (1865-1948) – left £3,217,839. Land and mineral owner.
The holder of an ancient title (see previous section) and known as the "King of Lancashire" for his vast landed and mineral wealth – 68, 942 acres worth £163,273 p.a. in 1883 he was the son of Frederick, 16th Earl of Derby (1841-1908, *q.v.*), who left £1,101,000. He was educated at Wellington College, served as an officer in the Boer War (despatches twice), and married Lady Alice, daughter of the 7th Duke of Manchester. He was a significant figure in the Conservative party, serving as a Tory M.P. from 1892 till 1906, and holding Cabinet office as Postmaster-General 1903-05, and as Secretary of State for War, 1916-18 and 1922-29. He also served as Ambassador to

France from 1918-20, and was Lord Lieutenant of Lancashire. He lived at Knowsley Hall, Prescot, Lancashire and at Derby House, Stratford Place, Middlesex.

68. William Henry Smith, 3rd Viscount Hambleden (1903-48) – left £3,088,066. Multiple newspaper and bookstall retailer.
The descendant of the W.H. Smith (1825-91, left £1,773,388, *q.v.*) whose family founded the famous bookstall and bookshop chain, he was the son of William Henry Danvers Smith, 2nd Viscount Hambleden (1868-1928, left £2,700,998, *q.v.*), and was educated at Eton and at New College, Oxford. In 1928 the family firm became a limited company, with him as Chairman and the holder of all Ordinary Shares. He died at only forty-five, leaving his heirs to pay the astronomical death duties of the time, which weakened the family's control of the firm. He was married to (Hon.) Patricia, Viscountess Hambleden (1904-94, left £1,618,659), daughter of Reginald, 15th Earl of Pembroke; she was Lady of the Bedchamber to Queen Elizabeth the Queen Mother. They lived at The Manor House, Hambleden, Buckinghamshire and at 20 Devonshire Place, Marylebone.

69. Jane Cowen (1856-1942) – left £1,991,262. Inherited a colliery and firebrick fortune in Co. Durham.
The unmarried daughter of Joseph Cowen, M.P. (1829-1900, left £501,973), a wealthy firebrick and clay retort manufacturer, newspaper proprietor, and colliery owner at Blaydon-on-Tyne near Gateshead, Co. Durham, she lived with her unmarried brother Joseph Cowen (1857-1942, left £1,489, 624, *q.v.*) at Stella Hall, Blaydon-on-Tyne. She died at ninety-one. She was awarded an OBE in 1918 for her war relief work, and, with her brother, established a school to train disabled soldiers and sailors.

70. Henry Lithgow (1886-1948) – left £1,960,035. Shipbuilder at Port Glasgow.
The son of the millionaire shipbuilder William Todd Lithgow (1854-1908, left £1,000,237, *q.v.*), shipbuilder at Port Glasgow, he was educated at the Glasgow Academy and was in lifelong partnership with his brother Sir James Lithgow, 1st Bt. (1883-1952, left £436,961). The pair developed their family firm, Russell & Co., into one of the very largest shipbuilders in the UK. Between 1920 and 1939 they built over one million tons of merchant ships, despite very difficult economic conditions. They were also involved in steel manufacturing and many other business ventures, and were notable benefactors of the Church of Scotland. Our man's heirs had to pay well over £1 million in death duties on his estate. Lithgow lived at Drums, Langbank, Renfrewshire.

71. Henry Oxley (1869-1948) – left £1,543,533, banker and company director in Leeds.
The son of James Walker Oxley (1834-1928, left £2,774,541, *q.v.*), a Partner in the Leeds bank of W. Brown & Co., he was educated at the Leys School and at Gonville and Caius College, Cambridge, and became a Partner in W. Brown & Co., as well as a director of steel manufacturing firms and other businesses. Like his father, he is surprisingly obscure, and little information exists about his career. The Leys School in Cambridge was established in 1875 as a public school for Methodists, suggesting that he was a Wesleyan. He lived at Spenfield, Weetwood, Leeds.

72. Samuel Ernest Palmer, 1st Baron Palmer (1858-1948) – left £1,014,558. Biscuit manufacturer at Reading and in London.

A member of the famous Quaker biscuit manufacturing family of Reading, Berkshire and London, he was the son of Samuel Palmer (1820-1903, left £1,334,830), one of three brothers who founded Huntley & Palmer, which became the largest firm of biscuit makers in the world, he was educated at Malvern College, and was a director of the family firm. He was also Deputy Chairman of the Great Western Railway from 1900 until 1948. Palmer served as High Sheriff of the County of London in 1924-25. He is best known, however, as one of the great patrons of music and musical education in Britain, and was a founder of the Royal College of Music and its Vice-President. He was awarded a baronetcy in 1916 and was created 1st Baron Palmer in 1933, the first person awarded a peerage for services to music. His son Ernest, 2nd Baron Palmer (1882-1950) left £206,098. Samuel Palmer lived at 10 Grosvenor Crescent, Belgravia.

73. Eleanor Williamson, Dowager Countess Peel (1871-1949) – left £4,274,902. Inherited a linoleum fortune made in Lancaster.

The daughter of the "linoleum king", James Williamson, 1st Baron Ashton (1842-1930), who made a fortune of £10,501,902 by manufacturing linoleum in Lancaster, in 1899 she married William Robert Wellesley Peel, 2nd Viscount and 1st Earl Peel (1867-1937, left £82,711), a descendant of Sir Robert Peel, 1st Bt. (1750-1830), the first cotton millionaire, and of Sir Robert Peel, 2nd Bt. (1788-1850), the Prime Minister. Her husband, educated at Harrow and at Balliol College, Oxford, served as a Liberal Unionist in 1900-06 and 1909-12, when he succeeded his father as 2nd Viscount Peel. He held Cabinet posts in 1922-24, 1924-29, and 1931-32. He was created 1st Earl Peel in 1929. He is probably best known for heading the Peel Commission of 1936-37, the first body to recommend the partitioning of Palestine. He also served as Chairman of James Williamson & Co., his father-in-law's linoleum firm. In later years the Dowager Countess Peel lived at Hendersyde Park, Kelso. Their son Arthur, 2nd Earl Peel (1901-69) left £747,070.

74. William Hulme Lever, 2nd Viscount Leverhulme (1888-1949) – left £2,987,755. Soap and household goods manufacturer at Port Sunlight, Cheshire and elsewhere.

The son of the famous manufacturer of soap and household products William Hesketh Lever, 1st Viscount Leverhulme (1851-1925, left £1,625,409, q.v.), he was educated at Eton and at Trinity College, Cambridge, and became Chairman of Lever Brothers and Unilever, as well as of Knowles Ltd., cotton spinners of Bolton. He served as High Sheriff of Cheshire in 1923-24, and was President of the London Chamber of Commerce, 1931-34. He was also Pro-Chancellor of Liverpool University in 1932-36. He was succeeded by his son Philip, 3rd Viscount Leverhulme (1915-2000). Our man lived at Thornton Manor, Thornton Heath, Cheshire.

75. Wyndham Raymond Portal, 1st Viscount Portal (1885-1949) – left £2,122,239. Paper banknote manufacturer at Whitchurch, Hampshire.

Of Huguenot descent, since the eighteenth century the Portals had a monopoly on the manufacture of paper banknotes, which they produced at Laverton Mills, Whitchurch, Hampshire. As paper money became more common than coins in the twentieth century, they became even wealthier From 1920 they were also allowed to make banknotes for other nations, and now do so for eighty different countries. Our man was the son of Sir William Wyndham Portal, 1st Bt. (1850-1931, left £159,380), of the family banknote firm. His mother Florence (d. 1931), was the daughter of St. Leger Glyn, the son of the banker George Carr Glyn, 1st Baron Wolverton (1797-1873, left £1,000,000, *q.v.*). Our man was educated at Eton and at Christ Church, Oxford, and was a Lieutenant-Colonel commanding the Household Battalion in France during the First World War (DSO; despatches four times). He served as Managing Director of Portal Ltd., the family firm, from 1919-31, when he became its Chairman. He was also the Chairman of Wiggins Teape Ltd., and of other companies. In 1934 he was the head of a government committee which produced a Report on Distressed Areas. In 1940-42 he was Chairman of the Coal Production Company, and, from 1942-44, First Commissioner of Works. He became known for expediting the making of prefabricated houses on a large scale. He was created a Viscount in 1945. He lived at Laverstoke House, Whitchurch, Hampshire. (Air Marshal) Charles Portal, 1st Viscount Portal of Hungerford (1893-1971, left £85,438), Chief of the Air Staff 1940-45, was a distant relative.

76. Kathleen Mary Christina Hamilton Rees-Mogg (*née* Wills) (1884-1949) – left £1,787,398. Inherited a tobacco fortune earned in Bristol.

Another member of the very wealthy Wills family of Imperial Tobacco of Bristol, she was the daughter of Sir Frederick Wills, 1st Bt. (1838-1909, left £2,918,115). She married, first in 1909, Dr. Edward Henry Douty, M.D. (d. 1911, left £2700), a physician. She married secondly, in 1922, (Lt. Col.) Graham Beauchamp Coxeter Rees-Mogg (1881-1949, left £244,339), a veterinarian and a Governor of the Royal Veterinary College. (Her second husband was not closely related to William Rees-Mogg, Baron Rees-Mogg (1928-2012), Editor of the *Times*, 1967-81, or to his son, Jacob Rees-Mogg, M.P. (b.1969), the Conservative Cabinet minister.) Her only son, the son of her first husband, Gilbert Edward Frederick Douty (d. 1938), is listed in the probate calendar of 1951 as having left £1,002,379, with the note that there was an earlier probate in 1938. However, no one of his name is listed in the probate calendar for 1938 or any other date prior to 1951. For this reason, he has not been included with the 1938 millionaires. Our lady lived at The Manor House, Clifford Chambers near Stratford-on-Avon, Warwickshire and at Flat 5, 23 Queen's Gate Gardens, SW7.

77. Evan Frederick Morgan, 2nd Viscount Tredegar (1893-1949) – left £1,719,137. Land and colliery owner.

The son of Courtenay Charles Evan Morgan, 1st Viscount Tredegar (1867-1934, left £2,369,686, *q.v.*), he was educated at Eton and at Christ Church, Oxford. In 1883 his forebear owned 39,157 acres worth £60,000 p.a. in Monmouthshire, Glamorganshire, and other counties, as well as lucrative coal mines. A well-known eccentric, he converted to Roman Catholicism and was chamberlain to two Popes, but was also a serious occultist, hailed by Aleister Crowley. He served as a Lieutenant in the First World War. During the Second World War, he worked for MI8 monitoring carrier pigeons, but was court-martialled for revealing secrets about them to two Girl Guides. He appears as a character in several novels of the period. He lived at Tredegar Park, Newport, Monmouthshire and at Honeywood House, Oakwood Hall, Dorking, Surrey.

78. William Worthington Worthington (*sic*, 1871-1949) – left £1,529,007. Brewer at Burton-on-Trent.

The son of Albert Octavius Worthington (1844-1918, left £1,356,975, *q.v.*), Chairman of Worthington & Co., brewers of Burton-on-Trent, he was educated at Charterhouse and at New College, Oxford, and continued in the family firm. In 1901 he married Lady Muriel, daughter of the 8th Earl of Aylesford. Worthington lived at Maple House near Lichfield, Staffordshire.

79. Arthur Charles Churchman, 1st Baron Woodbridge (1867-1949) – left £1,361,076. Tobacco manufacturer at Ipswich.

The son of the tobacco manufacturer Henry Charles Churchman (d. 1888, left £54,999) and educated at the Ipswich School, he went into partnership with his brother William (later Sir William, 1st Bt.) Churchman (1863-1947, left £1,102,720, *q.v.*) in a new cigarette firm, W.A. & A.C. Churchman, of Ipswich. It later became part of Imperial Tobacco; our man served as a Vice-Chairman of British-American Tobacco. He served as a Lieutenant-Colonel in the First World War, and was a Conservative M.P. from 1920-29 as well as Mayor of Ipswich 1901-02. Churchman was created a baronet in 1917 and awarded a peerage, as 1st Baron Woodbridge, in 1932. He lived at Abbey Oaks, Sproughton near Ipswich, Suffolk and at Kingston House, Princes Gate, SW7.

80. Lavinia Clarissa Keene (*née* Stevens) (1863-1949) – left £1,347,910. Widow of an insurance company director of High Holborn, London.

She was born in Mile End, Stepney in 1863, the daughter of George William Stevens (c. 1836-99, left £250), a printer of Leytonstone, Essex who, in 1891, employed four men and eight boys. In 1888 she married John Henry Keene (1864-1931, *q.v.*), then a company secretary but later a director of and leading figure in the Pearl Insurance Company of High Holborn, London and a millionaire. Childless, they were notable philanthropists. The astronomical rates of death duty in place at the time meant that no less than £937,663 of her estate of £1,347,910 was taken by the state in taxes. She lived at Carlton House, Galleywood, Chelmsford, Essex.

81. James Frazer (1864-1949) – left £1,131,388. Ship stores merchant in Northumberland.

The son of James Frazer (1826-87, left £43,600), a provision merchant in North Shields, Northumberland, he was born in Co. Antrim and went into business with his brother Anthony Strong Frazer (1865-1921, left £207,153) as ship stores merchants, with business premises at North Shields, Newcastle-upon-Tyne, and Tynemouth, all in Northumberland. Little is known of his career, but he probably also owned urban properties in these cities. He and his brother were unmarried. A third brother, Joseph Strong Frazer (d. 1939, left £354,251) apparently owned a similar business in Cardiff. Our man's addresses were given in his entry in the probate calendar as 35 Clive Street, North Shields; 25 Queen Street, Newcastle-upon-Tyne; and 19 Percy Gardens, Tynemouth, all in Northumberland.

82. Stephen Powys, 6th Baron Lilford (1869-1949) – left £1,100,737. Landowner.

The younger son of Thomas, 4th Baron Lilford (1833-96, left £53,278), he succeeded his brother John, 5th Baron Lilford (1863-1945, left £1,333,797, *q.v.*), but died only four years later. Our man was educated at Harrow and at Trinity College, Cambridge. The family owned land in Northamptonshire, Cheshire, and near Preston, Lancashire; £940,317 of his probated estate of £1,100,737 was in the form of settled land. Little is known about his career. He was succeeded by his second cousin George, 7th Baron Lilford (1931-2005). Our man lived at Lilford Hall, Oundle, Northamptonshire and at 5 Harrowby Court, Harrowby Street, Bryanston Square, Marylebone.

83. Joseph Henry Jacobs (1867-1949) – left £1,080,545. Shipowner in the City of London.

Born in Swansea, the son of Chapman Jacobs (1828-87), a pawnbroker and later a shipowner in London, he became a shipbroker and shipowner in London, in partnership with his brother John

Isaac Jacobs (1855-1917), shipowner, at 10 Mark Lane, City of London. His brother, who left £860,027, was Chairman of the Oil Carriers' Association and was married to the daughter of Sir Adolph Tuck, Bt. The family was Jewish. Our man lived at 4 Cambridge Terrace, Regent's Park, and at Woodland Court, Chesham Bois, Buckinghamshire.

84. Walter Runciman, 1st Viscount Runciman of Doxford (1870-1949) – left £1,038,335. Shipowner in Newcastle-upon-Tyne.

The son of Walter Runciman, 1st Baron Runciman (1947-1937, left £2,406,854, *q.v.*), a millionaire shipowner in Newcastle-upon-Tyne, he was educated at South Shields High School and at Trinity College, Cambridge. He became head of Moor Lines, his father's firm, and was Deputy Chairman of the Royal Mail Steam Packet Co., and of other companies, and served as President of the Chamber of Shipping. Runciman is best known as one of the more prominent political figures of his day. He served as Liberal, later National, M.P. in 1899-1900, 1902-18, 1924-29, and 1929-37, when he succeeded to the peerage. He was made 1st Viscount Runciman of Doxford in the same year, 1937. He held a variety of Cabinet posts between 1908 and 1939, including President of the Board of Trade in 1914-16 and 1931-37. In 1938 he was sent by the Government on the so-called "Runciman Mission" to Prague to adjudicate between the Czech government and the Sudeten Germans. His wife, Hilda *née* Stevenson (1869-1956, left £54,284) has an entry in the *ODNB* as a "politician". He lived at Doxford Hall, Chathill, Northumberland. His son, Walter, 2nd Viscount Runciman of Doxford (1900-89) left £1,792,084.

85. Charles Stewart Henry Vane-Tempest-Stewart, 7th Marquess of Londonderry (1879-1949) – left £1,021,755. Landowner.

From one of the wealthiest landed families, who in 1883 owned 50,323 acres worth £100,118 p.a., mainly in Co. Durham, where they owned extensive collieries, and in Co. Down (see previous section), he was the son of Charles, 6th Marquess of Londonderry (1852-1915, left £500,000), and was educated at Eton and at Sandhurst. He served as a Conservative M.P. from 1906-15 and held Cabinet office as First Commissioner of Works, 1928-29 and 1931, Secretary of State for Air 1931-35, and Lord Privy Seal and Leader of the Lords in 1935. He held many honorary positions as Chancellor of the Queen's University Belfast and of Durham University, and held important posts in the government of Northern Ireland. He became notorious as the so-called "friend of Hitler" in the 1930s, and, in particular, of Herman Goering, and held no Cabinet posts after 1935. He was also Lord Lieutenant of Co. Durham from 1928. He lived at Londonderry House, Park Lane, Mayfair and at Mt. Stewart in Northern Ireland.

Chapter 5: The Largest Estates Left in the UK, 1950-1979

1950–1959

Although relatively peaceful and prosperous, the decade from 1950 through 1959 was also marked by a continuation of the very high rates of taxation of the previous decade, the decade of World War Two and of the "Austerity" period of the Labour government. These very high rates of taxation were applied most strongly to death duties. One predictable result was that there estate duty avoidance almost certainly occurred at levels unseen in the past. Death duties in fact became widely known as a "voluntary tax"- although it will be seen that many wealthy persons volunteered to pay it. Estate duty avoidance was of course, not as easy as it seemed, as *inter vivos* gifts had to be paid more than four or five years(later seven years) before the death of the testator in order to avoid death duties. Before the internet it was also very difficult to transfer large amounts of money abroad to tax havens without attracting the attention of the Inland Revenue. The usual number of family quarrels and jealousies also no doubt acted as a brake on a millionaire giving his or her money away long before the reading of their will.

It will be seen that, strikingly, levels of great wealth were extraordinarily low by the standards of wealthholding in Britain during the past thirty years or so- in part because of the effects of inflation on the value of the pound, but also because the levels of wealth owned by the "Rich List" super-rich have grown to previously unimaginable levels.

In contrast to the previous chapters in this book about the very rich, which included all millionaires (and, up to 1880, all half-millionaires), the post 1950 lists presented here are for the ten to twelve largest estates left in Britain in a five-year span, in descending order. There would appear to be a surprising number of engineering fortunes and the like, with many fewer great landowners and merchant bankers than in the past. A number of those whose wealth is discussed here were very difficult to trace, and left little evidence about their careers. Many inherited great wealth from previous millionaires whose lives are discussed in this work.

1950–1954

1. Hugh Richard Arthur Grosvenor, 2nd Duke of Westminster (1879-1953) – left £10,703,656. Urban property and landowner.
The grandson of Hugh Lupus Grosvenor, 1st Duke of Westminster (1825-99), who left £594,229 in personalty but far more in urban and rural land, and the son of Victor, Earl Grosvenor (1853-84, left £5086), he was the owner of the ground rents of most of Mayfair, Belgravia, and Pimlico, as well as land in Cheshire, Flintshire and elsewhere. In a previous chapter, the Grosvenors were

credited with being the second wealthiest landowners in Britain in the nineteenth century, behind only the first Duke of Sutherland (but ahead of his successors). Owner of many of the wealthiest districts in London, the Duke's fortune only rose still further during his lifetime. According to his entry in *Who's Who*, he "owns about 30,000 acres in Cheshire and Flintshire, besides an estate in Scotland and 600 acres in London." The 2nd Duke was educated at Eton and served as an ADC to Viscount Milner during the Boer War, and also served as an officer in the First World War (DSO). He was known from childhood as "Bend Or," for a racetrack and as a pun on a component of his coat of arms. The Duke was married four times, in addition to a string of mistresses including "Coco" Chanel. An extreme right-wing anti-semite and admirer of Hitler, he travelled between Grosvenor House in Mayfair, his London mansion at the time, and Eaton Hall, his mansion in Cheshire, in a private train, with a separate fleet of seventeen Rolls-Royces to transport his goods and staff. His heir was his cousin, William, 3rd Duke of Westminster (1894-1963), who was born with brain damage, and left only £15,287. Our man's probate valuation, of £10.7 million, included an estimate of £5 million for settled land. These figures appear to have been considerable underestimates, as a total of £18 million was paid by his executors in death duties between 1953 and 1964, suggesting that he was actually worth £25-30 million. In order to pay the death duties on his estate, his properties in Pimlico had to be sold off, leaving him with only the ground rents of Mayfair and Belgravia to pay the bills. In later life, his London residence was at Bowdon House, Davies Street, W.1.

2. Hastings William Sackville Russell, 12th Duke of Bedford (1883-1953) – left £5,792,253. Urban property and landowner.

The son of Herbrand, 11th Duke of Bedford (1858-1940, left £4,651,371, *q.v.*), he was educated at Eton- which he hated and did not mention in his entry in *Who's Who*- and at Balliol College, Oxford. His family owned the ground rents of much of Bloomsbury and surrounding areas, in addition to 86,335 acres worth £141,793 p.a. in eleven counties (see previous section). Our man became an Evangelical Christian and a pacifist. He refused to serve in the First World War; as a result, his father refused to speak with him for twenty years. In 1935 his wife sued him for the restoration of conjugal rights; in 1939 he disinherited his son. A pathetic figure in public life, from 1935-39 he was a member of the pro-Nazi "British People's Party," and during the Second World War had meetings with Nazi German representatives in Dublin about reaching a peace treaty in direct opposition to the policy of the Churchill government, which seriously considered (but did not) intern him for the duration of the War. He died in October 1953 from what was described by the Coroner as "accidentally inflicted" gunshot wounds. The Duke's traditional residence was at Woburn Abbey, Bedfordshire. In later life his address was given as Crowholt, Woburn, Bedfordshire. He (inevitably) quarrelled with his son and successor, John, 13th Duke of Bedford (1917-2002), such that the son's first job in 1938 was as a rent collector. The new Duke wrote a well-known account of his family, *A Silver-Plated Spoon* (1959), opened a safari park at Woburn Abbey, and became a tax exile in Monaco.

3. John Arthur Dewar (1891-1954) – left £3,271,516. Distiller in London, in Perth, and elsewhere in Scotland.

The son of Charles Dewar (1858-1933, left £28,496), of Great Massingham Abbey, King's Lynn, Norfolk, a brother of the multi-millionaire whisky distillers Lord Forteviot (1856-1929, *q.v.*) and of Lord Dewar (1864-1930, *q.v.*), he was educated at the Aldenham School, and fought in the First World War. He joined the family firm, one of the largest whisky distillers in the world, and became its Managing Director and Chairman. He operated from the London headquarters of the firm, Dewar House in the Haymarket, rather than in Scotland. He lived at Dutton Homestall, East Grinstead, Sussex.

4. Joseph Aaron Littman (1898-1953) – left £3,264,167. Property developer in London.

One of the earliest and most successful of the post-World War Two London property developers, he was born in Russian Poland. His father Mayer Littman and his family emigrated to New York around 1913. They lived in the Bronx; he was naturalised as an American citizen in 1918. In New York, he worked as a doll importer at 475 Broadway. In the early 1920s, for reasons which are unclear but probably related to his marriage, he moved to London, working in a ladies' hat shop owned by his wife's family on High Road, Kilburn. He bought several properties in the area, and then devised and developed the "sale and leaseback" system, by which he managed to convince financial institutions to buy properties on his behalf and then lease them back to him on 99 or 999 year leases, which he sublet on short-term lease, the size of the rentals increasing over time. An entirely self-made man, Littman bought only existing properties and shops, including many on Oxford Street. By the late 1940s he had a property rent roll of £375,000 p.a. He died at the age of fifty-four of lung cancer. His son Louis Littman (1925-87), a Cambridge-educated solicitor, established the important publishing series the Littman Library of Jewish Civilisation, and left £27,529,809. Our man lived at Woodberry House, Winnington Road, Finchley, Middlesex.

5. John Dane Player (1864-1950) – left £2,501,622. Cigarette and tobacco manufacturer in Nottingham.

His father, John Player (1839-84, left £43,802), pioneered the pre-packaging of tobacco and tobacco products under a brand name, rather than selling tobacco loose from jars, as had been done before. He named one brand of his cigarettes "Gold Leaf," and, for another brand, "Jack's Glory," adopted the familiar picture of a British sailor as the brand's icon. He also relied on extensive advertising, which resulted in great brand loyalty. Our man was educated at Nottingham High School, and, with his brother William Goodacre Player (1866-1959, left £1,606,739), headed the family company, John Player & Sons, which became a component of Imperial Tobacco in 1901. Their firm, based in Nottingham, greatly prospered, and employed 5,000 workers in 1928, and was noted as an enlightened employer which treated its workers well. He was made a Freeman of Nottingham in 1934. Player lived at Fernleigh, Alexandra Park, Nottingham.

6. Charles Henry Wyndham, 3rd Baron Leconfield (1872-1952) – left £2,136,439. Landowner.

In 1883, his forebear owned 109,935 acres worth £88,112 p.a. in Sussex, Yorkshire, Cumberland, Co. Clare, and elsewhere (see previous section). He was the son of Henry, 2nd Baron Leconfield (1830-1901, left £1,861,959, *q.v.*). His mother Lady Constance (d. 1934), was the sister of the 5th Earl of Rosebery, the Prime Minister. He was educated at Winchester and served at a Temporary Captain in the Life Guards Reserve, 1915-17. Leconfield was Lord Lieutenant of Sussex from 1917 till 1949 and served as Chairman of the West Sussex County Council. He lived at Petworth House, Petworth, Sussex, at Cockermouth Castle, Cumberland, and at 9 Chesterfield Gardens, Mayfair. His relative John Wyndham (1920-72), who succeeded as 6th Baron Leconfield, was a close associate of Harold Macmillan, and was created 1st Baron Egremont in 1963. The author of *Wyndhams and Children First* (1968), he left £1,576,519.

7. Dame Margaret, Baroness Strickland (*nee* Hulton, 1868-1950) – left £2,066,264. Sister of a Manchester newspaper millionaire.

The daughter of the Manchester newpaper proprietor Edward Hulton (1838-1904, left £558,904) and the sister of the Manchester newspaper multi-millionaire Sir Edward Hulton, 1st Bt. (1869-1925, *q.v.*) who left £3,795,125, in 1926 she married, as his second wife, Gerald Strickland, 1st Baron Strickland (1861-1940, left £15,517), who was both a British M.P. and Prime Minister of Malta from 1927-32. In his remarkable career, he had previously served at different times as Governor of Tasmania, Western Australia, and New South Wales, and was made a peer in 1928. Descended on her mother's side from the Maltese nobility, she was, like her parents and her husband, a Roman Catholic, and lived mainly in Malta for the rest of her life, although she left a very large estate in England, and had residences at 5 Holland Park W11 and at Sizergh Castle, Westmorland. She was made a DBE in 1937. She died at the Villa Bologna, Malta, where her husband had lived.

8. Sir Arthur Munro Sutherland, 1st Bt. (1867-1953) – left £2,013,170. Shipowner in Newcastle-upon-Tyne.

The son of the Newcastle-upon-Tyne shipping merchant Benjamin John Sutherland (d.1909, left £43,294), he was educated at the Royal Grammar School, Newcastle-upon-Tyne, and entered his father's shipping company at an early age. He began a separate cargo shipping firm, Sutherland Steam Ship Co., and was a director of coal exporting and other companies. From 1920 till 1925 he was the owner of the *Newcastle Chronicle* newspaper. A Wesleyan Methodist and a teetotaler, he was a noted philanthropist of his home city, paying most of the costs of establishing medical and dental schools at the local university. He served as Lord Mayor of Newcastle-upon-Tyne in 1918-19, and was created a knight in 1920 and a baronet in 1921. Sutherland lived at Thurso House, Fernwood Road, Newcastle-upon-Tyne, at 38 Sandhill in that city, and at Hethpool Wooles, Northumberland.

9. James Voase Rank (1881-1952) – left £1,622,916. Flour manufacturer in Hull and in the City of London.

The son of Joseph Rank (1854-1943, left £70,954) who owned flour mills in Hull, he was educated at Hymers College, Hull and at Weston College, Harrogate. He became a wheat buyer for his father's firm in Hull, which became Joseph Rank Ltd. in 1899, and then a director in 1907, and later its Managing Director. He was very significant in establishing a reserve of wheat in the UK during the Second World War. Although a strict Methodist who gave an estimated £3.5 million to Methodist causes, he bred racehorses as well as pedigree dogs. In 1904 he moved the corporate headquarters of his firm from Hull to 22 Leadenhall Street and to the Old Corn Exchange, both in the City of London. His firm is now a component of Rank Hovis McDougall. His brother Joseph Arthur Rank, 1st Baron Rank (1888-1972), who was both a flour miller and a major film producer (*q.v.*) left £5,993,323. James Voase Rank lived at Ousborough, Godstone, Surrey.

10. William Ewart Berry, 1st Viscount Camrose (1879-1954) – left £1,480,686. Newspaper proprietor at Fleet Street, London and elsewhere.

One of three brothers who became major British "Presslords," he was born in Merthyr Tydfil, the son of John Mathias Berry (d. 1917, left £23,842), an estate agent. His brothers were, remarkably, also both created peers: (Hugh) Seymour Berry, 1st Baron Buckland (1877-1928, left £1,116,448, *q.v.*) and (James) Gomer Berry, 1st Viscount Kemsley (1883-1968, left £310,866). Camrose left school at fourteen and became a journalist. In 1901 he established the *Advertising World*. His fortune was made during the First World war, when he published the series *The War Illustrated*, which sold 750,000 copies. In 1916 he bought the *Sunday Times*, serving as its Editor-in-Chief until 1937; he also purchased the *Financial Times* in 1919. He followed this up by buying or owning many provincial newspapers, such as the *Western Mail*. In 1927 Camrose bought his first Fleet Street paper, the *Daily Telegraph*, serving as its Editor-in-Chief until 1937. He received a baronetcy in 1921, a peerage as 1st Baron Camrose in 1929, and was promoted to 1st Viscount Camrose in 1941. His son (William) Michael Berry (1911-2001) was Editor-in-Chief of the *Daily Telegraph* from 1954 till 1986. Camrose lived at Hackwood Park, Basingstoke, Hampshire. While less well-known than other "Presslords" like Northcliffe and Beaverbrook, he and his brothers were just as influential and successful.

11. Sir James Caird, 1st Bt. (1864-1954) – left £1,418,716. Shipowner and meat importer in the City of London.
The son of James Caird (d. 1914, left £9291), a solicitor in Glasgow, he was educated at the Glasgow Academy. In 1878 he became an East India merchant with William Graham & Co. of Glasgow, and, in 1889, came to London as manager of the Scottish Shire Line. He became a leading shipowner in the City of London, operating from 112 Fenchurch Street and later from Bevis Marks House. He was also Chairman of the Smithfield & Argentine Meat Co., and of other companies. Caird is chiefly known for providing most of the funding to establish the National Maritime Museum in Greenwich, which opened in 1937. During the 1920s, he also provided the funding to repair *HMS Victory*, Nelson's flagship, and other ships associated with Trafalgar. He was given a baronetcy in 1928, and declined the offer of a peerage in 1937. Caird lived at The Well House, Arthur Road, Wimbledon, Surrey.

1955-1959

1. James Armand Edmond de Rothschild (1878-1957) – left £11,622,759. Merchant banker in the City of London and in Paris.
From the French branch of the celebrated merchant banking family, Jimmy Rothschild (as he was known) was born in Paris, the son of Edmund James de Rothschild (1845-1934), and was educated at the Lycée Louis-le-Grand, Paris, and at Trinity College, Cambridge. He served in the British Army during the First World War as a Major, mainly in Palestine, and was naturalised as a British subject in 1920. He was a Partner in Rothschild's Bank in both the City of London and in Paris. He served as a Liberal M.P. from 1929 until 1945, and, from 1940-45, was Parliamentary Secretary to the Ministry of Supply. A successful racehorse owner, he, also like other members of his family, was a leading Zionist, and was President of the Palestine Jewish Colonisation Association. His wife, Dorothy Mathilde *nee* Pinto (1895-1988), left £94,117,964 at her death, the largest estate in nominal terms left in England and Wales up to that time. She also donated the funds to the Israeli government to build the Knesset Building in Jerusalem, and donated their country estate,

Waddesdon Manor at Waddesdon, Buckinghamshire, to the National Trust. They also lived at 27 St. James's Place, SW1.

2. Sir Alfred Edward Herbert (1866-1957) – left £5,336,052. Machine tool manufacturer in Coventry.

The son of William Herbert (d. 1908, left £21,562), a building contractor and farmer in Leicester, he was educated at the Stoneygate House School, Leicester. At eighteen he was apprenticed to a turner and fitter in Coventry, and, in 1887, became the manager of a small engineering firm there and then formed a machine tool manufacturing firm, Alfred Herbert Ltd., as a Partner with his brother William Henry Herbert (d. 1911, left £195,902). It imported machine tools, especially from America, and also manufactured them from its factory in Coventry. It became a limited liability company in 1994. The firm became the largest and most highly regarded in the UK, and employed 3800 workers in 1938. Herbert served as Controller of Machine Tools during the First World War, and was knighted in 1917. Herbert was a notable philanthropist of Coventry, and a model employer. He was constantly innovating, and introduced a tape-controlled production machine, a forerunner of computer control, when he was in his eighties. He lived at Dunley Manor, Hampshire.

3. George Alan Hamilton Wills, 1st Baron Dulverton (1880-1956) – left £4,268,271. Tobacco manufacturer in Bristol.

Yet another member of the immensely wealthy Wills family, he was a younger son of Sir Frederick Wills, 1st. Bt. (1838-1909, left £2,918,115, *q.v.*) of W.D. & H.O. Wills and then of Imperial Tobacco, of Bristol. His early life is somewhat obscure. *Who's Who* states that he was educated at Magdalen College, Oxford. In the 1901 Census (when he was twenty or twenty-one, and presumably at Oxford), he was stated to be a "play actor" of 55 Eardley Crescent, Brompton. He served in the First World War as a Lieutenant-Colonel (despatches). In 1914 he has married Victoria, daughter of (Rear-Admiral) Sir Edward Chichester, 9th Bt. Wills became President of Imperial Tobacco and was created 1st Baron Dulverton in 1929. Many of his relatives were millionaires and were awarded titles. He lived at Batsford Park, Moreton-in-Marsh, Gloucestershire and at 26 Wilton Crescent, SW1.

4. Gladys Meryl Yule (1903-57) – left £4,070,551. Inherited a mercantile fortune made in Calcutta, India.

The daughter of Sir David Yule, 1st Bt. (1858-1928), who left £348,039 in the UK but was said to be worth between £8 million and £15 million in India at the time of his death. Yule had been born in Edinburgh, but went to Calcutta to work for his uncle, and developed two of the largest business firms in India, Yule Catto & Co., founded with Thomas Catto, 1st Baron Catto (1879-1959), and Andrew Yule & Co. These were multi-purpose firms whose activities ranged from producing cotton goods and jute to inland shipping and coal. Yule was knighted in 1912 and made a baronet in 1922. In 1900 he married his cousin Annie (1874-1950, left £523,199), daughter of Andrew Yule of Calcutta. In Britain, she was one of the driving forces in the early British cinema, and, with our lady, their only child, bred racehorses at their country house, Hanstead Manor near St. Albans, Hertfordshire. They also built the *Nashlin*, the largest private yacht in the world, which was 300 feet long and had a crew of fifty-one. It does not appear that Gladys Yule had any involvement in business life.

5. Sir William Douglas Weir, 1st Viscount Weir (1877-1959) – left £3,304,393. Machinery manufacturer in Glasgow.

The head of G. & J. Weir, machinery manufacturers of Glasgow, he was the son of the founder of the firm, James Weir (1842-1920, left £564,500), of Over Courance, Dumfries-shire. Our man's paternal grandmother was the child of Robert Burns's illegitimate daughter. He was educated at Allan Glen's School in Glasgow and at Glasgow High School, and was apprenticed to his family firm. He became a director in 1898, Managing Director from 1902-15, and Chairman from 1910-53. The firm made condenser pumps, distillery machinery, and other engineering equipment of this type. Weir had a significant public career. He was Director of Aircraft Production, 1917-18, and Secretary of State for the RAF, 1917-18. Weir was also a director of Lloyd's Bank, ICI, Shell, and other companies; his advice was always highly regarded in the public and business worlds. He was knighted in 1917, and created 1st Baron Weir in 1918 and 1st Viscount Weir in 1938. He lived at Eastwood Park, Giffnock, Renfrewshire.

6. Horace Moore (1894-1959) – left £2,770,487. Multiple retailer in Yorkshire.

Very little could be traced about Horace Moore, described as a "multiple retailer," who was born and died in Keighley, Yorkshire. His father Frederick Moore (1860-1951, left £56,417) was an architect. In the 1939 UK Register, our man was described as a "director of companies." He lived at 43 Banks Lane, Riddlesden, Keighley, Yorkshire. His brother Frederick William Moore (1890-1966, left £831,008) was described in the 1939 Register as a "director of public companies since retiring as a practicing architect." It is possible that our man and his brother were involved in property development in Yorkshire.

7. Maurice Egerton, 4th Baron Egerton of Tatton (1874-1958) – left £1,717,673. Landowner; also a landowner in Kenya.

The son of Martin, 3rd Baron Egerton of Tatton (1845-1920, left £94,356), he was a landowner in Cheshire and Lancashire. In 1883 his father owned 11,559 acres worth £32,490 p.a. Our man's education is unlisted in any reference book, although he did serve as a Lieutenant-Commander in the RNVR in the First World War. He moved to Kenya, where he was an extensive landowner, and where he built a stately home resembling one in England; he died in Kenya. He was also known as a leading amateur aviator – he had met the Wright brothers – and was a motor car enthusiast and a naturalist. He died without direct heirs. His title became extinct, and his English mansion, Tatton Park in Knutsford, Cheshire, was left to the National Trust. He had also previously had a residence in London at 9 Seymour Place, Mayfair.

8. William Goodacre Player (1866-1959) – left £1,606,739. Tobacco manufacturer in Nottingham.

A partner with his brother John Dane Player (1866-1950, left £2,501,622, *q.v.*) in John Player & Sons, cigarette manufacturers of Nottingham, which became part of Imperial Tobacco. Like his brother he was educated at Nottingham High School. He was a notable philanthropist of the Anglican Church, and lived at Whatton Manor, Whatton-in-the-Vale, Nottinghamshire, about ten miles from Nottingham.

9. Sir Duncan Watson (1873-1959) – left £1,414,116. Electrical engineering good

manufacturer and motorcycle manufacturer in London.

Born in Glasgow, the son of Joseph Watson, a grain merchant, he was educated at Hutchison's Grammar School in Glasgow; at the Glasgow and West of Scotland Technical College; and at King's College, London. He moved to London, and founded Duncan Watson Electrical Engineers Ltd., whose offices were at 62 Berners Street, near Oxford Street. The firm made electrical light fittings and appliances, vacuum cleaners, and similar consumer goods. He was also Chairman of Harley-Davidson Ltd., the motorcycle manufacturers. Watson served as Mayor of Marylebone in 1919-20 and was a Governor of the Regent Street Polytechnic. He was knighted in 1927. He lived at Scammels Corner, Blackbrook near Dorking, Surrey.

10. William George West (1882-1959) – left £1,313,033. Builder, probably in Lancashire and Cheshire.

Almost nothing can be found about the wealthy builder William George West. He may be the man of this name who was born at Everton, Lancashire in November 1882, the son of Thomas West, a plasterer. He probably worked in the area of Liverpool and Cheshire, but this is unclear. His address in later life was 16 Carrwood Road, Bramhall, Cheshire.

11. Rupert Evelyn Beckett (1870-1955) – left £1,202,345. Banker in Leeds and in the City of London and newspaper proprietor in Leeds.

The son of William Beckett (1826-90, left £460,426), head of a long-established bank in Leeds and an M.P., and the brother of the banker Sir (William) Gervase Beckett (1866-1937, left £1,034,163, *q.v.*), he was educated at Eton and at Trinity College, Cambridge. He became a Partner in the family bank in 1892, working at Doncaster, and then was a director of its main branch at Leeds, becoming its Senior Partner. His bank became a part of the Westminster Bank, and he served as Chairman of the Westminster Bank (now NatWest) in London from 1931 to 1950. He was also the Chairman of the *Yorkshire Post* newspaper and of other concerns. He was highly regarded as an expert on finance, and gave advice to several Chancellors of the Exchequer. He lived at Stone House, Moor Allerton, Leeds and in a permanent apartment at the Park Lane Hotel in Mayfair, where he died.

1960-1969

In the 1960s, the levels of top wealth left by Britain's richest men and women were still remarkably low by today's standards, with an estate of £2.5 million placing its owner among the wealthiest in the UK; no estates were left of more than £11 million. To an unknown but almost certainly significant extent, this reflected the ever-increasing volume of deliberate estate-duty avoidance and other means of tax avoidance. However, these figures were also almost certainly an accurate reflection of reality, reflecting the many years of astronomical levels of taxation, the difficulties in transferring wealth internationally before electronic transfers existed, and the relative lack of lucrative investment opportunities in the UK. The people on this list include many in traditional areas of inherited wealth, such as the great landowners noted here, but the list also reflects a more "modern" look, with the manufacturers and proprietors of automobiles, modern consumer durables, household products, and retail chains also present. Top levels of wealth would begin to escalate dramatically, in part because of inflation, but also because of lower rates of taxation and world-wide trends.

1960–1964

1. Bernard Sunley (1910-64) – left £5,204,864. Property developer and investment banker in London and elsewhere.

One of the wealthiest of the property developers who emerged after the Second World War, he was the son of John Sunley (probably 1884-1963, left £120) of Catford, who began as a "muck shifter with a pony and cart" to become a florist and fruiterer. Educated at St. Anne's School, Hanwell, Middlesex, to the age of fourteen, he founded an earth moving firm, Blackwood Hodge Ltd., which also sold motorcycles, and then founded Bernard Sunley & Sons, large-scale builders. On his marriage license in 1931 he stated that his occupation was a "landscape contractor." Without any training in finance, he then branched out to found the Bernard Sunley Investment Trust, and also Sunley Homes. His firms built offices in the West End and in the Bahamas, as he became one of the richest men in England. Sunley unsuccessfully contested Ealing South as a Conservative at the 1945 general election. In the year prior to his death he is said to have given £500,000 to charity. He died of a heart attack at fifty-four. He lived at 25 Berkeley Square, Mayfair and at 26 Harley Road, Hampstead.

2. Howard Samuel (1914-61) – left £3,848,222. Property developer and publisher in London.

Another of the very wealthy post-war property developers in London, he was the son of Henry Samuel (d. 1963, left £39,611), the head of the jewellery chain H. Samuel. He was educated at St. Paul's School and served in World War Two as a private. With his brother Basil Samuel, he founded Basil & Howard Samuel, Surveyors, and later, Great Portland Estates, which became one of the largest of London property developers. He was assisted by the fact that his cousin Harold Samuel (1912-87) was the head of Land Securities, another great property development firm. Harold Samuel was knighted in 1963 and created Baron Samuel of Wych Cross in 1972; at his death he left £26,227,352. Howard Samuel differed from most millionaire plutocrats in that he was a supporter of the left wing of the Labour party, a friend of Aneurin Bevan, and, remarkably, a director of the *Tribune* and the *New Statesman*. He was also a publisher, the head of Associated Publishers, and a well-known collector of rare books. He died at forty-seven while swimming in Greece near Athens, where he suffered a heart attack. Samuel lived at 72 Elm Park Road, Chelsea SW3.

3. William Lawrence Stephenson (1880-1963) – left £3,490,209. Head of a multiple retail firm (Woolworths), headquartered in London but with branches throughout the UK.

Born in Scarborough, the son of Frederick James Stephenson (1853-1932, left £592), described in the 1901 and 1911 Censuses as a "foreman French polisher," he was educated in Hull and apprenticed to a general merchant in Birmingham, where he was responsible for purchasing goods for the firm. In 1904 he met Frank Woolworth, the head of the famous American chain of inexpensive retailers, and, in 1909, joined the Woolworth management when it opened its first shops in the UK. He became head of UK Woolworth in 1923, when it had 100 stores in Britain; by 1933, it owned 529 stores, in virtually every large town in the country, and was a household name, based on the principle of mass-producing cheap goods. Its headquarters were on Marylebone Road, London. During the Second World War, Stephenson served as Director-General of Equipment in the Ministry of Aircraft Production. He was also a director of Phoenix Assurance and other companies, and retired in 1948. He was a noted yachtsman. In 1930 he lived at The White Lodge, Bishops Avenue N2, and later at Rudheath, 112 Canford Cliffs Road, Bournemouth.

4. William Richard Morris, 1st Viscount Nuffield (1877-1963) – left £3,252,764. Automobile manufacturer in Oxford.

Frequently described as "the most famous industrialist of his age," William Morris, Lord Nuffield was the son of Frederick Morris (1849-1916, left £74), a farm bailiff of Oxford, and was educated at Cawley Village School, Oxford to age fifteen. He was apprenticed to a bicycle maker in Oxford, and then set up a cycle repair and later a bicycle making business; he also made motorcycles. From 1909 he ran an automobile repair business in Oxford and then, from 1912, manufactured automobiles as Morris Motors in Oxford; he served as its Chairman from 1919 until 1952. The firm made 20,000 cars in 1923 and built one-third of all UK-produced cars in the 1930s. His firm merged with Austin Motors in 1951 to become the British Motor Corporation. Morris transformed Oxford from a seat of learning with "dreamy towers" to a major industrial centre. He is best known for the incredible philanthropy, giving away no less than £30 million, two-thirds of which went to educational and medical causes. He was the founder of Nuffield College, Oxford, one of the few Oxbridge colleges named for a living person of the modern period. As a result of his generosity, a man who had no formal education past the age of fifteen, when he was apprenticed to a local bicycle maker, received honorary degrees from Oxford and seven other universities, was an Hon. Fellow of two Oxford Colleges, a Fellow of the Royal Society, and a Fellow of the Royal College of Surgeons. He was made a baronet in 1929, and then 1st Baron Nuffield in 1934, and 1st Viscount Nuffield in 1938. In 1958 he was made a Companion of Honour (C.H.). In his youth he was a champion cyclist. Nuffield's total wealth – £30 million given away, £3.3 million left for probate – puts him in the same class as Sir John Ellerman, 1st Bt. (1862-1933, *q.v.*) as a leviathan of wealth. He lived at Nuffield Place, Nuffield, near Henley-on-Thames, Oxfordshire.

5. (Hon.) Eleanor Georgiana Shelley-Rolls (1872-1961) – left £2,670,289. Landowner.

The daughter of John Allan Rolls, M.P. (1837-1912, left £249,776), of The Hendre near Monmouth, who was created 1st Baron Llangattock in 1912 and of (Hon.) Georgiana (1837-1923, left £57,730), daughter of Sir Charles Fitzroy Maclean, 9th Bt., in 1898 she married Sir John Shelley (later Shelley-Rolls), 6th Bt. (1871-1951, left £662,878), a grand-nephew of the poet Shelley. In 1883 her father owned 4,082 acres worth £3,710 p.a. in Monmouthshire, while her husband's forebear owned 6,500 acres worth £7,300 p.a. in Devon. These were relatively low figures, yet of our lady's probated estate of £2.7 million, £1,978,000 was in the form of settled land. She was known as a campaigner for women in engineering and was one of the founders of the Women's Engineering Society. She was also a keen hot-air balloonist. Her brother (Hon.) Charles Stewart Rolls (1877-1910, left £30,936) was the co-founder of Rolls-Royce. She lived at South Lodge, Knightsbridge SW7.

6. Joan Campbell (1887-1960) – left £2,238,870. Landowner and urban property owner in London.

The granddaughter of George Douglas Campbell, 8th Duke of Argyll (1823 – 1900, left £92,158), who in 1883 owned 175,114 acres worth £50,842 p.a. in Argyllshire and Dumbartonshire, she was the daughter of Lord George Campbell (1850-1915, left £33,399) and of Sybil (1860-1947, left £106,739), daughter of James Brace Alexander. She was unmarried, but was the lesbian companion of Margaret Emily "Pat" Dansey (d. 1959, left £20,902). Both were members of the Bloomsbury Group, and were friends of Virginia Woolf and Vita Sackville-West. Her wealth apparently derived in large part from her inheritance of urban land in the Bryanston Square area of London, although this is not entirely clear. She lived at 2 Bryanston Square, Marylebone and at Wythburn Court, Seymour Place W.1.

7. Mathilda Marks Kennedy (*nee* Marks) (1895-1964) – left £2,212,904. Inherited part of a famous multiple retailer, based in London.
The daughter of Michael Marks (1859-1907, left £31,113), the Russian-born co-founder of Marks & Spencer, the celebrated multiple retailer founded in Manchester but later based in London, and the sister of Simon Marks (1888-1964), Chairman of Marks & Spencer from 1916 until 1964, who was knighted in 1944 and created 1st Baron Marks of Broughton in 1961. (He left £1,830,935, just below the lowest valuation given here of persons deceased in 1960-64). In 1950, at the age of fifty-five, she married for the first time Terence Frank Kennedy (1907 in New York – 1997). The corporate headquarters of M & S was at Michael House, 37-67 Baker Street, London. A noted philanthropist, she was the founder of Mathilda Marks-Kennedy School, now in Mill Hill. She lived at 32 Upper Brook Street, W.1, and at Barton St. Mary, East Grinstead, Sussex.

8. Sir Jeremiah Colman, 2nd Bt. (1886-1961) – left £2,130,521. Inherited a mustard and starch fortune based in Norwich.
The son of Sir Jeremiah Colman, 1st Bt. (1859-1943, left £1,832,069, *q.v.*), the head of Reckitt & Colman, mustard and starch manufacturers of Norwich, he was educated at Winchester and at Trinity College, Cambridge. He was a director of Reckitt & Colman Holdings, and a J.P. of Hampshire and Surrey. He lived at Malshanger, Basingstoke, Hampshire.

9. Sir Henry Philip Price, 1st Bt. (1877-1963) – left £2,049,164. Men's clothing multiple retailer in Leeds and nationally.
In 1907, Price opened a tailor's shop in Leeds, which he developed into the "Fifty Shilling Tailors" chain, with branches throughout the country, especially in the North- at its peak it had 399 branches. It sold men's suits for £2.50, the equivalent of about £200 today. In 1953 the chain was sold to the United Drapery Stores, which renamed it John Collier. It continued to exist as a well-known chain until the 1980s. Price was the son of Joseph Price, a hosier and hatter of Headingley, Leeds. Our man was Chairman of the Executive Committee of the National Liberal Council, 1952-53, and one of the founders of the Royal Institute of International Affairs. He was made a knight in 1937 and a baronet in 1953. He lived at Wilbraham House, Wilbraham Place, Sloane Square W1., and at Wakehurst Place, Ardingly Sussex. Price left Wakehurst Place to the nation; it is now Kew Gardens' Millenium Seed Bank, an important national botanic institution.

10. Sir Maurice Bloch (1883-1964) – left £2,044,000. Distiller in Glasgow.
Born in Kovno, Lithuania, then in Russia, he came to Dundee around 1890 with his family. His

father Elias Bloch (1845-96, estate unlisted) was a "picture dealer" in Dundee. Bloch attended the Harris Academy in Dundee. His family was naturalised in 1910. With his brother, he established Bloch Brothers (Distillers) Ltd., first in Dundee and then in Glasgow. It was sold in 1954. Bloch was a leader of the Jewish community in Glasgow, and a notable philanthropist. He had the unenviable task of contesting the Gorbals constituency as a Conservative in the Parliamentary elections of 1929, 1931, and 1935, of course without success. He received a knighthood in 1937. A J.P. of Glasgow from 1921 till 1949, he was removed from this position when he was mentioned in the Lynskey Tribunal of 1948-49, which investigated alleged corruption in the Board of Trade, despite the fact that he was neither prosecuted for or convicted of any wrongdoing. He lived at 39 Newark Drive, Pollokshields, Glasgow.

10. Henry Edward Lyons, 1st Baron Ennisdale (1877-1963) – left £1,919,680. Insurance broker in the City of London.

One of the most mysterious of wealth holders and of newly created hereditary peers, he is described in reference works as the son of "John Edward Lyons of Ennis, Co. Clare." His father was indeed John Edward Lyons (c. 1852-1904, left £300), who was born in Chatham, Kent, and was a trumpeter with the 9th Lancers; he was described in the 1891 Census as a "musician," and in the 1901 Census as a "musician (Loyds)," whatever that means, of 92 Eland Road, Shaftesbury Park in Battersea. He had no known connection with Ireland. Our man was born in Battersea. His education is not given in any source. In reference works, he is described as a Major General during the First World War, but it is unclear if this is correct. He did serve in both the Boer War and the First World War. His career is similarly shrouded in mystery, although he was connected with Morgan Lyons & Co., Lloyds insurance brokers, of 149 Leadenhall Street, City of London. Lyons was given a baronetcy in 1937 and was created 1st Baron Ennisdale in 1939. The reasons for his high honours are similarly opaque, although he was a member of the executive of the Liberal National Party (the pro-tariff "Simonites" who abandoned Free Trade in 1931 and joined the National government); the implication is that he financially supported this small but powerful political grouping, and was rewarded. He was given his peerage in July 1939. Newspapers then had more important matters to report on, and his elevation to the Lords was apparently not questioned or explained. He was a member of the Lords for twenty-four years, but never spoke there at any time. Childless, his peerage died with him, although he did receive some publicity when his estate was probated and showed him to have been one of the richest men in England. In 1930 he lived at 19 Park Street, Grosvenor Square, Mayfair, and later at 29 St. James's Street SW1, and at Baynards Park, Cranleigh, Surrey.

11. Edward George Spencer-Churchill (1876-1964) – left £1,890,710. Landowner.

The grandson of the sixth Duke of Marlborough and the son of his younger son Lord Edward Spencer-Churchill (1853-1911, left £49,929), and of Augusta Warburton (d. 1941, left £29,027), he was educated at Eton and at Magdalen College, Oxford. He was a cousin of Sir Winston Churchill, and was a military officer who joined the Grenadier Guards in 1899. He served in the Boer War, winning two medals, and in the First World War (MC). Spencer-Churchill served as High Sheriff of Gloucestershire in 1924-25, and was a Trustee of the National Gallery from 1943-50. He apparently inherited land from relatives on his mother's side, as in 1883 the Duke of Marlborough owned 23,511 acres worth £36,557 p.a., and would almost certainly not have left a vast amount to a younger son. He lived at Northwick Park, Blockley, Gloucestershire.

12. Christopher William Hutley (1908-61) – left £1,875,785. Apparently a property developer, chiefly in Essex.

Little is known of the background or career of this rather mysterious millionaire. He was born in Ealing, the son of Christopher Hutley (1875-1942, left £900), of 30 Forest Drive, Theydon Bois, Essex. In 1911 our man was described in the Census as a "house carpenter (Bean Desert Hall)" (*sic*) of Longdon, Staffordshire, and in the 1939 Register as a "chartered secretary." In 1937 he lived at The Oaks, Hartford Road, Epping, Essex, and later at 29 Parkside, Westcliff-on-Sea, Essex." At his death, he was described as a property developer, and apparently was connected with the development of residential estates in Essex.

1965–1969

1. Guy Anthony Vandervell (1898-1967) – left £10,950,160. Automobile engine bearing manufacturer at Acton, Middlesex.

"Tony" Vandervell, as he was known, was the son of Charles Anthony Vandervell (1870-1955), founder of Lucas CAV, which manufactured diesel fuel-injection equipment and electrical equipment in London. He was very successful, and left £262,158. His son was a despatch rider during the First World war, and had been a motorcycle rider from the age of fifteen. He established Vendervell Products, with a factory at Western Avenue, Acton, which made "Thin Wall" engine bearings and other products. He became known as the financial backer of British racing car teams, employing such drivers as Stirling Moss. In 1958 his team won six of the eleven Formula One races held that year. At his death, his heirs attempted to avoid paying death duties and were involved in a well-known legal case, *Vandervell v. Inland Revenue Commissioners (1967)*, which they lost. He lived at Brockhurst Park, Stoke Poges, Buckinghamshire and at 21 Sloane Avenue SW3.

2. Sir (Alfred) Chester Beatty (1875-1968) – left £7,181,000. Mining engineer around the world; his central office was in the City of London.

Born in New York, the son of John Cumming Beatty, and educated at Westminster School in Dobbs Ferry, New York and then at the Columbia University School of Mines and at Princeton University, he became a consulting engineer with the Guggenheim Exploration Co., which developed silver and copper mines in Mexico and, especially, in Rhodesia. He then established his own mining company, the Selection Trust Co., whose premises were at One London Wall, City of London. He initially shared his office with Herbert Hoover, also a mining engineer and later the 31st President of the United States of America. Beatty's new firm developed mines all over the world, from Serbia and Siberia to, in particular, Northern Rhodesia. Remarkably, Beatty never visited most of the countries in which his mines were located, giving accurate supervision from London. He became a naturalised British subject in 1933 and was knighted in 1954. From 1950 he lived in Dublin, Ireland. He is also well-known for his remarkable collection of Indian and Persian miniatures, ancient manuscripts, and Impressionist paintings, which he left to the Irish nation. It is now housed in a museum and library at Dublin Castle. In 1956 he was made an Honorary Citizen of Ireland. In London he lived at Baroda House, 24 Kensington Palace Gardens, and in Ireland at 10 Ailesbury Road, Ballsbridge, Dublin. His son Alfred Chester Beatty (d.1983) left £12,454,317.

3. Charles Leonard Arnold (1885-1969) – left £5,829,618. Electrical plug and socket manufacturer in Edmonton, London.

The inventor of the 3-pinned safety socket, now ubiquitous in the UK, he was born in Peckham, the son of Charles Fearnely Arnold (1847-1912, left £2360), a flour salesman who lived at East Dulwich when he died. Our man was educated at the South London Telegraph Training College, and served in World War One as a captain (despatches). Before that war, he was a partner with Charles Reginald Belling (see below), who founded Belling & Co. to make electrical fires. When Arnold became a soldier, he sold his interest in the firm to Belling. In 1919, he established the Heavy Current Electric Accessories Co., later known as MK Electric, of Wakefield Street, Edmonton N.18, which manufactured his safety sockets. He remained Chairman of the firm until 1968. Arnold lived at 66 The Ridgway, Enfield Chase, Enfield.

4. Gerald Hugh Grosvenor, 4th Duke of Westminster (1907-67) – left £5,489,000. Urban property owner in London and landowner.

The son of (Capt.) Lord Hugh William Grosvenor (1884-1914, left £32,347), who was killed in action in France in the First World War, he was educated at Eton and at Sandhurst, and succeeded his cousin as Duke of Westminster in 1963. One of the richest men in Britain, the owner of most of the ground rents of Mayfair and Belgravia, as well as land in Cheshire, he held the title for only four years. He had joined the 9th Lancers in 1926, and was a Lieutenant-Colonel in the Lancers during World War Two, winning the DSO in 1942. He served as Exon of the Queen's Bodyguard from 1952-64, and was then Lord Steward of the Queen's Household, 1964-67. P.C., 1964. He served as High Sheriff of Cheshire in 1959-60. The Duke lived at Saighton Grange, Chester. He was succeeded by his brother Robert, 5th Duke of Westminster (1910-79).

5. William Pleydell-Bouverie, 7th Earl of Radnor (1895-1968) – left £4,552,599. Landowner.

The son of Jacob, 6th Earl of Radnor (1868-1930, left £387,653), he was educated at Harrow and at the Royal Agricultural College, Cirencester. In 1883 his forebear owned 24,870 acres worth £42,900 p.a. in Wiltshire, Kent, and Berkshire, plus lands in London. Our man served in the First World War (wounded). He was Chairman of the Forestry Commission, 1952-63, the Official Verderer of the New Forest, 1964-66, and Lord Warden of the Stannaries, 1933-65. He was made a Knight of the Garter in 1960. Lord Radnor lived at Longford Castle, Salisbury, Wiltshire. He was succeeded by his son Jacob, 8th Earl of Radnor (1927-2008).

6. Kenneth Peter Allpress (1917-68) – left £4,500,000. Civil engineering contractor, based in London.

The son of William Peter Allpress (1881-1946), a civil engineer who founded the William Press (sic) Group in 1913, he was born in Guildford, Surrey, and was educated at St. John's College, Cambridge. He became head of the firm, which was mainly concerned with laying pipelines. On passenger ship manifests, he was described in 1951 as a "contractor," and in 1954 as a "civil engineering contractor." In 1948 his business premises were at 32 Old Queen Street, Westminster. Very little has been written on his company, which operated internationally. His widow, Mary Joyce Allpress, nee Evans (1918-84) left £2,231,328. He lived at Wolvers, Reigate, Surrey.

7. Charles Reginald Belling (1884-1965) – left £2,845,459. Electrical goods manufacturer at

Enfield, London and Burnley, Lancashire.

The pioneer manufacturer of the type of electrical heaters found in many British homes, he was born in Bodmin, Cornwall, the son of Thomas Samuel Belling (1837-88, estate unlisted), a dentist, and was educated at Burts Grammar School, Lostwithiel, at the Crossley School, Halifax, and at technical colleges. He was apprenticed in 1903 to Crompton & Co. of Chelmsford. In 1912 with Charles Leonard Arnold (see above) he established a firm to manufacture electrical heaters, and invented the more efficient firebar heater. In 1913 he opened a large factory to produce his goods at Edmonton, and moved to Enfield in 1924, where his firm, Belling & Co., employed 500 workers. In 1955 he opened another factory at Burnley, Lancashire, his firm also producing electrical cookers and other products. He died at sea on a cruise near the Bahamas. His wife Cicely (d. 1992) left £484,062. Belling lived at Owl Hall Farm, Cattlegate Road, Enfield, Middlesex.

8. Francis Bernard Winham (1900-67) – left £2,654,337. Property developer in London.

Little is known of the career of Francis Bernard Winham, a very successful post-war property developer in London. He was the son of Charles Alfred Winham (1867-1938, estate unlisted), described in the 1911 Census as a "collector of King's (*sic*) taxes and house agent" of Croydon, Surrey, where his son was born, and of Frances Alice *nee* Dewey (1869-1950, left £552). He was married to Gwendoline Dorothy *nee* Ashton (1908-2003), and lived at 103A Park Street, W1. His brother George Alfred Winham (1897-1967) was a Roman Catholic priest in Uckfield, Sussex.

9. Urban Huttleston Rogers Broughton, 1st Baron Fairhaven (1896-1966) – left £2,485,191. Inherited a petroleum and investment fortune from his American grandmother.

From a very unusual background, Urban Broughton was born in Fairhaven, Massachusetts. He was the son of Urban Hanlon Broughton (1857-1929, left £104,923), born in England to a family who moved to America, where he was a civil engineer. He was installing sewerage piping at the home of the American millionaire Henry Huttleston Rogers, who had made a vast fortune as an associate of John D. Rockefeller of Standard Oil, and was also a successful investor, when he married Rogers's newly widowed daughter, Cara Leland Duff (1868-1939, left £725,050). Urban Hanlon Broughton and his family moved back to the UK, where he became a Conservative M.P. from 1915-18, and purchased a mansion at 37 Park Street, Mayfair and an estate at Park Close, Englefield Green, Surrey. He was to have been awarded a peerage in 1929 but died before it could be announced. The peerage was then granted to his son, our man, as 1st Baron Fairhaven, who in the meantime had inherited an estimated $12.5 million (£2.5 million) from his maternal great-grandmother. Our man was educated at St. Paul's School in Concord, New Hampshire and then at Harrow and Sandhurst. He served in the First Life Guards from 1916-24 and as a Liaison Officer with the Red Cross in the Second World War. He was known as a racehorse owner and an art collector of note. In 1961 a second hereditary barony, also as Baron Fairhaven, was conferred upon him, with a special remainder to his brother Henry, later 2nd Baron Fairhaven (1900-73, left £2,162,173), as our man was unmarried. In 1928 his father had given Ashridge House to the Conservative party and in 1929 his mother bought the land around Runnymede, where Magna Carta was signed, and donated it to the nation. Our man lived at Anglesey Abbey, Lode, Cambridgeshire, at 16 St. James's Square SW1, and at 37 Grosvenor Square W1.

10. Roland Hoopes Parker (1888-1967) – £2,358,765. Executive at F.W. Woolworths,

multiple retailers throughout the UK.

Like William Lawrence Stephenson (see above) he was an executive with F.W. Woolworths, the consumer products and goods retailers with branches throughout the UK, from its headquarters in Marylebone. He was born in Wilmington, Delaware, the son of Joseph Warner Parker (1859-1947), a life insurance salesman, and was brought to England around 1910 by F.W. Woolworth, the firm's founder, as an importer and buyer of products sold in its shops. He was the firm's Chief Buyer in Britain for the rest of his career. In an application for a passport in 1915, he was described as a "travelling importer for F.W. Woolworth," and on his US draft card in 1917, as a "Superintendant chain of stores." He also had property in Rhodesia and South Africa. His British-born wife, Emily Laura *nee* Marriott (1897-1987) left £4,833,651. They lived at Flat 81, Grosvenor House, Park Lane W1.

1970–1979

The 1970s show a clear increase in the maximum size of great fortunes. This trend began even before Margaret Thatcher was first elected as Prime Minister in 1979 and marginal rates of taxation were systematically reduced, and continued unabated until the present, such that the levels of great wealth indicated here now seem ludicrously low, even taking inflation into account. This process will also be discussed in the next section. The later 1970s also show the great growth in the value of land and property, with six of the top ten estates probated in 1975-79 being left by traditional hereditary landowners or by property developers. This trend would also continue, although new forms of entrepreneurship, especially in computing and information technology, would also come to the fore around the world.

1970–1974

1. Sir John Reeves Ellerman, 2nd Bt. (1909-73) – left £53,238,370. Shipowner and newspaper owner in the City of London.

The only son of Sir John Reeves Ellerman, 1st Bt. (1862-1933, *q.v.*), shipowner who was Britain's richest man and left £37 million, he was educated at Malvern College, where he wrote an anti-sport novel, *Why Do They Like It?* using the name E.L. Black. At the age of twenty-four, when his father died, he became Britain's richest man and had to pay £20 million in death duties. He inherited his father's shipping company, Ellerman Lines, of 19-21 Moorgate, City of London, and was also, like his father, a major investor in the Fleet Street press. Although lacking his father's business genius, he was by all accounts a competent company chairman. Elllerman Lines became one of the first shipping companies to use containerisation on a major scale, and he modernised its routes and ships. His major interest, however, was in natural history, and he became probably the world's greatest expert on the rodent family, producing many monographs and learned articles on this subject, including a three-volume, 1500-page work on *Families and Genera of Living Rodents* (1940-49). In 1933 he married Esther (d.1984), daughter of Clarence De Sola of Montreal, from a Jewish family. (Because of their surname and vast wealth, the Ellermans were often assumed to be Jewish, but they had no Jewish ancestry.) Like his father, he was also frequently attacked in the Beaverbrook press, apparently because of an old quarrel between Lord Beaverbrook and the first baronet. Our man lived at Chalfont St. Giles, Buckinghamshire and in a permanent suite at the Dorchester Hotel on Park Lane (which he presumably had little trouble in booking, since he owned the hotel). He also spent increasing time in a seaside mansion at Cape Town, South Africa. He died at sixty-three, without children or, apart from his wife and sister, the writer "Bryher," with whom he was not on speaking terms, any close relatives; his shipping assets were reorganised as a charitable trust, now known as The John Ellerman Foundation. His estate of £53 million was by far the largest, in nominal terms, ever left in the UK up till then.

2. Felix Donovan Fenston (1915-70) – left £12,670,566. Property developer in London.
One of the wealthiest of the post-war property developers, chiefly in London, he was born in Paddington. His father Joseph Fenston (1889-1963, left £204,825) was born as Joseph Feinstein in Switzerland and was naturalised in 1913. He was described as a theatrical impresario, but, according to the 1939 UK Register, was then an "iron and metal merchant." He married Mona Theresa Donovan (1895-1928), of Irish descent. (Our man was buried as an Anglican.) Felix Fenston was educated at the Regent Street Polytechnic and at the College of Estate Management, and worked as an estate agent; in the 1939 UK Register, he was described as a "surveyor." He served as a Corporal during World War Two, but during the War lost a leg in a motorcycle accident. After the War he began as a property developer with an office on Piccadilly but then worked from his home, 19 Hill Street, Mayfair. Fenston introduced several novel means of property finance, and was in partnership with the (notorious) property developer Harry Hyams, but fell out with him. Most of Fenston's activities involved office rebuilding in London; in 1959, he was said to be worth £4 million. He had a wide variety of interests, some unexpected, such as his establishment of a museum of heraldry. Married three times, he died of a heart attack at fifty-five on a train between Inverness and London. He lived at 19 Hill Street, Mayfair at Ockham Park, Surrey, and at a Manor House near Guildford.

3. (Albert Edward) Harry Meyer Archibald Primrose, 6th Earl of Rosebery (1882-1974) – left £9,941,699. Landowner and inherited merchant banking wealth in the City of London.
The son of Archibald Primrose, 5th Earl of Rosebery (1847-1929, left £1,641,706, *q.v.*), landowner and Prime Minister 1894-95 and of Hannah (d. 1890, left £764,883), daughter of Baron Meyer de Rothschild of the great merchant banking family, he was educated at Eton and Sandhurst. In 1883 his father's family owned 32,411 acres worth £36,479 p.a. in Midlothian and six other counties. His father had been created 1st Earl of Midlothian in the UK peerage – Rosebery was a title in the Scottish peerage – in 1911 – so our man was also 2nd Earl of Midlothian. He served in the Grenadier Guards in the First World War (wounded, DSO, despatches), and was Captain of the Surrey XI cricket team. Rosebery served as Secretary of State for Scotland in Churchill's Conservative government in 1945, and was Lord Lieutenant of Midlothian, 1929-64 and Chairman of the National Liberal Party, 1945-47. He was made a Knight of the Thistle in 1947. Rosebery lived at Mentmore Towers, Leighton Buzzard, Bedfordshire, which he inherited from the Rothschilds, and at Dalmeny House, West Lothian.

4. (Joseph) Arthur Rank, 1st Baron Rank (1888-1972) – left £5,993,323. Wholesale flour miller and cinema producer and theatre chain owner based in London and Hull.
J. Arthur Rank, as he was known, was the son of Joseph Rank (1854-1943), who developed a

nation-wide flour milling business based in Hull, where our man was born. He was educated at the Leys School in Cambridge, a Methodist public school; our man was a devout Methodist throughout his life, and entered the film business in part to counteract the allegedly debasing nature of Hollywood films. He served in the First World War as a Captain in the Royal Field Artillery. Our man's brother, who had headed the business, James Voase Rank (1881-1952. *q.v.*) left £1,632,916. After his death, he became head of the family flour milling business, serving as its Chairman from 1952-69. Its corporate headquarters were at 107-112 Leadenhall Street, City of London. It had been incorporated in 1933, with a market value of £7 million. In 1917 he had married (Hon.) Laura (d. 1971, left £823,741), daughter of Sir Horace Marshall, 1st Baron Marshall of Chipstead (d. 1936), a Methodist businessman who left £182,151. Our man's flour business later became part of Rank Hovis McDougall. In the late 1930s Rank entered a totally new field, becoming probably the most important movie producer of his time in the UK, with Rank's iconic symbol at the beginning of his films, a strongman banging an enormous gong, becoming universally known. Rank made such famous British films as *Henry V, Hamlet, Great Expectations,* and *Kind Hearts and Coronets,* from its studios at Pinewood and at Ealing. The firm also owned the Odeon cinema chain and other associated businesses. In 1952 he was created 1st Baron Rank. He lived at Sutton Manor, Scotney, Hampshire.

5. Hugh William Osbert Molyneux, 7th Earl of Sefton (1898-1972) – left £5,242,848. Landowner.

The son of Osbert, 6th Earl of Sefton (1871-1930, left £1,758,376, *q.v.*), he was educated at Harrow and at Sandhurst. The family owned valuable land in and near Liverpool and in Lancashire. He was an officer in the Royal Horse Guards from 1917-30, serving in the First World War. He served as an Aide-de-Camp to the Governor-General of Canada in 1919, to the Viceroy of India in 1936, and was Lord-in-Waiting to the King, 1936-7. Sefton also served at Lord Mayor of Liverpool in 1944-45. He was a noted racehorse owner and was Chairman of the Stewards of the British Jockey Club. In 1941 he married Josephine (1907-80, left £7,607,168); they were close friends of the Duke and Duchess of Windsor. He died without heirs and the title became extinct. Lord Sefton lived at Croxteth Hall, Liverpool, at Abbeystead, Lancashire, and at Grosvenor Cottage, Culross Street, Mayfair.

6. (Hon.) Olive Cecilia (*nee* Paget), Lady Baillie (1899-1974) – left £4,360,976. Inherited oil and banking money from her American ancestors.

She was the daughter of Almaric Paget, 1st Baron Queenborough (1861-1949, left £255,276), of Canfield Place, Hatfield, Hertfordshire, a right-wing Conservative M.P. from 1910 till 1917, who was given a peerage in 1918; his great-grandfather was Henry Paget, 1st Marquess of Anglesey, who commanded the Cavalry at Waterloo. Her mother was Pauline Payne Whitney (1874-1916, left £220,920), of the very wealthy Whitney family of New York, involved in oil and banking, who were estimated to be worth $100 million. Our lady inherited $2 million from her mother shortly before her death and millions more from other members of the Whitney family. She was educated in France and served as a nurse during the First World War. She was married three times and divorced twice. Her second husband, Arthur Wilson-Filmer (1895-1968), of the wealthy Wilson ship owning family, in 1926-27 bought Leeds Castle at Maidstone, Kent, which she kept after their divorce in 1930. Her third husband, married in 1931, was Sir Adrian William Maxwell

Baillie, 6th Bt. (1898-1947), a Conservative M.P. from 1931-35 and 1937-45. She spent a fortune repairing and upgrading Leeds Castle, where she lived – and which, confusingly, is located in Kent, not in Yorkshire – where she acted as a major Society hostess, entertaining a wide variety of people ranging from the Prince of Wales and Mrs. Simpson to Douglas Fairbanks and to von Ribbentrop, then the German Ambassador to the UK. A chain smoker, she was in an oxygen tank in her last years. There is a biography of her by Alan Bignall, *Lady Baillie of Leeds Castle* (2007). Her inheritance of vast American wealth was somewhat similar to that of Lord Fairhaven (see above), although her father was also a product of the British aristocracy.

7. Harold Keith Salvesen (1897-1970) – left £4,116,000. Shipowner and whale oil proprietor in Edinburgh.
The son of Theodore Emil Salvesen (1863-1942), shipowner of Edinburgh and whale oil proprietor, he was educated at the Edinburgh Academy and at University College, Oxford in PPE. He was then a Fellow of New College and taught economics; his pupils included Hugh Gaitskell and Richard Crossman. Our man always regarded himself as a Labour supporter, although he opposed nationalisation. During the First World War he was a Captain in the Indian Army (despatches). After teaching at Oxford, he joined the family firm of ship owners established by his grandfather Christian Salvesen (1823-1911), of Norwegian descent, who left £209,384, and became its Chairman in 1945. The millionaire ship owner Frederick Salvesen (18 70-1933, *q.v.*) was his uncle. One of his firm's main activities was in whaling, now illegal and regarded with horror. He lived at Inveralmond, Cramind, Edinburgh.

8. Francis John Wallis (1913-72) – left £3,163,193. Proprietor of a supermarket chain based in Rainham, Essex.
Little has been written about the proprietor of the F.J. Wallis chain of supermarkets, founded after the Second World War by Francis John Wallis. He was the son of Frederick John Wallis, about whom little could be traced, and Millicent Agnes *nee* Pooles (1884-1975, left £7783. In 1968 his firm had thirty-eight stores, with its headquarters at Rainham, Essex. In 1977, after his death, it was sold to International Stores. In 1939 he was described in the UK National Register as a "manager- bakery and provisions," of Ilford, Essex. He died in a small plane which crashed in the Pyrenees along with another executive of a grocery chain. Wallis lived at Wallsgrove House, High Beech, Loughton, Essex.

9. Edward Bishop Boughton (1881-1972) – left £2,932,716. Automobile and aircraft parts manufacturer in Leamington, London, etc.
The son of a grocer in Aylesbury, William Rutland Boughton (1841-1905, estate unlisted) he was a motor engineer in Coventry, and then, in 1920, the founder and head of the Automotive Parts Co., located in Leamington and at 3 Berners Street, London, which made automobile brakes and aircraft parts. It held many patents. He later added the Purolator oil filter company to his firm, and had factories at Bolton and Liverpool. In the 1939 UK Register he was an "engineer-mechanical and company director." Boughton lived at Towngate, Fairmile Lane, Cobham, Surrey. He was the brother of the well-known composer Rutland Boughton (1878-1960), who was also a long-time member of the British Communist party. Rutland Boughton left only £1329, suggesting that our man was not generous to his radical brother.

10. Eileen Daphne Solvia (*sic*) Rogerson (*nee* Joel) (1907-74) – left £2,874,078. Inherited a gold and diamond fortune from South Africa and the City of London.

The daughter of the "Randlord" Solomon Barnato Joel (1865-1931, left £1,000,000, *q.v.*), of the very wealthy Joel/Barnato family of diamond and gold millionaires; her father had also been Chairman of the Johannesburg Stock Exchange and had his financial offices at 10/11 Austin Friars, City of London. Her mother was Ellen *nee* Ridley (d. 1919). She was born in London and, in 1931, married Frank Leslie John Rogerson (1902-87, left £2,178,102), who was a Flight Lieutenant in the RAF in the Second World War, and was then a stockbroker in London. They lived at Guildenhurst Manor, Billingshurst, Sussex.

11. Yvonne Studd-Trench-Gascoigne (1919-73) – left £2,837,959. Landowner.

The daughter of Sir Alvary Douglas Frederick Trench-Gascoigne (1893-1970, left £472,711) of Lotherton Hall, Yorkshire and 66 Bishops Avenue N2, an old Etonian career diplomat who was Consul-General at Tangier, Morocco during the Second World War, where he rescued Jews fleeing Hitler, and then the Political Representative of the UK in Japan, 1946-51, and finally Ambassador to the USSR, 1951-53, who was knighted in 1947. In 1883 the family of his father Frederick Richard Trench-Gascoigne (1851-1937, left £688,977) owned 19,355 acres worth £16,339 p.a. in the West Riding, Argyllshire, Co. Limerick, etc. Our lady inherited Lotherton Hall near Leeds from him. The family property included collieries in the West Riding. In 1952 she married (Flight Lieutenant) Charles Kynaston Studd (1895-1959, left £2,720), of a landed family which in 1883 owned 4,243 acres worth £4452 p.a. in England and Scotland. Our lady lived at 126 Sloane Street SW1 and at Diptford Court by Totnes, Devon. She died in Santa Barbara, California at the age of fifty-three.

12. Miriam Sieff, Lady Marks of Broughton (1894-1972) – left £2,744,894. Wife and sister of the founders and heads of Marks & Spencer, multiple retailers.

The daughter of Ephraim Sieff (1863-1936, left £242,116), Lithuanian-born textile manufacturer of Manchester, and the sister of Israel Sieff, Baron Sieff (1889-1972, left £164,808), in 1915 she married her brother's business partner Simon Marks, 1st Baron Marks of Broughton (1888-1964, left £1,830,935), whose sister had married her brother Israel Sieff. Marks & Spencer was in the process of emerging as probably the foremost multiple retail chain in the UK, a legendary household name, famous for its high-quality goods. Like other members of her family, she was a notable philanthropist and a significant figure in the Zionist movement. Her nephew Sir Marcus Sieff, later Baron Sieff of Brimpton (1913-2001, left £4,657,846) was Chairman of the firm from 1972 until his death, and was given a life peerage in 1980. She lived at Titlarks Farm, Sunningdale, Surrey.

13. George Herbert Cross (1884-1972) – left £2,192,096. Property developer in London.

As with many property developers, little is known of his career. He was born in Islington, the son of John Cross (1840-1914, left £5135), a butcher who lived in Peckham at the time of his death. In the 1911 Census, our man was described as an "estate agent" of Randolph House, Coventry Street, N W1, possibly his business address. In the 1939 National Register, he was described as a "landowner" of Salisbury, Wiltshire. In 1913 he married Gertrude Alice Boden (b.1890), from whom he was divorced in 1924. At the time of his death Cross was living at The Dower House,

Compton Chamberlayne, Salisbury, Wiltshire.

14. Henry Rogers Broughton, 2nd Baron Fairhaven (1900-73) – left £2,162,173. Inherited a petroleum and investment fortune from his American grandmother.
The younger brother of Urban Broughton, 1st Baron Fairhaven (1896-1966, left £2,485,191, *q.v.*), he succeeded to his peerage by special remainder, with his wealth derived from the same sources. He was educated at Harrow and at Sandhurst. He was an army officer from 1919 until 1933 and during the Second World War. He lived at South Walsham Hall, Norwich and at 56 Eaton Place SW1.

1975-1979

1. Count Antoine Edward Seilern (1901-78) – left £30,836,261 in England. Inherited banking and newspaper wealth in the USA and an art collector in London.
From the Austrian nobility, the son of Count Carl Seilern und Anspang (1866-1940) of Vienna and Antoinette Woerishoffer (1875-1901, left £33,345 in England), who died a few days after he was born, he inherited a fortune from his maternal grandmother, Anna Woerishoffer (1850-1931) of Vienna and New York, whose family were bankers in New York and owned America's German-language newspaper the *New Yorker Staats-Zeitung*. He studied engineering in England and then art history at Vienna University. Seilern moved to England permanently in 1939 and served as an interpreter in the Royal Artillery during the Second World War. Apart from the American money he inherited, Seilern built up one of the greatest private art collections of modern times in England, which included 32 paintings by Rubens and 12 by Tiepolo, among many others. Seilern was respected in the art world as an erudite writer on art, as well as a great collector, and produced several volumes describing his art works. He left his entire collection to the Courtauld Gallery, now located at Somerset House on The Strand. His enormous probate valuation almost certainly included the value of his art collection. He lived in a mansion at 56 Princes Gate, SW7 and in Salzburg, Austria.

2. William Thomas George Wentworth-Fitzwilliam, 10th Earl Fitzwilliam (1904-79) – left £11,776,640. Landowner.
The son of George Charles Wentworth-Fitzwilliam (d. 1935, left £120,380), a great-grandson of the 5th Earl Fitzwilliam, he was educated at Eton and at Magdalene College, Cambridge, He served in the Second World War (American Bronze Star), and was a MFH. He was Chairman of the Milton (Peterborough) Estates Co. In 1883 the Earl Fitzwilliam of that time (see previous section) owned 115,743 acres worth £138,801 p.a. in Yorkshire, Co. Wicklow, etc. Our man succeeded a distant cousin, Eric, 9th Earl Fitzwilliam (1883-1952, left £94,227). He died without male heirs and the title became extinct. He lived at Wentworth Woodhouse near Rotherham, Yorkshire and at Milton Hall, Peterborough, Cambridgeshire, two of the largest private residences in the UK.

3. Thomas William Edward Coke, 5th Earl of Leicester (1908-76) – left £11,576,876. Landowner.

The son of Thomas, 4th Earl of Leicester (1880-1949, left £362,181), he was educated at Eton and Sandhurst, and served as an officer in the Scots Guards from 1938. From 1952 till 1956 he was a Lieutenant-Colonel in the Home Guard. He was an Extra Equerry to King George VI, 1937-52 and then to Queen Elizabeth II from 1952. In 1931 he married Lady Elizabeth Yorke (1912-85, left £406,411), daughter of the 8th Earl of Hardwicke and Lady of the Bedchamber to the Queen, 1955-73. His heir was his cousin, Anthony, 6th Earl of Leicester (1909-94). Our man lived at Holkham Hall, Holkham, Leicestershire.

4. Sir Richard James Boughey, 10th Bt. (1925-78) – left £5,956,143. Landowner.
The son of Sir George Menteth Boughey, 9th Bt. (1879-1959), an official in the Indian Civil Service who left only £888, he was educated at Eton, and served as a Lieutenant in the Coldstream Guards in 1943-46. He was High Sheriff of Sussex in 1964-65, and Liaison Officer to the Ministry of Agriculture, 1965-71. In 1883 his predecessor owned 10,975 acres worth £16,715 p.a., chiefly in Staffordshire. How our man became so wealthy is unclear: he owned residences in Sussex and Hampshire which must have come into the family after 1883, but the enormous size of his probated estate was unexpected, especially as his father left only a trivial sum. His son and successor, Sir John, 11th Bt. (b. 1959) is a medical practitioner who was educated at what is now the University of Zimbabwe. Our man lived at Ringmer Park, Sussex and at The Old Rectory, Quarley, Hampshire.

5. Joseph Sunlight (1889-1978) – left £5,714,422. Property developer and architect in Manchester and Cheshire.
Born in Belorussia, he came as an infant with his parents to Manchester in 1890. His father, Joseph Schimschlavitch (1864-1945, left £201) changed his name to "Sunlight" and was a cotton merchant in Manchester. Our man was educated at a private school at Kingston-upon-Thames, then trained as an architect in Manchester, and built houses and offices in and near Manchester. His art deco Sunlight House, built in 1932-33, fourteen stories high, was said to be the first skyscraper in the north of England. Sunlight's most notable building was the South Manchester Synagogue at Fallowfield, built in Moorish style. Most anomalously, Sunlight served as Liberal M.P. for Shrewsbury in 1923-24, when the vote was split between the three main parties, and the Liberals managed to elect M.P.s in some solidly Tory seats. This was the only time after 1885 that the seat was not won by the Conservatives. Sunlight was one of the wealthiest property developers to operate in the north of England rather than in the London area. His offices were at 14 Victoria Square, Manchester; he lived at Hallside, Knutsford, Cheshire. Rather unexpectedly, he has an entry in the *ODNB*.

6. Arnold Cass Lycett Wills (1906-78) – left £4,806,369. A tobacco fortune in Bristol.
A member of the enormously wealthy Wills family of Imperial Tobacco of Bristol, he lived at a time when cigarette smoking was known to be gravely harmful, and was restricted in many ways. Despite this, he left one of the larger fortunes of the time. He was the grandson of Sir Edward Payson Wills 1st Bt. (1834-1910, left £2.6 million, *q.v.*) and the son of Arnold Stancomb Wills (1877-1961, left £889,947), and was educated at Harrow and at Cambridge. He served as a Captain in the 24th Lancers during the Second World War, and was High Sheriff of Northamptonshire in 1935-6. Wills was a First Class cricketer for Northamptonshire, and lived at Thornby Hall, Northampton.

7. William Arthur Henry Cavendish-Bentinck, 7th Duke of Portland (1893-1977) – left £4,391,476. Landowner.

One of the wealthiest landed families, in 1883 his predecessor owned 183,199 acres worth £88,350 p.a. in Nottinghamshire, Ayrshire, Northumberland, and six other counties (see previous section). He was the son of William, 6th Duke of Portland (1857-1943, left £210,916) and was educated at Eton. He was a Lieutenant in the Royal Horse Guards, and then served as a Conservative M.P. in 1922-43, when he succeeded to the title. He held office as a Junior Lord of the Treasury in 1928-29 and 1931, and was Lord Lieutenant of Nottinghamshire, 1939-62. He died without male heirs, and the title (as an earl, not a duke) passed to a distant relative, Ferdinand, 8th Earl of Portland (1888-1980), who lived in Kenya and left £30,016 in England. Our man's main residence was at Wellbeck Woodhouse, Worksop, Nottinghamshire.

8. Philip Edward Rose (1926-77) – left £4,277,635. Property developer and investment banker in London.

Little could be traced about Philip Edward Rose. He was probably the son of Jack Rose (*nee* Rosenberg, 1895-1979), who left £186,823, and Sarah *nee* Cohen (1902-71), although this is not entirely clear. Our man was a property developer and investment banker in London, although the details are unclear. He was born in the St. Pancras district of London and lived at 28 Crawford Street W1 when he died, aged fifty-one, in 1977. After his death his family established the Rose Foundation, named for him and Jack Rose, a relative, which gives small grants for building projects in London.

9. Robert Walter Houchin (1916-78) – left £4,136,118. Manufacturer of aviation ground support equipment at Ashford, Kent.

The son of Robert Thomas Houchin (1890-1961, left £43,408), a farmer of Ruckings, Kent, in the 1939 UK Register he was described as an "electrical/mechanical engineer." Our man received a pilot's license in 1950. He became the head of Houchin Aviation of Ashford, Kent, which manufactured diesel-driven aviation ground support equipment and other aviation equipment. He was a Churchwarden of St. Mary's Anglican Church at Hinxhill near Ashford, Kent, where he has a memorial plaque. His firm closed down in 2014. He lived at Hinxhill Court, Hinxhill, Ashford, Kent.

10. Edmond Cecil Harmsworth, 2nd Viscount Rothermere (1898-1978) – Newspaper proprietor in London.

The son of the press-lord Harold Harmsworth, 1st Viscount Rothermere (1868-1940, left £335,308, *q.v.*) and the nephew of Alfred Harmsworth, 1st Viscount Northcliffe (1865-1922, left £5.2 million, *q.v.*), he was educated at Eton. His father and uncle are often said to have founded modern populistic journalism by establishing the *Daily Mail* in 1896. Our man served in the First World War, in which two of his brothers were killed, and was ADC to Lloyd George in 1919 at the Paris Peace Conference. From 1919-29 he served as a Conservative M.P. – he was first elected aged twenty-one – and became Chairman of the *Daily Mail* and head of Associated Newspapers Ltd. from 1932 to 1971. He was also Chairman of the Newspaper Proprietors Association from 1934 to 1961. Rothermere also had other economic interests such as paper manufacturing. A well-known member of London "Society," he was a friend of Mrs. Simpson, and it was he who suggested to Stanley Baldwin that Edward VIII be allowed to enter into a morganatic marriage with her, in which she did not become Queen; the suggestion was rejected. Rothermere was married three times. His second wife, Ann Charteris, Lady O'Neill, whom he married in 1945, divorced him in 1952 to marry Ian Fleming, the author of the James Bond novels. An indication of how incredibly the size of large personal fortunes have expanded since the 1970s is that his heir Vere Harmsworth, 3rd Viscount Rothermere (1925-98) left £60,219,897. Our man lived at Daylesford near Chipping Norton, Oxfordshire and at 11 South Audley Street, Mayfair.

Chapter 6: Wealth in Contemporary Britain

1990–2020

1990 saw the earliest of the *Sunday Times Rich Lists*. There was at least one previous attempt, in 1969, to create a list of Britain's richest people. It differed from the probate valuations in that families as well as individual persons were sometimes included, as was the case with more recent "Rich Lists." All such lists give alleged information about living persons and families, not about the recently deceased. The probate valuations are based on actual financial records submitted to the Principal Probate Registry, while the *Rich Lists* are always based on estimates made by those claiming to know the actual facts, but which are not based on personal financial records. On 31 March 1969 the *Daily Express* newspaper published a list of Britain's richest men and families. According to it, there were five fortunes said to be worth £100 million or more, those of Garfield Weston, the Canadian born head of Associated British Foods, said to be worth £200 million; the Pilkington glass family (£200 million); Lord Cowdray, petrol and engineering (£150 million); Sir John Ellerman, shipping (£150 million); and the Moores football pools family (£125 million). It is not possible to know how accurate these estimates were, or how extensive was the authors' research, but Sir John Ellerman (*q.v.*) died in 1973, leaving £53 million, about one-third of the newspaper's estimate. As he had no children, it is likely that his probate valuation was more or less accurate.

On the first *Sunday Times Rich List,* that of 1990, the ten wealthiest persons and families were as follows (with comments):

1. H.M. The Queen – £6,700 billion, with Prince Charles credited with a further £200 million.
The real wealth of The Queen and Royal Family are shrouded in mystery, and a wide range of estimates can be found. *Forbes* magazine claimed in 2021 that the Royal Family was worth $28 billion, about £20 billion, while the 2015 *Rich List* estimated her wealth at only £275 million. Apart from secrecy, difficulties arise from determining what belongs to the Queen in a personal capacity, what is owned by the Crown, the institution of Britain's monarchy, and what is owned by the British government. For instance, could Her Majesty sell Buckingham Palace? Almost certainly not, but no one ever looks too closely at the actual legal status of the Queen's possessions, and probably could not do so. It seems that most recent claims about the wealth of the Royal Family have lowered the estimated size of their wealth, but apart from the Royals no one knows the truth. The only member of the Royal Family who is included in this work was the 1st Duke of Fife (d. 1912, *q.v.*), who had been 6th Earl of Fife when he married the daughter of the future King Edward VIII, and left £1 million. Lord Mountbatten (1900-79) left £2,196,949. It is also notable

that although the Queen's estimated wealth appeared as the greatest UK fortune in the initial 1990 List, she does not appear near the top in more recent Lists.

2. Gerald Grosvenor, 6th Duke of Westminster – £4,200 billion. Urban property and land.

Regarded as the richest aristocrat, and the owner of much of the ground rents of Mayfair and Belgravia, Gerald, 6th Duke of Westminster (1951-2016) actually left the extraordinary sum of £616,400,000 for probate, although most of the Grosvenor wealth is tied up in trusts.

3. Gad and Hans Rausing – £2,040 billion. Food packaging.

The Swedish inventors of the plastic milk carton, Gad (1922-2000) and Hans (1926-2019) Rausing have long been regarded as among the richest businessmen in Britain.

4. Garfield Weston – £1,674 billion. Foods and bread.

The Canadian-born Garfield Weston (1927-2002) left £24,303,868 in England when he died. His father, Canadian-born Willard Garfield Weston (1898-1979), who founded the firm, left £93,423 in England.

5. The Moores family – £1,670 billion – football pools.

Sir John Moores (1896-1993) left £10,208,599 at his death; his brother Cecil Moores (1902-89) left £1,996,440.

6. Lord Sainsbury and David Sainsbury – £1,568 billion. Supermarkets.

Alan, Baron Sainsbury (1902-98) left £10,208,599; his brother Sir Robert Sainsbury (1906-2000) left £1,154,413. But Simon David Davans Sainsbury (1930-2006), of the family's next generation, left no less than £298,254,479. The present head of the family is David, Baron Sainsbury of Turville (b. 1940).

7. Lord Samuel Vestey and Edmund Vestey – £1,420 billion. Meat production and sales (Dewhursts).

Of Vesteys of the previous generation who have died, William Vestey, 1st Baron Vestey (1859-1940) left £261,515; his brother Sir Samuel Vestey, 1st Bt. (1866-1953) left £175,082; and Samuel, 2nd Baron Vestey (1882-1954) left £737,738.

8. Sir (John) Paul Getty II – £1,350 billion. Petroleum.

Getty (1932-2003), the American-born oil king, left £202,208,206 in England.

9. (Ian) Robert Maxwell – £1,100 billion – Publishing.

The disgraced publisher and financier, who lived from 1923 till 1991, is not listed in the probate calendars. He has an entry in the *ODNB*, which describes him as a "publisher and swindler."

10. Charles Feeney – £1,020 billion. Duty free shops.

The American Charles Feeney (b. 1931), probably the least known person on this list, invented the airport duty free shops. He is famous for his frugal lifestyle – he is said to carry his papers and goods with him in a plastic bag – and is said to have given $8 billion to charity. If these figures are accurate, they show an extraordinary increase in the scale of great wealth, compared with even the most recent lists of probate valuations. It is also clear that some astronomical sums have been left for probate in recent decades, despite death duties being known as a "voluntary tax."

* * *

The next *Sunday Times Rich List* to be examined here is that of 2005, fifteen years after the earliest one. According to it, the ten largest individual and family fortunes in the UK were as follows:

1. Lakshmi Mittal – £14,800 billion. Steel manufacturing and metals.
The Indian-born Lakshmi Mittal (b. 1950) attended Calcutta University, the son of a small steel manufacturer. He is the head of ArcelorMittal, the world's largest steel manufacturer. He lives in London.

2. Roman Abramovich – £7,500 billion. Petroleum and resources; also football.
Born in Russia, where his Jewish family suffered under Stalin, after the fall of Communism he was close to Yeltsin and other post-Soviet leaders. He owns MillhouseLLC and is best known in the UK for his ownership of the Chelsea football club. An international man, he became an Israeli citizen in 2018, and owns a mega-mansion in New York City.

3. Hugh, 7th Duke of Westminster – £5,600 billion. London property and land.
Born in 1991, the present owner of immensely valuable property in Mayfair and Belgravia (among other things) was educated at Ellesmere College in Shropshire and at Newcastle University, neither being the scholastic institutions one might expect. Despite massive death duties paid on the estates of previous Dukes, they appear as rich as ever, as astronomical rises in London property values have offset any losses.

4. Hans Rausing and family – £4,950 billion. Food packaging.
As noted, Hans Rausing (1926-2019) and his family, of Swedish descent, invented the plastic milk carton and other modern forms of food packaging. He lived in Wadhurst, East Sussex.

5. Sir Philip and Christina Green – £4,850 billion. Retail chains.
Born in 1952 and knighted in 2006, Sir Philip was the son of Simon Green, a property developer who died young. He left school at fifteen with no GCE 'O' Levels, and built up a retailing empire that includes Arcadia. He lives in Monaco and in a permanent suite in a London hotel.

6. Oleg Vladimirovich Deripaska – £4,375 billion. Aluminium and energy groups.
A Russian "Oligarch," he was the son of a farmer and was educated at Moscow State University.

7. Sir Richard Branson – £3,000 billion. Transport and mobile phones, etc. etc.
By far the most famous person on this list, a colourful self-publicist, it may be surprising to learn that he was the son of a barrister in Blackheath whose family had for several generations been connected with the East India Company, and was educated at Stowe, the exclusive public school. Born in 1950 and head of the Virgin Group, he received a knighthood in 2000.

8. Kirsted and Jorn Rausing – £2,575 billion. Food packaging; investments.
Other members of the Swedish-origin food packaging billionaires. Kirsted (b. 1952) Rausing is the owner of the Lanwades Stud.

9. David and Simon Reuben – £2,400 billion. Property and metal trading.
Born in Bombay to a Baghdadi Jewish family, David (b. 1941) and Simon (b. 1944) Reuben came to London in the 1950s and became billionaires in metal trading and property.

10. Roddy Fleming and family – £1,500 billion. Finance.
A descendant of Robert Fleming (1845-1933, *q.v.*), the merchant banker who left £2.2 million, Roddy Fleming was born in 1954 and is the head of Fleming Family & Partners, investment bankers. He is also related to Ian Fleming, the author of the James Bond novels.

It will be seen that most of the persons on this list are themselves migrants to the UK at one or were at two generations remove. Britain has always welcomed high achieving business migrants, as the names of the rich in this work, based on the probate data since the early nineteenth century, shows.

* * *

Moving on to 2021, the *Rich List* for 2021 includes many, but not all, of the richest persons and families found on the 2015 list. Only those not included on the 2015 *Rich List* will be commented about here.

1. Sir Leonard Blavatnik – £23 billion. "Investments, music, and media," according to the *Sunday Times*.
Born in 1958 in Odessa in the Ukraine, he came to the US around 1980, and heads Access Industries. Like the holdings of many today, his company is a conglomerate of businesses in various fields. He lives in a mansion in Kensington Palace Gardens, and was knighted in 2017 for his charitable bequests.

2. David and Simon Reuben – £21.5 billion.

3. Sri and Gopi Hinduja and family – £17 billion. Banking and manufacturing conglomerate.
The brothers Sri (b. 1936) and Gopi (b. 1940, with several other brothers living in India and elsewhere, head an international syndicate heavily involved in finance and manufacturing. These two brothers live in a mansion in Carlton House Terrace in St. James's, London.

4. Sir James Dyson and family – £16.3 billion.

5. Lakshmi Mittal and family – £14.7 billion.

6. Alisher Usmanov – £13.4 billion. Metal mining and investments.
Born in Uzbekistan in 1954, Alisher Usmanov heads businesses heavily involved in mining and

related industries in Russia, and in finance. He is known as a great philanthropist. He lives in a listed house in Highgate in North London

7. Kirsten and John Rausing – £13 billion.

8. Roman Abramovich – £12.1 billion.

9. Charlene de Cavarlho-Heineken and Michel de Carvalho – £12.0 billion. Brewing and related industries.

Twin sisters born in 1955, they inherited much of the stock in the Heineken brewing company and are involved in related companies in the drinks industry.

10. Guy, George, Alannah, and Galen Weston and family – £11 billion.

The Duke of Westminster currently sits at twelfth place, now worth £10.05 billion. Only three other landed and titled aristocrats appear among the one hundred wealthiest persons in the UK on the 2021 *Rich List*: the Earl Cadogan (24th richest, worth £6.37 billion); Baroness Howard de Walden (46th richest, worth £3.72 billion); and Lord Portman and family (82nd place, worth £2.6 billion). Each of these are primarily London property owners rather than the owners of agricultural land. The 100th richest person on the 2021 *Rich List* is a Thor Bjorgolfsson, involved in finance and investment, worth £1.6 billion. On an international scale, the British super-rich hardly make a dent. According to the same issue of the *Sunday Times Rich List*, not a single one of the one hundred richest persons or families in the world is British. The list is headed by the Walton family of the United States, worth £166.8 billion. At £23 billion, Sir Leonard Blavatnik just misses the top one hundred, slightly below Number 100, William Ding Lei, a Chinese online game mogul, worth £23.9 billion.

The largest fortune on the 2021 List, £23 billion, is the equivalent of about £200 million in pounds of the 1809-1914 period. The largest probated estate in the UK in this period was worth about £11 million, although the Duke of Westminster was probably worth about £13.5 million. If accurate estimates, today's UK super-rich appear vastly wealthier, at least on paper, than those of the nineteenth century, although apart from the Royal Family, probably no one today has the lifestyle of a senior landed aristocrat of the nineteenth century, with their armies of servants and their multiple stately homes and London mansions.

A Note on Sources

The probate valuation which form the basis of most of this book were derived from several sources. Prior to 1858, wills and letters of administration in England and Wales were probated in the Ecclesiatsical Courts, of which there were a great many. The most important was the Prerogative Court of Canterbury (which was actually located in the City of London, not in Canterbury), known as the "P.C.C.," where most wealthy estates were probated. The identities of the wealthholders in this study were taken from literally going through every Probate Act Book between 1809 (when these sources begin in a usable form) and 1858, and abstracting the names and other information about the largest estate-leavers. This was also done with the probate records of the Prerogative Court of York, and of the Lancashire Consistory Court, held at Preston. The same process was also done for the largest Scottish estates, from the manuscript sources held in Edinburgh.

From 1858, all wills and letters of administrations left in England and Wales were probated in a civil court, the Principal Probate Registry, located for many years at Somerset House on the Strand in London (although there were many local courts), and published annually in the so-called Probate Calendars. Again, I personally went through all of these from 1858 until 1914, and abstracted the names and other information about the testator from them. I went through a similar process with the printed annual Scottish probate calendars, which exist from 1876, and for the Irish probate calendars, which exist from 1858 until 1922. From 1901 until the 1980s, the *Daily Mail Year Book,* an annual publication, published lists of all large estates left in the previous year; these have been used as the basis for the twentieth century valuations. Information on all estates of £100,000 or more (not £500,000 or £1,000,000 or more) left between 1809 and 1869 has been produced by me and published by EER in the series of volumes titled *Who Were the Rich?* A number of the annual *Sunday Times Rich Lists,* the first of which appeared in 1990, have been used in the final chapter of this work.

Information about the largest landowners in the United Kingdom outside of London is available in John Bateman, *The Great Landowners of Great Britain and Ireland,* originally published in 1883, and republished, with an Introduction by David Spring, by Leicester University Press in 1971. Similar information, although based on different sources, about the largest landowners in London in the 1890s, can be found in Peter H. Lindert, *"Who Owned Victorian England?: The Debate Over Landed Wealth and Inequality,"* in *Agricultural History,* Vol. 61 (4), 1987, pp. 25-52. Information on the largest landowners in Great Britain and Ireland around 2000 has been collected and published by Kevin Cahill, in his *Who Owns Britain: The Hidden Facts Behind Landownership in the UK and Ireland* (Canongate, Edinburgh, 2001). These have been used in the chapters in this book on the great landowners.

* * *

1860-1869 Index

A

Abbot, John George   130
Abdy, Sir William, 7th Bt.   124
Abramovich, Roman   303, 305
Adair, Alexander   112
Agnew, Sir William, 1st Bt.   192
Agnew, Thomas   157
Aird, Sir John, 1st Bt.   195
Airedale, 1st Baron (James Kitson)   195
Alexander, Henry Browne   159
Allen, Thomas   111
Allendale, 1st Baron (Wentworth
    Beaumont)   85, 187
Allendale, 1st Viscount,
    Wentworth   215
Allhusen, Christian   169
Allpress, Kenneth Peter   290
Ames, John   131
Ancaster, Earls of   71
Anderson, Sir Kennth, 1st Bt.   258
Angerstein, John Julius   106
Anglesey, Marquesses of   35
Arden, 2nd Baron, Charles   116
Arkwright, Peter   128
Arkwright, Richard   114
Armstrong, 1st Baron (William
    George Armstrong)   178
Arnold, Charles Leonard   290
Ashton, 1st baron (James
    Williamson)   232
Assheton-Smith, George William
    Duff   183

Attwood, Benjamin   141
Attwood, Matthias   128

B

Bailey, Sir Joseph, 1st Bt.   123
Baillie, (Hon.) Olive, Lady   294
Baird, Alexander   126
Baird, Alexander   128
Baird, George   138
Baird, James   135
Baker, John   103
Bald, John   159
Barbour, George   207
Barbour, Robert   228
Baring, Thomas   133
Baring family   89
Baron, Bernhard   229
Barrow, Richard   128
Bass, Michael Thomas   151
Bates, Joshua   127
Baxter, Sir David, 1st Bt.   133
Bearsted, 1st Viscount (Marcus
    Samuel)   222
Beasley, Charles   215
Beatty, Sir Chester   289
Beauchamp, 1st Earl (William
    Lygon)   103
Beaumont, John   166
Beauvoir, (Revd.) Peter   104
Beckett, Rupert Evelyn   284
Beckett, Sir Gervase, 1st Bt.   249
Beckett, William   126

Beddington, Maurice 176
Bedford, 11th Duke of, Herbrand 254
Bedford, 12th Duke of, Hastings 278
Bedford, 8th Duke of, William 139
Bedford, Dukes of 8
Beecham, Sir Joseph, 1st Bt. 202
Behrens, Solomon Levi 140
Beit, Alfred 184
Belling, Charles Reginald 290
Bentinck, Lord William Cavendish 138
Benyon, James Herbert 244
Berners, John Anstruther 241
Bibby, Frank 215
Bibby, Frank Brian 231
Bibby, James Jenkinson 174
Birkin, Sir Thomas Isaac, 1st Bt. 212
Bischoffscheim, Henri Louis 188
Blackwell, Thomas Francis 187
Blavatnik, Sir Leonard 304
Bloch, Sir Maurice 287
Bolckow, Henry William 146
Boone, Charles 103
Booth, Sir Charles, 3rd Bt. 173
Boughey, Sir Richard, 10th Bt. 298
Bourne, Stanley 258
Bowlby, Edwin Salvin 181
Boyd, Thomas Lunham 236
Boyne, Viscounts 44
Brady, Anthony 199
Branson, Sir Richard 303
Brassey, Henry Arthur 170
Brassey, Thomas 133
Bridges, Thomas 131
Bridgewater, 7th Earl of, John 106
Brocklehurst, John 137
Brocklehurst, Thomas 137
Brocklehurst, William 232
Brook, Edward 182
Brotherton, 1st Baron (Edward Brotherton) 234
Broughton, Edward Bishop 295
Brown, Sir Alexander Hargreaves, 1st Bt. 212
Brown, Sir William, 1st Bt. 127

Browning, Henry 164
Brownlow, 3rd Earl, Adelbert 210
Brownlow, Barons 46
Buccleuch and Queensberry, 6th Duke of, William 199
Buccleuch and Queensberry, 7th Duke of, John 245
Buckland, 1st Baron (Henry Berry) 228
Bullough, John 170
Burton, 1st Baron (Michael Arthur Bass) 189
Bute, 3rd Marquess of, John 179
Bute, Marquesses of 27
Butler, Charles 192
Butler, Hubert Lavie 249
Buxton, Sir Edward, 2nd Bt. 122

C
Cadbury, George 214
Cadogan, 6th Earl, Gerald 239
Cahn, Sir Julien, 1st Bt. 263
Cain, Sir William Ernest, 1st Bt. 219
Caine, Nathaniel 146
Caird, Sir James, 1st Bt. 281
Campbell, Colin 162
Campbell, Joan 286
Campbell, Robert 162
Camrose, 1st Viscount (William Ewart Berry) 280
Candamo, Don Pedro de 129
Carr, Ellis 235
Cassel, Sir Ernest Joseph 209
Cavarlho-Heineken, Charlene and sister 305
Cave, Charles 163
Cavendish, (Hon.) Henry 101
Cayzer, Sir Charles, 1st Bt. 201
Chapman, David Barclay 170
Charrington, Charles Edward 247
Charrington, Spencer 183
Churchman, Sir William, 1st Bt. 270
Clanricarde, 2nd Marquess of, Hubert 201
Clanricarde, 2nd Marquess of, Hubert 86

Clark, Sir George Smith, 1st Bt. 245
Clark, Stewart 187
Clayton, Nathaniel 168
Cleveland, 1st Duke of (William Vane) 114
Cleveland, 2nd Duke of, Henry 127
Cleveland, 4th Duke of, Harry 170
Cleveland, Dukes of 38
Cliff, Stephen 227
Coats, Andrew 233
Coats, Archibald 197
Coats, Daniel 213
Coats, James 196
Coats, Peter 198
Coats, Sir James, 1st Bt. 198
Coats, Thomas 151
Coats, William Allan 221
Coats, William Hodge 227
Cockerline, Sir Walter Herbert 256
Cohen, Harold Leopold 246
Cohen, Louis 156
Cohen, Louis Samuel 213
Cohen, Rex David 228
Cohen, Stanley Samuel 262
Collins, Brenton Halliburton 217
Colman, Geoffrey Russell 244
Colman, Jeremiah 160
Colman, Russell James 268
Colman, Sir Jeremiah, 1st Bt. 257
Colman, Sir Jeremiah, 2nd Bt. 287
Combe, Charles 208
Constantine, Joseph 212
Conyngham, 2nd Marquess of, Francis 144
Cook, Frank Henry 237
Cook, Sir Francis, 1st Bt. 180
Cook, Sir Frederick Lucas, 2nd Bt. 208
Cook, William 132
Cook, Wyndham Francis 184
Cookson, William Isaac 164
Coope, Octavius Edward 163
Cooper, Sir George Alexander, 1st Bt. 254
Copestake, Sampson 141

Cotterell, Thomas 125
Coulthurst, William Matthew 145
Courtauld, George 208
Courtauld, Samuel 156
Courtauld, Samuel 271
Courtauld, Sir William Julien, 1st Bt. 255
Coutts, Thomas 105
Cowdray, 1st Viscount (Weetman Pearson) 223
Cowen, Jane 272
Cowen, Joseph 257
Cowper, 7th ear, Thomas 184
Craig, James 179
Craig-Sellar, Gerard Henry 230
Crawford, Archibald Inglis 255
Crawshay, George 141
Crawshay, Richard 102
Crawshay, Richard 124
Crawshay, Robert Thompson 137
Crawshay, William 111
Crawshay and Bailey, Barons Glanusk 96
Crigoe-Colmore, William 204
Cross, George Herbert 296
Crossley, Joseph 132
Crossman, Douglas 265
Cruddas, William Donaldson 197
Crystal, William James 210
Cubitt, Thomas 115
Cunliffe, Roger 173
Cunliffe-Brooks, Sir William, 1st Bt. 179
Cunliffe-Owen, Sir Hugo, 1st Bt. 269
Cunninghame, Alexander 130
Currie, Sir Donald 190

D

Dalziel of Wooler, 1st Baron (Davison Dalziel) 225
Daresbury, 1st Baron (Gilbert Greenall) 250
Dartmouth, Earls of 53
Davey, Thomas Ruding 252

Davidson, Henry 108
Davies, Edward 175
De Casariera, Thomas, Marquess 155
De Mier y Feran, Don Gregorio 137
De Murrieta, Cristobal 131
Denison, William Joseph 115
Dent, Thomas 139
Derby, 15th Earl of, Edward 171
Derby, 16th Earl of, Frederick 189
Derby, 17th Earl of, Edward 271
Derby, Earls of 20
Deripaska, Oleg 303
De Savillano, Maria, Marquessa 157
De Stern, David, Viscount 135
De Stern, Herman, Baron 152
Deuchar, James 224
Devonport, 1st Viscount (Hudson
    Kearley) 240
Devonshire, 6th Duke of, William 122
Devonshire, 7th Duke of, William 169
Devonshire, 8th Duke of, Spencer 188
Devonshire, Dukes of 14
Dewar, 1st Baron (Thomas Dewar) 233
Dewar, John Arthur 278
Dick, Quintin 122
Donaldson, Robert 162
Douglas-Hamilton, Edith 223
Downshire, Marquesses of 40
Drake del Castillo, Santiago 139
Dreyfus, Dr. Henry 260
Dudley, 1st Earl of (William Ward) 152
Dudley, Earls of 32
Dulverton, 1st Baron (George Alan
    Wills) 282
Dunbar, Duncan 123
Duncombe, (Hon.) and (Ven.)
    Augustus 154
Dunkels, Anton 194
Dunn, David Guthrie 240
Dunn, Sir William, 1st Bt. 197
Dunraven and Mt. Earl, 4th of,
    Windham 221
Durant, Richard 147
Durham, 2nd Earl of, George 147

Durham, 3rd Earl of, John 226
Durham, 4th Earl of, Frederick 231
Durham Earls of 76
Dysart, 7th Earl of, Lionel 135
Dysart, 8th Earl of, William 243
Dysart, 9th Earl of, William 87
Dyson, Sir James and family 304

E
Easton, Emily Matilda 199
Easton, John 154
Eckstein, Sir Friedrich, 1st Bt. 234
Egerton of Tatton, 4th baron,
    Maurice 283
Eldon, 1st Earl of (John Scott) 113
Eldon, 3rd Earl of, John 221
Ellerman, Sir John Reeves, 1st
    Bt. 99, 238
Ellerman, Sir John Reeves, 2nd
    Bt. 292
Ellesmere, 4th Earl of, John 261
Ellis, Wynne 142
Ennisdale, 1st Baron (Henry
    Edward Lyons) 288
Eno, James Crossley 200
Evans, Joseph 166
Evans-Bevan, Evan 230
Ewing, James 119
Eyre, Thomas Joseph 129
Eyres, Samuel 124

F
Fairhaven, 1st Baron (Urban
    Broughton) 291
Farihaven, 2nd Baron, Henry 297
Faringdon, 1st Baron (Alexander
    Henderson) 242
Farquhar, Alfred 226
Farquhar, Harvie Morton 165
Farrer, Gaspard Oliver 268
Feeney, Charles 302
Feilden, James Hawley 262
Fenston, Felix Donovan 293
Fenwick, George John 199

Ferrari, Raphael, Duc de 145
Feversham, 1st Baron (Charles Duncombe) 117
Fielden, John Ashton 258
Fielden, Joshua 163
Fielden, Samuel 154
Fielden, Thomas 125
Fife, 1st Duke of (Alexander Duff) 197
Fife, Dukes of 74
Findlay, Sir John Ritchie, 1st Bt. 235
Fitzwilliam, 10th Earl of, William 297
Fitzwilliam, 6th Earl, William 180
Fitzwilliam, Earls 28
Fleming, Robert 239
Fleming, Roddy and family 304
Fletcher, James 152
Fletcher, John 142
Flower, Sir Charles, 1st Bt. 112
Forman, William Henry 125
Forteviot, 1st Baron (John Dewar) 229
Foster, James 119
Foster, John 193
Foster, William 151
Foster, William Henry 218
Foster, William Orme 176
Fowler, Sir George Jefford 250
Frazer, James 275
Freake, Sir Charles James, 1st Bt. 160
Fry, Conrad Penrose 255
Fry, Joseph Storrs 198
Fry, Roderick James 265
Furness, 1st Baron (Christopher Furness) 196
Furness, 1st Viscount (Marmaduke Furness) 253
Fyfe-Jamieson, James 231

G
Gardner, Henry 147
Garton, Charles Henry 240
Garton, Sir Richard Charles 240
Garvey y Capdepon, Don José 197
Getty, Sir John Paul 302
Gibbs, William 142

Gladstone family 98
Glanely, 1st baron (William James Tatem) 257
Glentanar, 1st Baron (George Coats) 204
Godman, Joseph 141
Goldsmid, Frederick David 129
Goldsmid, Sir Francis, 2nd Bt. 135
Goldsmid, Sir Isaac Lyon, 1st Bt. 116
Goldsmid, Sir Julian, 3rd Bt. 174
Goldsmid family 96
Gooch, Charles Cubitt 166
Gooch, Sir Daniel, 1st Bt. 166
Goschen, William Henry 129
Gosling, Robert 132
Gosling, William 111
Graham, Christopher North 166
Grant, Sir Alexander, 1st Bt. 249
Grant, Sir Robert McVitie, 2nd Bt. 270
Gray, Sir William 175
Green, Sir Philip and Christina 303
Greenall, Sir Gilbert, 1st Bt. 172
Greenwell, Sir Walpole Lloyd, 1st Bt. 207
Greffulhe, Count Louis-Charles 166
Greffulhe, Count Urbain 148
Greffulhe, Jean-Louis 130
Gretton, 1st Baron (John Gretton) 268
Gretton, Frederick 227
Gretton, John 176
Greville, (Hon.) Dame Margaret 257
Grimthorpe, 1st Baron (Edmund Denison-Beckett) 183
Guest, Sir Josiah John, 1st Bt. 119
Guests, Barons and Wimborne, Viscounts 94
Guinness, Sir Benjamin Lee, 1st Bt. 124
Gurney, Hudson 124
Gurney, Samuel 121
Guthrie, Sir Connop, 1st B t. 264

H
H.M. Queen Elizabeth II 301
Hambleden, 3rd Viscount, William 272

Hambledon, 2nd Viscount, Frederick 226
Hambro, Baron Charles 146
Hambro, Sir Everard, 1st Bt. 219
Hamilton-Fellowes, Margaret 221
Hammersley, Hugh 117
Hanbury, Robert 158
Hanbury family 98
Hardy, Charles 130
Hardy, John 120
Hardy, Sir John, 1st Bt. 154
Hargreaves, John 143
Hargreaves, William 167
Harmsworth, Sir Hildebrand, 1st Bt. 231
Harrison, Charles Willis 248
Harrison, Sir Heath, 1st Bt. 242
Harrison, Thomas Fenwick 202
Harrison, William Edward 248
Hartley, Sir William Pickles 214
Haslam, Sir Alfred Seale 224
Hatfeild, Gilliat 186
Hatfeild, Gilliat Edward 256
Hatton, James 149
Haworth, Jesse 163
Heath, Cuthbert Eden 253
Henderson, George Edward 248
Henry, Alexander 126
Herbert, Sir Alfred Edward 282
Hermon, Edward 155
Herring, George 185
Hertford, 7th Marquess of, Robert 138
Hewetson, Henry 113
Heywood, Anna Maria 163
Heywood, John Pemberton 135
Heywood-Lonsdale, Arthur Pemberton 174
Hickman, Sir Alfred, 1st Bt. 193
Hignett, Lawrence 261
Hill, Philip Ernest 260
Hillingdon, 1st Baron (Charles Henry Mills) 175
Hillingdon, 2nd Baron, Charles 207
Hills, Frank Clarke 170

Hindlip, 1st Baron (Henry Allsopp) 163
Hinduja, Sri and family 304
Hirsch, Marurice, Baron de 173
Hobson, William 116
Hodgson, John 156
Hodgson, Kirkman Daniel 148
Hodgson, William 152
Holcroft, Si r Charles, 1st Bt. 202
Holford, Robert 110
Holland, Harriet, Lady 107
Hollenden, 1st Baron (Samuel Morley) 230
Hollond, Edward John 104
Hollond, William 110
Holloway, Thomas 158
Hood, Sir Joseph, 1st Bt. 237
Hope, Henry 105
Hornby, Charles Harry 268
Hotham, 2nd Baron, Beaumont 138
Houchin, Robert Walter 299
Houston, Dame Fanny 246
Howard de Walden, 8th Baron, Thomas 267
Hubbard, Charles Heman 264
Hulton, Sir Edward, 1st Bt. 219
Hutchison, Thomas Holt 206
Huth, John Frederick 128
Hutley, Christopher William 289
Hyde, Sir Charles, 1st Bt. 257

I

Ilchester, 5th Earl of, Francis 184
Innes, Jane 111
Inns, Jeremiah 265
Inverclyde, 3rd Baron, James 206
Isaacson, Frederick Wootton 176
Ismay, Thomas Henry 177
Iveagh, 1st Earl of (Edward Cecil Guinness) 222

J

Jackson, Sir Charles James 216
Jacobs, Joseph Henry 275

Jardine, Andrew 150
Jardine, Sir Robert, 1st Bt. 184
Jardine, Sir Robert, 2nd Bt. 223
Jersey, 8th Earl of, George 216
Jessop, Thomas 165
Joel, Dudley Jack 256
Joel, Isaac Barnato 254
Joel, Solomon Barnato 238
Johnston, Jonas Foster 154
Johnstone, James 147
Joicey, 1st baron (James Joicey) 246
Joicey, Edward 148
Joicey, John 156
Jones, Joseph 156
Jones, Robert 103
Jones, William Charles 159
Jones-Gibb, Thomas 158
Joynson, William 142

K

Keen, Arthur 201
Keene, John Henry 237
Keene, Lavinia Clarissa 275
Kemble, Henry 121
Kemp-Welch, John 160
Kennedy, Mathilda Marks 287
Kensington, Barons 63
Knight, John Messer 155
Knowles, Robert Millington 218

L

Lambert, Charles 144
Lambton, William Henry 129
Landau, Baron Horaz von 182
Langworthy, Edward Ryley 134
Lansdowne, 5th Marquess of, Henry 224
Lansdowne, 6th Marquess of, Henry 246
Lansdowne, 7th Marquess of, Charles 263
Larnach, Sydney 218
Latymer, 5th Baron, Francis 216
Laverton, Abraham 161

Lawson, Lionel 148
Lea, Charles Wheeley 175
Leconfield, 2nd Baron, Henry 180
Leconfield, 3rd Baron, Charles 279
Leconfield, Barons 45
Lee, Richard 121
Lees, James 138
Lees, Thomas Evans 148
Leicester, 5th Earl of, Thomas 297
Leigh, John Blundell 143
Leigh, John Shaw 138
Le Marchant, Francis Charles 234
Leschallas, John 146
Leven and Melville, 10th Earl of, Alexander 167
Leven and Melville, 11th Earl of, Ronald 186
Leverhulme, 1st Viscount (William Hesketh Lever) 220
Leverhulme, 2nd Viscount, William 273
Levy, Sir Albert 249
Lewis, Samuel 179
Lewis-Hill, Ada Hannah 186
Leyland, Christopher 118
Leyland, Thomas 108
Lilford, 4th Baron, John 264
Lilford, 6th Baron, Stephen 275
Lithgow, Henry 272
Lithgow, William Todd 189
Littman, Joseph Aaron 279
Llangattock, 2nd Baron, John 202
Loder, Giles 133
Loeffler, Johann Carl 185
Londonderry, 7th Marquess of, Charles 276
Lonsdale, 2nd earl of, William 140
Lonsdale, Earls of 79
Love, Joseph 134
Low, Andrew 161
Loyd, Arthur Thomas 263
Loyd, Edward 127
Loyd, Lewis 122
Ludlow, Baroness, Alice Sedwick 263

Lyde, Lionel 119
Lyle, Sir Archibald, 2nd Bt. 266
Lyne-Stephens, Stephens 126

M
Macfarlane, James 156
Mackenzie, Edward 149
Mackinnon, Duncan 205
Malcolm, Neil 112
Manners, Ernest John 261
Mansfield, Earls of 59
Manton, 1st Baron (Joseph
    Watson) 214
Maple, Sir John Blundell, 1st Bt. 181
Marcus, Maurice 214
Marjoribanks, Edward 131
Marks of Broughton, Miriam,
    Lady 296
Marling, Sir Samuel, 1st Bt. 157
Marryat, Emma Grace 224
Martin, James 147
Marx, Hermann 269
Masham, 2nd Baron, Samuel 203
Masham, 3rd Baron, John 218
Mason, James Francis 231
Matheson, Sir Alexander, 1st Bt. 164
Matheson family 95
Maxwell, Robert 302
McCalmon, Robert 150
McCalmont, Harry Leslie 181
McCalmont, Hugh 153
McClean, John Robinson 141
McEwan, William 198
McGarel, Charles 144
Melchett, 1st Baron (Alfred
    Mond) 235
Menzies, William Dudgeon 262
Merry, James 146
Meux, Sir Henry, 2nd Bt. 157
Michelham, 1st baron (Herbert
    Stern) 206
Milburn, Charles Thomas 212
Mildmay, Alfred 261
Miles, Philip John 115

Miller, Alexander 213
Miller, Sir Robert, 1st Bt. 153
Miller, Thomas 128
Mills, Henry Trueman 239
Mills, John Remington 136
Mills, Joseph Trueman 216
Mills, Samuel 118
Mills, Sir Charles, 1st Bt. 140
Mills, Thomas 126
Mittal, Lakshmi 303, 304
Molyneux-Cohan, William 251
Mond, Ludwig 190
Montagu, Andrew 85, 172
Montefiore, Abraham 107
Montefiore, Joseph Mayer 155
Moore, George 145
Moore, Horace 283
Moores family 302
Morgan, Junius Spencer 168
Morley, Howard
Morrison, Alan 155
Morrison, Charles 189
Morrison, Ellen 190
Morrison, Hugh 236
Morrison, James 115
Morrison, James and family 92
Morrison, Mary Anne 164
Morrison, Walter 209
Moses, Henry 145
Mountain, Henry Stanford 270
Mount Stephen, 1st Baron
    (George Stephen) 210
Moyne, 1st Baron (William
    Edward Guinness) 261
Mundey, Thomas Clement 143
Muntz, George Frederick 121
Muntz, George Frederick 176

N
Nairn, John 227
Napier, Montague Stanley 236
Neumann, Sir Sigmund 201
Newcastle, 7th Duke of, Henry 227
Newcastle, Dukes of 65

Newton, Susannah Houblon — 113
Nixon, John — 177
Norfolk, Dukes of — 61
Norman, Charles Loyd — 167
Normanton, 2nd Earl of, Welborne — 131
Northcliffe, 1st Viscount (Alfred Harmsworth) — 211
Northumberland, 2nd Duke of, Hugh — 103
Northumberland, 4th Duke of, Algernon — 128
Northumberland, 7th Duke of, Henry — 205
Northumberland, 8th Duke of, Alan — 233
Northumberland, 9th Duke of, Henry — 255
Northumberland, Dukes of — 17
Nuffield, 1st Viscount (William Richard Morris) — 286

O
Ogilvie, Alexander — 161
Ormrod, Peter — 143
Ormston, Robert — 157
Orr-Ewing, Sir Archibald, 1st Bt. — 172
Overstone, 1st Baron (Samuel Jones Loyd) — 84,150
Ovey, Richard — 142
Oxley, Henry — 272
Oxley, James Walker — 225

P
Page, Henry — 172
Palmer, 1st Baron (Samuel Ernest Palmer) — 272
Palmer, Charles Herbert — 248
Palmer, Samuel — 182
Park, James Smith — 210
Parker, Roland Hoopes — 291
Parkinson, Frank — 266
Parsons, Sir Charles — 237
Payton, Ernest Leopold — 267

Pearce, Sir William, 1st Bt. — 153
Pease, Edward — 155
Pease, Gurney — 140
Peckover, Algernon — 172
Peckover, William — 146
Peel, Eleanor, Countess Dowager — 273
Peel, Jonthan — 112
Peel, Sir Robert, 1st Bt. — 109
Peel, Sir Robert, 1st Bt. — 91
Pembroke, 11th Earl of, George — 108
Pembroke and Montgomery, Earls of — 57
Penn, John — 136
Pennant, George Hay Dawkins — 117
Penrhyn, 1st Baron (Edward Douglas-Pennant) — 161
Penrhyn, Barons — 82
Perrins, James Dyson — 164
Perry-Herrick, William — 144
Petter, George William — 165
Phillimore, 2nd Baron, Godfrey — 269
Pickering, Warley — 220
Platt, John — 140
Player, John Dane — 279
Player, William Goodacre — 283
Plymouth, 2nd Earl of, Ivor — 259
Pope, Edwin — 226
Portal, 1st Viscount (Wyndham Portal) — 273
Portland, 4th Duke of, William — 120
Portland, 5th Duke of, John — 136
Portland, 7th Duke of, William — 299
Portland, Dukes of — 24
Portman, 7th Viscount, Gerald — 271
Portman, Viscounts — 30
Povia, Count de, Henrique — 111
Price, Sir Henry Philip, 1st Bt. — 287
Priestman, Sir John, 1st Bt. — 256
Pulteney, (Revd.) Richard — 142

Q
Queensbury, 4th Duke of, William — 102
Quilter, Sir William Cuthbert, 1st Bt. — 194
Quilter, William — 165

R

Radcliffe, Henry 210
Radnor, 7th Earl of, William 290
Ralli, Alexandra 182
Ralli, Eustratios 159
Ralli, Peter 244
Ralli, Peter Pantia 131
Ralli, Sir Lucas, 1st Bt. 236
Ralli, Stephen Augustus 181
Rank, 1st Baron (Arthur Rank) 293
Rank, Joseph Voase 280
Rankin, Robert 137
Raphael, Edward Louis 182
Raphael, George Charles 186
Raphael, Henry Lewis 176
Raphael, Louis Edward 200
Ratcliff, Richard 175
Rausing family 302, 303, 304, 305
Reckitt, Francis 203
Reddihaugh, Frank 251
Reddihaugh, John 217
Rees-Mogg, Kathleen 274
Reuben, David and Simon 304
Revelstoke, 2nd Baron, John 229
Rhondda, 1st Viscount (David
    Alfred Thomas) 205
Ricardo, David 105
Richmond, Gordon, and Lennox,
    Dukes of 50
Rickards, Charles Hilditch 162
Riddell, 1st Baron (George Riddell) 241
Robartes, 1st Baron (Thomas
    Agar-Robartes) 157
Robinson, John Peter 173
Rogerson, Eileen Daphne 296
Ropner, Sir Robert, 1st Bt. 217
Rose, Philip Edward 299
Roseberry, 5th Earl of, Archibald 230
Roseberry, 6th Earl of, Harry 293
Rothermere, 2nd Viscount,
    Edmond 299
Rothschild, (Hon.) Nathaniel De 215
Rothschild, 1st Baron (Nathan
    Mayer Rothschild) 200

Rothschild, Alfred Charles de 204
Rothschild, Alice Charlotte de 211
Rothschild, Baron Adolphe de 178
Rothschild, Baroness, Emma
    Louisa 244
Rothschild, Baron Ferdinand 175
Rothschild, Baron Leopold de 202
Rothschild, Baron Lionel Nathan 136
Rothschild, Baron Mayer 134
Rothschild, Baron Nathan de 133
Rothschild, James Armand de 281
Rothschild, Nathan James De 156
Rothschild, Nathan Mayer 110
Rothschild, Sir Anthony, 1st Bt. 134
Rothschild family 97
Royden, Sir Thomas Bland, 1st Bt. 203
Runciman, 1st Baron (Walter
    Runciman) 247
Runciman of Doxford, 1st
    Viscount (Walter Runciman) 276
Rundell, Philip 102
Russell, Jesse 104
Rutland, Dukes of 41
Ryland, Louisa Anne 167
Rylands, Enriquetta 188
Rylands, John 153

S

Sainsbury, John James 228
Sainsbury, Lord and David 302
Salting, George 190
Salting, Millicent Emily 217
Salvesen, Frederick 239
Salvesen, Harold Keith 295
Samuel, Howard 285
Samuel, Samuel 241
Samuel, Samuel Moses 141
Sassoon, Sir Philip, 3rd Bt. 251
Savill, Walter 194
Scarlett, Dame Charlotte 165
Schiff, Sir Ernest Frederick 206
Schilizzi, John Stefanovitch 188
Schilizzi, Zanni 162
Schroder, Baron Sir John, 1st Bt. 191

Schuster, Leo — 139
Scott, Samuel — 125
Scott, Sir Edward Henry, 5th Bt. — 158
Scott, Sir Samuel, 2nd Bt. — 118
Scott, Sir Walter, 1st Bt. — 192
Scribbans, John Henry — 243
Scrutton, Frederick — 247
Seafield, Earls of — 55
Sebag-Montefiore, Sir Joseph — 182
Sefton, 6th Earl of, Osbert — 234
Sefton, 7th Earl of, Hugh — 294
Seilern, Count Antoine — 297
Selkirk, 6th Earl of, Dunbar — 161
Shelley-Rolls, (Hon.) Eleanor — 286
Shrewsbury, 15th Earl of, Charles — 108
Shuttleworth, Alfred — 221
Shuttleworth, Joseph — 158
Silver, Henry — 192
Singer, Washington Merritt — 242
Smith, George — 145
Smith, John — 250
Smith, Samuel George — 127
Smith, Samuel George — 178
Smith, Seth — 125
Smith, Sir Prince, 1st Bt. — 213
Smith, Thomas Valentine — 185
Smith, William Henry — 169
Smyth, (Hon.) Esmé — 266
Smyth, Sir John, 4th Bt. — 118
Soames, Arthur Gilstrap — 242
Sofer-Whitburn, Charles Joseph — 194
Somes, Joseph — 117
Southey, Thomas — 148
Sowerby, John — 106
Sparrow, William Henry — 130
Spencer, 5th Earl, John — 193
Spencer, 6th Earl, Charles — 213
Spencer-Churchill, Edward — 288
St. Albans, Duchess of, Harriot Mellon — 114
St. Oswald, 2nd Baron, Rowland — 207
Stanley, Lord, Edward — 250
Steinkopff, Edward — 186
Stephens, John James — 107

Stephenson, William Lawrence — 285
Stern, James — 180
Stewart-Clark, Sir John, 1st Bt. — 218
Strahan, Andrew — 111
Straker, John — 160
Strakosch, Sir Henry Edouard — 258
Strickland, Margaret, Baroness — 280
Strutt, Anthony Radford — 144
Strutt, George Henry — 173
Strutt, George Herbert — 229
Studd-Trench-Gascoigne, Yvonne — 296
Sturdy, William — 187
Sumner, Francis James — 159
Sunley, Bernard — 285
Sunlight, Joseph — 298
Sutherland, 1st Duke of (George Leveson-Gower) — 109
Sutherland, 2nd Duke of, George — 123
Sutherland, 3rd Duke of, George — 171
Sutherland, 4th Duke of, Cromartie — 199
Sutherland, Dukes of — 1
Sutherland, Sir Arthur Munro, 1st Bt. — 280
Sutton, Sir Richard Vincent, 6th Bt. — 206
Sutton, William Richard — 178
Swaythling, 1st Baron (Samuel Montagu) — 195

T
Talbot, Christopher Rice Mansel — 168
Talbot, Emily Charlotte — 204
Tarn, William — 144
Tasker, Joseph — 126
Tate, Sir Ernest, 3rd Bt. — 252
Tate, Sir Henry, 1st Bt. — 177
Tate, Sir William Henry, 2nd Bt. — 211
Taylor, Seth — 203
Tennant, Sir Charles, 1st Bt. — 185
Tetley, Henry Greenwood — 209
Tew, Edward — 145
Thellusson, Barons Rendlesham — 99
Thistlethwaite, Alexander — 200

Thistlethwayte, Thomas 118
Thomasson, John Penington 183
Thompson, Samuel Henry 171
Thompson, William 120
Thornton, Richard 124
Thornton, Thomas 137
Thwaytes, Ann 130
Thwaytes, William 112
Tibbitts, William Fox 224
Tredegar, 1st Viscount (Courtenay
    Morgan) 240
Tredegar, 2nd Viscount, Evan 274
Tunno, John 104
Turner, Charles 143

U
Usmanov, Alisher 304

V
Vagliano, Alcibiades 217
Vagliano, Panaghi 180
Vandervell, Guy Anthony 289
Vaughan, Philip Henry 203
Vernon-Wentworth, Thomas
    Frederick 181
Vestey, Lord Samuel and Edmund 302
Vivian, William Graham 197

W
Waddilove, Sir Joshua Kelly 208
Walker, Edward 140
Walker, Sir Andrew Barclay, 1st Bt. 171
Walker, Sir James, 1st Bt. 151
Walker, Thomas Andrew 167
Walker, Vyell Edward 185
Wallace, Sir Richard, 1st Bt. 48, 169
Wallis, Francis John 295
Wallis, Frank 267
Wandsworth, 1st Baron (Sydney
    James Stern) 196
Waring, Charles 164
Watney, James 151
Watney, James 152
Watney, Vernon James 226

Watson, Annie Lucy 247
Watson, Sir Duncan 283
Watson, Sir William George, 1st Bt. 233
Weir, 1st Viscount (William
    Douglas Weir) 283
Weir, William 198
Wellcome, Sir Henry Solomon 245
Wellington, 1st Duke of (Arthur
    Wellesley) 120
Wentworth, Frederick Vernon 162
Wernher, Sir Julius, 1st Bt. 195
Wertheimer, Asher 204
West, Richard Thornton 136
West, William George 284
West, William Thornton 137
Westminster, 2nd Duke of, Hugh 277
Westminster, 2nd Marquess of,
    Richard 132
Westminster, 4th Duke of, Gerald 290
Westminster, 6th Duke of, Gerald 302
Westminster, 7th Duke of, Hugh 303
Westminster, Dukes of 4
Weston, Garfield and family 301, 305
Wharrie, Mary Woodgate 248
Wharton, William Henry 251
Wheatley, Charles Joshua 259
Wheatley, Joshua Hirst 220
Whitaker, Joseph 160
White, James 159
Whitelaw, Alexander 149
Whiteley, William 187
Whittingstall, Elizabeth 107
Whittingstall, George 105
Wigan, Edward 120
Wigan, Henry 161
Williams, (Revd.) James 139
Williams, Benjamin Bacon 139
Williams, John Michael 149
Williams, Michael 122
Williams, Sir Howell Jones 252
Willoughby de Broke, 16th Baron,
    Henry 119
Wills, Arnold Cass 298
Wills, Arthur Stanley 243

Wills, Frederick Noel 222
Wills, Henry Herbert 211
Wills, Henry Overton 193
Wills, Michael Desmond 259
Wills, Sir Edward Payson, 1s t Bt. 191
Wills, Sir Fredrick, 1st Bt. 190
Wills, Sir George Alfred, 1st Bt. 225
Wills, Sir George Vernon, 2nd Bt. 237
Wills, Walter Melville 256
Wilson, George 147
Winans, William Louis 174
Winham, Francis Bernard 291
Winterbottom, George Harold 243
Winterbottom, William Dickson 219
Winterstoke, 1st Baron (William Henry Wills) 194
Wise, Francis 150
Wolverton, 1st Baron (George Carr Glyn) 133

Wolverton, 2nd Baron, George 153
Wood, Daniel 165
Wood, James Marke 189
Wood, Samuel 165
Woodbridge, 1st Baron (Arthur Churchman) 275
Woolavington, 1st baron (James Buchanan) 243
Worthington, Albert Octavius 205
Worthington, William 274
Wright, Francis 134
Wrigley, Thomas 149
Wythes, George 150

Y

Yapp, William Johnston 266
Yarborough, Earls of 49
Yates, Peter 262
Yule, Gladys Meryl 282